AIRLINES
WORLDWIDE

More than 360 Airlines Described and Illustrated in Colour

B I HENGI

MIDLAND
An imprint of
Ian Allan Publishing

Airlines Worldwide – 4th edition
© 2003 NARA-Verlag and Midland Publishing

ISBN 1 85780 155 5

First published in 2003 by
NARA-Verlag, Postfach 1241, D-85388 Allershausen,
Germany, as 'Fluggesellschaften Weltweit' 5th edn.

English language edition published 2003 by
Midland Publishing
4 Watling Drive, Hinckley, LE10 3EY, England.
Telephone: 01455 254 490   Fax: 01455 254 495
E-mail: midlandbooks@compuserve.com

Midland Publishing is an imprint of
Ian Allan Publishing Ltd

Worldwide distribution (except North America):
Midland Counties Publications
4 Watling Drive, Hinckley, LE10 3EY, England.
Telephone: 01455 254 450   Fax: 01455 233 737
E-mail: midlandbooks@compuserve.com
www.midlandcountiessuperstore.com

North American trade distribution:
Specialty Press Publishers and Wholesalers Inc.
39966 Grand Avenue, North Branch, MN 55056, USA
Telephone: 651 277 1400   Fax: 651 277 1203
Toll free telephone: 800 895 4585
www.specialtypress.com

Design concept and layout
© 2003 NARA-Verlag and Midland Publishing

Printed in China via World Print Ltd.

Front cover illustrations:
Josef Krauthäuser
Ken Petersen *(and opposite page)*
Florian Morasch
Frank Schorr

Rear cover: Daniel Klein; Jan-Alexander Lück

Title page: The end of an era! Concorde was in
service with Air France and British Airways for
over 27 years. (Air France)

AIRLINES
WORLDWIDE
More than 360 Airlines Described and Illustrated in Colour

This book is an English-language version of the successful German 'Fluggesellschaften Weltweit', now in its fifth edition, and is the fourth edition to appear in its English language guise.

It aims to give an overview and illustrate about 360 of the world's leading or more interesting airlines, including smaller national operators, with their history, routes, aircraft fleet and operations.

It cannot set out to be a comprehensive guide to every operator; adding together all the scheduled airlines, holiday and charter and local service operators gives an answer in the region of 5,000, which if included, would clearly result in a very large and extremely expensive publication.

The German edition was compiled by B I Hengi, edited by Josef Krauthäuser and published in Summer 2003. It has been translated, edited and updated by Neil Lewis so that it is as current as possible at press-time in September 2003.

Fleet quantities, and especially details of aircraft on order for future delivery, must be regarded as approximate only. With aircraft being delivered, retired, temporarily stored, loaned to associate operators, or leased between operators every day, it is impossible to be definitive. We have omitted some small aircraft which may be in an airline's fleet for training, communications or other purposes and are not in general passenger or airfreight service.

Likewise, what are termed as future orders in some circles can range from genuinely firm and fully signed-up contracts, through options, 'rolling options' to such nebulous things as letters of intent for up to 15 years hence! However we have done our best to ensure that the information in these pages is as up-to-date as possible and forms a valid and useful guide to the operations of the airlines described.

Since the last edition was published, there have been considerable changes in the air transport industry, not least influenced by the tragic events of 11th September 2001, wars in Afghanistan and Iraq, and to a lesser extent, general recession, all of which have led to significant downturn in traffic, storage of aircraft and even airline failures. Low-cost airlines have continued to proliferate, and all in all this edition is markedly different from the last. As usual, all of the photographs for this edition are new, and airline website address have been added.

We hope that you will enjoy this book, and welcome your comments for future editions.

Midland Publishing
September 2003

Contents

Introduction. 3
Contents 4

ABX AIR. 6
ACES COLOMBIA. 7
ADRIA AIRWAYS. 8
AEGEAN AIRLINES. 9
AERIS 10
AER LINGUS 11
AERO CALIFORNIA 12
AEROCARIBE 13
AERO CONTINENTE 14
AEROFLOT 15
AEROFLOT DON. 16
AEROLINEAS ARGENTINAS 17
AERO LLOYD 18
AEROMEXICO. 19
AEROPOSTAL. 20
AIR ALGERIE 21
AIR ATLANTA ICELANDIC 22
AIR BALTIC 23
AIR BERLIN 24
AIR BOSNA 25
AIR BOTNIA. 26
AIR BOTSWANA 27
AIR CANADA 28
AIR CANADA JAZZ 29
AIR CHINA. 30
AIR CONTRACTORS. 31
AIR DOLOMITI. 32
AIR EUROPA 33
AIRFAST INDONESIA 34
AIR FRANCE 35
AIR GABON. 36
AIR GREENLAND 37
AIR INDIA. 38
AIR JAMAICA 39
AIR KAZAKSTAN. 40
AIR KORYO 41
AIR LITTORAL 42
AIR LUXOR 43
AIR MACAU. 44
AIR MADAGASCAR. 45
AIR MALAWI 46
AIR MALTA 47
AIR MARSHALL ISLANDS. 48
AIR MAURITANIE 49
AIR MAURITIUS 50
AIR MOLDOVA 51
AIR NAMIBIA. 52
AIR NAURU 53
AIR NEW ZEALAND 54
AIR NIPPON 55
AIR NIUGINI 56
AIR NOSTRUM 57
AIR ONE 58
AIR PACIFIC 59
AIR PHILIPPINES 60
AIR PLUS COMET. 61
AIR SEYCHELLES. 62
AIR TAHITI. 63
AIR TAHITI NUI 64
AIR TANZANIA 65
AIR TCHAD 66

AIR TRAN AIRWAYS 67
AIR TRANSAT 68
AIR TRANSPORT INTERNATIONAL . . . 69
AIR 2000 70
AIR VANUATU 71
AIR ZIMBABWE. 72
AJT – AIR INTERNATIONAL 73
ALASKA AIRLINES 74
ALBANIAN AIRLINES 75
ALITALIA 76
ALLEGRO AIR. 77
ALL NIPPON AIRWAYS 78
ALOHA AIRLINES 79
ALPI EAGLES 80
AMERICAN AIRLINES. 81
AMERICAN EAGLE AIRLINES 82
AMERICA WEST AIRLINES. 83
AMERIJET INTERNATIONAL 84
ANTONOV AIRLINES 85
ARIANA AFGHAN 86
ARKIA ISRAELI AIRLINES 87
ARMENIAN AIRLINES 88
ARROW AIR 89
ASERCA 90
ASIANA 91
ATA-AMERICAN TRANS AIR. 92
ATLANTIC AIRLINES. 93
ATLANTIC SOUTHEAST AIRLINES . . . 94
ATLANT-SOYUZ AIRLINES 95
ATLAS AIR. 96
ATLASJET INT'L AIRWAYS 97
AUGSBURG AIRWAYS 98
AURIGNY AIR SERVICES 99
AUSTRALIAN AIRLINES 100
AUSTRIAN AIRLINES 101
AVIACSA 102
AVIANCA COLOMBIA. 103
AVIATECA 104
AZERBAIJAN AIRLINES 105
AZZURRA AIR 106

BAHAMASAIR 107
BANGKOK AIRWAYS 108
BAX GLOBAL 109
BELAIR AIRLINES 110
BELAVIA-BELARUSSIAN AIRLINES . . 111
BIMAN BANGLADESH 112
BINTER CANARIAS. 113
BLUE PANORAMA 114
BMI BABY 115
BMI – BRITISH MIDLAND INT'L 116
BOURAQ AIRLINES 117
BRAATHENS. 118
BRITANNIA AIRWAYS 119
BRITISH AIRWAYS 120
BRITISH AIRWAYS CITIEXPRESS . . . 121
BUFFALO AIRWAYS. 122
BWIA INTERNATIONAL 123

CAMEROON AIRLINES. 124
CARGOLUX. 125
CATHAY PACIFIC 126
CAYMAN AIRWAYS 127
CCM AIRLINES 128

CEBU PACIFIC AIR 129
CHAMPION AIR 130
CHANNEL EXPRESS AIR SERVICES . 131
CHINA AIRLINES 132
CHINA EASTERN 133
CHINA NORTHERN AIRLINES 134
CHINA NORTHWEST AIRLINES. 135
CHINA SOUTHERN AIRLINES 136
CHINA SOUTHWEST AIRLINES 137
CHINA XINJIANG AIRLINES 138
CHINA YUNNAN AIRLINES 139
CIMBER AIR 140
COMAIR 141
CONDOR FLUGDIENST 142
CONTINENTAL AIRLINES. 143
CONTINENTAL EXPRESS 144
COPA PANAMA 145
CORSAIR 146
CROATIA AIRLINES 147
CSA – CZECH AIRLINES 148
CUBANA DE AVIACION 149
CYPRUS AIRWAYS. 150

DANISH AIR TRANSPORT 151
DELTA AIR LINES 152
DEUTSCHE BA. 153
DHL AIRWAYS 154
DRAGONAIR. 155
DRUK AIR 156
DUTCH BIRD. 157
DUTCH CARIBBEAN AIRLINES 158

EASYJET AIRLINE 159
EDELWEISS AIR 160
EGYPT AIR 161
EL AL ISRAEL AIRLINES. 162
EMIRATES. 163
ERA AVIATION 164
ESTONIAN AIR 165
ETHIOPIAN AIRLINES. 166
EURALAIR 167
EUROCYPRIA AIRLINES. 168
EUROPEAN AVIATION AIR CHARTER 169
EUROWINGS 170
EVA AIR. 171
EVERGREEN INT'L AIRLINES 172
EXCEL AIRWAYS 173

FALCON AIR 174
FAR EASTERN AIR TRANSPORT – FAT 175
FEDEX. 176
FINNAIR 177
FIRST AIR 178
FISCHER AIR 179
FLY BE 180
FREEDOM AIR INTERNATIONAL. . . . 181
FRONTIER AIRLINES 182
FUTURA INT'L AIRWAYS 183

GARUDA INDONESIA. 184
GERMANIA 185
GERMANWINGS. 186
GHANA AIRWAYS. 187
GOL TRANSPORTES AEREOS 188

GULF AIR 189
GULFSTREAM INT'L AIRLINES 190

HAINAN AIRLINES 191
HAPAG LLOYD FLUG 192
HAPAG LLOYD EXPRESS 193
HAWAIIAN AIR 194
HORIZON AIR 195

IBERIA 196
IBERWORLD AIRLINES 197
ICELANDAIR 198
INDIAN AIRLINES 199
IRAN AIR 200
IRAN ASEMAN AIRLINES 201

JAL EXPRESS 202
JALWAYS 203
JAPAN AIRLINES 204
JAT AIRWAYS 205
JET AIRWAYS 206
JETBLUE AIRWAYS 207
JETSGO 208
JTA – JAPAN TRANSOCEAN AIR 209

KENYA AIRWAYS 210
KITTY HAWK AIRCARGO 211
KLM-CITYHOPPER 212
KLM ROYAL DUTCH AIRLINES 213
KMV – KAVKAZSKIE MINERALNYE VODY 214
KOREAN AIR 215
KRAS AIR 216
KUWAIT AIRWAYS 217
KYRGHYZSTAN AIRLINES 218

LAB – LLOYD AEREO BOLIVIANO . . . 219
LACSA 220
LAM 221
LAN CHILE 222
LAO AIRLINES 223
LAUDA AIR 224
LIAT 225
LIBYAN ARAB AIRLINES 226
LITHUANIAN AIRLINES 227
LOT – POLISH AIRLINES 228
LTE – INTERNATIONAL AIRWAYS . . . 229
LTU INTERNATIONAL AIRWAYS 230
LUFTHANSA 231
LUFTHANSA CARGO 232
LUFTHANSA CITYLINE 233
LUXAIR 234

MAERSK AIR 235
MAHAN AIR 236
MALAYSIA AIRLINES 237
MALEV – HUNGARIAN AIRLINES . . . 238
MANDARIN AIRLINES 239
MARTINAIR 240
MAT – MACEDONIAN AIRLINES 241
MEA – MIDDLE EAST AIRLINES 242
MERIDIANA 243
MERPATI 244
MESABA AIRLINES 245
MEXICANA 246
MIAMI AIR INTERNATIONAL 247
MIAT – MONGOLIAN AIRLINES 248
MIDWEST EXPRESS 249
MONARCH AIRLINES 250

MONTENEGRO AIRLINES 251
MYANMA AIRWAYS 252
MY TRAVEL AIRWAYS 253

NATIONAL JET SYSTEM 254
NATIONWIDE AIRLINES 255
NICA AIRLINES 256
NIPPON CARGO AIRLINES – NCA . . . 257
NORTH AMERICAN AIRLINES 258
NORTHERN AIR CARGO 259
NORTHWEST AIRLINES 260
NORWEGIAN AIR SHUTTLE 261
NOUVELAIR TUNISIE 262
NOVAIR 263

OLYMPIC AIRWAYS 264
OLYMPIC AVIATION 265
OMAN AIR 266
ONUR AIR 267

PAKISTAN INT'L AIRLINES 268
PAN AM 269
PEGASUS 270
PGA – PORTUGALIA 271
PHILIPPINES 272
PLUNA 273
POLAR AIR CARGO 274
POLYNESIAN 275
PULKOVO 276

QANTAS 277
QATAR AIRWAYS 278
REGIONAL AIRLINES 279

RIO-SUL 280
ROYAL AIR MAROC 281
ROYAL BRUNEI 282
ROYAL JORDANIAN 283
ROYAL NEPAL AIRLINES 284
RYANAIR 285
RYAN INTERNATIONAL AIRLINES . . . 286

SATA 287
SAUDI ARABIAN AIRLINES 288
SCANDINAVIAN – SAS 289
SCENIC AIRLINES 290
SHANGDONG AIRLINES 291
SHANGHAI AIRLINES 292
SHOROUK AIR 293
SIBERIA AIRLINES 294
SICHUAN AIRLINES 295
SILKAIR 296
SINGAPORE AIRLINES 297
SKY AIRLINES 298
SKYSERVICE AIRLINES 299
SKYWAYS 300
SKYWEST AIRLINES 301
SLOVAK AIRLINES 302
SN – BRUSSELS AIRLINES 303
SOBELAIR 304
SOUTH AFRICAN AIRWAYS 305
SOUTHEAST AIRLINES 306
SOUTHWEST AIRLINES 307
SPANAIR 308
SPIRIT AIRLINES 309
SRILANKAN 310
STAR AIRLINES 311
STERLING EUROPEAN AIRLINES . . . 312

SUDAN AIRWAYS 313
SUN COUNTRY AIRLINES 314
SUN EXPRESS 315
SURINAM AIRWAYS 316
SWISS INTERNATIONAL AIRLINES . . 317
SYRIANAIR 318

TAAG ANGOLA AIRLINES 319
TACA INTERNATIONAL AIRLINES . . . 320
TAJIKISTAN AIRLINES 321
TAM 322
TAME – LINEA AEREA DEL ECUADOR 323
TANGO 324
TAP AIR PORTUGAL 325
TAROM 326
THAI AIRWAYS INTERNATIONAL 327
THOMAS COOK AIRLINES 328
TNT AIRWAYS 329
TRANSAERO AIRLINES 330
TRANSASIA AIRWAYS 331
TRANSAVIA AIRLINES 332
TRANS MALDIVIAN AIRWAYS 333
TRANS MERIDIAN AIRLINES 334
TRANSPORTES AEREOS DE
    CABO VERDE 335
TRANS STATES AIRLINES 336
TRAVEL SERVICE AIRLINES 337
TUNISAIR 338
TURKISH AIRLINES 339
TYROLEAN AIRWAYS 340

UNKRAINE INT'L AIRLINES 341
UNITED AIRLINES 342
UNITED EXPRESS 343
UPS AIRLINES 344
URAL AIRLINES 345
US AIRWAYS 346
US AIRWAYS EXPRESS 347
USA3000 348
UZBEKISTAN AIRWAYS 349

VARIG BRASIL 350
VASP 351
VIA – AIR VIA BULGARIAN AIRWAYS . 352
VIETNAM AIRLINES 353
VIRGIN ATLANTIC 354
VIRGIN BLUE 355
VIRGIN EXPRESS 356
VLM 357
VOLARE AIRLINES 358

WDL AVIATION 359
WESTJET AIRLINES 360
WIDEROE 361
WORLD AIRWAYS 362
XIAMEN AIRLINES 363
YEMENIA 364
ZHONGYUAN AIRLINES 365
ZIP 366

Airport abbreviations/codes 367
Airline three-letter codes 376
International aircraft registration
    prefixes 380

Boeing 767-281 N791AX (Josef Krauthäuser / Phoenix)

ABX AIR

Airborne Air Park, 145 Hunter Drive, Wilmington
Ohio, 45177 USA, Tel. 937-3823838
E-mail: mail@abxair.com, www.abxair.com

Three- / Two- letter code	IATA No.	Reg'n prefix	ICAO callsign
ABX / GB	832	N	Abex

Airborne Freight began business at the end of the 1940s, importing flowers from Hawaii. These were flown principally into California, where they were sold. Midwest Air Charter of Elyria, Ohio specialised during the 1970s in courier flights for banks and for Airborne Freight Corp, using small aircraft such as the Aerostar, Beech 18, Piper Aztec and Lear Jet, to which five SE.210 Caravelles were added in 1978. A year later Airborne took over Midwest and thus acquired its own flight division. Airborne Express was granted FAA certification in April 1980 and expanded quickly. Alongside the Caravelle the NAMC YS-11 was introduced as a fast turboprop. From its own airport at Wilmington Airpark, where it has one of the largest package sorting facilities in the USA, more and more destinations in the USA were being served. DC-9s replaced the ageing Caravelles and quickly became the prevalent type in the fleet. In 1983 43000 tonnes of freight were forwarded. Longer distance routes and increasing amounts of freight led to the introduction to service in 1984 of the Douglas DC-8. The Airbus consortium offered a freighter version of the A300 as a replacement for the older aircraft in the fleet, but it was decided to adopt the Boeing 767-200 freighter conversion instead. The first of these came into service during the second half of 1997, and further examples are being added. In March 2003 DHL acquired the Airborne Express Ground Operation; this led to the splitting of Airborne Express from the independent ABX Air Inc. The aviation operation of Airborne Express was thus renamed and is also completely independent. ABX Air has numerous contracts to provide services for DHL and for other freight and express parcel companies.

Routes

Scheduled freight services to over 140 destinations within the USA. Canada and the Caribbean are also served.

Fleet

27 Boeing 767-200
20 Douglas DC-8/61/63/63F
72 Douglas DC-9-10/30/40

Airbus A320-233 VP-BVB (Frank Schorr / Miami)

ACES COLOMBIA

Calle 49, No.50-21 Piso 34, Ed del Cafe,
Medellin 6503, Columbia, Tel. 4-56-053,
Fax. 4-2511677, www.avianca.com

Three- / Two- letter code	IATA No.	Reg'n prefix	ICAO callsign
AES / VX	137	HK	Aces

The private Aerolineas Centrales de Colombia – ACES – was originally set up in August 1971 and was owned by the United Coffee Growers' Association. Regional services were begun on 1st February 1972 from its base at Medellin to Bogota and Manizales, using a Saunders ST-27. From September 1976 services were added to smaller airports, using the de Havilland DHC-6 Twin Otter. In order to build up a wider network, it was felt necessary to acquire jet aircraft. Boeing 727-100s were acquired from Eastern Air Lines and flew for ACES from 1981. The ST-27 continued in use until 1987, when it was replaced

by the Fokker F.27. By this time, the route network extended to over 20 domestic destinations and would be built up even further. In 1991 a wide-ranging fleet renewal was initiated; ATR 42s gradually replaced the F.27s and the older examples of the Boeing 727-100 were exchanged for newer-build aircraft. The first international scheduled service was to Miami on 1st July 1992. The build-up of this route saw the employment of further Boeing 727-200s, leased in 1994 and 1995. ACES was given the task of carrying letters and packages by the postal authorities, and charter flights were operated to many destinations in the Caribbean. From

the beginning of 1998 further fleet renewal was instituted, and the first Airbus A320, arrived as a replacement for the Boeing 727s. In a move to improve the efficiency of Columbian air transport in general, in May 2002 Aces Columbia, SAM and Avianca Columbia were all merged into the Summa alliance. Though the well-known names are retained for the time being, operations are centrally managed. A new colour scheme became evident from the end of 2002. Continuing difficulties during mid-2003 mean that many regional routes are being dropped and the ATR 42s returned to their lessors.

Routes

Apartado, Armenia, Bahia Solana, Barrancabermeja, Barranquilla, Bogota, Bucaramanga, Cali, Cartagena, Condoto, Cucuta, Fort Lauderdale, Ipiales, Lima, Manizales, Medellin, Miami, Monteria, Nuqui, Ocana, Otu, Panama City, Puerto Plata, Punta Cana, Quito, San Juan, Santo Domingo.

Fleet

8 Airbus A320
4 ATR 42-300
5 ATR 42-500
3 De Havilland DHC-6 Twin Otter

Airbus A320-231 S5-AAC (Josef Krauthäuser / Munich)

ADRIA AIRWAYS

Kuzmiceva 7, 1001 Ljubljana, Slovenia
Tel. 61-313366, Fax. 61-323356
E-mail: prc@adria.si, www.adria.si

Three- / Two- letter code	IATA No.	Reg'n prefix	ICAO callsign
ADR / JP	165	S5	Adria

Adria Airways was founded in 1960 in Yugoslavia and began mostly charter operations in March of the following year, the initial fleet consisting of four Douglas DC-6Bs which were obtained from KLM. During 1969 the airline became a part of the activities of the Interexport trading company, resulting in a swift change of name to Inex Adria Airways. In 1970, using new Douglas DC-9-32 aircraft, the first scheduled services were flown from Ljubljana to Belgrade. From 1985 Inex flew also for the first time to Munich, this being in the form of scheduled services to Ljubljana. Alongside these schedules charter flights were also undertaken for various tour operators. With the delivery of the first of three Airbus A320s during 1989 the company changed the colour scheme of its aircraft and reverted to its original name. All of the shares were now in the hands of the government. Civil unrest in Yugoslavia forced a halt to operations from October 1991 until January 1992. During 1992 Adria became the flag carrier of the newly independent state of Slovenia, after it had separated from Yugoslavia. A part-privatisation of the company followed in 1996 and the first Canadair Regional Jets were brought into service during 1998.

The fleet was optimised for the lower demand, which entailed the phasing out of the DC-9s and Dash 7s which had been in use. Likewise, the route network was redefined. After many years of confrontation, the political situation in the region has improved, as have relations with Serbia and this led to the establishment of direct flights between Belgrade and Ljubljana from December 2002. The most important European destination, however, is Frankfurt; hence there is close co-operation with Lufthansa.

Routes

Amsterdam, Belgrade, Brussels, Copenhagen, Dubrovnik, Frankfurt, Istanbul, Ljubljana, London-Gatwick, Moscow, Munich, Ohrid, Paris, Podgorica, Pristina, Sarajevo, Skopje, Split, Vienna and Zürich as scheduled services, Charter flights from many European airports to destinations in Croatia and Slovenia, and emigrant workers' flights.

Fleet

3 Airbus A320
5 Canadair Regional Jet

Avro RJ 100 SX-DVD (Stefan Schlick / Corfu)

AEGEAN AIRLINES

572 Vorliagmenis Avenue 16451 Athens, Greece,
Tel. (210) 9988350, www.aegeanair.com
E-mail: wwwcontac@aegeanair.com

Three- / Two- letter code	IATA No.	Reg'n prefix	ICAO callsign
AEE / A3	–	SX	Aegean

Aegean Aviation was founded in 1987 by Antonius and Nikolaos Simigdalas. As Greece's first privately-owned commercial aviation company, it was granted its Air Operators Certificate by the country's aviation authorities in 1992; this allowed unrestricted worldwide charter operations with two Learjets. In March of 1999, the introduction of new investors, amongst them the Vassilakis Group, led to the founding of Aegean Airlines. Two factory-fresh Avro RJ 100s were put into service from May of that year on Greek domestic routes from its base and home airport at Athens-Hellenikon, moving from 2001to the newly-constructed Eleftherios Venizelos airport. During the first year of operation, the network was increased and a third Avro RJ was added to the fleet. The local operator Air Greece, with its fleet of three ATR 72 and a Fokker 100, was taken over during December 1999. In this way Aegean Airlines was able to expand rapidly, so that 10 destinations on the Greek islands and mainland were being served, the passenger numbers climbed steeply and the airline moved into the position of becoming a competitor to the state-supported Olympic Airways. A further merger took place in March 2001 when the airline joined with Cronus Airlines, which had been around since 1994. Cronus Airlines was active on a scheduled and charter basis with several Boeing 737s and concentrated on European services, notably to Germany. After the takeover the aircraft wore the dual titling 'Cronus Aegean' for a while but since 2002 this has been simplified to just Aegean Airlines. As well as scheduled services, several of the aircraft are employed on charter work for a number of tour operators throughout the year. It is planned eventually to standardise the fleet on the Boeing 737.

Routes

Athens, Alexandroupolis, Chania, Cologne, Corfu, Düsseldorf, Frankfurt, Heraklion, Ioannina, Kavala, Munich, Mykonos, Mytilini, Rhodes, Rome, Stuttgart, Thessaloniki.

Fleet

3 ATR 72
6 Avro RJ 100
3 Boeing 737-300
5 Boeing 737-400

Boeing 737-36E F-GNFD (Albert Kuhbandner / Salzburg)

AERIS

1-BP 44, 31702 Blagnac, France
Tel. +33561167600, Fax. +335561167699
www.aeris.fr

Three- / Two- letter code	IATA No.	Reg'n prefix	ICAO callsign
AIS / SH	–	F	France Charter

Founded in 1990 as Air Toulouse, this airline has had a rather chequered history over several years. In its year of foundation, Air Toulouse began scheduled services with two SE.210 Caravelles to London Gatwick and Bristol from its Toulouse base. However, this was terminated after barely a year of flying and Air Toulouse went into a bankruptcy. The intervention of new investors permitted a new start to be made as Air Toulouse International. Again it was the Caravelle that was chosen for initial operations, but in 1993 the airline's first Boeing 737-200 came into service. Scheduled services were operated as well as charter work. During 1997 the last of the Caravelles was retired, replaced by further Boeing 737-200s which had been added during 1995 and 1996. Wide-ranging changes in the management took place, with yet again new investors and changes in the business structure. The Aeris Group, well supported by banks and investment companies, came on the scene during the summer of 1999 and this resulted in further decisive changes. The scheduled services were dropped and the old Boeing 737-200s were exchanged for newer 737-300s. Henceforth efforts were concentrated on charter services, with capacity being offered principally in the European market. The aircraft colour scheme was changed and the name Aeris introduced. The airline also benefited from the demise of Aero Lyon, from which several long-distance routes were taken over from summer 2002, necessitating the lease of a Boeing 767-300; a further example was added later in the year. Since May 2003 a subsidiary, Aeris Express has been active in the low-cost market. The airline's main base is at Toulouse-Blagnac, where it has its own maintenance facilities, but it also has a secondary base at Brest.

Routes

Agadir, Ancona, Brest, Cancun, Dakar, Djerba, Lyon, Marrakech, Marseilles, Munich, Nantes, Paris-CDG, Puerto Plata, Tenerife, Toulon, Toulouse.

Fleet

5 Boeing 737-300
2 Boeing 767-300

Airbus A330-301 EI-SHN (Jan Alexander Lück / Shannon)

AER LINGUS

P.O.Box 180, Dublin Airport, Ireland
Tel. 1-8862222, Fax. 1-8863832, E-mail:
groups@aerlingus.com, www.aerlingus.ie

Three- / Two- letter code	IATA No.	Reg'n prefix	ICAO callsign
EIN / EI	053	EI	Shamrock

On 22nd May 1936 Aer Lingus Teoranta was set up for regional and European services, and in 1947 Aerlinte Eireann Teoranta for international routes. From 1960, the two were closely integrated as the state-owned Aer Lingus – Irish International Airlines. Flights began using a de Havilland DH.84 from Baldonnel airfield near Dublin to Bristol on 27th May 1936. Soon there were flights to London, Liverpool and to the Isle of Man. During the war, only the Shannon-Dublin-Liverpool route was flown, with a single DC-3. In 1947 the purchase of seven Vickers Vikings signalled a new beginning, but these were sold in 1948 and DC-3s became the backbone of the fleet. Vickers Viscounts arrived in 1954, Fokker Friendships from 1958 and services were developed to many European destinations; from 1965 the BAC One-Eleven was used. For the transatlantic services, beginning with New York in 1958, Lockheed Constellations were flown, with Boeing 720s taking over from 1960 and the Boeing 747 from 1971. In the mid 1980s Aer Lingus entered a crisis; overcapacity had to be eliminated, and a re-organisation took place which also meant a fleet renewal. Boeing 737-200s, later replaced by newer models, formed the mainstay of the fleet, and Shorts 360s and Fokker 50s were ordered. BAe 146s, first acquired in 1995, are now being withdrawn. In March 1994 the first of the airline's Airbus A330-300s flew to New York for the first time, ousting the 747s, and the A321 started to replace the 737s from mid 1998. Aer Lingus joined the 'oneworld' alliance from June 2000. The Airbus 320 also joined the fleet in this year. Aer Lingus was hit particularly hard by the 2002 airline crisis, notably with its US services. However, the airline is working its way out of the crisis, though not without having seen strikes and route and fleet reductions.

Routes

Amsterdam, Barcelona, Birmingham, Boston, Bologna, Brussels, Chicago, Cork, Dublin, Düsseldorf, Edinburgh, Faro, Frankfurt, Geneva, Glasgow, Jersey, Lisbon, London-Heathrow, Los Angeles, Madrid, Malaga, Manchester, Milan, Munich, New York, Nice, Paris, Prague, Rome, Shannon, Vienna and Washington. Additionally charter flights are operated to over 15 European destinations on a seasonal basis.

Fleet

4 Airbus A320
6 Airbus A321
8 Airbus A330
6 BAe 146-300

3 Boeing 737-400
8 Boeing 737-500

Douglas DC-9-32 XA-TNT (Josef Krauthäuser / Los Angeles LAX)

AERO CALIFORNIA

Aquiles Serdan No.1995, La Paz, Baja California 23000, Mexico, Tel. 112-26655, Fax. 112-53993 www.aerocalifornia.de

Three- / Two- letter code	IATA No.	Reg'n prefix	ICAO callsign
SER / JR	078	XA	Aerocalifornia

The company was founded in 1960 and operated as an air taxi concern with several Cessnas and Beech 18s. Until the 1980s the indestructible Douglas DC-3 was also part of the fleet, which was expanded from 1982 by the acquisition of a Douglas DC-9-15. Aero California was at first only active in its own neighbourhood, Baja California, and flew charters, but also scheduled services, between La Paz, Tijuana and Hermosillo. These schedules were carried out using a Convair 340; further routes were added over the years. At the end of the 1980s it was decided to undertake a careful expansion and more DC-9s were acquired, enabling the propeller-driven types to be gradually phased out. At the beginning of 1990 a scheduled service was inaugurated to Los Angeles in the USA. Since 1995, when the last of the Cessnas and Beech 18s were retired, the fleet has been all-jet. As well as scheduled services, Aero California also offers charter services to the country's tourism centres. Outside Mexico, only Los Angeles and Tucson in the USA are served; several flights each day connect Los Angeles with destinations in Baja California and other Mexican provinces, as well as the capital, Mexico City. A close co-operation with American Airlines has existed for some years. Aero California has its own maintenance centre in La Paz, where work is also undertaken for other airlines.

Routes

Augascalientes, Chihuahua, Ciudad Juarez, Ciudad Obregon, Ciudad Victoria, Colima, Culiacan, Durango, Guadalajara, Hermosillo, La Paz, Leon, Loreto, Los Angeles, Los Mochis, Manzanillo, Matamoros, Mazatlan, Merida, Mexico City, Monterey, Puebla, Puerto Vallarta, San Jose Cabo, San Luis Potosi, Tampico, Tepic, Tijuana, Torreon, Tucson, Veracruz, Villahermosa.

Fleet

11 Douglas DC-9-10
11 Douglas DC-9-30

Douglas DC-9-31 XA-ABR (Richard Schmaus / Mexico City)

AEROCARIBE

Paseo de Montejo 500-B, 9700 Merida
Yucatan, Mexico, Tel. 9249500, Fax. 9281810
www.aerocaribe.com

Three- / Two- letter code	IATA No.	Reg'n prefix	ICAO callsign
CBE / QA	723	XA	Aerocaribe

The Yucatan peninsula, popular with tourists, did not have as well-developed an infrastructure in the 1970s as it has today. It was possible to fly to Merida from abroad or directly from Mexico City, but the regional centres were not so well developed and the connections by bus or train took hours. As a result, business interests from Merida and the region set up Aerovias Caribe in order to provide regional air services. The first flight took place in 1975, using a Convair 440 to Uxmal. Further regional centres were added, and two further 440s with which to operate them. A connection to Mexico City was established. At this time Cancun was being established as a tourist destination and gained its own airport, and so services were begun here too. At the end of the 1970s Aerovias Caribe adopted its current name. Fokker F.27s replaced the Convair 440s and by the end of 1989 the fleet consisted of F.27s and FH-227s. During 1978 Aero Cozumel was established in the town from which it takes its name and used Britten-Norman Islanders to operate principally a profitable route between Cancun and Cozumel. The demand for this was very strong and Fokker F.27 were used to supplement the Islanders. Though the two airlines flew independently, they had the same owner. During 1990 both operators were bought by Mexicana, from whom in December 1993 Aerocaribe received its first Douglas DC-9-15. When in 1996 the Cintra Group bought Mexicana and instituted some reorganisation, Aerocaribe and Aero Cozumel became partners in the Mexicana Inter Regional programme. From 1998 Aerocaribe received several BAe Jetstreams and further Douglas DC-9s; the older -15s are now replaced by -31s. Aerocaribe flies under Mexicana flight numbers, but largely retains its independence; the aircraft are in their own colours.

Routes

Acapulco, Austin, Cancun, Chetumel, Ciudad de Carmen, Cozumel, Escondido, Flores, Havana, Huatulco, Merida, Mexico City, Monterrey, Oaxaca, Palenque, Playa del Carmen, San Christobal, Veracruz.

Fleet

6 BAe Jetstream 32
1 Fokker/Fairchild FH-227
8 Douglas DC-9-30

Boeing 767-219 CC-CJP, now OB-1766 (Thomas Kim / Miami)

AERO CONTINENTE

Jr.Bolgnesi 125, Piso16 Miraflores, Lima, Peru
Tel. 51-12424260, Fax. 51-13324618
www.aerocontinente.com.pe/

Three- / Two- letter code	IATA No.	Reg'n prefix	ICAO callsign
ACQ / N6	929	OB	Aero Continente

Aero Continente S.A. was founded on 4th January 1992 in Tarapoto by the Gonzales family. The San Martin regional government gave tax concessions to companies being established in the region. Initially the airline aimed to look after the air transport needs of a government oil support company, whose depots were often in out-of-the-way locations which could only realistically be serviced by air. The first aircraft was a Boeing 737-200, and operations were begun with this on 25th May 1992. Following the deregulation of air transport in Peru at the end of 1992 Aero Continente expanded its services and for the first time offered scheduled services. The fleet was expanded with two more 737s and a 727 and the company's base moved to the Peruvian capital, Lima. Here the company was also able to carry out maintenance in its own hangar. The company continued to develop positively and more aircraft were needed. Further 727s, a Fokker F.28, Antonov An 24 and even Lockheed TriStars were brought into the fleet over the years. Aero Continente was especially able to benefit from the failures of other companies in finding opportunities to expand its own operations. Service to Miami was commenced in 1999 with a leased Boeing 757, this being replaced during the early part of 2000 with two Boeing 767s, which were also used to create more international routes. A subsidiary company has been established in Chile, in co-operation with local investors.

Routes

Arequipa, Ayacucho, Bogota, Buenos Aires, Cajamarca, Caracas, Chiclayo, Cuzco, Guayaquil, Iquitos, Juliaca, Lima, Miami, Piura, Pucallpa, Quito, Santo Domingo, Santiago, Tacna, Talara, Tarapoto, Trujillo, Tumbes.

Fleet

5 Boeing 727
14 Boeing 737-200
3 Boeing 767-200
3 Fokker F.28
1 Fokker F.27

Ilyushin IL-96-300 RA-96011 (Martin Kühn / Frankfurt)

AEROFLOT

Leningradsky Prospect 37a, 125167 Moscow, Russia, Tel. 70957529071, Fax. 70957529071
E-mail: aeroflot@russia.net, www.aeroflot.org

Three- / Two- letter code	IATA No.	Reg'n prefix	ICAO callsign
AFL / SU	555	RA	Aeroflot

Aeroflot was formed in 1923 as Dobrolet, becoming Aeroflot in 1932, and evolving into the world's largest air transport undertaking. In line with the political status in the Soviet Union, the development of air transport took a different direction from that in the West. Until 1991, Aeroflot dominated in all aspects of aviation activity, but then with the political changes in the Soviet Union, everything altered. The former Aeroflot directorates became independent, and many established their own companies. Likewise the newly-independent countries set up their own airlines, taking over former Aeroflot aircraft. During the course of 1993, a new Aeroflot, comparable to western airlines, emerged, taking on the name of Aeroflot-Russian International Airlines (ARIA). All non-airline services were delegated to independent companies. Only a small part of the former fleet was taken over, and for the first time western aircraft were used, with the lease of five Airbus A310-300s, delivered to Aeroflot from July 1992. Whereas previously services had been operated based on other criteria, now the motivation was only that of successful business. That held true also for aircraft procurement, and from 1996 other western types, much more efficient than their former Soviet counterparts were acquired; these included Boeing 737s, 767s, 777s and the DC-10. During 1997 Aeroflot was partially privatised, with 51% of the shares remaining with the government, the rest being spread among about 15,000 employees. In mid-2000, the shareholders agreed to drop 'International' from the title in view of increasing domestic success, so the airline is now known as Aeroflot – Russian Airlines. The IL-62 was retired mid 2003 after 36 years of service. Airbus A320 deliveries commence late 2003; by 2005 all the old Russian types should have been withdrawn.

Routes

Aeroflot flies to about 160 destinations in over 100 countries in Europe, America, Asia and Africa, and within Russia.

Fleet

		Ordered
11 Airbus A 310-300	6 Ilyushin IL-96-300	20 Airbus A320
6 Boeing 767-300ER	2 Douglas DC-10-40F	
2 Boeing 777-200ER	12 Tupolev Tu-134	
10 Boeing 737-400	21 Tupolev Tu-154	
12 Ilyushin IL-86		

Tupolev Tu-154M RA-85640 (Ralf Lücke / Düsseldorf)

AEROFLOT DON

Sholokova Prospekt 272, Rostov-na-Donu,
Russia, Tel. 8632-525079, Fax. 8632-520567
www.aeroflot.org

Three- / Two- letter code	IATA No.	Reg'n prefix	ICAO callsign
DNV / D9	733	RA	Donavia

Following the break-up of the Soviet Union, the former national airline Aeroflot was also divided into many individual companies, with new airlines being created from the majority of the former Aeroflot directorates. All had the same objective – economic change and the path from central direction to a style of market economy. Only a few of the new airlines in Russia managed to make this U-turn in the way they operate. Donavia was established as a joint stock company in 1993 by the employees of the former Aeroflot directorate in Rostov on Don. The employees owned 51% of the shares, with the balance held by the state. Partly in co-operation with the new Aeroflot, Donavia succeeded in establishing a well-ordered scheduled service network, using aircraft, principally Tupolev Tu-154s, which had been inherited from Aeroflot. The routes are largely domestic, though there are several international services. Donavia was also successful in freight and charter business, especially to the Gulf and Middle East. After the fragmentation of air transport in Russia following the break up of the Soviet Union, and the initial proliferation of smaller airlines, there has been some move towards rationalisation, and thus during 2000 Aeroflot-Russian Airlines took over this successful company and chose Aeroflot Don as the new operating name.

Routes

Dubai, Düsseldorf, Ekatarinenburg, Frankfurt, Irkutsk, Istanbul, Khaborovsk, Krasnoyarsk, Moscow, Neryungri, Novy Urengoy, Novosibirsk, Omsk, Rostov, Sharjah, St.Petersburg, Surgut, Tashkent, Tel Aviv, Tyumen, Vladivostok, Yerevan.

Fleet

2 Antonov An-12
3 Tupolev Tu-134
9 Tupolev Tu-154

Boeing 737-287 LV-JMY (Ken Petersen / Buenos Aires-AEP)

AEROLINEAS ARGENTINAS

Bouchard 547, 1063 Buenos Aires, Argentina
Tel. 01-3173000, Fax. 01-3173585
www.aerolineas.com.ar

Three- / Two- letter code	IATA No.	Reg'n prefix	ICAO callsign
ARG / AR	044	LV	Argentina

Aerolineas Argentinas was created as the new national airline by the amalgamation of four smaller companies, Aeroposta, ALFA, FAMA and Zonda in May 1949 at the instigation of the Argentinian transport ministry. These four airlines brought in their fleets of aircraft such as Douglas DC-3s and DC-4s which were used on internal services and from March 1950 also to New York. In 1959 the de Havilland Comet 4B made its debut on international routes, until in 1966 the first of ten Boeing 707s was delivered. Boeing 747s took over the New York route for the first time in 1976 and from 1977 were also used for services to

Europe. For the short and medium length routes, Boeing 727s and 737s, and the Fokker F.28 were brought into use. At the beginning of the 1990s these were supplemented with MD-80s and three Airbus A310s were used for a short while for US services. In 1993, Iberia acquired a 20% shareholding in the company, increased to 83% in 1995. The balance was held by employees and the government. During the Summer of 1996 a hub was set up at Miami, from where Boeing 727s would fly connecting flights to Canada and the Caribbean. The Airbus A340 was introduced in 1999 for long-haul services. During 1998 Iberia, which

was having financial difficulties, was obliged to reduce its shareholding to 10%, at which point American Airlines took 8.5%. During 2001, the airline found itself under bankruptcy protection; after several months of service interruption the Spanish investor group Marsan took shares in the ailing company, which with fresh capital was able to take to the air again. Austral, which had been majority-owned by Aerolineas Argentinas, was integrated, and during 2002 a European hub was set up at Madrid. ARG works closely with Aeroflot, Aerosur, American Airlines, Iberia, Malaysian and Qantas through various alliances.

Routes

Asuncion, Auckland, Bahia Blanca, Bogota, Buenos Aires, Caracas, Catamarca, Comodoro Rivadavia, Cordoba, Corrientes, El Calafate, Esquel, Florianopolis, Formosa, Iguasu, La Paz, Lima, London, Madrid, Mar del Plata, Mendoza, Mexico City, Miami, Montevideo, New York, Paris, Porto Alegre, Punta del Este, Rio de Janeiro, Rio Gallegos, Rio Grande, Rome, Santiago, Sao Paulo, Sydney, Tucuman, Ushuaia.

Fleet

Fleet		Ordered
4 Airbus A340-200	6 McDonnell Douglas MD-80	6 Airbus A340-600
6 Boeing 747-200		
26 Boeing 737-200		

Airbus A320-232 D-ALAA (Stefan Schlick / Arrecife)

AERO LLOYD

Lessingstrasse 7-9, 61440 Oberursel, Germany.
Tel. 06171-625347, Fax. 06171-6549
E-mail: info@aerolloyd.de, www.aerolloyd.de

Three- / Two- letter code	IATA No.	Reg'n prefix	ICAO callsign
AEF / YP	633	D	Aero Lloyd

Aero Lloyd Flugreisen GmbH is a private airline, set up on 20th December 1980, and which started operations in March 1981 with three SE 210 Caravelle 10Rs. The name harks back to the pioneering time of civil aviation in Germany in the 1920s. At first, charter flights were operated to popular destinations in the Mediterranean. The tour operator Air Charter Market also contributed to the utilisation of the aircraft, and has been a shareholder in the airline over the years. From May to July 1982 a DC-9-32 was in service. The company entered an expansion phase from 1986, when the first MD-80 was introduced. Over the years up to 22 MD-82/83/87s were used. In addition to charter flights, these have been used on scheduled services, which Aero Lloyd began from Summer 1988. As well as internal German services, there were routes to London, Paris and Zürich. However, Aero Lloyd withdrew from the scheduled market in 1992, after Lufthansa had taken a holding in the airline. The final DC-9-32 left the fleet at the end of 1993 and a pointer to the future was given with the order from Airbus of the A320. The capital structure of the company was also changed, the majority now being held by a bank. The first new Airbus A320, in a new, modern colour scheme, arrived in January 1996 at Aero Lloyd's main Frankfurt base; the airline has a second base at Munich. A changeover to a homogeneous Airbus fleet has been undertaken, with the first of the A321s delivered in 1998, and the process completed by the end of 2000. Whereas in earlier years the airline concentrated on flying from Germany only, more and more flights are being conducted from neighbouring countries. From 2003 Aero Lloyd Austria, a subsidiary, is serving the Austrian market with services from Vienna, Linz and Salzburg.

Routes

Adana, Agadir, Alicante, Almeria, Ankara, Antalya, Araxos, Arrecife, Bergen, Brindisi, Bodrum, Cairo, Calvi, Catania, Chania, Corfu, Dalaman, Dubrovnik, Faro, Fuerteventura, Funchal, Heraklion, Hurghada, Ibiza, Istanbul, Izmir, Jerez, Kalamata, Karpathos, Kavala, Kefalonia, Kos, Lamezia Terme, Las Palmas, Luxor, Malaga, Malta, Monastir, Murcia, Mykonos, Mytilene, Naples, Olbia, Palermo, Palma de Mallorca, Paphos, Preveza, Reuss, Reykjavik, Rhodes, Samos, Santorini, Sharm el Sheik, Skiathos, Split, Tel Aviv, Tenerife, Thessaloniki, Varna, Zakynthos.

Fleet

10 Airbus A320-200
11 Airbus A321-200

McDonnell Douglas MD-83 XA-SXJ (Josef Krauthäuser / Las Vegas)

AEROMEXICO

Paseo de la Reforma 445, 06500 Mexico City
Mexico, Tel. 1334000, Fax. 1334619, E-mail:
info@aeromexico.com, www.aeromexico.com

Three- / Two- letter code	IATA No.	Reg'n prefix	ICAO callsign
AMX / AM	139	XA	Aeromexico

The current Aerovias de Mexico, commonly known as Aeromexico, has been active since 1st October 1988. Its predecessor of the same name, which had its origins going back to 1934, was declared bankrupt by its owners, the Mexican government, at the beginning of 1988 and was compelled to cease operations. A consortium of Mexican business interests acquired control and services re-started to thirty domestic destinations and five cities in the United States. A fleet renewal programme brought the airline back up to acceptable international standards and passenger figures improved steadily. Aeromexico is a shareholder in the country's other national airline, Mexicana and in 1990 also acquired Servicos Aereos Litoral. The company is privately owned, with 25% of the shares held by the Mexican pilots' union. The apparently permanent state of business crisis in Mexico has its effects on the airline's operations; in 1995 routes to Europe were cut back and all the DC-10s sold. At home, increasingly unprofitable domestic routes also had to be abandoned. A financial restructuring in 1995 brought the company back on course. During 1998 services to Europe were recommenced with Madrid and Paris and the fleet was augmented with several Boeing 757s, 767s and MD-80s. There are alliances with Aerocaribe, Aerolitoral, Aeromar, Air France, Delta Air Lines, Mexicana and United Airlines. Aeromexico is also a member of the Skyteam alliance. In association with Delta Airlines and Air France, Aeromexico also serves a freight centre at Paris Charles de Gaulle airport.

Routes

Acapulco, Aguascalientes, Atlanta, Campeche, Cancun, Chicago, Chihuahua, Ciudad Juarez, Ciudad Obregon, Colima, Culiacan, Dallas/Fort Worth, Durango, El Paso, Guadalajara, Guaymas, Guerro Negro, Hermosilio, Houston, Ixtapa, Las Vegas, La Paz, Leon, Lima, Loreto, Los Angeles, Los Mochis, Madrid, Manzanillo, Matamoros, Mazatlan, Merida, Mexicali, Mexico-City, Miami, Monclovia, Monterrey, Morella, New Orleans, Ontario, Orlando, Paris, Phoenix, Puerto Vallarta, Queretaro, Reynosa, Salt Lake City, San Antonio, San Diego, San Jose Cabo, Santiago, Sao Paulo, Tampico,Tijuana, Tucson, Veracruz, Villahermosa.

Fleet

9 Boeing 757-200	30 McDonnell Douglas MD-82/88
5 Boeing 767-200/300	14 McDonnell Douglas MD-87
14 Douglas DC-9-32	

Boeing 727-224 N79749 (Josef Krauthäuser / Miami)

AEROPOSTAL

Avenida Paseo Colon, Torre Polar Oueste, Piso 22
Plaza Venezuela, Caracas 1050, Venezuela
Tel. 058-0212-7086211, Fax. 058-0212-7826323
E-mail: corporativa@aeropostal.com, www.aeropostal.com

Three- / Two- letter code	IATA No.	Reg'n prefix	ICAO callsign
LAV / VH	152	YV	Aeropostal

Still under French influence, the Compagnie Générale Aeropostal was founded in 1930. It was a part of the South American network which the French had built up in several countries on the continent. Following takeover of the company by the national government, the name was changed to Linea Aeropostal Venezolana. At first only regional destinations were served, but from 1953 the leap across the Atlantic was made. Lisbon, Madrid and Rome were served via Bermuda and the Azores. During 1957 Aeropostal grew by taking over TACA of Venezuela and further

expanded its operations to cover the whole of Venezuela, using Douglas DC-3s, Martin 2-0-2s and for the overseas routes Lockheed L-1049 Constellations. After the founding of the national airline VIASA in 1960, all route licences for services outside the country were handed over to VIASA. Aeropostal held 45% of the capital of the new airline and also provided staff. HS-748s and from 1968 Douglas DC-9s were used for the domestic services. More DC-9s were added right up until 1994, when the company filed for bankruptcy. The financial difficulties faced by Venezuela were a negative

influence on the fortunes of all the country's airlines and in Aeropostal's case were to be resolved by a privatisation. The sale to Alas de Venezuela was completed at the end of 1996 and by February 1997 the new, privatised company was flying under the old name. Again DC-9s formed the major part of the fleet, with several leased Airbus A320 and in addition two Airbus A310s were used, as the company profited from the bankruptcy of VIASA. There is close co-operation with Air Europa, including a codeshare to Madrid flown by an Air Europa Boeing 767.

Routes

Aruba, Barbados, Barcelona, Barquisemeto, Bogota, Caracas, Curacao, Guayaquil, Havana, Lima, Maiquetta, Manaus, Maracaibo, Maturin, Miami, Panama City, Porlamar, Port of Spain, Puerto Ordaz, Quito, San Antonio, Santo Domingo, Valencia.

Fleet

6 Boeing 727-200
23 McDonnell-Douglas DC-9/30/50
3 Douglas DC-9-20

7 Douglas DC-9-30
12 Douglas DC-9-50

Boeing 737-6D6 7T-VJT (Martin Kühn / Frankfurt)

AIR ALGERIE

1, Place Maurice Audin, Algiers, Democratic
Republic of Algeria, Tel. 664822, Fax. 610553
E-mail: contact@airalgerie.dz, www.airalgerie.dz

Three- / Two- letter code	IATA No.	Reg'n prefix	ICAO callsign
DAH / AH	124	7T	Air Algerie

The Compagnie Générale de Transport Aérien was created in 1946 while Algeria was still under French rule. It was merged with the Compagnie Air Transport to form the present Air Algerie on 22nd May 1953. Douglas DC-4s and Lockheed Constellations were used on routes including those to Paris and Marseilles. Air Algerie received its first jet equipment, the SE210 Caravelle in December 1959. In 1972 the airline was nationalised and in 1974 the first Airbus A300B4 was taken over from TEA. After the retirement of the Caravelles, the most prevalent types in the fleet were Boeing 727s and 737s, with the first Airbus A310 arriving in 1984. A period of slow growth and fleet renewal took place, marked in 1990 by the delivery of the first Boeing 767, and since then not too much has changed, though some of the older 737s are being replaced now by the new generation models of the same type. Air Algerie undertakes government flying, for instance agricultural work, for which a large number of helicopters and smaller fixed wing aircraft are available. For numerous transport tasks, including services to desert locations, Air Algerie flies the civilianised version of the military Lockheed Hercules freighter. Recent years have been marked by fleet renewal. In May 2002 Air Algerie received the first of five Boeing 737-600s, series -800s having been delivered in the preceding two years. Alliances are being developed with Royal Air Maroc and Tunis Air, the airlines of Algeria's neighbouring countries.

Routes

Adrar, Agades, Algiers, Alicante, Amman, Bamako, Barcelona, Batna, Bechar, Bejaja, Berlin, Biskra, Bordj Badji Mokhtar, Brussels, Cairo, Casablanca, Constantine, Dakar, Damascus, Djanet, El Golela, El Oued, Forli, Frankfurt, Geneva, Ghardaia, Hassi Messaoud, Illizi, In Amenas, In Salah, Istanbul, Jijef, Lille, London, Lyon, Madrid, Marseilles, Mascara, Moscow, Niamey, Nice, Nouakchott, Oran, Ouagadougou, Ouargla, Paris, Prague, Rome, Sharjah, Tamanrasset, Tbessa, Tiaret, Timimoun, Tindouf, Touggourt, Toulouse, Tunis.

Fleet

2 Airbus A310-200	3 Boeing 767-300
11 Boeing 737-200	7 Fokker F.27-400
5 Boeing 737-600	2 Lockheed L-382 Hercules
7 Boeing 737-800	
8 Boeing 727-200	

Boeing 747-200 TF-ABG (Gerhard Schütz / Munich)

AIR ATLANTA ICELANDIC

P.O.Box 80, IS-270 Mosfellsbaer, Iceland
Tel. 5667700, Fax. 5667766
E-mail: admin@airatlanta.is, www.airatlanta.is

Three- / Two- letter code	IATA No.	Reg'n prefix	ICAO callsign
ABD / CC	318	TF	Atlanta

On 10th January 1986 Captain Arngrimur Johannsson and his wife founded Air Atlanta Icelandic as a specialist wet-lease operator, i.e. the provision of aircraft inclusive of crews and other services. The first contract was for the use of a Boeing 707 for Caribbean Airways, flying the route from London to Barbados. In August 1988 a second Boeing 707 was brought into use, this time on behalf of Air Afrique. Under this leasing arrangement, Islamic pilgrims were flown for the first time to Saudi Arabia for the Hadj, a lucrative business where the company became well-established. In May 1991 came the first widebody,

a Lockheed L-1011 TriStar, and two years later the first three Boeing 747s were entered on the Icelandic register. These were employed for several years by Saudia, now Saudi Arabian Airlines. Air Atlanta also started operating its own charter series from 1993 and the fleet continued to expand. Boeing 737-200Fs were brought into use for freight work, and a Boeing 737-300 was used in June 1995 to open up a scheduled service from Iceland to Berlin. The British and African markets proved to be especially profitable for Air Atlanta. The TriStars were used particularly on behalf of British tour operators. The

TF- registered aircraft were seen however over the years in the service of many companies including Air India, Tunis Air, Caledonian or Monarch. During 1999 several of the TriStars and the Boeing 737 were taken out of service and further second-hand Boeing 747-100/200/300s acquired. The remaining L1011s were replaced in 2001 by Boeing 767s. A UK subsidiary was established in 2003 based at Manston. Air Atlanta aircraft fly under wet-lease arrangements for (and in the colours of) Excel Airways, Virgin Atlantic and Iberia.

Routes

As a wet-lease specialist, Air Atlanta's aircraft are to be seen operating schedules or charters for other airlines. On its own account, the company operates only some charter series from Iceland to the Mediterranean and Canary Isles.

Fleet

 1 Boeing 747-100
15 Boeing 747-200
 2 Boeing 747-300
 3 Boeing 757-200
 8 Boeing 767- 200/300

Avro RJ 70 YL-BAN (Author's collection)

AIR BALTIC

Riga Airport, Riga LV1053, Latvia
Tel. 207379, Fax. 207659
E-mail: info@airbaltic.lv, www.airbaltic.lv

Three- / Two- letter code	IATA No.	Reg'n prefix	ICAO callsign
BTI / BT	657	YL	Air Baltic

Baltic International was founded in 1992 by Texan businessmen and Latavio-Latvian Airlines. The independent subsidiary company carries out flights into neighbouring western countries. Alongside Tupolev Tu-134s, a DC-9 was also introduced into the fleet on a loan basis in 1993, but this was substituted by a Boeing 727 from 1995. As the company was not developing satisfactorily, a radical cure was decided upon and in September 1995 Baltic International was merged with Latvian Airlines to create a new national airline Air Baltic. The Latvian government owned the majority, 51% of the capital, with the rest shared by Baltic International USA, SAS and two investment firms. Using a Saab SF 340 a fresh start was made and in Spring 1996 three Avro RJ 70s were received. The Latvian government also promised that the airline would be allowed to take over the routes of Latavio, but the legal processes in this country are not the quickest, and so the dissolution of Latavio did not come about until 1998. In January 1999 SAS took over the shareholding of Baltic International USA. During this year also, three Fokker 50s were introduced to replace the Saab 340s, which had been deemed to be too small, and the last of which left the fleet in 2001. The route network was harmonised with SAS and other partners including Estonian Air and Lufthansa. As well as the scheduled services, various charters are also undertaken.

Routes

From Riga to Frankfurt, Copenhagen, Hamburg, Helsinki, Kiev, London, Stockholm, Tallinn, Vilnius and Warsaw.

Fleet

3 Avro RJ 70
4 Fokker 50

BAe-146-300 D-AWBA (Jan-Alexander Lück / Hamburg)

AIR BERLIN

Flughafen Tegel, 13405 Berlin, Germany,
Tel. 030-41012781, Fax. 030-4132003
E-mail: info@airberlin.de, www.airberlin.de

Three- / Two- letter code	IATA No.	Reg'n prefix	ICAO callsign
BER / AB	745	D	Air Berlin

Air Berlin USA was set up in July 1978 as a wholly-owned subsidiary of the American company Leico. The first charter flights took off from Berlin in April 1979, using a fleet of US-registered Boeing 707s. Until the reunification of Germany on 3rd October 1990, only airlines of the victorious nations from the Second World War were allowed to fly to Berlin. Air Berlin offered charter flights with specific departure times between Berlin and Florida. However, this service, with a stopover in Brussels, was only operated from October 1980 until October 1981. From that time, Air Berlin flew a single Boeing 737-300. A 167-seater

Boeing 737-400 came into service from April 1990, and this variant became the sole type in the growing fleet for several years. After reunification Air Berlin became more active in charter work, and in April 1991 a German company, Air Berlin GmbH & Co Luftverkehr KG was set up to take over the business. Thus registered under German law, it was not restricted to Berlin departures only. From 1994 to1996 the fleet was quickly expanded, and early delivery positions were secured for the for the 'new generation' Boeing 737-800 model. The delivery of the first of these in May 1998 also marked a change in the livery of Air

Berlin's aircraft. 1998 also marked the introduction of the so-called 'shuttle flights', at first to Majorca but which were so successful that other departure and destination airports were added in following years. During 2002 Air Berlin introduced low-cost flights to several destinations such as London, in spite of the escalating competition in this sector, and now offers services from almost all German airports. From early 2003 WDL, with its BAe 146s, was engaged to offer services from Mönchengladbach and Dortmund. The fleet renewal with Boeing 737-800s should be completed by the end of 2003.

Routes

Charter and scheduled flights from 20 German airports to Agadir, Alicante, Almeria, Antalya, Arrecife, Athens, Corfu, Dalaman, Djerba, Faro, Fuerteventura, Funchal, Heraklion, Hurghada, Ibiza, Jerez, Kos, Larnaca, Las Palmas, London, Luxor, Mahon, Malaga, Monastir, Palma de Mallorca, Paphos, Rhodes, Samos, Santa Cruz, Tenerife, Thessaloniki, Zakynthos.

Fleet

31 Boeing 737-800
 5 Boeing 737-400
 2 Boeing 737-700
 3 BAe 146-100/200

McDonnell Douglas MD-81 T9-AAC (Bastian Hilker / Düsseldorf)

AIR BOSNA

Kasindolska 136, 7100 Sarajevo, Bosnia-Herzegovina, Tel. 33-464921, Fax. 33-464829
E-mail: airbosna@bih.net, www.airbosna.ba

Three- / Two- letter code	IATA No.	Reg'n prefix	ICAO callsign
BON / JA	995	T9	Air Bosna

The national carrier of the Republic of Bosnia-Herzegovina was established in 1994. As the country was still embroiled in a civil war, only occasional flights could be undertaken, a Cessna 550 Citation business jet being used for the transportation of government officials and VIPs. In May 1996 it became possible to offer service to Sarajevo for the first time, using a leased Yak-42. At first there were sporadic charters, but from 1997 scheduled services to Sweden, German and Turkey were established. A further Yak-42 was added to the fleet from 1999; however, the Yak was not the preferred type to offer services up to Western standard. In 2001 Air Bosna was in a position to lease an MD-81, a more modern aircraft with which to open up new routes. Two Airbus A319s were ordered from the manufacturer, but the financing has proved to be a difficulty. New routes to Budapest and London were inaugurated in 2003 and a Boeing 737-200 leased in to provide additional capacity. Charter flights are undertaken as well as the scheduled services.

Routes

Amsterdam, Budapest, Düsseldorf, Frankfurt, Istanbul, London-LGW, Mostar, Oslo, Rome, Sarajevo, Stockholm.

Fleet	Ordered
1 McDonnell Douglas MD-81	2 Airbus A319
1 Boeing 737-200	
1 CASA 212	
1 Yakovlev Yak-42	

Avro RJ 85 OH-SAH (Author's collection)

AIR BOTNIA

P.O. Box 168, 01531 Vantaa, Finland
Tel. 358 20585 6000, Fax. 358 20585 6001
E-mail: airbotnia@sas.se, www.airbotnia.fn

Three- / Two- letter code	IATA No.	Reg'n prefix	ICAO callsign
KFB / KF	142	OH	Botnia

Air Botnia was founded in 1988 in Seinäjokige. A Cessna 402 and an Embraer 120 Bandeirante were used to commence service from Helsinki during 1989, during which year a further Embraer 120 was acquired and additional Finnish domestic routes established. Between 1993 and 1995 the earlier fleet was exchanged for five Jetstream 32s. After ten years of successful growth, in 1998 SAS-Scandinavian Airlines acquired all of the shares in Air Botnia. The fleet was completely changed over to five Saab 340s, and additionally the Fokker F.28 was acquired, the airline's first jet type.The F.28

enabled services to the Scandinavian capitals, Oslo, Stockholm and Copenhagen, to be undertaken. Also, on routes which SAS's own aircraft could not operate optimally, Air Botnia's more economical aircraft were used. Air Botnia was set up as a regional airline, with the principal objective of delivering passengers from the Finnish market into SAS hubs. To do this, Air Botnia benefitted from operational and logistical support from SAS, particularly through booking and codeshare arrangements. During 2001 the fleet was again completely renewed; Saab 200s replaced the smaller

Saab 340s and in place of the Fokker 28s, the Avro RJ 85 was brought into service. The first route outside Scandinavia, to Brussels from Helsinki, was started in 2002. Air Botnia is planned to become an all-jet airline and in August 2003 agreed to take the last four Avro RJs built; the two RJ85s and two RJ100s had been stored awaiting a customer since production ceased and are now to be delivered in November 2003.

Routes

Brussels, Copenhagen, Düsseldorf, Gothenburg, Helsinki, Oslo, Oulu, Stockholm, Tampere, Turku, Vasa.

Fleet

5 Avro RJ 85
5 Saab 2000

ATR 42 A2-ABB (Bastian Hilker / Harare)

AIR BOTSWANA

P.O.Box 92, Gabarone, Botswana
Tel. 267-352812, Fax. 267-374802
www.airbotswana.co.bw

Three- / Two- letter code	IATA No.	Reg'n prefix	ICAO callsign
BOT / BP	636	A2	Botswana

Air Botswana was set up as the national airline by a presidential decree of July 1972. After Botswana National Airways (1966-1969) and Botswana Airways (1969-1972), Air Botswana took over operations on 1st August 1972 with Fokker F.27s and Britten-Norman Islanders. A fleet renewal programme began in 1988, with the replacement of the F.27s by new ATR 42s. At the end of 1989 Air Botswana received its first jet, a BAe 146-100. There is close co-operation with Air Zimbabwe and for several routes a joint venture agreement is in place. In a dramatic incident in October 1999, the airline's whole fleet of three ATR 42s was destroyed, when the pilot of one of these aircraft committed suicide by crashing his aircraft onto the other two which were on the ground. Services were maintained using leased aircraft, with three replacement ATR 42-500s being delivered as replacements before the end of 1999. These ATRs were then purchased in 2001. As a result of domestic political crisis in neighbouring Zimbabwe resulting a a drop in tourism, Air Botswana has been afflicted by a reduction in services and is orienting itself more towards South Africa. In the long term, a privatisation of the state-owned airline is being considered.

Routes

Domestic routes from Gabarone to Francistown, Kasane, Limpopo, Maun, Maputo, Maseru. Internationally Harare, Johannesburg, Luanda, Victoria Falls and Lusaka are served.

Fleet

3 ATR 42-500
1 BAe 146-100

Airbus A319-114 C-FYKC (Daniel Klein / Toronto)

AIR CANADA

Place Air Canada Montreal, Quebec H2Z 1X5
Canada, Tel. 514-4225000, Fax. 514-4227741
E-mail: contact@aircanada.ca, www.aircanada.ca

Three- / Two- letter code	IATA No.	Reg'n prefix	ICAO callsign
ACA / AC	014	C	Air Canada

The Canadian government set up Trans-Canada Airlines (TCA) on 10th April 1937;it was administered by Canadian National Railways (CNR). Service began on 1st September between Vancouver and Seattle, with a Lockheed 10A. The build-up of an internal network was TCA's primary concern in the following years. April 1939 saw the first Vancouver-Montreal flight, and shortly afterwards TCA flew from Montreal to New York. During the war, regular service was provided from Canada to Scotland using converted Lancaster bombers. Post-war the DC-3, the Constellation, Canadair North Star, Bristol 170,

Vickers Viscount and Vickers Vanguard were all used. On 1st April 1960 the first jet, a DC-8 entered the fleet. During 1964 the name Air Canada was adopted, and in 1967 the DC-9 was added. Air Canada expanded worldwide and introduced its first widebody in 1971 – the Boeing 747. Lockheed TriStars were also added, being replaced by the Boeing 767. During 1988 a partial privatisation took place. Acquisition of the Airbus A320 from early 1990 continued the fleet renewal and marked the introduction of a new colour scheme. Newest types in the long-range fleet are the Airbus A340, used for Asian routes since 1994,

and the A330, which have largely replaced the 747s. Air Canada is closely associated with Continental Airlines in the USA. At the end of 1999, Air Canada, with support from Star Alliance partners, took over Canadian Airlines. The regional subsidiaries, Air BC, Air Ontario, Air Alliance, Air Nova, NWT-Air, and those of Canadian have all been merged in 2002 to form an independent operation, Jazz. Air Canada was particularly badly affected by the events of 11 September 2001 and the Iraq war, with staff and fleet reductions. On 1st April 2003 the airline entered bankruptcy protection.

Routes

Extensive route network in Canada, USA and the Caribbean, plus routes to Europe and Asia.

Fleet

48 Airbus A319	58 Boeing 767-200/300
52 Airbus A320	3 Boeing 747-200
15 Airbus A321	4 Boeing 747-400
8 Airbus A330	25 Canadair CRJ100ER
12 Airbus A340	20 Douglas DC-9-32

BAe 146-200A C-GRNV (Thomas Kim / Toronto)

AIR CANADA JAZZ

310 Goudey Drive, Halifax Intl. Airport, Enfield
Nova Scotia, B2T 1E4, Tel. 902-8735000
Fax. 902-8734901, www.flyjazz.ca

Three- / Two- letter code	IATA No.	Reg'n prefix	ICAO callsign
JZA / QK	983	C	Transcan

In January 2001, Air BC, Air Ontario, Air Nova and Canadian Regional Airlines were all merged into Air Canada Regional. The reorganisation of the whole Air Canada group had become necessary following the takeover of Canadian Airlines during 1999. The two airlines, who had previously been engaged in close competition, both had extensive regional networks, with smaller companies engaged as partner airlines. In some cases Air Canada or Canadian Airlines had at some time taken financial interests in these partners or acquired them completely. Air BC came into being in 1980 as a result of amalgamation of some smaller operators on the Canadian west coast. From 1988 it became an Air Canada Partner and in the mid-1990s Air Canada took complete ownership. Air Ontario originated from the province of that name and came into being in 1987 from the amalgamation of Austin Airways and Air Ontario Ltd, formerly Great Lakes Airlines. Air Ontario operated principally from the convenient Toronto Island Airport to destinations in the region and the neighbouring USA. Likewise Air Ontario became a 100% subsidiary of Air Canada. Air Nova began service with three DHC-8-100s in 1986, based at Halifax and concentrating its services in the north east of Canada. In 1991 it took over Air Alliance and became one of the largest of the Canadian regional carriers. Canadian Regional Airlines came into being in 1991 with the merger of several companies who had until then flown on behalf of Canadian Pacific or Pacific Western. After the fusion of all four of these constituent companies had been achieved in 2002, the new name of Air Canada Jazz was adopted. Many of the aircraft are still in their 'old' colours, with repaint to be undertaken over time.

Routes

Jazz serves more than 70 regional and smaller destinations in Canada and the neighbouring US states.

Fleet

10 BAe 146-200
10 Canadair Regional Jet
52 De Havilland DHC-8-100
26 De Havilland DHC-8-300

Boeing 737- 89L B-2643 (Jan Alexander Lück / Beijing)

AIR CHINA

100621 Capital Intl. Airport, Beijing
People's Republic of China, Tel. 1-4563220
Fax. 1-4563348, www.airchina.com

Three- / Two- letter code	IATA No.	Reg'n prefix	ICAO callsign
CCA / CA	999	B	Air China

Air China International was set up by the Civil Aviation Administration of China (CAAC) in July 1988 as an independent division, responsible for operating international services. Some aircraft were painted with Air China titling, but others were loaned from CAAC as required. New routes were added from the end of 1992 to Vienna, freight services to Los Angeles and in 1993 to Copenhagen. The fleet and route network are continually expanding. Thus in 1997 Airbus A340 and in 1998 Boeing 777s were acquired to replace older Boeing 747/747SPs. A significant

new service approved in mid-1997 following the handover by Britain of Hong Kong to China was a direct service from Hong Kong to London, the first by a mainland Chinese airline, and in direct competition with the established carrier Cathay Pacific. The delivery of the first of the new generation Boeing 737-800s in April 1999 was a noteworthy marker in the renewal of the short and medium-haul fleet, and at the turn of the millennium the older 747s were phased out, replaced by 747-400s. Air China works closely with Ariana, Austrian, Finnair, Korean Airlines

and Tarom and, likewise, there is a code-share agreement in place with Northwest since May 1998. Along with Lufthansa, the airline also has a shareholding in the Ameco maintenance organisation in Beijing. The Chinese authorities have indicated that they wish to see a consolidation of the country's now diverse airlines, and Air China is one of the airlines designated to lead one of three major groups; the Air China Group will encompass China Southwest Airlines and the China National Aviation Corporation and should be fully merged by 2005.

Routes

Anchorage, Atlanta, Bangkok, Chicago, Copenhagen, Frankfurt, Fukuoka, Hiroshima, Ho Chi Minh City, Hong Kong, Karachi, Kuwait, London, Los Angeles, Melbourne, Milan, Moscow, Osaka, Paris, Rome, San Francisco, Seoul, Singapore, Stockholm, Sydney, Tokyo, Ulaanbataar, Vancouver, Vienna, Zürich, plus over 50 Chinese domestic destinations.

Fleet

1 Airbus A319
3 Airbus A340-300
4 BAe 146-100
10 Boeing 777
16 Boeing 747-400

22 Boeing 737-300
4 Boeing 737-700
12 Boeing 737-800
9 Boeing 767-200/300ER

Ordered

6 Boeing 737-700
7 Airbus A319

Boeing 727-200 EI-HCC (Author's collection)

AIR CONTRACTORS

The Plaza, New Street, Swords Co, Dublin, Ireland
Tel. 353-18121900, Fax. 353-18121919, E-mail:
info@aircontractors.com, www.aircontractors.com

Three- / Two- letter code	IATA No.	Reg'n prefix	ICAO callsign
ABR / AG	914	EI	Contract

The origins of this airline can be traced back to 1972, when Air Bridge Carriers was set up at East Midlands Airport. Operations began with regular flights from East Midlands to the Channel Islands using Argosy 102 freighters, which carried fresh vegetables, fruit and newspapers, plus general freight. The fleet grew to four Argosies, but then in 1976 ABC received its first Vickers Vanguard freighter and increased its scope of operations. Non-stop flights to the Middle East became possible. A second Vanguard was added in 1979. Air Bridge Carriers was at the forefront of operators at the beginning of the development of

overnight express services in Europe, flying during the early 1980s for TNT, Federal Express or UPS throughout Europe. Capacity was augmented by the acquisition of Boeing 727s and Lockheed Electras. During 1992 the company name was changed to Hunting Cargo Airlines, as the parent Hunting Group repositioned some of its subsidiaries, and as a further part of this re-organisation, the operating base and headquarters were moved to Ireland. A new era was marked by the introduction of the first Airbus A300-B4 freighter. In 1998 Compagnie Maritime Belge (51%) and Safair (49%) acquired all the

shares, as the Hunting Group divested itself of its air transport activities, and the name was changed again, this time to Air Contractors. South African-based Safair brought in its three Hercules and the Brussels and East Midlands hubs were further developed. One of the L-100 Hercules is specially equipped and stands ready for worldwide oilspill operations. From 2001 further Airbus A300s were added, and fly mostly on overnight work for DHL and FedEx. An ATR 42 was acquired late in 2002, enabling the company to offer a smaller aircraft where required.

Routes

Principally, from its hubs at Brussels and East Midlands, package flights within Europe on behalf of DHL or FedEx, plus worldwide ad hoc charters.

Fleet

3 Airbus A 300-B4
1 ATR 72
3 Boeing 727-200
2 Lockheed L-100 Hercules

Canadair CRJ200LR I-ADJA (Josef Krauthäuser / Munich)

AIR DOLOMITI

Via Aquilera 45, 34077 Ronchi dei Legionari
Trieste, Italy, Tel. 481-474479, Fax. 481-477711
E-mail: service@airdolomiti.it, www.airdolomiti.it

Three- / Two- letter code	IATA No.	Reg'n prefix	ICAO callsign
DLA / EN	101	I	Dolomiti

Established in January 1988, Air Dolomiti started operations in May 1991 with a de Havilland Canada Dash 8 on the Trieste-Genoa route. Further Italian domestic services were added quickly. From November 1992 Air Dolomiti flew its first international route, from Verona to Munich. Verona developed into a minor hub for the company, with numerous connecting flights. With the acquisition of the ATR 42 from 1994, the Dash 8s left the fleet, and a new colour scheme was adopted. The airline has worked closely with Lufthansa since 1995 in sales and marketing and is a Lufthansa Partner, with several joint flights.

Thus Munich has developed as the most important airport for Air Dolomiti, and passengers from northern Italy have connections here to Lufthansa services. More direct flights were offered and, in order to provide these, the ATR 42 fleet was steadily increased in size. In addition, since 1996 the airline has had an alliance with the Swiss airline Crossair, and the Basle-Rome service is operated jointly. Seasonal and charter flights are operated as well as schedules to Italian holiday regions and to Sardinia. With the introduction of the larger, 64-seater, ATR 72 in 1998, Air Dolomiti not only took the opportunity to upgrade the

interior of their aircraft, but also adopted a new colour scheme. More ATR 42-500s, with more powerful and yet quieter engines have also augmented the fleet over recent years, and the airline's first jet type, the Canadair Regional Jet 200 was added from March 2001 for the longer routes. The airline has its own maintenance facility.

Routes

Amsterdam, Alghero, Ancona, Bari, Barcelona, Berlin, Bologna, Brussels, Cagliari, Corfu, Florence, Frankfurt, Geneva, Genoa, Madrid, Milan, Munich, Naples, Olbia, Paris, Pisa, Trieste, Tortoli, Turin,Venice, Verona, Vienna.

Fleet	Ordered
10 ATR 42-500	2 ATR 72-500
7 ATR 72-500	1 Canadair CRJ200
5 Canadair CRJ200	

Boeing 767-3Q8 EC-HKS (Hans-Willi Mertens / Madrid)

AIR EUROPA

Gran Via Asima 23, 07009 Palma de Mallorca
Spain, Tel. 178111, Fax. 431500,
www.g-air-europa.es

Three- / Two- letter code	IATA No.	Reg'n prefix	ICAO callsign
AEA / UX	996	EC	Air Europa

Air Europa is one of the profitable remainders of the former multinational organisation Air Europe, and was set up in June 1986 on the island of Majorca. The airline, registered as Air Espana SA, was at formation 75% owned by two Spanish banks and 25% by the British company ILG, until the time of the latter's failure in 1991. It started flights on 21st November 1986 with a Boeing 737-300. The first flight was from London-Gatwick to Palma de Mallorca, which is also Air Europa's base. Air Europe and Air Europa had an identical livery and fleet of Boeing 737s and 757s with aircraft switched between the carriers to meet their needs at different times of the year. After the failure of its British partner, several tour companies and banks took over Air Europa's shares, enabling operations to continue. During 1991 Air Europa acquired three Boeing 757-200s for use on long-range routes. Boeing 767s were used briefly during 1994/5 but these larger aircraft were found to be inflexible in their operation and they were exchanged for more Boeing 757s. Since 1995 Air Europa has found success as a scheduled service operator, initially in competition with Iberia and from 1998 as a franchise partner.

Additionally, the 767 has returned to the fleet, operating long-range routes on behalf of Iberia, to whom several 757s are also leased. The airline's own regional carrier, Air Europa Express, was established in 1996, and this operated principally to the Balearics. A takeover of Air Europa by Iberia failed in January 2001, and later in that year the route network was radically changed and the Air Europa Express operation terminated.The Boeing 737 has always formed an important part of Air Europa's fleet, and these have been updated over the past years with the delivery of the new generation -800 series.

Routes

Alicante, Arrecife, Asturias, Athens, Barcelona, Bilbao, Caracas, Geneva, Granada, Havana, Ibiza, Las Palmas, London, Madrid, Malaga, Milan, Naples, New York, Palma de Mallorca, Paris, Punta Cana, Santiago de Compostella, Santo Domingo, Seville, Tenerife, Valencia, Valladolid, Vigo, Zaragoza, Zürich.

Fleet

2 Boeing 737-300
5 Boeing 737-400
3 Boeing 737-600
15 Boeing 737-800

3 Boeing 767-300

Boeing 737-230C PK-OCI (Author's collection)

AIRFAST INDONESIA

Kuningan Plaza, Menara Utara 305 Jl HR Rasuna Said
Kav, C11-14 Djakarta, Indonesia
Tel. 6221-5200696, Fax. 6221-5202557
E-mail: charter@airfast.co.id, www.airfastindonesia.com

Three- / Two- letter code	IATA No.	Reg'n prefix	ICAO callsign
AFE	–	PK	Airfast

Set up in 1971 as a joint venture between Indonesia and Australia, with the objective of offering passenger and cargo charters for the oil industry in Southeast Asia, flights started with Douglas DC-3s. As well as serving Indonesia the airline was also active in Malaysia, Papua-New Guinea, South Korea, the Philippines and in the Near East. Fokker F.27s and various light aircraft were used for services to the many small Indonesian islands. From 1982 the company was in private Indonesian ownership and in addition to its original remit, additional tasks such as offshore flights to oil rigs, aerial photography and earth resource survey flights were undertaken. Additionally there were all sorts of other special flights such as aerial logging and other heavy lift jobs with helicopters. Air rescue and medical care flights have also been taken over from the government. The main base is Jakarta, but there are others in Singapore and Kalimantan. The Indonesian business crisis which came during the late 1990s did not seem to affect Airfast unduly; indeed the company benefited in some areas from the fall in competition and the reduced activities of other companies. The passenger services were notably profitable. The fleet has however shrunk somewhat, with the retirement of several aircraft and helicopters, and the last remaining DC-3 was replaced by a Beech Queen Air.

Routes

Passenger and freight services for companies and undertakings within Indonesia, to Singapore, Malaysia, the whole South East Asian area and Australia.

Fleet

1 BAe HS-748	2 Bell 412
1 Beech Queen Air	3 Boeing 737-200
2 Bell 204	1 CASA-IPTN 212
4 Bell 206	3 de Havilland DHC-6 Twin Otter
3 Bell 212	1 Sikorsky S-58

Airbus A320-111 F-GFKE (Daniel Klein / Düsseldorf)

AIR FRANCE

45 rue de Paris, 95747 Roissy, France
Tel. 1-41567800, Fax. 1-41567029
E-mail: info@airfrance.fr, www.airfrance.fr

Three- / Two- letter code	IATA No.	Reg'n prefix	ICAO callsign
AFR / AF	057	F	Airfrans

On 30th August 1933 Air Orient, Air Union, CIDNA and SGTA merged to form the national airline Air France. By the outbreak of war, Air France had a leading position in Europe and North Africa, and operated to all France's colonies including Indochina. Post-war nationalisation saw Air France make a new start in 1946, initially using mainly French-built types such as the Breguet 763 and SE 161. In 1953 came the first jet, the Comet. More British aircraft, Vickers Viscounts, took over short and medium length routes, while long range routes were served by DC-4s and Lockheed Constellations. On 26th May 1959 the successful SE 210 Caravelle saw its first service with Air France. Boeing 707s and 747s replaced propeller-driven types on intercontinental routes. From May 1974 the Airbus A300 was used for the first time between Paris and London, and from 21st January 1976 Concorde was licensed for scheduled services. Naturally, the airline has been a strong supporter of Airbus, and though Boeing has a strong representation in the fleet, all of the Airbus products are used in significant numbers. The operations, routes and aircraft of Aéromaritime and UTA were integrated into Air France in 1992. By the mid 1990s the Air France Group was in deep crisis and restructuring was necessary; this led to a part privatisation. Air France has shareholdings in many other airlines and alliances with regional airlines operating for Air France as franchise partners. In September 1999 Air France joined Delta Airlines in founding the global Skyteam alliance. The most recent types introduced into the fleet are the A319 (1997), A321 (1997), A330 (2002) and Boeing 777 (1998), with Airbus A318s scheduled for delivery from 2003. The end for the prestigious Concorde came in 2003, but Air France is one of the first to order the new Airbus 380 widebody.

Routes

Air France has a worldwide route serving over 160 destinations, notably in former French colonies and overseas provinces. In Europe all major cities are served, many in association with franchise partners.

Fleet		Ordered
40 Airbus A319-100	33 Boeing 737-300/500	15 Airbus A318
62 Airbus A320-100/200	19 Boeing 747-200/400	10 Airbus A380-800
17 Airbus A321-100/200	5 Boeing 767-300ER	8 Airbus A330-300
14 Airbus A330-200	25 Boeing 777-200ER	15 Boeing 777-300
22 Airbus A340-200/300		

Boeing 767-266(ER) TR-LFH (Author's collection)

AIR GABON

B.P. 2206, Libreville
Gabon
Tel. 733018, Fax. 731156

Three- / Two- letter code	IATA No.	Reg'n prefix	ICAO callsign
AGN / GN	185	TR	Golf November

Formed in 1951 as Compagnie Aérienne Gabonaise, the airline began local services from Libreville with Beech and de Havilland aircraft. The airline was a founder member of Air Afrique and was a member of the consortium from 1961 to 1977. Though operating internationally through Air Afrique, Air Gabon always operated domestic services on its own account. In 1974 it acquired its first Fokker F.28, followed by another aircraft of the same type and a Boeing 737 in 1978. After leaving Air Afrique, Air Gabon obtained a Boeing 747-200 in late 1978 for use on scheduled services to Europe. During 1988 the airline underwent a reorganisation, which entailed a tightening up of the route network. A Fokker 100 was taken on in 1990, but traffic growth on its routes meant that in 1993 this would be exchanged for a Boeing 727. A Boeing 767 has also been leased, initially in 1996, to supplement the 747 on long-range routes, which now include London. For freight services an Antonov An-12 and Lockheed Hercules have been leased for a time. Air France is a 20% shareholder (the other 80% being held by the government), hence there is close co-operation. For the moment some of the older aircraft, including the F.28s, are stored and newer Boeings leased, while discussions take place between the government and Boeing for the wholesale renewal of the fleet with Boeing 747-400, 767-300 and Boeing 737-800s.

Routes

Abidjan, Bamako, Bangui, Bitam, Conakry, Cotonou, Dakar, Douala, Dubai, Fougamou, Franceville, Gamva, Johannesburg, Lagos, Lome, London, Luanda, Malabo, Marseilles, Mekambo, Moanda, Nairobi, Nice, Oyem, Paris, Point Noire, Port Gentil, Rome, Sao Tome.

Fleet

2 Boeing 737-200Adv	1 Boeing 747-200
1 Boeing 737-300	1 Boeing 767-200
1 Boeing 737-400	

Airbus A330-223 F-WIHL / OY-GRN (Olaf Jürgensmeier / Lemwerder)

AIR GREENLAND

Nuuk Airport, POB 1012, 3900 Greenland, Denmark, Tel. 299-343434, Fax. 299-327288, E-mail: info@airgreenland.gl, www.airgreenland.dk

Three- / Two- letter code	IATA No.	Reg'n prefix	ICAO callsign
GRL / GL	631	OY	Greenlandair

Groenlandsfly was founded in 1960 to ensure air services to the Arctic island of Greenland, a province of Denmark, much larger than its motherland yet sparsely populated. Shares in the company were taken by the government, Royal Greenland Trading, Kryolit Mining Co. and the state airline SAS. Initially a Douglas DC-4 was used for reconnaissance of the ice fields, and this was also available for transport tasks as required. For other tasks, PBY Catalinas were leased, as there were few airfields on Greenland and these could take to the water to reach some settlements. Godthaab (now known as Nuuk) and Sondre

Stromfjord were the only made-up airfields, also used for military purposes by NATO. The use of a number of helicopters appeared to be a suitable answer for the needs of some settlements.Though more costly to operate than fixed-wing aircraft, they are not dependent on airfields. Also especially suited were the de Havilland Canada DHC-6 Twin Otter and DHC-7 with their exceptional take-off and landing abilities; they could use short runways which may have loose gravel, or be covered in ice during Winter. Groenlandsfly's tasks cannot be compared with those of conventional airlines. In addition to

numerous smaller helicopters, 25-seat Sikorsky S.61s form part of the fleet and are an important asset for passenger transport. Ambulance, rescue and reconnaissance flights are all important duties of the airline. During 1998 a Boeing 757 was acquired and is used for holiday flights to Greenland, but also from Greenland to the USA, Canada and to Europe. This was supplemented in 2002 by an Airbus A330, at which time the new name Air Greenland and a new colour scheme were adopted.

Routes

Aasiaat, Alluitsup Paa, Copenhagen, Groennedaal, Ilulissat, Kangerlussuaq, Kulusuk, Maniitsoq, Nanortalik, Narsaq, Narsasuaq, Neerlerit Inaat, Nuuk, Paamiut, Pituffik, Qaarsut, Qaqortoq, Qasigiannguit, Qeqertarsuaq, Reykjavik, Sisimiut, Upernavik, Uummannaq are all served on a scheduled basis. Charter flights to the USA, as far as Florida, to Canada and the Mediterranean.

Fleet

1 Airbus A330-200
2 De Havilland DHC-6 Twin Otter 300
6 De Havilland DHC-7 Dash 7

1 Boeing 757-200

Boeing 747-437 VT-EVB (Ken Petersen / New York-JFK)

AIR INDIA

Air India Bldg. 218 Backbay Rec. Nairnam Point, Mumbai 40021, India, Tel. 022-2024142, Fax. 022-2024897
E-mail: info@airindia.com, www.airindia.com

Three- / Two- letter code	IATA No.	Reg'n prefix	ICAO callsign
AIC / AI	098	VT	Airindia

Air India's history can be traced back to July 1932 when Tata Sons Ltd operated a mail service between Bombay, Madras and Karachi using de Havilland Puss Moths. The name was changed to Tata Airlines in 1938 and to Air India on 29th July 1946, after independence. Regular flights to London via Cairo and Geneva commenced in 1948 with Lockheed Constellations. During 1953 all Indian air services were placed under state control. On 18th February 1960 Air India received its first Boeing 707, which was used to fly via Europe to New York. The first widebody, the Boeing 747, was delivered in 1971, and the type was used on services to London, Frankfurt and New York. Since August 1980 Air India has also been an Airbus operator, with the A300 replacing the Boeing 707s. 1989 was the year when India's flag carrier was restructured, with the aircraft being given a more modern colour scheme. At the end of 1993 Air India received its first Boeing 747-400, but notably in the 'old' colour scheme, as the new one was disliked by customers. Drastic cost-cutting measures at the end of the century led Air India to a reduction in size and the abandonment of several routes, including those to Frankfurt and Rome and to a reduction in the aircraft fleet. The long-awaited part privatisation has been pushed back more and more. Air India has a shareholding in Air Mauritius of just 3%, and is not a member of any of the major alliances. However, the airline co-operates with Air France, Air Mauritius, Malaysia Airlines and SAS, Singapore Airlines and other operators.

Routes

Abu Dhabi, Ahmedabad, Amritsar, Bahrain, Bangalore, Bangkok, Chennai, Chicago, Dar-es-Salaam, Delhi, Dharan, Doha, Dubai, Frankfurt, Goa, Hong Kong, Hyderabad, Jeddah, Kolkota, Kuala Lumpur, Kuwait, London, Mauritius, Moscow, Mumbai, Muscat, Nairobi, New York, Osaka, Paris, Riyadh, Singapore, Sydney and Tokyo.

Fleet

17 Airbus A310-300
 2 Boeing 747-300
 4 Boeing 747-200
 7 Boeing 747-400

Airbus A321-211 6Y-JMH (Stefan Schlick / Montego Bay)

AIR JAMAICA

72-76 Harbour Street, Kingston, Jamaica
Tel. 809-9223460, Fax. 809-9220107, E-mail:
info@airjamaica.com, www.airjamaica.com

Three- / Two- letter code	IATA No.	Reg'n prefix	ICAO callsign
AJM / JM	201	6Y	Juliett Mike

Air Jamaica was established by the government of the island nation (60% share), together with Air Canada (40%) in October 1968. It succeeded an earlier company of the same name established with the help of BOAC and BWIA in 1962 and which had operated a Kingston-New York service with leased aircraft since 1965. Using a DC-9 leased from Air Canada, who provided technical support, the new company started flights to Miami on 1st April 1969 and with a DC-8, likewise from Air Canada, to New York. From 1974 London became the sole European destination in the timetable, but this was discontinued after a few years.

The DC-8 proved too large for the company's needs and in 1983 was replaced by the Airbus A300. These were used for flights to the USA and Canada. Boeing 727s were used for short and medium haul routes in the Caribbean. The long-awaited privatisation finally came about in May 1994, with the government disposing of 75% of the shares. The subsequent reorganisation brought with it a new colour scheme and new aircraft. The London service was re-opened in 1996 using the Airbus A310 and during 1999 turned over to the more modern Airbus A340. Regional services were taken over in 1996 by a newly-established

100% owned subsidiary company. Air Jamaica Express flies Dornier 228s and de Havilland Canada Dash 8s to the island airports. With the delivery of new Airbus A320 and A321s in 1999, the last Boeing 727s and MD-80s were retired, giving Air Jamaica a modern all-Airbus fleet. There are co-operation agreements with Air Canada and Delta Air Lines and over the last two or three years routes to Canada and the USA have been notably increased, but Europe is also becoming increasingly important.

Routes

Atlanta, Baltimore, Barbados, Bonaire, Boston, Chicago,Curacao, Fort Lauderdale,Grand Cayman, Grenada, Havana, Houston, Kingston, London, Los Angeles, Manchester, Miami, Montego Bay, Nassau, Negril, New York, Ochos Rios, Orlando, Philadelphia, Port Antonio, Port au Prince, Santo Domingo, St. Lucia, Toronto.

Fleet

```
 4 Airbus A310-300
 3 Airbus A340-300
11 Airbus A320-200
 6 Airbus A321-200
```

Airbus A310-322 UN-A3101 (Author's collection)

AIR KAZAKSTAN

Ul Ogareva 14, Almaty 480079, Kazakstan
Tel. 3272-570116, Fax. 3272-572503
E-mail: mail@airkaz.com, www.airkaz.com

Three- / Two- letter code	IATA No.	Reg'n prefix	ICAO callsign
KZK / 9Y	452	UN	Air Kazakstan

State-owned Air Kazakstan emerged in 1996 from Kazakstan Airlines, which, likewise state-owned, had become bankrupt and was practically reorganised. Following independence from the former Soviet Union, Aeroflot's regional directorate was dissolved and about 15 new airlines set up, of which Kazakstan Airlines was the largest, and was recognized as the flag carrier of the new state. Numerous activities in both scheduled and charter work made the airline a candidate for its first Western aircraft types. Thus Boeing 757s, Boeing 747SPs and Boeing 767s all came into service, with the hope that passengers from Western Europe would make Almaty a hub for onward flights within Asia. After a few years, both the country and the airline faced financial crisis. Kazakstan Airlines was in practice dissolved, the leasing contracts for Western types terminated, the route network, aircraft fleet and employee numbers all drastically reduced. Consolidation was deemed to be an important aim, in order to prepare the airline for a partial privatisation. The country's leading bank took over half of the shares from the government and from the beginning of 2000 two Airbus A310s were leased again. Boeing 737-200s were also acquired to replace the oldest of the Tupolev Tu-134s and -154s. The Ilyushin 86s are mostly stored out of use.

Routes

Aktau, Aktyubinsk, Almaty, Astana, Atyrau, Baku, Bangkok, Beijing, Budapest, Delhi, Dubai, Frankfurt, Hanover, Istanbul, Karaganda, Kostanay, Mineralnye Vody, Moscow, Novosibirsk, Seoul, Sharjah, St. Petersburg, Tashkent, Tel Aviv.

Fleet

2 Airbus A310-300	6 Ilyushin IL-86
13 Antonov An-24	2 Tupolev Tu-134
3 Boeing 737-200	9 Tupolev Tu-154
3 Ilyushin IL-76TD	

Tupolev Tu-154 P-552 (Author's collection)

AIR KORYO

Sunan District, Pyongyang,
People's Republic of Korea
Tel. 37917, Fax. 4571, www.airkoryo.com

Three- / Two- letter code	IATA No.	Reg'n prefix	ICAO callsign
KCA / JS	120	P	Airkoryo

Air Koryo, formerly Chosonminhang Korean Airways (CAAK) is the state airline of the Democratic Republic of Korea (North Korea). It was formed in 1954 to succeed SOKAO, the joint Aeroflot – North Korean airline established in 1950, which started with Lisunov Li-2s and operated Ilyushin IL-12s and Antonov An-2s. With the founding of CAAK, the Soviet share of the airline and their aircraft were taken over, with IL-14s and later IL-18s coming into service. As the Soviet Union provided massive support to North Korea, only Soviet aircraft types were used; thus the first jet was a Tupolev Tu-154 delivered in 1975, with further examples following in 1979 and 1982. These were also used on long-range routes, such as to East Berlin or Prague, with intermediate fuel stops being necessary. With the delivery of the Ilyushin IL-62 came an aircraft properly suited to these longer stretches and it was possible to introduce non-stop service from Pyongyang to Moscow. In 1993 came a change, when Choson-minhang became Air Koryo. In addition to passenger services, freight flights are also undertaken, and Air Koryo fulfils other functions on behalf of the state, including responsibility for handling at all the airports in the country. Its main base is at the airport of the capital, Pyongyang. In the Autumn of 1996 a new scheduled service was initiated to Macau, and from 2000 a service to Shenyang appeared in the timetable. An agreement is in place with DHL International for co-operation in the carriage of documents and freight. As a result of lack of funds for replacements, several aircraft have been retired since 2001, with a consequent reduction in the fleet.

Routes

Regular services to Beijing, Macau, Moscow, Shenyang and Vladivostok. Charter flights to Eastern Europe and the former Soviet Union, regional services to Chongsin, Hamhun, Kaesong, Kilchu, Kanggyae, Sinuiju and Wonsan.

Fleet

5 Antonov An-24	2 Tupolev Tu-134B
2 Ilyushin IL-18	4 Tupolev Tu-154B
4 Ilyushin IL-62M	
3 Ilyushin IL-76MD	

ATR 42-500 F-GPYO (Josef Krauthäuser / Munich)

AIR LITTORAL

Le Millenaire II, 417 Rue Samuel Morse, 34961
Cedex 2, Montpellier, France, Tel.+33 467206720
Fax.+33 467641061, www.air-littoral.fr

Three- / Two- letter code	IATA No.	Reg'n prefix	ICAO callsign
LIT / FU	659	F	Air Littoral

Air Littoral was founded in Le Castellet in 1972 as a regional operator, beginning operations with two Britten-Norman Islanders from Montpellier to Nice. Air Littoral was also active on the island of Corsica, with several regional routes there. In 1976 the headquarters was moved to Montpellier and in 1981 the airline became the first regional carrier to establish a connection to Italy. For this service the Fokker F.27 was used. Besides that, the fleet now consisted of Beechcraft 1900s, Embraer 110s and Nord 262s. In 1985 Air Littoral became the world's first regional operator to introduce the new ATR 42, using it for a route

from Beziers to Paris. A merger in 1987 with Compagnie Aérienne du Languedoc brought about an increase in routes, aircraft and personnel. 1990 saw the company's first jet, the Fokker 100, and KLM came on the scene as an investor. The first Canadair Regional Jet's arrival in 1993 saw the retirement of the older propeller-driven types and the addition of further routes to Germany and Spain. This led in 1995 to the setting up of the first hub operation at Montpellier with a second later added at Nice. Further expansion came in 1998, when the SAir Group took over the KLM shareholding and codeshare

arrangements were put in place with Swissair and Sabena. However, this did not bring about the expected success and Air Littoral was caught up in SAir's deep financial troubles in 2000. A merger, planned by SAir, with Air Liberté and AOM to create the second largest airline in France, failed. New investors during 2001 provided an exit from the SAir group, and the fleet was rationalised around the Fokker 70, Canadair Regional Jet and ATR 42, but receivers were called in in August 2003 and a takeover is sought. There are partnership agreements with Air Algerie, Air One, Lufthansa, Spanair and Alpieagles.

Routes

Ajaccio, Algiers, Barcelona, Bastia, Beziers, Bologna, Bordeaux, Calvi, Figari, Florence, Lille, Lyon, Madrid, Marseilles, Montpellier, Munich, Nantes, Naples, Nice, Nimes, Paris, Rome, Strasbourg, Toulouse, Venice, Zürich.

Fleet

10 ATR 42-500
17 Canadair CRJ100
 5 Fokker 70

Lockheed L-1011 TriStar 500 CS-TMP (Martin Kühn / Palma de Mallorca)

AIR LUXOR

Air Luxor Plaza, Av.da Republica 101 Lisbon, Portugal, Tel. 1-210026890, Fax. 1-210026888
www.airluxor.com

Three- / Two- letter code	IATA No.	Reg'n prefix	ICAO callsign
LXR / LK	040	CS	Air Luxor

Established by the Mirpuri Group in 1988, Air Luxor was initially engaged in executive transport, and later in courier and air ambulance services. In 1997 a third string was added to the bow – holiday and charter flights. A Lockheed L-1011-500 TriStar was used amongst other things for regular charters to Macau. Other principal destinations were Paris, Lisbon and Faro, the USA and the Cape Verde Islands, with some of these points being converted to scheduled services from 1999. As the TriStar was too large and inflexible for some of these routes, Air Luxor took on a single Airbus A320. Thus the airline was in a much better position to compete in the European market, and during the summer months many more charter series were operated to Faro or Funchal. Air Luxor is now one of the few remaining users of the TriStar, and a Boeing 767 has been added as a long-term replacement type, though an Airbus A330 has been leased in from December 2002, with a second in use for the 2003 summer season. Air Luxor GB was set up during 2003 as a separate division based in Guinea-Bissau using an A320. As well as the regular charters, Air Luxor specialises in ad hoc and freight charters worldwide, and the executive jet activity continues, principally using Dassault Falcons, Raytheon Hawkers and Cessna Citation Vs.

Routes

Lisbon, Faro, Funchal, Paris, Sal; further ad hoc passenger and freight charters.

Fleet

6 Airbus A320
1 Airbus A330-300
1 Boeing 767-200ER
1 Lockheed L-1011-500

Airbus A319-132 B-MAL (Jan Alexander Lück / Hamburg)

AIR MACAU

P.O.Box 1910, Macau, China
Tel. 3966888, Fax. 396866,
www.airmacau.com.mo

Three- / Two- letter code	IATA No.	Reg'n prefix	ICAO callsign
AMU / NX	675	B-M	Air Macau

The first Airbus A321 for Air Macau landed on 5th November 1995 at the new airport at Macau, the Portuguese colony on China's doorstep. The official opening of the airport followed on 8th December with the handover of the aircraft to Air Macau. The airline had been formed a year earlier, in October 1994, and belongs to the predominantly Chinese Macon Aviation Services Company (MASC), which in turn is owned by CAAC and local investors. A small part of the capital is also owned by TAP-Air Portugal. Two Airbus A320s and two A321s were ordered from the leasing company ILFC and when they were delivered during 1996 they were put to work on regional routes. At the New Year 1999/2000 China took over control of Macau from Portugal, and granted it a special business zone status, as it had already done with Hong Kong. The registration prefixes of the aircraft were changed from the Portuguese CS- to China's B-, but otherwise the status of Air Macau is unaltered, as an agreement with the Chinese government ensures its place as the flag carrier for Macau until at least 2020. Financial circumstances have oriented the carrier towards China; there is no longer any Portuguese shareholding. Air Macau is in direct competition with Dragonair for passengers from Taiwan, a route which only these two carriers are permitted to serve. In mid-2003 discussions were taking place with a view to radically changing the airline, transforming it into a low-cost carrier.

Routes

Bangkok, Beijing, Chongqing, Fuzhou, Guilin, Haikou, Kunming, Kaoshiung, Manila, Nanjing, Ningbo, Qingdao, Shanghai, Taipei, Wuhan, Xiamen and Zhengzhou.

Fleet	Ordered
5 Airbus A319	2 Airbus A330
1 Airbus A320-200	
5 Airbus A321-100/200	
2 Boeing 727-200F	

Boeing 737-3Q8 5R-MFH (Jörg Dieter Zmich / Johannesburg)

AIR MADAGASCAR

31 Ave. de l'Independence, BP 437,
Antanaraivo, 101 Madagascar
Tel. 22222, Fax. 25728, www.air-mad.com

Three- / Two- letter code	IATA No.	Reg'n prefix	ICAO callsign
MDG / MD	258	5R	Madair

Air Madagascar was founded in January 1961, a year after the country became independent. It was set up by the government (51%), Air France (40%) and a predecessor company of the same name which had been in existence since 1947. Prior to 1st January 1962 it had been known as Madair. The first service was inaugurated on 20th October 1961 between Tananarive and Paris with a Douglas DC-7C operated on the carrier's behalf by the French carrier TAI. Air France's contribution to the airline was to bring in the domestic flights which it had previously provided along with the corresponding aircraft, DC-3s and DC-4s. The new airline's own first international route was via Djibouti and Marseilles to Paris, using the Boeing 707. In 1979 came the Boeing 747-200SCD, the first and only widebody in the fleet. The delivery of a Boeing 737-300 in 1995 allowed an expansion of regional routes, particularly in the south of Africa. New routes to Europe were also added, for example to Munich. During 1998 Air Madagascar added a Boeing 767-300 for long-range routes. Air Madagascar has its headquarters and maintenance base at the airport of the capital, Antananarivo. The airline co-operates closely with Air Mauritius and Air France, the latter having a 3% shareholding. The government of Madagascar is making preparations for the privatisation of the airline around 2005.

Routes

Ambanja, Ambatomainty, Ambilobe, Analalava, Antalaha, Antsiranana, Belo, Besalampy, Doany, Farafangana, Fort Dauphin, Johannesburg, Mahanoro, Mahe, Maintirano, Majunga, Mampikony, Manakara, Mananara, Mananjary, Mandritsara, Manja, Mauritius, Morafenobe, Morombe, Morondava, Moroni, Nairobi, Nossi-Be, Paris, Port Berge, Rome, Sambava, Singapore, Soalala, St.Denis, Ste.Marie, St. Pierre, Tambohorano, Tulear, Vatomandry, Vohemar.

Fleet

3 ATR 42-300	4 De Havilland DHC-6-300
2 Boeing 737-200	
1 Boeing 737-300	
1 Boeing 767-300ER	

ATR 42-320 7Q-YKQ (Bastian Hilker / Harare)

AIR MALAWI

4 Robins Road, P.O.Box 84 Blantyre, Malawi
Tel. 265-620811, Fax. 265-620042, E-mail:
enquiries@airmalawi.net, www.airmalawi.net

Three- / Two- letter code	IATA No.	Reg'n prefix	ICAO callsign
AML / QM	167	7Q	Malawi

Air Malawi was founded in 1964 by the government of the new state (formerly Nyasaland) upon achieving independence from Great Britain. Central African Airways was responsible for the operation of flights with the Douglas DC-3 and the management of the airline until 1967, when Air Malawi became self-sufficient. Regional routes were served with the Vickers Viscount, and the first jet equipment was the BAC One-Eleven with which routes from Blantyre to Salisbury (now Harare), Johannesburg and Nairobi were flown from 1972. A Vickers VC-10 was introduced on 3rd December 1974 for the London service. Vickers Viscounts, HS.748s, Britten-Norman Islanders and Shorts Skyvans were all in use until the early 1990s when more modern aircraft such as the ATR 42 and Boeing 737-300 joined the small fleet of the national carrier. There is close co-operation with Air Tanzania. A planned privatisation was delayed in May 2003 after the Malawi government rejected as South African Airways-supported bid. The main base is at Blantyre-Chileka, where the airline has its own maintenance facility, which also carries out overhauls for other operators. Air Malawi, with its own handling company Lihaco, is responsible for ground handling at Lilongwe and Chileka airports.

Routes

Blantyre, Chileka, Club Makokola, Dar-es-Salaam, Harare, Johannesburg, Karonga, Lilongwe, Lusaka, Mzuzu, Nairobi.

Fleet

1 ATR 42-300
1 Boeing 737-300

Boeing 737-300 9H-ADL (Florian Morasch / Amsterdam)

AIR MALTA

Luqa Airport LQA 05 Malta, Republic of Malta
Tel. 6229990, Fax. 6673241,
www.airmalta.com

Three- / Two- letter code	IATA No.	Reg'n prefix	ICAO callsign
AMC / KM	643	9H	Air Malta

Air Malta is the national airline of the island republic of Malta and has been in existence since 30th March 1973, when it was set up by order of the government. The first service was Malta-Rome from 1st April 1973. Air Malta has only ever used jet aircraft, initially leased British Airways Tridents, followed from 1st April 1974 by independent operations. The route network was built up and regular flights and charters were carried out to London, Amsterdam, Paris, Zürich, Munich, Cairo and Tripoli. Boeing 720s came into service, supplemented from 1978 by Boeing 737-200s, which later took over completely. Spring 1990 saw the arrival of two Airbus A320s, which also carried a new colour scheme introduced by the airline. From September 1994, Avro RJ 70s were added to the fleet, but these were disposed of to Azzurra Air (an Italian company in which Air Malta has a 48% interest) in mid-1998. Air Malta also has shareholdings in Mediterranean Aviation (Med Avia), which operates CASA 212s, and in Malta Air Charter, which links Malta with the small island of Gozo, using Mil Mi-8 helicopters. Boeing 737-300s have been added to the fleet steadily since 1993, but in Spring 2003 a fleet renewal programme decision went in favour of Airbus, and new A319s and A320s are expected to join the fleet during 2003-7 and 2004-8 respectively.

Routes

Abu Dhabi, Amsterdam, Athens, Bahrain, Barcelona, Beirut, Berlin, Birmingham, Brussels, Budapest, Casablanca, Catania, Cairo, Copenhagen, Damascus, Dubai, Dublin, Düsseldorf, Frankfurt, Geneva, Glasgow, Gothenburg, Gozo, Hamburg, Istanbul, Larnaca, Lisbon, London, Lyon, Manchester, Milan, Marseilles, Munich, Moscow, Oslo, Palermo, Paris, Prague, Rome, Stockholm, Stuttgart, Tel Aviv, Thessaloniki, Tripoli, Tunis, Vienna and Zürich.

Fleet	Ordered
4 Airbus A320-200	7 Airbus A319
2 Boeing 737-200	5 Airbus A320
7 Boeing 737-300	

Dornier Do228-212 MI-8504 (Author's collection)

AIR MARSHALL ISLANDS

P.O.Box 1319 Majuro 96960,
Marshall Islands
Tel. 6253731, Fax. 6253730

Three- / Two- letter code	IATA No.	Reg'n prefix	ICAO callsign
MRS / CW	778	V7	Marhallislands

In 1980 an independent state airline was established with the purpose of creating better air connections between the individual islands of the state territory and the main island of Majuro. It was known as the Airline of the Marshall Islands, with the current name being adopted in 1989. The first flights were with GAF Nomads, but these were augmented in 1982 with a single BAe 748. The primary route is from Majuro to Kwajalein, where an American missile base and air force facility is located. The GAF Nomads were replaced by Dornier Do 228s delivered in 1984 and 1985. In the mid-1990s a leased DC-8-62 was used to help build up a tourist infrastructure, concentrating principally on tourists from the USA. However, this service was abandoned after a short while, as the DC-8 was found to be too expensive to operate. The arrival of a Saab 2000 in 1995 marked the introduction of a new generation of regional aircraft to replace the older types. However, as production of the Saab has ceased and it was not totally suited to the needs of the airline, it was decided to switch instead to the Dornier 328, but on grounds of cost the delivery of these was deferred and the older aircraft continued to serve the airline's routes. However, a de Havilland Canada Dash 8-100 has been leased in from January 2003.

Routes

Ailuk Island, Airok, Auckland, Aur Island, Bikini Atoll, Brisbane, Ebon, Ine Island, Jabot, Jeh, Kwajalein, Liekip Island, Loen, Majkin, Mili Island, Namdrik Island, Tarawa, Woja and Wotje Island.

Fleet

2 Fairchild-Dornier Do 228
1 de Havilland Canada DHC-8

Boeing 737-7Q8 5T-CLK (Author's collection / Paris-CDG)

AIR MAURITANIE

B.P.41, Nouakchott 174
Islamic Republic of Mauritania
Tel. 522211, Fax. 53815, www.airmauritanie.mr

Three- / Two- letter code	IATA No.	Reg'n prefix	ICAO callsign
MRT / MR	174	5T	Air Mauritania

Mauritania's national carrier was established in September 1962 by the state to take over and expand the small network previously provided by Air France and UAT. Operations started in October 1963 with technical assistance and equipment, including Fokker F.27s, from the Spanish airline Spantax and the airline quickly built up its services, particularly in the important agricultural areas in the south of the country. By the mid-1980s international services were operated to Dakar and Las Palmas in addition to an extensive domestic network.The airline was owned by the government (60%), Air Afrique (20%) and UTA (20%).Two Fokker F.28s were brought into use in 1983, and the small fleet was renewed at the end of 1996 with the delivery of two ATR 42s, but at the end of 1998 these were returned to the lessor on cost grounds and the airline reverted to Fokker F.28 equipment. Flights to Gran Canaria and Casablanca are carried out in partnership with Iberia and Royal Air Maroc. During 2002 Air Mauritanie opened a service to Paris, but as the Fokker F.28 has insufficient range for this, a Boeing 737-700 was leased. A further 737-700 is planned to be leased from ILFC from March 2004. The airline's base is at the international airport in Nouakchott.

Routes

Abidjan, Aioun, Bamako, Casablanca, Cotonou, Dakar, Kiffa, Las Palmas, Paris-CDG, Nema, Nouadhibou, Nouakchott, Selibaby, Tidjikja and Zouerate.

Fleet	Ordered
1 Boeing 737-700	1 Boeing 737-700
2 Fokker F.28	

Boeing 767-23B(ER) 3B-NAK (Marcus Baltes / Frankfurt)

AIR MAURITIUS

Rogers House 5, President John Kennedy Street, Port Louis, Mauritius, Tel. 2087700, Fax. 2088331, www.air-mauritius.com

Three- / Two- letter code	IATA No.	Reg'n prefix	ICAO callsign
MAU / MK	239	3B	Airmauritius

Air Mauritius was set up on 14th June 1967, although until 1972 it functioned only as a handling agent. After the independence from Britain of Mauritius, there was a need for a national airline. With help from the government, from Air India, British Airways and additional support from Air France, operations were begun with a Piper PA-31 Navajo. The first destination in August 1972 was the island of Rodrigues, some 600km from the main island. In 1973, in co-operation with Air India and using its aircraft, a service to Bombay was inaugurated. Likewise flights were started to London, using aircraft leased on a daily basis, and with Air France to Paris. Only on 31st October 1977 did a Boeing 707 in Air Mauritius' own colours come into use. In April 1978 Rome was brought into the network, with Durban, Johannesburg, Nairobi and Antananaraivo following in 1981 and Jeddah and Zürich during 1983. A Boeing 747SP was leased from SAA in 1984 to provide non-stop service to Paris. From April 1987 further new destinations were Munich and Singapore. Flights were scheduled for several times weekly, as the popularity of Mauritius as a holiday destination was growing strongly. The Boeing 707s were replaced in 1988 by new Boeing 767s, but the bulk of the long-haul fleet is now made up of Airbus A340s, the first of which entered service in 1994. For shorter routes, ATR 42s are in use, the first of these having been delivered in 1986, supplemented since 2002 by the larger ATR 72.Also new from 2002 is the Airbus A319. Aircraft are maintained at the airline's own base at Sir Seewoosagur Ramgoolam International Airport.

Routes

Antananavivo, Brussels, Capetown, Chennai, Delhi, Dubai, Durban, Frankfurt, Geneva, Harare, Hong Kong, Jeddah, Johannesburg, Kuala Lumpur, London, Mahe, Manchester, Melbourne, Milan, Mumbai, Munich, Nairobi, Paris, Perth, Rodrigues, Rome, Singapore, St.Denise de la Reunion, St. Pierre de la Reunion, Vienna, Zürich.

Fleet

2 ATR 42-500
1 ATR 72-500
2 Airbus A319-100
5 Airbus A340-300

2 Boeing 767-200ER

Tupolev Tu-134A ER-65140 (Bastian Hilker / Larnaca)

AIR MOLDOVA

Airport, 277026 Chisinau, Moldova
Tel. 2-525502, Fax. 2-526051, E-mail:
office@airmoldova.md, www.airmoldova.md

Three- / Two- letter code	IATA No.	Reg'n prefix	ICAO callsign
MLD / 9U	572	ER	Air Moldova

The former Soviet Republic of Moldova, bordering on Romania, declared its independence in 1992 and decided that it needed its own national airline. As early as May 1992 a regular service from Chisinau (otherwise known as Kishinev) to Frankfurt was being operated. Tupolev Tu-134A and Tu-154s formed the fleet, supplemented by Antonov An-24s for regional routes. The airline also operates charter and freight services; the Antonov An-26 is used for these. As a result of considerable national and business difficulties during the late 1990s, the demand for air transport in the region fell. The Tu-154s were sold off, the rest of the fleet reduced and many routes curtailed. During 2001 a part-privatisation was successfully achieved, with 49% of the shares passing to a partly state-owned investment company. Western aircraft could now be leased and some of the Tu-134s retired; hence the addition of the Embraer Brasilia and 145s. The airline had been working in co-operation with Balkan Bulgarian Airlines until the latter's bankruptcy.The Russian airline Transaero, however, is a recent partner, with which there are codeshare arrangements on several routes. Air Moldova is also active in the holiday charter market, particularly during the summer season with flights to the resorts on the Black Sea coast.

Routes

Amman, Antalya, Athens, Beirut, Bucharest, Bourgas, Frankfurt, Istanbul, Larnaca, Minsk, Moscow, Paris, Sofia, Prague, Rostov, Thessaloniki, Varna, Vienna.

Fleet

6 Antonov An-24/26
1 Embraer EMB-120
1 Embraer EMB-145
7 Tupolev Tu-134A

Beechcraft 1900C V5-LTC (Josef Krauthäuser collection)

AIR NAMIBIA

P.O.Box 731, Windhoek 9100, Namibia
Tel. 061-223019, Fax. 061-221910, E-mail:
holidays@airnamibia.com.na, www.airnamibia.com.na

Three- / Two- letter code	IATA No.	Reg'n prefix	ICAO callsign
NMB / SW	186	V5	Namibair

aAlthough this airline was set up as early as 1947 it was only after Namibia, the former South West Africa, became independent that Air Namibia appeared as Namibia's national carrier. After its formation as South West Air Transport, regular flights from Windhoek to Swakopmuk with Douglas DC-3s began in 1948. Oryx Aviation was taken over in 1959 and the name changed to Suidwes Lugdiens. There was a further takeover in the late 1960s – the charter airline Namibair Pty. Ltd. The name of this airline was adopted in 1978 as the airline provided a number of scheduled domestic feeder services

to connect with SAA flights at Windhoek. It became the national airline in 1987. On 24th April 1990 Namib Air started regular services to Frankfurt using a Boeing 747SP and in 1993 the name was changed again, to Air Namibia. In this year also, a second Boeing 747SP was acquired from SAA and the network expanded. As well as international services, Air Namibia also provides regional service within southern Africa, for which Boeing 737-200s and Beech 1900s are used, and from mid-1996 new de Havilland DHC-8s, but the latter type proved too expensive to maintain and were dropped from the fleet after only a

short time. A replacement was sought for the 747SPs and in 1988 a Boeing 767-300 was leased. This aircraft also was used to introduce a new colour scheme, incorporating the colours of the Namibian national flag. The 767 was however replaced in October 1999 by a Boeing 747-400. Because of world recession, flights to Namibia have diminished; thus Air Namibia was looking for a new long-haul type. For several months in 2002 an Airbus 330 was leased, but the 747-400 came back into use in 2003. Air Namibia co-operates with LAM, LTU and SAA on its international services.

Routes

From Windhoek to Frankfurt, Capetown, Johannesburg, Keetmanshoop, Livingston, Luanda, Lüderitz, Lusaka, Maun, Mokuti Lodge, Ondangwa, Oranjemund,Rosh Pinah, Swakopmuk, Tsueb, Victoria Falls and Walvis Bay.

Fleet

3 Beechcraft 1900
2 Boeing 737-200Adv.
1 Boeing 747-400

Boeing 737-4L7 VH-RON (Frank Schorr / Brisbane)

AIR NAURU

P.O.Box 40 Nauru Intl. Airport, Republic of Nauru
Tel. 444-3168, Fax. 444-3173,
www.airnauru.com.au

Three- / Two- letter code	IATA No.	Reg'n prefix	ICAO callsign
RON / ON	123	C2	Air Nauru

Air Nauru was founded as flag carrier by the government of the Pacific island nation in1970, and inaugurated service on 14th February 1970 with a Dassault Mystère 20 to Brisbane. Further destinations were Honiara and in the following year Majuro in the Marshall Islands and Tarawa on the Gilbert Islands. A Fokker F.28 replaced the Mystère in January 1972 and with this new routes to Japan and Guam were started. Boeing 737s and 727s followed the Fokker F.28 into service in 1976; there followed further expansion until 1984 when there were four Boeing 737s and a Boeing 727 in use. However, the latter was taken out of service in 1985, thus allowing Air Nauru to operate a small homogeneous fleet. Additional routes were opened to Manila, Hong Kong, Auckland, Nadi, Taipei and Truk. Recession and falling passenger numbers led to a reduction in service and a shrinking of the network during the late 1980s. A marketing alliance was concluded with Air New Zealand and Qantas, which allowed the airline to concentrate only on its profitable routes. During 1993 the remaining fleet was exchanged for a single, modern Boeing 737-400, with other aircraft leased briefly to cover for maintenance. Air Nauru came under the authority of the Australian aviation authorities and briefly operated under an Australian licence, but in 2001 this was withdrawn because of safety lapses, leading to a suspension of services. Qantas put the thumbscrews on its partner and confiscated the sole aircraft for some weeks in response to unpaid lease and maintenance payments. During this time Qantas expanded its own activities in the Pacific area and took over other operators. Air Nauru, with the help of the government, was able to remedy its failings and regain its licence. The Boeing 737-400 was taken onto the Australian register.

Routes

Brisbane, Guam, Manila, Melbourne, Nadi, Pohnpei, Suva and Tarawa.

Fleet

1 Boeing 737-400

Boeing 747-419 ZK-NBU (Martin Bach / London)

AIR NEW ZEALAND

Private Bag 92007, Auckland 1020, New Zealand
Tel. 9-3662400, Fax. 9-3662401,
E-mail: info@airnz.co.nz, www.airnz.co.nz

Three- / Two- letter code	IATA No.	Reg'n prefix	ICAO callsign
ANZ / NZ	086	ZK	New Zealand

The present-day Air New Zealand goes back to 1939, when Tasman Empire Airways Ltd (TEAL) was formed as a joint British (20%), Australian (30%) and New Zealand (50%) company. Short S-30 flying boats were used for regular flights between Australia and Auckland. The flying boats were in use until 1954, and were then replaced by Douglas DC-6 landplanes. In 1961 the New Zealand government assumed full control. TEAL entered the jet era in 1965 with the purchase of three Douglas DC-8s and in that year also the name was changed to Air New Zealand. New routes to the USA were started and the domestic airline NZNAC (formed in 1945) was taken over on 1st April 1978. Larger DC-10s and Boeing 747s were added to the DC-8s, the last of which left the fleet on 1st September 1989. Frankfurt, apart from London the sole European destination, was first served on 31st October 1987. Boeing 747-400s and Boeing 767s were added to the fleet from 1992. ANZ has developed regional services, operated by fully-owned subsidiaries Mount Cook Airlines, Eagle Aviation and Air Nelson. During 1996 ANZ acquired 50% of the shares of the Australian airline Ansett, and in the same year the present colour scheme for the aircraft fleet was introduced. After protracted negotiations, ANZ, itself now 25% owned by Singapore Airlines, took over Ansett completely at the end of 1999, but then in 2001, with the breakup of Ansett, Air New Zealand encountered difficulties. A proposed takeover of the Singapore Airlines' shareholding by Qantas was controversial and so the government again took a share. On cost grounds, routes were dropped and older aircraft retired. Air New Zealand has been a member of the Star Alliance since March 1999.

Routes

Apia, Auckland, Brisbane, Cairns, Christchurch, Dunedin, Hong Kong, Honolulu, London, Los Angeles, Melbourne, Nadi, Nagoya, Norfolk Island, Noumea, Osaka, Papeete, Perth, Queenstown, Rarotonga, Singapore, Sydney, Taipei, Tokyo, Tongatapu, Wellington.

Fleet		Ordered
15 Boeing 737-300	10 Boeing 767-300ER	15 Airbus A330-200
8 Boeing 747-400		
3 Boeing 767-200ER		

Boeing 737-54K JA301K (Thomas Kim / Tokyo)

AIR NIPPON

3-5-10 Haneda Airport, Otak-ku, Tokyo 144-0041
Japan, Tel. 3-54621911, Fax. 3-54621950,
www.ana.co.jp

Three- / Two- letter code	IATA No.	Reg'n prefix	ICAO callsign
ANK / EL	768	JA	Ank Air

By the direction of the Japanese commerce ministry, the country's three leading airlines, Japan Air Lines, All Nippon Airways and TOA Domestic Airlines, established a regional operator called Nihon Kinkyori Airways Company. The objective of the new airline was to provide a second-level service, connecting the smaller population centres in the north and south of Japan with the business centres in the middle of the country. It was also tasked with connecting smaller and outlying islands with the air transport centres on the main island. De Havilland Twin Otters and NAMC YS-11 turboprops were used and passenger numbers grew quickly, necessitating the lease of Boeing 737-200s. The commercial make-up of the company changed over the years; first the state withdrew, and after several years All Nippon Airways took over the majority of the shares previously shared between the three mainland airlines. The name was changed to Air Nippon and the colour scheme of the aircraft changed to one closely resembling that of ANA. During the 1990s, Boeing 737-500s and Airbus A320s saw a fleet modernization, which was over time brought to a state of standardisation on the Boeings. Air Nippon Network is a subsidiary company and operates several routes on behalf of Air Nippon with DHC-6s and DHC-8s. The airline has access to aircraft from its parent company as required and for charter flights.

Routes

Amami O Shima, Aomori, Fukue, Fukuoka, Fukushima, Hachijo Shima, Hakodate, Hiroshima, Ishigaki, Iwami, Kagoshima, Kochi, Komatsu, Kumamoto, Kushiro, Matsuyama, Memanbetsu, Miyake Jima, Miyazaki, Monbetsu, Nagasaki, Nagoya, Nakashibetsu, Niigata, Odate Noshiro, Oita, Okinawa, Okushiri, Osaka, Oshima, Rebun, Rishiri, Saga, Sapporo, Sendai, Shonai, Takamatsu, Tokyo, Toyama, Tsushima, Wakkanai, Yonaga.

Fleet

2 Boeing 737-400
26 Boeing 737-500
3 NAMC YS-11

Boeing 767-319 ZK-NCE (Josef Krauthäuser collection)

AIR NIUGINI

ANG House, Jacksons Airport P.O.B. 7186, 7186 Boroko
Papua-New Guinea. Tel. 675-3273200, Fax. 675-3273482
E-mail: airniugini@airniugini.com.pg
www.airniugini.com.pg/

Three- / Two- letter code	IATA No.	Reg'n prefix	ICAO callsign
ANG / PX	656	P2	Niugini

Ansett, Qantas, TAA and the government of Papua New Guinea formed Air Niugini jointly in November 1973. With eight Fokker Friendships and twelve Douglas DC-3s, the new airline took over operations from Ansett and TAA on 1st November 1973, and carried these out in Australian-administered New Guinea until independence, which came about on 16th September 1975. Flights to Sydney and Singapore began in 1975; the international network of flights was extended to Honolulu using Boeing 707s. A leased Airbus A300B4 – in a wonderful, exotic colour scheme –

replaced the 707 from 1984. Air Niugini received the first of its own A310s at the beginning of 1989, with a second following late in 1990. DHC-7s were used only on internal routes, with Fokker Fellowships (the first of which arrived in 1977) and the A310s looking after the modest number of international routes.With the introduction of the de Havilland Dash 8 in1997, the older Dash 7s were retired. During 1999 Air Niugini leased an Avro RJ70 as a replacement for one of the older Fokker Fellowships, indicating the beginning of a fleet renewal for regional routes, but this has not

been carried through. The relatively expensive Airbuses have been returned to their leasing companies, as in early 2000 political and other circumstances led to a dramatic fall in passenger bookings. A Boeing 767 is now leased from Air New Zealand for the longer-range routes.

Routes

Alotau, Brisbane, Buka, Cairns, Daru, Goroka, Honiara, Hoskins, Kavieng, Kundiawa, Lae, Lihir Island, Madang, Manila, Manus Island, Mount Hagen, Osaka, Popondetta, Port Moresby, Port Vila, Rabaul, Singapore, Talasea, Tari, Tokyo, Vanimo, Wapenamanda, Wewak.

Fleet

1 Boeing 767-300
1 De Havilland DHC-8
8 Fokker F.28

Fokker 50 EC- GBH (Albert Kuhbandner / Madrid)

AIR NOSTRUM

Calle Francisco Valldecabres 31, 46940, Manises
Valencia, Spain, Tel. 96-1960200, Fax. 96-1960287
E-mail: informacion@airnostrum.es, www.airnostrum.es

Three- / Two- letter code	IATA No.	Reg'n prefix	ICAO callsign
ANS / YW	694	EC	Nostrum Air

Air Nostrum was formed in Spring 1994 in Valencia, with operations beginning in November of that year from Valencia to Barcelona, Bilbao, Ibiza and Palma de Mallorca. Three Fokker 50s were used, with a further three being acquired by June 1995. The route network was expanded with equal pace and soon encompassed almost all the major cities in Spain. Thus a further expansion beyond Spain's borders was logical. In May 1997 Iberia and Air Nostrum consummated a franchise agreement and Air Nostrum flew from then on as Iberia Regional in harmony with Iberia's schedules. The booking and reservations systems were accordingly facilitated, with through bookings possible, and the markings on the Air Nostrum aircraft changed correspondingly. The first ATR 72 arrived in 1997, as the Fokker 50 was becoming too small for some of the routes. Air Nostrum put its first jet into service in Spring 1998, the Canadair Regional Jet also allowing destinations in central Europe to be served for the first time. After Aviaco was merged into Iberia in 1999, there were further changes for Air Nostrum, with additional routes being transferred in. The de Havilland Canada DHC-8 was added to the fleet from 2001; it is seen as a replacement for the remaining Fokker 50s.

Routes

Alicante, Almeria, Asturias, Badajoz, Barcelona, Bilbao, Bologna, Casablanca, Frankfurt, Geneva, Granada, Hanover, Ibiza, La Coruna, Leon, London, Lyon, Madrid, Malaga, Marseilles, Melilla, Menorca, Murcia, Nice, Palma de Mallorca, Pamplona, Paris, Porto, Reus, San Sebastian, Santander, Santiago de Compostella, Seville, Tangier, Toulouse, Turin, Valencia, Valladolid, Vigo, Vitoria, Zaragossa.

Fleet	Ordered
5 ATR 72-500	1 Canadair CRJ200
20 Canadair CRJ200	10 De Havilland DHC-8-300
13 De Havilland DHC-8-300	
9 Fokker 50	

Boeing 737-3Y0 EI-CLZ (Andreas Witek / Graz)

AIR ONE

Via Sardegna 14, 00187 Rome, Italy
Tel. 06-478761, Fax. 06-4885913,
www.flyairone.it

Three- / Two- letter code	IATA No.	Reg'n prefix	ICAO callsign
ADH / AP	867	I	Heron

In Pescara in Italy in 1983 Aliadriatica was established as a flying school and air taxi operation. The majority of the business passed in 1988 to Gruppo Toto, an engineering company. At first the company structure and activities remained unaltered, but with the delivery of a Boeing 737-200 in 1994 Aliadriatica entered the airline charter business. In April of the following year, 1995, a scheduled service licence was granted and services were begun from Rome to Brindisi, Reggio Calabria and Lamezia Terme. When the company was given permission to operate on the attractive route from Rome to Milan in November 1995, it changed not only the colour scheme of the aircraft, but also the airline's name, to Air One. During 1996 Air One took over the flying operations of Fortune Aviation and expanded strongly. An alliance with the Qualiflyer Group of airlines lasted only briefly, and the airline remains independent, though a partner with Lufthansa and Air Littoral. An impressive route network has been built up, with over 1000 flights daily flown by the fleet which is standardised on leased Boeing 737s in order to keep costs low;. Charter business is also being actively undertaken, particularly carrying tourists from several countries to Italy during the holiday season.

Routes

Alghero, Bari, Bergamo, Bologna, Brindisi, Cagliani, Catania, Crotone, Genoa, Lamezia Terme, Lampedusa, Milan, Naples, Palermo, Pantelleria, Pescara, Reggio Calabria, Rome, Turin, Venice.

Fleet

3 Boeing 737-200
6 Boeing 737-300
14 Boeing 737-400
5 Boeing 737-800

Boeing 767-300ER DQ-FJC (Thomas Kim / Los Angeles)

AIR PACIFIC

P.O.Box 9266 Nadi Airport, Fiji
Tel. 720777, Fax. 720512,
E-mail: info@airpacific.com, www.airpacific.com

Three- / Two- letter code	IATA No.	Reg'n prefix	ICAO callsign
FJI / FJ	260	DQ	Pacific

Fiji's national airline began operations in September 1951 as Fiji Airways, using de Havilland DH.89 Dragon Rapides. With the support of the Australian airline Qantas and in close co-operation with them, the route network was extended. In 1957 Qantas took over Fiji Airways as a subsidiary. In 1959 de Havilland Herons were added to the fleet, before in 1960 Air New Zealand and BOAC each took over a third of the company. The fleet was refreshed in 1967 with HS.748s and Britten-Norman Trislanders.The first jet was introduced in March 1972, a BAC One-Eleven 400. The name of the airline was changed in 1971 to Air Pacific, and by 1972 the governments of Fiji, Kiribati, Tonga, Nauru and some private investors acquired a majority interest. Embraer Bandeirantes were acquired in 1980 for regional services. Increasing passenger demand resulted in the purchase of two ATR 42s in 1988, but these were given up in favour of an all-jet fleet of Boeing 737s, 767s and 747s, Air Pacific having withdrawn from the regional market in1995. During 1998 Qantas took over a further 28.5% of the capital and is now the largest shareholder. In the latter part of 1998, with the introduction of the 'new generation' Boeing 737-700, the airline's colour scheme was also changed. During1999 Air Pacific took delivery of two more 'new generation' 737s, this time -800s and thus has a very modern fleet. In 2001 the last 747-200 and some older 737s were dropped and the fleet temporarily reduced as this formerly peaceful region encountered business difficulties. In April 2003 a 747-400 was acquired from SIA and used to increase frequency to Los Angeles. Some routes, and a Boeing 737, are operated jointly with Royal Tongan, and other alliances are in place in association with Qantas to American Airlines, Air Vanuatu and Solomon Airlines.

Routes

Apia, Auckland, Brisbane, Christchurch, Honoira, Honolulu, Los Angeles, Melbourne, Nadi, Nukualofa, Suva, Sydney, Tokyo, Tongapatu, Vancouver, Vila, Wellington.

Fleet

1 Boeing 737-700
2 Boeing 737-800
2 Boeing 747-400
1 Boeing 767-300ER

Boeing 737-3Y0 EI-BZM (Author's collection)

AIR PHILIPPINES

R1 Hangar APC Gate 1, Andrews Ave, Nichols, Pasaay City, Philippines, Tel. 02-851 7601, Fax. 02-851 7922, E-mail: reservation@airphilippines.com.ph, www.airphils.com

Three- / Two- letter code	IATA No.	Reg'n prefix	ICAO callsign
GAP / 2P	211	RP	Orient Pacific

After the regulation of air transport in the Philippines was liberalised, new airlines were established quickly. In February 1995, under the leadership of businessman William Gatchalian and with financial participation from the Chinese airline U-Land Airlines and JAS-Japan Air System, Air Philippines was founded. Services were begun with the Boeing 737-200 in February on the Manila-Cebu route. Air Philippines promotes itself as a low-cost/no-frills airline and offers cheap ticket prices, especially compared with the previous airline monopoly situation. Routes within the Philippine islands were quickly built up and further 737-200s acquired. For operation on less well frequented routes and to smaller airports, several NAMC YS-11s were taken over from JAS. Lacking international services, Air Philippines was not in a position to have foreign currency income when the Philippines was hit by the Asian business crisis, yet the leasing costs on the aircraft had to be paid in hard currency. Thus U-Land came to the rescue with some of their MD-80s and flew some routes on Air Philippines' behalf. By the beginning of 2000 the situation had improved, and tourist traffic was returning to the country. Expansion followed in 2002 with a first international service to neighbouring Indonesia, with Air Philippines being confirmed as an additional national carrier. The airline also conducts regular charter operations, for example to Hong Kong or Brunei. Some regional services have been dropped, as the YS-11s are now retired, but generally frequencies have been increased and several Boeing 737s leased. The airline's base is at Subic Bay.

Routes

Bacolod, Cagayan de Oro, Cebu, Davao, Dumguente, General Santos, Iloilo, Kalibo, Laoag, Manado, Manila, Puerto Princesa, San Jose, Subic Bay, Zamboango.

Fleet

8 Boeing 737-200
2 Boeing 737-300

Airbus A310-300 EC- HFQ (Klaus Brandmaier / Zürich)

AIR PLUS COMET

Edificio Air Plus, Bahia de Pollensa 21-23, 28042
Madrid, Spain, Tel. 91 2036300, Fax. 91 3293511
E-mail: airplus@aircomet.com, www.aircomet.com

Three- / Two- letter code	IATA No.	Reg'n prefix	ICAO callsign
MPD / A7	–	EC	Aircomet

Founded in 1996, Air Plus Comet is owned by the Spanish Marsans group, which is particularly active in the tourism industry. Flights began in Spring 1997 using two Airbus A310s, operating from Madrid and Palma de Mallorca, with destinations principally in Central America and the Caribbean. The group also has interests in Argentina and has established a subsidiary, Air Plus Argentina, there, using aircraft passed from the parent company. Air Plus was also instrumental in the conversion of Aerolineas Argentinas into a private company and currently has a large shareholding in the Argentinean national airline. As well as charter services for the Marsans group, Air Plus Comet flies for many other tour operators, either as single charters or series. The airline has also been particularly active in conducting ad hoc flights on behalf of other airlines, on either a short or long term basis. In 2001 Air Plus Comet received a route licence for scheduled services from Madrid to New York. Its operating base is at Madrid-Barajas.

Routes

Aruba, Cancun, Cartagena, Havana, Isla Margarita, Madrid, Miami, New York, Palma de Mallorca, Puerto Plata, Varadero.

Fleet

5 Airbus A310-300

Boeing 767-3Q8(ER) S7-ASY (Klaus Brandmaier / Munich)

AIR SEYCHELLES

P.O.Box 386,Victoria Mahe, Seychelles
Tel. 381000, 381000, Fax. 225933, E-mail:
pro@airseychelles.com, www.airseychelles.com

Three- / Two- letter code	IATA No.	Reg'n prefix	ICAO callsign
SEY / HM	061	S7	Seychelles

In July 1979 the government of the Seychelles bought the two domestic airlines Air Mahe (formed in 1972) and Inter Island Airways (formed in 1976), in order to create Air Seychelles as the national airline. The routes and aircraft were also taken over. Britten-Norman Islanders and Trislanders were used for services to the individual islands. Tourism was heavily promoted, creating a demand for international services. On 1st November 1983, Air Seychelles began scheduled flights to London and Frankfurt with a weekly DC-10 flight, using an aircraft chartered from British Caledonian Airways. In November 1985 Air Seychelles took delivery of an Airbus A300B4 from Air France and put it to use on services to Amsterdam, Rome and Frankfurt. In 1989 a Boeing 707 temporarily replaced the Airbus, until the arrival of the first Boeing 767-200. A Boeing 757-200 was added in 1993, but the need for extra capacity resulted in its exchange for a larger Boeing 767-300 at the end of 1996. From the main island radiates a dense network of domestic services, flown principally by the Twin Otters. Further careful expansion has taken place, with the delivery of a second Boeing 767-300 during 2001 and the first Boeing 737-700, used for new routes to India, the Maldives and the Comores, in November 2001. Also in 2001, Munich was added as a second destination in Germany.

Routes

Dubai, Frankfurt, Dzauouzi, Johannesburg, London, Mahe Island, Male, Mauritius, Moroni, Mumbai, Munich, Nairobi, Paris, Praslin Island, Rome, Singapore, Zürich.

Fleet

2 Boeing 767-300ER
1 Boeing 737-700
3 de Havilland DHC-6 Twin Otter
1 Britten-Norman Islander

1 Shorts 360

ATR 72-500 F-WWLN (Author's collection / Toulouse)

AIR TAHITI

BP 314 Boulevard Pomare, Papeete Tahiti
Tel. 864011, Fax. 864069
www.airtahiti.pf

Three- / Two- letter code	IATA No.	Reg'n prefix	ICAO callsign
VTA / VT	135	F	Air Tahiti

Air Tahiti, which is partly in private ownership, was formed in 1953 to improve communications between the individual islands which make up the French overseas province. At that time it was called RAI – Reseau Aérien Interinsulaire. On 1st January 1970 the name was changed to Air Polynésie, after the French airline TAI (later to become UTA) had taken overt 62% of the shareholding. For many years the aircraft fleet consisted of Fokker Friendships and Britten-Norman Islanders, as well as Twin Otters. In January 1987, after UTA disposed of its interest in the company, the name was again changed to Air Tahiti. To demonstrate its new-found independence, with the introduction of the ATR 42 during that year, a new colour scheme was adopted. During 1992 and 1993 the larger ATR 72 was also brought into the fleet, and during the later part of the 1990s the older examples of the ATR 42 were replaced by new, more powerful ATR 42-500 models. A close association has been cultivated with Air France, which has a small shareholding in Air Tahiti. Air Tahiti itself has shareholdings in Air Archipels, Air Moorea and in Air Tahiti Nui. Since Air Tahiti Nui took over services to France from Air France, co-operation has increased and Air Tahiti provides connecting flights from Papeete.

Routes

Ahe, Anaa, Atuona, Bora Bora, Fakarava, Gambier, Hao, Hiva Oa, Huahine, Kaukura, Kauehi, Makemo, Mangareva, Manihi, Maupiti, Matavia, Moorea, Nuku Hiva, Papeete, Raiatea, Rangioroa, Rurutu, Takapoto, Takaroa, Tikehau and Tubuai.

Fleet

4 ATR 42-500
5 ATR 72-500
2 Fairchild-Dornier 228-200

Airbus A340-313(X) F-OJTN (Jan-Alexander Lück / Paris-CDG)

AIR TAHITI NUI

BP.1673, 98713 Papeete, Tahiti, Tel. 460202
Fax. 460290, E-mail: service@airtahitinui.com
www.airtahitinui.com

Three- / Two- letter code	IATA No.	Reg'n prefix	ICAO callsign
THT / TN	244	F	Tahiti Airlines

Given the importance of the income from inbound tourism to the economy, the major function of the international carrier for Tahiti is the development of this industry. This was spelled out by the government to future investors in a new international airline, when Air Tahiti Nui was founded in October 1996. The shares were broadly spread and include Air Tahiti with 10%; naturally this airline would benefit from offering its services around Tahiti to more tourists. As the most important markets are in Japan, the USA and the motherland of France, only long-range aircraft were under consideration and the Airbus A340 was chosen, beginning service in November 1998 from Papeete to Los Angeles. Further destinations, served initially on a weekly basis, were Osaka and Auckland. Two more A340s followed during 2002, allowing frequencies to be increased. An agreement was also concluded with Qantas for codeshare on the route from Sydney to Auckland. Los Angeles is the most important hub in the USA, barely eight hours flying time from Papeete, and with the Winter 2002/3 timetable, the Los Angeles flights were extended to Paris. A fourth A340 thus became necessary; Air Tahiti Nui has a very young fleet.

Routes

Auckland, Los Angeles, Osaka, Papeete, Paris, Tokyo.

Fleet

4 Airbus A340-300

Boeing 737-2R8C 5H-ATC (Bastian Hilker / Harare)

AIR TANZANIA

P.O.Box 543 Dar-es-Salaam, Tanzania
Tel. 051-38300, Fax. 051-46545
www.airtanzania.com

Three- / Two- letter code	IATA No.	Reg'n prefix	ICAO callsign
ATC / TC	197	5H	Tanzania

In January 1977, after the break-up of East African Airlines which had been a joint venture between Kenya, Uganda and Tanzania, there were practically no air services remaining in Tanzania. Thus in March 1977 Air Tanzania was formed by the government and with Fokker F.27s and a Boeing 737 services were begun from Dar-es-Salaam. During 1978 and 1979 a further Boeing 737 and, for regional services, several de Havilland Twin Otters were acquired. The departure points for international flights are Dar-es-Salaam and Kilimanjaro International Airport. A Boeing 767 was used for a short while during 1994/95, but this could not be fully utilised. In 1995 the Twin Otter was also withdrawn from the fleet and the regional network reduced on financial grounds. The procurement of more modern aircraft was also put back, but a Boeing 737-300 was leased in 1999 as a replacement for one of the -200 models. The airline became a participant (10%) in the multi-national Air Alliance in 1995; this initially operated a Boeing 747SP on international services. In 2002 the first step towards privatisation was taken with the offer of a first batch of shares; an objective of privatisation will be to finance fleet renewal. The Boeing 737-300 is no longer in use, but a Dornier 228 was leased from South Africa from February 2002 and the airline also has use of two DHC-8s from South African Express on a rotating basis as required. There is co-operation with Air Malawi, Kenya Airways and Gulf Air, with some routes being flown on a codeshare basis.

Routes

Aden, Dar-es-Salaam, Dubai, Entebbe, Harare, Jeddah, Johannesburg, Kigali, Kigoma, Kilimanjaro, Kinshasa, Lilongwe, Lindi, Lusaka, Mombasa, Moroni, Mtwara, Muscat, Musoma, Mwanza, Nairobi, Tabora, Zanzibar.

Fleet

2 Boeing 737-200
1 Dornier 228-200
2 Fokker F.27

Fokker F.27 TT-AAK (Author's collection)

AIR TCHAD

27 Avenue Charles de Gaulle, BP 168,
N'Djamena, Chad
Tel. 235-515090

Three- / Two- letter code	IATA No.	Reg'n prefix	ICAO callsign
HTT / HT	95	TT	Hotel Tango

Formed on 24th June 1966 by the Chad government (64% shareholding) and UTA as Compagnie Nationale Tchadienne, the new national airline began regional service with the indestructible Douglas DC-3 from Fort Lamy (nowadays called N'Djamena). A Douglas DC-4 was used to fly via Algiers to Paris, thus creating a quick connection to the former French colony. The state of civil war which existed more or less from 1975 in Chad hindered development of the route system, which could only really begin to be built up slowly following a 1982 peace accord between the conflicting factions. In spite of that a Fokker F.27 was bought in 1983, and a further example was received by way of a gift from neighbouring Libya, but was not registered in Chad. As a replacement for the elderly DC-3, a de Havilland DHC-6 Twin Otter came into service. As a result of its takeover of UTA, Air France became a shareholder in Air Tchad and there is co-operation between the two airlines. Today Air France has only a 2% holding, the balance being with the Chad government. Alongside the very modest scheduled services, Air Tchad uses its sole F.27 for charter and relief work.

Routes

Abecher, Bol, Bongor, Mao, Mongo, Moundou, N'Djamena, Pala and Sarh.

Fleet

1 Fokker F.27

Boeing 717-200 N956AT (Josef Krauthäuser / Fort Lauderdale)

AIR TRAN AIRWAYS

9955 Air Tran Blvd. Orlando, Florida 32827, USA
Tel. 407-2515600, Fax. 407-2515567
E-mail: mail@airtran.com, www.airtran.com

Three- / Two- letter code	IATA No.	Reg'n prefix	ICAO callsign
TRS / FL	332	N	Citrus

Air Tran Airways came into being in September 1997 by the merger of Valujet and Airtran. Valujet was set up in 1993 and expanded rapidly in the east and southeast of the USA. Some 20 destinations were served from Atlanta with Douglas DC-9s, and Valujet was the launch operator for the new McDonnell Douglas MD-95 (later to become the Boeing 717). The company's fortunes were badly damaged by a notorious crash in May 1996, after which the airline was grounded by the FAA. Though it emerged later that the company was not to blame for the accident, the image had been tainted and passengers were choosing to fly with other airlines. The re-started, though limited, services were again suspended voluntarily in June 1996, in order to allow stringent investigation by the FAA. A further re-start was made in November 1996 under new management and with a small fleet of DC-9s. Air Tran Airways was likewise set up in 1993, initially under the name Conquest Sun Airlines. Its base was in Orlando and it served several routes in Florida and the neighbouring states using Boeing 737-200s, changing name to Air Tran Airways in August 1994. Naturally, on the merger, it was decided to adopt the Air Tran name, and a new colour scheme was adopted with a prominent 'a' on the tailfin. Deliveries of the Boeing 717 began in the second half of 1999, marking the beginning of renewal of the whole fleet, and the retirement of the Boeing 737-200s. The network has expanded quickly, with annual passenger boardings increasing at around 25% and Air Tran is the largest user of the 717, with 73 in service by the end of 2003. In July 2003 it was announced that the airline will take 50 Boeing 737-700s from June 2004, with 50 options. The two Airbus 320s are operated by Ryan International from Summer 2003 to inaugurate Los Angeles services.

Routes

Atlanta, Akron, Baltimore, Bloomington, Boston, Buffalo, Chicago, Dallas/Forth Worth, Dayton, Denver, Flint, Fort Lauderdale, Fort Myers, Grand Bahamas, Greensboro/High Point, Gulfport/Biloxi, Hartford, Houston, Jacksonville, Kansas, Memphis, Miami, Milwaukee, Minneapolis, Moline, Myrtle Beach, New Orleans, New York, Newark, Newport News, Orlando, Pensacola, Philadelphia, Pittsburgh, Raleigh/Durham, Rochester, Savannah, Tampa, Washington, West Palm Beach, Wichita.

Fleet

		Ordered
20 Douglas DC-9-30	2 Airbus A320-200	23 Boeing 717-200
60 Boeing 717-200		50 Boeing 737-700s

Airbus A330-243 C-GGTS (Martin Kühn / Frankfurt)

AIR TRANSAT

11600 Cargo Rd A 1, Montreal Intl. Airport, Mirabel Quebec
J7N 1G9, Canada, Tel. 450-4761011, Fax. 450-4760338
E-mail: informations@airtransat.com, www.airtransat.com

Three- / Two- letter code	IATA No.	Reg'n prefix	ICAO callsign
TSC / TS	649	C	Transat

Set up in December 1986, Air Transat has become Canada's largest charter airline since Nationair ceased flying in 1992. Operations began in early 1987 with Boeing 727-200s. Its base is at Montreal (where the airline has its own maintenance facility), but Air Transat also serves Toronto, Quebec City, Halifax and Vancouver. The airline obtained its first Lockheed L-1011 TriStar in late 1987 for services to the Caribbean. During the summer seasons, Air Transat flies regularly to Europe, and during 1996 the airline took on further TriStars from Air Canada and Cathay Pacific. Boeing 757s have also been steadily added to the fleet since 1992, and the Boeing 727s phased out. New charter routes have also been established, including to Poland and Portugal. The pattern of destinations varies seasonally, with Europe being strong in the Summer, whilst in Winter the Caribbean and South America predominate. During 1999 Air Transat added three Airbus A330s. Also during 1999 the colour scheme of the aircraft was changed; there is now a star on the tailfin, instead of the former 'at' logo. There are scheduled services between Montreal and Paris, and Air Transat is a leading player with flights from Canada to Cuba, a favourite destination for Canadians. Additionally Air Transat controls some 20 tour companies in Canada, France and the USA. The fleet is being renewed, principally with Airbus types and by 2005 the last TriStar should have left the fleet. The airline has its own maintenance base at Montreal.

Routes

Air Transat flies to about 90 destinations in over 20 countries including Belgium, Canada, Columbia, Costa Rica, Cuba, Dominican Republic, France, Germany, Great Britain, Greece, Haiti, Honduras, Ireland, Italy, Jamaica, Martinique, Mexico, Nicaragua, the Netherlands, Panama, Poland, Portugal, St. Maarten, USA, Venezuela.

Fleet

    4 Airbus A330-200/300
    5 Airbus A310-300
    3 Boeing 757-200
   10 Lockheed L-1011 TriStar 100/500

Douglas DC-8-63F N788AL (Josef Krauthäuser / Miami)

AIR TRANSPORT INTERNATIONAL

3800 Rodney Parham Rd, Little Rock, ARK.72212
USA, Tel. 501-6153500, Fax. 501-6032093
E-mail: info@airtransport.cc, www.airtransport.cc

Three- / Two- letter code	IATA No.	Reg'n prefix	ICAO callsign
ATN / 8C	346	N	Air Transport

This cargo airline was founded in 1978 as US Airways, but changed its name after a few months to Interstate Airlines. Using Lockheed Electras and Boeing 727s it flew as an independent operator from Detroit's Willow Run airport. Numerous routes were flown, especially for the automobile industry, but also for the emerging overnight express parcels concerns. At the beginning of the 1980s the company gained a lucrative contract from UPS and was thus in a position to expand the fleet with Douglas DC-8s. The company headquarters and operating base were moved to Little Rock in Arkansas, though the

aircraft were based in various places. There was another change in 1988, when the current name was adopted. With the delivery of more DC-8s, the Electras were removed from the fleet, and fresh opportunities arose. Thus several DC-8s were flown exclusively for Burlington Express, who did not have their own airline operation. Additionally, many overseas charters were flown for the US military, especially to the Gulf region. On 1st October 1994 ATI took over ICX International Cargo Express and integrated their two Douglas DC-8s into their own fleet. There were thus about twenty DC-8-

63s and DC-8-71s at the airline's disposal when in 1998 ATI was sold to BAX-Global. Today ATI continues to operate charter and ad hoc flights in its own colours, but the majority of the fleet is in use on behalf of BAX-Global. In addition the airline specialises in animal transport, not bulk loads, but horses and valuable breeding stock. After several years of losses, ATI returned to profit in 2002.

Routes

Scheduled freight services on behalf of BAX-Global to about 50 US destinations from a hub at Toledo. Charter and ad hoc freight flights worldwide.

Fleet

8 Douglas DC-8-61/63F
12 Douglas DC-8-71/73F

Airbus A 321-211 G-OOAF (Richard Schmaus / Salzburg)

AIR 2000

Jetset House, Church Road, Lowfield Heath, Crawley, RH11 0PQ, Great Britain. Tel. 1293-518966, Fax. 1293-524642, www.air2000.com

Three- / Two- letter code	IATA No.	Reg'n prefix	ICAO callsign
AMM / DP	091	G	Jetset

The airline was formed in 1986 by the tour operator Owners Abroad, one of the leading British tour companies, for the purpose of operating intensive charter services outside London. The densely populated region in the north seemed to be perfect and Manchester was selected as the base. Commercial operations commenced with two leased Boeing 757s on 11th April 1987. During 1988, two further Boeing 757s were added, one of which was based in Glasgow. Restrictions imposed by Canadian law prevented the intended formation of a Canadian subsidiary (see Canada 3000). The first flights to Mombasa were carried out in the winter season 1988/89, and after the 757s were equipped to ETOPS standard there were also transatlantic flights to Newark, Boston and Orlando. In October 1990 Air 2000 was granted a scheduled air service licence for flights from the United KIngdom to Cyprus and services were finally launched in late 1993 from Gatwick to Larnaca and Paphos. Following regular additions of Boeing 757s to the fleet, the first two Airbus A320s arrived in April 1992. In 1995, Newcastle and Belfast were added to the operating bases and from 1996 flights were offered from Dublin. In addition to intensive charter flights, Air 2000 is also involved in the wet-leasing business and leases its aircraft, primarily in the quiet Winter periods, to Canada 3000 and other airlines. Air 2000 today belongs to the major tour operator First Choice Holidays, which in 1998 took over rival Unijet along with its airline Leisure International. During 1999 the Leisure fleet of Airbus A320/A321s and Boeing 767s was integrated. A new colour scheme was introduced from the 2002 summer season. Air 2000 Engineering is a subsidiary based in Manchester and at important destinations.

Routes

Schedules from: Alicante, Arrecife, Birmingham, Bristol, Cardiff, Faro, Glasgow, London-Gatwick, Malaga, Manchester, Newcastle, Larnaca, Palma de Mallorca, Paphos,Tenerife. Charters from ten British regional airports to the Mediterrannean, North Africa, Canada, Caribbean, Mexico, Kenya, Sri Lanka and Thailand. In Winter charters to the Alpine ski resorts.

Fleet

6 Airbus A320-200
6 Airbus A321
16 Boeing 757-200ER
3 Boeing 767-300ER

Ordered

1 Airbus A320-200

Boeing 737-3Q8 YJ-AV18 (Jörg Thiel / Sydney)

AIR VANUATU

P.O.Box 148, Port Vila, Vanuatu, Tel. 23838
Fax. 23250, E-mail: admin@airvanuatu.com.vu
www.airvanutau.com

Three- / Two- letter code	IATA No.	Reg'n prefix	ICAO callsign
AVN / NF	218	YJ	Air Van

Following independence in 1980, Air Vanuatu was set up as the national airline of this Pacific republic by Ansett Transport Industries and the local government in 1981, using the former New Hebrides Airways as a basis. Ansett held 40% of the shares. Using a leased Boeing 737-200, flights were begun in September 1981 from Vila to Australia, whence about 70% of the passengers come. In November 1987 the government acquired the balance of the shares from Ansett. The airline entered a close co-operation with Australian Airlines, receiving aircraft and maintenance support. In 1989 Auckland and Adelaide were added to the route network. When Australian Airlines was absorbed into Qantas, it was decided to try to become self-sufficient,even though the sole Boeing 737 was provided by Qantas.There is close co-operation with local operator Vanair, with joint connecting flights. Thus in July 1995 an Embraer Bandeirante was acquired for regional services, though this was sold in 1998 in favour of a larger Saab 2000. This proved uneconomic, so was returned to the lessor after only a few months, and for regional flights Air Vanuatu rents DHC-8s or DHC-6s from Van Air. Air Vanuatu also works with other airlines in the region including Air Caledonie, Air Pacific, Qantas and Solomon Airlines. The base is at the Bauerfield airport, near Port Vila.

Routes

Aneityum, Aniwa, Auckland, Brisbane, Craig Crove, Dillons Bay, Emae, Espiritu Santo, Futuna, Gaua, Honiara, Ipota, Lamap, Lamen Bay, Longana, Lonorore, Maewo, Melbourne, Mota Lava, Nadi, Norsup, Noumea, Olpoi, Paama, Port Vila, Redcliffe, Sara, Sola, South West Bay, Sydney, Tanna, Togoa, Torres, Ulei,Valesdir, Walaha.

Fleet

1 Boeing 737-300

Boeing 737-2N0 Z-WPB (Bastian Hilker / Harare)

AIR ZIMBABWE

P.O.Box AP 1, Harare Airport, Harare, Zimbabwe
Tel. 4-575111, Fax. 4-796039
www.airzimbabwe.com

Three- / Two- letter code	IATA No.	Reg'n prefix	ICAO callsign
AZW / UM	168	Z	Zimbabwe

Air Zimbabwe was established on 1st September 1967 as a statutory body controlled by a board responsible to the Ministry of Transport as Air Rhodesia following the dissolution of the Central African Airways Corporation. CAA had served the three territories of Southern Rhodesia, Nyasaland and Northern Rhodesia for some 21 years. Due to the political situation, it was only possible to fly domestic routes and to neighbouring South Africa, until the present government took power and the airline was renamed Air Zimbabwe Rhodesia in 1978. Douglas DC-3s, Vickers Viscounts and Boeing 707/720s

were used. It was only from 1980 that the present Air Zimbabwe was able to develop into an airline with flights to neighbouring countries and to Europe. In 1983 it took over the cargo airline Affretair. Boeing 737-200s were acquired in the second half of the 1980s, and these remain with the airline today. The first Boeing 767s were delivered in 1989 and 1990 and in 1995 two Fokker 50s were acquired for shorter-range routes, but the latter were disposed of after only a couple of years. Also sold off were the older Boeing 707s and the BAe/HS-748, as well as Affretair in order to meet mounting losses. Since 1998 Air

Zimbabwe has operated only jets. The political decline and unsafe situation have decimated tourist interest in this once popular and flourishing country, with the result that the state airline has lost more than 80% of its tourist traffic. Routes to Europe have been practically abandoned and at least one 767 taken out of service, as there are no funds for maintenance or replacement. There are alliances with Air Botswana, Air Malawi, LAM and Qantas, and the airline's home base is at Harare-International.

Routes

Bulawayo, Dar-es-Salaam, Durban, Harare, Hwange National Park, Johannesburg, Kariba, Lilongwe, London, Luanda, Lusaka, Mauritius, Nairobi, Victoria Falls.

Fleet

1 BAe 146-200
3 Boeing 737-200
1 Boeing 767-200ER

Ilyushin IL-86 RA-86141 (Marcus Baltes / Frankfurt)

AJT – AIR INTERNATIONAL

Leningradsky Prospekt 37, Moscow, Russia
Tel. 095-1555495, Fax. 095-1556466
E-mail: avia@ajtair.msk.ru

Three- / Two- letter code	IATA No.	Reg'n prefix	ICAO callsign
TRJ / E9	766	RA	Turjet

AJT, Asian Joint Transport, was set up in 1991 and began operations in 1992. It was the first independent Russian airline to set up business after the dissolution of the old state-run monopoly, Aeroflot. The aircraft came from the residue of Aeroflot and initial operations were to the United Arab Emirates. The demand for consumer goods after the break-up of the Soviet Union was very strong amongst the Russian population and business people used the UAE as a prime source. Ilyushin IL-86s were added to the fleet and five of these widebodies were at AJT's disposal. Further aircraft were used on a long or short term rental basis to meet changing demand. Vnukovo Airlines took a share of the growing airline, which had also started to operate charters to Turkey and into Western Europe. Initially Antalya in Turkey and Rimini in Italy were favourite destinations. AJT's home base is Moscow Shermetyevo.

Routes

Charter flights within Russia, to the Middle East, Europe, North Africa and the Far East.

Fleet

4 Ilyushin IL-86
2 Tupolev Tu-154

Boeing 737-700 N626AS (Josef Krauthäuser / Las Vegas)

ALASKA AIRLINES

P.O.Box 68947, Seattle Washington 98168, USA
Tel. 206-431-7040, Fax. 206-431-5558
E-mail: info@alaskaair.com, www.alaskaair.com

Three- / Two- letter code	IATA No.	Reg'n prefix	ICAO callsign
ASA / AS	027	N	Alaska

Alaska Airlines traces its history back to the formation of McGhee Airways in 1932, which merged with Star Air Service in 1934. This airline then became Alaska Star Airlines in 1943, after the airlines Pollack Flying Service, Mirow Air and Laverny Airways were all taken over. With these purchases the airline had over 75% of Alaska's air traffic under its control. In 1944 the present name was adopted. In addition to scheduled services, Alaska Airlines was particularly active in the charter business. Alaska's aircraft participated in the Berlin Airlift and, later, in support of the Korean War. The first route from Alaska to Seattle

was inaugurated in 1951. In 1960 Convair 340s and DC-6s were acquired to replace the DC-3s previously used. On 1st February 1968 Alaska Airlines bought Cordova Airlines and on 1st April of that year, Alaska Coastal Airlines. In an allusion to the opening of the large oilfields, the airline's first jet aircraft were also dubbed 'Golden Nugget Jets'. In 1970 charter flights from Fairbanks to Khabarovsk in the USSR were flown for the first time. During the early 1980s the colour scheme was altered; on the tailfin, a smiling Eskimo appeared. Alaska became the first customer to order the new extended-range MD-83,

ordering nine aircraft in 1983. There were further purchases of airlines in 1986: Jet America and Horizon Air, the latter becoming a feeder operator for Alaska. The network was extended to California and Mexico, and western Canada was served from Seattle. In 1992 direct services to neighbouring Siberia were initiated. In 1996 Alaska made headlines by ordering Boeing 737-400s instead of the MD-90s which had been on option. The latest generation of 737s are in course of delivery, with the first -700 arriving in May 1999, and the larger 737-900 from April 2001.

Routes

Anchorage, Aniak, Astoria, Bellingham, Bethel, Billings, Boise, Burbank, Butte, Calgary, Cold Bay, Cordova, Dutch Harbor, Edmonton, Fairbanks, Fresno, GlacierBay, Helena, Juneau, Ketchikan, Kodiak, Kotzebue, La Paz, Las Vegas, Los Angeles, Los Cabos, Mazatlan, Nome, Oakland, Ontario, Orange County, Palm Springs, Phoenix, Portland, Prudhoe Bay, Puerto Vallarta, Reno, San Diego, San Francisco, San Jose, Seattle, Sitka, Spokane, Valdez, Vancouver and Yakutat are amongst many destinations served by Alaskan.

Fleet

		Ordered
9 Boeing 737-200Adv.	9 Boeing 737-900	3 Boeing 737-700
40 Boeing 737-400	32 McDonnell Douglas MD-82/3	4 Boeing 737-900
20 Boeing 737-700		

BAe 146-200 ZA-MAL (Bastian Hilker / Frankfurt)

ALBANIAN AIRLINES

Rruga Mira Peza 2, Tirana, Albania
Tel. 42-28461, Fax. 42-35162
www.flyalbanian.com

Three- / Two- letter code	IATA No.	Reg'n prefix	ICAO callsign
LBC / LV	639	ZA	Albanian

Since the major political changes of the 1990s, there has been an increasing need for an independent Albanian airline. Business restrictions in the country however would only allow for the existence of a state-supported venture. During 1992, with help and know-how provided by Austria's Tyrolean Airways, Albanian Airlines was set up. The Albanian partner was the government-owned Albtransport, which already had experience in bus and lorry transport. Operations began in May 1992 using a DHC-8 from Tirana to Vienna, Zürich, Frankfurt and Rome. However, after only a short time Tyrolean withdrew its support and shareholding, and with it went the sole aircraft. In 1995 MAK Albania, a subsidiary of the Kuwaiti Kharafi Group, took up a shareholding in Albanian, whose services had been at a standstill. A Tupolev Tu-134 was leased from Hemus Air in Bulgaria and put to use on scheduled and charter flights. On a seasonal basis, either another Tu-134 or a Tu-154 was also rented. However with increasing restrictions being imposed on both of these types at Western airports, it was decided in 2001 to acquire the airline's first BAe 146. In February 2003 this was augmented by a second aircraft, this time a series 300.

Routes

Bologna, Frankfurt, Istanbul, London-Gatwick, Pristina, Rome, Tirana, Zürich.

Fleet

1 BAe 146-200
1 BAe 146-300
1 Yakovlev Yak-40

Airbus A321-112 I-BIXG (Josef Krauthäuser / Madrid)

ALITALIA

Viale Alessandro Marchetti 111,
00148 Rome, Italy
Tel. 65622020, Fax. 65624733, www.alitalia.it

Three- / Two- letter code	IATA No.	Reg'n prefix	ICAO callsign
AZA / AZ	055	I	Alitalia

Alitalia (Aerolinee Italiane International) was founded on 16th September 1946 by the Italian government, BEA and several Italian companies. Operations began on 5th May 1947 using Fiat 612s, SIAI Marchetti SM 95s and Avro Lancastrians, with the first international flight, to Buenos Aires, taking place in 1948. In 1950 DC-4s were acquired, and in 1953 Convair 340/440s and DC-6s. The first jet was a DC-8 in 1960. Alitalia's further development was preceded by its merger with LAI in 1957 when it also became the national airline. Vickers Viscounts and Caravelles were acquired for short and medium haul,

the latter being replaced from August 1967 by DC-9s. The first Boeing 747 was delivered on 13th May 1970, and the DC-10 in February 1973. During the late 1970s Alitalia's aircraft orders caused something of a furore with the manufacturers, as Airbus A300s and DC-10s were ordered in addition to Boeing 727s and 747s; some orders had to be cancelled however. Since then, the trend has been one of fleet standardisation for cost reasons. For its intercontinental flights, Alitalia acquired MD-11s from 1992 onwards, and older DC-9s were replaced by the Airbus A321, the first of which was delivered in

March 1994. Another newcomer during 1995 was the Boeing 767, and 777s have largely replaced the 747-200s, now used for freight only. Subsidiary ATI was integrated in 1994. Part of the fleet is operated by 'Alitalia Team' with different cost structures as a cost-saving measure. Alitalia Express, a 100%-owned subsidiary, is responsible for regional services. It was planned for Alitalia to merge with the Dutch airline KLM, but this was all broken off abruptly in June 2000 and Alitalia is a member of the Sky Team alliance. Domestically, there is co-operation with Azzurra, Alpi Eagles, Meridiana, and Minerva.

Routes

Alitalia has a dense network of services to over 130 destinations on all continents; in Europe alone over 50 airports are served.

Fleet

5 Airbus A319
11 Airbus A320
24 Airbus A321-100
4 Boeing 747-200

12 Boeing 767-300
6 Boeing 777-200
90 McDonnell Douglas MD-82
8 McDonnell Douglas MD-11

Ordered

7 Airbus A319
3 Boeing 777-200

Boeing 727-200 N728FV (Stefan Schlick / Barbados)

ALLEGRO AIR

Jose Benitez 2709, Obispado, Monterey NL, 64060
Mexico, Tel. 52833399938, Fax. 5283339940
www.allegroair.net/

Three- / Two- letter code	IATA No.	Reg'n prefix	ICAO callsign
GRO / LL	902	XA	Allegro

Allegro Lineas Aereas was set up in Monterey, Mexico in October 1992 by private investors. In December of that year the first DC-9-15 in Allegro colours operated its first services to Cancun. During the first year of services, the airline concentrated its efforts on domestic destinations, leasing in several aircraft for some months during the high season. It is noteworthy that these came especially from European airlines; high season here is from mid-December to the end of February, a slack time for aircraft employment in Europe. From 1994 numerous charters were also operated from the USA and Canada to Mexican destinations and to the Caribbean. Contracts with tour operators such as Sunjet or Funjet who specialised in the Caribbean made entry into this lucrative market possible. This expansion meant that Allegro took on larger aircraft, the Boeing 727-200 and expanded its DC-9 fleet. Service to Las Vegas marked the airline's entry into the US scheduled domain, but the main activity remained in charter traffic for the important US market, with services offered to many cities. The fleet grew steadily to suit the market demand. During 2000 12 Boeing 727-200s were in use, but from 2001 these have been slowly withdrawn and in the long term are being replaced by MD-80s, with the entire changeover scheduled to be completed by 2005.

Routes

Acapulco, Atlanta, Cancun, Cozumel, Dallas-DFW, Guadalajara, Las Vegas, London Ontario, Mazatlan, Merida, Mexico City, Miami, Monterey, New York, Newark, Oakland, Orlando, Puerto Vallarta, Punta Cana, Tijuana, Vancouver.

Fleet

5 Boeing 727-200
8 Boeing MD-82/3

Boeing 747-481 JA8962 (Danniel Klein / Frankfurt)

ALL NIPPON AIRWAYS

3-3-2, Haneda Airport, Ota-Ku, Tokyo 144-0041, Japan, Tel. 3-54350333, Fax. 3-54350903
www.ana.co.jp

Three- / Two- letter code	IATA No.	Reg'n prefix	ICAO callsign
ANA / NH	205	JA	All Nippon

All Nippon Airways is Japan's largest airline on the basis of number of passengers carried. Formed in December 1952 as Japan Helicopter and Aeroplane Transport Company, scheduled services began in 1953. It merged in 1958 with Far East Airlines to form All Nippon Airways. The most important route at that time was Tokyo-Osaka. The network of routes was continuously expanded using Convair 340s and 440s. In July 1961 two new aircraft types were introduced at the same time, the Fokker F.27 and the Vickers Viscount 828. By taking over three regional airlines, Fujita in 1963, Central Japan in 1965 and Nagasaki

Airlines in 1967, All Nippon grew rapidly. Jet service with Boeing 727s was offered for the first time between Tokyo and Sapporo in 1964. In December 1973 the Lockheed TriStar became the first widebody with the airline. The Boeing 747SR gave ANA – as it also did with other Japanese companies – a jumbo jet with particularly closely-spaced seating, making it possible to carry around 500 passengers on short routes. Continuing fleet renewal brought in the Boeing 767 from mid-1984, the Airbus A320 from 1990 as well as the Boeing 747-400. Overseas routes were opened up relatively late by ANA, from March 1986, the

first destination being Guam. Services to the USA and Australia soon followed with Beijing added in 1987, Seoul in 1988 and London in 1989. Fukuoka, Osaka and Tokyo are ANA's main hubs. There has been impressive re-equipment in progress since 1997, bringing in Boeing 777s and Airbus A321s, and newer model 747s to replace the old. Since 1998 ANA has been aligned with the Star Alliance, with formal membership from October 2000 and has shareholdings in Air Japan, Air Nippon, Air Nippon Network, Fair and Nippon Cargo Airlines. It also often applies brightly painted special colour schemes.

Routes

ANA flies over 35 domestic routes and international services to Bangkok, Beijing, Chicago, Dalian, Frankfurt, Guam, Ho Chi Minh City, Hong Kong, Honolulu, Kuala Lumpur, London, Los Angeles, Mumbai, New York, Paris, Qingdao, San Francisco, Seoul, Shanghai, Shenyang, Singapore, Sydney, Tianjin, Vienna, Washington, Xiamen.

Fleet		Ordered
21 Airbus A320	23 Boeing 747-400	3 Airbus A321
7 Airbus A321	26 Boeing 777-200	14 Boeing 777-300
58 Boeing 767-200/300		
11 Boeing 747-200/SR		

Boeing 737-76N N741AL (Henry Tenby / Vancouver)

ALOHA AIRLINES

P.O.Box 30028 Honolulu 96820, USA
Tel. 808-8364210, Fax. 808-8333671, E-mail:
mail@alohaair.com, www.alohaair.com

Three- / Two- letter code	IATA No.	Reg'n prefix	ICAO callsign
AAH / AQ	327	N	Aloha

Aloha Airlines was set up as Trans Pacific Airlines Ltd on 9th June 1946 and non-scheduled operations began in July of that year. In the first three years of the airline's existence it operated passenger and cargo charters in the Hawaiian islands. In common with many airlines starting out at this time, its first aircraft type was the Douglas DC-3. The first scheduled flight was on 6th June 1949. The company changed its name to Aloha Airlines in November 1958. Fairchild F.27s replaced the DC-3s from June 1959 and in 1963 the larger Vickers Viscounts followed. Altogether Aloha acquired three Viscounts and six F.27s. Its

first jet aircraft was also a British product; on 29th April 1966 Aloha started scheduled flights from Honolulu to Maui with BAC One-Elevens. A step towards standardising the fleet was taken with the purchase of the first Boeing 737s in 1969. Due to the very short flight times between the islands, the 737s have very high utilisation figures. In 1980 Aloha Island Air was created as a subsidiary company operating DHC- 6 Twin Otters and now the DHC-8. With the delivery of the first of the Boeing 737-400s in early 1993 came a change of colour scheme; since then, the Boeing 737 has been the only type in the fleet.

During 1999 Aloha opened a route to the Marshall Islands. Other destinations in the Pacific include Kwajalein and Johnston Island. As a replacement for the older 737-200s, Aloha took delivery at the end of 1999 their first 737-700, and this was used on 28th February 2000 to inaugurate a route to Oakland, California, the airline's first service to mainland America. Further US destinations were added with Las Vegas and Santa Ana. A merger was planned with Hawaiian Air in January 2002, but this was abandoned in March of that year.

Routes

Hana, Hilo, Honolulu, Hoolehua, Johnston Island, Kahului, Kapalua, Kauai, Kona, Kwajalein, Lanai City, Las Vegas, Majuro, Oakland, Santa Ana.

Fleet

18 Boeing 737-200Adv.
11 Boeing 737-700

Fokker 100 I-ALPW (Andreas Witek / Graz)

ALPI EAGLES

Via E.Mattei 1, 30020 Marcon, Italy
Tel. 041-5997777, Fax. 041-5997708
www.alpieagles.com.i

Three- / Two- letter code	IATA No.	Reg'n prefix	ICAO callsign
ELG / E8	789	I	Alpi Eagles

Alpi Eagles belongs to one of the world's most famous aerobatic display teams, who have entertained crowds with their shows throughout the world. From this privately-financed venture developed a department to offer commercial and business flights. The Alpi Eagles were successful in this and thus the idea was conceived to offer scheduled and charter flights with larger aircraft. In 1996 two Fokker 100s were acquired, retaining the Alpi Eagles name even though the display team were by then no longer active. The two aircraft were used to launch scheduled services from May 1996, from a base at Venice- Marco Polo Airport. Agreement was reached with Alitalia for the takeover of several routes, and for others to be operated on a codeshare basis. In 1998 a new colour scheme was adopted, with further Fokker 100s being acquired in 1997 and 2000. As well as the scheduled services, charters, ad hoc and series, are undertaken.

Routes

Athens, Barcelona, Cagliari, Catania, Madrid, Naples, Palermo, Paris-CDG, Rome, Venice, Verona.

Fleet

8 Fokker 100

Boeing 737-823 N904AN (Josef Krauthäuser / Miami)

AMERICAN AIRLINES

P.O.Box 619616 DFW Intl. Airport Dallas, Texas 75261-9616, USA, Tel. 817-9671234, Fax. 817-9674318
E-mail: customerrelations@aa.com, www.aa.com

Three- / Two- letter code	IATA No.	Reg'n prefix	ICAO callsign
AAL / AA	001	N	American

American Airlines came into being on 13th May 1934. Before the DC-3, created to the specifications of American, came into use, Curtiss Condors were mainly used. In 1945 AOA, an airline specialising in flights to Europe, was taken over, but sold on to PanAm in 1950 and American concentrated solely on the American market. The airline was one of America's aircraft manufacturers' most important partners in the period that followed: the DC-7, Convair 240 and 990, Lockheed L-188 Electra and DC-10 all emerged from specifications and orders placed by American. The DC-7 was used from November 1953 to start the transcontinental non-stop service from New York to Los Angeles. Six years later, American's first jet, the Boeing 707 took over. BAC One-Eleven 400s and Boeing 727 also featured in the extensive fleet. In 1970 the widebody era began with the Boeing 747, followed by the DC-10 from August 1971. Also in 1971 American took over Trans Caribbean Airways and its extensive network in this region. After deregulation in1978 American grew even larger, taking over AirCal in1987. Numerous routes were acquired from other companies, paving the way for extensive expansion of routes to the Far East, South America and Europe. During 1984 regional services were consolidated under the 'American Eagle' banner (see page 82). An extensive fleet renewal plan has seen the introduction of the Boeing 777 and 737-800 from 1999. In the west of the USA, Reno Air was bought in 1998 and its fleet and routes integrated during 1999. The famous TWA was acquired after its failure in 2000 and integrated by the end of 2001. American was directly affected by the events of 11 September 2001, losing two aircraft to terrorism and since then has been badly affected by business downturn. American co-operates closely with British Airways, and both are leading members of the Oneworld alliance.

Routes

Over 160 destinations worldwide and in the USA, with major hubs at Dallas/Fort Worth, Chicago, and Miami. Including American Eagle brings the total to over 280 destinations.

Fleet

		Ordered
29 Airbus A300-600	43 Boeing 777	42 Boeing 737-800
77 Boeing 737-800	56 Fokker 100	5 Boeing 767-300
153 Boeing 757-200	360 McDonnell Douglas MD-82/3	3 Boeing 777
83 Boeing 767-200/300		

Embraer ERJ-135LR N729AE (Thomas Kim / Toronto)

AMERICAN EAGLE AIRLINES

4333 Amon Carter Blvd. MD 5494, Forth Worth, Texas 76155, USA, Tel. 972-4251520, Fax. 972-4251518, www.aa.com

Three- / Two- letter code	IATA No.	Reg'n prefix	ICAO callsign
EGF / AA	-	N	Eagle Flight

On behalf of American Airlines, a franchise system, American Eagle, was set up on 1st November 1984, with the previously independent Metroflight. Smaller airports were to be brought into the hub and spoke system, starting with a hub at Dallas/Fort Worth. 19-seat Swearingen Metros formed the initial fleet. On 1st December that year, Chapperal Airlines was brought into the system. Flights operated under American's 'AA' flight numbers and the aircraft painted in a unified colour scheme, closely resembling that of American. During 1985 AV Air in Raleigh-Durham and Simmons Airlines in Chicago also joined in, and a year later Air Midwest in Nashville and Command

Air in New York. At other hubs such as San Jose or San Juan, Wings West or Executive Air carried out these feeder flights. However, the system had its weaknesses, and Air Midwest went into bankruptcy, but was bought out by American's holding company, the AMR Corporation. Likewise, it was necessary to acquire AVAir and Simmons in order not to endanger the whole system. A new hub was set up at Miami by Flagship Airlines with ATR 42s. Wings West and Command Airways were also integrated, to save them from financial disaster. During the mid-1990s American Eagle suffered heavy losses, brought about by the

purchase of larger aircraft and poor business conditions. Rationalisation of the fleet was called for and it was concentrated on the Saab 340 and ATR 42/72. The previously independent companies were all brought into AMR ownership with the purchase of Business Express in 1998, making American Eagle Airlines the world's largest regional carrier with over 15 million passengers. In 1999 the Embraer ERJ-145 was the first jet for the airline, which slowly phased out its propeller types. The smaller RJ 135 and RJ 140 have been delivered in large numbers, with all of the ATR 42s and ATR 72s being transferred to American Connection partners.

Routes

Over 130 destinations throughout the USA, and in Canada, the Caribbean and the Bahamas are served.

Fleet		Ordered
15 Canadair CRJ700	95 Saab SF 340	7 Embraer ERJ-145
40 Embraer ERJ-135		86 Embraer ERJ-140
52 Embraer ERJ-140		10 Canadair CRJ700
56 Embraer ERJ-145		

Boeing 737-3B7 N328AW (Josef Krauthäuser / Phoenix)

AMERICA WEST AIRLINES

4000 East Sky Harbor Blvd. Phoenix, Arizona 85034, USA
Tel. 602-6930800, Fax. 602-6935546
E-mail: customer.advocate@americawest.com
www.americawest.com

Three- / Two- letter code	IATA No.	Reg'n prefix	ICAO callsign
AWE / HP	401	N	Cactus

America West Airlines is one of the younger and more dynamic of the major American airlines, having only been formed after the 1978 deregulation. Formed in February 1981, America West started flights from its Phoenix base on 1st August 1983, adding a major hub at Las Vegas and a smaller one at Columbus, Ohio. In only six years, the fleet grew from the initial three Boeing 737s to over 90 aircraft; with the new routes and destinations the number of employees also rose, all with a stake in America West Airlines in the form of shares. Initially, as the name suggests, the airline operated only in the west of the USA, but as the years passed the network was

expanded to all the states as well as to Canada and Hawaii, the latter with Boeing 747s from November 1989. In 1991, America West was the first US airline to use the Airbus A320. From 27th June1991, it flew under Chapter 11 bankruptcy protection with a reduced fleet, unprofitable routes were dropped and an economy programme brought in. This was successful, the carrier emerging from Chapter 11 in August 1994. Continental and Mesa Airlines acquired 25% of the shares. The present colour scheme was introduced in1996. To replace the ageing fleet of Boeing 737-200s America West decided upon the Airbus A319, the first aircraft being

delivered in October 1998. There were takeover negotiations with United during 1999, but the outcome was negative, and so AW is concentrating on building up the company with its own resources. Desert Sun Airlines, a subsidiary of Mesa Airlines and Freedom Airlines operate as America West Express. In 2003 the Columbus hub was dropped as more and more flights operate directly from Phoenix and Las Vegas to the east coast. Las Vegas has been built up more, following the 2002 collapse of National Airlines.

Routes

From main bases at Phoenix and Las Vegas, about 120 destinations in the USA, Canada and Mexico, for example. Acapulco, Guaymas, Hermosillo, Ixtapa, Manzanillo, Mazatlan, Mexico City, Monterey, Puerto Vallarta.

Fleet		Ordered
50 Airbus A320-200	14 Boeing 757-200	17 Airbus A320
32 Airbus A319-100		
10 Boeing 737-200Adv		
39 Boeing 737-300		

Boeing 727-233F N395AJ (Josef Krauthäuser / Fort Lauderdale)

AMERIJET INTERNATIONAL

498 SW 34th Street, Fort Lauderdale FL 33315, USA, Tel. 954-3590077, Fax. 954-3597866
www.amerijet.com

Three- / Two- letter code	IATA No.	Reg'n prefix	ICAO callsign
AJT / M6	810	N	Amerijet

Amerijet International was set up in 1974 and initially provided only cargo and express goods flights using Learjets and Cessna 401s. In 1985 the first three Boeing 727s were acquired and further examples of this type followed in 1988 and 1989, enabling charter, sub-charter and ad hoc freight flights to be undertaken. A combi version of this aircraft (Boeing 727-100C) was used when the airline moved into the passenger charter business as well as ambulance and cargo flights. Amerijet flies regular scheduled cargo flights on behalf of DHL and Burlington, both cargo specialists. In 1993 scheduled flights started for

the first time to Guyana. As the market for medium range freight aircraft had become thin, in 1996 five former PanAm Boeing 727s which had been stored for years in the Mojave Desert were bought. Some were taken into service with the airline after extensive overhaul at its base; others serve as spares sources. In 1998 operations and the company maintenance base were moved from Miami to nearby Fort Lauderdale. In June 2001 Amerijet sought Chapter 11 bankruptcy protection, and by December, after a successful reconstruction and with fresh capital and new equipment available, was able to make a new

beginning. The remaining six Boeing 727s are equipped with winglets and modern electronics and should be suitable for several more years of service. As well as scheduled services, the airline flies a lot of perishable goods, for instance meat, fish, vegetables and flowers and is always ready for worldwide ad hoc charters.

Routes

Antigua, Aruba, Barbados, Barcelona, Belize-City, Cancun, Curacao, Domenica, Fort de France, Fort Lauderdale, Georgetown, Grenada, Kingston, Maracaibo, Merida, Mexico City, Miami, Porlamar, Port au Prince, Porlamar, Port of Spain, Puerto Plata, San Juan, Santo Domingo, St.Kitts, St.Lucia, St. Maarten, St.Vincent.

Fleet

6 Boeing 727-200 F

Antonov An-124-100 UR-82009 (Albert Kuhbandner / Munich)

ANTONOV AIRLINES

Ul.Tupoleva 1, 252062 Kiev, Ukraine
Tel. 380-444430018, Fax. 380-444426124, E-mail:
office@antonov.kiev.ua, www.antonovaircargo.com

Three- / Two- letter code	IATA No.	Reg'n prefix	ICAO callsign
ADB / GS	–	UR	Antonov

One of the most famous aircraft design bureaus in the former Soviet Union was that named for its founder, Oleg Antonov. Outstanding aircraft such as the An-2, with over 20,000 built, were penned by the bureau, notably famous for its line of transport aircraft built from the 1950s and 1960s, including the An-8, An-10, An-12 and the impressive turboprop An-22 heavy transport. There followed the An-24/26, An-30/32 and the first jet, the An-72. Then there are the world's largest jet transports, the An-124 Ruslan and its derivative, the six-engined An-225 Mriya. In 1989 an agreement was reached with the British cargo airline HeavyLift for the use of an An-124 for worldwide charter operation. HeavyLift would rent the aircraft, inclusive of pilots, navigators and loading crews as required.The positive response and the demonstrated demand for this capacious transport led the Antonov Design Bureau to seek their own licence to operate the aircraft. Thus Antonov Airlines became the nation's cargo flag carrier by government decree. Antonov Airlines, with its numerous and diverse cargo charters, is always attracting media attention, for instance with the transport of 135 ton generators from Dusseldorf to Delhi, or support of the Paris-Dakar car rally. Antonov Airlines also flies for the United Nations and for foreign air forces when the need for such large freighters arises.

Routes

Worldwide ad hoc freight charters.

Fleet

3 Antonov An-12	1 Antonov An-74
1 Antonov An-22	7 Antonov An-124
1 Antonov An-26	1 Antonov An-225
2 Antonov An-32	

Airbus A300B4 YA-BAB (Oliver Köstinger / Sharjah)

ARIANA AFGHAN

P.O.Box 76 Ansari Watt, Kabul, Afghanistan
Tel. 873-762523844, Fax. 873-76252384
E-mail: flyariana@mail.com, www.flyariana.com

Three- / Two- letter code	IATA No.	Reg'n prefix	ICAO callsign
AFG / FG	255	YA	Ariana

Ariana Afghan Airlines Co Ltd. was founded on 27th January 1955 as a new national airline. The Indian company Indama Corp. provided the first Douglas DC-3 aircraft and held 49% of the shares. This holding was acquired in 1956 by Pan American World Airways, which expanded the airline considerably. International routes to Delhi and Beirut were quickly put in place, with the Beirut route being extended via Ankara and Prague to Frankfurt. Douglas DC-4s and, later, DC-6s were used. In 1963 its operational base was moved to Kabul from Kandahar, and 1967 saw Bakhtar Afghan Airlines formed to begin

taking over Ariana's domestic services. In 1968 Ariana took on its first jet, a Boeing 727, followed by a DC-10-30 in September 1979. Following the invasion of Afghanistan by Soviet troops over Christmas 1979, flight operations collapsed. The DC-10 was sold after suffering damage in a rocket attack and Soviet-built aircraft were added to the fleet. All operations were integrated into Bakhtar, which became the new national carrier, in October 1985, but by February 1988 the name had been changed back to its present form. During the ten years of the war, there were flights only to Moscow and Prague, and

occasionally to Berlin-Schönefeld, primarily to transport casualties for treatment. Gradually air transport was returning to normal, though the political situation was far from stable. Karachi in Pakistan was used as an alternative base for a while, but operations moved back to Kabul from 1998. A further setback came with the 2002 US-led war against the Taliban, during which six of the eight remaining aircraft were destroyed, but a sort of normality has returned and the fleet restored by gifts of Airbus A300s from India in 2002 and the acquisition of 727s from American Airlines and 747-200s from United in Spring 2003.

Routes

Amritsar, Delhi, Dubai, Frankfurt, Herat, Islamabad, Istanbul, Jeddah, Kabul, Mazar Sharif, Sharjah, Teheran.

Fleet

3 Airbus A300B4
6 Boeing 727-200
2 Boeing 747-200

Boeing 757-236 4X-BAZ (Josef Krauthäuser / Amsterdam)

ARKIA ISRAELI AIRLINES

P.O.Box 39301, Dov Airport, Tel Aviv 61392
Israel, Tel. 3-6902222, Fax. 3-6991390
E-mail: arkiaclick@arkia.co.il, www.arkia.co.il

Three- / Two- letter code	IATA No.	Reg'n prefix	ICAO callsign
AIZ / IZ	238	4X	Arkia

After the foundation in 1948 of the state of Israel and its airline El Al to serve Europe and the USA, there was also a need for an air service to Eilat. Road conditions across the desert to this Israeli outpost, which at that time consisted only of a small settlement and a military post, were dire. El Al and Histradut, the most important trades union, each took 50% of the shares of Eilata, which was set up late in 1948. On 28th February 1950 the airline carried out its official first flight from Tel Aviv to Eilat, using a Curtiss C-46 from El Al, which with two DH.89 Dragon Rapides formed the fleet. The airline's name was changed to Arkia

Israeli Airlines in September 1950, and subsequent expansion called for more and larger aircraft; several DC-3s and Beech 18s replaced the Dragon Rapides during the 1950s. With the opening of the first hotels in Eilat, passenger traffic increased. Handley Page Dart Heralds were acquired and for the first time Arkia flew internationally, to Cyprus. After the Six Day War in 1967 the occupied Sinai peninsula with Sharm-el-Sheik and Santa Katharina were added to the network. Between 1969 and 1974 Arkia took on Vickers Viscounts and in 1972 took a holding in Kanaf-Arkia Airlines, another domestic operator. In 1979 the airline was

privatised. Boeing 737-200s were added from 1981 and used on charter flights; domestic schedules were passed to DHC-7s and moved to Dov airport near the city of Tel Aviv. Increasing tourist traffic drove further expansion. Boeing 707s augmented the 737s until 1998, and in 1999 a fleet renewal began with the introduction of ATR 72s and Boeing 757-200s. A revised aircraft colour scheme was introduced with the delivery of the first 757, and Arkia was among the first to order the new, stretched 757-300. Arkia is the owner of over 30 Boeing aircraft, leased out principally in the USA, a lucrative business for the airline.

Routes

Scheduled services to Amman, Eilat, Haifa,Tel Aviv, Jerusalem, Rosh Pina and Kiryat Shmona. Frequent charters to Western Europe, East Africa and Thailand.

Fleet

3 ATR 72-500
1 Boeing 757-200
2 Boeing 757-300
5 de Havilland Canada DHC-7-100

Airbus A320-200 EK-32001 (Marcus Baltes / Frankfurt)

ARMENIAN AIRLINES

Zvartnots Airport, 375042 Yerevan, Armenia, Tel. 2-225444, Fax. 2-243152
www.armenianairlines.am

Three- / Two- letter code	IATA No.	Reg'n prefix	ICAO callsign
RME / R3	956	EK	Armenian

In 1993 the government of this newly independent republic took the initiative and took over the former Aeroflot Directorate in Armenia. The former Soviet republic, where business was once thriving, was at war with the neighbouring republic of Azerbaijan over the Nagorny-Karabakh territory, as a result of which the delivery of raw materials and energy from its neighbour were cut off. Armenia was dependent on these supplies and since the start of hostilities, business and living conditions had declined. Accordingly the development of air services was to be laborious. Even though the Aeroflot Directorate had carried a meagre two million passengers, the new airline could only manage a third of that number. Nevertheless, the airline has operated profitably, as there are countless expatriate Armenians who use the flights regularly. These expatriates could also provide a source of capital for a planned privatisation. Agreements have been made with KLM and Air France which should support the development of the company, especially as Armenia's capital, Yerevan, is an attractive tourist city. The business situation has not been good during the 1990s, and the hoped-for privatisation has not been progressed; in fact the fleet and route network have been trimmed. The delivery of a leased Airbus A310 in July 1998 was a step in the direction of fleet renewal, but this was returned in 2003 and an Airbus A320 leased instead, painted in new colours with 'Armenian International Airlines' titles. The company is to be reorganised and eventually relaunched when new investors can be found.

Routes

Adler, Aleppo, Amsterdam, Anapa, Ashkhabat, Athens, Dubai, Ekaterinburg, Frankfurt, Istanbul, Kiev, Kharkov, Krasnodar, Mineralnye Vody, Moscow, Novgorod, Novosibirsk, Odessa, Paris, Samara, St.Petersburg, Tabriz, Tashkent, Teheran, Volgograd, Yerevan.

Fleet		Ordered
1 Airbus A320-200	5 Tupolev Tu-134	2 Tupolev Tu-204
2 Antonov An-24	5 Tupolev Tu-154	
1 Antonov An-32		
2 Ilyushin IL-86		

Douglas DC-8-62F N791AL (Josef Krauthäuser / Miami)

ARROW AIR

2000 NW 62 Ave. Bldg.711, Miami FL 33122, USA
Tel. 305-8716606, Fax. 305-8714232
E-mail: sales@arrowair. com, www.arrowair.com

Three- / Two- letter code	IATA No.	Reg'n prefix	ICAO callsign
APW / GW	–	N	Big A

The name Arrow Airways was used in 1946 by a charter airline which existed only until 1954. However in 1980 the airline was reactivated and it started cargo charters on 26th May 1981, later undertaking passenger work, using Boeing 727s, DC-8s and DC-10s. The chequered history of Arrow Air came to an end in Spring 1995 when the FAA grounded the airline for safety reasons. After several months of reorganisation, services were re-started. In 1999 it was taken over by its direct competitor in Miami, Fine Airlines, though initially the two airlines continued to operate independently. Frank and Barry Fine had started the freight airline bearing their name in Miami at the beginning of 1992 and began operations that September with a flight to South America. Over the years more than 15 DC-8s were used by Fine for services to Central and South America. In September 2000 Fine Airlines placed itself under Chapter 11bankruptcy protection. The reconstruction plan envisaged a merger of Arrow Air and Fine, and a reduction of the fleet to save costs. Several aircraft were stored in the deserts of California or Arizona. With the aid of an investment bank, which in 2002 set up Arrow Air Holdings, it was possible to emerge from the bankruptcy situation. A new management team was installed and the name Arrow Air re-adopted. The fleet of mothballed DC-8s was slowly reactivated and joined by L-1011 TriStars on services again to Central and South America and the Caribbean. At the beginning of 2003 Arrow Air Holdings took over the assets of Air Global International (AGI) which is also active in the South American freight market with leased Boeing 747s. Arrow Air uses in Miami a large clearance centre for perishable goods – vegetables, flowers and fish – which is also used by other companies.

Routes

Freight flights to destinations in Central and South America and the Caribbean such as Columbia, Costa Rica, Ecuador, El Salvador, Guatemala, Honduras, Nicaragua, Panama, Peru, Puerto Rico, Trinidad and Venezuela.

Fleet

12 Douglas DC-8-61/62/63
 3 Lockheed L-1011

Douglas DC-9-31 YV-716C (Ralf Lücke / Porlamar)

ASERCA

Avda Bolivar Norte,Piso 8, Valencia 2002
Venezuela, Tel. 41-237111, Fax. 41-220210
www.asercaairlines.com

Three- / Two- letter code	IATA No.	Reg'n prefix	ICAO callsign
OCA / R7	717	YV	Aserca

Founded in 1991, Aserca-Aerolineas Regional del Centro from Valencia in northern Venezuela acquired two Douglas DC-9s from Midway Airlines with which to begin operations in 1992, initially to the holiday island of Margarita which lies off the north coast. Several Cessna 402s were also in the fleet for air taxi operations. The company was successful and so during 1993 and 1994 acquired more DC-9s and expanded further. As well as the capital Caracas, most of the important towns in Venezuela were soon being offered direct service from the country's second-largest city. During 1998 Aserca received its first MD-90 and took on a 70% shareholding in Air Aruba. Aserca also has a shareholding in the regional airline Santa Barbara, which flies ATR 42s. By way of fleet renewal, Boeing 737-800s were ordered to replace older DC-9s, with the first two aircraft being delivered in 1999. The consequences of the World Trade Center attack were felt by airlines in the Caribbean. Air Aruba became bankrupt and Aserca faced mounting financial difficulties. Several aircraft on lease were returned to their owners, others were stored out of service and the fleet renewal programme went by the board. A few unprofitable routes were dropped and the number of employees reduced. Today Aserca is set up as a low-cost airline operating well-supported services, principally with the old and inexpensive DC-9s. Though restricted to domestic services in the early years, the route network now encompasses the Caribbean region.

Routes

Aruba, Barcelona, Barquisemento, Caracas, Las Piedras, Lima, Maracaibo, Maturin, Porlamar, Puerto Ordaz, Punta Cana, San Antonio, Santo Domingo, Valencia.

Fleet

3 Boeing 737-200
13 Douglas DC-9-30

Boeing 747-48E HL7423 (Marcus Baltes / Frankfurt)

ASIANA

P.O.Box 9847 KangseoKu, Ose Dong, Seoul 135270
Republic of Korea, Tel. 02-6695099, Fax. 02-6695130
E-mail: asianacr@asiana.co.kr, www.asiana.co.kr

Three- / Two- letter code	IATA No.	Reg'n prefix	ICAO callsign
AAR / OZ	988	HL	Asiana

The economic boom of the 1980s in South Korea and the great mobility of the Koreans led to the formation of this airline. It was originally formed by the Kumho Industrial Group as Seoul Air International and started operations in December 1988, initially on domestic routes only. This restriction was soon lifted and international routes opened in 1989, first to Fukuoka in neighbouring Japan. Nagoya and Tokyo followed swiftly as well as other Korean domestic points; these were served with ten Boeing 737-400s. In 1990 routes to Hong Kong and Bangkok were added as well as new aircraft type, the Boeing 767. New routes to Los Angeles, San Francisco and New York from 1992 brought the Boeing 747-400 into the fleet and in December 1994 the first all-cargo jumbo, a Boeing 747-400F was introduced. The investment required was colossal, and for the decade beginning 1996 about 60 new aircraft, from Airbus as well as Boeing, were ordered or on option, with deliveries commencing in 1998. The leap to Europe was made in 1995 with a regular service to Brussels and Vienna, with London added at the end of 1996 and Frankfurt in 1997. The Asian financial downturn of the late 1990s put a damper on growth, with flights to Europe being particularly affected. By 2000 though, Asiana was again on a slow expansion path and acquiring new aircraft. The Football World Cup in Korea and the opening of the new Seoul airport both gave impetus. In March 2003 Asiana became a member of the Star Alliance.

Routes

Amsterdam,Anchorage, Bangkok, Beijing, Boston, Brussels, Chejudoo, Chengdu, Chicago, Chinju, Delhi, Djakarta, Frankfurt, Fukuoka, Guam, Guangzhou, Guilin,Harbin, Hiroshima, Ho Chi Minh-City, Hong Kong, Kuala Lumpur, Kwangju, Los Angeles, London, Macau, Manila, Matsuyama, Miyazaki, Mokpo, Nagoya, Nanjing, New York, Okinawa, Osaka, Pohang, Pusan, Saipan, San Francisco, Seattle, Sendai, Seoul, Shanghai, Shenzen, Singapore, Sydney, Taegu, Takamatsu, Tashkent, Tokyo, Toyama, Ulsan, Xian, Yosu.

Fleet

9 Airbus A321-100/200
22 Boeing 737-400
3 Boeing 737-500
13 Boeing 767-300

13 Boeing 747-400/-400F
4 Boeing 777-200ER

Ordered

8 Airbus A321
18 Airbus A330
3 Boeing 747-400
2 Boeing 767
4 Boeing 777

Boeing 737-700 N312TZ (Josef Krauthäuser / Fort Lauderdale)

ATA-AMERICAN TRANS AIR

P.O.Box 51609 Indianapolis, Indiana 46251, USA
Tel. 317-2474000, Fax. 317-2407091
E-mail: service@ata.com, www.ata.com

Three- / Two- letter code	IATA No.	Reg'n prefix	ICAO callsign
AMT / TZ	366	N	Amtran

American Trans Air is the largest charter operator in the United States, though in recent years it has moved more into the scheduled service market also. It was founded in 1973 in Indianapolis, Indiana and started flying for Ambassadair Travel Club, using a Boeing 720. In 1981 permission was granted by the Federal Aviation Administration for American Trans Air to operate as a charter airline. Further Boeing 707s were acquired and in 1982 DC-10s and Boeing 727s were added. As there was an acute shortage of second hand DC-10s on the worldwide airliner market, a switch was made to a fleet of Lockheed

L-1011 TriStars, and this type along with the 727 replaced the Boeing 707s, the older examples of the 727 being in turn replaced with Boeing 757s from 1992 onwards. A particularly vigorous expansion took place from 1993 to 1995 and a new, bright colour scheme was adopted, along with a change of name to ATA. After a short lull during the second part of the 1990s, expansion resumed and in 1999 the airline Chicago Express, equipped with BAe Jetstream 31s and Saab 340s for feeder services, was bought. ATA's first scheduled service destination in Europe was Dublin, from 1998. Fleet renewal began in

2001 with Boeing 757-300s in place of the older TriStars and Boeing 737-800s for the Boeing 727; the last 727 left the fleet in 2002. A fresh new colour scheme was introduced with the delivery of the first 737-800.The airline has a large maintenance complex at Indianapolis, and a further important hub at Chicago Midway. As well as its now extensive scheduled service network, ATA remains true to its origins and is active with military and civil charter work.

Routes

Cancun, Chicago, Dallas/Fort Worth, Dayton, Denver, Dublin, Fort Lauderdale, Fort Myers, Honolulu, Indianapolis, Las Vegas, Los Angeles, Maui, Milwaukee, Montego Bay, New York, Orlando, Phoenix, San Francisco, San Juan.

Fleet	Ordered
16 Boeing 757-200	10 Boeing 737-800
12 Boeing 757-300	
35 Boeing 737-800	
15 Lockheed L-1011	

Lockheed L-188C Electra G-LOFC (Stefan Schlick / Saarbrücken)

ATLANTIC AIRLINES

Coventry Airport, Coventry, CV8 3AZ, Great Britain
Tel. 0247-6882634, Fax. 0247-6307703, E-mail:
sales@atlanticairlines.co.uk, www.atlanticairlines.co.uk

Three letter code	IATA No.	ICAO Callsign
AAG/KI	-	Atlantic

In 1969 the air taxi company General Aviation Services was founded in Jersey in the Channel Islands. With a Cessna 310, all sorts of tasks were flown, from passengers to freight. Eventually the purchase of several Douglas DC-3s was made, and the company changed its name to Air Atlantique in 1974. The base was moved from Jersey to Coventry in 1984, and in 1986 the British government's attractive pollution control contract and their DC-3s were taken over from Harvest Air. Spectacular actions became increasingly common in the North Sea area during maritime patrol and oil pollution work following incidents to oil rigs or tankers. In 1987 the fleet was increased with the acquisition of a DC-6 for special charter use. In 1994 the company was reorganised into separate groups: Atlantic Cargo is responsible for freight charter and in 1994 received three Lockheed Electras; Air Atlantique Reconnaissance was responsible for maritime patrol and Pollution Control and had at its disposal aircraft with radar and infra-red equipment, but this division has now been sold and the pollution control is operated under contract by Air Atlantique. The two DC-6s have also now been adapted with a 'quick-fit' palletised system so that they can be readily converted from freighters to sprayers on demand. Atlantic Airways was set up for passenger charter work, and here the DC-3s have a special role for airshow work, pleasure and special flights. The newest division in the group is Air Atlantique Historic Flight, whose aim is the restoration, maintenance and operation of historic aircraft. The group has extensive freight contracts and often uses wet-leased aircraft from other airlines, including Brasilias, with Tupolev 204s in prospect.

Routes

Ad hoc freight and passenger charters, maritime patrol and pollution control.

Fleet

1 ATR 42	2 Douglas DC-3
3 Cessna 310	2 Douglas DC-6
3 Cessna 404	
1 Fairchild Swearingen Metro III	
7 Lockheed L-188 Electra	

Canadair CRJ200ER N906EV (Tony Stork / Baltimore)

ATLANTIC SOUTHEAST AIRLINES – ASA

100 Hartsfield Central Parkway, Suite 800
Atlanta, GA 30354 USA, Tel. 404-7661400
Fax. 404-2090162, www.delta.com

Three- / Two- letter code	IATA No.	Reg'n prefix	ICAO callsign
CAA / EV	862	N	Chandler

Atlantic Southwest Airlines – ASA was founded in March 1979 and in June of that year began its first services from Atlanta. De Havilland Canada DHC-7s, Embraer EMB-110 Bandeirantes and Shorts 360s were used. The company was successful from the outset and grew steadily, so that by 1981 over 150,000 passengers were being carried to around 20 destinations. In order to finance further expansion the company went to the stock exchange in 1982. Thus provided with additional capital, it was possible to take over a competitor, Southeastern Airlines, on 1st April 1993. In 1984 the important decision was taken to co-operate with Delta Air Lines, not only in unified marketing, but with ASA as a participant in the newly formed Delta Connection feeder system. With the delivery of the newer and faster Embraer 120 Brasilia during 1985 it was possible to phase out the Shorts 360s and the fleet continued to expand. Larger aircraft such as the ATR 42 in 1983 and the BAe 146 in 1985 were introduced from the two hubs at Atlanta and Dallas for longer routes. The BAe 146 was the airline's first jet type and in future this form of power would have the advantage in equipment choice. Thus in 1997 Canadair Regional Jet 200s were added, to replace Brasilias and with the aim in time of achieving a homogeneous fleet structure. These have been joined by the lengthened RJ 700 version, with delivery from 2001. Likewise the ATR 42s were replaced by the larger ATR 72. Over time, Delta took on more and more shares in ASA-Holdings and by 1999 ASA became a fully-owned, though independently operating, subsidiary, bound into to all Delta's alliances. This is reflected in the colour scheme, which is as Delta Connection, with only a small ASA logo. All of ASA's maintenance is carried out in its own facilities at Dallas and Atlanta.

Routes

From its two major hubs at Atlanta and Dallas a total of about 80 cities and towns in the south-east and midwest of the USA are served.

Fleet	Ordered
19 ATR 72-200	25 Canadair CRJ700
45 Embraer EMB-120	
85 Canadair CRJ200	
20 Canadair CRJ700	

Ilyushin IL-86 RA86062 (Marcus Baltes / Frankfurt)

ATLANT-SOYUZ AIRLINES

10/2 Nikolskaya Ul. Moscow 103012, Russia
Tel. 095-9239717, Fax. 095-9214360, E-mail:
info@atlant-soyuz.ru, www.atlant-soyuz,ru

Three- / Two- letter code	IATA No.	Reg'n prefix	ICAO callsign
AYZ / 3G	411	RA	Atlant Soyuz

During June 1993 a new joint stock company was registered in Moscow with the name Atlant-Soyuz Airlines. The Ukrainian airline Atlant and other investors were the shareholders. It was planned to operate freight flights, but in addition passenger services from Moscow. The aircraft were taken over from Aeroflot and operations were begun in the same month as the company was formed. Atlant-Soyuz Airlines also established a scheduled service between Chklakovsky and Magadan using Ilyushin IL-62s or Tupolev Tu-154s, and charter flights were made particularly to the shoppers' paradise of the Middle East, for instance to Dubai or Abu Dhabi in the United Arab Emirates. The company's IL-76s are often seen at airports in Western Europe operating freight charters. The Ilyushin IL-96 is also a freight version and was delivered to the airline in 1999. Atlant-Soyuz is the second largest freight airline in Russia. Passenger charters are undertaken to Turkey, Italy and other European destinations.

Routes

Abu Dhabi, Chklakovsky, Dubai, Magadan, Moscow, Simferopol are served on a scheduled basis. Additionally there are worldwide freight and passenger charters.

Fleet

12 Ilyushin IL-76
1 Ilyushin IL-86
1 Ilyushin IL-96-300

Boeing 747-243B N516MC (Martin Kühn / Frankfurt)

ATLAS AIR

2000 Winchester Avenue, Purchase, New York, NY 10577-2543, USA, Tel. 914-7018000, Fax. 914-7018053 E-mail: info@atlasair.com, www.atlasair.com

Three- / Two- letter code	IATA No.	Reg'n prefix	ICAO callsign
GTI / 5Y	369	N	Giant

In 1992 Atlas Air was formed in New York by Atlas Holdings, a sister company of Aeronautics Leasing, as a freight-only carrier, and since then has grown rapidly. With a fleet of Boeing 747 freighters Atlas Air operates worldwide. Regular flights operate from New York to Hong Kong via Anchorage and via Khabarovsk in Russia back to New York. As well as its own scheduled services, Atlas Air has flown regular freight charters for other well-known airlines including for example Alitalia, British Airways, Cargolux, China Airlines, FedEx, Iberia, KLM, Lufthansa, SAS and Thai, leasing them both crews and aircraft, sometimes on long-term contract and painted in the customer airline's colours. In 1996 five Boeing 747s were taken over from Fed Ex, but as there are few freighter 747s on the market, pure passenger aircraft have had to be acquired and converted to freighters for the airline. Thus for example the entire 747-200 fleet of Thai International was acquired and converted from 1997. Thus the fleet has grown quickly and the first of 12 new-build 747-400Fs entered service from mid-1998. In July 2001 Atlas took over its competitor Polar Air Cargo. Atlas Air's base is at New York's JFK International Airport; a further important departure point, especially for services to South America, is Miami.

Routes

Scheduled, charter and ad hoc freight flights. Atlas Air flies on behalf of Alitalia, British Airways, China Southwest, Lufthansa, SAS and other companies.

Fleet

```
 4 Boeing 747-200SF
 3 Boeing 747-300SF
16 Boeing 747-400UF
```

Boeing 757-225 TC-OGB (Albert Kuhbandner / Munich)

ATLASJET INTERNATIONAL AIRWAYS

Zümrütova Mah. Sinanaglu Cad. 35 / 1-2, 07160
Antalya, Türkey, Tel. +902423100450
E-mail: atlas@atlasjet.com, www.atlasjet.com

Three- / Two- letter code	IATA No.	Reg'n prefix	ICAO callsign
OGE / 2U	610	TC	Atlasjet

Several Turkish charter airlines were forced out of business during 2000 and 2001 and this left a gap, particularly in the German market, for economical capacity. The tour operator Öger Tours was particularly affected, and so under the aegis of Öger Holdings, Atlasjet International Airways was established in Antalya on 14th March 2001. The new charter airline took to the skies from 1st June 2001 with two Boeing 757-200s. Its headquarters and base are at Antalya, the fastest growing airport in Turkey. Initially flights were restricted to services from German airports to destinations in Turkey, but after this bedding-in phase came the delivery of a second Boeing 757-200 and an expansion of services to include Switzerland, France, Italy and Israel. As well as the tourist flights for Öger Tours, there are also numerous charters for expatriate Turkish workers. There has also been an increase in work on behalf of other tour operators, and in 2002 Atlasjet was involved for the first time in seasonal pilgrim flights to Saudi Arabia. Development plans up to 2006 call for a doubling of the fleet and an expansion of flights to include Russia, Scandinavia and Great Britain.

Routes

Adana, Amsterdam, Ankara, Antalya, Basle, Berlin-SXF,Bodrum, Bremen, Cologne, Dalaman, Dresden, Düsseldorf, Erfurt, Frankfurt, Gaziantep, Hamburg, Hanover, Istanbul, Izmir, Leipzig, Lyon, Milan, Munich, Münster, Paderborn, Paris-CDG, Stuttgart, Tel Aviv, Vienna, Zürich.

Fleet

3 Boeing 757-200

De Havilland DHC-8-402 D-ADHB (Albert Kuhbandner / Munich)

AUGSBURG AIRWAYS

Beim Glaspalast 1, 86153 Augsburg, Germany
Tel, 0821-270970, Fax. 0821-27097199, E-mail:
reservations@augsburgair.de, www.augsburgair.de

Three- / Two- letter code	IATA No.	Reg'n prefix	ICAO callsign
AUB / IQ	614	D	Augsburg Air

From 1979 Interot Air Service maintained a regular charter service on behalf of the Haindl Paper Company and Interot Internationale Spedition using the company aircraft, a Beech 200 Super King Air. From 1986 this was licensed as a scheduled service. A second King Air was added from Autumn 1987 to provide service to Hamburg. The demand for these services from Augsburg was good, so that in September 1988 the acquisition of a Beechcraft 1900 Airliner was warranted, with a second following in May 1989. Interot obtained its licence as a scheduled service operator in December 1989 and this

offered new perspectives for the future. A leased de Havilland Canada DHC-8 was put into service on the Düsseldorf route from October 1990; three aircraft of this type were ordered firm. The reunification of Germany brought with it new destinations from Augsburg, and a change of name to Interot Airways. After the opening of the new Munich airport, Augsburg was seen as an alternative to this, and new routes were opened to London and Cologne. From 1st January 1996 the name was changed again to Augsburg Airways and the aircraft colour scheme was changed. Effective from the Winter

1996/97 timetable, Augsburg Airways became a Lufthansa franchise partner under the Team Lufthansa banner and began flying for the national airline for the first time from Munich and other German regional airports. Thus the aircraft are in Lufthansa colours with only a small sticker announcing the actual operator. A changeover of the fleet to the quieter and more powerful Dash-8Q is in progress, but because of poor business conditions, Augsburg dropped most of the routes from its Augsburg base early in 2003 and began cost-reduction measures; some aircraft were leased out.

Routes

Berlin, Cologne, Düsseldorf, Frankfurt, Hamburg, Leipzig, Munich and other destinations on behalf of Team Lufthansa.

Fleet

```
 2 De Havilland DHC-8-200
 2 De Havilland DHC-8-300
10 De Havilland DHC-8-300Q
 5 De Havilland DHC-8-400QC
```

BN-Trislander G-JOEY (via Hans-Willi Mertens / Jersey)

AURIGNY AIR SERVICES

La Panque Lane, States Airport,Forest, Guernsey, Channel Islands GY8 ODT, Great Britain, Tel. 1481-66444, Fax. 1481-66446, E-mail:sales@aurigny.com www.aurigny.com

Three- / Two- letter code	IATA No.	Reg'n prefix	ICAO callsign
AUR / GR	924	G	Ayline

For more than 30 years Aurigny Air Services has been an institution on the British Channel Isles. It was set up on 1st March 1968 and began its inter-island services with two Britten-Norman Islanders between Guernsey, Jersey and Alderney. The small airline developed rapidly in the first couple of years, so that by 1970 eight Islanders were in use. A larger aircraft type was required, and the answer to this problem came also from Britten-Norman, who developed the three-engined Trislander, the first of which was delivered to Aurigny in July 1971. This unpretentious yet dependable aircraft proved to be ideal and has formed the mainstay of the fleet ever since that time. The route network was extended to northern France and the south of England. In 1987 Aurigny concluded a contract with the British Post Office to carry letters between the islands and to London-Gatwick and East Midlands. Aurigny also undertakes ambulance flights as required. During 1990 the company took delivery of its first turboprop type, a Shorts 360. In July 1999 the airline received the first of two Saab SF 340s. When KLM UK dropped its Guernsey services, Aurigny took over the Stansted route, using two more Saab 340s. An ATR 42 was used to give greater capacity for the 2002 summer, and the first jet, a BAe 146 acquired in Spring 2003 for services to Stansted and Manchester. During summer 2003 British Airways dropped their Gatwick service and the island government acquired the airline in a controversial move, designed to ensure the continuity of essential air connections to the mainland. An ATR 72 has been leased briefly for Aurigny to fly this Gatwick link.

Routes

Alderney, Bristol, Cherbourg, Dinard, East Midlands, Guernsey, Jersey, London-Stansted, Manchester, Southampton.

Fleet

1 BAe 146
8 Britten Norman Trislander
1 Shorts 360
4 Saab SF 340

Boeing 767-338 VH-OGK (Frank Schorr / Sydney)

AUSTRALIAN AIRLINES

Airport C 5, Mascot, NSW 2020, Australia
Tel. 2-96913636, Fax. 2-96913277
www.australianairlines.com.au

Three- / Two- letter code	IATA No.	Reg'n prefix	ICAO callsign
AO / –	–	VH	Australian Airlines

Following the collapse of Ansett Airlines late in 2001, there was a gap in the market for tourist flights in Australia. Ansett's flights had always been well patronised, especially by Japanese tourists. Qantas Airways therefore in February 2002 announced that it would set up an new tourist airline. A name was quickly found since, when Australian Airlines had been merged into Qantas in 1993, the rights to the name had been retained. Plans were formulated for Boeing 767 operations, with the operating licence being granted at the beginning of October, allowing the first flight to take place on 27th October 2002 from Cairns to Nagoya. Initially four Boeing 767-300s were transferred from Qantas to Australian Airlines; they were repainted in an attractive colour scheme, with a kangaroo on the fin. Within only a few months many new routes were inaugurated and in May 2003 the fleet was supplemented with two further 767s. In the medium term, it is planned for Australian to operate 12 aircraft, and also to undertake some domestic services.

Routes

Cairns, Denpasar, Fukuoka, Goldcoast, Hong Kong, Kota Kinabalu, Melbourne, Nagoya, Osaka, Singapore, Sydney, Taipei.

Fleet

6 Boeing 767-300

Airbus A320-214 OE-LBO (Marcus Baltes / Frankfurt)

AUSTRIAN AIRLINES

Postfach 50, 1107 Vienna, Austria
Tel. 1-17660, Fax. 1-17664230
E-mail: contact@aua.com, www.aua.com

Three- / Two- letter code	IATA No.	Reg'n prefix	ICAO callsign
AUA / OS	257	OE	Austrian

Austrian Airlines was set up on 30th September 1957 and began operations on 31st March 1958 on the Vienna-London route using Vickers Viscounts leased from shareholder Fred Olsen. A short time later, services also began to Frankfurt, Zürich, Paris, Stuttgart and Rome. In February 1960 AUA bought its own Vickers Viscount 837s. In April 1963 the Caravelle entered service. Domestic routes were still being served by the DC-3s, which were however replaced in 1966 by HS.748s. During 1969 AUA underwent a reorganisation with unprofitable routes and the entire

domestic network being dropped. The DC-9 was ordered, entering service in 1971. Two attempts to launch long-range services with Boeing 707s, the first in association with Sabena in 1969, were abandoned in 1973. From 1975 DC-9-51s were ordered and AUA was one of the launch customers for the MD-81. From 1988, MD-87s, with extended range, were also added to the fleet. The third attempt at long-range services in 1989 was more successful and began with services to Tokyo and New York, using Airbus A310s. Three new types entered the fleet during 1995: the

Fokker 70, Airbus A321 and Airbus A340, all of which displayed a new colour scheme. Fleet changes during 1999 were the introduction of the Airbus A330 and the beginning of the replacement of the MD-80s by the Airbus A320 and A321. During 1999 Austrian broke away from its long-term 'Qualiflyer' partner Swissair and joined the Star Alliance from March 2000. Lauda Air and Tyrolean are now 100% owned; the latest member of the group is Rheintalflug, taken over in 2002 and integrated into Tyrolean. Austrian has a shareholding in Ukraine International.

Routes

Abu Dhabi, Altenrhein, Amman, Amsterdam, Ankara, Athens, Barcelona, Beijing, Beirut, Belfast, Berlin, Bratislava, Brussels, Budapest, Bucharest, Cairo, Copenhagen, Cologne, Damascus, Dublin, Düsseldorf, Frankfurt, Gothenburg, Graz, Hamburg, Hanover, Istanbul, Kiev, Larnaca, Linz, London, Milan, Minsk, Montreal, Moscow, Munich, New York, Odessa, Osaka, Oslo, Ostrava, Paris, Prague, Salzburg, Sofia, Stockholm, Stuttgart, Tashkent, Tbilisi, Teheran, Tel Aviv, Timisoara, Tokyo, Toronto, Vienna, Vilnius, Washington, Warsaw, Zagreb, Zürich.

Fleet

Fleet		Ordered
8 Airbus A320	3 Fokker 70	7 Airbus A319
6 Airbus A321-100	5 McDonnell Douglas MD-82/83	5 Airbus A321
4 Airbus A330-200	4 McDonnell Douglas MD-87	
4 Airbus A340-200/300		

Boeing 737-219 XA-NAV (Josef Krauthäuser / Las Vegas)

AVIACSA

Hangar 1, Zona C Col. Aviacion Gral, CP 15520
Intl.Airport Mexico-City, Mexico, Tel. 55-57169005
Fax. 55-57583590, www.aviacsa.com.mx
E-mail: serve_abordo@aviacsa.com.mx

Three- / Two- letter code	IATA No.	Reg'n prefix	ICAO callsign
CHP / 6A	095	XA	Aviacsa

Consorcio Aviacsa SA was founded in June 1990 with swift progress being made to licensing, so that operations could begin on 20th September 1990 with a BAe 146. Later in the same year a second 146 was added and the network was expanded. Two Fokker 100s were added in 1991 but in 1994 the existing fleet, which was no longer really suited to the airline's needs, was exchanged for Boeing 727-200s. In this same year Aviacsa also started charter work. DC-9s joined the fleet in 1997. During 1999/2000 almost the whole of the Air New Zealand Boeing 737-200 fleet was taken over. In 2000 a company reorganisation took place, with new owners and a new corporate image. Services were started to neighbouring Texas, specifically Houston, and further expansion in the USA has seen the addition of Las Vegas and, from April 2003, Chicago.

Routes

Acapulco, Cancun, Chetumal, Chicago, Ciuad de Mexico, Guadalajara, Hermosilo, Houston, Las Vegas, Leon, Merida, Mexicali, Monterrey, Morelia, Oaxaca, Tapachula, Tijuana, Tuxtla Gutierrez, Villahermosa.

Fleet

19 Boeing 737-200
 8 Boeing 727-200
 2 Douglas DC-9-15

Boeing 767-300ER N535AW (Ken Petersen / New York – JFK)

AVIANCA COLOMBIA

Av. Eldorado 93-30 Piso 4, Bogota 1, Columbia
Tel. 1-4139511, Fax. 1-4138716, E-mail:
informacion@avianca.comwww.avianca.com.co

Three- / Two- letter code	IATA No.	Reg'n prefix	ICAO callsign
AVA / AV	134	HK	Avianca

The Sociedad Colombo-Alemanos de Transportes Aereos (SCADTA) was set up on 5th December 1919 and started flights from the port of Barranquilla on 12th September 1920. Initially Junkers F-13s were used for the route to Puerto Berrio. Destinations in neighbouring Ecuador and Venezuela were served with Junkers W34s. In 1930 Pan American acquired an 80% interest in SCADTA, took over the international flights itself and exchanged the German aircraft types for American ones. On 14th June 1940 SCADTA became Aerovias Nacionales de Colombia (Avianca) and merged with Servicio Aereo Colombiano, which had operated a small network since its foundation in 1933. In 1947 Avianca flew to Miami and two years later to New York also, using Douglas DC-4s. This type was also used to Europe – Paris and Lisbon. On 17th April 1953 Lockheed Constellations were used to begin service to Hamburg and to Frankfurt in the following year. Jet aircraft, Boeing 707s and 720s, were acquired for international routes from 1962. Avianca was the first South American airline to purchase 727s, and the first went into service in April 1966. From 1971 Zürich was added to the European destinations. The Boeing 747 was delivered in November 1976 and since 1988 the 767 has also been used; likewise older 727s have been replaced with 757s. Avianca has been in Colombian ownership since 1978, and itself owns over 90% of the shares in SAM-Colombia. Its base is at the Eldorado airport at Bogota. Together with Aces and Sam-Colombia, since May 2002, Avianca has been building up the Summa alliance, into which all the companies will be merged even though flying under their own names. From September 2002 the aircraft colours are changing to reflect this alliance.

Routes

Arauca, Aruba, Barranquilla, Bogota, Bucaramanga, Buenos Aires, Cali, Caracas, Cartagena, Cucuta, Curacao, Guatemala-City, Guayaquil, Lima, London, Los Angeles, Madrid, Manizales, Medellin, Mexico City, Miami, New York, Panama-City, Pasto, Pereira, Popayan, Quito, Rio de Janeiro, San Andres, San Jose, Santa Marta, Santiago, San Pedro Sula, San Salvador, Sao Paulo, Tegucigalpa.

Fleet

4 Boeing 767-200ER	6 Fokker 50
2 Boeing 767-300	13 McDonnell Douglas MD-83
5 Boeing 757-200	

Boeing 737-200 N121GU (Hans-Willi Mertens / Miami)

AVIATECA

Avienda Hincapie 12-22, Aeroporto La Aurora,
Guatemala City, Guatemala, Tel. 3310375
Fax. 3347846, www.groupotaca.com

Three- / Two- letter code	IATA No.	Reg'n prefix	ICAO callsign
GUG / GU	240	TG	Aviateca

On 14th March 1945 the airline Empresa Guatemalteca de Aviacion SA (Aviateca) was set up by the government, to take over the operations of PAA-financed Aerovias de Guatemala SA, which had been founded in 1939. DC-3s were used to continue the services, with Douglas DC-6Bs being added in 1961, allowing an expansion of the route network to Miami, New Orleans and other destinations. The first jet was a leased BAC One-Eleven in 1970. In 1974 the airline was renamed as Aerolinas de Guatemala and two Boeing 727s were added to the fleet. From 1989 Aviateca also flew two leased Boeing 737-200s, and further examples were acquired up until 1995. TACA held 30% of the shares and as a result there was co-operation in scheduling and aircraft use. During 1998 the co-operation was intensified, as Aviateca became a member of Grupo TACA, which is building up a network of airline operations in South and Central America. The aircraft livery was changed accordingly to reflect membership of the group. The airline is also a member of the Latin Pass marketing alliance in which most of the region's airlines participate to try to counterbalance the US airlines. The airline's base is at Guatemala – La Aurora, and there is a subsidiary company, Inter, which operates Cessna Grand Caravans on domestic services.

Routes

Flores, Guatemala City, Managua, Merida, Mexico City, Miami, New Orleans, Panama, San Jose, San Salvador.

Fleet

2 Boeing 737-200Adv.

Tupolev Tu-154B-2 4K-85548 (Hans-Willi Mertens collection)

AZERBAIJAN AIRLINES

11 Azadlig Avenue, 370109 Baku, Azerbaijan
Tel. 12-934434, Fax. 12-985237
E-mail: azal@azal.az, www.azal.az

Three- / Two- letter code	IATA No.	Reg'n prefix	ICAO callsign
AHY / J2	771	4K	Azal

In 1992 the government of the new republic of Azerbaijan in Baku brought into being the Azerbaijan Airline Concern, organised in three divisions. Azal Avia is responsible for passenger transport; it is the national flag carrier and flies under the name of Azerbaijan Airlines. The Soviet-built aircraft were taken over from the former Aeroflot division, and some older western aircraft, Boeing 707s and 727s, were also acquired. The Tupolev Tu-134s and 154s will be phased out slowly and have already been partly supplanted by the Boeing 757, which were delivered in mid-2000 especially for use on routes to central Europe.

Further development of the company however is dependent on the country's political situation. At the end of the 1990s re-organisation was carried out, and some of the older An-26s, and several Tu-134s and 154s were retired. International oil companies have been granted licences in the region, and Azerbaijan Airlines is benefiting from the resulting increased traffic, with two further Boeing 757-200s added. Freight operations have also been on the upturn, and the airline (through its sister company Azal Cargo) has acquired additional Ilyushin IL-76s to meet this demand

Routes

Adana, Aleppo, Aktau, Ankara, Baku, Bishkek, Chelyabinsk, Dubai, Ekaterinburg, Frankfurt, Gyandzha, Istanbul, Kiev, London, Moscow, Nakhichevan, Odessa, Paris, St. Petersburg, Tbilisi, Teheran, Tel Aviv, Trabzon, Urumqi, Voronezh.

Fleet

2 Boeing 727-200
4 Boeing 757-200
11 Ilyushin IL-76
8 Tupolev Tu-134B

4 Tupolev Tu-154B/M
5 Yakovlev Yak-40

BAe RJ 85 EI-CNI (Gerhard Schütz / Munich)

AZZURRA AIR

Via Paleocapa 3D, 24122 Bergamo, Italy
Tel. 035-4160311, Fax. 035-4160300
E-mail: info@azzurraair.it, www.azzurraair.it

Three- / Two- letter code	IATA No.	Reg'n prefix	ICAO callsign
AZI / ZS	864	I	Azzurraair

Azzurra was set up at the end of 1995 with logistical and financial support from Air Malta. Co-founders on the Italian side were IMS International and Medio Credito Centrale. Services began about a year later in December 1996 from Azzurra's base at Bergamo, using BAe Avro RJ 85s seconded from Air Malta. From the outset there was a partnership arrangement with Alitalia, and several routes were taken over in the AI-Express System; thus flights were operated from Milan-MXP. Further RJ 85s and the smaller RJ 70s augmented the fleet from 1998, and from the 1999 summer season the airline offered charter flights, for which a Boeing 737-300 was leased, with an order being placed at the same time with Boeing for two 737-700s. When these were delivered, they were employed on scheduled services as well as charters. By 2002 the fleet had grown to seven Boeing 737-700s. During 2003 Azzurra received its first Airbus A320-200. All Azzurra's aircraft are leased in, and registered in Ireland.

Routes

Alghero, Berlin, Bilbao, Copenhagen, Düsseldorf, Florence, Frankfurt, Hamburg, Milan, Munich, Porto, Rome, Stuttgart, Thessaloniki, Valencia, Vienna, Zürich.

Fleet

2 Airbus A320-200
7 BAe RJ 70/85
7 Boeing 737-700

Boeing 737-275 C6-BGL (Josef Krauthäuser / Fort Lauderdale)

BAHAMASAIR

P.O. Box N4881 Nassau, Bahamas,
Tel. 3778451, Fax. 3778550,
www.bahamasair.com

Three- / Two- letter code	IATA No.	Reg'n prefix	ICAO callsign
BHS / UP	111	C6	Bahamas

Bahamasair was established on 18th June 1973, just prior to Bahamian independence from Britain, and immediately took over the domestic routes of Out Island Airways and the domestic routes of Flamingo Airlines to become the national airline. Among the early aircraft used were HS.748s and BAC One-Elevens. Bahamasair's main routes are those from Nassau and Freetown and Miami in Florida, only 45 minutes flying time away. The One-Elevens were replaced from 1976 by three Boeing 737-200s from 1976, and two Boeing 727-200s followed for routes to New York and Boston. There was close

co-operation with Eastern Airlines, before the US airline collapsed. Several of the older HS.748s were replaced by more modern de Havilland Canada DHC-8s from 1990, with the last 748 leaving in 1996. The use of jet aircraft, and their maintenance costs, proved to be too expensive, and as a result, in 1992 Bahamasair took all the jets out of service and replaced them with turboprops. However, this move left the significant market to the east of the USA open to its competitors, until in 1995 it was again decided to lease a Boeing 737. During 1997 two further 737s were added, and these operate

flights several times a day to Miami, Orlando and Fort Lauderdale. Shorts 360s were acquired between 1995 and 1997 and used for shorter range trips within the Bahamas, but de Havilland Canada Dash 8s now look after the inter-island traffic.

Routes

Andros Town, Arthurs Town, Bimini, Crooked Island, Deadmanns Cay, Fort Lauderdale, Freeport, George Town, Governors Harbour, Grand Turk, Inagua, Mangrove Cay, Marsh Harbour, Miami, Nassau, North Eleuthera, Orlando, Providenciales, Rock Sound, San Andros, Stella Maris, Treasure Cay, West Palm Beach.

Fleet

2 Boeing 737-200
5 de Havilland DHC-8-300

Boeing 717-238 HS- PGO (Josef Krauthäuser collection)

BANGKOK AIRWAYS

99 Moo 14 Viphavadee Rangsit Rd. Ladyao, Chatuchak, Bangkok 10900, Thailand, Tel. 66-22655678 Fax. 66-22655500, E-mail: info@bangkokair.co.th, www.bangkokair.co.th

Three- / Two- letter code	IATA No.	Reg'n prefix	ICAO callsign
BKP / PG	829	HS	Bangkok Air

Set up in 1985 by the owner of Sahakol Air, an air-taxi company which had been formed in 1968 to operate between Bangkok and the tourist resorts of Samui Island and other points, Bangkok Airways started operations with an Embraer Bandeirante in January 1986. A Piper PA-31 Navajo was used also, though the company was still licensed only as an air-taxi operator and flew tourists to smaller resorts. An order for two Saab 340As was announced in September 1986 but did not come to fruition. During 1989 and 1990 however the fleet was augmented with the delivery of the de Havilland DHC-8 and a scheduled service licence was granted. The Dash 8s were replaced during 1994/95 with two ATR 72s. In addition Shorts 360s were used on services to the smaller island airports. Permission was forthcoming in 1992 for the first international route, to Phnom Penh, and in 1993 for the first time Mandalay in neighbouring Myanmar was served. Further ATR 72s and ATR 42s strengthened the fleet as passenger numbers grew, and Bangkok Air was fortunate in not being badly affected by the Asian business crisis. The airline's first jets, two Boeing 717s were added during 2001 and their greater range allowed the addition of services to Laos, Singapore and China. Two further 717s have since been added, and the ATR fleet mostly rolled over to new ATR 72-500s. The airline's home base is at Don Muang Domestic Airport in Bangkok, where it has its own maintenance facility.

Routes

Bangkok, Chiangmai, Da Nang, Ho Chi Minh City,Hua Hin, Jinhong, Koh Samui, Luan Prabang, Phnom Penh, Phuket, Ranong, Siem Reap,Singapore, Sukhothai, Utapao, Xian.

Fleet

12 ATR 72-200/500
 4 Boeing 717-200

Douglas DC-8-71F N822BX (Andre Littmann / Frankfurt)

BAX GLOBAL

16808 Armstrong, Irvine, California 92714, USA
Tel. 419-867991, Fax. 419-8670138, www.baxworld.com
E-mail: customerrelations@baxworld.com

Three- / Two- letter code	IATA No.	Reg'n prefix	ICAO callsign
BUR / 8W	–	N	–

This undertaking was founded in 1971 as Burlington Air Express and specialises in the express transport of all kinds of freight, and offering customers a complete logistical service. The key to success here is in having one's own delivery organisation. Consideration to having an in-house airline operation had been given for some years, as competitors such as DHL, Federal Express and UPS were already owning their own aircraft. Thus from 1985 Boeing 707s and DC-8-62/63s started to appear in the colours of Burlington Air Express, though in truth the company had shied away from forming its own air operation, and instead was leasing aircraft and crews from Southern Air Transport (707) or Rosenbalm Aviation (DC-8). As well as operating its own schedules, some ad hoc freight flights were carried out. Over the years the size of the fleet grew and Boeing 727s, and other operators of these aircraft, were introduced. In 1998 the company, which by now had changed its name to BAX-Global, acquired ATI- Air Transport International which already operated several DC-8s for Burlington/BAX. When required, other aircraft are leased in from operators such as Gemini Cargo or Kittyhawk.

Routes

Around 80 destinations are served on a regular basis in the USA, Canada and Mexico.

Fleet

3 Boeing 727-200
4 Douglas DC-8-63F
8 Douglas DC-8-71F

Boeing 757-2G5 HB-IHS (Author / Zürich)

BELAIR AIRLINES

Postfach, 8058 Zürich-Flughafen, Switzerland
Tel. 2118787, Fax. 2118130, www.bel-airlines.com
E-mail: info@belair-airlines.com

Three- / Two- letter code	IATA No.	Reg'n prefix	ICAO callsign
BHP / 4T	–	HB	Belair

The Hotelplan Group, with its Marken, Esco, Hotelplan and M-Travel brands, is the largest tour operator in Switzerland. For many years Hotelplan had been a customer of Swissair and its charter subsidiaries Crossair and Balair. An opportunity arose to operate an MD-80 in the striking colour scheme of a fast food restaurant chain, and to operate it exclusively for Hotelplan to holiday destinations. That was at the end of the 1990s and Hotelplan took over from the loss-making Balair two aircraft, which it passed to the Swissair group to operate under the well-known name. When in 2001 the SAir Group reached financial crisis, Hotelplan reacted very quickly and set up its own operation using the similar name Belair. Balair employees were also taken on and, after a short suspension of the operating licence, were able to continue where Balair had left off. The change of colour scheme and name on the aircraft did not entail great financial hardship, simply changing the 'a' for an 'e', with no further alteration! From Autumn 2002 Belair leased a Boeing 767-300 for longer-range routes.

Routes

Antalya, Arrecife, Bangkok, Basle, Calgary, Catania, Chaldiki, Djerba, Faro, Geneva, Goa, Heraklion, Keflavik, Kos, Jerez de la Frontera, Las Palmas, Luxor, Malaga, Monastir, Palma de Mallorca, Phuket, Puerto Plata, Punta Cana, Reuss, Rhodes, Samos, San Francisco, Santa Cruz, Sharm el Sheik, Tenerife, Vancouver, Varna, Zakynthos, Zürich.

Fleet

2 Boeing 757-200
1 Boeing 767-300

Tupolev Tu-154M EW-85703 (Albert Kuhbandner / Paris-CDG)

BELAVIA-BELARUSSIAN AIRLINES

Ul. Neminga 14, 220004 Minsk, Belarus
Tel. 17-2292424, Fax. 17-2292383
E-mail: info@belavia.by, www.belavia.by

Three- / Two- letter code	IATA No.	Reg'n prefix	ICAO callsign
BRU / B2	628	EW	Belarus Avia

A new national airline for Belarus was formed in November 1993; Belavia took over the aircraft, assets and routes of the former Aeroflot Directorate, as happened in other former Soviet republics, and continued its services. It was only much later that businesslike thinking and practices came to be applied, as financial resources were now much more limited. With many services into western and northern Europe, the airline tried to earn as much foreign currency as possible. The standards of service and reliability of the fleet were important marketing considerations and co-operation with western partners showed success after only a few years. A modernisation of the fleet is planned over time, with new Russian equipment such as the Tupolev Tu-204 and Ilyushin IL-114 being considered as well as western types. First, however, Minskavia was merged with Belavia in 1998. In 2001 the fleet was brought into line with the realities of the overall business situation, which entailed a reduction in aircraft. However, new routes were opened and numerous charter flights operated. Belavia has now ordered two Boeing737-500s, with the intention of shortly developing services to Western Europe.

Routes

Adler/Sochi, Astana, Baku, Berlin, Chelyabinsk, Frankfurt, Hurgada, Istanbul, Kaliningrad, Kiev, Krasnodar, Larnaca, London, Minsk, Moscow, Paris-CDG, Prague, Riga, Rome, Samara, Shannon, Simferopel, St.Petersburg, Stockholm, Tashkent, Tbilisi, Tel Aviv, Vienna, Warsaw.

Fleet	Ordered
3 Antonov An-24	2 Boeing 737-500
9 Tupolev Tu-154	
7 Tupolev Tu-134	
4 Yakovlev Yak-40	

Airbus A310-325 S2-ADE (Bastian Hilker/ London-LHR)

BIMAN BANGLADESH

Zia International Airport, Kurmitol, Dacca 1206, People's Republic of Bangladesh, Tel. 9560151, Fax. 863005
E-mail: dcsbiman@bdbiman.com, www.bimanair.com

Three- / Two- letter code	IATA No.	Reg'n prefix	ICAO callsign
BBC / BG	997	S2	Bangladesh

After Bangladesh split away from Pakistan, a new state airline was set up on 4th January 1972 to represent the state of Bangladesh (formerly East Pakistan) to the outside world. Flights started on 4th February 1972 with scheduled services to Chittagong and several other domestic points using a Douglas DC-3 leased from the Bangladesh Air Force. The DC-3 was soon replaced by Fokker F.27s. The first international flights were between Dhaka and and Calcutta. From January 1973 scheduled flights to London began, using two leased Boeing 707s. Two Fokker F.28s were added to the fleet in 1981, and the Boeing 707s left the fleet when DC-10-30s arrived from Singapore Airlines in 1983. In August 1990 the first BAe ATP was introduced to update the regional fleet, and in 1996 two Airbus A310s were acquired, principally for use on Asian services. The ATPs and a DC-10 left the fleet in 1998.The government was intending to sell 40% of the shares in Biman to other airlines by the end of 2000 and hoped to obtain stronger management and better co-operation in doing so, but this has not come to fruition. In order to motivate the employees, they are also to receive 9% of the shares. At the turn of the century new aircraft strengthened the fleet, with Airbus A310-300s arriving in 2002 as well as Boeing 737-300s, The ATPs were brought back into service briefly, but are now stored awaiting sale, along with most of the F.28s; these types are expected to be replaced by either the ATR 72 or Dash 8 – Q400s.

Routes

Abu Dhabi, Bahrain, Bangkok, Brussels, Chittagong, Cox's Bazaar, Dacca, Delhi, Dubai, Doha, Frankfurt, Hong Kong, Jeddah, Jessore, Karachi, Kathmandu, Kolkota, Kuala Lumpur, Kuwait, London, Mumbai, Muscat, New York, Paris, Rajshahi, Riyadh, Rome, Saidpur, Singapore, Tokyo, Yangon.

Fleet

4 Airbus A310-300
2 Boeing 737-300
6 Douglas DC-10-30
1 Fokker F.28

ATR 72-201 EC-FKQ (Stefan Schlick / Arrecife)

BINTER CANARIAS

Aeropuerto de Gran Canaria, P.O.B.50, 35230 Telde, Gran Canaria, Spain, Tel. 928-579601, Fax. 928-579604, www.bintercanarias.com

Three- / Two- letter code	IATA No.	Reg'n prefix	ICAO callsign
IBB / NT	474	EC	Canarias

In January 1988, Iberia, Spain's state airline, set up Binter Canarias in order to reorganise regional Spanish flights to the Canary Isles from mainland Spain, previously operated by Aviaco. The brief hops to the islands were uneconomic for Iberia's jets and so in mid-1988 Binter Canarias started operations with a CASA CN-235. Later in the same year, another aircraft was required, with two more in Spring 1989, followed by the first ATR 42s in the Autumn of that year. However, the latter were only used for a short time before being replaced with the larger ATR 72. For a new route from Tenerife to Funchal on Madeira DC-9-32 jets were leased from the parent company, and these were also used on other routes. In 1997 the last of the CASA CN-235s was retired from service. After various reorganisations within the parent Iberia group, Binter since 1999 is again concentrating on those tasks for which it was set up – flights between the Canary Isles – and uses only ATR 72s. During 2000 over two million passengers were carried for the first time, with a further growth shown in the following year.

Routes

Binter Canarias maintains scheduled services within the Canary Isles, including El Hierro, Lanzarote, Tenerife, Gran Canaria, Fuerteventura, La Gomera and La Palma.

Fleet

12 ATR 72

Boeing 767-3G5 EI-CZH (Jan-Alexander Lück / Paris-CDG)

BLUE PANORAMA

Via Corona Boreale n 86, Pelazzina D, 00050 Fiumicino,
Italy, Tel. 06-65508203, Fax. 06-65508555
E-mail: commerciale@bluepanorama.com
www.blue-panorama.com

Three- / Two- letter code	IATA No.	Reg'n prefix	ICAO callsign
BPA / BV	004	I	Blue Panorama

Blue Panorama was set up in 1998 by the Italian tour operator Astra Travel, which in turn belongs to the Distal & ITR Gruppe, which amongst other things is active in the field of aircraft handling. Late in 1998 Blue Panorama received its first aircraft, a Boeing 737-400 from Hapag Lloyd, and operations were begun to destinations all over Europe. Naturally services were flown for the parent tour operator, but in addition there were ad hoc charters for other airlines and for other tour operators. In 1999 further Boeing 737-400s were added, with additional aircraft being leased in from other operators during the summer season. Two

Boeing 767-300s were taken on from the LTU fleet during 2002, allowing Blue Panorama to start services to longer-range destinations including Denpasar, which was reached via a technical stop in Bangkok. The Boeing 767s were also used to the Caribbean area during the 2002 winter season, to destinations including Cancun, Punta Cana and Varadero. Codeshare agreements were put in place for these flights to Cuba with the Cuban national airline and the Boeing 767-300 used for these flights was given additional Cubana markings. Blue Panorama was also involved as a shareholder with the

Libyan government in the setting up of Afriqiyah Airways. The Italian airline was responsible for the airline's operations, using two Boeing 737-400s. The home base is at Rome's Fiumicino airport.

Routes

Blue Panorama flies domestic and Europe-wide charters, and additionally to Northern Africa, Asia and the Caribbean.

Fleet

5 Boeing 737-400
2 Boeing 767-300

Boeing 737-5Q8 G-BVZH (Gerhard Schütz / Munich)

BMI BABY

P.O.Box 737 bmibaby, Castle Donington, Derbyshire, DE74 2SB, Gt Britain, Tel. 01332-854000, Fax. 01332-854662
E-mail: babytalk@bmi-email.com, www.bmibaby.com

Three- / Two- letter code	IATA No.	Reg'n prefix	ICAO callsign
BMA / BD	236	G	Baby

The long-established British airline, British Midland, was obliged to follow the 'low-cost/no-frills' trend late in 2001, when it became apparent that the pieces were being put in place for the establishment of a low-cost division. These plans came to fruition on 17th January 2002 with the founding of BMI Baby (pronounced 'be my baby'). When operations began on 23rd March 2002, the original colour scheme chosen for the aircraft raised a smile. Passengers liked 'the baby' and it grew strongly. East Midlands was the departure point for the first set of destinations, but since then further hubs have been created at Cardiff, Manchester and Teesside, with a total of 45 routes stemming from the four bases, offering over 600 flights a week. Likewise the fleet has grown in harmony with the expanding network; initially BMI Baby took on a pair of Boeing 737-300 seconded from the parent airline, but this has been increased with the establishment of each new hub. The fleet consists purely of 737s, in order to keep costs to a minimum.

Routes

Alicante, Amsterdam, Barcelona, Belfast, Bergamo, Brussels, Cardiff, Cork, Dublin, East Midlands, Edinburgh, Faro, Geneva, Glasgow, Ibiza, Jersey, Malaga, Manchester, Munich, Nice, Palma de Mallorca, Paris, Pisa, Prague, Toulouse.

Fleet

5 Boeing 737-300
5 Boeing 737-500

Airbus A320-200 G-MIDR (Albert Kuhbandner / Amsterdam)

BMI – BRITISH MIDLAND INT'L

Donington Hall, Castle Donington, Derbyshire DE74 2SB, Great Britain, Tel. 854000, Fax. 854662
E-Maill: communications@flybmi.com, www.flybmi.com

Three- / Two- letter code	IATA No.	Reg'n prefix	ICAO callsign
BMA / BD	236	G	Midland

Originally set up as a flying school in 1938, the airline operation was begun in 1947 as Derby Aviation, changed to Derby Airways in 1953, then British Midland in 1964. Schedules were flown from Derby, Birmingham and Manchester, using DC-3s, Handley Page Heralds, BAC 1-11s, Vickers Viscounts and Boeing 707s. In 1965 the airline moved base from Derby to the new East Midlands Airport, which is still the main base and maintenance centre. In addition to scheduled services and charters, in the 1970s BMA was also successful with aircraft leasing. Bought in 1968 by an investment group, it became privately owned again in 1978 under managing director Michael Bishop, and has flourished since then. British Midland is a main shareholder in Manx Airlines and Loganair; the Airlines of Britain Group, formed in 1987 and in which SAS had a 40% stake, acts as holding company for all three airlines. The retirement of the DC-9 fleet came with the delivery of the Fokker 100 in April 1994 and the Fokker 70 in 1995. Backbone of the 1990s fleet was however the Boeing 737, flying mainly from Heathrow, where BMA is a major operator, but fleet additions since 1998 have concentrated on the Airbus A320/321. By taking over Aberdeen-based Business Air, British Midland Commuter was created, and this subsidiary now operates a fleet of Embraer 145s, BAe 146s and Saab 340s. In 1997 the Airlines of Britain Group was reorganised and renamed British Midland; Lufthansa replaced SAS as a major investor and British Midland became part of the Star Alliance in July 2000. A330s were ordered for the resumption of long-distance services from April 2001; along with these came a revised colour scheme and minor name revision. During 2002 BMI Baby was set up as a low-cost division (see page 115).

Routes

Aberdeen, Alicante, Amsterdam, Belfast, Birmingham, Bristol, Brussels, Budapest, Cardiff, Chicago, Copenhagen, Dublin, East Midlands, Edinburgh, Esbjerg, Faro, Glasgow, Guernsey, Humberside, Jersey, Leeds/Bradford, Liverpool, London-Heathrow, Malaga, Manchester, Milan, Nice, Palma de Mallorca, Paris, Prague, Teeside, Venice, Warsaw, Washington.

Fleet

11 Airbus A320
10 Airbus A321
 2 Airbus A330

5 Boeing 737-400/500
6 Fokker 100

Boeing 737-200 PK-IJM (Thomas Kim / Singapore)

BOURAQ AIRLINES

P.O.Box 2965, Jalan Angkasa 1-3, Jakarta Pusat 10720
Indonesia. Tel. 21-6295364, Fax. 21-6298651
E-mail: info@bouraq.com, www.bouraq.com

Three- / Two- letter code	IATA No.	Reg'n prefix	ICAO callsign
BOU / BO	666	PK	Bouraq

PT Bouraq Indonesian Airlines is a private company founded in the middle of 1970. With three Douglas DC-3s it flew from Jakarta to Banjarmasin, Balikpapan and Surabaya. In the following year it was able to re-equip with turboprops in the form of the NAMC YS-11. Britten-Norman Islanders were used to provide services to destinations well away from the main cities, mostly where only grass strips were available. Later came Fokker Friendships, Dornier Do 28s and HS.748s, and the Vickers Viscount replaced the DC-3s from 1980. The tasks for the airline were many and varied and freight and charter flights were also undertaken, including some to Malaysia, Thailand and to Manila. In 1973 Bouraq founded a subsidiary company Bali Air, which established its own network using aircraft provided by the parent company. As the turboprop fleet was showing its age, the transition to jets was slowly made. The Boeing 737-200 was used for the first time in 1993, with further examples added in 1994 and 1995. The Asian business downturn of the late 1990s brought expansion plans to an abrupt end. Bouraq was obliged to drop some routes and to shrink its fleet, with several aircraft being taken out of service and sold. It was decided to concentrate on the major routes which were flown with jets, with the smaller regional routes being passed over to subsidiary Bali Air, which uses its own BAe HS.748s. Three MD-82s have been added to the Bouraq fleet during the latter part of 2002. There is a co-operation agreement with Philippine Airlines.

Routes

Balikpapan, Bandung, Banjarmasin, Batan, Batu Besar, Berau, Denpasar, Jakarta, Manado, Medan, Palembang, Palu, Pangkalpinang, Pontianak, Samarinda, Semarang, Singapore, Surabaya, Tarakan, Tawau, Ujung Pandang, Yogyakarta.

Fleet

7 Boeing 737-200Adv.
3 McDonnell Douglas MD-82

Boeing 737-705 LN-TUF (Klaus Brandmaier / Innsbruck)

BRAATHENS

Okseneyveien 3, 1330 Oslo, Norway
Tel. 67-597000, Fax. 67-591309,
www.braathens.no

Three- / Two- letter code	IATA No.	Reg'n prefix	ICAO callsign
BRA / BU	154	LN	Braathens

Ludvig G Braathen, a Norwegian ship owner, formed his airline, Braathens South America and Far East Air Transport on 26th March 1946 and began operations with Douglas DC-4s. As is apparent from the name, the airline operated charters to South America and Hong Kong. On 5th August 1949 a scheduled service from Oslo via Amsterdam-Cairo-Basra-Karachi-Bombay-Calcutta-Bangkok to Hong Kong was introduced, but the route was taken over by SAS in April 1954. From 1952 a route network was also built up in Norway, at first with de Havilland Herons and from 1958 with Fokker F.27s. The first jet

aircraft, Boeing 737s came in 1969; the F.27s and Douglas DC-6s were replaced by Fokker F.28s. During 1984 Braathens took on its first widebody, a Boeing 767, but it was sold again because it was not being well-enough used. The introduction of the new Boeing 737-400/500 models provided Braathens with a very modern and homogeneous fleet, which is kept updated. Each year Braathens carried as many passengers as the entire population of Norway, about 4.5 million. In 1997 KLM acquired a 30% holding in Braathens S.A.F.E. In the later part of 1997 competitor Transwede was bought, and this then operated as

Braathens Sweden. A further acquisition in 1998 was Malmö Aviation. With the delivery of the first of the new Boeing 737-700s in April 1998, Braathens adopted a new corporate identity, dropping the old 'S.A.F.E.' suffix and trading briefly as Braathens Malmö Aviation. Major competitor SAS saw an opportunity and late in 2001 acquired a majority shareholding in Braathens by the purchase of KLM's shares. Another reorganisation took place with Malmö Aviation again becoming independent and Braathens flying principally in Norway, mostly on charter and freight work. The main bases are at Oslo and Stavanger.

Routes

Aberdeen, Alesund, Alicante, Amsterdam, Bardufoss, Barcelona, Bergen, Billund, Bodo, Evenes, Gothenburg, Halmstad, Harstadt/Narvik, Haugesund, Jonköping, Kristiansand, Kristiansund, London, Longyearbyen, Lulea, Malaga, Molde, Murmansk, Newcastle, Oslo, Roros, Stavanger, Stockholm, Svalbard, Tromsö, Trondheim, Umea. Charter flights throughout Europe.

Fleet

13 Boeing 737-700
15 Boeing 737-500
 5 Boeing 737-400

Boeing 767-304 G-OBYE (Martin Kühn / Palma de Mallorca)

BRITANNIA AIRWAYS

Luton Airport, Bedfordshire LU2 9ND, Great Britain
Tel. 1582-424155, Fax. 1582-458594, E-mail: webrelations
@uk.britanniaairways.com, www.britanniaairways.com

Three- / Two- letter code	IATA No.	Reg'n prefix	ICAO callsign
BAL / BY	754	G	Britannia

From modest beginnings, Britannia has grown into the largest charter airline in the world. On 1st December 1961 Euravia (London) was set up, and it started operations on 5th May 1962 with an L-1049 Constellation under contract to Universal Sky Tours, then the principal shareholder. When a Bristol Britannia 102 was commissioned on 6th December 1964, the present name for the airline was also adopted. The Thomson Organisation, one of the larger tour operators, took over the company on 26th April 1965, and Boeing 707s were used for charter flights to Hong Kong, Kuala Lumpur and other long-range destinations,

but the airline withdrew from long distance work from 1973 to 1985, as the Boeing 737, the sole type in the fleet for many years, was not suited. Boeing 757s and the larger 767, the first of which was delivered in February 1984, restored this capability. In 1988 Orion Airways was bought when Thomson's acquired its parent company, Horizon Travel, and six Boeing 737-300s were integrated. With the delivery of more 757s the number of 737s, which had totalled 34 in 1989, was reduced, until the last one left the fleet in 1994. During 1997 Britannia established a German subsidiary; Britannia Deutschland uses four 767s on long-range tour

flights from several German airports. Likewise in Sweden in 1998 tour operator Fritidsresor and its airline Blue Scandinavia were taken over and this now flies as Britannia AB. In order to be able to offer smaller aircraft, Airbus 320s were leased for the 1999 season, and from Spring 2000 the Boeing 737 returned, with the latest model -800s added to the fleet. In May 2000 parent company Thomson accepted a takeover offer from the German concern Preussag, whose tourist activities are bundled into the TUI Group. From early 2002 Britannia aircraft have been appearing in a revised mainly blue 'World of TUI' group livery.

Routes

Worldwide charter flights from about 20 airports in Great Britain, to the Caribbean, USA, within Europe and to the Canary Isles and Africa.

Fleet

21 Boeing 757-200
 4 Boeing 767-200ER
10 Boeing 767-300ER
 2 Boeing 737-800

Airbus A319-131 G-EUPL (Josef Krauthäuser / Madrid)

BRITISH AIRWAYS

P.O.Box 365, Harmondsworth, UB7 0GB
Great Britain, Tel. 20-87385050, Fax. 20-87389947
www.british-airways.com

Three- / Two- letter code	IATA No.	Reg'n prefix	ICAO callsign
BAW / BA	125	G	Speedbird

British Airways is the result of the amalgamation on 1st April 1972 of BEA and BOAC, after a government decision to bring British aviation interests under state ownership. The predecessors of British Airways can be traced back to the founding of Imperial Airways after the First World War. Until 1974 BEA and BOAC were still apparently operating separately; the merger became visible on the aircraft during 1974. In 1988 the second largest, privately-owned, airline, British Caledonian was taken over, after British Airways had been partly privatised in 1984. A major re-equipment programme was begun in 1989, with the aim of replacing older aircraft with a more homogeneous fleet. During 1992 and 1993 British Airways acquired a stake in US Air, then in the Australian airline Qantas and in the French airline TAT, in Air Mauritius and set up Deutsche BA. For the symbolic amount of one pound, Gatwick-based airline Dan Air with its routes and aircraft was taken over. Individual profit centres were created in 1993, and thus came about the regional operations BA-

Manchester and BA-Birmingham. In 1995 British Asia Airways was formed for operations to Taiwan. On 11th November 1995 BA received its first Boeing 777, signalling the start of replacement of some of the older examples from the extensive 747 fleet. During this year also BA began building Gatwick up as a second major base. The latter part of the 1990s was also noteworthy for BA's moves towards franchised operations for shorter-haul services. Brymon Airways, City Flyer Express (both now fully owned), GB Airways, Maersk, Loganair and Manx Airlines (the latter two now merged as British Regional Airlines) all participate in these arrangements, which have also been extended outside to South Africa, where Comair is a partner. Air Liberté and TAT in France were also acquired and merged, and operated in BA colours, but proved loss-making and was sold to SAir in 2000. A major agreement with American Airlines was planned to lead to a merger, but regulatory difficulties obstructed this for so long that it is now on ice; however, the

co-operation is strong and is the cornerstone of the expanding Oneworld alliance. A spectacular development in mid-1997 was the introduction of the controversial new colours, with tailfins decorated in artworks from various countries; however from mid-1999 all new aircraft are being painted in the Union Flag variant only. During 1998 BA not only completed its acquisition of franchise partner City Flyer Express, but also set up a low-cost subsidiary Go Fly, based at Stansted. Fleet plans for the future were signalled by orders for over 100 of the Airbus 318/319/320, which will more or less replace the 737s and 757s, where the entire fleet has been sold to DHL for freight conversion. BA was badly affected by the 11 September events, given its numerous transatlantic services. Even the prestigious Concorde services were losing money. Various routes were dropped and aircraft placed into storage; all 747-200s and 737-200s were parked in the USA awaiting sale. Long-range routes are increasingly served by the Boeing 777 fleet. / *continued*

Avro RJ 100 G-CFAH (Albert Kuhbandner / Hanover)

BRITISH AIRWAYS CITIEXPRESS

Three- / Two- letter code	IATA No.	Reg'n prefix	ICAO callsign
BAW / BA	–	G	British

In order to save costs, in 2002 BA merged its regional divisions (including Birmingham and Manchester) and Brymon Airways with CitiFlyer to form the new British Airways Citiexpress Ltd, the UK's largest regional airline. In a concerted move with Air France, it was also announced that Concorde services were to cease from late summer 2003, citing rising support and spares costs as the principal reason. Permission for codeshare with American Airlines was finally granted in March 2003, with the exclusion of London routes Development of the competition and

of low-cost airlines also had its effect on British Airways. Go Fly was sold to EasyJet and loss-making Deutsche BA was also to have been sold to EasyJet, but this latter deal fell apart early in 2003, and it was later sold for a nominal sum to a German investment group. BA is looking for every opportunity for cost-saving and is optimistic that it will remain Europe's largest airline. British Mediterranean Airways, GB Airways, Loganair and Maersk Air are active franchise partners with a total of over 60 aircraft, though the latter airline, subject of a management buyout from the

Danish parent company in mid-2003 and a change of name to Duo Airways, is in the process of severing its BA ties. Fast-growing Eastern Airways, a Jetstream operator, has been added during 2003. In South Africa, Comair acts as a BA franchise partner, offering nationwide services. All the aircraft of Citiexpress and the franchise partners are painted in British Airways colours and fly under BA flight numbers, with the obligatory sticker announcing the true operator.

Routes

British Airways flies worldwide to over 130 destinations, or over 250 including those serve by franchise partners.

Fleet

27 Airbus A320-200
33 Airbus A319-100
20 Boeing 767-300
56 Boeing 747-400
51 Boeing 737-400/500
15 Boeing 757-200
43 Boeing 777-200ER

6 ATR 72
21 BAe 146-100/200/300
13 BAe ATP
12 BAe Jetstream 41
10 De Havilland DHC-8-300
28 Embraer ERJ-145

Ordered

6 Airbus A319
10 Airbus A320
10 Airbus A321

Douglas DC-4 C-FIQM (Josef Krauthäuser collection)

BUFFALO AIRWAYS

1000 Buffalo Drive, Hay River, NW Territories X0E 0R9
Canada, Tel. 403-8743333, Fax. 403-8743572, E-mail:
ops@buffaloairways.com, www.buffaloairways.com

Three- / Two- letter code	IATA No.	Reg'n prefix	ICAO callsign
BFL / J4	–	C	Buffalo

This Northern Canadian company was founded in 1959 in Fort Smith. Its principal field of operations is in supply flights in the North West Territories and the Yukon. Several helicopters and smaller aircraft types were used. However the ideal aircraft for most of these varied tasks is the ubiquitous Douglas DC-3, built around 1942, and brought into service here in 1979. At the beginning of the 1980s a regional scheduled service was begun, serving Hay River, Uranium City and Chipewyan. The DC-3s are operated with wheeled undercarriages in Summer and on skis in the Winter, an advantage of one of the few aircraft of this size which can be used to such remote and snow-covered places.Over the course of time, and following the relocation of the company to its present base at Hay River, further DC-3s and the larger DC-4 were added to the fleet, along with another veteran, the Curtiss C-46 Commando. Not surprisingly, Hay River is now a place of pilgrimage for propliner enthusiasts. Aerial firefighting duties are also undertaken, using four specialist Canadair CL-215 fire-bombers, on behalf of the North West Territories government as the first line of defence against forest fires. For these tasks some Consolidated PBY Cansos are also kept available.

Routes

Schedules to Yellowknife, and ad hoc, charter, freight and special flights in the region.

Fleet

3 Curtiss C-46 Commando
9 Douglas DC-3/C-47
8 Douglas DC-4/C-54
4 Canadair CL-215

3 Consolidated PBY-5A
2 Beech King Air

Boeing 737-8Q8 9Y-BGI (Josef Krauthäuser / Miami)

BWIA INTERNATIONAL

Administration Buildg. Intl. Airport Port of Spain, Trinidad and Tobago, Tel. 809-6693000, Fax. 809-6643540, www.bwee.com

Three- / Two- letter code	IATA No.	Reg'n prefix	ICAO callsign
BWA / BW	106	9Y	West Indian

BWIA began operations on 17th November 1940 with a Lockheed Lodestar between Trinidad and Barbados. Two further Lodestars were added in 1942 and charters were begun for US military personnel. In 1947 BWIA was sold to BSAA, but a new airline with the old 'BWIA' name was set up in 1948. Five Vickers Vikings were used to serve almost all the major Caribbean islands. In June 1949 BSAA was merged into BOAC, thus BWIA became a BOAC subsidiary and took over some routes and aircraft. Four Vickers Viscounts were added in 1955 and in 1960 leased Bristol Britannias were first used to fly to London via New York. In 1961 the government of Trinidad and Tobago bought back 90% of the shares from BOAC, and the final 10% in 1967. BWIA used Boeing 727s for the first time to Miami in 1965, replacing the Viscounts. On 14th December 1968, Boeing 707s were first used on the New York route; flights to London-Heathrow started in 1975. A merger with Trinidad and Tobago Air Services, brought a change of name to BWIA International. The first Lockheed TriStar arrived in Trinidad on 29th January 1980. In 1994 the company was part-privatised, with the Acker Group and local investors participating; along with this went a fundamental reorganisation. Routes were dropped, with London the only European destination to survive. Aircraft procurement policy was strange: new Boeing 757s and 767s were ordered, to replace the predominantly MD-83 fleet, but dropped in favour of A340s and A321s; the 340s were cancelled and only the 321s arrived but operated only very briefly from late 1996. Eventually 737-800s were chosen, with deliveries from December 1999. Early in 1999 two DHC-8s were received for a new regional division BWee Express, but this was disbanded after only a short life in 2002. For long-range routes BWIA settled on the Airbus A340-300 as the replacement for the TriStars.

Routes

Antigua, Barbados, Caracas, Georgetown, Grenada, Kingston, London, Miami, New York, Port of Spain, St.Kitts, St. Lucia, St.Maarten, Tobago, Toronto.

Fleet

2 Airbus A340-300
7 Boeing 737-800

Boeing 767-33A TJ-CAC (Albert Kuhbandner / Paris-CDG)

CAMEROON AIRLINES

BP 4092, Ave. General de Gaulle, Douala, Cameroon
Tel. 237-2230304, Fax. 237-2230732, E-mail: infos@
cameroon-airlines.com, www.cameroon-airlines.com

Three- / Two- letter code	IATA No.	Reg'n prefix	ICAO callsign
UYC / UY	604	TJ	Camair

Cameroon Airlines was set up on 26th July 1971 by the Cameroon government in order to be in a position to withdraw from the multinational airline Air Afrique; its interest in the consortium ended on 2nd September 1971. In setting up the new national airline, the privately-owned Air Cameroun and its regional network was also taken over. Operations began in November 1971 with flights between Douala and Yaounde, using Boeing 737s. A Boeing 707 was acquired from Air France for long-distance services and was used to Paris via Rome. In 1982 it was replaced by the airline's sole widebody, a Boeing 747. New Boeing 737-300s were introduced between August 1997 and October 1998, allowing the older 737-200s to be retired and the fleet thus modernised. During 2001 and 2002 the Boeing 757 was added for regional and medium-haul routes and the Boring 767-300 for long-range services. Air France now owns just 4% of the capital; the rest remains with the government. There is close co-operation with Nigeria Airways, Air Affretaires Afrique, Air France, Air Gabon and Oman Air. With its own maintenance and base facilities in Douala, Cameroon Airlines has the infrastructure to look after its own aircraft.

Routes

Abidjan, Brazzaville, Cotonou, Douala, Garoua, Harare, Jeddah, Johannesburg, Kigali, Kinshasa, Lagos, Libreville, London, Malabo, Maroua, Nairobi, N'Djamena, Ngaoundere, Paris, Yaounde.

Fleet

3 Boeing 737-300
1 Boeing 747-200
3 Boeing 757-200
2 Boeing 767-300

Boeing 747-4R7F LX-LCV (Stefan Schlick / Luxembourg)

CARGOLUX

Luxembourg Airport P.O.Box 591
2015 Luxembourg, Tel. 42111, Fax. 435446
E-mail: info@cargolux.com, www.cargolux.com

Three- / Two- letter code	IATA No.	Reg'n prefix	ICAO callsign
CLX / CV	172	LX	Cargolux

Cargolux Airlines International SA, Europe's largest scheduled all-cargo airline, was set up on 4th March 1970. The shareholders were Luxair SA, the Icelandic airline Loftleidir and the Swedish shipping concern Salenia AB. Operations began in May 1970 with a Canadair CL-44. Altogether five CL-44s were used, augmented in 1971 by a Douglas DC-8-61. In 1973 the first Boeing 747-200C was acquired. The Salenia and Loftleidir shares were taken over by Luxair in the late 1970s, and then in 1992 Lufthansa took a shareholding in Luxair, and thereby also in Cargolux. However, more than 40% of the shares are owned by various Luxembourg banks. The first Boeing 747-400F in the world, a cargo aircraft of the latest generation, was delivered in November 1993, with a second following at the beginning of 1994 as Cargolux's services to the USA and South-East Asia were strengthened. There is a code-share agreement with China Airlines, with an exchange of freight space on the Taipei-Luxembourg route, and similar codeshares have been put into place with other airlines. During 1997 SAir Logistics, a part of the Swissair group, acquired Lufthansa's shareholding in Cargolux, but with the collapse of the SAir Group, this shareholding passed to the new Swiss Cargo. From 1997 to 1999 the fleet was converted fully to the Boeing 747-400F, making the company one of the most modern freight concerns in the world, and also one of the most profitable. In addition to its air operations, Cargolux offers a trucking service within Europe for Luxembourg-originating freight.

Routes

Abidjan, Abu Dhabi, Accra, Auckland, Baku, Bangkok, Beirut, Bogota, Calgary, Curitiba, Damascus, Dubai, Guadalajara, Hong Kong, Houston, Huntsville, Johannesburg, Karachi, Komatsu, Kuala Lumpur, Kuwait, Los Angeles, Luxembourg, Madras, Manila, Melbourne, Miami, Nairobi, New York, Rio de Janeiro, San Francisco, Sao Paulo, Santiago, Seattle, Seoul, Sharjah, Shanghai, Shannon, Singapore, Taipei, Teheran.

Fleet	Ordered
12 Boeing 747-400F	1 Boeing 747-400F

Boeing 777-267 B-HNC (Hans-Willi Mertens / London)

CATHAY PACIFIC

8 Scienic Road, Cathay Pacific City, Lantau, Hong Kong, China, Tel. 27475000, Fax. 28106563, E-mail: enquiry@cathaypacific.com, www.cathaypacific.com

Three- / Two- letter code	IATA No.	Reg'n prefix	ICAO callsign
CPA / CX	160	B-H	Cathay

Cathay Pacific Airways Ltd. was set up on 24th September 1946 and began by connecting Shanghai via Hong Kong and other stops to Sydney, using a Douglas DC-3. In 1948 the Swire Group bought its way into the airline, acquiring 45% of the capital (increased to 70% by 1980), and in 1959 the BOAC subsidiary Hong Kong Airways was taken over. From April 1959 the fleet, which had included DC-6s from the early 1950s, was updated with Lockheed L-188 Electras, and three years later Convair 880s. These were supplemented by Boeing 707s until the decision was made to acquire the first widebody, the Lockheed TriStar, used to open up new routes in the Middle East. As a British company, Cathay wanted to be able to serve London, and to do this Boeing 747s were bought, and the first service to London took place on 17th July 1980. In addition to London, Frankfurt was added in 1984, and these quickly converted to non-stop services with the delivery of the new 747-300s, which had longer range. Fleet renewal at Cathay is a continuing process with the Boeing 747-400 (1989), Boeing 777 (1996), Airbus A330-300 (1995), Airbus A340 (1996) and Airbus 340-600 (2003). The airline also introduced a new colour scheme from Autumn 1994. With the changed political situation in Hong Kong, the Swire Group sold part of its Cathay shares to Chinese investors. The airline, always seen as one of the most successful, was hit by the Asian business crisis and in 1998 made a loss for the first time ever. As a member of the Oneworld alliance the company is however a strong partner in the Far East, even in the face of local difficulties such as the 2003 SARS outbreak. Cathay Pacific has shareholdings in Dragon Air (17.8%) and Air Hong Kong (75%).

Routes

Adelaide, Amsterdam, Auckland, Bahrain, Bangkok, Brisbane, Cairns, Cebu, Colombo, Delhi, Denpasar, Djakarta, Dubai, Frankfurt, Fukuoka, Ho Chi Minh, Hong Kong, Johannesburg, Karachi, Kuala Lumpur, London, Los Angeles, Manila, Melbourne, Mumbai, Nagoya, New York, Osaka, Paris, Penang, Perth, Riyadh, Rome, San Francisco, Sapporo, Seoul, Singapore, Surabaya, Sydney, Taipei, Tokyo, Toronto, Vancouver.

Fleet

		Ordered
20 Airbus A330-300	7 Boeing 747-400F	3 Airbus A330-300
15 Airbus A340-300	19 Boeing 747-400	
3 Airbus A340-600	5 Boeing 777-200	
4 Boeing 747-200F	9 Boeing 777-300	

Boeing 737-205 VP-CAL (Stefan Schlick / Montego Bay)

CAYMAN AIRWAYS

P.O.Box 1101, Georgetown, Grand Cayman, Cayman Islands, Tel. 9498200, Fax. 9497607, www.caymanairways.com

Three- / Two- letter code	IATA No.	Reg'n prefix	ICAO callsign
CAY / KX	378	VP-C	Cayman

Cayman Airways Ltd. was formed in July 1968 to take over the business of Cayman Brac Airways Ltd, which in turn had been set up by the Costa Rican airline LACSA. LACSA owned 49% of the shares in Cayman Airways until December 1977 when the airline came under the control of the Cayman government. Operations began to Jamaica and Miami with BAC One-Elevens. Britten-Norman Trislanders were used for the Cayman inter-island services, linking Grand Cayman, Brac and Little Cayman. Boeing 727-200s replaced the One-Elevens, and a Douglas DC-8 which had been in service during the 1970s. During 1989 the first leased Boeing 737-400s were brought into the fleet to replace the Boeing 727s, but in 1993 operations were scaled down as the 737-400 proved to be too large and expensive. Since that time the airline has concentrated on providing services to Jamaica and to several destinations in the USA and has been using Boeing 737-200s. There is an agreement with United Airlines, which provides technical and administrative support to Cayman Airways.

Routes

Cayman Brac, Grand Cayman, Houston, Kingston, Miami, Montego Bay, Orlando, Tampa.

Fleet

3 Boeing 737-200Adv.

Airbus A319 F-GYFM (Author's collection / Paris-Orly)

CCM AIRLINES

Aeroport de Campo dell 'Oro, BP 505, 2200
Ajaccio Corsica, France, Tel. 4-95290500
Fax. 4-95290505, www.ccm-airlines.com

Three- / Two- letter code	IATA No.	Reg'n prefix	ICAO callsign
CCM / XK	146	F	Corsica

On the French Mediterranean island of Corsica on 6th January 1989 Compagnie Corse Mediterranée was established. The shareholders, along with airlines Air France and TAT, were various local companies and several banks. The new airline was charged with meeting regional needs, and to provide service to the motherland, with more routes to the smaller cities. Corse Mediterranée began flight operations in June 1990 using two ATR 72s from Ajaccio to Bastia and Calvi. More ATR 72s and Fokker 100s were added to the fleet during 1992 and 1993, and services to Marseilles, Rome and Strasbourg were also introduced. In addition to its scheduled operations, Corse Mediterranée also undertook extensive series of charters, principally from the French mainland to destinations in the southern Mediterranean area. As a result of the takeover of shareholder TAT by British Airways in 1997, there were some changes to the company structure and in 2000 came a change of name of the airline to CCM Airlines. The first Airbus A319 for CCM was delivered late in 2002 and it displayed a new colour scheme for the airline. More A319s are being added, with the last of the Fokker 100s expected to have left the fleet by the end of 2003.

Routes

Ajaccio, Bastia, Bordeaux, Basle-Mulhouse, Calvi, Figari, Lille, Lyon, Marseilles, Nantes, Nice, Paris-Orly, Strasbourg.

Fleet

2 Airbus A319
6 ATR 72
4 Fokker 100

Boeing 757-236 RP-C2714 (Pierre Alain Petit / Manila)

CEBU PACIFIC AIR

30 EDSA Corner Pioneer, Mandalayong City, Metro Manila 5506, Philippines, Tel. 2-6371810, Fax. 2-6379170, E-mail: feedback@cebupacificair.com.ph, www.cebupacificair.com.ph

Three- / Two- letter code	IATA No.	Reg'n prefix	ICAO callsign
CEB / 5J	203	RP	Cebu Air

Following deregulation of air transport in the Philippines in 1995, one of the many new start-up airlines which emerged was Cebu Pacific Air. Many investors were tempted to invest in an airline with the chance to enter into competition on lucrative routes which had previously been monopolised by the state. So it was with JG Summit Holding, a concern owned by the Gokongwei family, and Cebu's operations were able to begin in March 1996. Using four Douglas DC-9-32s flights were from Manila to Cebu, at high frequency and with low fares, following the pattern seen to be so successful in the United

States. After only a year of operation, Cebu Pacific took on three more DC-9-32s and had carried over a million passengers. As well as the primary route, six further destinations were added. However in February 1998 a grounding by order of the government put a stop to further rapid expansion. Following the crash of one of its aircraft, Cebu Pacific Air was being viewed in a poor light, and only after a close examination of its whole flight operation was it able to resume services again at the end of March 1998. As a consequence of the Asian business downturn,

expansion was now slower than it had been, yet the fleet has continued to expand, with three more colourfully-painted DC-9-32s being added during 1999. This also adorned the first of the Boeing 757s which joined the fleet in November 2001. Since late 2002 Cebu Pacific has added services to Seoul in South Korea from both Cebu and Subic.

Routes

Bacalod, Butuan, Cagayan d Oro, Cebu, Clark, Davao, Dumaquete, Iloilo, Kalibo, Manila, Porto Princesa, Roxas, Seoul, Subic, Tacloban, Zamboango.

Fleet

16 Douglas DC-9-31/32
 3 Boeing 757-200

Boeing 727-290 N295AS (Josef Krauthäuser / Las Vegas)

CHAMPION AIR

8009 34th Ave. South Suite 500, Bloomington, Minnesota
55425-1674 USA, Tel. 612-8148700, Fax. 612-8148799
E-mail: Info@ChampionAir.com, www.championair.com

Three- / Two- letter code	IATA No.	Reg'n prefix	ICAO callsign
CCP / MG	–	N	Champion Air

Champion Air is a successor to the former MGM Grand Air, which was known for its luxuriously outfitted Douglas DC-8s and Boeing 727s. MGM's clientele consisted of stars of entertainment, sport, music and their associates and entourages; the level of luxury and privacy appealed to the very wealthy more than the idea of travelling by regular airlines. However, in 1994, when this type of flying was no longer proving to be profitable, MGM sold a part of its operation to Front Page Tours, which specialised in the transport of sports teams and their fans to events such as the Super Bowl or the Kentucky Derby. The change of name to Champion Air took place at the same time as the takeover of the licence from MGM in 1995. More Boeing 727s were acquired for the planned expansion of the company. When the new company encountered difficulties in 1997, the shares were acquired by Carl Pohland (60%) and Northwest Airlines (40%) and Champion Air was reorganised as a charter company catering for the needs of the general public. The fleet was expanded with more Boeing 727s to carry out its new tasks. The company's headquarters was moved from Salt Lake City to Minneapolis, where the aircraft were maintained by Northwest Airlines.

The airline now works closely with major tour companies including Adventure Tours in Dallas, MLT Vacations in Minneapolis and Worry Free Vacations.

Routes

Aruba, Cancun, Cozumel, Denver, Detroit, Grand Cayman, Kingston, Las Vegas, Los Cabos, Minneapolis/St.Paul, Nassau, Oklahoma City, Phoenix, Punta Cana, Puerte Vallarta, San Jose, St.Louis, Tulsa.

Fleet

14 Boeing 727-200

Fokker F.27 G-CEXA (Daniel Klein / Bournemouth)

CHANNEL EXPRESS AIR SERVICES

Bldg. 470 Bournemouth Intl. Airport, Christchurch Dorset BH23 6SE, Great Britain, Tel. 1202-597600 Fax. 1202-573512, www.channel-express.co.uk E-mail: charters@channel-express.co.uk,

Three- / Two- letter code	IATA No.	Reg'n prefix	ICAO callsign
EXS / LS	839	G	Channex

Express Air Service began operations from its home base at Bournemouth in 1978 with a small fleet of Handley Page Heralds. The Channel Islands were provided with their daily needs, and cut flowers formed the return loads. During the summer season, passengers were also carried, though that was not a profitable exercise. Contracts for the carriage of mail made more aircraft necessary, and the fleet grew to eight aircraft. In 1983 the name was changed by the addition of 'Channel'. The whole fleet of Heralds were modified and updated, but in the mid 1990s this process could not be economically

sustained on the ageing airframes, and the Fokker F.27 was introduced gradually as a replacement. The last Heralds left the fleet in 1998 after 20 years service for the type. In order to be able to handle other freight contracts, especially express parcels, Lockheed L-188 Electras were introduced, able to carry palletised cargo which gives the advantage of reducing loading and turnaround times. The more capacious and longer-range Electras were used on new international routes until retired in 2003. With the delivery of the airline's first Airbus A300B4 freighter in 1997, new possibilities were

opened for Channel Express. Long-term contracts with DHL led to the acquisition of more Airbus A300B4 freighters during 1998 and 1999. Channel Express is in the position of being able to react to customers' special needs and also flies ad hoc charters and on a wet-lease basis for other companies. Thus passenger charter work is carried out with Boeing 737-300s, and Jet 2 was set up in 2003 as a low-cost operator within the group, operating from Leeds/Bradford with 737s provided by the parent.

Routes

Bournemouth, Bristol, Brussels, Cologne/Bonn, Coventry, Dublin, East Midlands, Edinburgh, Guernsey, Jersey, London-Gatwick, Liverpool, Luton, Newcastle, Nuremberg, Stansted see regular freight services. Passenger charters in Europe, notably to the Mediterranean holiday resorts.

Fleet

4 Airbus A300B4 Freighter
4 Boeing 737-300
7 Fokker F.27

Boeing 737-809 B-18609 (Thomas Kim / Bangkok)

CHINA AIRLINES

131, Nanking East Rd. Taipei 104, Republic of China, Tel. 02-27152233, Fax. 02-27155754, www.china-airlines.com

Three- / Two- letter code	IATA No.	Reg'n prefix	ICAO callsign
CAL / CI	297	B	Cal

On 16th December 1959 some former members of the Chinese Nationalist Air Force set up CAL. Consolidated PBY Catalina flying boats were initially used for charters. Domestic scheduled services were also operated using Douglas DC-3s and Curtiss C-46s. In 1965 the airline became the official flag carrier of the Republic of China and in December 1966 Lockheed Constellations were used to start a scheduled service to Saigon, primarily to transport members of the US armed forces and cargo to Vietnam. During 1967 services to Hong Kong and Tokyo were also started, using two new

Boeing 727s. 1970 saw the first trans-Pacific flight to San Francisco, via Tokyo and Honolulu. CAL took delivery of its first widebody, a Boeing 747, in 1975, and this was followed from June 1982 by the Airbus A310 for regional services. In 1983 a route to Amsterdam was inaugurated, the only destination in Europe for many years, because of political considerations. MD-11s and Boeing 747-400s were acquired, to replace older aircraft. With Mandarin Airlines and Formosa Air, CAL had powerful subsidiaries, which were in sharp competition with private enterprises. The airline also has a

shareholding in FAT-Far Eastern Air Transport. The current colour scheme was introduced in October 1995. During 1999 Formosa Air was merged with Mandarin and there was a substantial reorganisation within the group. New Boeing 737-800s were introduced from the later part of 1998 and the MD-11s transferred to Mandarin. Likewise the older Boeing 747-200s which had been used as freighters were replaced by new 747-400Fs. Two A330-200s are on lease until new A330-300s are delivered. The airline's base is at the Chiang Kai Chek airport in Taipei.

Routes

Abu Dhabi, Amsterdam, Anchorage, Atlanta, Bangkok, Chicago, Colombo, Dallas/Forth Worth, Delhi, Denpasar, Djakarta, Frankfurt, Fukuoka, Guam, Ho Chi Minh City, Hong Kong, Honolulu, Kaohsiung, Kuala Lumpur, Los Angeles, Luxembourg, Manchester, Miami, Nagoya, Nashville, New York, Okinawa, Penang, Phuket, Rome, San Francisco, Singapore, Sydney, Taipei, Tokyo.

Fleet		Ordered
12 Airbus A300-600	11 Boeing 737-800	4 Airbus A330-300
2 Airbus A330-200		5 Boeing 737-800
7 Airbus A340-300		3 Boeing 747-400F
2 Boeing 747-200F		
26 Boeing 747-400/400F		

Airbus A319-112 B-2331 (Jan-Alexander Lück / Beijing)

CHINA EASTERN

2550 Hongqiao Rd, Intl. Airport, 200335 Shanghai, People's Republic of China, Tel. 21-62686268 Fax. 21-62686039, www.ce-air.com

Three- / Two- letter code	IATA No.	Reg'n prefix	ICAO callsign
CES / MU	781	B	China Eastern

In December 1987 China Eastern Airlines separated from CAAC, and assumed responsibility for its flights from Shanghai, initially using a fleet of ten MD-82s shared with China Northern Airlines. A flourishing international airline has developed from the former CAAC regional directorate. Using MD-11s delivered during 1992/93, routes were opened to the USA and Europe. Chinese-assembled MD-82s formed the backbone of the modern fleet, augmented by Airbus A310s from 1987. Even during CAAC times the Shanghai district had used western aircraft such as the Shorts 360,

DHC-8, Lockheed Hercules and BAe 146, though only in small numbers. With the upsizing of the fleet came an expansion of the network. Hong Kong, Nagoya and Seoul were served with Airbuses, and from 1996 delivery of new Airbus A340-300s allowed the addition of further destinations in Europe, including Munich. On the route from Shanghai to Seoul there is a codeshare arrangement with Asiana; other partners are Air France and American Airlines. During 1997 the loss-making China General Aviation was taken over. Fokker 100s were replaced by Airbus A320s during

1998/99. Regular freight services are flown to the USA, using the MD-11. China Eastern Airlines has two main bases: Hongqiao airport in Shanghai concentrates on international flights, while domestic services are also flown from Nanchang. The centre for all other operations, which include agricultural aviation and spraying, using Yunshuji Y-5s, is at Hefei.The government-ordained merger of China Eastern, China Northwest Airlines and China Yunnan Airlines will in time lead to a single company led by China Eastern.

Routes

Bangkok, Beijing, Changsha, Cheju, Chengdu, Chicago, Dalian, Fukuoka, Fuzhou, Guangzhou, Guilin, Haikou, Hong Kong, Hongzhou, Hefei, Huangyan, Jinan, Jinjiang, Kunming, Los Angeles, Madrid, Munich, Nagasaki, Nagoya, Nanchang, Nanjing, Okayama, Osaka, Paris, Pusan, San Francisco, Seoul, Shanghai, Santou, Shenzen, Singapore, Sydney, Tokyo, Tunxi, Wenzhou, Wuhan, Xiamen, Xian, Yantai, Zhengzhou, Zhoushan.

Fleet		Ordered
10 Airbus A300-600	4 Boeing 737-700	14 Airbus A330-200
1 Airbus A340-600	2 Boeing 737-800	4 Airbus A340-600
26 Airbus A320	3 McDonnell Douglas/SAIC MD-82	
10 Airbus A319	9 McDonnell Douglas/SAIC MD-90	
5 Airbus A340-300	6 McDonnell Douglas MD-11	
10 Boeing 737-300		

McDonnell Douglas MD-90-30 B-2254 (Jan-Alexander Lück / Beijing)

CHINA NORTHERN AIRLINES

Dongtha Airport, Shenyang, Liaoning 110043,
People's Republic of China, Tel. 24-8294231,
Fax. 24-8294433, www.cna.com.cn

Three- / Two- letter code	IATA No.	Reg'n prefix	ICAO callsign
CBF / CJ	782	B	China Northern

This airline from the furthest northern regions of the People's Republic of China was set up in 1988, taking on the mantle of the former CAAC Shenyang administration. Its home base is at the Shenyang-Taoxin airport. Yunshuji Y-7s and MD-82s form the main body of the fleet; indeed China Northern is the largest user of the MD-82 in China. Included in this fleet are MD-82s assembled in China by SAIC under a licence agreement with McDonnell Douglas. As well as scheduled and charter flights, Mil-8 helicopters are used for industrial work and for various other tasks including heavy lifting and the

erection of masts. In 1993 two Airbus A300-600s were leased and proved to be successful in service, so that six further examples were ordered, entering service during 1994-95. A further licence-building arrangement was agreed with McDonnell Douglas, this time for the MD-90, and China Northern was the first airline to receive finished examples. In Spring 1996 the airline operated its first international route, from Shenzento the new airport at Macau. Charter flights are now also operated to Japan, Korea and other points in South East Asia. MD-90s are also operated on behalf of partner company Beiya Air. Late in

2002 the Chinese aviation authorities declared that China Northern was to be merged with China Southern Airlines, during the period 2003/4. In the meantime China Northern continues to operate independently.

Routes

Beijing, Changchun, Changhsa, Chengdu, Chongqing, Dalian, Dandong, Fuzhou, Guangzhou, Gulyang, Haikou, Hangzhou, Harbin, Hefei, Hong Kong, Jilin, Jinan, Kunming, Lianyungang, Macau, Nanjing, Niigata, Ningbo, Pyongyang, Qingdao, Sapporo, Seoul, Shanghai, Shantou, Shenyang, Shenzen, Tianjin, Urumqi, Wenzhou, Wuhan, Xiamen, Xian, Yangi, Yantai, Zhengzhou and Zhuhai.

Fleet		Ordered
6 Airbus A300-600	10 Yunshuji Y-7	6 Airbus A321-200
4 Airbus A321-200	24 McDonnell Douglas/SAIC MD-82	
44 Yunshuji Y-5	13 McDonnell Douglas MD-90	

Airbus A310-222 B-2303 (Jan-Alexander Lück / Beijing)

CHINA NORTHWEST AIRLINES

2 Feng Hao Road, 710082 Xian, Shanxi
People's Republic of China, Tel. 29-8702021
Fax. 29-8702027, www.cnwa.com

Three- / Two- letter code	IATA No.	Reg'n prefix	ICAO callsign
CNW / WH	783	B	China Northwest

The former CAAC regional directorate of Xian has been flying under the name of China Northwest Airlines since 1989 and has the task of operating regional scheduled and charter flights, as well as the agricultural and forestry work, for which the Yunshuji Y-5 sprayers are used. The fleet which was taken over from CAAC was based in Lanzhou and Xian and still consisted of Soviet-designed aircraft, mainly Tupolev Tu-154s. China Northwest has a modern maintenance centre at the new Xian-Xianyang airport. Conditions were therefore right for a successive replacement of the fleet with aircraft up to western standards. Thus in 1990/91, BAe 146s were delivered for regional services as a replacement for the Antonov An-24, and in the following year Airbus A300-600s and A310s were brought into service. Further fleet renewal took place with the delivery of the first Airbus A320 in November 1997; these had replaced the Tupolev Tu-154s by the end of 1999. Two Tupolev Tu-204s have been ordered for delivery during 2004. In the planned mergers of Chinese airlines to form larger units, China Northwest is to merge with China Eastern over the next couple of years. Until this is achieved, all the airlines continue to fly under their existing company names. China Northwest has an 80% shareholding in Nanjing Airlines, which operates two Yunshuji Y-7s from Nanjing

Routes

Beijing, Changsha, Chengdu, Chongqing, Dalian, Dayong, Dunhuang, Fukuoka, Fuzhou, Guangzhou, Guilin, Guiyang, Haikou, Hangzhou, Harbin, Hiroshima, Jiayugan, Kunming, Lanzhou, Lianyungang, Nagoya, Nanchang, Nanjing, Niigata, Ningbo, Okinawa, Qingdao, Sapporo, Seoul, Shanghai, Shantou, Shenyang, Shenzen, Urumqui, Wenzhou, Wuhan, Wuyishan, Xian, Xiamen, Xining, Yantai, Yinchuan, Zhanjiang, Zhuhai.

Fleet		Ordered
3 Airbus A310-200	10 BAe 146-100/300	2 Tupolev Tu-204
3 Airbus A300-600	11 Yunshuji Y5	
13 Airbus A320		

Boeing 777-21B(ER) B-2058 (Albert Kuhbandner / Amsterdam)

CHINA SOUTHERN AIRLINES

Baiyun Intl.Airport, 510406 Guangzhou
People's Republic of China, Tel. 20-86681818
Fax. 20-86665436, www.cs-air.com

Three- / Two- letter code	IATA No.	Reg'n prefix	ICAO callsign
CSN / CZ	784	B	China Southern

In common with other Chinese airlines, China Southern stems from the 1989 reorganisation of CAAC. Based in Guangzhou, it became China's second largest international airline, with spectacular growth. In a two-year period alone, over $600 million was invested in the fleet. Thus from 1990 Boeing 737s, 757s and more recently 767s were being delivered continually. China Southern was the first Chinese company to take delivery of the up-to-the-minute Boeing 777 from 1995, for its long-range routes. During 1996 China Southern also set up its own 'business airline', equipped with LearJets. Twenty Airbus A320s were ordered in 1997, the first Airbuses to be sold directly to a Chinese operator, thus it became possible to retire all the former Soviet-built types and older Boeing 737-200s. In addition to its airline operations, China Southern also undertakes other diverse flying tasks including agricultural aviation and offshore work, and uses various light aircraft and helicopters for these. The airline also has shareholdings in other Chinese airlines: Guangxi Airlines (60%), Guihou Airlines (60%), Shantou Airlines (60%), Xiamen Airlines (60%), Zhuhai Helicopter (100%) and Zhuhai Airlines (100%). The new generation Boeing 737-800 was added from 2002, and Airbus A319s on lease from May 2003. China Southern is one of the three airlines designated to lead new consolidated groups in the air transport industry, and as a first step, it acquired Zhongyuan Airlines (see page 365) in mid-2000, though this continues in independent operation. China Northern and Xinjiang Airlines are to be merged in during 2003/4.There are alliances and codeshare arrangements with Delta Air Lines and United Airlines.

Routes

Amsterdam, Anchorage, Bangkok, Beihai, Changchun, Changde, Changsha, Changzhou, Chengdu, Chicago, Chongqing, Dalian, Dandong, Dayong, Djakarta, Fukuoka, Fuzhou, Guangzhou, Guilin, Guiyang, Haikou, Hangzhou, Hanoi, Harbin, Hefei, Ho Chi Minh City, Hong Kong, Jilin, Jinan, Jinjiang, Jinzhou, Jiujiang, Kuala Lumpur, Kunming, Lianyungang, Liuzhou, Los Angeles, Manila, Melbourne, Mudanjiang, Nanchang, Nanjing, Nanning, Nantong, Nanyang, Ningbo, Osaka, Penang, Phnom Penh, Qingdao, Sanya, Seoul, Shanghai, Shantou, Sharjah,Shasi, Shenyang, Shenzen, Singapore, Surabaya, Sydney, Taiyuan, Tianjin, Tunxi, Urumqui, Weiha, Wenzhou, Wuhan, Xian, Xiamen, Xuzhou, Yichang, Yiwu, Zhanjiang, Zhengzhou, Zhuhai.

Fleet		Ordered
4 Airbus A319-100	18 Boeing 757-200	13 Boeing 737-800
20 Airbus A320-200	10 Boeing 777-200	
26 Boeing 737-300	2 Boeing 747-400F	
12 Boeing 737-500		
7 Boeing 737-800		

Boeing 757-2Z0 B-2837 (Jan-Alexander Lück / Beijing)

CHINA SOUTHWEST AIRLINES

Shuangli Airport, Chengdu 610202, People's Republic of China, Tel. 28-5703361, Fax. 28-57043673
E-mail: info@cswa.com, www.cswa.com

Three- / Two- letter code	IATA No.	Reg'n prefix	ICAO callsign
CXN / SZ	785	B	China Southwest

China Southwest was founded in October 1987 to take over the activities of the former CAAC regional administration. Initially the fleet consisted of the inherited types – Antonov 24s, Boeing 707s and Tupolev Tu-154s, but soon no less than 20 Boeing 737-300s and various propeller-driven types were serving over 30 destinations from Chengdu-Shuangliu airport. Other hubs were at Chongqing and Guiyang. The fleet grew quickly as did the network, including more and more international destinations. Hong Kong, Bangkok, Kathmandu and Singapore were all served from

1989. Particularly noteworthy was the route over 'the roof of the world' from Chengdu to Lhasa in Tibet. Freight operations were carried out using the former CAAC Boeing 707s, though the number of this type in service reduced as new Boeing 757s were delivered from 1992 onwards. This fast-growing company, which carries over six million passengers each year, has its maintenance base at the airport at Chengdu and is building up its staff and experience as Boeing specialists. However, the airline is not quite an all-Boeing operator, having taken delivery of Airbus

A340s from December 1998 and has ordered the Tupolev Tu-204 for delivery from 2004. Whether delivery of these will actually take place in view of the scheduled merger with Air China during 2003/4 is uncertain, and bearing in mind also the undoubted popularity of the new generation Boeing 737-600/700/800 series in China.

Routes

Bangkok, Beihai, Beijing, Changsa, Chengdu, Chongqing, Dalian, Fuzhou, Guangzhou, Guiyang, Guilin, Haikou, Hangzhou, Hefei, Hong Kong, Kunming, Lhasa, Lanzhou, Longdongbao, Luoyang, Nanchang, Nanjing, Nanning, Ningbo, Qingdoa, Shanghai, Shantou, Shenzen, Singapore, Urumqi, Wenzhou, Wuhan, Xian, Xiamen, Xichang, Xining, Xuzhou, Yantai, Yichang, Zhanjiang, Zhangjiajie, Zhengzhou.

Fleet		Ordered
3 Airbus A340-300	6 Boeing 737-800	3 Tupolev Tu-204
14 Boeing 737-300	13 Boeing 757-200	4 Boeing 737-600
6 Boeing 737-600		

ATR 72-500 B-3027 (Thomas Kim / Beijing)

CHINA XINJIANG AIRLINES

Diwobao Intl. Airport, Urumqi, Xinjiang 830016,
People's Republic of China
Tel. 991-3801703, Fax. 991-3711084

Three- / Two- letter code	IATA No.	Reg'n prefix	ICAO callsign
CXJ / XO	651	B	Xinjiang

Xinjiang Airlines was founded in 1985, its forbear being the CAAC Xinjiang regional administration. It is owned 50% each by CAAC and the regional government of Xinjiang. This far western region of China borders on Kyrgyzstan, Mongolia and India, and many places are not quickly accessible other than by air. Thus it is no surprise that for such routes the de Havilland Canada DHC-6 Twin Otter was introduced into service from February 1985. Xinjiang Airlines acquired a further Western type, the Boeing 737-300, during 1993 and 1994; these were used for international services to Islamabad and Hong Kong. For the high-frequency scheduled service to Beijing, three 350-seat Ilyushin IL-86 widebodies were acquired at the end of 1993, and at that time the name of the airline was also changed to China Xinjiang Airlines. The fleet has been regularly updated: from August 1997 the Twin Otters were replaced with the larger ATR 72, and Boeing 757s, first delivered in April 1998, have replaced the older Russian types. Three of the new generation Boeing 737-700s are on order, with delivery expected from March 2001. At the behest of the Chinese government, China Xinjiang is to be merged with China Southern Airlines to form one of China's three future major airline groupings. Until this amalgamation is consummated, the airline continues in its present form, with its principal operating and maintenance base at Urumqi.

Routes

Aksu, Almaty, Beijing, Changsha, Chengdu, Chongqing, Dalian, Fuyun, Guangzhou, Guilin, Harbin, Hong Kong, Hotan, Islamabad, Jinan, Karamy, Kashi, Korla, Kunming, Kuqa, Lanzhou, Moscow, Novosibirsk, Qiemo, Qingdao, Shanghai, Shenyang, Shenzen, Tianjin, Xian, Xiamen, Yinning, Zhengzhou.

Fleet

5 ATR 72
2 Boeing 737-300
4 Boeing 737-700
9 Boeing 757-200

3 Ilyushin Il-86

Canadair CRJ200 B-3070 (Klaus Brandmaier / Munich)

CHINA YUNNAN AIRLINES

Wujiabao Airport, Kunming, Yunnan 650200
People's Republic of China, Tel. 871-7112999
Fax: 871-7151509, www.chinayunnanair.com

Three- / Two- letter code	IATA No.	Reg'n prefix	ICAO callsign
CYH / 3Q	592	B	Yunnan

Like almost all Chinese airline companies, Yunnan has its origins in CAAC, in this case the Yunnan regional administration. It became independent in July 1992 and began a daily Boeing 737-300 service from its base at Kunming-Wujiabao to Beijing and Shanghai. From 1993, international flights were introduced to Bangkok and Singapore. Until mid-1996 the fleet had consisted of Boeing 737-300s only, but was then expanded by the addition of two 263-seat Boeing 767-300s in order to accommodate steeply rising passenger numbers. The 767s took over on popular routes including those to Beijing and Bangkok. The

latest model of the 737, the -700 came into service with China Yunnan at the beginning of 1999. For shorter routes China Yunnan also acquired the Canadair CRJ200, with deliveries during 2002. As with all the other companies which originated from the old CAAC, China Yunnan Airlines is to be re-consolidated into one of the three new major groups. It will join China Northwest Airlines in merging with China Eastern Airlines, but for the moment continues its own operations as before.

Routes

Bangkok, Baoshan,Beihai, Beijing, Changchun,Changsha, Chengdu,Dali City, Dalian, Fuzhou, Guangzhou, Guilin, Guiyang, Haikou, Hangzhou,Harbin, Hefei, Jinan, Kuala Lumpur, Kunming, Lijiang, Luxi, Macau, Seoul, Shanghai, Shenzen, Singapore, Vientiane, Wuhan, Xian, Xiamen, Xuzhou, Yibin, Yichang, Zhanjiang, Zhengzhou, Zhuhai.

Fleet

12 Boeing 737-300
 4 Boeing 737-700
 3 Boeing 767-300ER
 6 Canadair CRJ200

ATR 42-500 OY-CIK (Albert Kuhbandner / Munich)

CIMBER AIR

Sonderborg Airport, 6400 Sonderborg, Denmark, Tel. 74-422277, Fax. 74-426511, E-mail: marketing@cimber.dk, www.cimberair.dk

Three- / Two- letter code	IATA No.	Reg'n prefix	ICAO callsign
CIM / QI	647	OY	Cimber

Cimber Air was founded by Ingolf Nielsen in 1950 when he took over Sonderjyllands Flyvelskab and remains largely in the hands of the Nielsen family. At first air taxi operations were carried out, often from the airline's Sonderborg base to Copenhagen. At the end of 1963 Cimber Air was awarded a scheduled service licence for this route. Nord 262s were brought into use and the radius of service was extended to Germany with flights to Hamburg and Kiel. During 1971 SAS, Maersk and Cimber Air together formed a new company called Danair, which took on all of their domestic services. More Nord 262s and from 1975 VFW 614s were brought into use; Cimber Air was the launch customer for the latter type. The limited opportunities in the Danish market led Cimber Air to look abroad for work; the airline flew services on behalf of Saudi Arabian Airlines and for DLT, the precursor of today's current Lufthansa Cityline. In order to do this a German subsidiary company was founded in Kiel. Fokker F.27s and F.28s were used on the various routes, until in 1989 the ATR 42, an optimal aircraft for the company's needs, became available. This type, and the larger ATR 72, formed the entire fleet for some years, until Canadair Regional Jets were added from July 2000. Co-operation with Lufthansa was built up especially around the time of German reunification at the beginning of the 1990s and today Cimber Air is a member of the Team Lufthansa operation, with some aircraft flown in Team Lufthansa colours. In order to facilitate further expansion, SAS took a shareholding during 1998. Through its co-operation with Lufthansa and SAS, Cimber Air benefits from numerous activities of the Star Alliance.

Routes

Aalborg, Aarhus, Berlin, Bremen, Brussels, Cologne/Bonn, Copenhagen, Dublin, Esbjerg, Frankfurt, Helsinki, Karup, Kiel, Luxembourg, Montpellier, Munich, Nice, Nuremberg, Roenne, Sonderborg, Vienna, Warsaw.

Fleet

9 ATR 42
5 ATR 72
2 Canadair CRJ200

Canadair CRJ100ER N927CA (Josef Krauthäuser / Miami)

COMAIR

P.O.Box 75021, Cincinnati Intl. Airport, Ohio 45275, USA, Tel. 859-7672550
Fax. 859-7672278, www.comair.com

Three- / Two- letter code	IATA No.	Reg'n prefix	ICAO callsign
COM / OH	886	N	Comair

Comair began regional services in March 1977 with a Piper Navajo between Cincinnati and Cleveland. The larger Embraer EMB-110 Bandeirante came into service from 1981, with more destinations being added. The addition of Shorts 360s, Swearingen Metros and in 1984 Saab 340s were indicative of the expansion to meet increasing demand. At the beginning of 1984 some 30 points were being served from Cincinnati and the airline was already a major regional carrier. In September 1984 Comair became a partner in the newly-created 'Delta Connection' system, under which marketing banner Delta brought together the feeder and regional services which had previously been operated by individual airlines under their own identities. Delta took a 20% shareholding in Comair. In 1989 Comair Holdings Inc. was formed to bring together the by now substantial activities of the group. From 1988 the Embraer 120 Brasilia, a fast turboprop, was introduced; Comair was a launch customer. Likewise it was a substantial launch customer for the Canadair Regional Jet, which began deliveries in 1993 and was the airline's first jet. In October 1999 Delta Air Lines took over all the shares in Comair. More Canadair Jets continued to be acquired and the propeller-driven types were phased out, so that the airline now has an all-jet, indeed an all-CRJ, fleet. Comair became one of the first users of the new lengthened 70-seater Canadair Regional Jet 700 model when deliveries began in September 2002.

Routes

From major hubs at Cincinnati and Orlando to 85 destinations in 30 US states, as well as points in Canada and the Bahamas.

Fleet

115 Canadair CRJ100
40 Canadair CRJ200
16 Canadair CRJ700

Ordered

17 Canadair CRJ200
11 Canadair CRJ700

aBoeing 767-330 D-ABUZ (Marcus Baltes / Frankfurt)

CONDOR FLUGDIENST

Am Grünen Weg 3, 65440 Kelsterbach, Germany
Tel. 06107-939 0, Fax. 06107-939520, E-mail:
information@condor.de, www.thomascook-flug.de

Three- / Two- letter code	IATA No.	Reg'n prefix	ICAO callsign
CFG / DE	881	D	Condor

Condor was the traditional charter subsidiary of German flag-carrier Lufthansa. Set up in 1955 as Deutsche Flugdienst GmbH, German Federal Railways, two shipping companies and Lufthansa were the shareholders. The first aircraft were Vickers Vikings. After considerable initial successes, it suffered a setback in 1959 and was completely taken over by Lufthansa with state aid, thus avoiding bankruptcy. In 1961 Lufthansa bought the Condor Luftreederei (formed in 1957) from the Oetker group and merged it with DF to form the new Condor Flugdienst GmbH. Vickers Viscounts were bought in 1961 and two Fokker F.27s in 1963;

in 1965 the first Boeing 727 entered service. By 1968 Condor had an all-jet fleet, and added examples of the Boeing 747-200 in 1971 and 1972; these were used to open new routes to the USA and Bangkok. During the late 1970s, the first oil crisis resulted in excess capacity being reduced; the smaller DC-10-30 replaced the 747s on long-range routes. Boeing 737-300s and Airbus A310s were used from 1987, and from 1989 the Boeing 757 was added as a 727 replacement. To meet increased demand, and additionally to operate scheduled flights for Lufthansa for a while, the fleet was increased. In 1995 Condor took shareholdings in various tour operators, to ensure

getting their business for its flights. In 1997 Condor Berlin, a low-cost subsidiary was set up, with Airbus A320s. Condor was the launch customer for the lengthened Boeing 757-300, with the first delivery in 1999, when the DC-10s were retired. To the dismay of many workers and customers, the well-known Condor name was given up in 2002. Tour operator Thomas Cook, also the owner of the British airline JMC, applied its own colours and titling to the aircraft for the 2003 season, with the addition on Condor aircraft of 'powered by Condor' wording.

Routes

Over 60 destinations worldwide, including the USA, Caribbean, Middle and Far East, India, Nepal and the usual Mediterranean holiday spots, the Canary Isles, Cape Verde, Northern Africa, Mauritius, Seychelles and Kenya.

Fleet

12 Airbus A320
16 Boeing 757-200
13 Boeing 757-300
 9 Boeing 767-300ER

Boeing 757-224 N29124 (Josef Krauthäuser / Fort Lauderdale)

CONTINENTAL AIRLINES

1600 Smith Street, Houston Texas 77002, USA
Tel. 713-324-5000, Fax. 713-24-2087, E-mail:
corpcomm@coair.com, www.continental.com

Three- / Two- letter code	IATA No.	Reg'n prefix	ICAO callsign
COA / CO	005	N	Continental

Continental can trace its history back to July 1934 as the southwest division of Varney Speed Lines; it changed name to Varney Air Transport on 17th December 1934 and in 1937 to Continental Air Lines. A network was established using various Lockheed aircraft, mainly in the western USA. Post-war, Convair 240s, DC-6s and DC-7Bs and Vickers Viscounts were used. Pioneer Airlines was taken over in 1954. Boeing 707s began 'Golden Jet' flights on 8th June 1959. The first 747 entered service on 18th May 1970, with the DC-10 following two years later. In October 1981 Texas International acquired a stake in Continental, and the two merged

in October 1982, using the Continental name. 1983 brought enormous financial problems and Chapter 11 bankruptcy protection. Aircraft and routes were dropped and it emerged from Chapter 11 in 1986. In February 1987, the parent company bought PeoplExpress, New York Air and Frontier and all were merged into Continental, but not without difficulty, as Chapter 11 was again used from December 1990 to May 1993. With a new colour scheme, the airline was ready to move on to the next crisis; in 1994 a low-cost division was set up 'Continental Light' but after losing millions it was abandoned. In the late 1990s a major re-equipment

programme was begun with the introduction of the Boeing 777 and 737-800, to replace the DC-10s and Boeing 727s. Boeing 757s and 767s were also added. The US airline crisis led Continental to institute many economies from 2001 to 2003; older aircraft were stored in the desert, routes dropped and new aircraft deliveries deferred. Northwest Airlines has a 14% holding in Continental and Continental itself has shareholdings in America West, COPA, Continental Express and Gulfstream International. Continental Express, a 100% subsidiary, operates from several hubs to many regional destinations (see page 144).

Routes

Continental has an intensive US domestic network, serving over 120 destinations. Additionally international services cover a further 65 cities abroad.

Fleet

120 Boeing 737-300/500
36 Boeing 737-700
86 Boeing 737-800/900
45 Boeing 757-200/300
10 Boeing 767-200

16 Boeing 767-400
19 Boeing 777-200
20 McDonnell Douglas MD-80

Ordered

115 Boeing 737-700/800/900
11 Boeing 757
9 Boeing 777

Embraer EMB-120 N51726 (Josef Krauthäuser / Tampa)

CONTINENTAL EXPRESS

1600 Smith Street, Houston Texas, 77002 USA
Tel. 713-3242639, Fax. 713-3244914
www.continental.com

Three- / Two- letter code	IATA No.	Reg'n prefix	ICAO callsign
BTA / CO	565	N	Jetlink

In 1956 Vercoa Air Service was founded and later renamed as Britt Airways. Its network in the US midwest served many smaller towns, centred on its base at Terre Haute, Indiana. Beech 99s, Swearingen Metros,Fairchild F.27s and FH-227s and later BAC One-Elevens were used. Flights were also operated on behalf of Allegheny and Piedmont on newly created commuter routes. The airline was taken over in 1986 by PeoplExpress, but PeoplExpress in turn was taken over by the Texas Air

Corporation in 1987. Britt Airways was then sold off, but continued to operate as an independent undertaking and was one of the companies which then operated feeder flights for Continental Airlines. From January 1989 these were brought under the banner of Continental Express and over time the aircraft were updated; in place of the Metros came Embraer EMB-120 Brasilias. After the airline was taken over by Continental in the early 1990s, ATR 42s and Beech 1900s were introduced. As launch

customer for the Embraer Regional Jets, Continental Express received its first RJ-145s as soon as late 1996, becoming the first operator to bring them into scheduled service, from the beginning of 1997. Delivery of the first of the smaller RJ 135s followed in late 1999. The last Beech 1900s were retired in 2001, followed by the ATR 42, so that Continental Express becomes an all-jet operator. The main hubs for Continental Express are Cleveland, Denver, Newark and Houston.

Routes

Abilene,Akron, Albany, Alexandria, Allentown, Amarillo, Atlanta, Baltimore, Baton-Rouge, Birmingham, Boston, Brownsville, Buffalo, Burlington, Charlestown, Charlotte, Chicago, Cincinnati, Cleveland, Colorado Springs, Columbus, Corpus Christi, Dallas/Fort Worth, Dayton, Denver, Detroit, El Paso, Erie, Flint, Fort Wayne, Grand Rapids, Greenville, Gulfport/Biloxi, Harlingen, Harrisburg, Hartford, Houston, Huntsville, Indianapolis, Jacksonville, Kalamazoo, Kansas City, Knoxville, Lake Charles,Lansing, Laredo, Little Rock, Louisville, Lubbock, Memphis, Midland/Odessa, Milwaukee, Minneapolis,Mobile, Monroe, Nashville, New York, Oklahoma City, Omaha, Ottawa, Philadelphia, Pittsburgh, St.Louis, Syracuse, Tampa, Tampico. Toledo, Toronto, Vail, Waco, Washington, Wichita.

Fleet	Ordered
15 Embraer EMB-120	30 Embraer ERJ-135
45 Embraer ERJ-135	50 Embraer ERJ-145
145 Embraer ERJ-145	

Boeing 737-71Q HP-1369CMP (Josef Krauthäuser / Miami)

COPA PANAMA

Apartado Postal 1572, Panama City 1, Panama
Tel. 2272522, Fax. 2271952,
www.copaair.com

Three- / Two- letter code	IATA No.	Reg'n prefix	ICAO callsign
CMP / CM	230	HP	Copa

The Compania Panamena de Aviacion SA – COPA – was formed on 21st June 1944. As was the case with many other South and Central American airlines, Pan American Airways (holding 32% of the shares) was behind the formation, in association with business people from Panama. Scheduled services to neighbouring countries commenced on 15th August 1947 with Douglas DC-3s. A Convair 240 was added to the fleet in 1952. Until the time when jet aircraft were introduced, an HS.748 and Lockheed L-188 Electra were in service with COPA. During 1971 Pan American sold its shareholding in the airline to the Panamanian government. Domestic services were discontinued from 1981, but international services were expanded, with Mexico City being added from 1991 and Cali, Montego Bay and Puerto Rico in 1992. In 1995 service to the Dominican Republic was added. An event of significance in the airline's recent development took place in 1998 when Continental Airlines acquired 49% of the capital, setting the scene for a close commercial co-operation. A fleet renewal was begun with the delivery of the first Boeing 737-700 in May 1999. With the introduction of the new type, a new colour scheme which has strong similarities to that of Continental, was adopted. By 2005 all of the Boeing 737-200s should have been withdrawn and COPA will have an ultra-modern fleet. The Panama-Tocumen Airport is both the most important hub and home base for COPA, and houses the airline's maintenance base.

Routes

Barranquilla, Bogota, Buenos Aires, Cali, Cancun, Caracas, Cartagena, Guatemala-City, Guayaquil, Havana, Kingston, Lima, Los Angeles, Managua, Medellin, Mexico City, Miami, Montego Bay, Orlando, Panama City, Port au Prince, Quito, San Jose, San Juan, San Pedro Sula, San Salvador, Santiago, Santo Domingo, Sao Paulo.

Fleet	Ordered
8 Boeing 737-200Adv. 12 Boeing 737-700	8 Boeing 737-700

Boeing 737-4B3 F-GFUH (Daniel Klein / Münster-Osnabrück)

CORSAIR

24 rue Saarinen, Silic 221, 94528 Rungis Silic Cedex, France, Tel. 1-49794979, Fax. 1-49794968, www.corsair.fr

Three- / Two- letter code	IATA No.	Reg'n prefix	ICAO callsign
CRL / SS	923	F	Corsair

Formed in 1981 as Corse-Air International, the airline started operations on 1st July 1981 and acquired four SE.210 Caravelles. Charters were operated from Paris and Ajaccio, within Europe and to Northern Africa. A characteristic feature of the fleet was a striking head with a headband painted on the tailfins of the aircraft. The first Boeing 737s were taken on in 1987, marking the start of a fleet replacement programme and during 1990 the first Boeing 747 was added. After a leading French tour operator, Nouvelles Frontières, took a stake in the airline in 1991, the airline's name was changed to its present form, and a new colour scheme was adopted for the aircraft. Traffic rights were obtained for a greater range of destinations, including flights to the French overseas territories, and Corsair developed into one of the larger charter operators. More long range routes continued to be added from 1994 to 1997, and in 1999 the first new Airbus A330 was introduced, the first new generation aircraft to replace the Boeing 747SPs on these long-range services. A further A330 was added at the beginning of 2000. Two Boeing 737-400s are operated on charter work exclusively for Nouvelles Frontières. With the TUI group taking over Nouvelles Frontières, Corsair has become a sister company of Hapag Lloyd and Britannia. An example of the new co-operation within the group is the lease of a Britannia Boeing 767-300 to Corsair from 2003. It is intended to replace the Boeing 747-200s and -300s with series -400s between 2005 and 2007.

Routes

Abidjan, Ajaccio, Amman, Athens, Bamako, Barcelona, Bari, Bastia, Cairo, Calvi, Cayenne, Cotonou,Dakar, Djerba, Dublin, Fagernes, Faro, Fort de France, Funchal, Hanover, Havana, Heraklion, Hurghada, Istanbul, Keflavik, Larnaca, Lisbon, Lome, Los Angeles, Luxor, Malaga, Male, Marrakech, Mombasa, Palma de Mallorca, Papeete, Pont a Pitre, Porto, Rome, San Francisco, St.Denis, St. Louis, St. Martin, Santo Domingo, Tenerife, Touzeur,Venice.

Fleet		Ordered
2 Airbus A330-200	1 Boeing 767-300	2 Airbus A330-200
2 Boeing 737-400		
5 Boeing 747-300		
1 Boeing 747SP		

ATR 42-300 9A-CTT (Author /Zürich)

CROATIA AIRLINES

Savska Cesta 41, 1000 Zagreb, Croatia
Tel. 1-6160066, Fax. 1-6176845,
www.croatiaairlines.hr

Three- / Two- letter code	IATA No.	Reg'n prefix	ICAO callsign
CTN / OU	831	9A	Croatia

After the break-up of Yugoslavia, the Republic of Croatia was formed in the north of the country, with Zagreb as its capital. The national airline formed in 1989 was initially called Zagal-Zagreb Airlines and used Cessna and Piper light aircraft, but it took on the present name in 1990. The scheduled services formerly operated by JAT were taken over, using DC-9s from Adria Airways and operations commenced on 5th May 1991 between Zagreb and Split. As a result of the United Nations embargo and continued fighting, the airspace over the country was closed from September 1990 until 1st April 1992. After it was re-opened, Croatian Airlines expanded its operations, using Boeing 737-200s. From 1993, ATR 42s also came into use for internal and short-range international flights. With the opening of airports at Mostar and Sarajevo in Summer 1996, these points were also served. A fleet renewal with factory-fresh Airbus A320s and A319s began in 1997, allowing the older Boeing 737s to be retired, and giving Croatia one of the youngest fleets in Europe. In addition to scheduled services, there are also special flights for expatriate Croatian workers, as well as holiday charters for the Adriatic tourist market, which is coming back to life, partially by the efforts of the airline's own tour company which has been formed for this purpose. As a result of considerable reorganisation of routes entailing the dropping of some destinations, the airline has achieved profitability. There are co-operation agreements with Air France, Alitalia, CSA, Iberia, Lufthansa, LOT-Polish Airlines and THY-Turkish Airlines.

Routes

Amsterdam, Berlin, Bol, Brussels, Dubrovnik, Düsseldorf, Frankfurt, London, Manchester, Mostar, Munich, Osijek, Paris, Prague, Pula, Rijeka, Rome, Sarajevo, Skopje, Split, Tel Aviv, Vienna, Zadar, Zagreb and Zürich.

Fleet

4 Airbus A319-100
3 Airbus A320-200
3 ATR 42-300
1 BAe 146-200

Boeing 737-55S OK-XGD (Daniel Klein / Düsseldorf)

CSA – CZECH AIRLINES

Ruzyne Airport 16008 Prague, Czech Republic
Tel 2-20111111, Fax. 2-20562266,
E-mail: okplus@csa.cz, www.csa.cz

Three- / Two- letter code	IATA No.	Reg'n prefix	ICAO callsign
CSA / OK	064	OK	CSA Lines

CSA was founded on 6th October 1923 and flew its first service from Prague to Bratislava with a Hansa Brandenburg Aero A-14. In the mid-1930s the exclusively domestic service was expanded internationally with a Prague-Bratislava-Vienna-Zagreb route, and connections to Romania and the USSR followed. By the mid-1930s CSA was one of the leading European airlines. However, closure was enforced by the war from 1938 to 1946. A new start was made in 1947 with the Douglas DC-3, but following political change in 1948 came the influx of Soviet technology, and CSA flew Ilyushin IL-12s and -14s, and from 9th December 1957, the Tupolev Tu-104A, with which service to Jakarta was introduced. The IL-12s were replaced by Ilyushin IL-18s and a schedule to Havana initiated for political reasons. For long-range routes the Ilyushin IL-62 was acquired in 1969 and in 1970 New York and Montreal were first served. The Tu-134A was employed for many years on European routes, but gradually replaced from April 1988 with Tu-154Ms. The major political change during 1989 made it possible for the first time in 40 years to order Western aircraft. Airbus A310-300s were thus delivered in 1990 to replace the IL-62s. Since then the fleet has been constantly renewed and upgraded, with ATR 72s added from 1992, ATR 42s from March 1996, Boeing 737-500s from March 1997 and 737-400s from April 1998. Following the division of the former Czechoslovakia into two republics, a change of name (from 26th March 1995) and a new colour scheme were introduced. By the end of the 1990s the last of the Tupolevs had been retired. CSA joined the Sky Team alliance in 2001.

Routes

Abu Dhabi, Amsterdam, Athens, Bahrain, Bangkok, Barcelona, Beirut, Belgrade, Berlin, Bologna, Bratislava, Brno, Brussels, Bucharest, Cairo, Copenhagen, Damascus, Dubai, Dublin, Düsseldorf, Edinburgh, Frankfurt, Geneva, Gothenburg, Hamburg, Hanover, Helsinki, Istanbul, Karlovy Vary, Kiev, Kosice, Larnaca, London, Madrid, Manchester, Milan, Montreal, Munich, New York, Nice, Oslo, Paris, Poprad/Tatry, Prague, Riga, Rome, Sofia, Split, St.Petersburg, Stockholm, Stuttgart, Tel Aviv, Toronto, Vienna, Warsaw, Zagreb, Zürich.

Fleet

3 Airbus A310-300	11 Boeing 737-400
5 ATR 42-300	12 Boeing 737-500
4 ATR 72-200	

Yakovlev Yak-42 CU-T1285 (Jan Alexander Lück / Havana)

CUBANA DE AVIACION

23-64 Vedado Havana 4, Republic of Cuba
Tel. 334949, Fax. 334056,
www.cubana.cu

Three- / Two- letter code	IATA No.	Reg'n prefix	ICAO callsign
CUB / CU	136	CU	Cubana

Staunchly socialist Cuba has had its doors open for tourists for several years, ever since tourism was recognised as a valuable source of foreign currency. Thus Cubana Ilyushin IL-62s have been seen from time to time at European airports. Empresa Consolidada Cubana de Aviacion was set up on 27th June 1961 by the new Cuban government, taking over and reorganising its predecessor Compania Cubana de Aviacion SA and merging in several smaller airlines. At that time the inherited fleet consisted of British and American built aircraft such as Constellations, Britannias and

Viscounts, but after the imposition of a trade embargo by the USA, Soviet types were brought into use, with IL-14s, IL-18s, An-12s and An-24s arriving between 1961 and 1967. In 1974 Cubana's first jet, an IL-62, arrived and went into service in November between Havana and Madrid. Following the collapse of the Warsaw Pact, services were increased to non-communist countries, some flown with wet-leased DC-10s. The acquisition of six Fokker F.27s from Aviaco in 1994 was another sign of the easing of relations, and was also marked by the introduction of a new colour

scheme. From November 1998, Airbus A320s were added, and the total of Soviet built types has been steadily declining. In the medium term, Cubana has need for more new aircraft, as the average age of the fleet and its heavy demand for maintenance militates against keeping the older types flying. As an interim measure, pending a hoped-for relaxation of a now rather outdated US embargo on the delivery of new aircraft, various types have been used on wet lease from several airlines.

Routes

Baracoa, Bayamo, Camaguey, Cancun, Caracas, Cayo Largo, Ciego de Avila, Cienfuegos, Cordoba, Fort de France, Guantanamo, Guatemala City, Havana, Holguin, Kingston, Las Tunas, Mendoza, Mexico City, Montego Bay, Montevideo, Montreal, Nassau, Nueva Gerona, Paris, Punta Cana, Santiago, Santiago de Cuba, Santo Domingo, Sao Paulo, Varadero.

Fleet

7 Antonov An-24	4 Ilyushin IL-62
5 Yakovlev Yak-42	2 Ilyushin IL-76
2 Fokker F.27	5 Tupolev Tu-154

Airbus A319-132 5B-DBO (Martin Kühn / Frankfurt)

CYPRUS AIRWAYS

21 Alkeou Street Engomi 1903 Nicosia, Cyprus
Tel. 2-663054, Fax. 2-663167
www.cyprusair.com.cy

Three- / Two- letter code	IATA No.	Reg'n prefix	ICAO callsign
CYP / CY	048	5B	Cyprus

Cyprus Airways was set up on 24th September 1947 by British European Airways, Cypriot business interests and the government. BEA Douglas DC-3s were used to start operations to Athens on 6th October 1947. Other routes were added to Haifa, Istanbul, Rome, Beirut and Cairo. The airline took delivery of the first of its own DC-3s in April 1948 and was thus able to operate its own services. During 1950 BOAC took over 23% of the shares, though these were sold in 1959 to the Cypriot government. Vickers Viscounts opened the London route in the 1950s after BEA, on behalf of Cyprus Airways, began the world's first sustained turboprop passenger service on 18th April 1953 when a Viscount flew from Heathrow to Nicosia. Cyprus gained independence in August 1960 and BEA signed a deal with Cyprus Airways in 1961 to operate its services, initially for a five year period, with BEA aircraft. The arrangement finally ended in 1969, in which year Cyprus took delivery of its first jets, two Hawker-Siddeley Tridents bought from BEA in November. In July 1974 Cyprus Airways had to cease operations, as Turkish troops occupied Nicosia airport and a Trident was destroyed in fighting. However, on 8th February 1975 the first Boeing 707 took off from the new base at Larnaca in the south of Cyprus. BAC One-Elevens were acquired from 1978 to 1980 and in 1984 came the first Airbus A310, with the first A320 following in mid-1989. A subsidiary company, Eurocypria Airlines, was founded in 1990, using A320s for charter work. A new colour scheme was introduced in 1991 and is still in use. For several years Cyprus Airways operated an almost unchanged network, but expansion was evident from 2002, with two new types joining the fleet, the first Airbus A330 in the autumn and two A319s in the spring, all displaying a further new colour scheme.

Routes

Amman, Amsterdam, Athens, Bahrain, Beirut, Birmingham, Brussels, Damascus, Dubai, Düsseldorf, Frankfurt, Heraklion, Jeddah, Kuwait, Larnaca, London, Manchester, Milan, Moscow, Munich, Paphos, Paris, Riyadh, Rome, Salzburg, Tel Aviv, Thessaloniki, Vienna, Warsaw and Zürich.

Fleet

2 Airbus A319
8 Airbus A320
2 Airbus A330-200
4 Airbus A310-200

ATR 42-300 OY-JRJ (Andreas Witek / Graz)

DANISH AIR TRANSPORT

P.O.Box 80 6580 Vamdrup, Denmark
Tel. 75-583777, Fax. 75-583722
E-mail: sales@dat,dk, www.dat.dk

Three- / Two- letter code	IATA No.	Reg'n prefix	ICAO callsign
DTR / DX	–	OY	Danish

Husband and wife team Kirsten and Jesper Rungholm set up their own airline, Danish Air Transport in 1989 in Kolding. Jesper Rungholm was a pilot, who also flew rescue helicopters for the Danish Navy. Using a Shorts SC.7, otherwise known as the flying shoe-box, as their first equipment, operations were begun in April 1989. Anything that would fit in the aircraft would be carried, including horses, postal sacks and packages, and spares for vehicles and other aircraft. DAT also provided the support and general transport aircraft for the famous Paris-Dakar car rally. The company achieved positive growth and further aircraft including the Beech 99 and Beech 1900 were added to the varied fleet, which could also be described as colourful. The extensive use of red, blue, green and yellow marked out the individuality of DAT. Additional investors joined the Rungholm family and this financed the acquisition of larger aircraft, ATR 42s and ATR 72s. DAT has its own scheduled service network between Denmark, Norway and Sweden, though flying only from Stockholm-Arlanda in Sweden. Some of these services are government-subsidised. Charter and holiday flights are flown principally with the ATRs. Aircraft are leased to other companies on both a short and long term basis. The main operating and maintenance base remains at Kolding.

Routes

Aalborg, Arvidsjaur, Bergen, Billund, Esbjerg, Floro, Gällivan, Hemavan, Lyckelle, Oslo, Stavanger, Stockholm.

Fleet

7 ATR 42
3 ATR 72
1 Beech 99
3 Beech 1900

1 Shorts SC-7
1 Saab 340

151

Boeing 737-832 N3750D (Stefan Schlick / Montego Bay)

DELTA AIR LINES

Hartsfield Atlanta Airport, Georgia 30320-6001
USA, Tel. 404-7152600, Fax. 404-7155876
www.delta.com

Three- / Two- letter code	IATA No.	Reg'n prefix	ICAO callsign
DAL / DA	006	N	Delta

Delta Air Lines is not only one of the largest airlines in the USA, but also one of the oldest, tracing its history back to Huff Daland setting up in 1924 at Monroe, LA to spray cotton fields in the Mississippi Delta. The name Delta Air Services was taken in 1928. A Travelair was used on the first scheduled passenger service on 17th June 1929 from Dallas to Jackson. The company was sold to the Aviation Corporation in 1930 and became Delta Air Corporation. By 1940 the fleet consisted of ten Lockheed Electras and five DC-3s. In 1953 Delta merged with Chicago & Southern Airlines, Northeast Airlines was taken over in 1972 and

finally Western Airlines was acquired in 1987; thus the network and fleet were continually expanded. In 1959 DC-8s, in 1960 Convair 880s and in 1965 DC-9s were brought into service, with Delta being a launch customer in each case. Widebodies, Boeing 747s from 1970-1977, and DC-10s from 1972-1975 were also used before the airline settled on the Lockheed TriStar. During 1978 began transatlantic service, to London, with Frankfurt added a year later. In November 1991, the ailing Pan Am was bought and all its routes and aircraft integrated. Delta Express, a low-cost division serving about 20 destinations, was

established in October 1996. In Spring 1997 Delta signed an exclusive 20-year fleet acquisition plan with Boeing, and as a result, two new types, the 737-800 and 777 were added from 1998 to replace the older 737-200s and Lockheed TriStars. It is also a launch customer for the Boeing 767-400. A further acquisition at the beginning of 1999 was ASA-Atlantic Southwest Airlines, which provides feeder services as 'Delta Connection'. In 2003 a new low-cost division called Song was set up and the last of the 727s retired; the remaining MD-11s are all in store. Delta was a founding member of the Sky Team alliance.

Routes

Delta Air Lines flies to over 260 destinations, mostly in the USA, but in excess of 40 internationally.

Fleet

Fleet		Ordered
38 Boeing 737-200Adv.	21 Boeing 767-400	60 Boeing 737-800
26 Boeing 737-300	8 Boeing 777-200	5 Boeing 777-200
71 Boeing 737-800	14 McDonnell Douglas MD-11	
121 Boeing 757-200	120 McDonnell Douglas MD-88	
15 Boeing 767-200	16 McDonnell Douglas MD-90	
87 Boeing 767-300/300ER		

Boeing 737-329 D-ADIE (Albert Kuhbandner / Munich)

DEUTSCHE BA

Wartungsallee 13, 85356 Munich-Flughafen, Germany, Tel. 089-97591 500, Fax. 089-97591 503, www.flydba.com

Three- / Two- letter code	IATA No.	Reg'n prefix	ICAO callsign
BAG / DI	944	D	Speedway

Delta Air of Friedrichshafen was set up by the Scholpp transport group in Stuttgart in March 1978 and started flights between Friedrichshafen and Stuttgart with a DHC-6 Twin Otter in April 1978, as well as from Friedrichshafen to Zürich. In 1982 a Swearingen Metro III was added to the fleet. A second Metro III was added in 1984 as well as a Dornier 228, which was used on the route from Friedrichshafen to Oberpfaffenhofen. In 1985 Delta Air was converted into a private limited company, with the involvement of the Swiss airline Crossair. In May 1987 it was given the status of a scheduled airline and from that time

flew some routes with Saab 340s, added to the fleet in 1986, on behalf of Lufthansa. In March 1992 three German banks bought 51% of the shares and British Airways the remaining 49% stake in Delta, and the name was changed to Deutsche BA on 5th May 1992. The new airline used not only Saab 340s, but also Boeing 737-300s, introducing the Saab 2000 and Fokker 100 from 1995. The company headquarters moved to Munich from 1st January 1995, and in 1997 the regional operations were sold and the company withdrew from the operation of propeller-driven types, the fleet being standardised on the

Boeing 737-300 alone. A new colour scheme was introduced, following the British Airways' example of artistic tail adornment. As a subsidiary of BA, Deutsche BA became a member of the Oneworld alliance. In 2001 EasyJet bought a purchase option in BA's loss-making subsidiary, but early in 2003 this was allowed to lapse. During 2002 Deutsche BA had changed its structure and positioned itself more as a low-cost company, moving away from the British Airways image, and with a new colour scheme. On 2nd June 2003 the airline was sold for a nominal sum to a German investor group.

Routes

Berlin, Cologne/Bonn, Düsseldorf, Hamburg, Malaga, Munich, Nice, Stuttgart; charter flights principally to the Mediterranean holiday areas.

Fleet

16 Boeing 737-300

Boeing 757-236(SF) G-BIKM (Gerhard Schütz / Munich)

DHL AIRWAYS

P.O.Box 75122, Cincinnati Ohio 45275, USA
Tel. 606-2832232, Fax. 606-5251998,
www.dhl.com

Three- / Two- letter code	IATA No.	Reg'n prefix	ICAO callsign
DHL / ER	423	N	Dahl

DHL Airways was an enterprise of the internationally represented DHL Worldwide Express, which was founded in 1969. The DHL name stems from the first letters of the surnames of the three founders. Initially its task was the carriage of courier packages between California and Hawaii, carried on scheduled flights, and then on other routes within the USA. In time, as the volume of business grew, the company started to use its own smaller aircraft such as the Swearingen Metro II or Cessna 402 on selected domestic routes. At the beginning of the 1980s business had grown so much that packages were carried on their own aircraft only and within the USA there were 12 hubs and 76 so-called gateways, where freight could be accepted – not only small and express packages. DHL now has 16 international hubs worldwide. Boeing 727s have formed the bulk of the fleet, with DC-8s for long-range routes, and even a helicopter for service in New York. Other operators fly on behalf of DHL, for example European Air Transport of Belgium, for various European services. For the expanding Asia market DHL has a Chinese partner in Sinotrans and similarly there are regional partners in several other countries. With the delivery of the first Airbus A300B4 in April 1999 DHL both initiated fleet renewal and added capacity. The majority shareholding was acquired in 2002 by Deutsche Post World Net and this resulted in some substantial changes in the business operations and a new colour scheme. The Boeing 757-200(SF)s operated by DHL Air Ltd have increased in prominence. In the US, DHL chief executive John Dasburg led an investor group to buy out the whole airline, in order to resolve a problem over a perceived foreign ownership of the business, which has caused difficulties with competitors.

Routes

Scheduled freight services within the USA and internationally to over 160 destinations on all continents.

Fleet

7 Airbus A300B4F
1 Bell 206-L1 Longranger
30 Boeing 727-100/200
10 Boeing 757-200SF
8 Douglas DC-8-73F

Boeing 747-312(SF) B-KAB (Bastian Hilker / Amsterdam)

DRAGONAIR

22F. Devon House, Taikoo Place 979 Kings Rd,
Quarry Bay, Hong Kong, Tel. 25901328
Fax. 25901333, www.dragonair.com

Three- / Two- letter code	IATA No.	Reg'n prefix	ICAO callsign
HDA / KA	043	B-H	Dragonair

Dragonair began its activities in 1985, mainly to serve destinations in the People's Republic of China from Hong Kong. The airline, a wholly-owned subsidiary of Hong Kong Macau International Investments, started operations with two Boeing 737-200s, though during the first year the aircraft were often grounded as a result of strong opposition from Cathay Pacific. However over the next few years some scheduled routes were awarded to Dragonair and several more Boeing 737s were leased as the network was expanded. From 1989 destinations other than in the People's Republic of China were

served and a charter division established. It was also in 1989 that China International Trust and Investment and the Swire Group, owners of Cathay Pacific, acquired most of the shares in Dragonair. In mid-1990 a Lockheed L-1011 TriStar was acquired from Cathay Pacific. When the first Airbus A320 was delivered in late 1992, a new aircraft colour scheme was adopted. Four Airbus A330s were introduced in 1995/96 as replacements for the TriStars, and these have been augmented by the delivery of further Airbus types, giving the airline a modern fleet. In 1998 and 1999 Airbus A321s were also leased, to

add further services to Chinese destinations following the return of Hong Kong to Chinese sovereignty and the opening of the new Hong Kong airport. After this move Dragonair also entered into the airfreight business, using Boeing 747 freighters obtained from Cathay Pacific. This business is to be developed over the coming years; thus Airbus A300 freighters are on order and it is anticipated that the 747F fleet will be tripled by 2008.

Routes

Beijing, Changsa, Chengdu, Chongqing, Dacca, Dalian, Dubai, Fuzhou, Guilin, Haikou,Hangzhou, Hiroshima, Hong Kong, Kaohsiung, Kota Kinabalu, Kunming, Nanjing, Osaka, Phnom Penh, Phuket, Qingdao, Sendai, Shanghai, Wuhan, Xian, Xiamen.

Fleet	Ordered
8 Airbus A320-200	3 Airbus A320-200
4 Airbus A321-200	2 Airbus A321-200
9 Airbus A330-300	6 Airbus A300-600F
3 Boeing 747F	

BAe 146-100 A5-RGD (Josef Krauthäuser/Bangkok)

DRUK AIR

P.O.Box 209 Thimpu, Kingdom of Bhutan
Tel. 827-1856, Fax. 827-1861, www.drukair.com
E-mail: drukair@druknet.bt

Three- / Two- letter code	IATA No.	Reg'n prefix	ICAO callsign
DRK / KB	787	A5	Royal Bhutan

Druk Air was established as the national airline on 1st April 1981 by decree of the King of Bhutan. After the infrastructure for air traffic had been prepared – it was necessary to build an airport near to the capital – a Dornier 228 began services with a flight to Calcutta on 12th February 1983. In mid-1983 a second aircraft of the same type was acquired. Charters were flown on behalf of the Indian domestic carrier, Vayudoot, on routes in eastern India. When a BAe 146 was delivered, the young airline entered the jet age; the new type allowed an expansion of the network and the addition of service to more distant destinations. The first new route was to Bangkok, where passengers from Europe change aircraft to fly to Bhutan with Druk Air. The BAe 146 is also at the disposal of the King of Bhutan for his personal use. With the delivery of a further BAe 146 in December 1992 the Dorniers were sold and the fleet became all-jet. During the tourist season from May to October Druk Air operates special 'Sky Kingdom' flights, which show off the tiny Kingdom of Bhutan from a fantastic perspective, flying amongst the Himalayan peaks and offering unique panoramas. Outside the tourist season, one of the BAe 146s is sometimes leased out. Druk Air works in co-operation with Thai International, who carry out major aircraft overhauls and training of personnel. There is an intention to replace the 146s with Airbus A319s.

Routes

Bangkok, Dacca, Delhi, Kathmandu, Kolkota, Paro, Yangon.

Fleet

2 BAe 146-100

Boeing 757-200 PH-DBA (Stefan Schlick / Arrecife)

DUTCH BIRD

P.O.Box 75798, 1118ZX Schiphol, the Netherlands
Tel. 20-6055800, Fax. 20-6055810
E-mail: pos@dutchbird.nl

Three- / Two- letter code	IATA No.	Reg'n prefix	ICAO callsign
DBR / 5D	–	PH	Dutchbird

Dutch Bird is the newest charter airline from the Netherlands, founded in Amsterdam in Spring 2000 by Bimoss Holding. Using two leased Boeing 757-200s acquired from the German airline Condor, operations were begun in November 2000. Dutch Bird works with all the larger Dutch tour operators and is also available for ad hoc charter work. The principal departure airport is Amsterdam, but services are also flown from Maastricht and Groningen. Fortaleza in Brazil has been the most exotic destination thus far for a charter series. Mostly, it is the traditional Mediterranean resorts which are served, with the addition of the Caribbean in the winter. Since August 2002 Dutch Bird acts as the official carrier for the famous Ajax Amsterdam football club. New-build Airbus 320s are being added, the first delivered in April 2003 and the second a month later, with the first commercial operation on 4th April from Groningen to Faro.

Routes

Antalya, Arrecife, Cancun, Chania, Corfu, Faro, Fortalezza, Fuerteventura, Heraklion, Hurghada, Karpatos, Kos, Lefkas, Lesbos, Malaga, Monastir, Palma de Mallorca, Puerto Vallarta, Rhodes, Samos, Sharm el Sheik, Tenerife, Zakynthos.

Fleet

2 Airbus A320-200
3 Boeing 757-200

McDonnell Douglas MD-82 PJ-SEF (Frank Schorr / Miami)

DUTCH CARIBBEAN AIRLINES

Hato Aeroport, Willemsstad, Curacao
Tel. 98394201, Fax. 9839 4300, E-mail:
hernandezf@fly-dca.net, www.flydca.net

Three- / Two- letter code	IATA No.	Reg'n prefix	ICAO callsign
DCA / K8	559	PJ	Dutchcaribbean

Following the financial failure of Air ALM on 1st November 2001, the government of this Dutch island province had to address quickly the question of the establishment of a new airline. Tourism is an essential to the economy of the island and without direct service to its important markets, visitor numbers would decline rapidly. It thus supported the expansion of Dutch Caribbean Express, which had begun operations in July 2001. Using two DHC-8s, services were conducted to the neighbouring islands and to Caracas. An investment programme was set up and with the availability of new capital the first DC-9 and MD-82 were acquired. The objectives of the airlines were as described in its name. Using the MD-82, scheduled services were recommenced to Miami, in time for the important Christmas holiday season. Air ALM had served these routes daily. In spite of the general world crisis, the war in Iraq and other apparent obstacles, DCA also worked to set up a connection with Amsterdam and this was begun on 1st May 2003, using a Boeing 767-300, leased from and operated on behalf of DCA by Sobelair. The DHC-6s and DHC-8s are operated by Dutch Caribbean Express.

Routes

Amsterdam, Aruba, Bonaire, Caracas, Coro, Curacao, Kingston, Los Piedras, Maracaibo, Miami, Paramaraibo, Port-au-Prince, Port of Spain, Santo Domingo, St. Maarten, Valencia.

Fleet

1 Boeing 767-300
3 Douglas DC-9-31
3 McDonnell Douglas MD-82
2 De Havilland DHC-6

2 De Havilland DHC-8-300

Boeing 737-73V G-EZJK (Florian Morasch / Amsterdam)

EASYJET AIRLINE

Luton Intl. Airport, Luton LU2 9LS
Great Britain, Tel. 1582445566,
Fax. 1582443355, www.easyjet.com

Three- / Two- letter code	IATA No.	Reg'n prefix	ICAO callsign
EZY / U2	–	G	Easy

In October 1995 Stelios Haji-Ioannou, a member of the Greek shipping line family, set up this new airline in London. EasyJet was the first British airline to follow the low-cost model which had been proved in the United States. The airline began services from London-Luton to Glasgow three times daily, only a month after its formation. Using two leased Boeing 737-200s and foreign cockpit crews, EasyJet was initially without its own operator's certificate. Two weeks later, services were begun to Edinburgh. After some start-up difficulties, new services were added, but there was a shortage of aircraft in the fleet to accomplish all this and the company had to take time to stabilise the situation before proceeding. New Boeing 737-300s in 148-seat configuration were ordered and introduced from 1996, with deliveries on a monthly basis. Amsterdam became the first foreign destination from Spring 1996. During 1997 the airline was granted its own operating licence and created a second hub at Liverpool. A majority of the shares in TEA Switzerland was acquired, and this airline renamed as EasyJet Switzerland; it too operates Boeing 737-300s. Competitor Go Fly (also a 737 operator with bases at Stansted, East Midlands and Bristol) was bought from British Airways in 2001 and integrated. An option to acquire Deutsche BA was also purchased from British Airways, but this was allowed to lapse in 2003. New model Boeing 737-700s are in course of delivery to EasyJet; deliveries commenced in October 2000. However, a change of fleet direction was signalled with an order for 115 Airbus A319s, for delivery from 2004 to 2007. Further expansion is on the cards, especially in France, where a bid was made for former Air Lib slots in Paris.

Routes

Aberdeen, Alicante,Amsterdam, Athens, Barcelona, Belfast, Bilbao, Bologna, Bristol, Copenhagen, East Midlands, Edinburgh, Faro, Geneva, Glasgow, Ibiza, Inverness, Liverpool, London-Gatwick/Luton/Stansted, Lyon, Madrid, Malaga, Milan, Munich, Naples, Palma de Mallorca, Paris-CDG, Prague, Rome, Toulouse, Venice, Zürich.

Fleet	Ordered
44 Boeing 737-300	115 Airbus A319
27 Boeing 737-700	6 Boeing 737-700

Airbus A330-243 HB-IQZ (Author / Zürich)

EDELWEISS AIR

Postfach, 8055 Zürich-Flughafen, Switzerland
Tel. 1-8165060, Fax. 1-8165061, E-mail:
office@edelweissair.ch, www.edelweissair.ch

Three- / Two- letter code	IATA No.	Reg'n prefix	ICAO callsign
EDW / 8R	945	HB	Edelweiss

On 19th October 1995 a new charter company was set up in the Zürich area, with the Kuoni travel company and the Greek airline Venus as the shareholders. It was set up as a joint stock company and could therefore take on further participants; the capital was raised to 3.5 million Swiss francs on the acquisition of aircraft in December 1995. At the end of January 1996 the first McDonnell Douglas MD-83 arrived, with the second following at the end of March. In the words of the officials at Kuoni Reisen AG, the main shareholder after the departure of Venus, Edelweiss tries to be an airline which offers a very Swiss atmosphere. The attractive colour scheme corresponds with the name and features a stylised version of the Swiss national flower. Beginning in the 1996 summer season, flights were operated to the traditional Mediterranean holiday resorts and to European cities. Good service and punctuality led to success, and a further MD-83 was acquired. From February 1999 the fleet was changed over to factory-fresh Airbus A320s, with three aircraft being delivered by June 1999. Edelweiss also has ambitions in the long-haul tour market and to this end, an Airbus A330-200 was delivered to Zürich late in 2000. With this increased seating capacity Edelweiss has been able to serve destinations in the Caribbean, Africa and the Indian Ocean.

Routes

Antalya, Arrecife, Cancun, Catania, Colombo, Corfu, Djerba, Eilat, Faro, Fuerteventura, Geneva, Heraklion, Holguin, Hurghada, Ibiza, Kos, Larnaca, La Palma, Las Palmas, London, Mahon, Malaga, Male, Marsa Alam, Miami, Mombasa, Monastir, Mykonos, Naples, Olbia, Orlando, Palermo, Palma de Mallorca, Puerto Plata, Punta Cana, Rhodes, Santorini, Sharm el Sheik,Tenerife, Varadero,Vienna, Zürich.

Fleet	Ordered
3 Airbus A320-200	
1 Airbus A330-200	

Airbus A340-212 SU-GBN (Albert Kuhbandner / Munich)

EGYPT AIR

International Airport, Cairo, Egypt
Tel. 2-2454400, Fax. 2-3901557,
www.egyptair.com.eg

Three- / Two- letter code	IATA No.	Reg'n prefix	ICAO callsign
MSR / MS	077	SU	Egyptair

Misr Airwork was founded on 7th June 1932 and services began in July 1933 with de Havilland Dragons. In 1949 the then wholly Egyptian-owned operation was renamed Misrair. Following a political union between Egypt and Syria in February 1958, Misrair was renamed United Arab Airlines and in December 1958, Syrian Airways was merged into UAA, which used Comet 4Bs and Vickers Viscounts. However, in September 1961, Syria withdrew. Egypt carried on alone under the UAA name, but in 1964 Misrair was revived as a domestic

airline, and then was brought together with UAA on 10th October 1971 to form the new Egypt Air. For political reasons UAA/Egypt Air flew Soviet types in the 1960s and 1970s, including An-24s, IL-18s, IL-62s and Tu-154s. In April 1975 the airline switched over to Airbus A300s and Boeing 737s. Boeing 707s followed for longer-range work, and later 747s as well. An extensive fleet replacement began with Boeing 767s and Airbus A300-600s in 1989. In 1991 Airbus A320s followed for short and medium-range routes. Late in 1996 the Airbus A340 was

introduced as an eventual replacement for the Boeing 747, and the introduction of the 340 also brought a new colour scheme for the airline. The Boeing 777 was added from 1997, completing the fleet renewal. However, at the turn of the century the process was begun again, with Egypt Air becoming a launch customer for the very long-range Airbus A340-600, deliveries of which commenced March 2003. ATR 42s were added on lease from the end of 2002. Re-equipment is to continue with A330s ordered early in 2003, for delivery in 2004/5.

Routes

Abidjan, Abu Dhabi, Abu Simbel, Accra, Addis Ababa, Aden, Al Ain, Aleppo, Alexandria, Algiers, Amman, Amsterdam, Asmara, Assuit, Aswan, Athens, Bahrain, Bangkok, Barcelona, Beirut, Berlin, Brussels, Budapest, Cairo, Capetown, Casablanca, Copenhagen, Damascus, Dhakla, Doha, Dubai, Düsseldorf, Frankfurt, Gaza, Geneva, Hamburg, Hurghada, Istanbul, Jeddah, Johannesburg, Khartoum, Kiev, Kuwait, Lagos, Larnaca, Lisbon, London, Los Angeles, Luxor, Madrid, Malta, Manchester, Manila, Milan, Mombasa, Moscow, Mumbai, Munich, Muscat, Nairobi, New York, Osaka, Paris, Riyadh, Rome, Sanaa, Sharjah, Sharm el Sheik, Singapore, Stockholm, Sydney, Taba, Tokyo, Tunis, Vienna, Zürich.

Fleet

7 Airbus A300-600
2 Airbus A300F
8 Airbus A320-200
4 Airbus A321-200
3 Airbus A340-200

5 ATR 42-500
2 Boeing 747-300
4 Boeing 737-500
5 Boeing 777-200ER

Ordered

5 Airbus A320
7 Airbus A-330-200

Boeing 777-258(ER) 4X-ECC (Ken Petersen / New York-JFK)

EL AL ISRAEL AIRLINES

P.O.Box 41 Ben Gurion Airport 70100 Tel Aviv, Israel, Tel. 3-9716111, Fax. 3-9716040, www.elal.co.il

Three- / Two- letter code	IATA No.	Reg'n prefix	ICAO callsign
ELY / LY	114	4X	ElAl

El Al took the initiative after the founding of the State of Israel and started building up services with aircraft belonging to the Israel Air Force. These were and are vital to Israel, which is surrounded by potential enemies. The aircraft used after the airline was formally established on 15th November 1948 were Curtiss C-46 Commandos and Douglas DC-4s (C-54s). Operations began on 31st July 1949 with services to Switzerland and Paris, with London added later in the year. A regular service to New York was established as soon as 1950 using Lockheed Constellations. Bristol Britannias were acquired in 1957 and the change to jets began in 1960, initially with leased Boeing 707s; indeed 707s and 720s were to be the backbone of the fleet for many years. In 1971 the first Boeing 747 arrived; in 1983 767s replaced 707s, followed in 1987 by 757s. During the mid-1980s El Al was restructured as the danger of economic collapse was threatening, and with a view to eventual privatisation. New Boeing 747-400s were introduced during 1994 and 1995, lowering the average age of the fleet. With the delivery of new Boeing 737-700s and -800s in 1999 a new colour scheme was adopted by the airline; Boeing 777s were added from 2001. Some overcapacity was eliminated, and 757s passed to North American, an airline in which El Al has a holding. El Al remains in state ownership, as investors are not forthcoming and the risk is difficult to ascertain, with less tourists being inclined to visit Israel. Some aircraft are loaned to another Israeli airline, Arkia, on a seasonal basis and Boeing 747 freighters operate for CAL Cargo Airlines.

Routes

Almaty, Amsterdam, Athens, Atlanta, Bangkok, Barcelona, Beijing, Berlin, Brussels, Budapest, Bucharest, Cairo, Chicago, Delhi, Dnepropetrovsk, Düsseldorf, Eilat, Frankfurt, Geneva, Hong Kong, Istanbul, Johannesburg, Kiev, Krakow, Lisbon, London, Los Angeles, Madrid, Marseilles, Miami, Milan, Minsk, Moscow, Mumbai, Munich, Nairobi, New York, Odessa, Ovda, Paris, Prague, Rome, St.Petersburg, Tel Aviv, Toronto, Vienna, Warsaw, Zürich.

Fleet

4 Boeing 747-400	6 Boeing 757-200
2 Boeing 747-200	2 Boeing 737-700
2 Boeing 747-200F	4 Boeing 737-800
6 Boeing 767-200	4 Boeing 777-200

Airbus A330-200 A6-EKV (Oliver Köstinger / Dubai)

EMIRATES

P.O.Box 686, Dubai, United Arab Emirates
Tel. 4-2951111, Fax. 4-2952001, www.emirates.com
E-mail: media.relations@emirates.com

Three- / Two- letter code	IATA No.	Reg'n prefix	ICAO callsign
UAE / EK	176	A6	Emirates

This independent state airline was formed in 1985 with political and financial support of the council of the seven independent emirates and the reigning head of government, the Emir of Dubai. The first aircraft, a Boeing 727 and Airbus A300, were leased from Pakistan International Airlines, who also gave assistance with establishing the airline under a management agreement. The first service was on 25th October 1985 to Karachi in Pakistan, and India was also served from the outset. In 1986 Dacca, Colombo and Cairo were added, with the first European routes starting from 1987, to London, Frankfurt and Istanbul.

Newly-delivered Airbus A310s were used here, with further examples being added in 1988 and 1990. The larger Airbus A300-600 was ordered however, and the last two Boeing 727s withdrawn from the fleet in 1995. Emirates has seen purposeful expansion, but always with caution in new markets. In 1996 a new service to Melbourne was added, using the new Boeing 777, first delivered in June 1996. Emirates operates a very modern fleet, consisting only of widebody aircraft. From 1999 further fleet renewal has taken place, with Airbus A330s and Boeing 777s replacing the A310s and A330-600s. Even in the face of

world problems, including the Iraq war, Emirates continues to expand and be successful. It is a launch customer for the new Airbus 380, with no less than 45 on order and extensive orders for further Airbus and Boeing aircraft announced in mid-2003.There is a codeshare agreement with SriLankan Airlines, in which company Emirates has a 25% shareholding,and other co-operation and codeshares with United Airlines, Thai Airways International, British Airways and South African Airways. Emirates remains independent, and seeks no alliance memberships.

Routes

Abu Dhabi, Amman, Athens, Bahrain, Bangkok, Beirut, Birmingham, Cairo, Casablanca, Chenai, Colombo, Damascus, Dammam, Dar-es-Salaam, Delhi, Dacca, Djakarta, Doha, Dubai, Düsseldorf, Entebbe/Kampala, Frankfurt, Hong Kong, Islamabad, Istanbul, Jeddah, Johannesburg, Karachi, Khartoum, Kuala Lumpur, Kuwait, Lahore, Larnaca, London, Male, Malta, Manila, Manchester, Mauritius, Melbourne, Milan, Mumbai, Munich, Muscat, Nairobi, Nice, Osaka, Paris, Peshawar, Riyadh, Rome, Sanaa, Singapore, Sydney, Teheran, Tripoli, Zürich.

Fleet	Ordered	
1 Airbus A310-300	8 Airbus A340-500	45 Airbus A380
28 Airbus A330-200	18 Airbus A340-600HGW	2 Airbus A380F
21 Boeing 777-200/300		26 Boeing 777-300ER

Convair 580 N569JA (Lutz Schönfeld / Anchorage)

ERA AVIATION

6160 Carl Brady Drive, Anchorage, Alaska, 99502-1801 USA, Tel. 907-2484422, Fax. 907-2668383, E-mail: airlineinfo@eraaviation.com, www.era-aviation.com

Three- / Two- letter code	IATA No.	Reg'n prefix	ICAO callsign
ERH / 7H	808	N	Erah

ERA Aviation is an important undertaking, known not only for its extensive operations in Alaska, but also for its wide-ranging activities in support of exploration and oil production in the Gulf of Mexico. Founded in 1948, ERA was taken over in 1967 by the Houston, Texas-based Rowan Companies, who are active in the oil and natural gas production business. ERA is organised into several divisions, for instance ERA Helicopters Alaska Division, or the Gulf Coast Division. Then there was Jet Alaska, later known as ERA Jet Alaska, which mainly flew ad hoc and freight charters, but also passengers, mostly Alaska Pipeline building workers. In 1983 scheduled services were also being operated, and ERA's individual activities were brought together. Using DHC-6 Twin Otters, DHC-7s and Convair 580s ERA Aviation flew on behalf of Alaska Airlines from Anchorage and Bethel. The DHC-7s were replaced by the de Havilland Canada DHC-8, with the first being delivered in 1990. The Convair 580 is especially suited to Alaskan operations, and more examples have been acquired. ERA flies under Alaska Airlines flight numbers, but operates its aircraft in its own colour scheme. Two Douglas DC-3s are used for special flights and appear in ERA Classic Airlines colours. ERA Flightseeing conducts charter flights for tourists, using these DC-3s as well as other aircraft and helicopters.

Routes

Anchorage, Bethel, Chefornak, Chevak, Cordova, Eek, Goodnews Bay, Homer, Hooper Bay, Iliamna, Kenai, Kipnuk, Kodiak, Kongiganak, Kwigillingkok, Mekoryuk, Mountain Village, Newtok, Nightmute, Pilot Station, Platinium,Quinhagak, Scammon Bay, St.Marys, Toksook Bay, Tuntutuliak, Tununak, Valdez, Whitehorse.

Fleet

9 De Havilland DHC-6 Twin Otter
3 De Havilland DHC-8
5 Convair 580
2 Douglas DC-3

Fokker 50 ES-AFM (Daniel Hustedt / Hamburg)

ESTONIAN AIR

2 Lennujaama Str. Tallinn 11101, Estonia
Tel. 6401100, Fax. 6312740,
E-mail: ov@estonian-air.ee, www.estonian-air.ee

Three- / Two- letter code	IATA No.	Reg'n prefix	ICAO callsign
ELL / OV	960	ES	Estonian

Estonian Air was set up by the government of the newly independent state of Estonia on 1st December 1991 and declared to be the country's flag carrier. The first scheduled service, to Helsinki, started in the same month using Tupolev Tu-134s inherited along with Yak-40s and An-12s from Aeroflot. Further routes, especially within Scandinavia, were established in quick succession. In 1995 the state privatisation commission permitted conversion into a public company. 34% of the capital remained with the government; the rest is with private investors led by the Danish airline Maersk Air, who now give considerable management assistance. The first step after privatisation was the disposal of several Tupolev Tu-134s and the acquisition of two Boeing 737-500s decorated in a new, modern colour scheme, along with an expansion of the route network. The main base is in the Estonian capital of Tallinn, where the airline also has maintenance facilities. As well as scheduled services, seasonal charters are conducted throughout Europe. There are co-operation agreements with Air Botnia, Finnair and SAS. Estonian Air now operates only Western-built aircraft, the last Yak-40s having been replaced on regional routes in 1998 by two Fokker 50s supplied by Maersk. As well as the scheduled services, the Boeing 737s are used for charters to the Mediterranean in association with tour operators.

Routes

Amsterdam, Brussels, Copenhagen, Frankfurt, Hamburg, Helsinki, Kiev, London-Gatwick, Minsk, Moscow, Oslo, Paris, Riga, Stockholm, Tallinn, Vilnius.

Fleet

3 Boeing 737-500
1 Fokker 50

Boeing 737-260 ET-AJB (Josef Krauthäuser collection)

ETHIOPIAN AIRLINES

P.O.Box 1755, Bole Airport, Addis Ababa, Ethiopia
Tel. 1-612222, Fax. 1-611474, www.flyethiopian.com
E-mail: webmaster@flyethiopian.com

Three- / Two- letter code	IATA No.	Reg'n prefix	ICAO callsign
ETH / ET	071	ET	Ethiopian

Ethiopian Airlines was set up on 26th December 1945 by proclamation of the emperor at the time, Haile Selassie, to develop international services and to establish connections from the capital to communities in isolated, mountainous regions, where little or no surface transport existed. Scheduled flights started on 8th April 1946 with five Douglas DC-3s. The first service was between Addis Ababa and Cairo. A management contract was concluded with the American airline TWA assuring long-term support; this lasted until 1970. Douglas DC-6Bs were used to operate regular flights to the first European destination, Frankfurt, from June 1958, followed by Athens, Rome, Paris and London. Boeing 720 jets were introduced from 1962, followed by further 707s and 720s. The first Boeing 727 arrived in December 1981 and Boeing 767s replaced the 707s and 720s from 1984. The DC-3s were augmented with Twin Otters, and phased out with the delivery of ATR 42s from 1989. From 1993, new Boeing 757s replaced the 727s. After some years of relative stagnation, partially brought about by the country's poor economic position and the war with Eritrea, the company acquired some Fokker 50s from September 1996 onwards and a Boeing 767-300ER, which was used at the beginning of 1998 to open up services to New York and Washington. During 1999 a further Boeing 767-300ER was leased. In autumn 2002 Ethiopian announced a fleet renewal plan, again in favour of Boeing. 737-700s are to replace the -200s and 777s to be added for long-range routes. In 2002 the airline carried over a million passengers, added a further 767-300 and started services to new destinations including Hong Kong and Amsterdam.

Routes

Over 40 domestic routes and internationally to Abidjan, Abu Dhabi, Accra, Amsterdam, Bahrain, Bamako, Bangkok, Beijing, Beirut, Dakar, Dar-es-Salaam, Delhi, Djibouti, Dubai, Entebbe, Frankfurt, Harare, Hong Kong, Jeddah, Johannesburg, Karachi, Khartoum, Kigali, Kilimanjaro, Kinshasa, Kuwait, Lagos, Lilongwe, Lome, London, Luanda, Lusaka, Mumbai, Muscat, Nairobi, Ndjamena, New York, Niamey, Riyadh, Rome, Sanaa, Tel Aviv, Washington.

Fleet

Fleet		Ordered
2 ATR 42-300	4 Boeing 767-300ER	5 Boeing 737-700
3 De Havilland DHC-6	5 Boeing 757-200	2 Boeing 767-300
2 Lockheed L-100-30 Hercules	2 Boeing 737-200Adv.	3 Boeing 777
1 Boeing 707-320	5 Fokker 50	
2 Boeing 767-200ER		

Boeing 737-85F F-GRNB (Josef Krauthäuser / Paris-CDG)

EURALAIR

Aeroport de Paris, Le Bourget, Zone Nord, 93350
Le Bourget, France, Tel. 1-49346200, Fax. 1-49346300
E-mail: aviation_commerciale@euralair.com
www.euralair.com

Three- / Two- letter code	IATA No.	Reg'n prefix	ICAO callsign
EUH / RN	–	F	Euralair

In 1962 at Toussus-le-Noble, near Paris, the S.E.R.V.I.C.E. co-operative was set up by aircraft owners with the objective of renting out their aircraft for business or pleasure trips. This worked out advantageously, with the result that more aircraft could be taken on. From this co-operation in 1966 came Euralair, with its headquarters at Le Bourget. Two Fokker F.27s formed the basis to start charter flights in 1968. Contracts were in place with CNRO, a state-run social organisation set up to give affordable holidays to working families. In each year,1971 and

1972, an SE.210 Caravelle was added and these replaced the F.27s. Contrasted with Air France or Air Inter, these were flown with a two-man crew. As Euralair was in the same charter pool with Air France, this led to pressure from the Air France pilots' union, resulting in Euralair leaving the pool. With the introduction of the Boeing 737-200 in 1979, the Caravelle era came to an end. By 1983, when Air France no longer had three-crew cockpits, Euralair was able to return to the charter pool. From 1988 two BAe 146s were added and from 1991 came scheduled services from Paris

to Madrid. A shareholding taken in Air Liberté in exchange for shares and slots, was sold off when British Airways acquired the latter carrier. Long-term contracts with two tour operators were the basis for the acquisition of a new Boeing 737-800, for which type Euralair was the first user in Europe. An Airbus A310-300 was used from 2002 on behalf of NAS Air Mali. Euralair is active in airport services, business aircraft operation and leasing and in 2001 set up Horizon as the charter arm for the Boeing 737-800.

Routes

Charter flights for tour operators Frog and Go Voyages to domestic holiday destinations, the Mediterranean and Northern Africa.

Fleet

1 Airbus A310-300
5 Boeing 737-800

Boeing 737-8Q8 5B-DBV (Florian Morasch / Munich)

EUROCYPRIA AIRLINES

P.O.Box 40970, CY-6308 Larnaca, Cyprus
Tel. 4-658000, Fax. 4-658008, E-mail:
sales@eurocypria.com.cy, www.eurocypria.com.cy

Three- / Two- letter code	IATA No.	Reg'n prefix	ICAO callsign
ECA / UI		5B	Eurocypria

On 12th June 1991,Cyprus Airways set up a subsidiary company called Eurocypria Airlines. The objective of the new airline was to offer attractive charter prices to tour operators for holidays on Cyprus, and to make the island tempting for new types of holidaymaker. Until then, Cyprus had attracted overwhelmingly English tourists because of the former links and the historical sights and beauty of the island, but few of the beach-loving tourists from other parts of Europe. More and more tourists discovered Cyprus during and after the Gulf War. The new airline began operations in March 1992 using Airbus A320s seconded from the parent company Cyprus Airways. The fleet of three 174-seat Airbus A320s remained unaltered for several years, flying all over Europe, including to some of the smaller airports.The destinations in Cyprus are Larnaca and Paphos, both in the Greek sector of the divided island. The company was reorganised at the beginning of 2003, and the fleet replaced by brand new winglet-equipped Boeing 737-800s, the first of which was delivered in March 2003.

Routes

Aalborg, Alesund, Basle, Bergen, Berlin-SXF, Birmingham, Bristol, Brussels, Chania, Cairo, Copenhagen, Corfu, Cork, Dresden, Dublin, East Midlands, Edinburgh, Gothenburg, Graz, Hamburg, Hanover, Leipzig, London-Gatwick, Luela, Malmö, Manchester, Munich, Oreboe, Oslo, Prague, Rhodes, Salzburg, Stavanger, Trondheim, Vienna, Zakinthos, to Larnaca and Paphos.

Fleet

4 Boeing 737-800

Boeing 747-236B G-BDXJ (Daniel Klein / Bournemouth)

EUROPEAN AVIATION AIR CHARTER – EAL

European Aviation House, Bournemouth Intl. Airport
Christchurch, Dorset, BH23 6EA
Tel. 01-202 581111, Fax. 01-202578333
E-mail: info@eaac.co.uk, www.eaac.co.uk

Three- / Two- letter code	IATA No.	Reg'n prefix	ICAO callsign
EAL / E7	158	G	Eurocharter

European Aviation set up European Aviation Air Charter in September 1993. European Aviation had been active since 1989, establishing itself as a specialist in airline charter, executive air charter, engineering, crew training and airline support. It had taken 20 BAC One-Elevens on their retirement from British Airways and 16 of these were passed to European Aviation Air Charter for their use. The base was established at Bournemouth (where the One-Elevens had been built) even though the company headquarters was in Ledbury. Here EAL built up an enormous spares operation, especially for the One-Eleven, but also covering the Airbus A300 and Boeing 737-200. All the One-Elevens flying in recent years have been kept in the air thanks to EAL and its ability to deliver necessary spares. As the One-Eleven was driven out of service in Europe, EAL acquired 737-200s. These were used for charter series for tour operators as well as one-off operations as well as for lease to other airlines. One of the 737s was also equipped as a VIP aircraft. A few Boeing 747-200s being retired by British Airways were also acquired in 2002 and can be seen at various airports, especially in support of Formula One car racing. They transport the 'racing circus' and many fans from race to race. EAL is closely associated with, and a main sponsor of, the Minardi team. The 747s are also used for holiday charters, notably from the UK to Florida. Some of EAL's aircraft have started to appear in a new colour scheme during the summer of 2003.

Routes

Charter flights, ad-hoc and subcharters for tour companies take the aircraft to destinations worldwide.

Fleet

8 Boeing 737-200
5 Boeing 747-200

Canadair CRJ200ER D-ACRF (Klaus Brandmaier / Munich)

EUROWINGS

Flugplatz 21, 44319 Dortmund, Germany
Tel. 0231-92450, Fax. 0231-9245102, E-mail:
postkasten@eurowings.de, www. eurowings.de

Three- / Two- letter code	IATA No.	Reg'n prefix	ICAO callsign
EWG / EW	104	D	Eurowings

Eurowings stems from the amalgamation from 1st January 1993 of NFD-Nürnberger Flugdienst and RFG-Regional airline. Majority shareholder, Albrecht Knauf, had proposed a concentration and work-sharing by the two companies, and the logical result was a combined operation. At the same time a new colour scheme was introduced for the combined fleet. NFD and RFG both had extensive regional networks from Dortmund and Nuremberg, using ATRs, Fairchild Metros and Dornier 228s. A BAe 146-200 QT was also used as a pure freighter on behalf of TNT, but its adaptable characteristics meant that it could also be used for passengers from 1995; it was used for busier scheduled routes and for charter work. EWG entered the tour market strongly from Autumn 1995 with the formation of its own tour company Eurowings Flug. Two A319s were ordered from Airbus for this purpose, and were used for the first time during the 1997/98 season. As well as operating its own scheduled services with a fleet now made up mainly of BAe 146s and ATR 42s and 72s, Eurowings flies on behalf of other companies on a codeshare basis. There are co-operation agreements with Air France, KLM and Northwest Airlines, offering passengers good connections to these companies' international routes in Amsterdam and Paris. More Airbus A319s were added during 1998 and 1999, and used mainly for charter work, but in 2002 formed the basis of the fleet of Germanwings, a low-cost operation set up by Eurowings. In 2000 Lufthansa took a 25% shareholding, since when the airlines have co-operated closely and Eurowings takes part in the Lufthansa frequent flier programme 'Miles & More'. The airline is not only principally based at Dortmund, but also at Nuremberg, where there are extensive overhaul and maintenance facilities.

Routes

Amsterdam, Barcelona, Berlin, Bilbao, Birmingham, Bologna, Bordeaux, Bremen, Brussels, Budapest, Cologne/Bonn, Dortmund, Dresden, Düsseldorf, Frankfurt, Friedrichshafen, Geneva, Hamburg, Hanover, Katowice, Leipzig, London, Lyon, Marseilles, Milan, Munich, Münster/Osnabrück, Naples, Nice, Nuremberg, Paderborn/Lippstadt, Paris, Stuttgart, Toulouse, Turin, Vienna, Warsaw, Wroclaw, Zagreb, Zürich.

Fleet		Ordered
10 ATR 42-300/500	13 Canadair CRJ100/200	12 Canadair CRJ200
16 ATR 72-200/500		
10 BAe 146-200		

Boeing 747-400F N416MC (Ken Petersen / New York-JFK)

EVA AIR

376 Hsin-nan Road, Sec. 1 Luchu, Taoyuan Hsien 338, Republic of China, Tel. 3-3515151, Fax. 3-3510005, www.evaair.com.tw

Three- / Two- letter code	IATA No.	Reg'n prefix	ICAO callsign
EVA / BR	695	B	Evaair

In March 1989 Evergreen, the largest container shipping line in the world, set up its own airline. However, state-imposed conditions, quarrels concerning the airline's name (confusion with the names of other companies) and the non-immediate availability of new aircraft prevented the new airline from starting operations straightaway. Finally, EVA Air started flights on 1st July 1991. It used Boeing 767-300ERs on routes to Bangkok, Manila, Hong Kong and Seoul. Vienna was served from November 1991 and London from April 1993. There are also important connections to the USA, with the first trans-Pacific service

starting from Taipei to Los Angeles in December 1992. Fast-growing EVA Air has become one of the top Taiwanese airlines and has acquired stakes in Makung Airlines and Great China Airlines, thus adding a regional dimension to its network. The first MD-11was delivered in Autumn 1994, and the fleet of Boeing 747-400s has also been built up. The first MD-11 freighter service took place in October 1995 from Taiwan to Amsterdam. New routes to Brisbane, Paris and San Francisco were also added. In 1996 there was a further acquisition of a domestic carrier, Taiwan Airlines which flew several Britten-Norman Islanders

and Dornier 228s, with seasonal services to Far Eastern holiday centres. Makung Airlines and Taiwan Airlines were merged to form Uni-Air and in 1998 took over the whole of EVA's regional services. In freight services, EVA has expanded dramatically, with aircraft leased long-term from other companies to boost capacity. The first A330-200 was delivered in July 2003; these will replace 767s on medium to long-haul routes. Boeing 777s are on order for delivery from 2006. EVA is also a shareholder in Air Macau, and has alliances with Air Canada, Air New Zealand, ANA, American Airlines, Ansett and Uni-Air.

Routes

Amsterdam, Anchorage, Atlanta, Auckland, Bangkok, Brisbane, Brussels, Chicago, Dallas/Fort Worth, Djakarta, Dubai, Fukuoka, Ho Chi Minh City, Hong Kong, Kaoshing, Kuala Lumpur, London, Los Angeles, Macau, Manila, Mumbai, New York, Osaka, Paris, Penang, Phnom Penh, San Francisco, Seattle, Seoul, Sharjah, Singapore, Surabaya, Sydney, Taipei, Tokyo, Toronto, Vancouver, Vienna.

Fleet

1 Airbus A330-200
4 Boeing 767-300ER
4 Boeing 767-200
2 Boeing 757-200

19 Boeing 747-400/400F
11 McDonnell Douglas MD-11/11F
1 McDonnell Douglas MD-90-30

Ordered

9 Airbus A330-200
15 Boeing 777-300

Boeing 747-121(SF) N480EV (Sebastian Poller / Frankfurt)

EVERGREEN INTERNATIONAL AIRLINES

3850 Three Mile Lane, McMinnville,OR 97128-9496, USA, Tel. 503-4720011, Fax. 503-4346492, E-mail: info@ evergreenaviation.com, www.evergreenaviation.com

Three- / Two- letter code	IATA No.	Reg'n prefix	ICAO callsign
EIA / EZ	494	N	Evergreen

Evergreen International Airlines is a division of Evergreen Aviation. This holding company also owns one of the largest helicopter companies in the USA, Evergreen Helicopters, as well as the famous Marana Airpark in Arizona, where large numbers of transport aircraft are parked when temporarily out of use. Here Evergreen also has an extensive maintenance facility and performs storage and overhaul work on most airliner types. Additionally, Evergreen has set up at McMinnville, its company headquarters, a noteworthy aviation museum, where several 'oldtimers' are kept in flying condition. The airline was set up on 28th November 1975 when Evergreen Helicopters acquired the operators' certificate from Johnson Airlines of Missoula. Operating as Johnson International, the company was founded in 1924 and was awarded one of the first supplemental certificates in 1957. Evergreen operates a domestic American cargo service on behalf of UPS and other companies but also has its own services to China and Hong Kong. In addition, aircraft are wet leased (i.e. inclusive of crew) to other operators. In 1995 the fleet was slimmed down and the Boeing 727s which had been in use were sold to a customer for re-engining.

Evergreen operates scheduled and ad hoc charter flights, both freight and passenger, and undertakes troop transportation for the United States Army. During the Gulf Crisis of 2002/3, Evergreen was especially busy moving troops and freight to the conflict areas.

Routes

Scheduled freight flights from Hong Kong to New York, Anchorage, Atlanta, Auckland, Chicago, Columbus, Honolulu, Los Angeles, Nadi, Pago Pago, San Francisco, Sapporo, Sydney, Taipei, Toledo. Worldwide ad-hoc charter flights.

Fleet

10 Boeing 747-100/200
 8 Douglas DC-9-15/30F

Boeing 737-800 G-XLAA (Stefan Schlick / Arrecife)

EXCEL AIRWAYS

Mitre Court, Fleming Way, Crawley, W Sussex RH10 9NJ, Great Britain, Tel. 01293-410727, Fax. 01293-410737
E-mail:sales@excelairways.com, www.excelairways.com

Three- / Two- letter code	IATA No.	Reg'n prefix	ICAO callsign
XLA / JN	–	G	Excel

Excel Airways took over the operating licence of Sabre Airways at the beginning of 2001. A renaming of the company was necessary however, because the similarly-named company which runs the international reservations system, had complained about possible confusion. Sabre had originally been founded in 1994, using Boeing 727s for charter work. In 1999 Boeing 737-800s were added to the fleet and operations were conducted on behalf of Libra Holidays, a British tour operator. The Libra Holidays group took a two-thirds shareholding in Excel Airways and took capacity. Excel made its first flight on 1st May 2001. The Sabre fleet of 737-800s was taken over and expanded, and Excel grew quickly in both size and popularity. Capacity was further increased with the Boeing 767-200, which are operated in co-operation with Air Atlanta, the Icelandic company, as are the recently-added Boeing 757s. Excel Airways is active in offering direct sale of seats to the public, something which is less actively pursued by other similar charter airlines. London-Gatwick and Manchester are the company's principal hubs, but it is also active from other UK airports, where aircraft are based.

Routes

Alicante, Arrecife, Athens, Bastia, Birmingham, Bristol, Chania, Corfu, Dalaman, East Midlands, Faro, Fuerteventura, Glasgow, Heraklion, Hurghada, Ibiza, Kavala, Kefalonia, Los, Larnaca, Las Palmas, Lesbos, Luxor, Mahon, Malaga, Malta, Mykonos, Newcastle, Palma de Mallorca, Olbia, Paphos, Preveza, Rhodes, Samos, Santorini, Sharm el Sheik, Skiathos, Thessaloniki.

Fleet

8 Boeing 737-800
3 Boeing 757-200
3 Boeing 767-200

Boeing 737-33A(QC) SE-DPB (Albert Kuhbandner / Salzburg)

FALCON AIR

P.O.Box 36, 23032 Malmö-Sturup, Sweden
Tel. 40-500500, Fax. 40-500149
E-mail: office@falconair.se, www.falconair.se

Three- / Two- letter code	IATA No.	Reg'n prefix	ICAO callsign
FCN / IH	759	SE	Falcon

Falcon Cargo Aviation was set up in 1986 in Gothenburg, specialising in freight charter and ad hoc domestic flights. Two Lockheed L-188C Electras were used. The sole owner was Kungsair Falcon AB, a company which had also been set up in Gothenburg, in 1966 and operated smaller aircraft on air taxi duties from Gothenburg and Stockholm. Falcon Cargo won a tender from the Swedish postal authorities for the transport of letters and small packages within Sweden. In 1987 the company moved its headquarters to Malmö, after Postbolagen had taken a 42% shareholding. The Swedish Post Office went on to acquire the balance of the shareholding in 1988. Three Boeing 737-300QCs were acquired from SAS in 1991, with SAS also providing the crews. At this point the Electras were sold. The great advantage of the QC version of the 737 is the ability to quickly convert from freight configuration to a passenger version, in which the seats, galleys and toilets are palletised and can be installed within a hour. Thus during the day the aircraft fly for SAS on passenger routes and during the night they are used for letters and packages. Various tour operators have also booked charter series; hence Falcon Air aircraft can be seen at holiday destinations within Europe. Since March 2003, a single ATR 42 has been added to the fleet on a lease basis, for freight work.

Routes

Angelholm/Helsingborg, Gothenberg, Malmö, Skelleftea, Stockholm,Sundsvall,Uemea are served on a scheduled basis for post or passengers. Charter flights within Europe.

Fleet

1 ATR 42-300
3 Boeing 737-300QC

Boeing 757-27A B-27015 (Wolfgang Juli / Phuket)

FAR EASTERN AIR TRANSPORT – FAT

No.5 Alley 123, Lane 405, Tun Hwa North Road
Taipei 105, Republic of China, www.fat.co.tw
E-mail: master@fat.co.tw

Three- / Two- letter code	IATA No.	Reg'n prefix	ICAO callsign
FEA / EF	265	B	

Far Eastern Air Transport Corporation – FAT was established in Spring 1957 by former military pilots and several business people. Operations began in July 1957 using Douglas DC-3s and Beech 18s, and for a long time only domestic services were flown. Handley Page Heralds, Vickers Viscounts and, as the first jet type, Caravelles were used. Using the Vickers Viscount, the first international services were flown to Hong Kong and Saigon. During the Vietnam War many special flights were also operated from Saigon to Taipei. Boeing 737-100s joined the fleet as replacements for the Viscounts, with more modern Boeing 737-200s following a couple of years later. At the beginning of the 1990s the fleet was converted to McDonnell Douglas MD-80s and the larger Boeing 757. FAT is today the largest regional airline in Taiwan and as well as scheduled services, it flies charters. China Airlines holds 10% of the shares in what is still a private company. Far Eastern was granted rights for direct flights into the People's Republic of China in 2002; these do however have to be flown via Hong Kong or Macau as entry points, continuing to their chosen destinations; this permission was at first used for charter services. Also in 2002, in August, two MD-90s were added to the fleet to supplement the MD-80s. The main operating and maintenance base is at the Sung San Airport at Taipei.

Routes

Chiayi, Hualien, Kaoshiung, Kinmen, Koror, Kota Kinabalu, Laoag, Macau, Makung, Phuket, Subic Bay, Tainan, Taipei, Taitung.

Fleet

7 Boeing 757-200
9 McDonnell Douglas MD-82/83
2 McDonnell Douglas MD-90

Airbus A310-222 N451FE (Josef Krauthäuser / Munich)

FEDEX

P.O.Box 727, Memphis TN 38134-2424, USA
Tel. 901-3693600, Fax. 901-3323772
E-mail: smunoz@fedex.co, www.fedex.com

Three- / Two- letter code	IATA No.	Reg'n prefix	ICAO callsign
FDX / FX	023	N	Fedex

Frederick W Smith set up Federal Express in June 1971; it began operations on 17th April 1973 using up to 60 Dassault Falcon 20s. In it was floated on the stock exchange and became a joint stock company. The FedEx system revolutionised the entire cargo market; shipments are distributed from a central hub in Memphis with US regional sorting centres, using the hub and spoke distribution system. After air cargo deregulation in November 1977, FedEx was also able to operate larger aircraft. They bought Boeing 727s in large numbers, and later DC-10s and Boeing 747s as well. During 1989 the Flying Tiger Line, which had been established and well-known for many years, was bought and its DC-8s and 747s integrated. Although only express shipments were forwarded at the beginning, other cargo is now transported. 1995 was a year of particular innovation, when FedEx opened its own hub at the former US military base at Subic Bay in the Philippines and in July started Asia One, the first overnight delivery service in Asia; from Subic the whole Asian region is accessible to FedEx. A second change in 1995 was the introduction of a new corporate identity with the adoption of the former colloquial acronym of FedEx as its official name. New Airbus A310 freighters carried the new colour scheme. Many A310s and A300s, DC-10s and MD-11s have been acquired from other airlines and converted to freighters by the world's largest airfreight carrier. Numerous smaller companies operate feeder services from smaller cities and towns on behalf of FedEx with Cessna Caravans, Fokker F.27s or Shorts 360s. At the end of 2001 FedEx was obliged by business recession, which had brought about overcapacity in the airfreight business, and the end for some companies, to place some aircraft in desert storage. The DC-10 conversion programme was also put on hold. Latest type in the fleet is the ATR 42; this will in time replace the F.27. The Airbus 380 has been ordered; deliveries start in 2008.

Routes

Federal Express serves over 160 US cities and worldwide over 180 countries on all continents. Hubs are in Memphis, Miami, Brussels, Paris and Hong Kong.

Fleet		Ordered
44 Airbus A300-605F	250 Cessna Caravan	10 Airbus A380-800F
51 Airbus A310	33 Fokker F.27	
8 ATR 42-300	88 Douglas DC-10	
129 Boeing 727-100/200	42 McDonnell Douglas MD-11	

Airbus A320-214 OH-LXB (Albert Kuhbandner / Innsbruck)

FINNAIR

Tietotie 11A, Airport, 01053 Vantaa, Finland
Tel. 9-81881, Fax. 9-8184401, www.finnair.com
E-mail: communications@finnair.com

Three- / Two- letter code	IATA No.	Reg'n prefix	ICAO callsign
FIN / AY	105	OH	Finnair

Finnair was set up on 9th October 1923 as Aero OY, the German company Junkers holding 50% of the shares. The first flight was from Helsinki to Tallinn on 20th March 1924 with a Junkers F-13. Until 1936, when airports were built in Finland, seaplanes were used. Flights to Berlin and Paris were added, but operations had to cease on 21st September 1944 until Spring 1945 when eight Douglas C-47s were bought from the USAAF. The first services were to Stockholm and Copenhagen. Convair 340s and 440s replaced the C-47s and a new service to Moscow in 1956 was followed by Frankfurt, Cologne, Basle and Geneva in 1957. The Caravelle was introduced at Finnair in 1960, marking the beginning of the changeover to jets. Kar Air, a private Finnish airline founded in 1957, was taken over in 1962. Douglas DC-8s were ordered for new long range services to the USA, with the first being delivered in 1969; these were also used on charters to the Mediterranean. In 1968 the name Finnair was adopted as the sole valid designation for the airline. DC-10-30s were delivered from 4th February 1975 and used primarily for flights to the American west coast, Tokyo and New York. For medium-range services Caravelles were replaced by DC-9s. The first MD-11 was acquired in December 1990. On economic grounds, Kar Air, which had operated independently, was integrated in 1993. Likewise, Finnaviation which had operated Saab 340s on domestic services, was integrated in 1996. During 1997 the Boeing 757-200 was added, and with it came a new colour scheme. Fleet renewal with the Airbus has been in continuous process since 1999, replacing the older Douglas DC-9s and MD-80s. Since September 1999 Finnair has been a partner in the Oneworld alliance.

Routes

Amsterdam, Bangkok, Barcelona, Beijing, Berlin, Brussels, Budapest, Copenhagen, Dublin, Düsseldorf, Frankfurt, Gothenberg, Hamburg, Helsinki, London, Madrid, Manchester, Milan, Moscow, Munich, New York, Oslo, Paris, Prague, Rome, St.Petersburg, Singapore, Stockholm, Stuttgart, Tallinn, Tokyo, Vienna, Vilnius, Warsaw, Zürich.Additionally to 25 domestic and 30 seasonal charter destinations in the Mediterranean and Canary Isles.

Fleet

Fleet		Ordered
9 Airbus A319-100	7 Boeing 757-200	2 Airbus A319
9 Airbus A320-200	5 McDonnell Douglas MD-11	2 Airbus A320
5 Airbus A321-100	14 McDonnell Douglas MD-82/83	2 Airbus A321
9 ATR 72-200	8 Douglas DC-9-51	

Boeing 727-44C C-GVFA (Gerhard Schütz / Munich)

FIRST AIR

Carp Airport, 3257 Carp Road, Carp Ontario
KOA ILO, Canada, Tel. 613-8393340,
Fax. 613-8395690, www.firstair.com

Three- / Two- letter code	IATA No.	Reg'n prefix	ICAO callsign
FAB / 7F	245	C	First

Bradley Air Services is Canada's largest independent regional carrier and provides scheduled charter and cargo flights from various points in Canada; the scheduled flights use the marketing name First Air. Having originally started out as Bradley Flying School in 1946, Bradley Air Services was set up in 1954 and started flight operations with Douglas DC-3s the same year. The first scheduled services were flown in the 1970s by DC-3s, followed from 1978 onwards by HS.748s, a type extremely well suited to operation in the extreme climatic conditions found where the company flies. Jets in the form of the Boeing 727 arrived in 1986, being used initially on the Frobisher Bay to Ottawa services. The operating profile is quite unusual; principally carrying freight in the far north of Canada and on to Greenland, but with the possibility of carrying passengers on some sectors. For this reason the aircraft are configured in combi versions. The main base is Ottawa, where the company has maintenance facilities, but there is a further base at Yellowknife, which is also the home of a subsidiary company, Ptarmigan Airways. Since 1995 First Air has been a part of the Makivik Corporation, a non-profit organisation of the Inuit people. During 1999, First Air took over Northwest Territorial Airways and their three Yellowknife-based Boeing 737-200s. The latest type in the fleet is the ATR 42, as a replacement for the BAe HS.748s. The first was delivered in November 2001, with two more following during 2002. The sole Lockheed Hercules is also a recent addition.

Routes

Broughton Island, Cambridge Bay, Cape Dorset, Clyde River, Edmonton, Fort Simpson, Gjoa Haven, Hall Beach, Hay River, Holman Island, Igloolik, Inukjuak, Iqaluit, Kangerlussaq, Kimmirut/Lake Harbour, Kugluktuk Coppermine, Kuujjuarapik, La Grande, Montreal, Nanisivik, Ottawa, Pangnirtung, Pelly Bay, Pond Inlet, Puvirnituq, Resolute Bay, Sanikiluaq, Taloyoak, Umiujaq, Whitehorse, Yellowkife.

Fleet

4 ATR 42	3 Boeing 737-200
1 Beech 99 Airliner	3 De Havilland DHC-6
3 BAe HS-748	1 Lockheed L100-30 Hercules
6 Boeing 727-200C/F	

Boeing 737-36N OK-FIT (Author's collection)

FISCHER AIR

Ruzyne Airport, 16008 Prague 6, Czech Republic
Tel. 2-20116170, Fax. 2-20115439
E-mail: info@fischer.cz, www.fischer.cz

Three- / Two- letter code	IATA No.	Reg'n prefix	ICAO callsign
FFR / 8F	–	OK	Fischer

Vaclav Fischer had led and built up a successful tour company for some years in Germany. As a result of the political changes and restoration of democracy and a free market in Czechoslovakia in the early 1990s, the Czech exile sold his German business and set out to repeat his success in his former homeland. Because there was strong demand for travel to Western countries, the business flourished. It was however difficult for tour operators to find sufficient aircraft capacity, as the state airline CSA was fully occupied looking after the needs of its own in-house tour company. Thus, without further ado, in 1996 Fischer set up his own airline. Using a leased 148-seat Boeing 737-300, operations began on 27th April 1997, full of optimism for the summer season. The first flight was from Prague to Palma de Mallorca. A further 737-300 was delivered in the same year to Prague, Fischer Air's base airport. Fischer co-operates with CSA and operates the Prague to Malta route as a codeshare. Since the airline otherwise flies exclusively for its own tour company, expansion has been careful. A third Boeing 737-300 was added to the fleet in March 1999. Departures from Poland, Slovakia and Hungary have been added, working with tour operators in these countries.

Routes

Malta and Prague are served on a scheduled basis in co-operation with CSA. Charter flights to the Mediterranean, Northern Africa, Canary Isles and Middle East.

Fleet

3 Boeing 737-300

De Havilland DHC-8-400Q G-JEDL (Josef Krauthäuser / Salzburg)

FLY BE

Exeter Airport, Exeter, Devon EX5 2BD, Great Britain, Tel.1392366669, Fax. 1392366151
E-mail: info@flybe.com, www.flybe.com

Three- / Two- letter code	IATA No.	Reg'n prefix	ICAO callsign
BEE / BE	267	G	Jersey

Jersey European Airways was founded on 1st November 1979 in order to bring together the operations of Intra Airways and Express Air Services. Intra Airways goes back to 1969, when several BUA pilots formed their own airline, using a DC-3 for services from Jersey to the other Channel Islands and Northern France and later to Ostend in Belgium. In 1974 a Britten-Norman Islander was added and a route to London-Gatwick opened. As well as the schedules, the airline had many charter and freight contracts, with six DC-3s in use at the time of the merger. Express Air Services had used several light aircraft for courier and passenger flights. Intra was bought by the Walker Group in 1983 and the two companies were brought together operationally. The small aircraft were replaced with Twin Otters and Embraer Bandeirantes, and with the start of a new schedule to Birmingham, the first Fokker F.27 was introduced. In 1989 the HS 748 turboprop was added. The company was not only active in and around the Channel Isles, but increasingly in mainland Great Britain; passenger routes such as Birmingham-Belfast were being added. Shorts 360s and BAe 146s joined the fleet. In July 2000 the company changed its name to British European Airlines. Several scheduled routes were taken over from Air France, for whom BEA flew as a franchise partner, with some aircraft painted in Air France colours. Hardly had the new name and identity been painted on the aircraft, than a further change came about in July 2002, to FlyBe-British European Airways, with a further change of colours. The fleet now consists principally of the 146s and Dash 8s and Birmingham is a major hub.

Routes

Aberdeen, Belfast, Birmingham, Blackpool, Bristol, Brussels, Cork, Dublin, Edinburgh, Exeter, Glasgow, Geneva, Guernsey, Isle of Man, Jersey, Leeds/Bradford, London-City, London-Gatwick, London-Heathrow, London-Luton, Malaga, Murcia, Newcastle, Shannon, Southampton, Toulouse, plus various charter and holiday flights.

Fleet

9 BAe 146-100/200
6 BAe 146-300
4 Canadair CRJ200
7 De Havilland DHC-8-200Q/300Q

4 De Havilland DHC-8-400Q

Boeing 737-3M8 ZK-FDM (Frank Schorr / Sydney)

FREEDOM AIR INTERNATIONAL

P.O.Box 109-698, Newpark Tower, 5 Short Street
Newmarket, Auckland 1001, New Zealand
Tel. 649 9126980, Fax. 649 9126998, E-mail:
contactus@freedomair.co.nz, www.freedomair.co.nz

Three- / Two- letter code	IATA No.	Reg'n prefix	ICAO callsign
FOM / –	–	ZK	Freeair

The Mount Cook Group was set up in 1995, to include Mount Cook Airlines and South Pacific Air Charters. At first charters were operated for various travel organisations, but then the name Freedom Air International was established as a low-cost arm of Air New Zealand Holdings, the parent company of the Mount Cook Group. A Boeing 737-300 came into use, initially for a twice-weekly service to the Fiji Islands and to provide scheduled service to Australia. A leased Boeing 757 was also used for a while on this service. At first several scheduled services within New Zealand were set up in competition with Air New Zealand and Ansett of New Zealand, then still in existence. Following the collapse of the Ansett Group, in Australia as well as in New Zealand, the whole Air New Zealand group was repositioned. For Freedom Air this meant a withdrawal from the domestic market and a concentration on services from New Zealand to Australia. This concentration was not however limited to departures from Auckland or Christchurch, but augmented with services from regional centres. Thus most flights today operate from secondary hubs, with the fleet and network being built up.

Routes

Auckland, Brisbane, Christchurch, Dunedin, Goldcoast, Hamilton, Melbourne, Palmerston North, Sydney, Wellington.

Fleet

4 Boeing 737-300

Airbus A319-111 N903FR (Tony Stork / Baltimore)

FRONTIER AIRLINES

7001 Tower Road, Denver, CO 80249, USA
Tel. 720-374-4200, Fax. 720-374-4375, E-mail:
info@flyfrontier.com, www.flyfrontier.com

Three- / Two- letter code	IATA No.	Reg'n prefix	ICAO callsign
FFT / F9	422	N	Frontierflight

Shortly after the opening of Denver's new airport Continental Airlines reduced its services there by 80%. To fill this vacuum local investors and business people created a new airline with the historic name of 'Frontier'. The first Frontier Airlines was formed, also in Denver, in 1948 and was active until 1986 when deregulation in the US airline industry led to the creation of mega-carriers, taking over the smaller companies; thus Frontier was absorbed into Continental and the name disappeared from the skies. So on 5th July 1994 the new Frontier, operating two leased

Boeing 737-200s, began service from Denver again, with service to Bismarck and Fargo. Two more Boeing 737s were leased in August 1994 and the network expanded. The tailfins of Frontier's 737s, which have gone on to include -300s as well as the original -200s, are decorated with attractive animal motifs. There is a marketing alliance with Continental Airlines, and to allow for future expansion the issue of further shares is planned, but it is a condition that no shareholder may own more than 10% of the shares. At the beginning of 2000 a bold step was taken for the future, with the

placing of orders for Airbus A318s and A319s. The 132-seat 319s began delivery from May 2001, while the 114-seat 318s saw the first delivery from July 2003. These all have a new colour scheme, but the colourful tail logos are retained. In the meantime further Boeing 737-300s have been leased to continue the airline's expansion, but Frontier is expected to be an all-Airbus operator by 2005. In February 2002 Frontier JetExpress was set up for regional flights.

Routes

Albuquerque, Atlanta, Austin, Baltimore, Boise, Chicago, Dallas/Fort Worth, Denver, El Paso, Fort Lauderdale, Fort Myers, Houston, Indianapolis, Kansas City, Las Vegas, Los Angeles, Minneapolis/St. Paul, New Orleans, New York-LGA, Oklahoma City, Orlando, Phoenix, Portland, Reno, Salt Lake City, San Diego, Sacramento, San Francisco, Seattle, Tampa, Tucson, Washington –DCA.

Fleet

17 Airbus A319
 2 Boeing 737-200
16 Boeing 737-300

Ordered

6 Airbus A318
5 Airbus A319

Boeing 737-86N EC-HHG (Author / Palma de Mallorca)

FUTURA INTERNATIONAL AIRWAYS

Gran Via Asima 17, Poligono Son Castello, 07009
Palma de Mallorca, Spain, Tel. 971-910700
Fax. 971-910701, www.futura-aer.com

Three- / Two- letter code	IATA No.	Reg'n prefix	ICAO callsign
FUA / FH	–	EC	Futura

Futura International Airways was set up in 1989 as a joint venture between the Irish airline Aer Lingus (initially with a 25%, later 85% shareholding) and Spanish investors. Based at Palma, its objective was to provide package tours from Ireland to Spain. In February 1990, flights started from Dublin to Palma de Mallorca with two Boeing 737-300s leased from Guinness-Peat Aviation. Services from other airports including Basle, Düsseldorf, Manchester, Munich and Vienna followed quickly. Larger Boeing 737-400s were acquired during 1991 and 1992. With the opening up of markets in the former Warsaw Pact states, Futura was able to take a slice of this business, and thus flies tourists from Hungary, Ukraine and Russia to Spain. During 1995 more Boeing 737-400s were added, with the -300s being traded in. Around 1.3 million passengers flew with Futura during that year. The expansion and development of the airline has continued, with the first of six new generation Boeing 737-800s being added in November 1999. This delivery also marked the introduction of a new subdued dark blue colour scheme in place of the former bright red and yellow.

Routes

Charter flights from Ireland, Israel, Great Britain, Germany, Austria, Ukraine, Hungary, Czech Republic, and Switzerland to Spain, especially Mallorca and the Canary Isles.

Fleet

5 Boeing 737-400
8 Boeing 737-800

Boeing 747-4U3 PK-GSH (Dominik Stapf / Frankfurt)

GARUDA INDONESIA

Jalan Merdeka Selastan 13, Jakarta 10110,
Indonesia. Tel. 21-3801901,
Fax. 21-3806652, www.garuda.co.id

Three- / Two- letter code	IATA No.	Reg'n prefix	ICAO callsign
GIA / GA	126	PK	Indonesia

On 26th January 1949, the official foundation date of Garuda, a DC-3 flew from Calcutta to Rangoon under the name of 'Indonesian Airways'. It was the first civil aircraft of the new Republic of Indonesia, but could not fly in Indonesia for political reasons. It was only after official independence at the end of 1949 that the airline was also installed by the government in Indonesia; however, at first, it needed assistance which came from KLM. The airline was nationalised in 1954. In addition to DC-3s, Convair 240/340s were used, plus Lockheed L-188 Electras from 1961. In 1963, de Kroonduif, an airline in the Indonesian part of New Guinea, was taken over. Convair CV990s were Garuda's first jets, and were used for a service to Amsterdam. They were replaced from 1968 by DC-8s. Sydney was served for the first time in 1969, via Bali, and DC-9s were also bought in that year, with some Fokker F.27s for domestic services. These were however sold from 1971 as F.28s were delivered. The first widebody was the DC-10-30, leased from KLM from 1973. Boeing 747s entered service in 1980, and were used to Frankfurt and London, with the first new MD-11 added in 1992. The Asian business crisis of the late 1990s hit Garuda hard, and there was a drastic reduction in staff, routes and aircraft. All the MD-11s and Airbus A300s were taken out of service and capacity almost halved. In early 2000, the situation stabilised somewhat, but the tourist industry had been badly affected. Since 2001 new airlines have been established in the Indonesian domestic market; these are more flexible and can offer cheap fares. Garuda is trying, as national carrier and with new and modern equipment, to regain influence in the region. There are codeshare agreements with KLM, China Airlines and Iberia and the airline has a shareholding in Merpati.

Routes

Adelaide, Amsterdam, Auckland, Balikpapan, Banda Aceh, Bangkok, Banjarmasin, Batam, Biak, Brisbane, Dammam, Darwin, Denpasar, Djakarta, Frankfurt, Fukuoka, Guangzhou, Hong Kong, Jayapura, Jeddah, Kuala Lumpur, London, Manado, Manila, Mataram, Medan, Melbourne, Nagoya, Osaka, Padang, Palembang, Pekanbaru, Perth, Pontianak, Riyadh, Semarang, Seoul, Singapore, Solo City, Surabaya, Sydney, Tokyo, Ujung Pandang, Yogyakarta.

Fleet		Ordered
6 Airbus A330-300	3 Boeing 747-400	18 Boeing 737-700
30 Boeing 737-300/400/500	5 Douglas DC-10-30	6 Boeing 777-200
4 Boeing 747-200	5 Fokker F.28	

Boeing 737-75B D-AGEU (Josef Krauthäuser / Munich)

GERMANIA

Flughafen Tegel, Gebäude 23, 13405 Berlin
Germany,Tel. 030-41013610, Fax. 030-41013615
www.germania.aero

Three- / Two- letter code	IATA No.	Reg'n prefix	ICAO callsign
GMI / ST		D	Germania

In 1986, exactly ten years after it had been set up, the SAT (Special Air Transport) airline changed its name to Germania. Operations had begun with a Fokker F.27, but switched to jets from September 1978 with three former LTU Caravelle 10Rs. As well as the Caravelles, the airline owned two Boeing 727s, but these were only flown in Germania's colours after the airline had been renamed. The Caravelles were replaced from 1989 onwards and the first Boeing 737-300s were acquired. Germania flew sub-charters for other airlines and for tour operators; some aircraft were flown in DFD colours.

Germania is particularly active out of Berlin, including scheduled services from Berlin to Heringsdorf/Baltic Sea. Six further Boeing 737-300s were brought into use from the Spring of 1992, at which point the colour scheme was also modified. The airline was taken over by the Hetzel travel company in 1995. Several aircraft were leased to Condor, but flown by Germania crews. Germania was one of the first to order the new generation Boeing 737-700 for its future equipment, and so in 1998 it received early deliveries, with the whole fleet having now been switched over to the latest model. Several aircraft fly with other

companies such as Hapag Lloyd Express. During early 2003 a number of Fokker 100s were acquired from US Airways, who were retiring the type, and these have joined 'Germania Express', a low-cost operation set up from 1st June 2003.

Routes

Charter flights from German airports principally to the Mediterranean, Northern Africa, Canary Isles, Turkey, and Madeira.

Fleet

14 Boeing 737-700
17 Fokker 100

Airbus A319-112 D-AKNF (Daniel Klein / Frankfurt)

GERMANWINGS

Terminalstrasse 10, Flughafen 51147 Cologne, Germany
Tel. 01805 955855, Fax. 02203 1027300, E-mail:
info@germanwings.com, www.germanwings.com

Three- / Two- letter code	IATA No.	Reg'n prefix	ICAO callsign
GWI / 4U	–	D	Germanwings

On 30th April 1990, after barely a year of operations, Germanwings succumbed to bankruptcy and was dissolved. However the shell of the company and the name were acquired by Deutsche Lufthansa AG and more than ten years after the inglorious bankruptcy, a new Germanwings was in business from autumn 2002. If the first Gemanwings had problems in its time, then parallels can be drawn with the new incarnation. The founder of Germanwings is Eurowings AG, a company in which Lufthansa has a shareholding and the airline is positioned in the low-cost, no-frills segment. Its main base and central hub is at Cologne/Bonn, where other companies are also developing a low-cost offering. The philosophy is to retaliate by keeping costs to a minimum, with modest salaries, low servicing costs and thus cheap fares. Therefore flights are only bookable over the internet, or via the call centre and only one way. Contrary to the low prices advertised, which are of limited availability, the real prices are usually far removed from the 'cheap airline' expectation. Prices comparable to those charged by Germanwings for routes such as Lisbon and London, are offered by the established airlines. Airbus A319s, augmented since mid-2002 by A320s leased from Lufthansa, form the fleet. Plans for further growth of the company seem to be unclear; it seems that this may only be a testing out of the marketplace to see if the product works. Unlike other low-cost airlines, flights are mostly conducted to the airports corresponding to the destination cities, with very little use of the cheaper, if somewhat distant, secondary airports.

Routes

From Cologne/Bonn to Barcelona, Berlin, Bologna, Budapest, Dresden, Edinburgh, Istanbul, Izmir, Lisbon, London, Madrid, Milan, Nice, Paris, Prague, Rome, Thessaloniki,Venice, Vienna, Zürich.

Fleet	Ordered
5 Airbus A319-100 4 Airbus A320-200	1 Airbus A319-100

Douglas DC-10-30 9G-ANA (Daniel Klein / Düsseldorf)

GHANA AIRWAYS

Ghana Airways Ave 9, P.O.Box 1636 Accra, Ghana, Tel. 21-773321, Fax. 21-777078, www.ghanaairways-usa.com

Three- / Two- letter code	IATA No.	Reg'n prefix	ICAO callsign
GHA / GH	237	9G	Ghana

With the support of BOAC, the government of Ghana set up its national airline on 4th July 1958, with the government having a 60% stake and BOAC 40%, to take over the operations of West African Airways Corporation in the British colony formerly known as the Gold Coast. Only 12 days later, on 16th July, a scheduled service to London began, using Boeing 377 Stratocruisers leased from BOAC. Domestic services were taken over from WAAC on 1st October 1958. The Stratocruisers were later replaced by Bristol Britannias. On 14th February 1961 Ghana took over sole control of the airline.

Soviet-built Ilyushin IL-18s were acquired as part of a further expansion, but these proved to be not very economical in use and all eight aircraft were returned to the manufacturer after a period. Ghana Airways' first jet was a Vickers VC-10, and for short-range routes, which had previously been flown by Douglas DC-3s, HS.748s were acquired. In 1983 the Douglas DC-10 was acquired for long-range routes, and regional services were flown with Fokker F.28s and Douglas DC-9s, but the F.28s were replaced by F.27s. In the long term, it is intended to expand regional services and to serve more points in

Europe; a further DC-10 was added in 1999. Poor management over several years has led to increasing difficulties, but this is planned to be alleviated during 2003 and a part-privatisation achieved. Interest has been shown by Nationwide Air and by South African Airways, but only if a majority shareholding is possible. The main base is at the international airport at Accra-Kotoka and there is co-operation with South African Airways.

Routes

Abidjan, Accra, Baltimore-Washington, Bamako, Banjul, Beirut, Conakry, Cotonou, Dakar, Douala, Dubai, Düsseldorf, Freetown, Harare, Johannesburg, Kuassi, Lagos, Lome, London, Monrovia, New York, Ouagadougou, Rome.

Fleet

3 Douglas DC-10-30
2 Douglas DC-9-51

Boeing 737-700 PR-GOM (Manfred Turek / Sao Paulo-CGH)

GOL TRANSPORTES AEREOS

Avenida Dom Jaime de Barros Camara 300, Planalto
09895-400 Sao Bernardo do Campo, Sao Paulo, Brazil
Tel. 11-43556500, Fax. 11-43556526, www.voegol.com.br

Three- / Two- letter code	IATA No.	Reg'n prefix	ICAO callsign
GLO / G3	–	PP/PR/PT	Gol Transporte

In spite of years of poor business conditions and, as a result, adverse prospects for domestic aviation, the Sao Paulo-based Grupo Aurea decided to set up its own airline. Negotiations with banks and leasing companies in 2000 led to success in the objective of setting up a low-cost airline in direct competition with Varig, Viasa, TAM and other companies. The model here was the US company Southwest Airlines, with internet and telephone bookings being the order of the day, plus, of course, the lowest possible cost base. The home base is at Sao Paulo – Congonhas, from where the first service was flown on 15th January 2001. Following the collapse of Transbrasil at the beginning of 2002, Gol was able to increase its offering, by taking over some of their routes. The fleet has grown steadily with factory-fresh Boeing 737-700s and 800s being added.

Routes

Belem, Belo Horizonte, Brasilia, Campinas, Curitiba, Florianopolis, Porto Alegre, Recife, Rio de Janeiro, Salvador, Sao Paulo, Vitoria.

Fleet

18 Boeing 737-700
 4 Boeing 737-800

Airbus A340-300 A4O-LF (Hans-Willi Mertens collection)

GULF AIR

P.O.Box 138 Manama, Bahrain
Tel. 322200, Fax. 330466
E-mail: info@gulfairco.com, www.gulfairco.com

Three- / Two- letter code	IATA No.	Reg'n prefix	ICAO callsign
GFA / GF	072	A4O	Gulfair

Gulf Air is the national carrier of the Gulf state co-operation of Bahrain, Qatar, the United Arab Emirates and Oman. The airline was set up as Gulf Aviation on 24th March 1950, with regional flights starting on 5th July 1950 with Avro Ansons. De Havilland Dove and Heron aircraft followed and DC-3s and Fokker F.27s were added, partly under British sponsorship. These were replaced from 1969 onwards with BAC One-Elevens. 1970 saw the start of regular flights to London with leased Vickers VC-10s. On 1st April 1974 the four states took over Gulf Aviation, giving the airline a new legal status and the present name of Gulf Air. Boeing 737s replaced the One-Elevens from 1977. For longer-range flights, Gulf Air used Lockheed L-1011 TriStars starting in 1976. Fleet renewal and expansion began with the arrival of the first Boeing 767-300ERs as replacements for the TriStars. As a result of the Gulf War, the renewal programme was halted, but re-started in 1993 with the delivery of the Airbus A320, with the last of the Boeing 737-200s being taken out of service during 1994/95. At the same time the long-range Airbus A340 was introduced, with the last of the TriStars leaving the fleet by the later part of 1996. Because member states have formed their own airline operations, Gulf Air has suffered from overcapacity, with the result that some aircraft have been leased out to other airlines, though new aircraft acquisition continues, with the Airbus A330 being added from June 1999. To mark the airline's 50th anniversary in 2000, some aircraft were painted in a special colour scheme. However, Gulf Air has continued to struggle, though a reorganisation during 2002/3 has shown improved results.

Routes

Abu Dhabi, AlAin, Amman, Athens, Bahrain, Bangkok, Beirut, Boston, Cairo, Casablanca, Chennai, Chicago, Colombo, Damascus, Dammam, Dar-es-Salaam, Delhi, Dharan, Djakarta, Doha, Dubai, Frankfurt, Glasgow, Hong Kong, Islamabad, Istanbul, Jeddah, Karachi, Kathmandu, Kuala Lumpur, Kuwait, Lahore, Larnaca, London, Los Angeles, Manchester, Manila, Melbourne, Miami, Milan, Mumbai, Muscat, Nairobi, New York, Paris, Rome, Riyadh, Sanaa, Zanzibar, Sharjah, Shiraz, Singapore, Sydney, Teheran.

Fleet

10 Airbus A320-200
 5 Airbus A340-300
 6 Airbus A330-300

9 Boeing 767-300

Beech 1900 Airliner N152GA (Hans-Willi Mertens / Fort Lauderdale)

GULFSTREAM INT'L AIRLINES

1815 Griffin Road, Dania Florida 33004, USA
Tel. 954-266-3000, Fax. 954-266-3030, E-mail:
hperez@gulfstreamair.com, www.gulfstreamair.com

Three- / Two- letter code	IATA No.	Reg'n prefix	ICAO callsign
GFT / 3M	449	N	Gulf Flight

As a former Eastern Air Lines captain, Thomas L Cooper had many years of experience in the business to draw on when he founded his own small non-scheduled airline in 1990. Using a Cessna 402 he offered air taxi services between Miami and Haiti. As the Haitian political situation became more and more unstable during 1991/92, and with the government making attacks against the population, Cooper moved his operations to the Bahamas. The signing of a codeshare agreement with United Airlines in May 1994 opened up new possibilities and called for larger

equipment. Beech 1900s were thus brought into use for United's feeder service. A similar agreement was negotiated with Continental Airlines and the route network and aircraft fleet doubled in only a few years. Shorts 360s were added to the fleet from 1996 and one of these aircraft, painted in a special Sandals Clubs colour scheme, was flown exclusively on behalf of the club. Cooper founded G-Holdings as an umbrella company, as other activities such as aircraft ground handling were undertaken. In 1998 Continental took a shareholding in Gulfstream International, and in

August 1998 G-Holdings took over the Fort Lauderdale-based Paradise Island Air, along with its fleet of de Havilland Canada DHC-7s. As one of the few US airlines allowed to fly to Cuba, Gulfstream flies the classic Miami-Havana 'Cuba Air Bridge' route, though declared as charters. There are codeshare agreements with Continental Airlines, Copa Airlines, Northwest Airlines and United Airlines. A feeder service is operated under the Continental Connection, in Continental colours.

Routes

Fort Lauderdale, Freeport, Havana, Key West, Marsh Harbor, Miami, Nassau, North Eleuthera, Orlando, Tampa, Treasure Key, West Palm Beach.

Fleet

25 Beech 1900D Airliner

Boeing 737-84P B-2647 (Thomas Kim / Beijing)

HAINAN AIRLINES

Haihang Devl. Buildg, 29 Haixiu Rd, Hainan Province
Haikou 570206, China, Tel. 898-679829, Fax.898-6798976
E-mail: mail@hnair.com, www.hnair.com

Three- / Two- letter code	IATA No.	Reg'n prefix	ICAO callsign
CHH / HU	880	B	Hainan

In 1989 the first private airline in China was founded as Hainan Joint Stock Air Enterprises, otherwise known as Hainan Tour and Aviation Services. The organisation of such a private venture and the overcoming of bureaucratic obstacles had taken several years. It is also noteworthy that for the first time, foreign investment was permitted, with a listing on the Shanghai stock exchange. The airline succeeded in beginning operations from 1993 with three Boeing 737s from its home base on the subtropical island of Hainan, which also gave its name to the airline from 1995. The popularity of the island of Hainan amongst the Chinese middle classes led to the addition of more destinations on the mainland and the acquisition of several business jets. For regional services Hainan took on some 15 Fairchild Metros. As well as the home base at the Meilan international airport, in which the airline is a 25% shareholder, Hainan has a hub at Ningbo. No Chinese airline grew as quickly as Hainan, with more Boeing 737-400s, and the then new model -700s and -800s being added in order to meet the growing demand. The regional fleet also grew steadily and was changed over to jet equipment. In1999 Hainan Airlines received its first Fairchild / Dornier 328 Jet, and at the other end of the fleet spectrum, the first of three Boeing 767-300s was added in November 2002; these are used on international services. Hainan has shareholdings in Changan Airlines, Deer Jet and Shanxi Airlines, with whom co-operation agreements are also in place.

Routes

Beihai, Beijing, Changsha, Chengdu, Chongqing, Dalian, Fuzhou, Guangzhou, Guilin, Guiyang, Haikou, Hailar, Hangzhou, Jinan, Jinjiang, Kunming, Lanzhou, Luoyang, Macau, Nanchang, Nanjing, Nanning, Ningbo, Qingdao, Sanya, Seoul, Shanghai, Shantou, Shenzen, Tianjin, Tongren, Ulanhot, Urumqui, Wuhan, Xian, Xiamen, Xilinhot, Xuzhou, Zhanjian, Zhuhai.

Fleet

19 Fairchild / Dornier 328 Jet	13 Boeing 737-800
3 Boeing 737-300	3 Boeing 767-300
8 Boeing 737-400	
3 Boeing 737-700	

Boeing 737-8K5 D-AHLR (Stefan Schlick / Corfu)

HAPAG LLOYD FLUG

Postfach 420240, 30662 Hanover, Germany
Tel. 0511-97270, Fax. 0511-9727494
E-mail: info@hlf.de, www.hlf.de

Three- / Two- letter code	IATA No.	Reg'n prefix	ICAO callsign
HLF / HF	617	D	Hapaglloyd

The well-known German shipping company Hapag-Lloyd set up the airline with its traditional name in July 1972. Flights started in March of the following year with three Boeing 727-100s acquired from All Nippon Airlines and the 727 fleet had increased to eight aircraft by 1979. After lengthy negotiations Bavaria-Germanair was taken over in late 1978. This takeover provided Hapag-Lloyd with various BAC One-Eleven and Airbus A300B4 aircraft. While the latter were integrated, the One Elevens were sold and new Boeing 737-200s ordered. A renewal of the fleet and its adaptation to future needs was decided in 1987. A total of six Airbus A300B4s were exchanged for Airbus A310s, and Boeing 737-400s were ordered, the first of which arrived at Hapag's Hanover base in Autumn 1990. With the introduction of the A310, the company was for the first time in a position to offer flights to the USA and the Caribbean. Hapag-Lloyd was the first to order the new Boeing 737-800 and from early 1999 had the first of these new aircraft at its disposal; now the airline has the most modern of the German charter fleets. Services are flown from all German airports, principally for the tour operator TUI, which is also a shareholder in Hapag-Lloyd. There is co-operation with Britannia Airways in the UK, and Nexos Air in Italy, both also members of the World of TUI, and in future a common fleet policy, especially for long-range equipment, can be expected. The TUI ownership has also been evident since early 2002 in the blue TUI house colours on the aircraft; the traditional names are sadly being lost. In autumn 2002 Hapag Lloyd Express was set up, a 100% subsidiary to operate scheduled services in the competitive 'low-cost' segment (see page 193).

Routes

Charter flights, principally from Germany, to the Mediterranean, the Canary Isles, and northern Africa.

Fleet

```
 4 Airbus A310-200
 2 Airbus A310-300
 3 Boeing 737-400
 3 Boeing 737-500
26 Boeing 737-800
```

Boeing 737-75B D-AGEP (Martin Bach, Cologne / Bonn)

HAPAG LLOYD EXPRESS

Benkendorffstr. 22b, 30855 Langenhagen, Germany, Tel. 0511-59000, Fax. 0511-59000-609 E-mail: info@hlx.com, www.hlx.com

Three- / Two- letter code	IATA No.	Reg'n prefix	ICAO callsign
HLX / X3	–	D	–

The first flight of Hapag Lloyd Express left Cologne for Berlin on 3rd December 2002. A Boeing 737-700, in a striking yellow colour scheme reminiscent of the New York taxi cab, rolled from the terminal to the runway and signalled the start of a new chapter in the era of the low-cost airline. It represented the realisation of the ambition of Europe's largest tour concern, TUI AG, to which the new airline belongs 100%, to have its own low-cost operation. Four Boeing 737-700s were used to start services to European destinations, with a further four aircraft of the same type added by March 2003. The list of destinations likewise expanded, with attractive cities joined by tourist points. Most services were flown from central airports and not, as is the case with many low-cost operators, distant regional locations. Even from the start, some destinations were served more than once a day. In addition to the first hub in Cologne/Bonn, from 1st April 2003 Hapag Lloyd Express set up a second hub at Hanover. It is anticipated that the fleet and number of destinations offered will expand continually over the coming years.

Routes

Berlin, Bilbao, Catania, Hamburg, London-Luton, Madrid, Manchester, Marseilles, Milan, Naples, Nice, Olbia, Pisa, Reuss, Rome-Ciampino, Valencia, Venice.

Fleet	Ordered
10 Boeing 737-700	2 Boeing 737-700

Boeing 767-33A(ER) N581HA (Thomas Kim)

HAWAIIAN AIR

P.O.Box 3008 Int.Airport Honolulu, 96820 Hawaii USA, Tel. 808-8353700, Fax. 808-8353690, E-mail: info@hawaiianair.com, www.hawaiianair.com

Three- / Two- letter code	IATA No.	Reg'n prefix	ICAO callsign
HAL / HA	173	N	Hawaiian

Hawaiian Air was founded in Honolulu on 30th January 1929 as Inter Island Airways by the Inter Island Steam Navigation Company. Flights started on 11th November 1929 between Honolulu and Hilo with Sikorsky S-36 amphibians, later replaced by larger Sikorsky S-43s. In 1941 the current name was introduced and operations changed over to Douglas DC-3s. Strong expansion in the tourist business and route additions led to the acquisition of larger aircraft such as the Convair 340 in 1952 and the Douglas DC-6 from 1958. In 1967 the airline moved over to jet equipment with the introduction of the Douglas DC-9-30. For charter flights to the American mainland, the Pacific and Europe, DC-8s were added to the fleet in 1983, followed in 1987 by Lockheed TriStars. As a result of financial problems, Hawaiian Air entered Chapter 11 bankruptcy protection in 1993, and sought new financial partners, with the whole company being reorganised. Initially DHC-7s were sold, DC-8s taken out of service, the TriStars exchanged for Douglas DC-10s and many routes dropped, but in September 1994 things had improved so that Chapter 11 protection could be left behind. A marketing agreement was agreed with American Airlines and there is close co-operation. Once the market had stabilised, more aircraft were acquired and flights to Papeete and Samoa offered. During 1999 new routes from Los Angeles to Maui and Kona were added; only Honolulu had been served with direct flights from the mainland before. Further DC-10-30s were added to the fleet and some shares were bought back by the company. From 2001, the entire DC-9 fleet was replaced by new Boeing 717s, also bringing in a new colour scheme. The DC-10s have also been replaced by Boeing 767s. Early in 2002 Aloha and Hawaiian planned to merge, but this plan fell by the wayside. Hawaiian was forced into Chapter 11 again in March 2003 and has been in dispute with Boeing over unpaid 717 and 767 lease fees.

Routes

Hilo, Honolulu, Hoolehua, Kahului, Kauai, Kona, Lanai City, Las Vegas, Los Angeles, Pago Pago, Papeete, Portland, San Diego, San Francisco, Seattle.

Fleet

16 Boeing 767-300
13 Boeing 717-200

Canadair CRJ700 N611QX (Thomas Kim)

HORIZON AIR

P.O.Box 48309 Seattle, Washington 98148
USA, Tel. 206-2416757, Fax. 206-4314696
www.horizonair.com

Three- / Two- letter code	IATA No.	Reg'n prefix	ICAO callsign
QXE / QX	481	N	Horizon Air

Horizon Air, part of the Alaska Air Group, has its origins in May 1981 when its first route was opened from Seattle to Yakima. With the purchase of Air Oregon, a small airline from the north west of the USA, in mid 1982, the way was set for Horizon to grow to become one of the largest regional operators in the USA. Swearingen-Fairchild Metros and Fokker F.27s came into service. In 1984 Horizon Industries went to the stock exchange in order to acquire the capital necessary for the further expansion of the airline. Following the acquisition of Transwestern Airlines the pace of expansion quickened. Within three years the passenger total quadrupled from 185,000 in the first year to well over half a million in 1984. Further growth came from the operation of feeder flights on behalf of both Northwest Airlines and Alaska Airlines. The first jet, a Fokker F.28, came into service in 1985 and as it was found to be well suited, more were acquired. In 1986 Alaska Group took over the majority shareholding, but left Horizon to operate as an independent company. More modern DHC-8s and Dornier Do 328s replaced the F.27s and Metros during the mid-1990s, but while the Do 228s did not come up to expectations with Horizon and were removed from the fleet, the number of DHC-8s grew steadily. Horizon was US launch customer for the DHC-8-Q400 from late 2000, and took on the longer version of the Canadair Regional Jet, the 700, from July 2002, presaging retirement of the F.28s. There are alliances which bring the benefit of marketing activities and bookings with Alaska Airlines, Northwest Airlines, TWA, Continental Airlines and KLM. The main base and central hub is Seattle, with further hubs in Boise, Portland and Spokane.

Routes

Arcata, Bellingham, Billings, Boise, Bozeman, Butte, Calgary, Edmonton, Eugene, Fresno, Great Falls, Helena, Idaho Falls, Kalispell, Kelowna, Klamath Falls, Lewiston, Medford, Missoula, North Bend, Palm Springs, Pasco, Pendleton, Pocatello, Port Angeles, Portland, Pullman, Redding, Redmont, Sacramento, San Jose, Seattle, Spokane, Sun Valley, Vancouver, Victoria, Walla Walla, Wenatchee, Yakima.

Fleet		Ordered
8 De Havilland DHC-8-100	16 Canadair CRJ700	14 Canadair CRJ700
28 De Havilland DHC-8-200	12 Fokker F.28	
15 De Havilland DHC-8-Q400		

Airbus A321-211 EC-HTF (Klaus Brandmaier / Amsterdam)

IBERIA

130 Calle Velazquez, 28006 Madrid, Spain
Tel. 91-5878787, Fax. 91-5857469, E-mail:
information@iberia.com, www.iberia.com

Three- / Two- letter code	IATA No.	Reg'n prefix	ICAO callsign
IBE / IB	075	EC	Iberia

The present-day Iberia was formed in 1940 by the merger of several companies. After the Spanish Civil War, German influence was still quite considerable, with Lufthansa holding 49% of the shares. In 1944 the Spanish government took over all the shares and ordered DC-3s to replace the Junkers Ju 52s. Iberia, as a pioneering European airline after the war, opened up important routes to Buenos Aires (1946), Caracas and San Juan (1949), Havana, New York and Mexico (1954), Bogota (1958), Santiago and further destinations in early 1960. South America is thus traditionally one of its most important markets.

DC-4s and Lockheed Constellations were used, and the first jet was the DC-8 in 1961. The Caravelle was acquired from 1962 for short and medium-haul flights; these were passed on to subsidiary Aviaco from 1967 and DC-9s acquired. The first widebody, the Boeing 747 arrived in October 1970; in 1972 Boeing 727s were bought and a year later DC-10-30. A large scale fleet renewal programme marked the 1990s. MD-87s, Boeing 757s and A320s replaced older DC-9s and 727s. Iberia also took shareholdings in other airlines including VIASA, Aerolineas Argentinas, Viva, Aviaco, Ladeco and Royal Air Maroc. In

1996 the Airbus A340 was introduced to replace DC-10s on long-range services. During 1999, Aviaco was integrated as a result of stronger domestic competition. More new aircraft introduced to replace Boeing 727s from 1999 were the Airbus A321 and in 2000 the A319. Airbus A340-600s, being delivered from 2003-2005, will oust the last Boeing 747s. Iberia was fully privatised in 2001, and shown on the Madrid stock exchange. Iberia became a member of the Oneworld alliance in September 1999, and there is co-operation with Air Nostrum, who fly regional services intensively on behalf of Iberia.

Routes

Strong domestic network to over 30 destinations, with main hubs in Madrid and Barcelona. Scheduled services to USA, Caribbean, South and Central America, the Middle East, Africa, and to major cities in within Europe.

Fleet

52 Airbus A320-200
 4 Airbus A319-100
 7 Airbus A321
18 Airbus A340-300
 3 Airbus A340-600

19 Boeing 757-200
 6 Boeing 747-200
18 McDonnell Douglas MD-87
14 McDonnell Douglas MD-88

Ordered

 5 Airbus A319
13 Airbus A321
 4 Airbus A340-300

Airbus A320-214 EC-IEQ (Stefan Schlick / Saarbrücken)

IBERWORLD AIRLINES

Gran Via Asima 23, 07009 Palma de Mallorca
Spain, Tel. 971-787940, Fax. 971-713184
E-mail: iberworld@iberworld.com, www.iberworld.es

Three- / Two- letter code	IATA No.	Reg'n prefix	ICAO callsign
IWD / TY	–	EC	Iberworld

The Spanish-based Iberostar-Group has been in the tourist and travel trade for over 70 years, and currently conducts business in over 23 countries. The group's interests encompass hotels and travel agencies and for many years it has been active as a worldwide holiday organiser. In 1998 it decided to set up its own airline, Iberworld Airlines. The inaugural flight from Palma de Mallorca to Bilbao took place on 12th April 1998, using an Airbus A320, the type which had been chosen to form the initial fleet. By the end of 1998 the airline was using four aircraft of this type. Company development went ahead quickly, helped along by the use of the airline's capacity by the travel companies within the group. The initial Spanish destinations were augmented by more and more points in Europe. For long-range services, especially to the winter destinations in the Caribbean, Iberworld received its first Airbus A310-300 in 1999, but this was replaced in February 2002 by the first Airbus A330-200. The fleet, which is maintained at the company's own base in Palma de Mallorca, continues to be expanded.

Routes

Alicante, Amsterdam, Arrecife, Athens, Barcelona, Bergen, Berlin, Bilbao, Birmingham, Brussels, Budapest, Cancun, Ciego de Avilla, Cork, Dublin, Düsseldorf, East Midlands, Frankfurt, Fuerteventura, Glasgow, Groningen, Hamburg, Helsinki, Ibiza, Las Palmas, Lisbon, London, Madrid, Malaga, Milan, Munich, Nantes, Paris, Prague, Puerto Plata, Punta Cana, Seville, Shannon, Valencia, Varadero, Vaxjo, Vigo, Vitoria, Zanzibar, Zürich.

Fleet

8 Airbus A320-200
2 Airbus A330-200

Boeing 757-208 TF-FIH (Josef Krauthäuser/Frankfurt)

ICELANDAIR

Reykjavik Airport, 101 Reykjavik, Iceland
Tel. 5050300, Fax. 5050391
E-mail: info@islandair.is, www.icelandair.is

Three- / Two- letter code	IATA No.	Reg'n prefix	ICAO callsign
ICE / FI	108	TF	Iceair

Icelandair, or Flugfelag Islands HF, was formed on the north coast of Iceland as Flugfelag Akureyar on 3rd June 1937 and began service to Reykjavik with a Waco YKS. In 1940 the headquarters of the airline was moved to the capital, Reykjavik and a Beech 18, two Dragon Rapides and another Waco YKS were bought. After the end of the Second World War, a scheduled service from Iceland via Prestwick to Copenhagen was set up for the first time in 1946. In April 1948 Flugfelag took delivery of its first Douglas DC-4, using it for a second route to London, with services to Germany added from 1955. In 1965 the present title

was adopted and Fokker F.27s brought into service; two years later came the first Boeing 727. Icelandair was set up in its present form on 20th July 1973 as the holding company for a merger of Flugfelag Islands and Loftleidir Icelandic Airlines, formed on 10th March 1944. Initially Icelandair flew domestic and European services and Loftleidir continued in its transatlantic role, in close co-operation, but from 1st October 1979 services were fully merged under the Icelandair name. In 1988, 836,000 passengers were carried. From 1989 the former Loftleidir DC-8s were replaced by Boeing 757s, and

the rest of the fleet was steadily renewed, principally with Boeing 737s. For regional services the Fokker F.27s were replaced with Fokker 50s. More Boeing 757s were added, including the stretched -300 with service entry in 2001; one of the 757s is a freighter, operated by separate division Icelandair Cargo. During 1999 a new colour scheme was adopted. Since 2002 Icelandair has operated an all-jet fleet, as the regional services and Fokker 50s have been passed over to subsidiary Flugfelag Islands.

Routes

Icelandic domestic services to 10 destinations. International routes from Reykjavik to Amsterdam, Baltimore, Barcelona, Boston, Copenhagen, Faroe Islands, Frankfurt, Glasgow, Gothenburg, Halifax, Hamburg, Helsinki, London, Milan, Minneapolis/St.Paul, New York, Orlando, Oslo, Palma de Mallorca, Paris, Stockholm. Charter flights to the Mediterranean, and on an ad hoc basis.

Fleet

11 Boeing 757-200ER
 1 Boeing 737-300
 2 Boeing 757-300

Airbus A320-231 VT-EPI (Jörg Thiel / Bangkok)

INDIAN AIRLINES

113 Gurdwara Rakabganj Road, New Delhi
110001, India, Tel. 11-3718951
Fax. 11-3711014, www.nic.in/indian-airlines

Three- / Two- letter code	IATA No.	Reg'n prefix	ICAO callsign
IAC / IC	058	VT	Indair

Indian Airlines Corporation was set up on 28th May 1953 by central government in Delhi and on 1st August 1953 formally acquired the routes and assets of eight independent airlines – Airways (India), Bharat Airways, Himalayan Aviation, Kalinga Airlines, Indian National Airways, Deccan Airways, Air India and Air Services of India. They were all nationalised and combined to form Air India and Indian Airlines, with Indian Airlines being responsible for regional services. The airline's first flights were on 1st August 1953 and it used DC-4s, Vickers Vikings and DC-3s. In 1957 these aircraft were partly replaced by Vickers Viscounts, and by the Fokker F.27 from May 1961 onwards. The airline's first jet was the Caravelle, acquired in February 1964. HS.748s manufactured under licence in India were also used, as were Airbus A300s, the first widebody for Indian. When the latest generation of aircraft, the Airbus A320, was introduced from the end of 1989, some operational problems arose which had an effect on flights and on passenger numbers. Indian Airlines' flights were divided on a regional basis, from Delhi, Calcutta, Madras and Mumbai (formerly Bombay). The airline was partially privatised in 1994, with a further offer of sale of shares in 1998 but the government retains 49% and has a strong influence. The airline would like to order 43 Airbus narrowbodies, but the application for approval has been stalled by the government for nearly two years. The regional carrier Vayudoot formed with Air India in 1981 and its Dornier 228s were integrated into Indian Airlines during 1996. Alliance Air is a subsidiary operating Boeing 737s within India, and there are co-operation agreements with Air France, Air India Druk Air and Srilankan.

Routes

Over 50 points in India are served regularly, and there are international services to Al-Fujairah, Bahrain, Bangkok, Colombo, Dacca, Doha, Karachi, Kathmandu, Kuala Lumpur, Male, Muscat, Ras al Khaimah, Sharjah, Singapore, and Yangon.

Fleet

  5 Airbus A300B4
37 Airbus A320-200
  3 Fairchild-Dornier 228

Airbus A300-605R EP-IBA (Josef Krauthäuser / Frankfurt)

IRAN AIR

P.O.Box 13185-775, Mehrabad Airport,
Teheran, Islamic Republic of Iran
Tel. 979111, Fax. 6003248, www.iranair.co.ir

Three- / Two- letter code	IATA No.	Reg'n prefix	ICAO callsign
IRA / IR	096	EP	Iranair

Iran Air came into existence in February 1962 as the result of the fusion of Iranian Airways and Persian Air Service, by order of the government of the day, and took over the routes and aircraft of both airlines. Iran Air had been established as a private company in 1944 and was known as Iranair. Persian, also in private hands, had begun freight services in 1955 with Avro Yorks. In 1965 Iran Air acquired Boeing 727s and used them to open new routes to London and Frankfurt. In March 1976 a Boeing 747SP began scheduled services to New York. The first Airbus A300s were brought into use during 1978, mainly on the much travelled routes to neighbouring countries. Political developments in the early 1980s following the Ayatollah Khomeini's rise to power in 1979, with the departure of the Shah, and the war lasting several years with neighbour Iraq brought many changes. Prior to 1979 Iran Air had been one of the world's fastest growing airlines, with over 100 weekly international departures from Teheran to nearly 30 destinations, but by the mid-1980s departures had reduced to less than 30 a week. However, from 1989 restructuring became possible and fleet modernisation began in September 1990 with the delivery of the first Fokker 100 for regional services. Further modernisation fell foul of the United States instigated economic embargo, but Airbus 310s have been acquired. In 1992, in co-operation with Tajikistan Airlines, a subsidiary company, Iran Air Tours was set up and this operates a fleet of Tupolev Tu-154s. There are co-operation agreements with Aeroflot, Austrian Airlines, Lufthansa, Malaysian Airlines and Syrianair.

Routes

Abu Dhabi, Ahwaz, Almaty, Amsterdam, Ardabil, Ashkabad, Bahrein, Baku, Bandar Abbas, Bandar Lengeh, Beijing, Buskihr, Cha-Bahar, Cologne/Bonn, Copenhagen, Damascus, Dacca, Delhi, Doha, Dubai, Entebbe, Frankfurt, Geneva, Gothenburg, Hamburg, Isfahan, Istanbul, Jeddah, Kabul, Karachi, Kerrnan, Kormanshar, Kuala Lumpur, Kuwait, Larnaca, London, Mashad, Moscow, Mumbai, Nairobi, Paris, Rome, Sary, Sharjah, Shiraz, Stockholm, Tabriz, Tashkent, Teheran, Tokyo, Vienna, Yazd, Zahedan.

Fleet

4 Airbus A300B2
2 Airbus A300-600
7 Airbus A310-200/300
3 Boeing 737-200
6 Boeing 727-200

3 Boeing 747-200
1 Boeing 747-100
4 Boeing 747SP
5 Fokker 100

Boeing 727-228 EP-ASB (Bastian Hilker / Dubai)

IRAN ASEMAN AIRLINES

P.O.Box 141748 Mehrabad Airport
Teheran 13145-1476, Islamic Republic of Iran
Tel. 21-6400257, Fax. 21-6404318, www.iaa.ir

Three- / Two- letter code	IATA No.	Reg'n prefix	ICAO callsign
IRC / EP	–	EP	Aseman

Following the revolution in Iran, in 1980 Iran Aseman Airlines was formed by state order from the merger of various smaller air taxi companies. Air Taxi founded in 1958, Air Service in 1962, Pars Air which had been in existence since 1969, and Hoor Asseman, all with their light aircraft formed the nucleus of the new company, which soon was using Fokker F.28s. The continuing war between Iran and Iraq was for a while a hindrance to the further development of the company, which operated only domestic services. There were no

scheduled routes however, but overwhelmingly charter and contract work for companies and state enterprises and institutions which had need of air services. During 1993 and 1994 there was a wholesale reorganisation, which led to the acquisition of further Fokker F.28s and ATR 42s and ATR 72s. In addition the airline equipped itself with four Boeing 727s. Iran Aseman Airlines, as it is now known, having dropped one of the 's's from its original name, has built up an extensive domestic network in Iran, and flies in addition, to neighbouring

countries in the Arabian peninsula. As well as Teheran, Shiraz is an important centre for the airline, with Dubai developing into a hub with several daily flights. During 1999 the company's fleet was updated with the delivery of the latest, more powerful model ATR 72-500.

Routes

Abadan, Ahwaz, Ardabai, Ashkabad, Bahrain, Bam, Bandar Abbas, Birjand, Bishkek, Bojnord, Bishier, Chah Bahar, Doha, Dubai, Dushanbe, Fasa, Gonbad, Hamadan, Isfahan, Kerman, Keramshah, Khorramabad, Kish, Kuwait, Lar, Mashad, Quetta, Rafsanjan, Ramsar, Sanandaj, Shiraz, Tabas, Tabriz, Teheran, Yazd, Zahedan.

Fleet

8 ATR 72-200/500
4 Boeing 727-200
2 Britten Norman Islander
6 Fokker F.28

Boeing 737-446 JA8991 (Josef Krauthäuser collection)

JAL EXPRESS

4-11 Higashi-Shinagawa, 2-chome Sinagawa-ku, Tokyo 1040, Japan, Tel. 6-68577378
Fax. 6-68577384, www.jal.co.jp/jex

Three- / Two- letter code	IATA No.	Reg'n prefix	ICAO callsign
JEX / JC	–	JA	Janex

Domestic air services have a particular significance in densely populated Japan. Over the last few years new, smaller airlines have established niche markets in competition with the former dominant carriers ANA/All Nippon, Japan Airlines and JAS. On several routes there have been strongly competitive battles, partly based on ticket prices. The established airlines had high operating costs which led ANA to pass over the operation of several flights to its subsidiary Air Nippon. Similarly, in April 1997, Japan Airlines was moved to set up its own low cost airline known as JAL-Express. Initially it used two Boeing 737-400s leased from the parent company, and began operations on 1st July 1998. The first route was Osaka-Miyazaki and this was flown several times daily. With the delivery of further 737-400s, operations were expanded, so that Kagoshima was also served from Osaka, again several times a day. JAL Express has the long term aim of creating an intensive domestic network, following the model established by similar low-cost/low-fare airlines in the United States and in Europe. Following the 2002 merger of JAL and JAS, there is some speculation over the future of JAL Express.

Routes

Akita, Fukuoka, Kagoshima, Kumamoto, Memambetsu, Miyazaki, Nagasaki, Nagoya, Oita, Okinawa, Osaka, Sapporo, Sendai, Tokyo.

Fleet

6 Boeing 737-400

Douglas DC-10-40 JA8544 (Josef Krauthäuser collection)

JALWAYS

2-4-11 Higashi-Shinagawa 2 chome, Shinagawa-Ku
Tokyo 140-8647, Japan, Tel. 3-54606830
Fax. 3-54606839, www.jalwys.co.jp

Three- / Two- letter code	IATA No.	Reg'n prefix	ICAO callsign
JAZ / JO	708	JA	J-Way

Japan Air Charter – JAZ was founded on 5th October 1990, with Japan Airlines as the majority shareholder, with over 80% of the capital. JAL also provided the aircraft, a DC-10-40 and a Boeing 747-200 on wet lease. Pilots and cabin personnel likewise came from JAL. The single-class layout was typically Japanese and the objective was to undertake numerous charter flights to Hawaii. What the Mediterranean is to the holidaying middle-Europeans, Hawaii is to the Japanese, six flying hours away. Other destinations were Bangkok and Guam. Over the next few years, the fleet was expanded and became more colourful, literally. In 1997 there was the first resort colour scheme which appeared on both the DC-10 and 747s. Japan Air Charter had taken on the role of leasing company for JAL. From 1st October 1999 the name was changed to JALWays. Likewise altered were the task of the company and its colour scheme. It flew charters no more, but took on for JAL flights to all holiday areas, as an independent company; this was also reflected in a change of cabin crew attire. JAL was able to use the capital freed up by this move and institute direct services to Los Angeles or San Francisco. Jalways' aircraft are provided and looked after by JAL, and its operating base is Tokyo-Narita.

Routes

Bangkok, Guam, Hiroshima, Honolulu, Kona, Niigata, Osaka, Saipan, Sapporo, Sendai, Tokyo.

Fleet

3 Boeing 747-200
2 Boeing 747-300
4 Douglas DC-10-40

Boeing 747-446 JA8904 (L. Mukrati / Tokyo)

JAPAN AIRLINES

Jal Building, Higashi Shinagawa 2-4-11
Shinagawaku, Tokyo 140, Japan
Tel. 3-54603121, Fax. 3-54603936, www.jal.co.jp

Three- / Two- letter code	IATA No.	Reg'n prefix	ICAO callsign
JAL / JL	131	JA	Japanair

JAL was set up on 1st August 1951 as Japanese Air Lines when civil aviation was reactivated in Japan after the Second World War. The first flight was from Tokyo-Haneda to Osaka with a leased Martin 202 on 25th October 1951. A year later the first flight with a DC-4 owned by the airline took place. In 1953 the DC-6 was introduced and 2nd February 1954 saw the first international flight from Tokyo to San Francisco; in August 1960 the DC-8 was introduced for this route. In the following year the Tokyo-London polar route and Paris/Copenhagen to Tokyo were opened with DC-8s. Convair 880s were introduced in 1962 and used for the first time to Frankfurt via South East Asia. In 1967 a round-the-world flight was established; the first flights over Siberia to Europe were in March 1970, saving several hours over the previous polar route. In the same year, on 1st July 1970, the Boeing 747 was introduced, at first on Pacific routes. The Douglas DC-10-40 was specially designed for JAL and used from the mid-1970s. New destinations were Zürich in 1979 and Düsseldorf from 1985, and there was expansion to the USA in the 1980s. The first Boeing 767 was brought into the fleet during 1987, and the airline privatised during the following year. The MD-11 was introduced from 1993, the Boeing 737-400 from 1995 and the Boeing 777 from 1996. JAL has holdings in Japan Asia, JALexpress, JALways and Japan Trans Ocean. It had an 8.5% holding in Japan Air System, but in 2002 acquired the rest and merged the two airlines under the JAL name, with a new corporate identity featuring the symbolic red sun on the fin. There is co-operation with many other carriers, especially through JAL's membership of the Oneworld Alliance.

Routes

Akita, Amami, Amsterdam, Atlanta, Bangkok, Beijing, Brisbane, Chicago,Dalian, Dallas/Fort Worth, Delhi, Denpasar, Djakarta, Frankfurt, Fukuoka, Fukushima, Geneva, Guam, Guangzhou, Hakodate, Hiroshima, Ho Chi Minh City, Hong Kong, Honolulu, Kagoshima, Kochi, Komatsu, Kona, Kuala Lumpur, Kumamoto, Las Vegas, London, Los Angeles, Manila, Matsuyama, Memphis, Mexico City, Milan, Moscow, Nagasaki, Nagoya, New York, Niigata, Obihiro, Oita, Okinawa, Osaka, Paris, Pusan, Qingdao, Rome, Saipan, San Francisco, Sao Paulo, Sapporo, Sendai, Seoul, Shanghai, Singapore, Sydney, Tianjin, Tokyo, Tukushima, Vancouver, Xian, Yamagata, Zürich.

Fleet

36 Airbus A300B2/B4/300-600	8 Douglas DC-10-40
31 Boeing 767-200/300	6 McDonnell Douglas MD-11
43 Boeing 747-400	26 McDonnell Douglas MD-81/87
34 Boeing 747-100/200/300	
27 Boeing 777-200/300	

Boeing 737-3H9 YU-ANF (Marcus Baltes / Frankfurt)

JAT AIRWAYS

Bulevar Umetnosti 16, 11070 Novi Beograd
Yugoslavia, Tel. 11-3114222, Fax. 11-137756
E-mail: sales@jat.com, www.jat.com/

Three- / Two- letter code	IATA No.	Reg'n prefix	ICAO callsign
JAT / JU	115	YU	JAT

The predecessor of JAT was Aeroput, founded in 1927, but this was forced to quit operations at the outbreak of the Second World War. JAT was then founded on 1st April 1947 and began operations with the DC-3. The jet era arrived with the Caravelle in 1963 and marked an expansion of services in Europe especially; destinations such as Moscow, Amsterdam and Stockholm could now be reached non-stop. In 1969 the DC-9 was introduced and a year later the Boeing 707, allowing service for the first time to the USA and Canada, plus additional destinations in the Far East and Australia. In 1974 the Caravelles were replaced by the Boeing 727,

and from 1978 the DC-10 succeeded the Boeing 707s. A further fleet renewal began in 1985 with the acquisition of the Boeing 737-300. However on 31st May 1992 JAT was forced to give up its international flights as a result of United Nations sanctions because of the political situation in what was by then the former Yugoslavia and the ongoing civil war in Bosnia. Services resumed on 6th October 1994; a new colour scheme was adopted and the 'Yugoslav Airlines' inscription added. Routes were flown from Belgrade to mainly European cities, but there was no demand for long-range routes and three DC-10s were sold; other

aircraft in the formerly extensive fleet were leased out or stored. No new aircraft have been delivered since 1991, when ATR 72s were added. JAT suffered further problems in 1999, when from March NATO was bombing some parts of Yugoslavia; a fresh embargo was imposed, but lifted in March 2000. JAT – Yugoslav Airlines changed its name to JAT Airways in 2003 and is again trying to build up its route network from its Belgrade base, concentrating on Europe and the Middle East, with a correspondingly configured fleet. The last DC-10 has been leased to Cubana. It is planned to replace the relatively old 737s with the Airbus A319 during 2004-5.

Routes

Amsterdam, Athens, Banjaluka, Beirut, Belgrade, Berlin, Bucharest, Cairo, Copenhagen, Damascus, Dubai, Düsseldorf, Frankfurt, Gothenburg, Hamburg, Hanover, Istanbul, Larnaca, London, Malta, Milan, Moscow, Paris, Podgorica, Prague, Rome, Skopje, Sofia, St.Petersburg, Stockholm, Stuttgart, Tel Aviv, Thessaloniki, Tivat, Trieste, Tripoli, Tunis, Vienna, Zürich.

Fleet	Ordered
3 ATR 72-200	8 Airbus A319
11 Boeing 737-300/400	
1 Douglas DC-10-30	

Boeing 737-45R VT-JAU (Mumbai / Gerhard Schütz collection)

JET AIRWAYS

SM Centre, Andheri-Kurla Road, Andheri
Mumbai, 400059 India, Tel. 91-22 8505080
Fax. 91-228505631, www.jetairways.com

Three- / Two- letter code	IATA No.	Reg'n prefix	ICAO callsign
JAI / 9W	589	VT	Jet Airways

India is the world's second most populous country, occupying almost all of the enormous Indian subcontinent. Thus the aircraft is, and will become increasingly, an important means of communication. Many years of restrictions on private companies and the monopoly situations enjoyed by the two state-owned companies Air India and Indian Airlines are being partially removed. For the last few years, more and more private companies have been allowed, including Jet Airways. This airline was founded in Mumbai in 1992 and began flying early in 1993, using the Boeing 737-300. In 1994 the airline was given permission for scheduled operations. From this point, company growth was swift and it has become the largest private airline in India. It has maintained a homogeneous fleet of Boeing 737s, including the current -700 and -800 models, but from 1999 ATR 72-500s were added for short routes. Aircraft are maintained at the company's own facility at the main base of Mumbai. Other important hubs are at Bangalore, Chennai, Delhi and Kolkota. All the subcontinent's major cities are served.

Routes

Ahmedabat, Aurangabad, Bagdogra, Bangalore, Bhavnagar, Bhopal, Bhubaneswar, Bhuj, Chandigarh, Chennai, Coimbatore, Delhi, Diu, Goa, Guwahati, Hyderabad, Imphal, Indore, Jaipur, Jammu, Jodphur, Jorhat, Khajuraho, Leh, Lucknow, Ludhiana, Madurai, Mangalore, Mumbai, Nagpur, Porbandar, Port Blair, Puna, Rajkot, Srinagar, Thiruvananthapuram, Tirupati, Trivandrum, Udaipur, Vadodara, Varanasi, Vishakhapatnam.

Fleet

8 ATR 72-500
8 Boeing 737-400
7 Boeing 737-700

14 Boeing 737-800
2 Boeing 737-900

Ordered

2 Boeing 737-800

Airbus A320-232 N505JB (Ken Petersen / New York)

JETBLUE AIRWAYS

8002 Kew Gardens Road, New York,11415, USA
Tel. 718-2867900, Fax. 718-2867950, E-mail:
dearjetblue@jetblue.com, www.jetblue.com

Three- / Two- letter code	IATA No.	Reg'n prefix	ICAO callsign
JBU / B6	–	N	Jetblue

David Neeleman, the founder of JetBlue, is not unknown in airline circles, having over some years led Morris Air to such considerable success that it was bought out by its mighty competitor, Southwest Airlines. After his time at Morris Air, Neeleman went on to be a success at Southwest, building up a reservations system, and also helping the Canadian airline West Jet to set up their operation. However the notion of having his own airline stayed with him and in 1998 the idea became a reality. First it was necessary to find investors willing to come up with the sum of $130 million, an amount which had

never before been raised for an airline start-up. Another feature of the plan was the aircraft choice; only factory-fresh aircraft were to be considered, and the choice fell in favour of Airbus. In April an order was placed for 82 A320s, all equipped with the latest 24-channel TV system, and leather seats. As an operating base and main departure point only New York's Kennedy Airport was on the agenda, since this was believed to offer the best market opportunities. Options were taken on 75 slots here. With the delivery of the first A320 in January 2000, JetBlue was ready for the off, and on 11th February the first

service took place, from New York to Fort Lauderdale. Services to Buffalo and Tampa quickly followed. JetBlue has grown quickly, and even the effects of 11 September seem to have been shortlived for this airline, with services now routing nationwide, and to Puerto Rico. Airbus 320 deliveries continue, to meet the ambitious expansion, and in June 2003, an order was announced for 100 Embraer 190s (plus 100 options) for delivery from August 2006 to 2011.

Routes

Atlanta, Buffalo, Burlington, Denver, Fort Lauderdale, Fort Myers, Las vegas, Long Beach, New Orleans, New York-JFK, Oakland, Ontario,Rochester, Salt Lake City, San Diego, San Juan, Seattle, Tampa, West Palm beach, Washington DC-Dulles.

Fleet	Ordered
45 Airbus A320-200	120 Airbus A320 100 Embraer 190LR

McDonnell Douglas MD-83 C-GKLK (Thomas Kim / Toronto)

JETSGO

7800 Chemin Cote du Liesse, St. Laurent, Quebec
H4T 1G1, Canada, Tel. 514-3447100, Fax. 514-7331376
E-mail: info@jetsgo.com, www.jetsgo.net

Three- / Two- letter code	IATA No.	Reg'n prefix	ICAO callsign
JGO / SG	–	C	Jetsetgo

After Air Canada had established Tango and Zip both as low-cost/no-frills operations to compete in the race for passengers with the well-established Westjet, in June 2002 another airline came on the scene. Michael Leblanc, well known in airline circles, having been the owner of Royal Airlines which had sold to Canada 3000 in 2001, brought Jetsgo into the marketplace in May 2002. Canada 3000 had been forced to accept grounding only a couple of months after 11 September and filed for bankruptcy. Bookings halted abruptly and for several days there was an embargo on flights in US airspace. Leblanc did not wish his sale proceeds sit in the bank and wanted to invest in the airline business again. With support from a major Canadian bank and from the Boeing Company, the Jetsgo Corporation was formed in Montreal in March 2002. Operations began on 12th June 2002 using three McDonnell Douglas MD-83s. Prices for one-way trips were mostly below those of the competition; there were no tickets and bookings made overwhelmingly through the internet (90%) or by telephone. Load factors exceeded 70%. Jetsgo did not restrict itself to the major centres of population, but also targeted destinations which Air Canada Jazz was serving with DHC-8s. During 2002 further MD-83s were added to the fleet, which was growing faster than had originally been envisaged. The route network also grew correspondingly, with some routes seeing enhanced service on a seasonally-dependent basis. The first routes to the USA are to New York and Fort Lauderdale, and these are to be followed by Las Vegas and to eslewhere in Florida at the end of 2003.

Routes

Calgary, Charlottetown, Edmonton, Fort Lauderdale, Gander, Goose Bay, Halifax, Montreal, Newark, Ottawa, Quebec-City, Saguenay, Saint John, St. Johns, Stephenville, Sydney NS, Thunder Bay, Timmins, Toronto, Winnipeg, Vancouver, Victoria.

Fleet

10 McDonnell Douglas MD-83

Boeing 737-4Q3 JA-8524 (Josef Krauthäuser collection)

JTA – JAPAN TRANSOCEAN AIR

3-24 Yamashita-cho, Naha-shi, Okinawa 900
Japan, Tel. 98-8572112, Fax. 98-8589396
www.jal.co.jp/jta

Three- / Two- letter code	IATA No.	Reg'n prefix	ICAO callsign
JTA / NU	353	JA	Jai Ocean

Southwest Airlines – SWAL was based at the airport at Naha, the capital of Okinawa, an island in the Ryukyu group which from 1945 until 1972 was under American control and administration. During the Second World War Okinawa had been occupied by the Americans. Occasional services had been provided by Air America, but for Japanese citizens there were certain restrictions. Thus on 22nd June 1967 a group of Okinawa business people set up their own airline. Support came from Japan Air Lines, who took a 51% shareholding, and a Convair 240 came into use from 1st July 1967. After a year a locally-produced NAMC YS-11 took over the services. The smaller islands in the archipelago were also served, using the de Havilland DHC-6 Twin Otter, which was able to cope with the short runways which were all that was available on some islands. At the beginning of the 1980s the first Boeing 737-200 came into service and was used to give service several times a day to Ishigaki, the most important route to the mainland. In July 1993 the airline's name was changed to Japan Trans Ocean Air. A year later JTA received the Boeing 737-400 as a more modern replacement for the older YS-11s. Ryukyu Air Commuter is a JTA subsidiary company, which uses de Havilland DHC-8s and Twin Otters to continue service to the smaller islands.

Routes

Aguni, Amami O Shima, Fukuoka, Fukushima, Hateruma, Ishigaki, Kagoshima, Kerama, Kitadaito, Kochi, Komatsu, Kume Jima, Matsuyama, Minami Daito, Miyako Jima, Nagoya, Nahe, Obihiro, Okayama, Osaka, Sapporo, Taramajima, Tokyo, Yonaguni Jima, Yoronjima.

Fleet

18 Boeing 737-400

Boeing 767-36N(ER) 5Y- KQZ (Albert Kuhbandner / Amsterdam)

KENYA AIRWAYS

Jomo Kenyatta Intl. Airport, P.O.Box 19002,
Nairobi, Kenya, Tel. 2-823000, Fax. 2-823488,
www.kenyaairways.com

Three- / Two- letter code	IATA No.	Reg'n prefix	ICAO callsign
KQA / KQ	706	5Y	Kenya

Following the collapse of the multi-national airline East African Airways, the flag carrier for Kenya, Tanzania and Uganda, in 1976, the Kenyan government was forced to set up its own airline. With the aid of British Midland Airways and using two leased Boeing 707s, services were begun from Nairobi to London, Frankfurt, Athens and Rome in February 1977, one month after the airline was formed on 22nd January 1977. The leased aircraft were replaced by the airline's own 707s, which in turn were replaced by more modern aircraft in the form of the Airbus A310 from 1986. Fokker 50s were introduced for shorter routes

from 1988. During the early 1990s the airline declined, earning a poor reputation for reliability and service, but the problem was tackled and reorganisation and rationalisation effected. In 1996 the airline was partially privatised with the participation of KLM, which took a 26% shareholding. In April 1997 a daily service to Amsterdam was started, to feed into the KLM network, and this close co-operation continues. During 1998 a new colour scheme was adopted for the aircraft, and the Fokker 50s phased out. Further Boeing 737s were added, making the fleet all-jet. At the beginning of 2000 Kenya Airways

leased a Boeing 767, and this type has now replaced the remaining A310s. New Boeing 737-700s are likewise replacing the older -200 series. Also in the early part of 2000, a subsidiary, Kenya Flamingo Airways, was set up to operate four Saab 340s on short range services. Both airlines are based at Nairobi's Jomo Kenyatta International Airport. Boeing 777s are on order, to join the fleet from 2004.

Routes

Abidjan, Accra, Addis Ababa, Amsterdam, Bujumbura, Cairo, Dar-es-Salaam, Douala, Dubai, Eldoret, Entebbe/Kampala, Frankfurt, Harare, Jeddah, Johannesburg, Khartoum, Kigali, Kinshasa, Kisumu, Lagos, Lilongwe, London, Lusaka, Mahe, Malindi, Mombasa, Mumbai, Nairobi, Yaounde, Zanzibar.

Fleet		Ordered
3 Boeing 737-200Adv.	5 Boeing 767-300	3 Boeing 777-200
4 Boeing 737-300		
4 Boeing 737-700		

Boeing 727-251F N278US (Josef Krauthäuser / Dallas-DFW)

KITTY HAWK AIRCARGO

P.O.Box 612787 1515 West 20th Street, DFW Airport
Dallas, Texas 75261, USA, Tel. 972-4566000
Fax. 972-4562277, E-mail: info@kha.com, www.kha.com

Three- / Two- letter code	IATA No.	Reg'n prefix	ICAO callsign
KHA / KR	798	N	Air Kittyhawk

After the merger of Kitty Hawk International with Kalitta American International in 1997, it was only a few years before the airline had to cease operations temporarily and seek Chapter 11 bankruptcy protection. Behind this were the effects of both 11 September and supervision of the fleet by the FAA. The aircraft were mostly mothballed at desert airports in Arizona and California. After a reorganisation of the Kitty Hawk Group, which has been in the transport business for many years, new investment and the overhaul of several of the Boeing 727Fs, Kitty Hawk was able to leave Chapter 11 in September 2002 and return to business. The new company using the well-known name was located in Fort Wayne, Indiana, where it has its own warehouse and forwarding centre. Every night aircraft converge from all parts of the USA, are unloaded and re-loaded and fly back to their points of origin. Thus Kitty Hawk flies everything from small packets to bulky goods in its specially adapted Boeing 727 freighters.

Routes

Atlanta, Baltimore, Boston, Buffalo, Charlotte, Chicago, Cincinnati, Cleveland, Dallas, Dayton, Denver, Detroit, El Paso, Erie, Fort Wayne, Grand Rapids, Hartford, Houston, Huntsville, Indianapolis, Jacksonville, Lexington, Los Angeles, Louisville, Memphis, Miami, Milwaukee, Minneapolis, Nashville, Newark, New York-JFK, Norfolk, Ontario, Orlando, Philadelphia, Pittsburgh, Portland, Rochester, San Diego, San Jose, Seattle, South Bend, Syracuse, Tampa, Toronto, Washington-Dulles.

Fleet

36 Boeing 727-200F

Fokker 50 PH-KVG (Stefan Schlick / Luxembourg)

KLM-CITYHOPPER

Postbus 7700, 1117 ZL Schiphol Oost, the Netherlands, Tel. 20-6492227, Fax. 20-6488154, www.klm.com

Three- / Two- letter code	IATA No.	Reg'n prefix	ICAO callsign
KLC / KL	195	PH	City

The present KLM-Cityhopper is the successor in name to NLM Dutch Airlines, which was set up in 1966 and started scheduled flights between Amsterdam, Eindhoven and Maastricht on 29th August 1966, using the proven Fokker F.27 Friendship. Regional international schedules began in 1974. In 1976 the name of the airline was changed to NLM Cityhopper and KLM acquired a majority interest. Another independent Dutch operator, Netherlines, was set up in 1984 and on 8th January 1985 began operations with Jetstream 31s between Amsterdam and Luxembourg, with further routes opened up from 1985 and 1988. By 1987, Netherlines was owned by the Nedlloyd Group, who also owned Transavia. In 1988, KLM decided to buy Netherlines with the intention of asking NLM, which operated F.27s and F.28s, to merge the airlines together to form the new KLM-Cityhopper, a 100% KLM subsidiary. Saab 340s and Fokker 50s were introduced at the beginning of the 1990s, with the first Fokker 70 delivered in Spring 1996, but the planned total of this type was not reached as a result of Fokker's demise. During 2002 KLM Cityhopper and KLM UK were organisationally combined, as part of a restructuring of the whole KLM group, with the objective of cost saving. KLM-Cityhopper is primarily responsible for regional feeder services and flies under KLM flight numbers. The airline's base is at Amsterdam-Schiphol, where the whole KLM infrastructure is used.

Routes

Aberdeen, Amsterdam, Basle, Berlin, Birmingham, Bologna, Bremen, Bristol, Brussels, Cardiff, Düsseldorf, Frankfurt, Glasgow, Hamburg, Humberside, Kristiansand, London, Luxembourg, Lyon, Malmö, Manchester, Munich, Newcastle, Nice, Norwich, Oslo, Paris, Rotterdam, Stavanger, Teeside, Toulouse, Turin, Venice, Verona.

Fleet

14 Fokker 100
20 Fokker 70
21 Fokker 50

Boeing 737-300 PH-BDG (Richard Schmaus / Munich)

KLM ROYAL DUTCH AIRLINES

P.O.Box 7700, 1117 ZL Amsterdam, Airport Schiphol, Netherlands, Tel. 20-6499123, Fax. 20-6493113, www.klm.com

Three- / Two- letter code	IATA No.	Reg'n prefix	ICAO callsign
KLM / KL	074	PH	KLM

Formed on 7th October 1919, KLM is one of the oldest operating airlines in the world. The first scheduled flights were Amsterdam to London on 17th May 1920. Mainly Fokker aircraft were used until the outbreak of war. In 1929 the route to Batavia (today called Jakarta) was opened, at that time the longest route. The first transatlantic link was to Curacao in 1934 and operations in the West Indies began in 1935. Douglas DC-2s were introduced in 1935, followed by DC-3s in 1936 and until 1940 KLM had one of the densest networks in Europe. After 1945, reconstruction commenced with DC-3s, with Convair 240s added from 1948; these were replaced by Convair 340s from 1953. The Vickers Viscount took over important routes in Europe from 1957 onwards, augmented by the Lockheed Electra from 1959. Overseas flights were initially flown by DC-4s, Lockheed Constellations, with DC-6s and DC-7s as the last of the propeller-driven aircraft. The first DC-8 was used to New York on 4th April 1960. Boeing 747s, introduced in 1971, and DC-10s took over the long-distance routes in the 1970s. For short and medium distances, KLM initially used DC-9s, which were then replaced by Boeing 737s (now in process of updating with new generation models) and augmented by Airbus A310s. KLM's present flagship is the Boeing 747-400 which has been used since May 1989. During 1993 KLM took a minority shareholding in Northwest Airlines and since then has worked closely with its US partner in the successful Wings Alliance. KLM has interests in ALM-Antillean, Kenya Airways, KLM Alps, Martinair, Transavia and KLM-Cityhopper. In 2002 the group was reorganised, the Buzz low-cost subsidiary being sold off, and decisions taken on re-equipment, including A330s from 2005. A revised colour scheme is also being introduced.

Routes

From its base at Amsterdam-Schiphol KLM operates an intensive European network, and internationally connects over 165 destinations on all continents. In co-operation with Northwest and other partners over 350 cities are served.

Fleet		Ordered
24 Boeing 747-400	12 Boeing 767-300	6 Airbus A330-200
6 Boeing 747-200 (several SUD)	10 McDonnell Douglas MD-11	10 Boeing 777-200
30 Boeing 737-300/400		
17 Boeing 737-800/900		

Tupolev Tu-204-100 RA-64016 (Bernhard Müller jun. / Salzburg)

KMV - KAVKAZSKIE MINERALNYE VODY

Mineralnye Airport –5, Mineralnye Vody,
Stavropol 357310, Russia, Tel. 86531- 58535
Fax. 86531- 57228, www.kmvavia.ru

Three- / Two- letter code	IATA No.	Reg'n prefix	ICAO callsign
MVD / KV	348	RA	Air Minvody

The provenance of KMV – Kavkazskie Mineralnye Vody, or Kavminvodyavia, as the airline is also known, is pretty much identical to that of other Russian airlines. Following the disintegration of Aeroflot, a new organisation was formed in Mineralnye Vody called Mineralnye Vody C.A.P.O and Aeroflot Mineralnye Vody Product & Flying Unit. Several thousand people were seeking gainful employment and operations began using aircraft from the former local Aeroflot directorate. As well as scheduled services, charter work was also undertaken, notably to countries in the Persian Gulf, which are particularly attractive to Russians for their shopping opportunities. The Mineralnye Vody area is also attractive to tourists and because of its many mineral springs it is known for its curative qualities. Thus the region is slowly prospering. A new Tupolev 204, the first of the new generation of Russian airliners, was acquired in 1998, and this was used in 1999 to operate the airline's first scheduled service to the west, to Munich. A second Tu-204 was added in mid-2000. KMV operates charter flights in the summer to holiday resorts in Turkey, Bulgaria and Italy, and in winter to the ski resorts of Austria, Switzerland and France.

Routes

Aleppo, Antalya, Athens, Chisinau, Chita, Ekaterinburg, Dubai, Istanbul, Khabarovsk, Krasnoyarsk, Larnaca, Malta, Mineralnye Vody, Moscow, Munich, Murmansk, Nizhnevartovsk, Niszhny Novgorod, Norilsk, Novosibirsk, Omsk, Salzburg, Samara, St. Petersburg, Sharjah, Surgut, Tel Aviv, Thessaloniki, Tyumen, Ufa, Uljanowsk, Varna.
.

Fleet

```
 5 Tupolev Tu-134
15 Tupolev Tu-154
 2 Tupolev Tu-204
```

Boeing 737-86N HL 7558 (Josef Krauthäuser collection)

KOREAN AIR

C.P.O.Box 864, Seoul, Republic of Korea
Tel. 2-6567114, Fax. 2-7752936, E-mail:
selpro@koreanair.co.kr, www.koreanair.com

Three- / Two- letter code	IATA No.	Reg'n prefix	ICAO callsign
KAL / KE	180	HL	Koreanair

The private company Hanjin Transport Group took over Korean Airlines, formed in 1962 and which had been state owned, and eight aircraft on 1st March 1969. Its international routes were to Hong Kong and Osaka. In 1973, KAL acquired its first Boeing 747, used from May 1973 for trans-Pacific services via Tokyo and Honolulu to Los Angeles. In the same year a weekly service to Paris started, the first destination in Europe, with Boeing 707s. The Airbus A300B4 came into service in 1975 and was used for the East Asian market; DC-10 deliveries also began in 1975. In 1984 the name Korean Air was introduced and the present colour scheme adopted. Korean Air developed to become one of the world's largest airlines, with services to all five continents, and a large fleet of dedicated freighters, including five passenger MD-11s converted in 1996/7. However, during the late 1990s, partly because of the Asian business crisis, and partly because of its own difficulties, KAL suffered a few turbulent years. Routes and fleet were reduced in order to contain losses, and a new management team was installed. By the first part of 2000 things were moving in the right direction and renewal and expansion of the fleet is in progress. In 2002 Seoul's new international airport at Inchon was opened, with Kimpo relegated to domestic services only. All the Fokker 100s and MD-80s were retired in 2001/2 and replaced with Boeing 737-800/900s. Airbus A380s are expected to join the fleet in 2007/9. Since 2002 Korean Air has been a member of the Skyteam alliance.

Routes

Akita, Amsterdam, Anchorage, Atlanta, Auckland, Bangkok, Beijing, Boston, Brisbane, Brussels, Cairo, Cheju, Cheong Ju, Chicago, Chinju, Christchurch, Colombo, Copenhagen, Dallas/Fort Worth, Delhi, Djakarta, Dubai, Frankfurt, Fukuoka, Ho Chi Minh City, Hong Kong, Honolulu, Jinan, Kangnung, Kuala Lumpur, Kunming, Kunsan, Kwangju, London, Los Angeles, Manila, Mokpo, Moscow, Mumbai, Nagasaki, Nagoya, New York, Okayama, Osaka, Paris, Penang, Pohang, Portland, Pusan, Qingdao, Rome, San Francisco, Sao Paulo, Sanya, Sapporo, Seoul, Shanghai, Shenyang, Singapore, Sokcho, Sydney, Tashkent, Taegu, Taipei, Tianjin, Tokyo, Toronto, Ulaanbaatar, Ulsan, Vancouver, Vladivostok, Washington, Wonju, Wuhan, Xiamen, Yantai, Yosu, Zürich.

Fleet

		Ordered
12 Airbus A300-600	10 Boeing 747-400F	7 Boeing 737-900
2 Airbus A300B4F	2 Boeing 747-300	3 Boeing 777-200
18 Airbus A330-300	2 Boeing 747-200	
24 Boeing 737-800/900	12 Boeing 777-200/300	
28 Boeing 747-400	4 McDonnell Douglas MD-11F	

Tupolev Tu-154M RA-85694 (Jannis Malzahn / Hanover)

KRAS AIR

Airport Krasnoyarsk, 663020 Krasnoyarsk, Russia
Tel. 3912-267563, Fax. 3912-660205
E-mail: krasair@krasair.ru, www.krasair.ru

Three- / Two- letter code	IATA No.	Reg'n prefix	ICAO callsign
KJC / 7B	499	RA	Krasnoyarskyair

As is the case with most Russian airlines, Kras Air has its origins in an Aeroflot directorate. The division covering the Krasnoyarsk region of Siberia was privatised in 1993 as Krasnoyarskie Avialinii. The local government took 51% of the shares, the balance being widely spread, including amongst the company's employees. A multitude of aircraft were taken over, which were used for various tasks. For a while the Douglas DC-10 was used. During its first years, Kras Air confined itself to domestic routes, but in the late 1990s it started to conduct charter flights to the Middle East and into Europe. Also, freight flights with

Ilyushin 76s to Dubai or Sharjah happened more often, and indeed these freighters could be seen in use at various airports around the world from time to time. Scheduled services to Seoul, Frankfurt and Hanover resulted, from 2002. The principal reason for this was that the airport at Krasnoyarsk was being promoted by the company as a hub for west-east traffic. Also in 2002, the company's first modern Tupolev Tu-204 was delivered; more are on order to replace some of the older Soviet-era types including the Tu-134 and IL-62. It is also intended to acquire western equipment in the fleet renewal process; thus the

airline's first Boeing 767-200 was delivered at the beginning of 2003 and set to work on the most important route from Krasnoyarsk to Moscow, where the Domodedovo airport is used. Charter and freight flights also originate from here.

Routes

Adler/Sochi, Almaty, Baku, Barnaul, Chita, Ekaterinburg, Frankfurt, Hanover, Irkutsk, Kaliningrad, Kermerovo, Khaborovsk, Kiev, Komsomolsk, Krasnodar, Krasnoyarsk, Mineralnye Vody, Mirnyj, Moscow, Norilsk, Novosibirsk, Omsk, Petropavlovsk, Poljarnij, Rostov, Samara, Seoul, St. Petersburg, Tashkent, Tomsk, Ufa, Ulan-Ude, Vladivostok.

Fleet		Ordered
2 Boeing 767-200	3 Tupolev Tu-134	2 Tupolev Tu-204
2 Ilyushin IL-62	17 Tupolev Tu-154	
8 Ilyushin IL-76	2 Tupolev Tu-204	
5 Ilyushin IL-86		

Airbus A340-313 9K-AND (Martin Kühn / Frankfurt)

KUWAIT AIRWAYS

P.O.Box 394, 13004 Safat,
Kuwait Tel. 4345555, Fax. 4314118
www.kuwait-airways.com

Three- / Two- letter code	IATA No.	Reg'n prefix	ICAO callsign
KAC / KU	229	9K	Kuwaiti

Kuwait Airways Corporation came into existence in 1953 as a national airline set up by local businessmen as Kuwait National Airways. Its first route was from Kuwait City to Basra, flown for the first time in 1954 with DC-3s. The present name was adopted in May 1958 when BOAC took over the management of the airline, which it continued until independence in 1962. Vickers Viscounts replaced the DC-3s and a de Havilland Comet 4C was used from 1964 on the routes to London, Paris and Frankfurt. The airline became wholly government-owned on 1st June 1963 and took over Trans Arabia. On 20th March 1966

the first of three HS Tridents was introduced; three Boeing 707s followed two years later and gradually took over all the routes. In 1978 Kuwait Airways acquired its first Boeing 747, and Airbus aircraft succeeded the Boeing 707s, with three Boeing 767s continuing the fleet renewal process from 1986. After the Iraqi occupation of Kuwait in summer 1991 flights were discontinued; some aircraft were destroyed, some were seized by Iraq, while others were transferred abroad for lease. However, Kuwait Airways did manage to maintain a very restricted service, operating out of Cairo, and after the ending of the

Gulf War, KAC resumed its services and rebuilt its fleet, with a modestly updated colour scheme, from 1993. By 1995 almost all of the fleet had been renewed, and the latest type added is the Boeing 777-200ER, the first of which was delivered in 1998. Services to Chicago and New York have also been commenced, routing via Amsterdam or London. The second Iraq conflict in spring 2003 did not result in the loss of aircraft, but the closing of airports and suspension of services has caused the airline to suffer major financial losses. Several Kuwait Airways aircraft are held at the disposal of the government.

Routes

Abu Dhabi, Alexandria, Amman, Amsterdam, Bahrain, Bangalore,Bangkok, Beirut, Cairo, Calcutta, Chennai, Colombo, Damascus, Damman, Dacca, Delhi, Doha, Dubai, Frankfurt, Geneva, Islamabad, Istanbul, Jeddah, Karachi, Kuwait, Lahore, Larnaca, London, Luxor, Manila, Mumbai, Muscat, New York, Paris, Riyadh, Rome, Singapore, Teheran.

Fleet

5 Airbus A300-600	2 Boeing 777-200ER
3 Airbus A310-300	
3 Airbus A320-200	
4 Airbus A340-300	

Tupolev Tu-154M EX-85762 (Bastian Hilker / Hanover)

KYRGHYZSTAN AIRLINES

720062 Bishkek, Manus Airport, Kyrghyzstan
Tel. 3312-257755, Fax. 3312-257162
www.kyrgyzair.de

Three- / Two- letter code	IATA No.	Reg'n prefix	ICAO callsign
KGA / K8	758	EX	Kyrgyz

Although independent since 1991, Kyrghyzstan has remained a member of the CIS. The former Aeroflot directorate was taken over to form the basis of the national airline and to develop future services. The transformed company was called Kyrgyzstan Aba Yoldoru National Airline, with Bishkek Air Enterprises as its major shareholder. It also has a subsidiary, Osch-Karakol Air Enterprises, located in the second major city in the country, Osch. Additionally the airline still works with Aeroflot for ticketing and marketing and as a codeshare partner. Furthermore, the company has responsibilities for government duties including ambulance and relief flights, for which a number of light aircraft and helicopters are maintained. Kyrghyzstan is one of the poorest states of the CIS; developing business relationships with neighbouring Kazakstan, Uzbekistan and China bring an increased need for air services in this remote region. As well as scheduled services, charter flights are operated and efforts are made to fill aircraft with cargo.The first service to Western Europe, to Frankfurt, was inaugurated in Summer 1996. In 1998 the airline acquired its first new aircraft, an Airbus A319 which was used on international services, including the inauguration of a service to Birmingham, but the aircraft was returned to its lessor on cost grounds after only a few months. Since then the old Soviet-era fleet has soldiered on, but Airbus A319s are on order again, and in July 2003 a service to London-Gatwick was begun, using a wet-leased Boeing 737-300.

Routes

Almaty, Baku, Beijing, Bishek, Chisinau, Delhi,Ekatarinenburg, Frankfurt, Istanbul, Hanover, Kaliningrad, Karachi, Karakol, Krasnoyarsk, London-Gatwick, Moscow, Novosibirsk, Omsk, Osch, Samara, Sharjah, St. Petersburg, Stuttgart, Tashkent and Ufa.

Fleet		Ordered
7 Antonov An-26/28: 1 Ilyushin IL-76TD 10 Tupolev Tu-154 5 Tupolev Tu-134	18 Yakovlev Yak-40	2 Airbus A319

Boeing 727-2K3 CP-1366 (Author's collection)

LAB – LLOYD AEREO BOLIVIANO

Casilla Correo 132, Cochabamba, Bolivia
Tel. 42-50736, Fax. 42-50766
www.labairlines.com

Three- / Two- letter code	IATA No.	Reg'n prefix	ICAO callsign
LLB / LB	051	CP	Lloyd Aereo

LAB was set up by German immigrants on 15th September 1925, following an historic proving flight with an imported Junkers F-13 on 25th July from Cochabamba to Sucre. A regular service with the F-13 began a few months later on 24th December between Cochabamba and Santa Cruz. The Bolivian government had a stake in the airline, which however encountered financial difficulties in 1928. Shares were sold to the Junkers company, which supplied three further F-13s to the airline. The route network was steadily extended as far as the Brazilian and Argentinian borders. Over the years further Junkers types

including W-34s and Ju-52s saw service with LAB. German influence disappeared in 1941 as a result of American pressure. The company was nationalised on 14th May 1941 and Lodestars were introduced after Panagra took an interest in operations. In 1948 Curtiss C-46s were added. The first DC-4s were used on the new route to Asuncion or Porto Vila, followed in 1961 by DC-6s. In the late 1960s LAB was reorganised and Fairchild FH-227s were acquired for regional routes as well as Lockheed Electras for international services. In 1970 the change was made to Boeing 727s, with flights to Miami being operated

for the first time from 1975. Further routes to Santiago and Caracas followed. Airbus A310-300s were introduced, the first in 1991 and a second in 1996. At the end of 1995 the Brazilian airline VASP took a 49% interest in LAB, one of the results of which was that the colour scheme was modified to resemble that of VASP. Early in 2000 VASP's financial situation had deteriorated, which meant that the shareholding in LAB was sold on again. A fleet renewal programme has now been started with the acquisition of Boeing 737-300s and 767-300s.

Routes

Arica, Asuncion, Bogota, Buenos Aires, Cancun, Caracas, Cobija, Cochabamba, Cordoba, Cuzco, Guayara, Havana, Iquique, La Paz, Lima, Magdalena, Manaus, Mexico City, Miami, Montevideo, Panama, Riberalta, Rio de Janeiro, Salta, San Joaquim, Santiago, Santa Cruz de la Sierra, Sao Paulo, Sucre, Tarija, Trinidad, Tucuman.

Fleet

1 Airbus A310-300
2 Boeing 767-300
8 Boeing 727-100/200
2 Boeing 737-300

1 Fokker F.27

Airbus A320-233 N941LF (Josef Krauthäuser/Miami)

LACSA

Apartado 1531, San Jose 1000, Costa Rica
Tel. 2316064, Fax. 2329185, E-mail:
prensa@taca.com, www.erupotaca.com

Three- / Two- letter code	IATA No.	Reg'n prefix	ICAO callsign
LRC / LR	133	TI	Lacsa

Pan American set up Lineas Aereas Costarricenses SA in December 1945 with the support of the government of Costa Rica and private interests. Some domestic routes were flown from June 1946, and its designation as national flag carrier in 1949 presaged the introduction of service to Miami from 1950. In use were Convair CV-440s, Curtiss C-46s and Douglas DC-6s. In 1952 TACA de Costa Rica, their only competitor in the country, was bought up. In 1967 LACSA acquired its first jet type, the BAC One-Eleven 400; these were replaced by Boeing 727s in late 1970. The airline's domestic network was transferred in September 1979 to subsidiary Servicios Aereos Nacionales (SANSA), which currently operates a fleet of Cessna 208B Caravans. A fleet acquisition programme for the 1990s saw the arrival of the first leased Airbus A320 at the end of 1990 and a total of six A320s are now in the fleet. TACA holds 10% of the shares, thus LACSA is a member of Grupo Taca. This became outwardly evident on the aircraft during 1999 when new colours were introduced in the group's style. Naturally there are co-operation agreements with the other members of the group, Aviateca, Nica, Taca and Avianca and additionally with the Summa alliance. The airline's base and major maintenance facility are at the airport at San Jose, where maintenance is also carried out.

Routes

Bogota, Caracas, El Salvador, Guatemala, Guayaquil, Havana, La Ceiba, Los Angeles, Managua, Mexico-City, Miami, Montreal, New Orleans, New York, Panama-City, Quito, San Jose, San Pedro Sula, San Salvador, Santiago, Tegucigalpa, Toronto.

Fleet

6 Airbus A320-200
2 Boeing 737-200Adv.

Boeing 737-2B1C C9-BAC (Josef Krauthäuser collection)

LAM

P.O.Box 2060, Maputo, People's Republic of Mozambique, Tel. 1- 465026, Fax. 1-422936, E-mail: linhadocliente@lam.co.mz, www.lam.co.mz

Three- / Two- letter code	IATA No.	Reg'n prefix	ICAO callsign
LAM / TM	068	C9	Mozambique

DETA – Direccao de Exploracao dos Transportes Aereos – was set up in August 1936 as a department of the railways and harbours and airways administration in Laurenco Marques (now Maputo), the capital at that time of Mozambique, which was under Portuguese administration. An airfield was set up on the outskirts of the city for the first time and DETA's first flight was on 22nd December 1937 to Johannesburg with a Junkers 52. De Havilland Moths and Dragonflies were also used, as were further Ju 52s, but these were replaced after the end of the Second World War by Douglas DC-3s. July 1962 saw the first use of Fokker F.27s and the arrival of two Boeing 737s in December 1969 heralded the beginning of the jet age for DETA. During the revolution in the 1970s, flights practically came to a standstill, but after Mozambique's independence in June 1975 and reorganisation, the national airline was reinvigorated and received a new name: LAM-Lineas Aereas de Mocambique. In 1993 a leased Boeing 767 came into use alongside Boeing 737-300s, and all displayed a new colour scheme. TAP-Air Portugal is an important partner for LAM and the Lisbon to Maputo route is jointly operated. The other routes to Europe were abandoned in 1995 on cost grounds. The latter part of the 1990s saw a slow improvement in business, partly due to the changes which have taken place in neighbouring South Africa. There are co-operation agreements (including technical and logistical assistance) in place with South African Airways and Air Zimbabwe. The long-term plan for privatisation of the airline has seen some progress with the issue of shares to employees, though the state still has an 80% holding.

Routes

Beira, Durban, Dzaoudi, Harare, Johannesburg, Lichinga, Maputo, Manzini, Nampula, Pemba, Quelimane,Tete, Vilanculos.

Fleet

4 Boeing 737-200Adv.
1 Boeing 767-200
2 Beech 200C
1 Beech 1900

Airbus A340-300 CC-CQA (Marcus Baltes / Frankfurt)

LAN CHILE

Estado 10, Piso 21, Casilla 147-D, Santiago de Chile, Chile, Tel. 2-6394411, Fax. 2-6383884
E-mail: info@lanchile.com, www.lanchile.com

Three- / Two- letter code	IATA No.	Reg'n prefix	ICAO callsign
LAN / LA	045	CC	Lan

LAN Chile, Linea Aerea Nacional de Chile, is one of the oldest airlines in South America. Set up on 5th March 1929 as Linea Aeropostal Santiago-Africa under the command of the Chilean Air Force, it initially provided mail flights. The airline was nationalised in 1932 when the present name was adopted. Lockheed Lodestars were used in 1948 to open a service to Buenos Aires, and then DC-6s to Miami from 1958. The SE 210 Caravelle was LAN's first jet aircraft, delivered from March 1964. In 1967 the Boeing 707 followed and was used to start a route to the Easter Islands and on to Tahiti. In 1974 the South Pole route was opened to Australia, LAN being the first airline to link the two continents. Three DC-10s were acquired in 1980 and used for services to the USA and Europe. Boeing 767s were added from 1986 and later replaced the DC-10s. In September 1989 LAN Chile was privatised and the Cueto family became the principal shareholder. Regional and national flights were further improved and extended from 1990 with leased BAe 146s. In 1996 the Cueto family also acquired the majority shareholding in Ladeco and there has been a sharing out of routes. Since 1998 there has been a close co-operation with American Airlines, which has led to LAN Chile becoming a member of the Oneworld alliance. The airline introduced a new corporate identity during 1999 and ordered 30 aircraft from Airbus to completely renew the short and medium haul fleet. Also during 2000 a subsidiary, LAN-Peru, was formed to allow expansion in the neighbouring country. At the end of 2001 Ladeco was closed and formed the basis for the new LAN Express. The first Airbus 340 was delivered late in 2002 for use on long-range routes to Europe and the USA and from mid-2001 the Airbus A320 started to replace the older Boeing 737-200s.

Routes

Antofagasto, Arica, Bogota, Buenos Aires, Cancun, Caracas, Cordoba, Frankfurt, Guayaquil, Havana, Houston, Iquique, La Paz, Lima, Los Angeles, Madrid, Mendoza, Mexico City, Miami, Montevideo, New York, New Orleans, Papeete, Paris, Puerto Montt, Punta Arenas, Punta Cana, Rio de Janeiro, Rio Gallegos, Salta, San Salvador, Santiago, Santa Cruz, Sao Paulo.

Fleet		Ordered
14 Airbus A320	12 Boeing 767-300	11 Airbus A319
4 Airbus A340-300		3 Airbus A320
8 Boeing 737-200		3 Airbus A340

Antonov An-24 RDPL-34005 (Romano Germann / Vientiane)

LAO AIRLINES

2, Rue Pang Kham, Vientiane, People's Republic of Laos Tel. 212057, Fax. 212056
www.mekongexpress.com/laos/

Three- / Two- letter code	IATA No.	Reg'n prefix	ICAO callsign
LAO / QV	627	RDPL	Lao

As a consequence of the Vietnam War, in which what was then the Kingdom of Laos was also involved, there were three airlines which were active in Laos in the early 1970s: Royal Air Lao, Lao Air Lines and Civil Aviation Co. The last of these was operated by the Pathet Lao movement, and this airline received help from North Vietnam. After the eventual takeover of power the remaining aircraft belonging to the airlines were brought together to form Lao Aviation, which was established on 19th January 1976 by the People's Republic of Laos and took over from Royal Air Lao as the national carrier. The fleet

consisted of Vickers Viscounts, Lockheed Hercules, Sikorsky S-58 helicopters, Douglas DC-3s and DC-4s. As there was no real need for domestic flights, and there was a lack of spare parts, these were sold or scrapped, and a new fleet built up favouring Soviet-built types. Flights between Vientiane and Bangkok and Hanoi were introduced and to Phnom-Penh, operated by Antonov An-24s. During the first part of the 1990s, Chinese-built aircraft came into favour, with the acquisition of small fleets of 17-seat Yunshuji Y12s and 52-seat Y7s. After the government allowed foreign investors to take a stake in 1995, an

ATR 72 and a Boeing 737 were acquired for international services, though the 737 was given up during the time of the Asian business downturn, the effects of which have constrained development and pushed back expansion plans.With help from Air France from 2002 there was further investment in aircraft and routes; the first A320 entered service in July 2003 and it is planned to add two more within four years. The Y 7s are being phased out. The Lao government is aiming to sell 60% of the loss-making airline, which changed name to Lao Airlines in mid-2003, to investors to allow modernisation and expansion.

Routes

Bangkok, Chiang Mai, Dien Bien Phu, Hanoi, Ho Chi Minh City, Houeisay, Kunming, Luang Namtha, Luang Prabang, Pakse, Phnom Penh, Siem Riap, Vientiane, Xieng Khouang, Yangon.

Fleet

1 Airbus A320	2 ATR 72-200
1 Antonov An-24	5 Yunshuji Y 12
1 Antonov An-74	2 Yunshuji Y 7

Boeing 737-6Z9 OE-LNL (Josef Krauthäuser / Munich)

LAUDA AIR

Postfach 56, 1300 Flughafen Wien-Schwechat,
Austria, Tel. 1-70000, Fax. 70074105,
www.laudaair.com

Three- / Two- letter code	IATA No.	Reg'n prefix	ICAO callsign
LDA / NG	231	OE	Laudaair

Lauda Air was established in April 1979 when Niki Lauda, the former Formula One motor racing champion, took over a licence to operate non-scheduled flights from Alpair. Operations started on 24th May 1979 with two Fokker F.27s. After a phase of restructuring and conversion into a joint stock company, the airline leased two Rombac One-Elevens from Tarom in 1985. Boeing 737-200s and -300s were added and later used to replace the One Elevens. At that time Lauda Air was flying primarily to Greece and to Spain. In 1986 the airline applied for a licence to operate scheduled flights to Australia, which it finally obtained in 1988, and in this year also it took on its first Boeing 767-300ER; a second followed in November 1989. Scheduled services to Sydney, Hong Kong and Singapore were expanded. The first European scheduled routes were begun in late 1990, from Vienna to London-Gatwick, and in the same year licences were obtained for international services which had previously been reserved for Austrian Airlines. In the Autumn, Lufthansa acquired a 25% share in Lauda Air via Condor, and this was increased to 39.7% in 1994. As a result, there was co-operation between the two airlines with Lauda flying to Miami and on some European routes on behalf of the German airline. In 1993 an Italian subsidiary, Lauda Air SpA was formed, operating from Milan. In March 1997 Austrian Airlines acquired half of Lufthansa's shares; Lauda Air has thus become integrated into the AUA Group and from the beginning of 2000, a member of the Star Alliance. The first Boeing 777 arrived in Autumn 1997; Boeing 737-600/700/800s have also been added. Frustrated founder Niki Lauda withdrew in November 2000; AUA took over the shares, and in time Lauda Air is set to become the charter arm of the group.

Routes

Agadir,Alicante, Bangkok, Cancun, Denpasar,Geneva, Graz, Innsbruck, Hamburg, Klagenfurt, Kuala Lumpur, Las Palmas, Linz, Lisbon, London, Madrid, Manchester, Melbourne, Miami, Milan, Munich,Nice, Phuket, Riga, Rome, Salzburg, Sofia, Split, Sydney, Tallinn, Tenerife, Timisoara, Verona, Vienna, Vilnius, Wroclaw, Yangon.

Fleet

3 Boeing 777-200ER	2 Boeing 737-600	3 Boeing 737-800
4 Boeing 767-300ER	2 Boeing 737-700	4 Canadair CRJ100
1 Boeing 737-300	4 Boeing 737-800	
1 Boeing 737-400		

De Havilland DHC-8-102 V2-LDP (Stefan Schlick / Barbados)

LIAT

P.O.Box 819 V.C.Bird Intl. Airport St.Johns, Antigua & Barbuda, Tel. 4620700, Fax. 4622682/4765, E-mail: connections@liatairlines.com, www.liatairline.com

Three- / Two- letter code	IATA No.	Reg'n prefix	ICAO callsign
LIA / LI	140	V2	Liat

Leeward Island Air Transport Services Ltd, LIAT for short, was set up in 1956 by two American businessmen, and started flights from Antigua to Montserrat with a Piper Apache. A year later LIAT became part of British West Indian Airways who took a 75% stake. Beech Bonanzas and de Havilland Herons were ideal aircraft for the short hops to other islands within the Virgin Islands. The first HS.748 was acquired on 1st February 1965. In November 1971 the British company Court Line Aviation took over the airline and introduced the BAC One-Eleven and Britten-Norman Islanders, but with the spectacular collapse of Court Line in August 1974, a rescue company was set up in November known as LIAT (1974) Ltd. Its participants were the governments of six Caribbean island states, with further states acquiring interests later on. The first de Havilland DHC-8s were bought in 1987, contributing to the expansion of the network. At the beginning of 1995 the last of the HS.748s left the fleet and in November 1995 the company was privatised, though some 30% remains under government control. During 1996/97 further Dash 8-300s were added and the Twin Otters retired. These Dash 8s were in turn replaced by larger and more powerful versions during 2002/3, with aircraft also taking on a new colour scheme. Another innovation was the setting up of the Caribsky alliance from 12th July 2002; LIAT and Air Caraibes are the founders, with Trans Island Airways and other smaller carriers joining later. The main operating and maintenance base is Antigua.

Routes

Anguilla, Antigua, Barbados, Barbuda, Beef Island, Caracas, Carriacou, Grenada, Dominica,Fort de France, Georgetown, Grenada, Martinique, Montserrat, Nevis, San Juan, St.Croix, St.Kitts, St.Lucia, St.Maarten, St.Thomas, St.Vincent, Tobago, Tortola, Trinidad and Union Island.

Fleet

5 De Havilland DHC-8-100
7 De Havilland DHC-8-300

Fokker F.28 Fellowship 4000 5A-DTH (Richard Schmaus / Malta)

LIBYAN ARAB AIRLINES

Haiti Street, P.O.Box 2555 Tripoli,
People's Republic of Libya
Tel. 21-3684829, Fax. 21-3614103

Three- / Two- letter code	IATA No.	Reg'n prefix	ICAO callsign
LAA / LN	148	5A	Libair

In September 1964 the merger of Libiavia and United Libyan Airlines resulted in the formation of the state-owned Kingdom of Libya Airlines. August 1965 saw the start of flights to Europe and North Africa as well as to the Middle East with two Caravelles. In 1969, Fokker F.27s were added to the fleet for domestic services and this year also saw political changes in the country following the September revolution, as a result of which the airline changed its name to Libyan Arab Airlines. Boeing 707s, 727s and later on, Airbus A310s were all added. However, political and trade sanctions meant that the western

built fleet could not be fully maintained and used and it was partly sold off. For this reason the fleet was expanded from 1990 onwards with Soviet-built types, specifically the Tupolev Tu-154M. An independent division, Libyan Arab Cargo, was active in the freight business with Ilyushin IL-76s and Lockheed L-100 Hercules. From 15th April 1992, United Nations imposed sanctions meant that Libyan Arab Airlines no longer had any rights to fly abroad, and was unable to buy aircraft spares; thus it was reduced to a modest domestic service only. To combat their inability to buy parts, several aircraft

were reduced to spares donors. However, sanctions were lifted in 1999 and several former supporters of sanctions were looking for good business in the re-equipment of the airline. Libyan Arab used wet-leased Airbus A320s as replacements for the Boeing 727s to restart several routes in Europe, also taking the opportunity to introduce a new colour scheme for their aircraft. Negotiations for fleet renewal have so far failed to come to fruition and so aircraft are being leased from sympathetic companies, notably Nouvelair International, who provide Algerian-registered Airbus A300s on wet-lease.

Routes

Al Bayda, Algiers, Amman, Benghazi, Casablanca, Damascus, Dubai, Frankfurt, Ghadames, Istanbul, Jeddah, Khartoum, London, Malta, Mersa Brega, Milan, Paris, Rome, Sebha, Tobruk, Tripoli.

Fleet

2 Airbus A300-600
2 Fokker F.27
5 Fokker F.28
3 Boeing 727-200

Saab 2000 LY-SBC (Josef Krauthäuser / Frankfurt)

LITHUANIAN AIRLINES

A.Gustacio 4, Vilnius Airport, 2038 Vilnius, Lithuania, Tel. 5-2301617, Fax. 5-2162159
E-mail: info@lal.lt, www.lal.lt

Three- / Two- letter code	IATA No.	Reg'n prefix	ICAO callsign
LIL / TE	874	LY	Lithuania

Lithuanian Airlines was the first airline to emerge in the Baltic republics which gained independence from the former Soviet Union; it started its own flights in 1991. The aircraft were taken over from the former local Aeroflot directorate. Lithuanian immediately turned its attentions towards western Europe and Scandinavia and started flights to these countries first. A leased Boeing 737 was first used to Copenhagen on 20th December 1991. The Hungarian airline Malev assisted in building up the airline and trained the pilots on 737s. In late 1992 Lithuanian was accepted into membership of IATA. With the delivery of further Boeing 737s, several Tupolev Tu-134s were sold and takers were also found for the Antonov 24s and Yakovlev 40s, thus rationalising the fleet. A new colour scheme was introduced in 1994. The final Tu-134s were taken out of service during 1997/98 when Saab 340s and 2000s were leased in. During 1999 the colour scheme was changed again. Late in 2001 Lithuanian Airlines took over Air Lithuania which operated Yak 40s and ATR 42s; the latter were kept for a while, but the Yaks sold. At the beginning of 2003 the government made a first tranche of shares available for sale, signalling the start of a privatisation process. In spring 2003, two Boeing 737-500s were taken on in place of 737-300s. There are co-operation agreements in place with Air Baltic, Finnair, LOT and Air Ukraine.

Routes

Amsterdam, Berlin, Brussels, Copenhagen, Frankfurt, Hamburg, Helsinki, Kiev, London, Madrid, Moscow, Paris, Prague, Stockholm, Tallinn, Vilnius, Warsaw.

Fleet

2 Boeing 737-500
2 Boeing 737-200
3 Saab 2000

Boeing 767-35D(ER) SP-LPA (Martin Kühn / Palma de Mallorca)

LOT – POLISH AIRLINES

Uliczka 17 Stycznia 39, 00906 Warsaw, Poland, Tel. 22-66066111, Fax. 22-8466409
E-mail: contact@lot.com, www.lot.com

Three- / Two- letter code	IATA No.	Reg'n prefix	ICAO callsign
LOT / LO	080	SP	LOT

Aero Lloyd Warsaw (subsequently Aerolot) and Aero T2 were united to form the future state airline Polskie Linie Lotnicze-LOT on 1st January 1929 by order of the government. Aero Lloyd had begun regular flights in September 1922 and started international services in 1925, while Aero had been formed in 1922. LOT Junkers F-13s flew to Vienna, Berlin. Moscow and Helsinki. A fresh start was made after the war with Soviet-built aircraft in 1946. While the Ilyushin IL-14 was part of the fleet in the 1950s, western aircraft such as the Convair 240 and Vickers Viscount were also used. Tupolev Tu-134 and Tu-154 jets were the mainstay of the short and medium-range fleet, while the Ilyushin 62M was used for long hauls. A return to western-originated equipment, to enable LOT to compete effectively with other western operators, was begun in 1989 with the acquisition of Boeing 767s. For regional routes ATR 72s were acquired from 1991, and Boeing 737s from 1993 to 1996 also signalling the departure of the last of the Russian-built jets. During 1997 LOT established Eurolot, a subsidiary for regional services with ATR 72s and 42s. LOT had become a joint stock company in December 1992 as a first step towards privatisation and in 1997 the SAir Group took over 37% of the shares, with the rest remaining with the Polish state. Employees have also been allowed to acquire shares and by 2003 this represented about 7% of the total. The SAir holding passed, after their collapse, to its successor company SAir Lines Europe BV. The first Embraer 145 jets arrived in 1999 for European services and these are to be joined by 170s from 2004. Since April 2002 LOT has been co-operating closely with Lufthansa and has joined in their frequent flyer programme. In 2003 LOT became a member of the Star Alliance.

Routes

Amsterdam, Athens, Bangkok, Barcelona, Berlin, Bratislava, Brussels, Budapest, Bydgoszcs, Chicago, Copenhagen, Damascus, Düsseldorf, Frankfurt, Geneva, Gdansk, Hamburg, Helsinki, Istanbul, Kaliningrad, Katowice, Kiev, Krakow, Larnaca, London, Lodz, Lyon, Madrid, Manchester, Milan, Minsk, Moscow, Munich, New York, Nice, Odessa, Oslo, Paris, Posen, Prague, Riga, Rome, Sofia, St.Petersburg, Stockholm, Szczecin, Tallinn, Tel Aviv, Vilnius, Warsaw, Vienna, Wroclaw, Zielona Gora, Zürich.

Fleet		Ordered
5 Boeing 767-200/300ER	14 Embraer ERJ-145	2 Boeing 737-800
10 Boeing 737-500		2 Embraer ERJ-145
9 Boeing 737-300/400		10 Embraer ERJ-170

Airbus A320-214 EC-IEP (Oliver Köstinger / Munich)

LTE – INTERNATIONAL AIRWAYS

Calle del Ter 27, 07009 Palma de Mallorca,
Spain, Tel. 475700, Fax. 478877
www.lte.es

Three- / Two- letter code	IATA No.	Reg'n prefix	ICAO callsign
LTE / XO	–	EC	Funjet

On 29th April 1987 LTE-Lineas Transportadores Espanola was set up in Palma de Mallorca. The instigators were the German charter airline LTU, who, through a Spanish/German company sought to even out the imbalance in Spanish tourism and the year-round disputes about allocations of traffic between Spanish and foreign airlines which went with it. It was also the intention to enter into other European charter operations and it was seen as important to be in a position to take advantage of an anticipated liberalisation of European markets. Two Boeing 757-200s were seconded from the LTU subsidiary LTS and used to begin operations from 1st November 1987. Initially the focus was on the Scandinavian markets, but from the time of German reunification there was also emphasis on airports in the former East Germany. When European moves for air transport liberalisation were put in place, the company was completely taken over by LTU, the aircraft were repainted in a typical LTU red and white scheme and the name was changed to LTE-International Airways. The SAir group took a shareholding in LTU, but with the Swiss parent's mounting financial problems, LTE was again put up for sale in 2001, amalgamation with LTU not seeming to be a viable solution. The company passed into the hands of a group of Spanish and Italian investors. The delivery of the first Airbus A320 in 2002 also marked the introduction of a new colour scheme. Two Airbus A321s were added in January and February of 2003.

Routes

Charter flights from many parts of Europe to destinations in the Mediterranean, especially Spain and the Canary Isles.

Fleet	Ordered
2 Airbus A320-200	3 Airbus A320-200
2 Airbus A321-200	
3 Boeing 757-200	

Airbus A330-322 D-AERQ (Josef Krauthäuser / Düsseldorf)

LTU INTERNATIONAL AIRWAYS

Halle 8, Flughafen, 40474 Düsseldorf, Germany, Tel. 0211-9418888, Fax. 0211-9418881 E-mail: internet@ltu.de, www.ltu.de

Three- / Two- letter code	IATA No.	Reg'n prefix	ICAO callsign
LTU / LT	266	D	LTU

LTU was formed as Lufttransport Union on 20th October 1965 by an Englishman Mr. Dromgoole, but the major partner, soon to become sole owner, was the Duisburg building contractor Conie; the present name was adopted in 1956. The first aircraft, Vickers Vikings were used until 1963. Also used were Bristol 170s, Fokker F.27s and DC-4s, until Caravelles began jet service in 1965. From 1969 LTU was one of the first charter airlines to use solely jets, with F.28 Fellowships joining the Caravelles from 1968. In 1973 came the first widebodies, Lockheed TriStars, and this type allowed LTU to make the

breakthrough to become Germany's largest charter airline. Eleven TriStars were used and enabled the airline to serve faraway holiday destinations. In 1989 LTU applied for a licence to operate as a scheduled carrier, and permission was granted for some routes from Autumn 1990 onwards. The delivery of the first MD-11 late in 1991 set a fleet renewal in motion, which culminated in 1996 with the delivery of A330s, the last TriStar leaving the fleet in May 1996. In Spring 1996 LTU took over Rheinland Air Service and LTU-Süd was integrated into the parent company. The airline was not performing well

financially and a restructuring announced in July 1997 meant that some long-haul routes were dropped and all the MD-11s taken out of service. The majority of the shares were acquired by the SAir Group which then again reorganised the whole LTU group, but in time brought it to the edge of financial collapse. New owners and management, including a local government interest, ensured survival. Subsidiary LTE was sold off in 2001, the fleet was harmonised and is to be all-Airbus after the last of the Boeing 757s are replaced by the Airbus A321s in course of delivery.

Routes

Agadir, Alicante, Almeria, Antalya, Araxos, Arrecife, Athens, Bangkok, Berlin, Bodrum, Brindisi, Bourgas, Cagliari, Cancun, Capetown, Catania, Chongqing, Cologne/Bonn, Colombo, Corfu, Dalaman, Djerba, Düsseldorf, Egilsstadir, Faro, Fort Myers, Frankfurt, Fuerteventura, Funchal, Genoa, Hamburg, Hanover, Heraklion, Holguin, Hurghada, Ibiza, Istanbul, Izmir, Jerez de la Frontera, Karpathos, Kavalla, Kos, Larnaca, Las Palmas, Leipzig, Lesbos, Los Angeles, Mahon, Malaga, Male, Malta, Miami, Mombasa, Monastir, Munich, Naples, Olbia, Orlando, Palma de Mallorca, Phuket, Puerto Plata, Punta Cana, Reykjavik, Rhodes, Rimini, Salzburg, Samos, Seville, St. Cruz, Stuttgart, Tabarka, Tenerife, Thessaloniki, Toronto, Varadero, Varna, Windhoek, Zakynthos.

Fleet		Ordered
12 Airbus A320-200	4 Boeing 757-200	2 Airbus A321
4 Airbus A321-200		2 Airbus A330
13 Airbus A330-200/300		

Airbus A319-114 D-AILU (Josef Krauthäuser / Munich)

LUFTHANSA

von Gablenz-Str 2-6, 50679 Cologne, Germany, Tel. 0221-826-0, Fax. 0221-8263818, www.lufthansa.com

Three- / Two- letter code	IATA No.	Reg'n prefix	ICAO callsign
DLH / LH	220	D	Lufthansa

The 'old' Lufthansa, founded in 1926, was liquidated by the victorious powers in the Second World War. In early 1950 the German government wished to reassert its air sovereignty by having an independent national airline. To this end Luftag was set up in 1953, and renamed after the old Lufthansa in 1954. The first flight with a Convair 340 was on 1st April 1955, and the first international flight was to New York on 8th June 1955 with a Lockheed Constellation. From 1960 Lufthansa began using the Boeing 707 on transatlantic routes; Boeing 720s were acquired for services to Africa and the Middle East. Lufthansa was the first customer outside the USA for the Boeing 727

for medium-distance routes from April 1964, and was also the first to order the 737, delivered from 1967. The era of the widebody arrived with the Boeing 747 in March 1970, with DC-10s and Airbus A300s following during the mid-1970s. Lufthansa is well known for its ongoing fleet renewal policy. In 1988 the Boeing 747-400 and the Airbus A320 were introduced, in 1993 the Airbus A340, 1994 the A321 (as launch customer) and in 1996 the smaller Airbus A319. During 1997 Lufthansa was fully privatised, with a wide distribution of share ownership. In the same year, in co-operation with United, SAS, Air Canada and Thai International Lufthansa founded the Star Alliance,

and in addition Lufthansa has direct shareholdings in Air Dolomiti, Eurowings, Lufthansa Cargo, Lufthansa Cityline, Luxair, SAS and Thomas Cook Airlines. There are franchise arrangements with other airlines who fly as 'Team Lufthansa' on behalf of Lufthansa on German internal and European routes: Air Littoral, Augsburg Airways, Cimber Air, and Contact Air. Lufthansa suffered large losses following the 11th September events and there is now strong competition in Germany and Europe from low-cost operators, which has resulted in Lufthansa cutting some aircraft and routes. Airbus A380s are on order for delivery from September 2007.

Routes

The Lufthansa network includes Europe, North and South America, Asia and Africa. Around 150 destinations in 100 countries are served directly.

Fleet

20 Airbus A319
36 Airbus A320-200
26 Airbus A321-100
6 Airbus A310-300
15 Airbus A300-600
5 Airbus A330-200
36 Airbus A340-200/300

39 Boeing 737-300
30 Boeing 737-500
4 Boeing 747-200
13 Boeing 747-400
2 Boeing 767-300

Ordered

10 Airbus A340
15 Airbus A380

Boeing 747-230B(SF) D-ABYZ (Oliver Köstinger / Sharjah)

LUFTHANSA CARGO

Flughafen, Bereich West, 60546 Frankfurt,
Germany, Tel. 01802020020, Fax. 01802747747
E-mail: ihcargo@dhl.de, www.lhcargo.com

Three- / Two- letter code	IATA No.	Reg'n prefix	ICAO callsign
GEC / LH	020	D	Lufthansa Cargo

Lufthansa Cargo Aktiengesellschaft was established on 1st January 1995 as a 100% subsidiary of Lufthansa, to take over its worldwide freight activities. Its predecessor was Lufthansa Cargo Airlines, one of the many restructurings with Lufthansa, and German Cargo Services GmbH. The latter owed its existence to the withdrawal in 1977 of an anachronistic statute which had until then forbidden full-freight charter in the Federal Republic. The driving force behind this change was Lufthansa, who were losing tons of freight to neighbouring countries. Thus on 10th March 1977 German Cargo Services GmbH was

founded in Frankfurt, making its first flight on 15th April 1975 with a Boeing 707 to Hong Kong. By mid-1979 four Boeing 707s were in use, such was the growth of the freight business. With the introduction of the Douglas DC-8, GCS's structure was altered, having until then been reliant on Lufthansa for the provision of crews and maintenance. It now employed its own pilots and had its own maintenance facility. German Cargo Services had four DC-8-73s in service, transporting everything which could travel by air and specialising particularly in services to Africa, South America and the Far East, as well as worldwide charters.

As a part of a reorganisation in 1994/95, the airline became Lufthansa Cargo. The first of the dedicated MD-11F freighters was delivered in mid 1998, and this type along with the Boeing 747-200F now forms the whole of the fleet.From March 2002 Lufthansa Cargo, SAS Cargo and Singapore Airlines Cargo formed the WOW-alliance, joined from April 2003 by JAL Cargo.

Routes

Worldwide freight flights, both scheduled and charters.

Fleet

 8 Boeing 747-200F
14 McDonnell Douglas MD-11F

Canadair CRJ700ER D-ACPI (Marcus Baltes / Frankfurt)

LUFTHANSA CITYLINE

Heinrich Steinmann Str. 51147 Cologne, Germany
Tel. 02203-5960, Fax. 02203-596801
E-mail: lh-cityline@dlh.de, www.lh-cityline.com

Three- / Two- letter code	IATA No.	Reg'n prefix	ICAO callsign
CLH / CL	683	D	Hansaline

DLT-Deutsche Luftverkehrs-Company mbH was set up in 1974 as a successor to OLT-Ostfriesische Lufttransport GmbH. A German internal network was operated on behalf of Lufthansa using Shorts 330s, DHC-6 Twin Otters and Hawker Siddeley HS.748s. When the airline was short of its own aircraft, WDL with F.27s and other companies with the Fairchild Metro filled the breach. In 1987 Embraer EMB-120s were introduced, but soon proved to be too small, as DLT expanded. Fokker 50s were ordered after Lufthansa took a financial interest in DLT and the available capital was increased. By 1990 over a million passengers a year were being carried, and the rate was climbing. In March came the change of name to Lufthansa Cityline and, following a reorganisation, another swift change of fleet to jet types. 50-seater Canadair Regional Jets were ordered, with the first being delivered in Autumn 1992. In 1994 Cityline received its first Avro RJ 85. Thus the airline was in a position to take over more routes from Lufthansa, which were not profitable for even their smallest jets. Lufthansa Cityline is today 100% owned by Lufthansa and participates in all marketing, ticketing and promotional programmes such as Miles & More. For the first time, on 1st July 2001, Cityline flew the new Canadair CRJ700 and has acquired more of these aircraft in place of the abandoned Dornier 728 regional jet, to which the airline had committed heavily as launch customer. Cityline's main base is at the Cologne/Bonn airport, where it also has maintenance and repair facilities.

Routes

Lufthansa Cityline flies to about 80 destinations in Germany and Europe on behalf of Lufthansa and using LH flight numbers.

Fleet	Ordered
18 Avro RJ85	10 Canadair CRJ700
34 Canadair CRJ100ER	
11 Canadair CRJ200	
20 Canadair CRJ700	

Boeing 737-5C9 LX-LGP (Dominik Stapf / Frankfurt))

LUXAIR

Bp 2203, 2987 Luxembourg Airport, Grand Duchy of Luxembourg, Tel. 4-7984281, Fax. 4-7984289 E-mail:info@luxair. www.luxair.lu

Three- / Two- letter code	IATA No.	Reg'n prefix	ICAO callsign
LGL / LG	149	LX	Luxair

The Société Luxembourgeoise de Navigation Aérienne, or Luxair as it is usually known, was set up in 1961 as Luxembourg Airlines with the support of the government, of banks and Radio Luxembourg, and with technical assistance provided by KLM. Regular services began on 2nd April 1962 with a Fokker F.27 serving Amsterdam, Frankfurt and Paris. Luxair started using Vickers Viscounts in 1966 and SE 210 Caravelles in March 1970. These were replaced in 1977 by Boeing 737s. Leased Boeing 707s were added to the fleet in 1980 for long-haul services. A single Airbus A300B4 was also used, but only for a short time as it proved too large for the airline's needs, and was exchanged for a Boeing 747SP which was then used on long-distance services, though these were abandoned from 1995. A fleet replacement programme began in 1989 with the delivery of the first Fokker 50s. Luxair Commuter is a subsidiary company, which served short-range destinations with Embraer 120s, but at the end of the 1990s this was integrated into Luxair. Embraer ERJ-145s were introduced from 1998 as a long-term replacement for the Fokker 50. Luxair has a 24.5% holding in Cargolux, while Lufthansa holds 13% of Luxair. There is co-operation with both Lufthansa and Air France.Orders were placed early in 2003 for new Boeing 737-700s for delivery in 2004. As well as its scheduled services, Luxair carries out a large number of charters.

Routes

Agadir, Alicante, Amsterdam, Arrecife, Athens, Barcelona, Berlin, Catania, Copenhagen, Djerba, Dublin, Faro, Florence, Frankfurt, Fuerteventura, Funchal, Geneva, Hamburg, Ibiza, Innsbruck, Las Palmas, Lisbon, London, Luxembourg, Luxor, Madrid, Malaga, Malta, Manchester, Marseilles, Metz, Milan, Monastir, Montpellier,Munich, Nice, Palma de Mallorca, Paris, Porto, Rome, Saarbrücken, Sharm el Sheik, Stockholm, Tenerife, Turin, Vienna.

Fleet		Ordered
2 Boeing 737-400	3 Fokker 50	2 Boeing 737-700
3 Boeing 737-500		
8 Embraer ERJ-145		

Canadair CRJ100 OY-MBO (Josef Krauthäuser collection / Frankfurt)

MAERSK AIR

Copenhagen Airport South, 2791 Dragoer
Denmark, Tel. 32-314444, Fax. 32-314490
E-mail: info@maersk-air.dk, www.maersk-air.com

Three- / Two- letter code	IATA No.	Reg'n prefix	ICAO callsign
DAN / DM	349	OY	Maerskair

The A.P. Moeller shipping company, owners of the Maersk shipping line, set up Maersk Air as a subsidiary in February 1969, intending it to operate purely as a charter business. Operations began in December 1969 with a Fokker F.27 and an HS.125. The young airline's urge to expand resulted in it taking over Falckair, a domestic airline, along with its routes to Odense and Aarhus in 1970. Air Business, another regional airline, was acquired in May 1983; it had been operating between Esbjerg and Stavanger. The route from Billund to Sonthad was opened with de Havilland DHC-7s and further

scheduled services connected Copenhagen with Billund and Ronne. As well as scheduled and charter flights, Maersk was doing increasing business in aircraft leasing. Thus several Boeing 737s were leased long-term to Deutsche BA. In July 1993 Maersk Air UK was founded to take over the activities of Birmingham European Airways; this became a British Airways franchise operation using principally Boeing 737s and Canadair Regional Jets supplied by the parent, but was sold off to its UK management in mid-2003 and renamed as Duo Airways. A further subsidiary is Star Air, which operates Fokker F.27s on regional

routes, and Boeing 727 and 757 freighters in Europe in UPS colours on behalf of the US package giant. Additionally, Maersk has close ties with Estonian, in which it has a 49% holding. Maersk was one of the first airlines to place an order for the new Boeing 737-700, with the first arriving in March 1998, allowing older 737-300s to be phased out. Canadair Regional Jets were added from May 2000.

Routes

Aalborg, Amsterdam, Athens, Billund, Brussels, Copenhagen, Dublin, Esbjerg, Faroe Islands, Frankfurt, Kristiansand, Lisbon, London, Nice, Odense, Paris, Ronne, Stockholm, Venice, Vojens. Seasonal charters to the Mediterranean, or to the Alpine winter resorts.

Fleet

11 Boeing 737-500
10 Boeing 737-700
 3 Canadair CRJ200

Airbus A310-304 EP-MHH (Bastian Hilker, Düsseldorf)

MAHAN AIR

Mahan Tower, 21 Azadeghan St, M.A. JenaH Express Way, Teheran, Tel. 9821-4070507-9, Fax. 9821-4070404
E-mail: fly@mahanair.ir, www.mahanairlines.com

Three- / Two- letter code	IATA No.	Reg'n prefix	ICAO callsign
IRM / W5	537	EP	Mahan Air

The Mola-Al-Movahedin organisation, already active in hotel management, set up its own charter airline, Mahan Air, in 1991. The headquarters were at Kirman, an industrial metropolis about 100 km south east of the Iranian capital. Because of business boycotts imposed by the USA, the airline was forced to turn initially to Russian equipment and used the Tupolev Tu-154 to begin operations. In spring 1992 many charter flights were undertaken to Saudi Arabia for the annual pilgrimages, but domestic services were also begun, especially to the capital Teheran,

initially as charters, but swiftly developed into scheduled services. Damascus in Syria was the first destination in an international network, which was quickly built up with new destinations in the Gulf area. More Tu-154s were acquired from the former Soviet Union, as were some Ilyushin 76s for freight work. At the end of the 1990s the administration and operations were moved to Teheran. During 1999 it became possible to acquire two Airbus A300s and these were used on international routes, doubling the available capacity. In 2002 the airline's own maintenance and

overhaul base, with associated training centre, was opened at Kirman; there is co-operation with Lufthansa and SOGERMA in maintenance activities. During 2002 Mahan Air also received Airbus A310s, and inaugurated service to Düsseldorf, its first destination in western Europe.

Routes

Antalya, Bahrain, Bandar Abbas, Bangkok, Colombo, Damascus, Delhi, Dubai, Düsseldorf, Isfahan, Jeddah, Kabul, Kirman, Kish, Male, Mashad, Muscat, Qeshm, Seoul, Sharjah, Shiraz, Teheran, Zahedan.

Fleet	Ordered
3 Airbus A300B4	2 Airbus A310
3 Airbus A310	
2 Tupolev Tu-154	

Boeing 777-2H6(ER) 9M –MRE (Gottfried Auer / Zürich)

MALAYSIA AIRLINES

Jalan Sultan Ismail Bangunan MAS, 50250 Kuala Lumpur Malaysia, Tel. 3-21610555, Fax. 3-21613472, E-mail: corpcomm@mas.com.my, www.malaysia-airlines.com.my

Three- / Two- letter code	IATA No.	Reg'n prefix	ICAO callsign
MAS / MH	232	9M	Malaysian

Malaysian Airline System Berhad came into existence on 3rd April 1971 after the former MSA (Malaysia-Singapore Airlines) was split up. Using nine Fokker F.27s and three Britten-Norman Islanders, Malaysian domestic services were operated. From 1974 London was served on a weekly basis with a Boeing 707, with further services to Amsterdam, Zürich and Frankfurt following shortly afterwards. In 1976 the first DC-10-30 was delivered and in1982 two Boeing 747-200s were added; these were used to add service to destinations in the USA from 1995. On 15th October 1987

MAS introduced a new colour scheme and 'System' was dropped from the name, following the sale by the government of its shares. MAS continued to expand worldwide and invested heavily in new technology and aircraft. Airbus A330s began arriving in 1994 as DC-10 replacements, with MD-11s following in 1994 and 1995. The airline's own freight division, MAS Cargo, operates dedicated MD-11 and 747-200F freighters. Regional destinations are served with Fokker 50s and DHC-6 Twin Otters. In 1997 the company took delivery of its first Boeing 777, replacing older Boeing

747-100s and DC-10s on the long-range services. The Asian business crisis of the late 1990s affected Malaysia Airlines; as with other companies in the area, routes were suspended and aircraft either sold or returned to their lessors. However, by the beginning of 2000, things had stabilised and Malaysian was set to continue its expansion. The last MD-11 left the fleet at the end of 2001: A330s and Boeing 777s now feature in the long-haul fleet.

Routes

Some 35 domestic destinations and services to Australia, Japan, Korea, Hong Kong, Indonesia, the Philippines, Thailand, Taiwan and the People's Republic of China. There are also services to the Middle East, South Africa, USA and Europe, to give a total of more than 110destinations worldwide.

Fleet		Ordered
12 Airbus A330-300	17 Boeing 747-400	3 Boeing 747-400
39 Boeing 737-400	15 Boeing 777-200ER	9 Boeing 777-200
1 Boeing 737-700	6 De Havilland DHC-6	
5 Boeing 747-200F	10 Fokker 50	

Boeing 737-4Q8 HA-LEZ (Gerhard Schütz / Corfu)

MALEV – HUNGARIAN AIRLINES

V, Roosevelt ter 2, 1051 Budapest, Hungary
Tel. 1-2353535, Fax. 1-2662759
www.malev.hu

Three- / Two- letter code	IATA No.	Reg'n prefix	ICAO callsign
MAH / MA	182	HA	Malev

Malev was originally established on 26th April 1946 as a joint Hungarian/Soviet undertaking with the title Maszovlet, with a fleet of eleven Lisunov Li-2s and six Polikarpov Po-2s. Flight operations began on 15th October 1946 on domestic routes and international flights began in the next year. On 25th November 1954 the Hungarian government took complete control and the airline adopted the name Magyar Legiközlekedesi Vollat (MALEV). When Ilyushin IL-18s were delivered in May 1960, flights started to European destinations such as Amsterdam, Vienna and Moscow. As Hungary's road system

developed, the need for domestic services declined and the last such flights operated in 1969. The Tupolev Tu-134 was the first jet aircraft in 1968, followed by the Tu-154 in 1973. Replacement of Soviet-built aircraft with Boeing 737s started in 1989 with Malev being one of the first eastern bloc countries to obtain western equipment. Likewise Boeing was the source for new long-range equipment, with 767s arriving from the end of 1992. The airline became a public limited company from 30th June 1992. Alitalia acquired 30% of the capital and started to work closely with Malev. During 1995 Malev received its first

Fokker 70s for shorter European routes and several of the older Tupolevs were sold off; a few were retained for charter work for a while. Ailing Alitalia was forced to sell its shares in 1998 and they were acquired by a consortium of Hungarian banks. There are co-operation and/or codeshare agreements with Air France, British Airways, CSA, Delta Air Lines, Moldavian and Tarom. Malev's base is at Budapest-Ferihegy airport, where there are major maintenance facilities for the growing fleet, which now centres around the most modern versions of the Boeing 737.

Routes

Amsterdam, Athens, Berlin, Beirut, Bologna, Brussels, Budapest, Bucharest, Cairo, Damascus, Debrecen, Dublin, Düsseldorf, Frankfurt, Geneva, Hamburg, Helsinki, Istanbul, Kiev, Larnaca, London, Madrid, Milan, Moscow, Munich, Odessa, Oslo, Paris, Prague, Prestina, Rome, Sarajevo, Skopje, Sofia, Split, St.Petersburg, Stockholm, Stuttgart, Tel Aviv, Thessaloniki, Tirana, Toronto, Tripoli, Vienna, Warsaw, Zagreb, Zürich.

Fleet		Ordered
7 Boeing 737-300	2 Boeing 737-800	6 Boeing 737-600
6 Boeing 737-400	2 Boeing 767-200ER	5 Boeing 737-700
2 Boeing 737-500	2 Canadair CRJ200	4 Boeing 737-800
2 Boeing 737-700	6 Fokker 70	

Fokker 100 B-12291 (Author's collection)

MANDARIN AIRLINES

134 Minsheng East Road, Sector 3, Taipei 105
Republic of China, Tel. 2-27171188,
Fax. 2-27170716, www.mandarinair.com

Three- / Two- letter code	IATA No.	Reg'n prefix	ICAO callsign
MDA / AE	803	B	Mandarin Air

In June 1991 the Kuos Development Corporation and China Airlines founded a joint venture airline, Mandarin Airlines, with China Airlines taking over complete ownership late in 1992. Mandarin used Boeing 747SPs, Boeing 747-400s and MD-11s to fly to Canada, Europe and Australia. A private airline called Yun Shin Airlines was established in May 1966, which later changed name to Formosa Airlines and operated domestic services; Dornier 228s, Fokker 50s and Saab SF 340s were used to destinations which were not suited to jet service. China Airlines had a 42% holding, later increased to 100%, in this company which was based at Taipei's Sung Shan city airport. In August 1999, Formosa Airlines and Mandarin Airlines were formally merged under the Mandarin Airlines identity. As part of this realignment, all the international long-range routes were taken over by China Airlines, leaving all the domestic services of the China Airlines group to be conducted by Mandarin Airlines; this reorganisation was completed by the end of 2001. As well as domestic destinations, Mandarin now serves some points in neighbouring countries, but it no longer needs the larger aircraft, which have left the fleet. The Boeing 737-800 was introduced from January 2001.

Routes

Cebu, Chi Mei, Chiang Mai, Denpasar, Green Island, Hualien, Kaohsiung, Makung, Macau, Phnom Penh, Orchid Island, Taichung, Taipei, Taitung, Yangon.

Fleet

3 Boeing 737-800
4 Dornier 228-200
7 Fokker 50
2 Fokker 100

Airbus A320-232 PH-MPE (Jan-Alexander Lück / Amsterdam)

MARTINAIR

Postbus 7507,1118 ZG Schiphol, Netherlands
Tel. 20-6011222, Fax. 20-6011303, E-mail:
sales@martinair.com, www.martinair.com

Three- / Two- letter code	IATA No.	Reg'n prefix	ICAO callsign
MPH / MP	129	PH	Martinair

Martin Air Holland, or to be precise Martin's Luchtvervoer Maatschappij NV, was founded on 24th May 1958 by Martin Schröder with a single Douglas DC-3. The airline was first called Martin's Air Charter until the present name was introduced in April 1968. Sightseeing and air taxi flights were provided. A smaller airline, Fairways Rotterdam, was taken over in January 1964. KLM acquired a 25% stake in the airline and further shares were sold to a shipping company, NedLloyd Reederei. Martinair acquired DC-7s, Lockheed Electras and DC-8s over time from KLM and used these types to go into the charter business in a big way. The first widebody to join the fleet was the DC-10 in 1973, and this was followed by Airbus A310s in 1984 and the first Boeing 747, a combi version, in 1988. Further fleet renewal continued and the Boeing 767 replaced the Airbuses, and the first MD-11 convertible freighter arrived at the end of 1994; this type was to replace the DC-10s. The word 'Holland' was dropped from the title in 1995. Using a modern fleet, Martinair continues to expand, and yet continues to undertake its traditional activities of aerial photography, survey, aerial advertising and air taxi work with a fleet of light aircraft. A Fokker 70 is also maintained and flown on behalf of the Dutch royal family. On 1st July 1998 KLM acquired NedLloyd's shares in Martinair and is thus now the sole owner, though the airline continues to operate independently. In late 1999 Air Holland's Boeing 757s were taken over. The latest aircraft in the fleet is the Airbus A320-200, the first of which was delivered to Amsterdam in April 2003 as a Boeing 757 replacement. Martinair's base and maintenance facility is at Amsterdam's Schiphol airport.

Routes

Aruba, Amsterdam, Calgary, Cancun, Caribbean, Edmonton, Havana, Holguin, Miami, Montego Bay, Orlando, Puerto Plata, Punta Cana, San Jose, Santo Domingo, Toronto, Vancouver, Varadero on a scheduled basis, plus charters to holiday destinations in the Mediterranean, USA, Canada, South-East Asia and freight flights worldwide.

Fleet		Ordered
2 Airbus A320-200	6 McDonnell Douglas MD-11	1 Airbus A320-200
4 Boeing 747-200		
5 Boeing 767-300ER		

Boeing 737-3H9 Z3-ARF (Jannis Malzahn / Hamburg)

MAT – MACEDONIAN AIRLINES

Vasil Glavinov 3, 9100 Skopje, Macedonia
Tel. 389-2292333, Fax. 389-2229576, E-mail:
systems@mat.com.mk, www.mat.com.mk

Three- / Two- letter code	IATA No.	Reg'n prefix	ICAO callsign
MAK / IN	367	Z3	Makavio

With the break-up of the former Yugoslavia into 'new' countries around its constituent parts, Macedonia came into being in 1991 with Skopje as its capital and major airport. The town of Ohrid also had its own airport. At the time of the formation of Macedonia, several airlines became active, with varying lifespans, and mostly operating old, Russian-designed types. As Greece was operating a blockade against inland Macedonia over the similarity of name with its own province of Macedonia, the port of Thessalonika in northern Greece was also closed for goods bound for Macedonia and the use of aircraft to transport essential goods was of heightened importance. On 16th January 1994 MAT-Makavio was founded; a company with shares was chosen, in order to be able to take in investment capital. Operations began on 23rd September 1994 using a Boeing 737-200, with the first flight from Skopje to Zürich. Further routes to western Europe followed. In 1997 a more modern Boeing 737-300 was acquired, and this also marked the introduction of the current colour scheme and the 'internationalisation' of the name, as in the meantime MAT had been designated as the national carrier. In 1999 a further Boeing 737-300 was added, and a DC-9 augmented this in 2002. MAT conducts charter flights, particularly at holiday times.

Routes

Amsterdam, Berlin, Düsseldorf, Frankfurt, Hamburg, Ohrid, Rome, Skopje, Stuttgart, Vienna, Zürich.

Fleet

2 Boeing 737-300
1 Douglas DC-9-32

Foto:Airbus A320 -232 F-OHLO (Author's collection)

MEA – MIDDLE EAST AIRLINES

P.O.Box 206, Beirut, Lebanon
Tel. 1-629250, Fax. 629260
E-mail: mea@mea.com.lb, www.mea.com.lb

Three- / Two- letter code	IATA No.	Reg'n prefix	ICAO callsign
MEA / ME	076	OD	Cedar Jet

MEA, whose full title is Middle East Airline SA, was founded in May 1945 as a private company by a group of Lebanese businessmen and started a service with a de Havilland Dragon Rapide between Beirut and Nicosia on 20th November and to Baghdad on 15th February 1946. In 1949 Pan American acquired a stake, replacing the Rapide with a DC-3 in order to provide more cargo capacity. Pan American withdrew in 1955, its stake being acquired by BOAC. Scheduled services started on 2nd October 1955 to London using Vickers Viscounts; Karachi and Bombay followed. The first jet type was the de Havilland Comet 4B, used on the London route from

6th January 1961. Further expansion came in March 1963 when joint development was agreed with Air Liban, which was fully merged into MEA along with its DC-6s and SE 210 Caravelles in November 1965. Air France became a shareholder. Boeing 707s came into service in 1968 and in 1969 Lebanese International Airways (LIA) together with its fleet, routes and staff was taken over. This merger was government-inspired as several of LIA's and MEA's aircraft had been destroyed by an Israeli attack on Beirut airport in 1968. Operations were badly affected by the civil war which went on for more than ten years, but MEA was the only airline

to maintain links with the outside world despite every adversity. Two leased A310s replaced the Boeing 707s. To revive the fortunes of the airline, Air France and an investment company again took shares, and a fresh start was made, with new colours introduced at the beginning of 1997. The fleet and Beirut airport's infrastructure were renewed. Airbus A320s and A321s were delivered, the three Boeing 747s were sold and more A310s ordered. The introduction of the A330-200 in May 2003 raises MEA's standards. The airline has its own frequent flier programme and is in close co-operation with Air France.

Routes

Abidjan, Abu Dhabi, Accra, Amman, Athens, Beirut, Cairo, Colombo, Dammam, Dubai, Frankfurt, Geneva, Istanbul, Jeddah, Kano, Kuwait, Lagos, Larnaca, London, Nice, Paris, Riyadh, Rome, Teheran.

Fleet

3 Airbus A310-300
1 Airbus A320-200
6 Airbus A321-200
3 Airbus A330-200

BAe 146-200 I-FLRE (Daniel Klein / Amsterdam)

MERIDIANA

Aeroporto Costa Smeralda, 07026 Olbia, Italy,
Tel. 0789-52600, Fax. 0789-52802,
www.meridiana.it

Three- / Two- letter code	IATA No.	Reg'n prefix	ICAO callsign
ISS / IG	191	I	Merair

Meridiana was the result of the strategic merger of the Italian airline Alisarda and the Spanish operator Universair in 1991. Until the Spanish airline Meridiana became bankrupt in late 1992, the two partners had co-ordinated their operations while remaining relatively independent. Alisarda was founded on 24th March 1963 in Olbia as an air taxi and general charter company using two Beech C-45s and began operations in that same year. Scheduled passenger services were added from 1st June 1966, initially with Nord 262s, later replaced by Fokker Friendships. Later, services took place to destinations in France, Switzerland and within Italy using DC-9s from 1975. Other destinations followed seasonally, such as Frankfurt or Munich, initially as charters but later as scheduled services. Two MD-82s were acquired in 1984 and the fleet of this type has gradually increased. A third-level operator, Avianova was established in 1986, but sold to the Alitalia group in 1991. On 1st September 1991 Alisarda changed its name to Meridiana and by 1992 it had become the largest privately-owned airline in Italy. Four BAe 146s were added in 1994. The main base is at Olbia and Florence is also being built up as a major hub in the network. Meridiana was expanding strongly, with new routes and aircraft being added each year, but the aviation industry crisis did not leave the airline unscathed; losses were made in 2001 and 2002, with routes being dropped and aircraft disposed of. As well as scheduled services, charters are also flown on behalf of various tour operators, and there is close co-operation with Alitalia.

Routes

Amsterdam, Barcelona, Bologna, Cagliari, Catania, Florence, Frankfurt, Geneva, Genoa, London, Milan, Munich, Naples, Nice, Olbia, Palermo, Paris, Pisa, Rome, Turin, Verona, Zürich.

Fleet

4 BAe 146-200
8 McDonnell Douglas MD-83
9 McDonnell Douglas MD-82

Fokker F.27 Friendship 500 PK-MFF (Hans Willi Mertens / Djakarta)

MERPATI

Jolan Angkasa 2, Kotak pos 323, Jakarta 10720
Indonesia, Tel. 21-4243608, Fax. 21-6540620
www.merpati.co.id

Three- / Two- letter code	IATA No.	Reg'n prefix	ICAO callsign
MNA / MZ	621	PK	Merpati

The Indonesian government founded Merpati Nusantara Airlines on 6th September 1962 to take over the network of internal services developed by the Indonesian Air Force. Initial operations started on 11th September 1962 connecting Jakarta with domestic points. In 1964, Merpati took over the routes previously operated by KLM subsidiary de Kroonduif, which had been flown by Garuda since 1962. This predecessor had been particularly active in West Guinea. Merpati has used a variety of aircraft types: DC-3, HS-748, Vickers Viscount, Vickers Vanguard, NAMC YS-11, Dornier 28, and Pilatus Porter. Numerous CASA aircraft manufactured in Indonesia under licence were also used, such as IPTN 235s, replacing older equipment. On 28th October 1978 the airline was taken over by Garuda, though Merpati continues to operate independently as a part of the group. When the first DC-9s arrived in Autumn 1990, new colours were introduced on the aircraft. The first Fokker 100 was introduced in 1993 and Boeing 737-200s taken on in 1994 as DC-9 replacements. Merpati has the densest route network in Indonesia and was on an expansion course until the 1998 political and economic crisis in the country. The general Asian crisis has also affected Indonesia especially badly, and there have been added problems with ethnic disputes and the plunge in the value of the currency, which is especially significant when leasing costs are to be paid in US dollars. Thus Merpati has been forced to return aircraft and drop routes. In 1999 there was discussion as to whether Garuda and Merpati should merge, but these ideas did not come to fruition and route and fleet cuts ensued until 2003; three quarters of the F.28s were sold. However, new Boeing 737-400s came into the fleet around the turn of the year 2002/3.

Routes

Ambon, Balikpapan, Bandar Lampung, Bandung, Batam, Bengkulu, Biak, Bima, Denpasar, Dilli, Djakarta, Jambi, Jayapura, Jogjakarta, Kuala Lumpur, Kupang, Mataram, Medan, Merauke, Padang, Palankarya, Palembang, Pekanbaru, Pontianak, Port Hedland, Sorong, Sumbawa, Surabaya, Tanjung Pinan, Ujung Padang.

Fleet

7 Boeing 737-200	7 Fokker F.28
3 Boeing 737-400	3 Fokker 100
6 De Havilland DHC-6 Twin Otter	9 ITPN-CN-235-10
9 Fokker F.27	7 ITPN-212 AB4/CC4 Aviocar

Saab 340 N 401BH (Josef Krauthäuser / Lansing)

MESABA AIRLINES

7501 26th Ave. South, Minneapolis, MN 55450
USA, Tel. 612-7265151, Fax. 612-7261568
E-mail: info@mesaba.com, www.mesaba.com

Three- / Two- letter code	IATA No.	Reg'n prefix	ICAO callsign
MES / XJ	582	N	Mesaba

In1944 Gary Newstrom bought an aircraft and set up his firm, Mesaba Aviation, in Coleraine, Minnesota; in 1950 the airline moved to nearby Grand Rapids. Not too much else is recorded until 1973, when Mesaba became active as a regional airline.Using a Beech 99 and other small aircraft a regional network was built up. A change of ownership to the Svenson company came in 1977 and from then on Mesaba developed continually. Airline deregulation also made it possible for the airline to fly outside Minnesota's state borders. Minneapolis/St.Paul became the new base and Mesaba had

contracts with North Central Airlines and its first codeshare agreement. Larger Swearingen Metros came into service. After the merger of North Central Airlines with Southern Airlines, flights continued on behalf of the new Republic Airlines. BAe Jetstream 31s joined the fleet, and later came Fokker F.27s. In 1983, for organisational reasons, Mesaba Aviation's operations were renamed as Mesaba Airlines. A further merger of Republic Airlines into Northwest Orient Airlines brought a new partnership from 1984 and a contract as the first Northwest Airlink Partner. Extensive further contracts with Northwest ensured Mesaba's

continued growth. More F.27s were acquired and then the DHC.8, in Northwest Airlink colours. Conquest Air was an acquisition in 1994, changing name to Air Tran, before ceasing operations in 1995. Saab 340s and BAe/Avro 85s joined the growing fleet in the mid-1990s. In 1995 all activities were brought under the Mesaba Holdings banner and two divisions formed, Northwest Airlink and Northwest Jetlink. New routes were added and a further hub in Detroit established. In time, the Saab 340s are expected to be replaced by Canadair Regional Jets.

Routes

Operating as Northwest Airlink and Jetlink Partner, Mesaba serves some 100 destinations in the northern states of the USA and neighbouring Canada.

Fleet

36 BAe /Avro RJ 85
49 Saab 340

Airbus A320-231 F-OHME (Stefan Schlick / Puerto Vallarta)

MEXICANA

Xola 535, Piso 30, Colonia de Valle 03100
Mexico City, Mexico, Tel. 5-4483096
Fax. 5-4483096, www.mexicana.com

Three- / Two- letter code	IATA No.	Reg'n prefix	ICAO callsign
MXA / MX	132	XA	Mexicana

The Compania Mexicana de Aviacion is one of the world's oldest airlines. It was founded on 12th July 1921 initially to fly wages to oilfields near Tampico, as transporting this money overland was no longer safe. The present name was adopted on 20th August 1924, and scheduled services began on 15th April 1928 between Mexico City and Tampico. From 1929 to 1968 Pan American had a majority interest in Mexicana. Aerovias Centrales was bought in 1935 and Transportes Aereos de Jalinco in 1955. In addition to DC-3s and DC-6s, Comet 4Cs were used on routes to Havana, Los Angeles

and New York starting in 1960. The Boeing 727 was introduced in 1966 and the DC-10 in 1981. The Mexican government became the major shareholder in 1982, but on 22nd August 1989 it became a private company. A necessary reorganisation involved changes to flight operations and the route network. Mexicana's relatively old fleet was augmented from mid 1991 with Airbus A320s and from 1992 by the smaller Fokker 100, and at this time a new colour scheme was introduced, with the tailfin of each aircraft being painted in a different hue. Mexicana has interests in various regional

operators including Aerocaribe, Aerocozumel (both of which operate a feeder system on behalf of Aeromexico), Aeromonterrey and Turboreactores. In 1996 Mexicana was acquired by the Cintra Group, whose portfolio of other companies includes former competitor Aeromexico. Newest aircraft for Mexicana is the Airbus A319, from the end of 2001, and the A320 fleet has been increased, allowing the retirement of the Boeing 727s. Mexicana is a participant in the Latinpass frequent flyer scheme and since early 2000, a member of the Star Alliance.

Routes

Acapulco, Bogota, Buenos Aires, Cancun, Caracas, Chicago, Ciuad del Carmen, Cozumel, Denver, Durango, Guadalahara, Guatemala, Havana, Hermosilo, Huatulco, Ixtapa, Ixtepec, Las Vegas, Leon, Los Angeles, Managua, Manzanillo, Mazatlan, Merida, Miami, Mexicali, Mexico City, Montreal, Monterrey, Morelia, New York, Nuevo Laredo, Oakland, Oaxaca, Orlando, Panama City, Puerto Vallarta, Saltillo, San Antonio, San Francisco, San Jose, San Jose Cabo, San Juan, San Luis Potosi, San Salvador, Santo Domingo, Tampico, Toronto, Veracruz, Villahermosa, Zacatecas.

Fleet		Ordered
12 Airbus A319-100	12 Fokker 100	8 Airbus A320
24 Airbus A320-200		2 Airbus A319
14 Boeing 727-200Adv.		
9 Boeing 757-200		

Boeing 737-81Q N733MA (Josef Krauthäuser / Fort Lauderdale)

MIAMI AIR INTERNATIONAL

5000 NW 36 Street, Ste. 307, Miami, Florida 33122 USA, Tel. 305-8763600, Fax. 305-87142222, E-mail: service@miamiair.com, www.miamiair.com

Three- / Two- letter code	IATA No.	Reg'n prefix	ICAO callsign
BSK / GL	–	N	Biscayne

As the collapse of Eastern Airlines was becoming more and more inevitable, a group of pilots, management and technical employees from Eastern decided in 1990 to set up their own company; thus in August 1990 Miami Air International was founded. Once licensing formalities were completed, operations began in October 1991, using the trusty Boeing 727 for charter work on behalf of several tour companies, including the largest cruise ship operator in the Caribbean. Most destinations were in the USA and there was also ad hoc work for incentive companies or for music and film industry stars. During the season, college sports teams and their supporters would be flown to away fixtures. An important customer however was the government; many Miami Air aircraft were used for troop transport missions, including to destinations outside the USA. Two presidential election candidates used Miami Air aircraft during their campaigns to crisis-cross the USA. In 2000 the 727 fleet was augmented by the first Boeing 737-800. The airline's tradition of naming each aircraft after outstanding employees was continued with the new type, but the colour scheme was slightly changed with the 737's arrival. A freight company took a shareholding in the airline in 2002; one of the 727s was converted as a freighter, expanding the company's activities. Further 737-800s were added during 2001 and 2002, though some have been leased out during the off-peak season, notably to Excel in the UK. Further expansion is planned up to 2005.

Routes

Charter flights within the USA, to the Caribbean and Mexico. Worldwide ad hoc charters.

Fleet	Ordered
4 Boeing 727-200	1 Boeing 737-800
4 Boeing 737-800	

Boeing 737-8CX EI-CXV (Marcus Baltes / Frankfurt)

MIAT – MONGOLIAN AIRLINES

Airport Buyant-Ukhaa 34, Ulaanbataar, People's Republic of Mongolia, Tel. 311333, Fax. 310238 E-mail: info@miat.com.mn, www.miat.com.mn

Three- / Two- letter code	IATA No.	Reg'n prefix	ICAO callsign
MGL / OM	289	JU	Mongolair

The airline, founded in 1956, has been known under a variety of names such as 'Mongolian Airlines', 'Mongoflot', or 'Air Mongol'. MIAT was built up with the aid of the USSR and Aeroflot. The first flight was on 7th July 1956 from Ulaanbaatar to Irkutsk using an Antonov 24. Initially equipment including Lisunov Li-2s (Soviet-built versions of the Douglas DC-3) was supplied by the Soviet airline, and international routes were opened up to Irkutsk, to connect with Aeroflot's service to Moscow, and to Peking, though this was soon withdrawn for lack of demand. The bulk of the fleet built up since the 1980s consists of

Antonov twin turboprops, but Chinese Yunshuji Y-12s were used from 1992. As part of a co-operation and development agreement, MIAT received a Boeing 727 from Korean Airlines in 1992, with two more following, allowing the disposal of the former Tupolev Tu-154s. As well as scheduled and charter flights, MIAT is tasked with other state functions including agricultural flying and air ambulance work. A leased Airbus A310 was taken on in May 1998 and this has been used for flights to Europe, which are valuable as a means of earning foreign exchange. The revised colour scheme which has been applied to

the Airbus is an outward sign of MIAT's steps forward into the modern era. In July 2002 a Boeing 737-800 was added on a long lease.

Routes

From Ulaanbaatar, destinations within Mongolia such as Darchan and Eerdenet are served. There are further services to Beijing, Frankfurt, Irkutsk, Moscow and Seoul. and charter flights to Korea, Japan, the Middle East and other destinations in China.

Fleet

```
 1 Airbus A310-300
14 Antonov An-24/26
 1 Boeing 737-800
 2 Yunshuji Y 12
```

McDonnell Douglas MD-82 N808ME (Josef Krauthäuser / Phoenix)

MIDWEST EXPRESS

6744 South Howell Ave, Oak Creek, Wisconsin 53154, USA, Tel. 414-5704080
Fax. 414-5700199, www.midwestexpress.com

Three- / Two- letter code	IATA No.	Reg'n prefix	ICAO callsign
MEP / YX	453	N	Midex

Midwest Express was established after deregulation in November 1983 as a subsidiary of KC Aviation, itself the established aviation division of Kimberley-Clark, the major paper products company, to provide passenger service in the Midwest and Southeast of the USA.The initial fleet was a DC-9 and Convair 580, but further DC-9s were soon added. Operations began on 29th April 1984 on the route Milwaukee-Boston. Over the following years a fleet of DC-9-10s and -32s was built up and routes extended to cover 20 cities including as far as Dallas and Los Angeles. During 1994/95 capital was increased to allow further expansion, and in 1995 a revised colour scheme was introduced. This steady expansion continued, and included the establishment of a subsidiary, Skyway Airlines, to provide feeder services to Midwest at its Milwaukee and Omaha hubs. The fleet remains firmly fixed to the DC-9 and its developments, but more modern MD-80s supplanted some of the older DC-9s, and from February 2003 the Boeing 717 (still a DC-9 development, despite the change of manufacturer name) is being delivered. The extended route network now reaches from Los Angeles to New York. There are alliances with American Eagle Airlines and USAirways Express. A feeder network has been built up by Skyways at Milwaukee, as Midwest Express Connection.

Routes

Appleton, Atlanta, Baltimore, Boston, Dallas/Fort Worth, Denver, Des Moines, Fort Lauderdale, Fort Myers, Kansas City, Las Vegas, Los Angeles, Milwaukee, New York, Omaha, Orlando, Philadelphia, Phoenix, San Francisco, Tampa, Washington-National.

Fleet		Ordered
7 Boeing 717-200	2 McDonnell Douglas MD-88	18 Boeing 717-200
4 Douglas DC-9-14/15		
15 Douglas DC-9-32		
11 McDonnell Douglas MD-81/82		

Boeing 757-2T7 G-MONE (Gerhard Schütz / Corfu)

MONARCH AIRLINES

Luton Airport, Luton Bedfordshire LU2 9NU
Great Britain, Tel. 1582-400000
Fax. 1582-411000, www.flymonarch.com

Three- / Two- letter code	IATA No.	Reg'n prefix	ICAO callsign
MON / ZB	974	G	Monarch

Monarch Airlines, the well-known British charter company, was founded on 5th June 1967 by Cosmos Tours. Flight operations started on 5th April 1968 with a Bristol Britannia flying between Luton and Madrid. Its initial Luton-based fleet consisted of two Britannias and its destinations were principally Mediterranean holiday resorts. In 1971 the first jet aircraft was acquired, a Boeing 720. BAC One-Elevens followed in 1975, Boeing 707s in 1978 and the first Boeing 737 in 1980. Its first Boeing 757, the first in Europe, arrived in 1983. Licences to operate scheduled services from Luton to

Mahon, Palma and Malaga were awarded in the mid-1980s and the first service to Mahon began on 5th July 1986. Long-haul charters to the USA were introduced from 1988. Apart from the charter business, Monarch has also been very active in aircraft leasing; for example, the entire Euroberlin fleet was leased from Monarch for some years. In 1990 Monarch received its first widebody, the Airbus A300-600, and the Boeing 737s were largely replaced by Airbus A320s from early 1993. Boeing 767s were acquired but leased to Alitalia. The first Airbus A321 was delivered in April 1997 and Airbus A330-200s in 1999 for

long-range routes. For the 2002 summer season Monarch unveiled a new colour scheme for their aircraft. The main operating and engineering base is at Luton, but operations are conducted also from Birmingham, Gatwick, Liverpool, Manchester and other British regional airports.

Routes

Scheduled flights from Manchester and London to Alicante, Faro, Gibraltar, Malaga, Palma de Mallorca and Tenerife, plus many charter flights, depending on season, to the Mediterranean, Alps, Caribbean, East Africa, Canada and the USA.

Fleet / Ordered

Fleet		Ordered
4 Airbus A300-600	7 Boeing 757-200/200ER	5 Airbus A321
4 Airbus A320-200		
5 Airbus A321-200		
2 Airbus A330-200		

Fokker 100 YU-AOK (Albert Kuhbandner / Zürich)

MONTENEGRO AIRLINES

Slobode 23, 81000 Podorica, Montenegro
Tel. 1-18224406, Fax. 1-246207, E-mail: commerce
@mgx.cg.yu, www.montenegro-airlines.cg.yu

Three- / Two- letter code	IATA No.	Reg'n prefix	ICAO callsign
MGX / YM	409	YU	Montenegro

Politics played a role in the formation of Montenegro Airlines since, after the dissolution of the former Yugoslavia, Montenegro found itself cut off from the air transport network. There was no national carrier, and the country would have to depend on other companies. Thus the government of Montenegro set up Montenegro Airlines in 1994, with shares taken by banks, the tourist industry or by quasi-government bodies. In spite of that the government still was obliged to take a 51% holding in order to retain control. It was around two years after the airline's formation that the first aircraft arrived in Podgorica; it was a Fokker F.28 and was used on the sparse network. The United Nations had a trade boycott in place against the rump of Yugoslavia, including Serbia and Montenegro as a consequence of Serbia's conflict with Bosnia-Herzegovina. This was lifted from 1999 and Macedonian Airlines could look to expansion. Thus late in 1998 a second F.28 was acquired. There were destinations in western Europe which could be served, which had populations of refugees or expatriate workers who would want to fly back to Montenegro. The airline's first Fokker 100 was delivered in 2000 and this was painted in new colours for the airline. Two more Fokker 100s were added in 2001 and 2002 to complete the current fleet, by replacing the F.28s. As well as its scheduled operations, Montenegro Airlines is active in charter work. The country's two airports at Podgorica and Tivat are served regularly.

Routes

Athens, Belgrade, Budapest, Düsseldorf, Frankfurt, Istanbul, Corfu, Ljubljana, Paris, Podgorica, Rhodes, Riga, Rome, Skiathos, Skopje, Tel Aviv, Tivat, Zürich.

Fleet

3 Fokker 100

Fokker F.28 Fellowship 4000 XY-AGA (Josef Krauthäuser collection)

MYANMA AIRWAYS

104 Kanna Road, Yangon,
Myanmar
Tel. 1-280710, Fax. 1-289583

Three- / Two- letter code	IATA No.	Reg'n prefix	ICAO callsign
UBA / UB	209	XY	Unionair

Originally established in 1948 by the Burmese government as the Union of Burma Airways, the airline changed its name in December 1972 to Burma Airways Corporation and finally on 1st April 1989 to Myanma Airways, reflecting the change of name of Burma to Myanmar. In between lie 40 years of flight operations, which started in 1948 with de Havilland Doves. These were followed by DC-3s and Vickers Viscounts and the introduction of domestic and international services. The first Fokker F.27 was delivered in October 1963. In 1969 a Boeing 727 replaced the Viscount on international routes. From the time of the delivery of the the first Fokker F.28 in 1977 the airline has used exclusively Fokkers. In 1993 a co-operation agreement was concluded with Highsonics Enterprises of Singapore, under which international routes would be flown by a joint company, Myanmar Airways International, which has been active since early 1994 with leased Boeing 737-300s, leaving Myanma Airways to concentrate on domestic routes only. The fleet continues to be Fokker-only, with three more second-hand F.27s and two F.28s added in 2001.

Routes

Akyab, Bhamo, Dawe, Heho, Kalemyo, Kawthaung, Kengtung, Khamti, Lashio, Loikaw, Mandalay, Maulmyne, Mong Hsat, Myeik, Myitkyina, Nyaung-u, Putao, Sittwe,Tachilek, Tandwe, Yangon.

Fleet

7 Fokker F.27
5 Fokker F.28

Boeing 757-225 G-PIDS (Martin Kühn / Palma de Mallorca)

MY TRAVEL AIRWAYS

Parkway Three, 300 Princess Rd, Manchester, M14 7QU
Great Britain, Tel. 161-2326600, Fax. 161-2326610
E-mail: info@mytravel.com, www.mytravel.com

Three- / Two- letter code	IATA No.	Reg'n prefix	ICAO callsign
MYT / VZ	727	G	Kestrel

One of the major British tour operators, Airtours, set up its own in-house airline in Manchester in 1990. It began operations in March 1991 with three MD-83s. The young company expanded quickly and acquired three further MD-83s in late 1991. During the Summer of 1993, Airtours' parent company took over its competitor Aspro Holidays, along with their airline Inter European Airways (formed in 1987) and its fleet consisting of Boeing 737s and 757s. For the 1994 season, the fleet was augmented with Airbus A320s and in addition two Boeing 767-300s were added for long-range services to holiday destinations in the USA

and Thailand. The arrival of the 767s also saw the introduction of a new colour scheme. The MD-83s were dropped from the fleet for the 1996 summer season and replaced with further A320s. During this year also, Airtours acquired the Danish travel concern Spies Holding, along with its airline Premiair, and in 1997 the Belgian tour operator Sun International, with its airline Air Belgium, was also added to the group. Having held a partial shareholding, Airtours is since mid-2000 the 100% owner of the German tour operator Frosch Touristik Gruppe, which set up its own airline Fly FTI in 1998, and for whom A320s

from the Airtours fleet were flying during 1999. Four Airbus A330s for use on long range routes were added to the growing fleet during 1999. From 1st January 2002 Airtours and Premiair were merged as MyTravel, with new house colours. An entry into the booming low-cost market was made from October 2002 with the establishment of Birmingham-based subsidiary MyTravel Lite (MYL), which uses A320s seconded from the parent.

Routes

Charter flights from Manchester, Birmingham, Cardiff, London-Gatwick, Glasgow, Liverpool, Newcastle, other UK cities and Scandinavia to favourite holiday destinations around the Mediterranean, Alps, Caribbean, USA, Thailand, Africa and Australia.

Fleet		Ordered
23 Airbus A320-200	3 Boeing 767-300 ER	4 Airbus A321
4 Airbus A321-200	4 Douglas DC-10	
7 Airbus A330-200/300		
6 Boeing 757-200		

De Havilland DHC-8-315 VH-JSQ (Jörg Thiel / Darwin)

NATIONAL JET SYSTEM

28 James Schofield Drive, Airport. Adelaide SA 5090, Australia, Tel. 8-81547000, Fax. 8-81547256, E-mail: info@nationaljet.com.au, www.nationaljet.com.au

Three- / Two- letter code	IATA No.	Reg'n prefix	ICAO callsign
NJS / NC	–	VH	National Jet

Founded in Adelaide in 1990, this company is in many ways not strictly an airline, but specialises more in the supply of aircraft and services packages. It all began with a Piper Navajo and an IAI Westwind. From 1992 expansion was the watchword with five BAe 146s delivered, flying scheduled services on behalf of Australian Airlink. For Australian Air Express freight flights were also undertaken and BAe 146QCs were added for use on the important overnight express package services. National Jet also operated on behalf of the Royal Australian Air Force, using specially equipped Learjets. An important sphere of activity has

been, and still is, the leasing of aircraft. A complete service is offered, from the creation to the day-to-day operation of an airline. Since 1993 a specially modified de Havilland DHC-8 has been operated for the Australian government on coastal surveillance missions. Similarly, National Jet gives important support in the search for natural resources in inland areas; under contract to mineral companies, employees and materials are flown to airfield sites located close by the mines. National Jet Italia started operations as a British Airways franchise in July 2000 using BAe 146-300s between

Rome and Palermo, but this was a very short-lived venture. In Australia some aircraft are employed on the Qantas Link regional system and several 146s operate for Australian Air Express on their freight express services. There is a single scheduled service, from Darwin to the new state of East Timor. National Jet Systems is now a subsidiary of the UK-based Cobham Group, having been acquired early in 2000.

Routes

Brisbane, Cairns, Christmas Island, Cocos Island, Darwin, Launceston, Learmonth, Mc Arthur River, Perth Tanami, Timka are regularly served. Charter flights and ad hoc freight flights are also undertaken.

Fleet

1 Avro RJ 70
20 BAe 146-100/200/300
5 De Havilland DHC-8-100/200/300

BAC 1-11-537GF ZS-NUI (Manfred Turek / Lanseria)

NATIONWIDE AIRLINES

P.O.Box 422, Lanseria Airport, Gauteng 1748, Republic of S Africa Tel. 11 701 3330, Fax. 11 701 3243, E-mail: info@flynationwide.co.za, www.flynationwide.co.za

Three- / Two- letter code	IATA No.	Reg'n prefix	ICAO callsign
NTW / CE	567	ZS	Nationwide Air

As the political situation in South Africa was slowly altering at the beginning of the 1990s, so there also developed the opportunity for new airlines, as the practical monopoly position enjoyed by South African Airways was not especially welcomed by industry. For political reasons also there was a need for new formations, as many African countries were lifting their previous restrictions on flights by South African aircraft. Companies such as Nationwide Air Charter, which had since the 1970s operated business and air taxi services from Lanseria Airport with Beech aircraft, expanded their operations. In

February 1994 a BAC One-Eleven was purchased and initially used on charter work. Business was good, and two further One-Elevens arrived in November 1994 in time for the beginning of the major travel season in South Africa. Flights to neighbouring countries, to Madagascar and to Mauritius were flown on behalf of several tour companies. The delivery of further One-Elevens allowed the commencement of scheduled services, at which point the airline's name was changed to Nationwide Airlines. From 1997 Boeing 727s strengthened the fleet, with Boeing 737s added from the end of 1998.

The era of the BAC One-Eleven in South Africa is rapidly coming to a close because of noise restrictions, and Nationwide has largely switched over to Boeing 737-200s. The company is not only active with scheduled and charter work, but in freight operations and in chartering aircraft to other companies. There are codeshare arrangements in place with various other airlines.

Routes

Capetown, Durban, East London, George, Johannesburg, Livingstone, Lusaka, Nelspruit, Port Elizabeth as schedules. Charter flights to neighbouring Namibia, Zimbabwe, to Kenya, the Comores, Seychelles and Mauritius.

Fleet

3 BAe/BAC 1-11-400/500
5 Boeing 727-100/200
8 Boeing 737-200

Boeing 737-200 N501NG (Author's collection)

NICA AIRLINES

P.O.Box 6018 Managua, Nicaragua
Tel. 2-631929, Fax. 2-631822
www.groupotacacom

Three- / Two- letter code	IATA No.	Reg'n prefix	ICAO callsign
NIS / 6Y	930	YN	Nica

Following the collapse of Aeronica there was no longer an international airline active in the still politically unstable Nicaragua. Soon after the elections in 1992 a new company was established with the help of TACA – Nicaraguenses de Aviacion SA – or NICA for short. The TACA Group held 49% of the shares, the rest being with private investors and the Nicaraguan government. In July 1992 it was possible to open the first service to Miami, using a leased Boeing 737-200. The main base is Managua, from where an internal network was also run with a CASA 212. As well as scheduled passenger services, charters and freight services are also flown. NICA is a participant in the frequent flier programme of TACA, LACSA and Aviateca. These companies are building a marketing alliance and the dominance of the TACA group is to be seen in the livery of the aircraft, which apart from the name is essentially that of TACA. NICA is able to call on aircraft from other group members according to demand.

Routes

Guatemala City, Managua, Miami, Panama City, Puerto Cabezas, San Jose, San Salvador.

Fleet

1 Boeing 737-200Adv.

Boeing 747-281F JA8167 (Josef Krauthäuser / Amsterdam)

NIPPON CARGO AIRLINES – NCA

Shiodome City Center 8F5-2, Higashi-Shinbashi
1-Chome, Minato-Ku, Tokyo 105-7108, Japan
Tel. 81-367355500, Fax. 81-367355535
E-mail: sales@nca.aero, www.nca.aero

Three- / Two- letter code	IATA No.	Reg'n prefix	ICAO callsign
NCA / KZ	933	JA	Nipponcargo

As a country oriented towards the export of technical and high quality wares, the transport of these goods is extremely important to Japan. Time is often a more important consideration than the transport cost, and this was in the minds of the founders of Nippon Cargo Airlines Ltd, formed on 21st September 1978. The shareholders included, amongst others, All Nippon Airways, Kawasaki Industries, Mitsui, Nippon Express, Bank of Tokyo, Tokyo Marine & Fire Insurance and 60 other subscribers. The objective was to build up a worldwide scheduled airfreight service. However, it took several years to overcome state-imposed restrictions for new airline start-ups; after all, state-owned JAL had a monopoly for international freight flights from Japan. After much controversy and strong pressure from within industry, the ministry responsible finally granted a licence for flights to the USA in 1985. For these to take place however, bilateral negotiations with the USA had to happen, since from their side the Americans wanted to see reciprocal rights for their airlines in Japan. From the outset, NCA used the Boeing 747F; several of these aircraft are equipped with the nose cargo door, facilitating the easy loading of containers or packages. The routes have been built up to match demand, and at some destinations NCA has its own warehouses and sorting centres.

Routes

Amsterdam, Anchorage, Chicago, Frankfurt, Guadelajara, Hong Kong, Kuala Lumpur,London, Los Angeles, Manila, Milan, New York, Osaka, San Francisco, Seoul, Shanghai, Singapore, Taipei, Tokyo.

Fleet

11 Boeing 747-200F

Boeing 757-28A N752NA (Josef Krauthäuser / Miami)

NORTH AMERICAN AIRLINES

Suite 250, Building 75, North Hangar Road, Jamaica, NY 11430, USA Tel. 718-6562650, Fax. 718-9953372, E-mail: acooper@northamericanair.com, www.northamair.com

Three- / Two- letter code	IATA No.	Reg'n prefix	ICAO callsign
NAO / XG	455	N	Northamerican

Dan McKinnon, formerly in charge of the CAB – Civil Aeronautics Board of the USA, formed North American Airlines in 1989. A shareholder – officially with 25% – was El Al Israel Airlines. The initial objective of the new airline was to provide connecting services to El Al flights to New York and Montreal. Thus El Al could eliminate its expensive New York - Los Angeles sector which was unprofitable since no domestic passengers could be carried because of the lack of IATA fifth freedom rights. Operations began on 22nd January 1990 using a Boeing 757-200 from New York's J F Kennedy airport, where the airline's

base had been established, to Los Angeles. From 1992 a McDonnell Douglas MD-83 was added to the fleet and from 1995 a further Boeing 757-200. As well as the New York to Los Angeles flights, charter operations were added on behalf of various tour operators. A further change to the fleet came with the delivery of Boeing 737-800s in August 1998 and February 1999, replacing the MD-83. Scheduled flights to Guyana were started in 1999 after Guyana Airways suspended its services including the connection to New York. Further scheduled services followed in 2002, to Puerto Rico and the

Dominican Republic, and Boeing 767-300s were added in place of the 737-800s. As well as schedules, worldwide charters are offered. Government work is also undertaken, be it troop transport, or movement of the presidential press corps.

Routes

From New York, schedules to Aquadilla, Georgetown, Los Angeles and Santo Domingo, plus worldwide charter flights.

Fleet

2 Boeing 767-300
5 Boeing 757-200

Douglas C-118A (DC-6F) N2907F (Lutz Schönfeld / Anchorage)

NORTHERN AIR CARGO

3900 West International Airport Rd, Anchorage, Alaska, 99502 USA, Tel.907-2433331, Fax. 907-2495190, E-mail: sales@northernaircargo.com, www.northernaircargo.com

Three- / Two- letter code	IATA No.	Reg'n prefix	ICAO callsign
NAC / NC	345	N	Yukon

Robert Sholton and Maurice Carlsen formed their small air transport company Sholton & Carlsen Inc. in Alaska in 1956 and began operations with two Fairchild C-82 Packets, Korean War survivors which had been demobbed by the US Air Force. The company's contracts also came mostly from the military. In the mid-1950s in Alaska, the DEW-Line (Defense Early Warning) was being built, a chain of radar stations stretching from Alaska to Greenland. Heavy materiel such as generators and other equipment was flown to places which at that time were well outside the reach of civilisation or roads. In addition

there were humanitarian flights, including those after the Good Friday earthquake of 1964, which saw the Packets in the front line of relief. In 1969 the first Douglas DC-6 arrived and over the following 25 years 14 of these indestructible propliners were used. Several had the swing-tail modification, allowing the whole tail section to be swung away from the aircraft for easy loading of bulky items. Northern Air Cargo has also been very active in providing transport for the oil and offshore industries in northern Alaska, flying essential freight in often difficult conditions. For many years NAC has served over 40

points in its so-called 'flagstop' service. It also has special contracts with companies concerned with the provision of daily necessities to Eskimo communities. In March 2003 NAC tried to take over the operating licence of the bankrupt National Airlines, with charter flights from Houston to Magadan in Russia in mind. With this licence, NAC could use larger aircraft such as the Boeing 757 to start passenger charter work.

Routes

Anchorage, Aniak, Barrow, Bethel, Dillingham, Dutch Harbor, Emmanek, Fairbanks, Fort Yukon, Galena, Iliamna, King Salmon, Kodiak, Kotzebue, McGreth, Nome, Prudhoe Bay, Red Dog, Seattle, St. George, St. Marys, St.Paul, Unalaklet, Whitehorse.

Fleet

3 Boeing 727-100F
14 Douglas DC-6 (C-118)

Airbus A319-114 D-AVWL, now N337NB (Jan-Alexander Lück / Hamburg-XFW)

NORTHWEST AIRLINES

5101 Northwest Drive, St. Paul, MN.55111-3034
USA, Tel. 612-7262331, Fax. 612-7263942
www.nwa.com

Three- / Two- letter code	IATA No.	Reg'n prefix	ICAO callsign
NWA / NW	012	N	Northwest

Founded on 1st August 1926 in Minneapolis/St.Paul as Northwest Airways, initial services were flown with a Stinson Post from Chicago to St.Paul. Regular passenger services began in 1933 with DC-3s. In 1934 Northern Air Transport was taken over and the name changed to Northwest Airlines. On 15th July 1947 the first polar route was opened with DC-4s; this was from Seattle via Anchorage to Tokyo and on to Manila and led to a change of name to Northwest Orient Airlines. Boeing Stratocruisers came into service for the South East Asia routes. Lockheed Constellations, DC-6s, DC-7s and Lockheed

Electras were the predominant types during the propliner era. Jets began to oust these from 1960, when the first DC-8s were delivered. First widebody was the Boeing 747, from 30th April 1970, followed by the DC-10-40 late in 1972. Northwest crossed the Atlantic in 1979, to Copenhagen and Stockholm, followed by London in 1980. Northwest's growth was solely internal until 1986 when Republic was acquired. In 1988 the old name Northwest Airlines was re-adopted and a re-structuring took place.The first Airbus A320s were delivered in late 1989, and ten years later the smaller A319 was introduced, but

Northwest also acquired a large fleet of second-hand DC-9s. In 2001 the cargo division became independent as Northwest Cargo; also in 2001 Boeing 757-300s were introduced. However, new aircraft have come more from Airbus of late, including the A330s which began delivery in 2003, introducing a new colour scheme for the airline. There is close co-operation with shareholder KLM, and feeder and regional services are flown as Northwest Airlink by other airlines including Mesaba and Express Airlines I, in which Northwest have shares. Northwest also has holdings in Champion Air and Continental Airlines.

Routes

Northwest serves over 250 destinations in more than 20 countries, including over 120 in the USA, with major hubs at Minneapolis, Memphis and Detroit. Feeder and regional services are flown in association with Northwest Airlink.

Fleet

		Ordered
66 Airbus A319	56 Boeing 757-200	12 Airbus A319
78 Airbus A320-200	10 Boeing 757-300	6 Airbus A320
1 Airbus A330-200	24 Douglas DC-10-30/40	9 Airbus A330-200
12 Boeing 727-200	167 Douglas DC-9-14/15/31/32	14 Airbus A330-300
20 Boeing 747-200		5 Boeing 757-300
16 Boeing 747-400		

Boeing 737-3K2 LN-KKF (Author's collection)

NORWEGIAN AIR SHUTTLE

Postbox 115, 1330 Fornebu, Norway
Tel.67593000, Fax. 67593001, E-mail:
post@norwegian.no, www.norwegian.no

Three- / Two- letter code	IATA No.	Reg'n prefix	ICAO callsign
NAX / DY	328	LN	Norshuttle

Though this airline was formed in 1993, at first it had no aircraft of its own but chartered them as required from fellow Norwegian airline Busy Bee, mostly Fokker 50s used on Braathens routes. Up to six leased Fokker 50s were used, but then from 2002 Norwegian Air Shuttle received its own Fokker 50, which was used for services from Stavanger to Newcastle, also flown on behalf of Braathens. Then in 2002 Norwegian changed strategy and set up as a low-cost/no-frills operator in competition with SAS and Braathens. Using leased Boeing 737-300s, services were offered from Oslo to various destinations in Norway. From April 2003 international services were offered, beginning with the well-frequented holiday spots in Spain and Portugal. The fleet was built up quickly, with further Boeing 737s leased.The aircraft are painted in an attractive colour scheme, each with the portrait of a famous Norwegian personality on the tailfin. Norwegian has its own maintenance base in Stavanger.

Routes

Andenes, Bergen, Bodo, Faro, Haugesund, Kristiansund, Lakselv, Malaga, Molde, Murcia, Oslo, Stavanger, Tromsoe, Trondheim.

Fleet

7 Boeing 737-300
6 Fokker 50

Airbus A320-214 TS-INB (Albert Kuhbandner / Paris-CDG)

NOUVELAIR TUNISIE

BP 66 Aéroport International H/B Monastir
Monastir 5000, Tunisia, Tel. 3-520671, Fax. 3-520666
E-mail: info@nouvelair.com.tn, www.nouvelair.com

Three- / Two- letter code	IATA No.	Reg'n prefix	ICAO callsign
LBT / BJ	–	TS	Nouvelair

The French airline Air Liberté established a subsidiary of the same name in Tunisia in 1990 and it began regular charter flights from Monastir for the summer season with a MD-83 supplied by the parent company. Destinations in the former East Germany, newly part of the unified country, were especially served, since Tunisia proved to be a leading holiday destination from here. Additional aircraft were made available from Air Liberté to meet additional demand. The company showed satisfactory development and another MD-83 was added in 1991. However, financial crisis overtook the parent and things

looked black for the Tunisian arm until it was sold in 1996 to the Tunisian Travel Service Group, a semi-governmental organisation. There was to be increased co-operation with Tunisair and with Air Liberté until the latter was sold to British Airways. With the sale of shares Air Liberté Tunisie became a company under Tunisian law and a renaming as Nouvelair Tunisie followed in March 1996. Hand in hand with the new name came a new colour scheme for the aircraft. Two further MD-83s were added in 1997 before it was decided to adopt the Airbus A320 as the airline's future equipment. The first two

aircraft were delivered in December 1999 and March 2000 to Monastir, which is the company's base and the departure point for most of its flights. Two further aircraft have been added and a new colour scheme adopted.

Routes

Typical of the operations of such charter airlines, Nouvelair flies holidaymakers from many European countries to Tunisia. Tunis, Monastir and Djerba are regularly served.

Fleet

4 Airbus A320-200
2 McDonnell Douglas MD-83

Airbus A330-223 SE-RBF (Author's collection / Frankfurt)

NOVAIR

Svaevägen 155, 11346 Stockholm, Sweden
Tel. 8-6738600, Fax. 8-6738605
E-mail: info@novair.se, www.novair.net

Three- / Two- letter code	IATA No.	Reg'n prefix	ICAO callsign
NVR / 1L	–	SE	Navigator

Stockholm-based Apollo Reser belongs to the largest tour operator in Scandinavia, in which the Swiss Kuoni group is a majority shareholder. The expanding group saw the need in 1997 to establish its own airline. Nova Airlines AB, or Novair took to the skies for the first time in autumn 1997 with flights to the Mediterranean holiday resorts and the Canary Isles. Equipment was the proven Lockheed L-1011 TriStar; it is a six hour flight from Stockholm or Oslo to Las Palmas, which means a long-range type. Novair had a total of three TriStars in use, flying additionally during the winter season to Phuket in Thailand, or Goa. The heavyweight TriStars were not however suited to all destinations and so Novair leased an Airbus A320. In spring 1999 Novair acquired a more flexible type in the form of the Boeing 737-800, which has the range to fly non-stop from Scandinavia to the Canary Isles. It is also able to use smaller airports and Novair is now able to offer service from more departure points in Sweden or Norway. In place of the well-worn, uneconomic TriStars in September and October 2000 came replacements, the Airbus A330-200. Early in 2003 the first A330 was seen in a new colour scheme, featuring the European flag on the tailfin. Novair's main base is at Stockholm-Arlanda airport.

Routes

Agadir, Antalya, Arrecife, Athens, Bourgas, Chania, Copenhagen, Corfu, Dalaman, Faro, Goa, Gothenburg, Heraklion, Hurghada, Karpathos, Larnaca, Las Palmas, Lulea, Malmö, Mykonos, Oslo, Palma de Mallorca, Phuket, Prevesa, Rhodes, Samos, Santorin, Sharm el Sheik, Skiathos, Stavanger, Stockholm, Tenerife, Thessaloniki, Trondheim, Umea, Vargas, Zakinthos.

Fleet

3 Boeing 737-800
2 Airbus A330-200

Airbus A340-313 SX-DFB (Albert Kuhbandner / Munich)

OLYMPIC AIRWAYS

96 Snygrou Ave. 11741 Athens, Greece
Tel. 1-9269111, Fax. 1-9267154, www.olympic-airways.gr
E-mail: customer-relations@olympic-airways.gr

Three- / Two- letter code	IATA No.	Reg'n prefix	ICAO callsign
OAL / OA	050	SX	Olympic

Olympic Airways was founded on 6th April 1957 by no less a person than Aristotle Onassis. The famous shipowner took over a state-owned airline called TAE Greek National Airlines which had been in existence since July 1951. By the time of the first oil crisis Onassis had turned Olympic into a modern airline, but the oil situation caused Olympic difficulties and it suspended operations for several months in 1974. In order to avoid complete bankruptcy, the Greek state intervened and took over Olympic from 1st January 1976. After a complete restructuring of the airline which involved the abandonment of unprofitable routes, things began to improve slowly. When flight operations began in April 1957, Olympic had a fleet of 13 DC-3s and a DC-4, with DC-6s added a year later. In 1960 leased de Havilland Comet 4Bs were added, with the Boeing 707 following in 1966. This type was used to start long-range services to New York, Johannesburg and Sydney. While still under the Onassis regime, the first Boeing 747 arrived. The Boeing 707s and 727s were replaced by 1992 with new Boeing 737-400s and Airbus A300-600s, and these new types were given an attractive new colour scheme. Olympic had been amassing huge losses, and planned privatisation failed while the EU commission and Greek government were in dispute about state subsidies. It is now planned to relaunch the airline as a new privately-owned company, Olympic Airlines. Airbus A340s replaced the 747s and from Spring 2000 Boeing 737-800s were added. In 2002 Olympic dropped its Australian routes, though strengthening its European offering, and retired the Boeing 737-200s. It also completed a move of base to the new Athens airport. Olympic has 100% holdings in Macedonian Airlines and Olympic Aviation (see page 265).

Routes

Alexandria, Amsterdam, Athens, Barcelona, Beirut, Belgrade, Berlin, Brussels, Bucharest, Budapest, Cairo, Copenhagen, Dubai, Düsseldorf, Frankfurt, Geneva, Heraklion, Istanbul, Jeddah, Johannesburg, Kalamata, Karpathos, Kavala, Kerkyria, Kiev, Kos, Kuwait, Larnaca, Lisbon, London, Madrid, Manchester, Marseilles, Milan, Montreal, Moscow, Munich, New York, Odessa, Paris, Prague, Rhodes, Rome, Skopje, Sofia, Strasbourg, Stuttgart, Tel Aviv, Thessaloniki, Tirana, Toronto, Vienna.

Fleet

4 Airbus A340-300
3 Airbus A300-600
2 Boeing 737-300
13 Boeing 737-400

ATR 72-202 SX-BIL (Jan Alexander Lück / Athens)

OLYMPIC AVIATION

96 Snygrou Ave. Athens, Greece
Tel. 1-9362681, Fax. 1-9883009
www.olav.gr

Three- / Two- letter code	IATA No.	Reg'n prefix	ICAO callsign
OLY / ML	898	SX	Olavia

Greece, with its numerous islands and its fragmented and mountainous mainland, is dependent not only on a dense network of ferry connections but also on properly functioning regional air services. In order to open up smaller islands to tourists and to save them having to endure long transfer times, Olympic Aviation was set up on 1st August 1971 with the objective of building up regional services. First of all, runways had to be laid, extended or repaired on many of the islands. As many runways did not have a hard surface, robust aircraft such as Shorts Skyvans and Dornier 228s were used. Initially the airline was privately-owned, but became government owned in 1974. Flights are operated to those places where parent company, Olympic Airways, cannot operate its larger aircraft, and in addition the airline operates as a feeder service to international flights at Athens. ATR 72s, introduced in 1992/93 are also used for charter services from European points directly to the Greek islands. The airline was one of the first to take delivery of the new Boeing 717, in December 1999, and the acquisition of this type marked its increasing involvement in European scheduled services. The major event in 2000 was the move to the new Athens airport, but a third Boeing 717 was also added. Olympic Aviation also operates a flying school and several helicopters; its own maintenance base specialises particularly in helicopter work.

Routes

Olympic Aviation serves more than 45 points in Greece and some 15 international destinations in Europe.

Fleet

7 ATR 72
6 ATR 42
3 Boeing 717-200
7 Dornier Do228-200

Boeing 737-7Q8 A4O-BS (Sebastian Hilker / Dubai)

OMAN AIR

P.O.Box 58, Seeb International Airport, Muscat
111, Oman, Tel. 968-519327, Fax. 968-510924
www.oman-air.com

Three- / Two- letter code	IATA No.	Reg'n prefix	ICAO callsign
OMA / WY	910	A4O	Air Oman

The government of Oman, along with Bahrain, Qatar and the United Arab Emirates are the owners of Gulf Air, the joint national carrier of these countries. Nonetheless the Omani state decided in 1981 to establish its own separate airline. This was brought about by the merger of Gulf Light Air and Oman International Services. As well as the Omani government, various private companies and business people became shareholders. Initially the new company was known as Oman Aviation Service and began operations during 1981, using Fokker F.27s. De Havilland DHC-6 Twin Otters and various helicopters were added. In the early years of the airline, only domestic destinations were served, but this changed with the delivery of the first Boeing 737-300 in 1991. A new colour scheme and the current name were introduced in 1993; in the same year the first international link was made, to Dubai. Further international services were added steadily, notably to the Indian subcontinent. Fleet renewal has been an ongoing process with Airbus A320s and ATR 42s. Up to four A320s and for a while an A310 were in use. However, a reappraisal of the route network and of the fleet was made in 1999, and new generation Boeing 737-800s and -700s were acquired for fleet unification and to reduce costs. The company employs about 2,500 workers, carries around a million passengers and has its main base and maintenance facility at Muscat's international airport.

Routes

Abu Dhabi, Al Ain, Beirut, Cairo, Chennai, Colombo, Dar-es Salaam, Dacca, Doha, Dubai, Jeddah, Karachi, Khasab, Kochi, Kuwait, Mombasa, Mumbai, Muscat, Salalah, Thirvananthapuram, Zanzibar.

Fleet

4 ATR 42-500
3 Boeing 737-700
3 Boeing 737-800

Airbus A300B4 TC-ONL (Josef Krauthäuser / Düsseldorf)

ONUR AIR

Senlikkoy Mah, Catal Sokak No.3, 34810
Istanbul,Turkey, Tel. 0212-6632300
Fax. 0212-6636054, www.onurair.com.tr

Three- / Two- letter code	IATA No.	Reg'n prefix	ICAO callsign
OHY / 8Q	–	TC	Onur Air

Founded in 1992, this airline is a subsidiary of the Turkish tour operator TK Air Travel. Operations began with factory-fresh Airbus A320s on 14th May 1993. As well as the usual charter and inclusive tour work, the airline also wanted to operate scheduled services. During the high season, further A320s were leased in to augment its own fleet. From early in 1994 Ten Tours took over Onur Air and placed it on a more stable financial footing. Radiating from its base at Istanbul, a network of Turkish domestic services was built up during the 1990s. Airbus A300s were acquired from January 1996, with A321s following later in the same year. A change of fleet policy took effect from early 1997, with the acquisition of an MD-88, which was used for the first time for the 1997 summer season to destinations where there were fewer passengers. The international popularity of Turkish holiday resorts has also brought about an increase in the number of flights to Eastern Europe. The need for larger aircraft has been met by the addition of Airbus A300s, with A300-600s arriving during 2002. Aircraft from other airlines are rented in to meet seasonal demand.

Routes

Amsterdam, Ankara, Antalya, Barcelona, Berlin, Billund, Birmingham, Bodrum, Bremen, Brussels, Cologne/Bonn, Copenhagen, Dalaman, Düsseldorf, Edinburgh, Frankfurt, Geneva, Istanbul, Izmir, Hamburg, Hanover, Helsinki, Leipzig, Liège, Linz, Liverpool, London, Manchester, Milan, Moscow, Munich, Münster/Osnabrück, Naples, Nuremberg, Paris, Prague, Rome, Salzburg, Stuttgart, Teeside, Tel Aviv, Vienna, Zürich.

Fleet

2 Airbus A320-200
2 Airbus A321-100
2 Airbus A321-300
5 Airbus A300B4
3 Airbus A300-600

5 McDonnell Douglas MD-88

Fokker F.27 Friendship 200 AP-BCZ (Oliver Köstinger / Sharjah)

PAKISTAN INT'L AIRLINES

PIA Building, Quaid-e-Azam Intl.Airport, Karachi 75200, Pakistan, Tel. 21-4572011, Fax. 21-4570419
E-mail: info@piac.com.pk, www.piac.com.pk

Three- / Two- letter code	IATA No.	Reg'n prefix	ICAO callsign
PIA / PK	214	AP	Pakistan

Pakistan Airlines was set up by the government in 1951 and began Super Constellation services on 7th June 1954, providing a valuable connection between East and West Pakistan. International routes to Cairo and London followed from February 1955 and on 10th March 1955 the airline was reorganised after formal amalgamation with Orient Airways, which had been founded in 1946 prior to the partitioning of India. Convair 240s and DC-3s were used for domestic and regional services, to be replaced by Vickers Viscounts and later HS Tridents. In 1960, long-range flights were taken over by

Boeing 707s, and in 1961 New York was served for the first time. The first widebody was the DC-10-30 in 1974. Two Boeing 747s were leased from TAP – Air Portugal in 1976 and later bought, with further 747s added during the 1980s. During 1971 many services had to be suspended due to the war situation and the secession of East Pakistan to become Bangladesh. After reorganisation, flight operations picked up again in late 1972 and abandoned routes including New York reinstated. The backbone of the fleet has been Airbus A310s for long-range routes and A300B4s for high-density short and medium

range routes. Regional services are looked after primarily by Fokker F.27s, the first of which was delivered as long ago as 1961. During 1999 PIA took on five Boeing 747-300s from Singapore Airlines, and a revised colour scheme was applied to these aircraft. The first of the old A300B4s was replaced by the newer A310-300 in 2002, when the last Boeing 707 freighter was also retired. Boeing 777-200s have been ordered for delivery from January 2004. The main base, with a large maintenance complex, is at Karachi, with important hubs at Islamabad, Lahore, Peshawar and Quetta.

Routes

Abu Dhabi, Almaty, Amsterdam, Athens, Bahrain, Bangkok, Beijing, Colombo, Copenhagen, Dacca, Delhi, Djakarta, Doha, Dubai, Frankfurt, Hong Kong, Islamabad, Istanbul, Jeddah, Karachi, Kathmandu, Kuala Lumpur, Kuwait, London, Manchester, Manila, Mumbai, Muscat, New York, Oslo, Paris, Riyadh, Rome, Shannon, Sharjah, Singapore, Tashkent, Tokyo, Toronto,Tripoli and over 30 domestic destinations.

Fleet

		Ordered
6 Airbus A310-300	7 Boeing 737-300	8 Boeing 777-200
8 Airbus A300B4	2 De Havilland DHC-6	
4 Boeing 747-200	10 Fokker F.27	
6 Boeing 747-300		

Boeing 727-225 N365PA (Josef Krauthäuser / Fort Lauderdale)

PAN AM

14 Aviation Ave, Portsmouth, New Hampshire, 03801 USA, Tel. 603-7662000, Fax. 603-7662094, E-mail: flypanam@flypanam.com, www.flypanam.com

Three- / Two- letter code	IATA No.	Reg'n prefix	ICAO callsign
PAA / PN	–	N	Clipper

On 4th December 1991 the long-established Pan American Airways ceased operations and went into liquidation. The historic name was sold, and after a few changes of ownership, passed in 1998 to Guildford Transportation Industries. The company's registered office was moved from Florida to Portsmouth and in June 1998 the Pan Am name was reactivated. Using several Boeing 727s, services were begun in December 1998 from the new home base of Pease International Tradeport in Portsmouth. Also located here is Pan Am Service, a subsidiary for fuelling and operations. Pan Am set out to serve niche destinations; thus Sanford in Florida was used as a jumping off point for the Caribbean. A further subsidiary is Boston-Maine Airways, which supports Pan Am's Clipper Service with feeder flights. During 2002 Pan Am acquired 24 Boeing 727s from the fleet of United Airlines; several of these were overhauled and fitted with winglets, while others were used as spares sources or leased out. As well as its scheduled services, Pan Am is active in the charter market, working particularly with golf and sports tour operators.

Routes

Aquadilla, Baltimore, Bangor, Belleville, Cumberland, Fort Lauderdale, Hagerstown, Manchester, Portsmouth, Sanford, San Juan, Santo Domingo, Worcester.

Fleet

20 Boeing 727-200

Boeing 737-86N TC-AAP (Albert Kuhbandner / Munich)

PEGASUS

23 Istasyon Caddeshi, TR-34800 Istanbul
Turkey, Tel. 212-6632931, Fax. 212-6635458
www.pgtair.com

Three- / Two- letter code	IATA No.	Reg'n prefix	ICAO callsign
PGT / PG	–	TC	Sunturk

At a time when tourism to Turkey was at a low ebb as a result of the Gulf conflict, in December 1989, Pegasus was set up by Aer Lingus. The new holiday airline began operations in April 1990. Tour operators and their potential customers were offered the latest in technology, in the form of the Boeing 737-400. Originally it was planned to use three aircraft from the outset, but because of the political situation, this did not come about. Nevertheless, with help from the parent company, the first season was successfully negotiated, and in 1992 the tourists started to return to Turkey. A further 737-400 was added and Pegasus also leased in two Airbus A320s and other aircraft for a time to meet peak-season demand. Development of the company continued satisfactorily and further aircraft were acquired. In 1994 the Istanbul-based Yapi Kreditbank took over the ownership from Aer Lingus, and Pegasus became a purely Turkish enterprise. During the Winter months, Pegasus aircraft could be seen in the Caribbean or in Canada, where they were leased out as there was a shortage of work for them in Europe. The fleet now consists almost entirely of the latest model, winglet-equipped Boeing 737-800s, the first of which was delivered to Pegasus in March 1999.

Routes

Charter flights from more than 60 airports, including those in Germany, Finland, France, Great Britain, Ireland, Israel, Italy, the Netherlands, Norway, Austria, Poland, Switzerland, Spain and other countries to Antalya, Bodrum, Dalaman, Izmir, and Istanbul in Turkey.

Fleet

 2 Boeing 737-400
14 Boeing 737-800

Fokker 100 CS-TPA (Author / Geneva)

PGA – PORTUGALIA

Aeroporto Lisboa, Rua C, Edif. 70, 1749-79 Lisbon, Portugal, Tel. 21-8425500, Fax. 21-8425623, E-mail: cc@pga.pt, www.pga.pt

Three- / Two- letter code	IATA No.	Reg'n prefix	ICAO callsign
PGA / NI	685	CS	Portugalia

Portugalia was founded as a regional airline on 25th July 1989 and nearly a year later, on 7th July 1990 it began operations with a Fokker 100. During the first two years, losses were made equivalent to about US$12 million, but 1993 showed a small profit. With the introduction of the sixth Fokker 100 in 1995 the colour scheme was slightly modified. Especially in holiday times, PGA is also active with charter work and serves Portuguese destinations, particularly Faro, from various European airports. In May 1997 PGA took delivery of its first Regional Jet from Embraer, an RJ-145 and put it into service on an expanded route network. During 1999 the SAir Group agreed to acquire from the 80% owner Espirito Santo a 42% shareholding in PGA and the airline's activities were realigned in anticipation of this being completed. However, the move was blocked in mid-2000 by the European Commission on competition grounds, and the SAir investment was withdrawn. There are co-operation agreements with Air France, Air Luxor and Regional Airlines and some routes are flown as codeshares. Portugalia has its operating and maintenance base in Lisbon.

Routes

Barcelona, Basle, Bilbao, Bologna, Brussels, Faro, La Corunha, Lisbon, Lyon, Madrid, Manchester, Marseilles, Milan, Nice, Porto, Stuttgart, Toulouse, Turin, Valencia, Valladolid, Vigo.

Fleet

8 Embraer ERJ-145
6 Fokker 100

Boeing 747-4F6 N753PR (Pierre Alain Petit / Manila)

PHILIPPINES

1, Legaspi Street, Makati, Metro Manila 1059,
Philippines, Tel. 632-8171234, Fax. 632-8136715
E-mail: rgeecd@pal.com.ph, www.philippineair.com

Three- / Two- letter code	IATA No.	Reg'n prefix	ICAO callsign
PAL/ PR	079	RP	Philippine

Philippine Air Lines was set up on 26th February 1941, but had to suspend operations at the end of the year as a result of the Japanese invasion. After liberation, PAL restarted services with five DC-3s on 14th February 1946. Far East Air Transport, which had routes to Hong Kong, Shanghai, Bangkok and Calcutta, was taken over with its five DC-4s in 1947. In the same year PAL began scheduled service to San Francisco, but in 1954 all international routes except Hong Kong were suspended. This allowed an expansion of domestic services to take place. In 1962, in co-operation with KLM, the San Francisco route was re-opened. From May 1966 BAC One-Elevens were introduced, and from 1969 Douglas DC-8s were used to start Amsterdam, Frankfurt and Rome services. In 1974 Air Manila and Filipinas were bought, and in this same year the first leased DC-10-30 arrived as a DC-8 replacement. Boeing 747s and Airbus A300 B4s were introduced in 1979 and with the arrival of Fokker 50s from1988 the older HS-748s were retired. Likewise The BAC One-Elevens were replaced by Boeing 737-300s. The newest jet in the fleet is the Airbus A340-300, introduced in 1996 alongside the Boeing 747-400s for long-range routes. Further re-equipment for the future was expected until 1998, when on 23rd September, Philippines was forced to cease operations, as a result of employees' strikes and the general Asian downturn. After a few weeks of difficult negotiations, service was restarted with a sharply reduced route network, fleet and staff. A programme of reorganisation and reconstruction is showing some success and it seems that PAL is on its way out of its crisis. Airbus Industrie Financial Service and other leasing companies are supporting the airline with new aircraft. There is a codeshare arrangement with KLM for flights to Amsterdam.

Routes

Abu Dhabi, Bacolod, Bangkok, Butuan, Cairo, Cagayan, Cebu, Cotabato, Dammam, Davao, Dipolog, Djakarta, Dubai, Doha, Fukuoka, Guam, Ho Chi Minh City, Hong Kong, Honolulu, Jeddah, Kuala Lumpur, Legaspi, Los Angeles, Manila, Melbourne, Osaka, Puerto Princesa, Pusan, Riyadh, Roxas, San Francisco, Seoul, Shanghai, Singapore, Tacloban, Taipei, Tokyo, Vancouver, Xiamen, Zamboango and other domestic destinations.

Fleet

3 Airbus A320-200
8 Airbus A330-300
4 Airbus A340-300
7 Boeing 737-300

3 Boeing 737-400
4 Boeing 747-400

Boeing 737-3Q8 CX-PUA (Manfred Turek / Buenos Aires-AEP)

PLUNA

Colonia 1013-1021, P.O.Box 1360 Montevideo
Uruguay, Tel. 2-980606, Fax. 2-921478, E-mail:
info@pluna.com.uy, www.pluna.com.uy

Three- / Two- letter code	IATA No.	Reg'n prefix	ICAO callsign
PUA / PU	286	CX	Pluna

Primeras Lineas Uruguayas de Navigacion Aerea – PLUNA – was founded in September 1935 by the Marquez Vaeza brothers. Operations began on 20th November 1936 with two de Havilland DH.90 Dragonflies. The company expanded and ordered a DH.86B, but then operations had to be suspended on 15th March 1943. After the end of the Second World War, the government of Uruguay acquired 83% of the airline's shares and on 12th November 1951 the remaining shares were also transferred to the state. Douglas DC-3s were used to operate to neighbouring countries, and a domestic network was set up. In addition to the DC-3s, de Havilland Herons and Vickers Viscounts were used. In late 1967 PLUNA took over the route network and aircraft belonging to CAUSA. The airline took on its first jet, a Boeing 737-200, late in 1969. Pluna's sole overseas route was a weekly service from Montevideo to Madrid; Boeing 707s were used on this route from 1982, but Pluna entered into a co-operation agreement with Spanair in 1993, whereby the Spanish airline operated the route with its Boeing 767s, as Pluna had no suitable aircraft of its own. This situation altered late in 1994, when Brazilian airline VARIG bought 51% of the shares in Pluna, thus bringing about the anticipated privatisation. Employees have also acquired shares, so that the Brazilian company now holds only 49%. Flights to Spain were restarted with a Douglas DC-10-30, painted in a new colour scheme. During 1998 the colours were again modified to more closely match those of Varig. Since the end of 2002 a Boeing 767 has been used, with Pluna operating the Madrid flight under its own auspices.

Routes

Asuncion, Buenos Aires, Cordoba, Madrid, Montevideo, Porto Alegre, Punta de Este, Rio de Janeiro, Rosario, Salvador deBahia, Santiago de Chile, Sao Paulo.

Fleet

4 Boeing 737-200Adv.
1 Boeing 737-300
1 Boeing 767-300ER

Boeing 747-46NF N451PA (JStefan Schlick / Luxembourg)

POLAR AIR CARGO

100 Oceangate Long Beach, California 90802, USA, Tel. 562-5287471, Fax. 562-4369333, E-mail: charter @polaraircargo.com, www.polaraircargo.com

Three- / Two- letter code	IATA No.	Reg'n prefix	ICAO callsign
PAC / PO	403	N	Polar Tiger

Polar Air Cargo was established in January 1993 and began scheduled freight services to Anchorage, Honolulu and New York in May 1993. Two Boeing 747-100 freighters were brought into service initially, with two more added later in the year. On 7th July 1994 the Federal Aviation Administration gave permission for the airline to carry out its own maintenance at its main base in New York and during the year more Boeing 747s were added, so that by the end of the year there were 12 in the fleet. Since then the purely 747 fleet, including -400Fs from late 2000, has continued to grow. Alongside FedEx and UPS, Polar has been one of the fastest growing cargo airlines, with worldwide scheduled and charter operations. The airline works with cargo agencies worldwide and offers a dependable service. The scheduled services to Europe, India, Africa and the Middle East were augmented with further new destinations from the mid 1990s. In 2001 Polar Air Cargo was taken over by competitor Atlas Air, but operations continue unaltered and independently, though the aircraft have received a revised colour scheme. There are co-operation agreements with Finnair and Air New Zealand.

Routes

Scheduled freight services to Amsterdam, Anchorage, Atlanta, Auckland, Cali, Chaborovsk, Chicago, Dubai, Gander, Glasgow, Helsinki, Hong Kong, Honolulu, London, Los Angeles, Manaus, Manchester, Manila, Melbourne, Miami, Nadi, New York, Santiago, Sao Paulo, Sapporo, Seoul, Singapore, Sydney, Taipei, and Tokyo, plus many ad hoc and charter flights worldwide for all types of freight.

Fleet

8 Boeing 747-200F
3 Boeing 747-300F
6 Boeing 747-400F

Boeing 737-8Q8 5W-SAM (Andreas Zeitler / Sydney)

POLYNESIAN

NPF Buildg. Beach Road, P.O.Box 599 Apia, West Samoa, Tel. 685-21261, Fax. 685-20023, E-mail: enquiries@ polynesionairlines.ws, www.PolynesianAirlines.com

Three- / Two- letter code	IATA No.	Reg'n prefix	ICAO callsign
PAO / PH	162	5W	Polynesian

After the collapse of its predecessor, Samoan Airlines, Polynesian Airlines Limited was founded on 7th May 1959. Its first service was from Apia to Pago Pago, using a Percival Prince. After the independence of Polynesia in 1962, further routes to the Cook Islands were opened on 5th July 1963 and a Douglas DC-3 was acquired. In 1968 Polynesian took on a Douglas DC-4 and from January 1972 onwards modern turboprops were acquired in the form of two HS.748s. Modernisation became possible after the state took a 70% stake in the airline and made more capital available. Polynesian entered the jet age in 1981 with the delivery of a Boeing 737, which in turn allowed the addition of new routes to Australia. Various smaller aircraft such as GAF Nomads, Britten-Norman Islanders and de Havilland Twin Otters were also used on regional routes. In the early 1990s Polynesian acquired the latest Boeing 737-300. A Boeing 767 leased from Air New Zealand followed in 1993; this was used for routes to the United States, but proved to be too large and was returned. There is close co-operation and a marketing alliance with Air New Zealand, with a codeshare agreement. Polynesian also co-operates with Qantas and Air Pacific. A new model Boeing 737-800 with winglets was delivered in autumn 2001 and featured a revised colour scheme. A further 737-800 joined it in 2002 and services have been resumed after a break of several years to Melbourne, Christchurch and to the USA.

Routes

Apia, Asau, Auckland, Brisbane, Christchurch, Fagolii, Hanan, Honolulu, Los Angeles, Maota Savail Island, Melbourne, Nadi, Nine, Pago Pago, Sydney, Tongatapu, Vila, Wellington.

Fleet

2 Boeing 737-800
2 De Havilland DHC-6 Twin Otter
1 BN-2 Islander

Ilyushin IL-86 RA-86094 (Marcus Baltes / Frankfurt)

PULKOVO

18/4 Pilotov Ul.196210 St.Petersburg, Russia
Tel. 812-1043462, Fax. 812-1043462
www.pulkovo.ru

Three- / Two- letter code	IATA No.	Reg'n prefix	ICAO callsign
PLK / FV	195	RA	Pulkovo

The former Leningrad Division of Aeroflot, just as with other former Aeroflot directorates, was recast into individual airline companies after the break up of the Soviet Union. Lacking any particular form of organisation, a non-scheduled operation was continued as Aeroflot. Only with the new formation of Aeroflot Russian International Airlines ARIA was the former state aviation reorganised. Thus in 1992 the Pulkovo Aviation Concern was established in St. Petersburg (formerly Leningrad), taking its name from its home base airfield of Pulkovo. Initially it took over the aircraft of the former Aeroflot division and flew both domestic and international routes on behalf of ARIA. After the concern renamed itself in 1996 as Pulkovo Aviation Enterprise and painted the aircraft in its own distinctive colours, it undertook a pruning of routes which had been unprofitable. Pulkovo still has a strategic alliance with Aeroflot-Russian Airlines and flies some routes on its behalf, under a sort of codeshare arrangement. Several new routes have been established from St. Petersburg to Western Europe. Pulkovo is also active in the charter and freight businesses, and is responsible for the management of its home airport and the provision of ground handling services there.

Routes

Adler/Sochi, Almaty, Amsterdam, Archangelansk, Baku, Barnaul, Berlin, Bishkek, Chelyabinsk, Copenhagen, Düsseldorf, Ekatarinenburg, Frankfurt, Gyandzha, Hamburg, Hanover, Helsinki, Irtusk, Kaliningrad, Karaganda, Kiev, Krasnodar, Krasnoyarsk, Mineralnye Vody, Moscow, Munich, Murmansk, Norilsk, Novosibirsk, Omsk, Petropavlowsk, Prague, Rostov, Samara, St.Petersburg, Stockholm, Surgut, Tashkent, Tbilisi, Tel Aviv, Tyumen, Ufa, Vienna, Vladivostok, Volgograd, Yerevan.

Fleet

8 Ilyushin IL-86
10 Tupolev Tu-134
24 Tupolev Tu-154

Boeing 737-476 VH-TJU (Frank Schorr / Brisbane)

QANTAS

Qantas Centre, 203 Coward Street, Sydney, NSW 2020, Australia, Tel. 2-96913636, Fax. 2-9693339, www.qantas.com.au

Three- / Two- letter code	IATA No.	Reg'n prefix	ICAO callsign
QFA / QF	081	VH	Qantas

Queensland and Northern Territory Aerial Service Ltd – QANTAS for short – was formed on 16th November 1920. Two Avro 504s were stationed at Longreach, initially for sightseeing and air taxi flights, and the first route from Charleville to Cloncurry was flown in November 1922. Qantas aircraft were also used to set up the famous Flying Doctor Service in 1928 and in the same year began the first scheduled air service in Australia, from Brisbane to Toowoomba. In co-operation with Imperial Airways, Qantas served the London-Brisbane route, with Qantas flying the last leg from Singapore to Brisbane from 1934, using Short Empire flying boats to Sydney from

1938. The airline was known as Qantas Empire Airways from 1934 to 1967. During the war, flights in Australia were almost halted, but post-war, Lockheed Constellations, DC-3s and DC-4s were all acquired. In 1947 the Australian government acquired a controlling interest and in 1953 Qantas took over British Commonwealth Airlines with its aircraft and routes to the USA. Boeing 707s were delivered from 1959, Boeing 747s from August 1971 and Boeing 767s from 1985, the latter also bringing a new aircraft livery. Australian Airlines, also state-owned, was integrated into Qantas from 1st November 1993, giving the airline a new domestic dimension,

having previously been responsible for international services only. Qantas has shareholdings in Airlink, Eastern Australian Airlines, Southern Australian Airlines and Sunstates Airlines; these airlines fly feeder services for the national carrier. British Airways took a 25% stake in Qantas in 1992; there is close co-operation, and Qantas is a founder member of the Oneworld Alliance. When Ansett failed in 2001, Australian commercial aviation was reshaped; Qantas took over Impulse Airlines and new domestic routes were added. The delivery of the first Airbus A330s in 2002 signalled the end of Boeing fleet dominance and A380s are on order for 2006.

Routes

Atlanta, Auckland, Bangkok, Buenos Aires, Chicago, Christchurch, Denpasar, Djakarta, Frankfurt, Ho Chi Minh City, Hong Kong, Honolulu, Johannesburg, London, Los Angeles, Manila, Memphis, Mumbai, Nadi, Nagoya, New York, Noumea, Osaka, Paris, Port Moresby, Queenstown, Rome, Shanghai, Singapore, Taipei, Tokyo, Wellington and more than 25 domestic destinations.

Fleet

		Ordered
4 Airbus A330-200	7 Boeing 747-200/300	9 Airbus A330
37 Boeing 737-300/400	30 Boeing 747-400	12 Airbus A380
19 Boeing 737-800	36 Boeing 767-200/300ER	

Airbus A300-622R A7-ABV (Albert Kuhbandner / Munich)

QATAR AIRWAYS

P.O.Box 22550, Doha, Qatar, Tel. 449-6000
Fax. 4621533, E-mail: info@qatarairways.com
www.qatarairways.com

Three- / Two- letter code	IATA No.	Reg'n prefix	ICAO callsign
QTR / QR	157	A7	Qatari

The Qatar government, though a shareholder in the multi-national Gulf Air, decided that it would like to have its own flag carrier, and as a result Qatar Airways was brought into being. It was founded on the personal initiative of the Emir in 1993. At first an Airbus A310 was leased and services commenced in January 1994 with a route to London. The initial choice of aircraft was obviously not a good one, and the Airbus was returned to its lessor and replaced by a Boeing 747SP in 1995. Likewise the pricing and route policies were obviously causing some difficulty, and the performance of the airline lagged behind

expectations. Boeing 727-200s were bought for use on regional services, a market which the airline wished to enter. A change in the management of the company in early 1997 however brought a change of direction; Qatar Airways was repositioned in the market and set out to become a quality carrier. New examples of the most modern aircraft were acquired, Airbus A300-600s for the longer routes and A320s for short and medium distances. Since then Qatar has expanded slowly and cautiously in new markets. Munich was added as a second European destination from 1999, in addition to London, but

Qatar's concentration is however in the Middle East and Asia, where the network has been expanded. The fleet has also grown with the addition of further A300-600s, and from 2002, new A330s. Qatar is the launch customer for the A340-600HGW (high gross weight), with two on order for early 2006 and eight options. These and other large Airbus orders (including the A380) will expand the fleet more rapidly, from its current two dozen to around sixty by the end of the decade.

Routes

Abu Dhabi, Amman, Bahrain, Bangkok, Beirut, Cairo, Colombo, Dacca, Damascus, Dammam, Doha, Dubai, Djakarta, Jeddah, Karachi, Kathmandu, Khartoum, Kuala Lumpur, Kuwait, Lahore, London, Male, Manchester, Manila, Mumbai, Munich, Muscat, Paris, Peshawar, Trivandrum.

Fleet		Ordered
7 Airbus A300-600	5 Airbus A330	4 Airbus A320
1 Airbus A319-100CJ		2 Airbus A330
11 Airbus A320		2 Airbus A380

Embraer ERJ-135ER F-GRGP (Josef Krauthäuser / Düsseldorf)

REGIONAL AIRLINES

Aéroport Nantes Atlantique, F-44345 Bouguenais Cedex, France, Tel. 2-40135300, Fax. 2-40135313 E-mail: contact@regional.com, www.regional.com

Three- / Two- letter code	IATA No.	Reg'n prefix	ICAO callsign
RGI / YS	977	F	Regional

The merger of Air Vendée and Airlec in 1992 brought a new airline, Regional Airlines, into being. Both constituent airlines were active regional operators in France, and operated between them Dornier 228s, Fairchild-Swearingen Metros and other smaller types. From Nantes, Rouen and Rennes Regional Airlines built up its network. Clermont-Ferrand is also an important hub for the company, providing good connecting services to other French cities. The fleet also grew steadily and was always kept relatively young; BAe Jetstream 31s in 1993, Saab 2000s from 1995 and Embraer Brasilias from 1997. In

1997 Regional acquired Deutsche BA's regional fleet of Saab 340s and Saab 2000s, as well as some routes. Regional was one of the first European customers for the new Embraer Regional Jet series. The first of these RJ-145s was brought into use in May 1997 between Clermont-Ferrand and Paris. The smaller RJ-135 arrived at the beginning of 2000 and replaced the Jetstreams. Air France took a shareholding in Regional Airlines quite early in its life, and has increased it so that the national airline now owns 70%. Two regional operators, Flandre Air and Protheus Air were merged with Regional from

1st April 2001. The route structure was reorganised and harmonised with Air France and its partners; Regional operates out of hubs in Paris, Lyon, Bordeaux and Clermont-Ferrand. In autumn 2001 the company name was changed to Regional Compagnie Aérienne Européenne.

Routes

Aberdeen, Ajaccio, Amsterdam, Angers, Angouleme, Barcelona, Basle/Mulhouse, Bastia, Biarritz, Bologne, Bordeaux, Brest, Brussels, Clermont-Ferrand, Dijon, Dublin, Düsseldorf, Geneva, Hanover, La Rochelle, Lille, Lisbon, London, Lorient, Lyon, Madrid, Milan, Montpellier, Nantes, Nice, Nuremberg, Paris, Pau, Perpignan, Poitiers, Porto, Rennes, Strasbourg, Stuttgart, Toulon, Toulouse, Turin, Venice, Zürich.

Fleet

14 Embraer EMB-120 Brasilia	6 Saab 2000
9 Embraer ERJ-135	
25 Embraer ERJ-145	

Boeing 737-76Q PR-SAA (Manfred Turek / Rio de Janeiro)

RIO-SUL

Avenida Rio Branco 85, CEP 20040-004 Rio de Janeiro, Brazil, Tel. 21-2168591, Fax. 21-2532044, www.voeriosul.com.br

Three- / Two- letter code	IATA No.	Reg'n prefix	ICAO callsign
RSL / SL	293	PT	Riosul

On 12th November 1976 the Brazilian government decree number 76590 imposed a new order on regional air transport. Five companies were contracted, each to build up regional air services in their allocated territories. Varig acquired shares in Top Taxi Aereo and thus in December 1976 formed Rio-Sul Servicos Aereos Regionais SA. The airline was allocated the southern area of Brazil and began building a network using Embraer 110 Bandeirantes. The Piper Navajos which had been taken over from Top Taxi were also used. The company showed satisfactory

development and in 1988 was in a position to order new Embraer 120 Brasilias, and these were put into service in the same year. In1992 the government changed its policy and allowed companies to expand beyond the regional boundaries which had been laid down in the 1976 decree. This gave the opportunity for the acquisition of new aircraft; the routes were longer and because of the size of the country could only be served by jets. Rio Sul received its first Boeing 737-500 in October 1992, with more following in the next few years and these were used to expand the

previous network. During 1995 Nordeste was taken over and their Fokker 50s integrated into the fleet. With the introduction of the Embraer ERJ-145 in 1998 Rio Sul set itself on track to operating a purely jet fleet; the Fokker 50s have now been phased out. The airline, now a 100% subsidiary of Varig Holdings, is based at Sao Paulo Congonhas International Airport.

Routes

Araguaina, Belem, Belo Horizonte, Brasilia, Campinas, Campos, Carajas, Cascavel, Caxias du Sul, Chapeco, Criciuma, Curitiba, Florianopolis, Goiania, Iguacu Falls, Ilheus, Imperatiz, Joinville, Lages, Livramento, Londrina, Maraba, Maringa, Navegantes, Passo Fundo, Pelotas, Porto Alegre, Porto Seguro, Recife, Ribeirao Preto, Rio de Janeiro, Rio Grande, Santa Maria, Santo Angelo, Sao Jose do Rio Preto, Sao Jose dos Campos, Sao Paulo, Toledo, Uberaba, Uruguaiana, Vitoria.

Fleet	Ordered
20 Boeing 737-300/500	15 Embraer ERJ-145
6 Boeing 737-700	
3 Embraer EMB-120 Brasilia	
16 Embraer ERJ-145	

Boeing 747-428 CN-RGA (Marcus Baltes / Frankfurt)

ROYAL AIR MAROC

Aéroport Arifa, Casablanca, Morocco
Tel. 02-311122, Fax. 02-442409, E-mail: info@
royalairmaroc.com, www.royalairmaroc.com

Three- / Two- letter code	IATA No.	Reg'n prefix	ICAO callsign
RAM / AT	147	CN	Royal Air Maroc

The name Royal Air Maroc was introduced on 28th June 1957, after Morocco had gained independence from Spain and France. The state-owned airline emerged from Société Air Atlas and Avia Maroc Aérienne, which together formed the Compagnie Chérifienne des Transports Aériens (CCTA) on 25th June 1953. At first there were only domestic services and some routes to France using Junkers Ju 52s but these were soon replaced by Douglas DC-3s. In 1957 a Lockheed Constellation came into use and was employed on the newly introduced international routes, including New York. In July 1958 Royal Air Maroc received its first Caravelle. Boeing 707s were bought in 1975 for long-distance services, and Boeing 727s were acquired from 1970 for regional and medium length routes. The next fleet replacement programme commenced in July 1986 with the delivery of the first Boeing 757, and the first of the ATR 42s arrived in March 1989 for use on domestic services. In 1993 RAM acquired a widebody, a Boeing 747-400, and also from Boeing in 1994 came the 737-400 to replace the 727s and older model 737s. The latest generation of Boeing 737 has also been ordered by Royal Air Maroc, with the first 737-700s and -800s both arriving during 1999. Latest type in the fleet is the Boeing 767-300, replacing the older 747-200s, and being used to expand longer-range services. The order for Airbus A321s for delivery from late 2003 is noteworthy, marking a move away from Boeing. The government owns almost all of the shares, though Air France and Iberia have small stakes. Air Algerie, Air France, Gulf Air, Iberia, Libyan Airlines, TAP Air Portugal, and Tunis Air all co-operate with Royal Air Maroc.

Routes

Abidjan, Abu Dhabi, Agadir, Algiers, Al Hoceima, Amsterdam, Athens, Bahrain, Bamako, Barcelona, Basle, Bordeaux, Brussels, Cairo, Casablanca, Conakry, Constantine, Dakar, Dhaklia, Dubai, Errachidia, Essaouria, Fez, Frankfurt, Gaza, Geneva, Jeddah, Johannesburg, Las Palmas, Laayoune, Libreville, Lisbon, London, Los Angeles, Lyon, Madrid, Malaga, Marseilles, Marrakech, Miami, Milan, Montreal, Nador, New York, Niamey, Nice, Nouakchott, Oran, Orlando,Paris, Quarzazate, Oujda, Rabat, Riyadh, Rome, Tangier, Tetuan, Toulouse, Tunis, Zürich.

Fleet

		Ordered
2 ATR 42-300	7 Boeing 737-800	8 Boeing 737-800
6 Boeing 737-200Adv.	1 Boeing 747-400	4 Airbus A321
6 Boeing 737-500	2 Boeing 757-200	
7 Boeing 737-400	2 Boeing 767-300ER	
5 Boeing 737-700		

Boeing 767-33A(ER) V8-RBL (Frank Fielitz / Frankfurt)

ROYAL BRUNEI

P.O.Box 737 Bandar Seri Begawan BS 8671,
Sultanate of Brunei, Tel. 2-240500, Fax. 2-244737
E-mail: feedback@rba.com.bn, www.bruneiair.com

Three- / Two- letter code	IATA No.	Reg'n prefix	ICAO callsign
RBA / BI	672	V8	Brunei

Royal Brunei Airlines was founded on 18th November 1974 as the national airline of Brunei Negara Darussalam and began operations on the Bandar Seri Bagawan to Singapore route on 14th May 1975. A few Boeing 737-200s were the mainstay of the fleet until three Boeing 757s were acquired, the first on 6th May 1986. When this aircraft was delivered Royal Brunei adopted an attractive new colour scheme, principally in yellow and white. A service to London Gatwick was flown by the 757s, but in order to be able to serve long-distance destinations non-stop, a leased Boeing 767 was acquired in June 1990, with the airline's own 767-300ERs following from 1992. The 757s took over some of the routes previously flown by the 737s, which were disposed of. An Airbus A340 delivered in 1993, although it wears Royal Brunei colours, is operated as the personal transport of the Sultan of Brunei. More Boeing 767s were added during 1993 and 1994, and in 1996 two Fokker 100s were acquired for regional routes, but these have now been sold. The airline is owned by the small, but rich state, and yet was still adversely affected by the Asian business crisis of the late 1990s so that as bookings reduced, expansion plans were shelved and the fleet and routes sharply reduced. From early 2000 the situation improved and stabilised. Two Airbus A319s were ordered at the end of 2002 and with their delivery in autumn 2003, the Boeing 757s are to be phased out.The airline has discussed with Airbus the acquisition of two Airbus A340-500s for long-haul services from summer 2004; this would allow non-stop to London, currently served via the Middle East. All this would fit in with the long term plan established in spring 2003, which calls for an expansion to a feet of 12 narrowbodies and 6 widebodies by 2013.

Routes

Abu Dhabi, Balikpapan, Bandar Seri Begawan, Bangkok, Brisbane, Darwin, Denpasar, Djakarta,Dubai, Frankfurt, Hong Kong, Jeddah, Kolkota, Kota Kinabalu, Kuala Lumpur, Kuching, Kuwait, London, Manila, Perth, Singapore, Shanghai, Surabaya, Taipei.

Fleet

2 Airbus A319
2 Boeing 757-200
8 Boeing 767-300ER

Airbus A310-304 JY-AGL (Albert Kuhbandner / Munich)

ROYAL JORDANIAN

P.O.Box 302 Amman 11118, Jordan
Tel. 6-5607399, Fax. 6-5672527, www.rja.com.jo
E-mail: rjmail@rja.com.jo

Three- / Two- letter code	IATA No.	Reg'n prefix	ICAO callsign
RJA / RJ	512	JY	Jordanian

On 8th December 1963, King Hussein declared the establishment of the Jordanian national airline Alia. It succeeded Jordan Airways, which itself had succeeded Air Jordan of the Holy Land two years previously. Alia (meaning high-flying) was named after King Hussein's daughter. Operations began from 15th December 1963 from Amman to Beirut, Cairo and Kuwait with two Handley Page Dart Heralds and a Douglas DC-7. In 1964 a second DC-7 was added to the fleet. With the introduction of the SE 210 Caravelle a European route to Rome was opened for the first time in 1965; Paris and London followed in

1966. The DC-7s were destroyed during the Israeli-Arab Six Day War and later replaced by Fokker F.27s. The Jordanian government assumed full control of the airline in 1968. In 1969 the network was expanded to include Munich, Istanbul and Teheran, followed by Frankfurt in 1970. In 1971 Alia acquired its first Boeing 707; the Caravelle was replaced in 1973 by Boeing 727s and in 1977 two Boeing 747s were bought. Flights to New York and Los Angeles began in 1984; Alia was the first of the Arab national carriers to fly schedules to the USA, using 747s. TriStars joined the fleet in 1981, and Airbus A310s

in 1986, along with a new colour scheme and the new name, Royal Jordanian. During the Gulf War of 1990/91 the airline suffered severe losses, so some aircraft had to be leased. From 1992 Berlin, Jakarta and Aden were served, and Athens reinstated. The arrival of the third Airbus A320 in March 1996 saw the retirement of the last Boeing 727. Likewise, the last TriStar left the fleet in 1999; the Airbus A340 had been acquired as a replacement, but proved too large and so were leased out. More A310-300s were added, but in 2002 the A340-200 came back into the reckoning, replacing several A310-200s.

Routes

Abu Dhabi, Aden, Al Ain, Algiers, Amman, Amsterdam, Ankara, Aqaba, Athens, Bahrain, Bangkok, Beirut, Berlin, Brussels, Cairo, Casablanca, Chicago, Colombo, Damascus, Dammam, Delhi, Detroit, Djakarta, Doha, Dubai, Frankfurt, Gaza, Geneva, Istanbul, Jeddah, Kolkota, Karachi, Kuala Lumpur, Kuwait, Larnaca, London, Madrid, Montreal, Mumbai, Muscat, New York, Paris, Riyadh, Rome, Sanaa, Shannon, Tel Aviv, Tripoli, Tunis, Vienna and Zürich.

Fleet		Ordered
8 Airbus A310-300	2 Boeing 707F	2 Airbus A340-200
3 Airbus A340-200		
5 Airbus A320-200		

BAe HS.748 Srs.2A 9N-AAV (Romano Germann / Kathmandu)

ROYAL NEPAL AIRLINES

RNAC Building, P.O.Box 401 Kantipath
Kathmandu, 711000 Nepal, Tel. 1-220757
Fax. 1-225348, www.royalnepal.com

Three- / Two- letter code	IATA No.	Reg'n prefix	ICAO callsign
RNA / RA	285	9N	Royal Nepal

Royal Nepal Airlines Corporation Limited was founded by the government on 1st July 1958, replacing Indian Airlines which had operated domestic services for some eight years on Nepal's behalf. External services to such points as Delhi and Calcutta continued to be operated by Indian Airlines until 1960 when Royal Nepal took over Douglas DC-3s and later Fokker F.27 Friendships, ideal aircraft for the harsh conditions of Nepal because they are so undemanding. Three HS.748s came into use in 1970, and the first Boeing 727 in June 1972. However, the airfield at mountainous Kathmandu had to be extended by that time, which was a difficult business; even today it is not possible for very large aircraft to take off and land there. The Boeing 727 was used to open service to Delhi. The acquisition of de Havilland Twin Otters in 1971 improved services to remote mountain villages with short runways. The delivery of the first Boeing 757s in 1987 and 1988 marked both a fleet replacement plan and an expansion of services to Europe; Frankfurt and London were both served for the first time from the 1989/90 Winter timetable. As demand on these international services to India and Europe grew, further 757s were added. From 1996 services to Shanghai in China and Osaka in Japan were also added. Royal Nepal planned the acquisition of further aircraft, but in 2001 the political situation in Nepal led to a cessation of flights to Europe and Singapore. The company had to overcome some financial scandals and disposed of some aircraft. However, from April 2003 service to Singapore was restored, and Kuala Lumpur added as a new destination; both countries waived landing fees.

Routes

Bangalore, Bangkok, Bharatpur, Biratnagar, Delhi, Hong Kong, Jomsom, Kathmandu, Kolkota, Kuala Lumpur, Lukla, Manang, Mumbai, Osaka, Pokhara, Shanghai, Singapore and to about ten other destinations in Nepal.

Fleet

2 Boeing 757-200
1 BAe HS.748
6 De Havilland DHC-6

Boeing 737-8AS EI-CSP (Martin Kühn / Hahn)

RYANAIR

Corporate Building Dublin Airport, Republic of Ireland, Tel. 1-8121212, Fax. 1-8121213
www.ryanair.com

Three- / Two- letter code	IATA No.	Reg'n prefix	ICAO callsign
RYR / FR)	224	EI	Ryanair

Founded in May 1985, Ryanair quickly became a competitor to Aer Lingus on its regional services and flights to Great Britain. No airline has served more points in Ireland, nine airports in all at one time, than Ryanair. It used ATR 42s and BAC/Rombac One-Elevens, and took over Aer Lingus routes from Dublin to Munich and Dublin to Liverpool. Dublin to Luton was also an important route in the early years. Starting from March 1994 the fleet was completely changed over from One-Elevens to Boeing 737-200s. Ryan Air UK was set up in 1995 as a wholly-owned subsidiary and operates from Stansted as a low-

cost airline. It has put established British airlines under pressure and has been a pioneer in cheap flights to Europe, with particular expansion since 1997. Secondary airports in the general area of business centres are the main destinations; this helps to keep operating costs as low as possible, and allows the ticket prices to be particularly attractive to passengers. Some of Ryanair's aircraft have been painted as 'logojets', carrying colourful advertising for cars, beer, newspapers or telephone services, as well as its scheduled services. Over the years the fleet of second-hand 737-200s has been built up,

but a switch to factory fresh 737-800s began in March 1999. In 2002 Ryanair started an offensive on the German market, establishing a second European hub at Hahn (the first is at Charleroi, Belgium), basing four Boeing 737s here. Other airports including Lübeck, Friedrichshafen or Altenburg and Niederrhein were added. In 2003 Ryanair acquired competitor Buzz from KLM, and integrated their services into its Stansted operations. Rapid expansion continues, with a large number of new Boeings in course of delivery.

Routes

Aarhus, Altenburg, Ancona, Berlin-SXF, Beauvais, Biarritz, Birmingham, Bournemouth, Brescia, Brest, Bristol, Carcassonne, Cardiff, Charleroi, Cork, Dinard, Dublin, Eindhoven, Florence, Genoa, Glasgow, Groningen, Hahn, Kerry, Knock, Kristianstad, Lamezia Terme, Leeds/Bradford, Liverpool, London-Stansted, Londonderry, Lübeck, Malmö, Manchester, Nimes, Oslo, Palermo, Perpignan, Rimini, St.Etienne, Stockholm, Teesside, Turin, Venice.

Fleet	Ordered
21 Boeing 737-200	110 Boeing 737-800
36 Boeing 737-800	

Boeing 757-25F G-JMCE (Stefan Schlick / Puerto Vallarta)

RYAN INTERNATIONAL AIRLINES

6800 West Kellogg, Wichita,KS 67209, USA
Tel. 316-9420141, Fax. 316-9427949,
E-mail: inquiries@flyryan.com, www.flyryan.com

Three- / Two- letter code	IATA No.	Reg'n prefix	ICAO callsign
RYN / HS		N	Ryan International

Ryan Aviation has been in existence since 1972 as an airline operating charter flights and began operations on 3rd March 1973 as DeBoer Aviation. Ryan International was a division of these operations until it was sold in 1985 to the PHH group. In February 1989 Ronald Ryan bought the company back and started an airfreight service from Indianapolis for the US Mail using eight DC-9s and nine Boeing 727s. The airline operates worldwide as a subcontractor for Emery Worldwide, using further Boeing 727s. Ryan sought to increase its activities in the Pacific, and a Boeing 727 is used to fly freshly caught fish from Saipan to Japan, and freight is flown between the islands of Micronesia. A Boeing 737-200 was made available to a tour operator for passenger flights from Cleveland and Cincinnati; this service was extended to Atlantic City in 1995 and switched to Airbus A320 operation. The fleet was also increased in that year by the acquisition of further Boeing 727s to meet demand. However, Ryan operates few aircraft in its own colours; most are painted in the colours of the particular client and only some small external lettering indicates the identity of the real operator. Aircraft are leased in and out as seasonal demand varies, with aircraft from European charter and holiday airlines sometimes seen during the European winter. In 2003 Ryan Air took on long-term contract for the operation of two Airbus A320s on schedules from Atlanta to Las Vegas and Los Angeles for Air Tran, and painted in their colours.

Routes

Passenger charters for, amongst others, Apple Vacations, Gold Transportation, Sun Trips, Sports Hawk, and Trans Global Tours to the Caribbean,South America, Canada and Europe. Intensive freight network in the USA for Emery and the United States Postal Service.

Fleet

6 Airbus A320
3 Boeing 737-200
2 Boeing 737-400
1 Boeing 737-800

2 Boeing 757-200
18 Boeing 727
2 Douglas DC-10-10

Boeing 737-3Q8 CS-TGP (Lutz Schönfeld / Palma de Mallorca)

SATA

Avenida Infante D Henrique 55-4, Ponta Delgada, Portugal, Tel. 296-209727
Fax. 296-209722, www.sata.pt

Three- / Two- letter code	IATA No.	Reg'n prefix	ICAO callsign
RZO / S4	331	CS	Air Azores

SATA Air Acores was founded as long ago as August 1941. Transatlantic flying boats would make a stop in the Azores, and the regional administration in the Azores saw air services as an alternative to seaborne ferries. However, at that time there were no land airports anywhere on the islands and so the infrastructure had to be painstakingly created. On 15th June 1947 the first flight took place, from Sao Miguel to Santa Maria. A seven-passenger Beech 18 was brought into service. Later aircraft used as services developed over the years were the Douglas DC-3, HS-748, Do 228 and BAe ATP. The company grew under the ownership of the regional government, which later established the SATA Group. In 1994 SATA took over Oceanair with its two BN-2 Islanders. In 1995 SATA acquired a Boeing 737-300 and began charter flights outside the archipelago. As Azores Express, or SATA Express services to Toronto, Montreal and Boston were undertaken. During 1998 SATA was awarded licences for scheduled services to Funchal and Porto. More Boeing 737-300s and Airbus A310-300s were leased in, with the latest A310 arriving with SATA International in April 2003. Services are being developed to include Brazil, the Dominican Republic, Canada and the USA.

Routes

Birmingham, Boston. Dublin, Funchal, Frankfurt, Glasgow, Innsbruck, Lisbon, Luxembourg, Manchester, Milan, Montreal, Palma de Mallorca, Oslo, Paris, Ponta del Gada, Porto, Port Seyma, Punta Cana, Rome, Toronto, Vienna.

Fleet

3 Airbus A310-300
1 Boeing 737-300
2 Boeing 737-400

Boeing 777-268 HZ-AKF (Albert Kuhbandner / Nice)

SAUDI ARABIAN AIRLINES

P.O.Box 620, CC181 Jeddah 21231, Saudi Arabia, Tel. 2-6860000, Fax. 2-6864552, www.saudiairlines.com

Three- / Two- letter code	IATA No.	Reg'n prefix	ICAO callsign
SVA / SV	065	HZ	Saudia

Saudi Arabian Airlines, the national carrier of the Kingdom of Saudi Arabia, was founded in late 1945 as the Saudi Arabian Airlines Corporation, but came to be known for most of its history as Saudia. Flights began from 14th March 1947 with Douglas DC-3s. In the early 1950s, five Bristol Freighter 21s, DC-4s and Convair 340s were used. The jet age began in April 1962 with the introduction of the Boeing 720B, which was used to start longer-distance services including Cairo, Karachi and Bombay, and in 1968 to London, Rome, Geneva and Frankfurt. In 1975 came the first widebody, the Lockheed TriStar, with the Boeing 747 added from June 1977. The always cautious expansion policy has led Saudia to become the leading airline in the Arab world, and with about 11 million passengers a year, one of the world's largest international airlines. The fleet age is kept low and aircraft manufacturers in the USA and Europe are always looking for lucrative fleet renewal contracts. As soon as a massive new order for US aircraft had been announced at the beginning of 1996, a new corporate image was introduced and applied as the aircraft were delivered, and the name changed from Saudia to the present style. Two new types were added from 1997, the McDonnell Douglas MD-90 and the MD-11 freighter, with Boeing 777s arriving from early 1998, replacing the last of the TriStars. Deliveries of further 777s, now the major type in the fleet, saw the retirement of the older 747-100s. Also operating in Saudi Arabian colours are the aircraft of the Saudi royal family and various government machines; these have their own VIP division. Saudi Arabian Airlines' base is at Jeddah, with further major operating bases at Riyadh and Dhahran.

Routes

Abu Dhabi, Addis Ababa, Alexandria, Algiers, Amman, Amsterdam, Ankara, Asmara, Athens, Bahrain, Bangkok, Beirut, Brussels, Cairo, Casablanca, Chennai, Colombo, Copenhagen, Dacca, Damascus, Delhi, Djakarta, Doha, Dubai, Frankfurt, Geneva, Gurayat, Houston, Islamabad, Istanbul, Jeddah, Johannesburg, Kano, Karachi, Khartoum, Kuala Lumpur, Kuwait, Lahore, London, Manila, Milan, Mumbai, Muscat, Nairobi, New York, Nice, Paris, Riyadh, Rome, Sanaa, Sharjah, Shararah, Singapore, Taipei, Teheran, Tokyo, Tunis,Washington and to about 25 domestic destinations.

Fleet

11 Airbus A300-600
12 Boeing 737-200Adv.
16 Boeing 747-100/200/300
 5 Boeing 747-400
23 Boeing 777-200
 4 McDonnell Douglas MD-11F
29 Mc Donnell Douglas MD-90

Airbus A321-232 OY-KBK (Marcus Baltes / Frankfurt)

SCANDINAVIAN – SAS

Frösundaviks Alle 1, 19587 Stockholm, Sweden
Tel. 8-7970000, Fax. 8-7971603
www.scandinavian.net

Three- / Two- letter code	IATA No.	Reg'n prefix	ICAO callsign
SAS / SK	117	SE/OY/LN	Scandinavian

SAS – Scandinavian Airlines came into existence on 1st August 1946 by the merger of DDL (Denmark), DNL (Norway) and ABA (Sweden), all of which were formed in the 1920s, except for DDL in 1918. Realisation that these three countries could not operate flights independently meant that plans from 1940 were revived. SAS started scheduled flights on 9th September 1946 with a DC-4 from Stockholm via Copenhagen to New York. A route to Buenos Aires was opened in 1946 and Bangkok from 1949. Johannesburg was added from 1953 with DC-6s. SAS's pioneering effort was to explore the polar routes to Los Angeles and Tokyo, which were opened on 15th

November 1954 and 24th February 1957 respectively. In Europe, Saab Scandias and Convair 440s were used in addition to DC-3s. SAS's first jet was the SE 210 Caravelle, first used in 1959 from Copenhagen to Beirut. The DC-8 followed in 1960 for intercontinental routes, replacing DC-6s and DC-7s. In early 1971 came the first widebody, the Boeing 747; DC-10s and Airbus A300B4s were added in the late 1970s. Structural changes in the company and adjustment of capacity led to the sale of the 747s and Airbus A300s in the mid-1980s. MD-80s and Boeing 767s were ordered. A few MD-90s were also added in the mid-1990s but the main type for

short and medium haul is now the Boeing 737, in various models, but principally the -600. The first of these was delivered in late 1998 and was the first aircraft to wear the new colour scheme. Recent orders, however, have favoured Airbus, with both the A321 and A340 being introduced in 2001. SAS is a member of the Star Alliance and has shareholdings in various other airlines including Air Baltic, Air Botnia, Braathens, British Midland, Cimber Air, Air Greenland, SAS Commuter, Skyways, Spanair and Wideroes. It took over and absorbed Linjeflyg in 1995. There is a cargo alliance with JAL Cargo, Lufthansa Cargo and Singapore Cargo.

Routes

Dense network in Scandinavia and to over 100 destinations in more than 35 countries in the rest of Europe, North America, Africa and Asia.

Fleet

12 Airbus A321-200
3 Airbus A330-300
7 Airbus A340-300
31 Boeing 737-600
5 Boeing 737-700

19 Boeing 737-800
9 Boeing 767-300ER
66 McDonnell Douglas
MD-81/82/83/87
8 McDonnell Douglas MD-90

Ordered

2 Airbus A330
3 Airbus A321
4 Boeing 737-800

De Havilland DHC-6-300 N233SA (Josef Krauthäuser / Grand Canyon)

SCENIC AIRLINES

2705 Airport Drive, North Las Vegas, Nevada 89032, USA, Tel. 702-6383300, Fax. 702-6383275 E-mail: info@scenic.com, www.scenic.com

Three- / Two- letter code	IATA No.	Reg'n prefix	ICAO callsign
SCE / YR	398	N	Scenic

The origins of the Scenic name go back to 1927. By that time, there were already organised sightseeing flights in operation to the Grand Canyon. By August 1929 there were newspaper advertisements in the Las Vegas press for round trips with Ford 4AT Trimotors, and Scenic Airways was one of the first companies in the USA to buy the type. Apparently two were used. This first Scenic Airways operated only until the end of 1930, when flights were stopped because of the critical business situation. The company which operates as Scenic Airlines today was established in 1967, at first operating pleasure flights around Las Vegas with small Cessnas. The demand led to the need for a larger aircraft, so again a Ford Trimotor (which can today be seen in an aircraft museum near the Grand Canyon) was brought into service. The de Havilland DHC-6 Twin Otter is well suited to sightseeing work, and the type came into use with Scenic in 1972. It has only two lines of seats, so a window is available for each of the 19 passengers; in the Scenic fleet the windows are specially enlarged. The high wing layout also gives uninterrupted downward views. Scenic Airlines has been a pioneer in this type of flying and has become a synonym for Grand Canyon flights. Several million tourists have experienced the canyon in this way. In 1997 Scenic had its own terminal constructed in the northern part of the Las Vegas McCarron airport, which also includes its own maintenance base and administration. A year later the company merged with Eagle Canyon Airlines, but retained the well known marketing name of Scenic Airlines. Since 2001 Scenic has held a licence for scheduled services.

Routes

Schedules to Ely, Grand Canyon, Las Vegas and Merced. Sightseeing flights to the Grand Canyon, Bryce Canyon, Monument Valley, Yosemite Park.

Fleet

  1 Beech 1900
20 De Havilland DHC-6
  3 Cessna 402
  5 Fokker F.27

Boeing 737-35N B-2995 (Jan-Alexander Lück /Beijing)

SHANGDONG AIRLINES

Er Huan East Road 5746 Lixa District, Jinan, Shandong
People's Republic of China, Tel. 531-5698666
Fax. 531-5698668, www.shandongair.com

Three- / Two- letter code	IATA No.	Reg'n prefix	ICAO callsign
CDG / SC	324	B	Shangdong

Shandong Airlines is a division of the Shandong Aviation Group Enterprises, set up by the provincial government in March 1994. The shares are quoted on the Shenzen and Hong Kong exchanges. Within the group as well as the airline are a tourist group, hangarage and maintenance, airport operations, freight and transport and numerous other businesses. There is even a business jet operation, Rainbow Jet.The airline began operations in autumn 1994, concentrating its services at first on the Shandong province, which with about 87 million inhabitants is comparable in size with Germany. The initial equipment was the Yunshuji Y-7, with the first Boeing 737-300 arriving in 1995. The whole fleet was quickly turned over to western equipment; thus Saab 340s replaced the Y-7s for regional services and the 737-300 fleet was steadily increased. During 2000 the first Canadair Regional Jet was added, and a pair of the stretched CRJ700 models are to be delivered late in 2003. Along with other Chinese provincial companies, Shandong Airlines founded the New Star Aviation Alliance in 1997; this encompasses various forms of co-operation and codeshares. During the autumn of 2003, talks were in progress with Air China with a view to the major taking a significant shareholding; this would result in Shandong being closely aligned with one of China's new 'big three' airlines.

Routes

Beijing, Changchun, Changsha, Chengdu, Chongqing, Dalian, Fuzhou, Guangzhou, Guilin, Haikou, Hangzhou, Hefei, Jinan, Juzhou, Kunming, Linyi, Nanchang, Nanjing, Nantong, Ningbo, Qingdao, Quinhuangdao, Shanghai, Shenyang, Shenzen, Tianjin, Tunxi, Urumqui, Wenzhou, Wuhan, Xian, Xiamen, Xuzhou, Yantai, Zhengzhou.

Fleet	Ordered
9 Boeing 737-300	2 Canadair CRJ700ER
10 Canadair CRJ200	
4 Saab 340	

Boeing 757-200 B-2809 (Olaf Bichel / Shanghai)

SHANGHAI AIRLINES

Faa Nr.212, Jiangning Road, 200040 Shanghai, People's Republic of China, Tel. 21-62558888, Fax. 21-62558885, www.shanghai-air.com

Three- / Two- letter code	IATA No.	Reg'n prefix	ICAO callsign
CSH / FM	774	B	Shanghaiair

As early as 1985 an airline was formed by the regional government of the Shanghai district. At that time it was not possible for aircraft to fly in their own colours, but it was the first airline in China to become independent from the all-embracing CAAC. Five Boeing 707s were used in CAAC livery on domestic services, but in 1988 one of these 707s appeared in Shanghai's own insignia. The airline's first Boeing 757 was delivered in August 1989 in the full colour scheme which is still in use today. Maintaining the all-Boeing fleet stance, 767s were introduced from 1994 and used for flights to Beijing and other major cities. Until 1997, Shanghai Airlines flew scheduled and charter flights only within the Peoples' Republic of China, but in that year it was given licences for international services, and began to fly to Bangkok, Hong Kong, Macau and Singapore. The fleet was further expanded and from 1998 the new generation Boeing 737-700 was added, with the 737-800 joining it from 2001. Also from 2001 a network of shorter routes was established, and to operate these came the first non-Boeing type, Canadair Regional Jets. The airline's base and home airport is Shanghai, and over 25% of its shares are privately-owned.

Routes

Beijing, Chengdu, Chongquing, Dalian, Fuzhou, Guangzhou, Guilin,Guiyang, Haiku, Hangzhou, Harbin, Hefei, Jinan, Jinghong, Jingjian, Jinzhou, Kaoshiung, Kunming, Lijang, Macau, Nanchang, Nanjing, Ningbo, Phnom Penh, Qingdao, Sanya, Shanghai, Shantou, Shenyang, Shenzen, Singapore, Taiyuan, Tianjin, Wehai, Wenzhou, Wuhan, Xiamen, Xian, Xining, Yantai, Yinchuan.

Fleet

3 Canadair CRJ200
7 Boeing 757-200
4 Boeing 767-300

8 Boeing 737-700
5 Boeing 737-800

Airbus A320-231 SU-RAA (Daniel Hustedt / Hamburg)

SHOROUK AIR

2, El Shaheed Ismail Fahmy, P.O.Box 2684
Heliopolis-Cairo, Egypt
Tel. 2-4172313, Fax. 2-4172311

Three- / Two- letter code	IATA No.	Reg'n prefix	ICAO callsign
SHK / 7Q	273	SU	Shorouk

Shorouk Air is a Cairo-based joint venture set up by Egypt Air and Kuwait Airways in 1992; the shares are held 51% and 49% respectively. Charter flights from Western Europe to Egypt were begun in the same year, as well as scheduled services in the Middle East, using a pair of new Airbus A320s. It was intended that Shorouk should operate cargo flights, particularly on behalf of Kuwait Airways, using Boeing 757-200PFs, but because of poor business results brought about by the effects of the Gulf War, the aircraft were not delivered. Similarly, Egyptian tourism has been badly affected by terrorist threats and attacks, causing visitors to stay away, and this has left Shorouk short of passengers. Thus the airline has turned its attentions to sub-charter work for other airlines including Air Sinai and Egyptair, especially at Hadj time, with many flights to Jeddah. A third A320 was however delivered to the airline at the end of 1999 and a fourth in 2001. Though one of these was leased out to another airline long-term, the charter network has been increased, and new destinations in Egypt added.

Routes

Scheduled services from Cairo to Beirut; charter flights from various points in Europe to Hurghada, Cairo, Luxor and Sharm al Sheik.

Fleet

4 Airbus A320-200

Ilyushin IL-86 RA-86105 (Jannis Malzahn / Hanover)

SIBERIA AIRLINES

Tolmachevo Airport, Ob-4, Novosibirsk 633115
Russia, Tel. 3832-599011, Fax. 3832-599064
E-mail: reklama@s7.ru, www.sibir.ru

Three- / Two- letter code	IATA No.	Reg'n prefix	ICAO callsign
SBI / S7	421	RA	Siberia Airlines

Aviakompania Sibir developed from the Tolmachevo State Enterprise, which was founded in 1992 in Ob, a town in the vicinity of Novosibirsk in Eastern Russia. As with most Russian airlines, its basis was in the former Aeroflot Novosibirsk division, from which it took over routes and aircraft. Moscow-Vnukovo and Novosibirsk-Tolmachevo were the two most important airports for the new airline, which also used the name Sibir and later Siberia Airlines. The company developed very positively, and alliances were set up with several other companies in Siberia including Chita Avia, Baikal and Novokuznetsk, with the intention that several smaller companies could be brought together under the Siberia Airlines name to mutual benefit and thus operate more profitably. As one of the more modern and well-organised airlines in the former Soviet Union Siberia is profitable and is able to finance the acquisition of new aircraft. The Tupolev Tu-204 was brought into use from December 1999 and the Tupolev Tu-154s and Ilyushin IL-86 have been modernised, as they are used on routes to Western Europe. During 2000 Sibir acquired shares in the almost bankrupt Vnukovo Airlines and took over their routes and several aircraft. In May 2001 the shareholders agreed to a merger. As well as its home airport at Tolmachevo, Irkutsk and Moscow-Vnukovo are important hubs in the airline's network. As well as its schedules, Siberia Airlines operates a large number of charters to Western Europe.

Routes

Adler/Sochi, Baku,Barnaul, Beijing, Bishek, Blagoveschensk, Bratsk, Chita, Dubai, Dushanbe, Düsseldorf, Frankfurt, Hanover, Irkutsk, Kemerov, Krasnodar, Mineralnye Vody, Moscow, Norilsk, Novokuznetsk, Novosibirsk, Omsk, Orenburg, Petropavlovsk-Kamchats, Samara, Seoul, Simferopol, Sharjah, St.Petersburg, Tashkent, Tel Aviv, Tianjin, Tomsk, Ufa, Ulan Ude, Urumqui, Vladivostok, Yakutsk,Yerevan.

Fleet

```
 1 Antonov An-26
12 Ilyushin IL-86
36 Tupolev Tu-154
 2 Tupolev Tu-204
```

Airbus A321-231 B-2371 (Thomas Kim / Beijing)

SICHUAN AIRLINES

9 Nan Sanduan Yihuan Road, Chengdu,
Sichuan 610041, People's Republic of China
Tel. 28-5551161, Fax. 28-5582641

Three- / Two- letter code	IATA No.	Reg'n prefix	ICAO callsign
CSC / 3U	–	B	Chuanghang

In 1986 the regional government of the Sichuan province of China perceived a need for its own airline. After bureaucratic squabbles with the mighty CAAC, the new airline was in a position to commence services in July 1988 with Yunshuji Y-7s. The first, and for a while only, service was from Chengdu to Wanxian on the Yangtse River. More Y-7s were added in 1990 and the company's own colours were applied to the aircraft. At the end of 1991 Tupolev Tu-154Ms were acquired for use on a new service to Beijing. Western aircraft in the form of three Airbus A320s leased from

ILFC appeared at the very end of 1995 and in early 1996, leading to a further expansion. In spite of this the airline is still only active within the confines of the Peoples' Republic of China, with no current plans for international routes. Late in 1997 the Xingxing alliance was formed, a co-operation between Sichuan Airlines, Hainan Airlines, Shandong Airlines, Shenzen Airlines, Wuhan Air and Zhongyuan Airlines. The delivery of new Airbus A320s and A321s during 1998 and 1999 has brought the fleet up to a modern standard. Sichuan was the first customer for the Brazilian Embraer EMB-145LR

regional jets, with the first of five aircraft delivered late in 2000. At the same time the last of the Tupolev Tu-154s was retired.

Routes

Beijing, Chengdu, Chongqing, Daxian, Guangzhou, Guilin, Haikou, Harbin, Jian, Kunming, Luzhou, Nanchong, Nanjing, Shanghai, Shantou, Shenzen, Wanxian, Wenzhou, Wuhan, Xichang, Yibin, Zhengzhou.

Fleet	Ordered
7 Airbus A320-200	2 Airbus A319
2 Airbus A321-200	
5 Embraer EMB-145	
4 Yunshuji Y-7	

Airbus A319-132 9V-SBB (Jan-Alexander Lück / Hamburg-Finkenwerder)

SILKAIR

P.O. Box 104, Changi Airport, Singapore
918144, Singapore, Tel. 65403160
Fax. 65420023, www.silkair.net

Three- / Two- letter code	IATA No.	Reg'n prefix	ICAO callsign
SLK / MI	629	9V	Silkair

Tradewinds Charters was founded in October 1976 as a subsidiary of Singapore Airlines to carry out its non-scheduled passenger flights. Its operations consisted of inclusive-tour work, oil-crew changes and ad hoc charters. Some flights were operated in the region from Seletar airport until 1988; it leased its aircraft from SIA as needed. Using MD-87s on scheduled flights to five destinations in Malaysia and Brunei, Tradewinds became Singapore's second scheduled airline operator. In 1991 the airline was renamed as Silkair. New routes were opened to Cebu, Medan, Phnom Penh and Ho

Chi Minh City. Apart from scheduled flights, the airline continued with its charter work from its base at Singapore's Changi airport. In 1990 the fleet was augmented by the Boeing 737, and for a short while Airbus A310s seconded from the parent company were also in use. Two Fokker 70s were acquired in 1995 for short-haul work, but both these and the 737s were to be ousted by a complete changeover of the fleet to exclusively Airbus A320s (first delivered in Autumn 1998) and A319s (first arrival Autumn 1999). Silk Air is moving more towards being a typical

holiday airline in response to demand from the tourist industry. As well as flights, the airline offers tour operators complete packages with hotels and sightseeing included.

Routes

Balikpapan, Cebu, Chengdu, Chiang Mai, Chittagong, Davao, Hyderabad, Kochi, Krabi, Kunming, Langkawi, Lombok, Macau, Manado, Medan, Padang, Palambang, Phnom Penh, Phuket, Siem Rap, Singapore, Solo City, Trivandrum, Xiamen, Yangon.

Fleet	Ordered
4 Airbus A319-100	4 Airbus A320
6 Airbus A320-200	2 Airbus A319

Airbus A340-313 9V-SJO (Thomas Kim / Singapore)

SINGAPORE AIRLINES

P.O.Box 501, 25 Airline Road, Singapore 819829, Tel. 5423333, Fax. 5455034, E-mail: mail@singaporeair.com, www.singaporeair.com

Three- / Two- letter code	IATA No.	Reg'n prefix	ICAO callsign
SIA / SQ	618	9V	Singapore

Singapore Airlines was formed on 28th January 1972 as the wholly government owned national airline to succeed the jointly-operated Malaysia-Singapore Airlines. Operations began on 1st October 1972, with Boeing 707s and 737s taken over from MSA, but in 1973 the changeover was quickly made to Boeing 747-200s. Since then Singapore Airlines has been one of those companies which is continually expanding. Concordes were used with British Airways on a joint London-Bahrain-Singapore route, but it was not a success and ended in 1980. More 747s were added, allowing expansion of routes to Australia, New Zealand, the USA and Europe. From 1979 there were daily flights via Honolulu to San Francisco. Airbus A310s were added from 1984 for Asian regional routes and Boeing 727s and 757s and DC-10s were also used, but the fleet was then rationalised around the 747 and A310. The first 747-400s were delivered in December 1988 and the first 747 freighter in 1989, with a new dedicated freight terminal opened at the new Changi airport in 1995. New Airbus A340-300s augmented the long-haul fleet, coming into service from Spring 1996; a year later the Boeing 777 was also introduced and further examples of this type have ousted the short-lived A340s, traded in to Boeing. That said, longer-range A340-500s are on order for 2004 delivery, as is the A380 as a launch customer for delivery from 2006. In April 2000 Singapore Airlines became a member of the Star Alliance. Silkair and Singapore Airlines Cargo are 100% subsidiaries, and since 1999 Singapore owns 49% of Virgin Atlantic. It also has shares in in Air New Zealand. The main base is at Changi airport.

Routes

Adelaide, Amsterdam, Athens, Auckland, Bandar Seri Begawan, Bangalore, Bangkok, Beijing, Brisbane, Brussels, Capetown, Chennai, Chicago, Christchurch, Colombo, Copenhagen, Dalian, Dacca, Dallas /Fort Worth, Delhi, Denpasar, Djakarta, Dubai, Durban, Frankfurt, Fukuoka, Guangzhou, Hakodata, Hanoi, Harbin, Hiroshima, Ho Chi Minh City, Hong Kong, Istanbul, Johannesburg, Jeddah, Jinan, Kathmandu, Kolkota, Kuala Lumpur, Lahore, Las Vegas, Los Angeles, London, Macau, Madrid, Manchester, Manila, Mauritius, Melbourne, Moscow, Mumbai, Nagoya, New York, Osaka, Paris, Perth, Rome, San Francisco, Seoul, Shanghai, Singapore, Sydney, Taipei, Tokyo, Vancouver, Wellington and Zürich.

Fleet		Ordered
9 Airbus A310-300	8 Boeing 777-300	4 Airbus A340-500
41 Boeing 747-400		10 Airbus A380
42 Boeing 777-200		22 Boeing 777-200

Boeing 737-85F TC-SKC (Klaus Brandmaier / Düsseldorf)

SKY AIRLINES

Caglayan Mah 2053, Sok No.42 Barynaklar, 7104
Antalya, Turkey, Tel. 242-3237576, Fax. 242-3237567
E-mail: yt@skyairlines.net, www.skyairlines.net

Three- / Two- letter code	IATA No.	Reg'n prefix	ICAO callsign
SHY / –	–	TC	Antalya Bird

The Turkish Kayi Group is internationally active in the tourist industry. With GTI-German Travel International it has a tour operator which is positioned to take advantage of the most popular market in Europe. The Riva Hotels are predominantly on the Turkish Riviera coast and attract good, middle-class business. Eagle Rent a car belongs to Turkey's largest private rental company. All of these activities were supported by the start of Sky Airlines on 12th April 2001, when a Boeing 737-400 flew from Antalya to Düsseldorf. The Kayi Group had planned its own airline since 2000. For many Europeans,

Turkey is one of their favourite holiday destinations. The group, based in Antalya, has on its doorstep the second largest Turkish airport, an ideal base, from which their Boeing aircraft fly to over 30 destinations. During its first year, Sky Airlines carried around 250,000 passengers, and that takes into account the difficulties following 11th September. It seems that the Iraq crisis also failed to deter tourists from taking their holidays in Turkey. Sky Airlines continues to invest in its fleet and during 2002 added the latest model Boeing 737-800. The aircraft are fitted out in an economical single-class layout.

They are also eyecatching to the observer because of their differently-coloured tailfins. Though at first the German market was the sole target, from 2002 Sky Airlines has been flying to Poland and Scandinavia.

Routes

Amsterdam, Antalya, Berlin, Bremen, Brussels, Cologne/Bonn, Copenhagen, Dortmund, Dresden, Düsseldorf, Erfurt, Frankfurt, Hamburg, Hanover, Helsinki, Katowice, Leipzig, London, Maastricht, Munich, Nuremberg, Oslo, Paris, Podzan, Rome, Stuttgart, Tel Aviv, Warsaw.

Fleet

3 Boeing 737-400
1 Boeing 737-800

Airbus A320-231 C-GTDK (Stefan Schlick / Montego Bay)

SKYSERVICE AIRLINES

31 Fasken Drive, Quebec, Ontario, M9W 1K6, Canada
Tel. 416-6795700, Fax. 416-6795710, www.skyservice.com
E-mail: communications@skyservice.com

Three- / Two- letter code	IATA No.	Reg'n prefix	ICAO callsign
SSV / 6J	884	C	Skytour

Skyservice was set up in 1994 as an air taxi and business flight company. Using several business jets, non-scheduled flights were operated in Canada and the United States. Charter flights for small groups were also undertaken, and for these a Jetstream 31 was available. From 1995 larger-scale seasonal charter flights were offered for the first time, and suitable aircraft leased in. The Airbus A320 was the favoured type, coming from ILFC and Monarch Airlines. Initially these activities were restricted to the Canadian wintertime, flying to the Caribbean and the warmer parts of the southern United States. However,

with the delivery of the airline's own first Airbus A330, this was all to change. The A330, the first of its type to be delivered to a North American operator, arrived in May 1997. During 1998 Airbus A320s were added to the airline's own fleet, which operated principally from Montreal and Toronto, and as demand dictated, further aircraft were leased in to provide additional capacity, for instance A320s from MyTravel or other European operators. Skyservice operated its first charters to Europe from 1997. The development of the company has gone in leaps and bounds, having been nearly trebled by 2003.

Skyservice works with Canada's leading tour operators, and does not take individual bookings. The aircraft are available for other charter work, for instance flights to sports events, exhibitions, conferences, incentive or advertising campaigns. They have also been seasonally leased out, notably to European operators during the summer.

Routes

Charter flights within Canada, to Europe, the Caribbean, Mexico and the USA. Ad hoc and ambulance flights to destinations worldwide.

Fleet

4 Airbus A319-200	2 Boeing 727-200
16 Airbus A320-200	
4 Airbus A330-300	

Embraer ERJ-145EP SE-DZA (Author / Zürich)

SKYWAYS

Box 1537, 58115 Linköping, Sweden,
Tel. 13-375500, Fax. 13-375501,
www.skyways.se

Three- / Two- letter code	IATA No.	Reg'n prefix	ICAO callsign
SKX / JZ	752	SE	Skyexpress

Avia was founded in Visby, on the Swedish island of Gotland in the Baltic, as long ago as 1939, and during the 1980s used Beech and Cessna light aircraft to offer non-scheduled services, including operations to the mainland. Many Swedes like to go to Gotland during the Summer, which was Avia's high season. Larger aircraft, Shorts 330s and 360s were acquired. In 1991 Avia took over Salair, integrated their Saab SF340 fleet and became known as Avia & Salair AB. Using Salair's licence, activities were expanded markedly and the headquarters was moved to Norrköping. More Saab 340s were added to the fleet, which moved to a new base at Linköping in 1993. The year also marked the change of name to Skyways AB, with the company receiving its own licence in this new name. During 1995 the first Fokker 50 joined the fleet, and the Shorts 360s were ousted. Another smaller company, Highland Air, was acquired in 1997. SAS took a 25% shareholding in Skyways from 1998, with flights then being on a codeshare basis. Some routes are served directly for SAS, especially where the SAS aircraft cannot be operated economically. In 1999 the Embraer 145 was introduced. Flying Enterprise, another Swedish regional, was taken over early in 2000, including their operations from the Bromma airport, convenient to Stockholm. In October 2000 the Skyways group was reorganised, and the operating names changed to Skyways Express and Skyways Regional. The two divisions operate their own networks. Skyways is also a successful leasing company.

Routes

Arvidsjaur, Borlange, Copenhagen, Dublin, Gallivare, Geneva, Götheborg, Halmstad, Hemavan, Hultsfred, Kiruna, Kramfors, Linköping, Lulea, Lycksele, Malmö, Manchester, Mora, Norrköping, Orebo, Oskarshamm, Skovde, Söderhamm, Stockholm, Storuman, Sundsvall, Sveg, Trollhättan, Vaasa,Vilhelmia, Visby, Zürich.

Fleet

 5 Embraer ERJ-145
17 Fokker 50
12 Saab 340

Canadair CRJ200ER N423SW (Josef Krauthäuser / Phoenix)

SKYWEST AIRLINES

444 South River Road, St.George Utah 84790
USA, Tel. 435- 6343000, Fax. 435-6343305,
E-mail: info@skywest.com, www.skywest.com

Three- / Two- letter code	IATA No.	Reg'n prefix	ICAO callsign
SKW / OO	302	N	Skywest

Skywest was established on 27th March 1972 in Salt Lake City, Utah, with services beginning just three months later with Swearingen Metros. After only a short time, routes were in place in the states of Arizona, Colorado, Idaho, California, Utah and Wyoming. A Californian competitor, Sun Aire was bought up in 1984. In 1986 new aircraft were acquired to meet new demands. During the mid-1980s the major US airlines were in the process of passing over the operation of regional services to smaller, established airlines. Thus Skywest became a partner for Delta Airlines, and introduced the modern 30-seater Embraer EMB-120 Brasilia turboprop. An extensive network was built up, radiating from Delta's important hub at Salt Lake City, and hand-in-hand with this was an expansion of the fleet with more Brasilias. The latter became the airline's standard type and had replaced the last of the Metros by 1989. The first Canadair Regional Jet joined the Skywest fleet at the beginning of 1994, and in time the whole fleet will consist of this type. A further partnership agreement was concluded with United Airlines in 1997, covering a regional service as United Express with hubs at Los Angeles, San Francisco, Portland and Seattle/Tacoma. This service has been developed successfully, with aircraft flying either in Delta Connection or United Express colours, though with the Skywest name visible on the aircraft. Nearly 9 million passengers a year are carried on about 1000 daily flights to around 100 destinations.

Routes

Albuquerque, Arcata, Bakersfield, Bellingham, Billings, Boise, Bozeman, Butte, Calgary, Carlsbad, Casper, Cedar City, Chico, Cody, Colorado Springs,Crescent City, Elko, Eugene, Fresno, Grand Junction, Helena, Idaho Falls, Imperial, Inyokern, Jackson, Las Vegas, Los Angeles, Medford, Merced, Missoula, Modesto, Monterey, Omaha, Ontario, Oxnard, Palm Springs, Pasco, Phoenix, Pocatello, Portland, Rapid City, Redding, Redmond, Reno, Sacramento, Salt Lake City, San Diego, San Francisco, San Jose, San Luis Obispo, Santa Ana, Santa Maria, Santa Rosa, Seattle, Spokane, St.George, Sun Valley, Twin Falls, Vancouver, Vernal, West Yellowstone, Yakima, Yuma.

Fleet	Ordered
19 Canadair CRJ100	35 Canadair CRJ200
40 Canadair CRJ200	
42 Embraer EMB-120 Brasilia	

Boeing 737-33A OM-AAD (Richard Schmaus / Munich)

SLOVAK AIRLINES

Trnavska cesta 56 82101 Bratislava, Slovakia
Tel. 2-44450096, Fax. 2-44450097, E-mail:
slovakairlines@sll.sk, www.slovak-airlines.sk

Three- / Two- letter code	IATA No.	Reg'n prefix	ICAO callsign
SLL / 6Q	921	OM	Slov Line

With participation by the Ministry of Transport and Telecommunications, on 24th June 1995 Slovenske Aeroline / Slovak Airlines was registered as a company. Alongside the Ministry, the Devin Group was a major shareholder in the new venture. There was initially discussion about which aircraft type should be chosen, with the Saab 340 or Saab 2000 preferred, but all these plans faltered because of the leasing costs, which were higher than had been anticipated. Then along came unfavourable political and business conditions in Slovakia, so that it was 1998 before operations were begun, using the Tupolev Tu-154, the first example of which was leased from the government. Two more 154s were added in July and September of 1998, again coming from government sources. The operational experiences in the early years were negative, and Slovak Airlines ceased flying. However, after a reorganisation, a new start was made. The sole scheduled service to Moscow was given up and the airline chose to specialise in charter and holiday flights. Slovak Air added a Boeing 737-300 to the three Tu-154s in 2002, and this has been augmented by a further two examples. A Boeing 757-200 was acquired in mid-2003 with the intention of expanding east-west services using Bratislava as a hub; services were begun to Birmingham in August 2003. Bratislava is the home airport, but the airport at Kosice in the east of the country is also used for charter flights.

Routes

Amritsar, Antalya, Birmingham, Bratislava, Bourgas, Chania, Gerona, Corfu, Dalaman, Ibiza, Hurghada, Kos, Kosice, Kovalla, Larnaca, Moscow, Monastir, Sharm el Sheik, Thessaloniki, Tivat, Zakynthos.

Fleet

1 Boeing 737-300
1 Boeing 757-200
3 Tupolev Tu-154M

BAe RJ 85 OO-DJT (Manfred Turek / Munich)

SN – BRUSSELS AIRLINES

Da Vincilaan 9, 1930 Zaventem, Belgium
Tel. 070351111 (Callcenter)
www.flysn.com

Three- / Two- letter code	IATA No.	Reg'n prefix	ICAO callsign
DAT / SN	082	OO	S-Tail

After the eventual collapse of Sabena World Airlines in January 2002, Belgium found itself without a national airline. The independent DAT-Delta Air Transport, in which Sabena had been a shareholder, was tasked with creating a new airline, SN-Brussels. Virgin Express was also expected to participate in the new company, but negotiations for this broke down. DAT's own fleet of BAe 146s was used in part to pick up where Sabena had left off. This was achieved without major problems, partly because DAT had already operated part of Sabena's European network before the collapse. Delta Air Transport had

begun operations from Antwerp in 1966. It used Convair 580, Fokker F.27, Embraer EMB120, Fokker 28 and BAe 146 aircraft over the years and came to fly extensively on behalf of Sabena to smaller locations regionally and in the northern part of Europe. DAT could do this more economically than Sabena, and the fleet size thus increased. After the takeover of the Sabena mantle, DAT's name was changed to SN Brussels Airlines, and several well-known elements of Sabena were also transferred. Three Airbus A340-300s came in Spring 2002 and were put to use on routes ton Africa. The first Airbus A319 also

joined the fleet in early 2003. In the meantime the network has grown to include around 50 destinations in Europe and Africa, thus partially filling the gap caused by Sabena's demise. There is a codeshare agreement in place with American Airlines on North Atlantic services.

Routes

Abidjan, Amsterdam, Athens, Banjul, Barcelona, Berlin, Bilbao, Birmingham, Bologna, Bordeaux, Bristol, Budapest, Bucharest, Conakry, Copenhagen, Dakar, Douala, Dublin, Düsseldorf, Edinburgh, Florence, Frankfurt, Freetown, Geneva, Glasgow, Gothenberg, Hamburg, Hanover, Helsinki, Kinshasa, Lisbon, London, Luanda, Lyon, Madrid, Manchester, Munich, Naples, Newcastle, Nice, Oslo, Rome, Stuttgart, Venice, Vienna, Zürich.

Fleet

3 Airbus A319-100
3 Airbus A330-300
32 BAe 146-100/200-RJ-85/100

Boeing 767-3BG(ER) OO-SLR (Manfred Turek / Brussels)

SOBELAIR

Building 45 Airport, 1930 Zaventem, Belgium
Tel. 2-7541211, Fax. 2-7541288,
www.sobelair.be

Three- / Two- letter code	IATA No.	Reg'n prefix	ICAO callsign
SLR / Q7	644	OO	Sobelair

Société Belge de Transports par Air SA was established on 30th July 1946 and operations began in the following year with a Douglas DC-3. The intention was to provide charter flights, mainly to the Belgian Congo, with DC-4s. In 1948 Sabena acquired a controlling interest in Sobelair. From 1957 to 1962 a domestic network of routes was set up using Cessna 310s on behalf of Sabena within the Congo to supplement the main services operated by the Belgian national carrier. As well as a DC-6, Sobelair also acquired ex-Sabena SE 210 Caravelles as its first jet aircraft. Up to 1960 the major activity had involved schedules between Belgium and the Congo (now Zaire) but from then on, the airline has been operating mainly charter flights for holidaymakers to the Mediterranean. After the last Boeing 707 was sold in 1988, Sobelair used only Boeing 737s. When Sabena introduced a new colour scheme in Spring 1993, Sobelair's aircraft adopted a similar livery. The first of two Boeing 767-300ERs was delivered to Sobelair in 1994, with the second in Spring 1996, thus allowing long-range services to be flown. As requirements changed seasonally, Sobelair leased aircraft in from Sabena and other carriers. After the takeover by the SAir group, Sobelair established the Leisure Alliance, together with Air Europe, Balair, LTU and Volare. However the bankruptcy of Sabena and Swissair brought financial difficulties to Sobelair, which had been operating profitably. New owners acquired the company in 2001, and allowed the independent company to move ahead. Careful expansion of the fleet and routes took place in 2002, which also saw the arrival of the first Boeing 737-800, and the addition of Johannesburg as a destination.

Routes

To destinations in the Mediterranean, Canary Isles, Northern Africa, Caribbean and various other charters and subcharters.

Fleet

2 Boeing 737-300
4 Boeing 737-400
2 Boeing 737-800
4 Boeing 767-300ER

Boeing 737-85F ZS-SJJ (Ken Petersen / New York)

SOUTH AFRICAN AIRWAYS

SAA Towers, P.O.Box 7778, Johannesburg 2000, Republic of South Africa, Tel. 11-9781127 Fax. 11-9781126, www.saa.co.za

Three- / Two- letter code	IATA No.	Reg'n prefix	ICAO callsign
SAA / SA	083	ZS	Springbok

South African Airways was founded on 1st February 1934 when Union Airways passed into government ownership. Operations started that day with a fleet of single-engined Junkers F-13s, later supplemented by a large number of Ju 52s and Ju 86s. Numerous routes were operated, including to Nairobi, until the outbreak of the Second World War. November 1945 saw the start of the 'Springbok' service to London, using DC-4s, DC-7s and Lockheed Constellations. The latter were also used to open a route to Perth in Australia in November 1957, and with the introduction of the Boeing 707 from 1960 this was

extended to Sydney. A further long-range route was opened to Rio de Janeiro in 1969. For political reasons, SAA had to restrict its European services to a few points only; many African nations refused flyover rights. In order to be able to operate direct flights, Boeing 747SPs and later 747-300s with extreme long ranges were ordered. Airbus A300s and Boeing 737s were acquired for regional and domestic routes, replacing Vickers Viscounts and other older types. The first Airbus A320 was delivered to SAA in 1991 and in the same year the Boeing 747-400. After the 1994 change of political regime, things

changed markedly; sanctions were lifted and it became possible for SAA to fly to any country, which resulted in new routes. Aircraft were painted in a new livery, based on the new national flag. A partial privatisation took place in 1999, with the SAir group taking 20% of SAA's capital, but on SAir's failure, the government retrieved its money from Switzerland. Fleet modernisation continues, with the Boeing 737-800 from May 2000, Airbus 340 and leased A330s. By 2005 the whole fleet will have been renewed. SAA has financial stakes in regional airlines SA Alliance Air, SA Airlink and SA Express.

Routes

Abidjan, Accra, Atlanta, Bangkok, Blantyre, Bulawayo, Cairo, Capetown, Dar es Salaam, Durban, East London, Fort Lauderdale, Frankfurt, Gabarone, Harare, Hong Kong, Johannesburg, Kinshasa, Lagos, Lilongwe, London, Luanda, Lusaka, Maputo, Mauritius, Maseru, Mumbai, Nairobi, Nelspruit, New York, Paris, Perth, Port Elizabeth, Sao Paulo, Sal, Windhoek, Zürich.

Fleet		Ordered
2 Airbus A330-200	2 Boeing 747SP	10 Airbus A319
3 Airbus A340-600	4 Boeing 747-300	15 Airbus A320
19 Boeing 737-200	8 Boeing 747-400	12 Airbus A340
21 Boeing 737-800	2 Boeing 767-200ER	
4 Boeing 747-200		

McDonnell Douglas MD-82 N418GE (Tony Stork / Baltimore)

SOUTHEAST AIRLINES

12600 S. Belcher Road, Suite 100, Largo FL 33774, USA, Tel. 727-5321632 Fax. 727-5301615, www.flyseal.com

Three- / Two- letter code	IATA No.	Reg'n prefix	ICAO callsign
SNK / –	–	N	Sunking

The famous 'sunking' symbol carried on the tailplanes of this company's aircraft stems from another airline, which was also based in Florida. National Airlines merged in 1980 with Pan American, with the name National and its marking passing into other hands. In 1992, Tom Kolfenbach founded Sun Jet International Airlines, with its home base at the St.Petersburg/Clearwater Airport. Operations began in 1993 with McDonnell Douglas MD-80s, with scheduled services to destinations right along the Gulf Coast and into the south-eastern USA. 1997 saw the former expansion terminated, when the company went into Chapter 11 bankruptcy protection. Operations shrunk markedly to just a few destinations and were for a time completely suspended. New investors brought fresh capital and so operations recommenced in 1999, under the newly-chosen name of Southeast Airlines. The company, which had purchased the rights to the sunking emblem, was to concentrate only on charter flights. Several large tour operators such as Apple Vacations became customers. Southeast Airlines developed as a reliable partner, and in 2002 restarted scheduled services, but this time sticking with smaller airports and seeking out niche markets ignored by other carriers. The fleet has again been built up and now consists of DC-9s and MD-82s and -88s.

Routes

Scheduled services to Allentown, Fort Lauderdale, Gulfport/Biloxi, Newburgh, Newark, Sanford, St. Petersburg/Clearwater, and in addition charter flights within the USA and to the Caribbean.

Fleet

8 Douglas DC-9-30
4 McDonnell Douglas MD-82/88

Boeing 737-3H4 N363SW (Tony Stork / Baltimore)

SOUTHWEST AIRLINES

PO Box 36611 Love Field, Dallas,TX 75235-1611
USA, Tel. 214-7924000, Fax. 214-792411,
www.southwest.com

Three- / Two- letter code	IATA No.	Reg'n prefix	ICAO callsign
SWA / WN	526	N	Southwest

This famous low-cost pioneer came on the scene on 15th March 1967 under the name of Air Southwest, but it was some time before operations actually began. The established airlines tried their utmost to prevent the troublesome newcomer from taking to the air, as the airline intended to rock the boat by setting up a 'one class service' with particularly low fares. Major legal controversy for many years concerned Southwest's use of Love Field airport in Dallas; other airlines and some local officials tried to force the carrier to use the more distant Dallas-Fort Worth Regional Airport, which was then quite small. In March 1971 the airline's name was changed to Southwest Airlines, and in June 1971 service was begun from Dallas to Houston and San Antonio. The airline acquired Muse Air on 25th June 1985, renaming it TranStar in 1986, but operations of the subsidiary ceased due to losses in 1987. After deregulation in the United States, Southwest's fortunes soared. Expanding from initial operations restricted to the state of Texas only, it covers a wide swathe of the continental USA, with a massive, unified fleet composed entirely of the Boeing 737 in various models, and carrying ever more passengers to more destinations year on year. Utah-based Morris Air was acquired in December 1993 and completely integrated in 1995, and the long-neglected area in the South-East of the USA and Florida was brought into the network from 1996. Fleet renewal has been in full flow with Boeing 737-700s being delivered from December 1997, and the East Coast area service has been strengthened, with a hub on Long Island. At the end of 2000 Southwest rolled out a new company livery, including more blue. While most US airlines have suffered badly and for a long period from 11 September, Southwest recovered quickly; stored aircraft were soon back in service and the airline continues to record profits.

Routes

Albuquerque, Amarillo, Austin, Baltimore, Birmingham, Boise, Burbank,Chicago, Cleveland, Columbus,Corpus Christi, Dallas, Detroit, El Paso, Fort Lauderdale, Harlingen, Hartford, Houston,Indianapolis, Jackson, Jacksonville, Kansas City, Las Vegas, Little Rock, Long Island Mcarthur, Los Angeles, Louisville, Lubbock, Manchester, Midland/Odessa, Nashville, New Orleans, Oakland, Oklahoma City, Omaha, Ontario, Orlando, Phoenix, Portland, Providence, Raleigh/Durham, Reno, Sacramento, Salt Lake City, San Antonio, San Diego, San Francisco, San Jose, Santa Ana, Seattle, Spokane, St. Louis, Tampa, Tucson, Tulsa, West Palm Beach.

Fleet

27 Boeing 737-200Adv.	150 Boeing 737-700
194 Boeing 737-300	
25 Boeing 737-500	

Airbus A320-232 EC-ICL (Stefan Schlick /Arrecife)

SPANAIR

Airport P.O.Box 50086, Palma de Mallorca
07000, Spain, Tel. 971-745020, Fax. 971-492553
E-mail: spanair@spanair.es, www.spanair.com

Three- / Two- letter code	IATA No.	Reg'n prefix	ICAO callsign
JKK / JK	680	EC	Spanair

The tour operators Vingresor AB and Scandinavia & Viajes Marsoms SA founded their own charter airline by the name of Spanair in 1987. It is based on the holiday island of Majorca. Operations commenced during March 1988 and a fleet of new MD-83s were leased from Irish Aerospace and Guinness Peat Aviation, primarily flying Scandinavian holidaymakers to the sunny beaches of Spain. Spanair also flies from UK and German airports and from Zürich and Salzburg and has increased its European coverage, and its fleet of MD-80 derivatives. When Boeing 767-300ERs were acquired in 1992 flights were also added to destinations in the USA, Mexico and the Caribbean. In addition to its basic charter business, from 1994 Spanair went into the scheduled service market from Madrid, Barcelona and other major cities and this part of the operation has seen steady growth, providing competition for Iberia. In order to provide the additional capacity for these services, the fleet has required expansion; new aircraft, Airbus A320s and A321s have been delivered from the later part of 2000. SAS became a shareholder and as a consequence Spanair has become a part of the Star Alliance family, with membership officially conferred from 1st April 2003. Scheduled services now account for around three-quarters of its flights, the balance being charters, almost all in Europe. Aebal, operating as 'Spanair Link' is a subsidiary using Boeing 717s on thinner routes, but using Spanair codes.

Routes

Alicante, Arrecife, Asturias, Barcelona, Bilbao, Copenhagen, Frankfurt, Fuerteventura, Hamburg, Helsinki, Ibiza, Las Palmas, London, Madrid, Malabo, Malaga, Menorca, Palma de Mallorca, Munich, Oslo, Santiago de Compostela, Seville, Stockholm, Tenerife, Valencia, Vigo and Vienna are all served regularly, plus many other charter destinations.

Fleet	Ordered
10 Airbus A320-200	2 Airbus A320
5 Airbus A321-200	1 Airbus A321
36 McDonnell Douglas MD-82/83/87	

McDonnell Douglas MD-83 N819NK (Josef Krauthäuser / Fort Lauderdale)

SPIRIT AIRLINES

2800 Executive Way, Miramar, Florida 33025
USA, Tel. 954-4477965, Fax. 954-4477979
E-mail: mail@spiritair.com, www.spiritair.com

Three- / Two- letter code	IATA No.	Reg'n prefix	ICAO callsign
NKS / NK	487	N	Spirit Wings

Tour operator Charter One was set up in 1980 and organised day and weekend trips to the gambling and entertainment paradise of Atlantic City from Chicago, Boston, Detroit and Providence. From 1984 the company also specialised in short trips to the Bahamas. Success led the tour operator to offer accompanied Caribbean tours from 1987 and the addition of Las Vegas to the programme. Aircraft were leased from various different companies for these operations. In 1990 Charter One bought a pair of Convair 580s and applied for a scheduled service licence, which was granted on 8th September,

allowing flights to Atlantic City to be started. In 1992 four DC-9-32s were leased and the name changed to Spirit Airlines. Florida was the declared objective and so services were offered from Boston, Chicago and Detroit to Miami, Fort Lauderdale, Fort Myers and Tampa. As the number of new services grew, so did the fleet and further DC-9-41 were added. The base was at Detroit and within a few months a move was made into larger premises. During 1996 services from Cleveland and Newark were added. The important New York market was tapped for the first time in 1998, and further Florida destinations were

added at Myrtle Beach, Melbourne and Orlando. MD-80s were also used for the first time, as the market for suitable used DC-9s was exhausted. Additional aircraft are also leased in on a seasonal basis. During 1999 Spirit also began flights from Detroit to Los Angeles, and a new headquarters was established at Miramar, Florida. Expansion has continued during 2001-2003, with investment in further aircraft and new routes to Denver and San Juan; frequencies have also been increased on existing routes. A completely new colour scheme for the aircraft has also been introduced.

Routes

Atlantic City, Chicago, Cleveland, Denver, Detroit, Fort Lauderdale, Fort Myers, Las Vegas, Los Angeles, Myrtle Beach, New York-LGA, Orlando, San Juan, Tampa, West Palm Beach.

Fleet

27 McDonnell Douglas MD-81/82/83
 6 Douglas DC-9-30/40

Airbus A340-311 4R-ADA (Albert Kuhbandner / London-LHR)

SRILANKAN

22-01 East Tower WTC, Echelon Square, Colombo 1, Sri Lanka, Tel. 94-735555, Fax. 94-735122
E-mail: ulweb@srilankan.lk, www.srilankan.lk

Three- / Two- letter code	IATA No.	Reg'n prefix	ICAO callsign
ALK / UL	603	4R	Srilankan

Air Lanka was set up on 10th January 1979 in order to continue the business of Air Ceylon, which had ceased operations in 1978. The airline was then 60% owned by the Sri Lankan government and 40% by local businesses. Management and technical assistance was supplied by Singapore Airlines. Operations started on 1st September 1979 with two Boeing 707s leased from SIA. The first TriStar owned by the airline flew from Colombo to Paris on 2nd November 1990; Zürich, Frankfurt and London soon followed. For a while a leased Boeing 747 was used to London Gatwick, but because of an unstable political situation in Sri

Lanka, passenger numbers were insufficient. The Boeing 737 was acquired for regional flights to India and the Maldives. A planned renewal of the long-distance fleet had to be postponed in 1993 as financing for the planned Airbus A340s was not initially possible. However this was in time arranged through an international banking consortium and in Autumn 1994 the first two A340s joined the fleet. Further examples followed in 1995 and 1995, replacing the TriStars. During 1999 Emirates took a shareholding in Air Lanka, which was restructured. The airline changed its name to SriLankan, at

the same time adopting a whole new corporate identity and aircraft colours. With the delivery of new Airbus A330s from 2000 new destinations including Berlin, Stockholm and Sydney were added, and other routes are now flown in codeshare with Emirates.On 24th July 2001a terrorist attack was made against the airport at Colombo, resulting in SriLankan having 50% of its fleet damaged or destroyed. Some routes had to be suspended, but Emirates loaned aircraft while replacements were obtained. With the apparent end of the conflict in the island, the airline is poised for further expansion.

Routes

Abu Dhabi, Bahrain, Bangalore, Bangkok, Bodhgaya, Chennai, Colombo, Damman, Delhi, Djakarta, Doha, Dubai, Frankfurt, Hong Kong, Karachi, Kochi, Kuwait, Kuala Lumpur, London, Male, Mumbai, Muscat, Paris, Riyadh, Rome, Singapore, Stockholm, Sydney, Tokyo, Trivandrum and Zürich.

Fleet	Ordered
2 Airbus A320-200	
4 Airbus A330-300	
4 Airbus A340-300	

Airbus A320-214 F-GRSD (Jan-Alexander Lück / Paris-CDG)

STAR AIRLINES

Immeubles Horizon, 10 Allee Bienvenue
93885 Noisy-le-Grand, France, Tel. 1-48159000
Fax. 1-48159010, www.star-airlines.fr

Three- / Two- letter code	IATA No.	Reg'n prefix	ICAO callsign
SEU / 2R	473	F	Starway

Star Europe, Société de Transport Aérien, was founded on 5th August 1995. The French tour operator Look Voyages wanted to be independent of other charter operators and to have its own airline. Thus, using a rented Boeing 737-200, Star Europe began operations from 22nd December 1995. Look Voyages is a French/Canadian business group which also owns Air Transat in Canada; the latter took a direct 23% shareholding in 1996 and thus has some influence at Star. For the 1996 season, Star Europe flew a pair of Boeing 737s, but then the fleet was changed over to the Airbus A320.

Along with this new equipment came a change of colour scheme and a modification of the name to Star Airlines. The company has continued to show satisfactory progress and growth and the fleet has grown to six A320s. The Airbus A330-200 has been introduced as the first widebody type, and this is used for long-range routes to Asia and the Caribbean. From 2003 the colour scheme has again been slightly modified, to more closely resemble that of Air Transat.

Routes

Charter flights within Europe, principally to holiday areas in the Mediterranean, and to North Africa, the Middle East, Asia and the Caribbean.

Fleet	Ordered
6 Airbus A320-200 1 Airbus A330-200	1 Airbus A330-200

Boeing 737-8Q8 OY-SEB (Jan-Alexander Lück / Malaga)

STERLING EUROPEAN AIRLINES

Copenhagen Airport, 2791 Dragoer, Denmark
Tel. 32-890000, Fax. 32-451412, E-mail:
sterling@sterling.dk, www.sterlingticket.com

Three- / Two- letter code	IATA No.	Reg'n prefix	ICAO callsign
SNB / NB	373	OY	Sterling

The name of Sterling has a certain resonance in the world of aviation, having originally been started as a charter company in Denmark in 1962 by an evangelical pastor for his tour company Tjaereborg, which offered Mediterranean holidays at attractive prices to many sections of the population, but especially to families. However, after thirty years of operation, the familiar airline failed in September 1993, when all rescue attempts failed and bankruptcy became inevitable. A new business took over the company mantle, including the name, which still had a competitive value. Operations recommenced in 1994 as Sterling European Airlines with several Boeing 727s, though flying exclusively on behalf of freight operator TNT. In 1996 the company was granted a passenger licence for the 727 and began flying holidaymakers again. During 1998, after new investors had taken shareholdings, this part of the business was strongly rebuilt. Boeing 737-300s and -500s as well as the new generation -800s (from June 1998) were leased in and flown under the marketing name of Sterling. The aircraft were painted in an attractive, colourful livery with a beach-ball logo on the fin and using different base colours for each aircraft, thus creating the holiday mood at the airport. Since 1999 Sterling European has been in the ownership of the Norwegian Fred Olsen group, who reorganised the company in 2002, setting it up as a low-cost airline, with a modified colour scheme. The operations to the Mediterranean remain largely unaltered, though Scandinavian destinations have been added.

Routes

Alicante, Barcelona, Bergen, Billund, Chania, Copenhagen, Funchal, Gothenburg, Las Palmas, Madeira, Malaga, Malmö, Milan, Nice, Oslo, Palma de Mallorca, Rome, Stavanger, Stockholm, Tenerife.

Fleet

2 Boeing 737-700
6 Boeing 737-800

Boeing 737-2J8C ST-AFK (Oliver Köstinger / Dubai)

SUDAN AIRWAYS

P.O.Box 253, Amarat Khartoum, Sudan
Tel. 11-47953, Fax. 11-472377
E-mail: info@sudanair.com, www.sudanair.com

Three- / Two- letter code	IATA No.	Reg'n prefix	ICAO callsign
SUD / SD	200	ST	Sudanair

Sudan Airways was founded in February 1946 by the Sudanese government as a subsidiary of Sudan Railways System and a contract was signed for technical and operational assistance from the British company Airwork. Domestic services began in July 1947 with a fleet of four de Havilland Doves. In November 1954, the first international service was the route to Cairo, which was served with Douglas DC-3s. On 8th June 1959 a scheduled service was opened via Cairo, Athens and Rome to London using Vickers Viscounts, and Comet 4Cs from 1962 onwards. The first Fokker F.27 was delivered in 1962

and the first de Havilland Comet on 13th November 1962. The second jet generation was introduced in 1972 in the form of the Boeing 707, which was used for regular flights to Europe. For domestic services mainly F.27s were used, replaced in Spring 1990 by modern Fokker 50s. Sudan Airways is also responsible for agricultural flying and other government work, and the small aircraft used for these duties and for training can sometimes also be used for short domestic routes. Civil unrest in the Sudan has had an effect on air traffic; however new aircraft have been introduced to the fleet, the Airbus A320, A310 and

A300-600 from 1993. These have been used on the sharply reduced international network. As Sudan has become more politically marginalised, services have declined and some aircraft were returned to their lessors at the end of the 1990s. The fleet thus consists mostly of older aircraft, owned by the airline, as for political and financial reasons Airbus is no longer willing to lease aircraft. Also US sanctions cause parts shortages. However, Antonov 24s are leased in, in Armenian marks, and during 2002 a new administration building was constructed, with other investments in the infrastructure.

Routes

Abu Dhabi, Amman, Asmara, Bangui, Cairo, Damascus, Dharan, Doha, Dongala, Dubai, El Fasher, El Obeid, Jeddah, Juba, Kano, London, Merowe, Nyala, Paris, Port Sudan, Riyadh, Sanaa, Sharjah, Tripoli, Wadi Halfar.

Fleet

4 Antonov An-24	2 Boeing 737-200
1 Airbus A300-600	
2 Boeing 707-300F	
2 Boeing 727-200	

Boeing 737-8Q8 N800SY (Ken Petersen / New York – JFK)

SUN COUNTRY AIRLINES

1300 Mendota Heights Rd, Mendota Heights
MN 55120, USA, Tel. 651-6813900,
Fax. 651-6813970, www.suncountry.com

Three- / Two- letter code	IATA No.	Reg'n prefix	ICAO callsign
SCX / SY	337	N	Sun Country

Sun Country was set up on 1st July 1982 in Minneapolis by a group of former employees of Braniff International Airlines, which had gone spectacularly bankrupt on 12th May 1982. After the issue of a licence as a charter operator in January 1993, flights were begun on 20th January with Boeing 727s and operating for MLT Tours. This organisation held 51% of the share capital, but this was given up in 1988 when the company underwent a fundamental reorganisation. In 1984 a scheduled service licence was issued and a route inaugurated between Minneapolis and Las Vegas. Further Boeing 727s were added to the fleet over the years as the company made good progress and flights were undertaken to Florida, Mexico and the Caribbean. In 1986 Sun Country took on its first widebody, a DC-10, and from 1994 the airline went into international charter services in a much bigger way, giving up its scheduled operations. From this time also the aircraft were painted into a new colour scheme. Additionally, aircraft were leased out to other operators from time to time. A further change of policy came in 1999, with a reorientation towards scheduled services again, but this time as a low-cost, low-fares operator, with various routes on offer from its Minneapolis base. The bulk of the fleet was made up of Boeing 727s, though some of these were 'Super 27' re-engined quiet versions. In December 2001 Sun Country suspended operations for a while, re-organised, and then started up afresh with new capital provided by new owners. The new fleet of Boeing 737-800s carried a new colour scheme and are used for services which are a mix of schedules and charters.

Routes

Abilene, Albuquerque, Anchorage, Cancun, Cedar Rapids, Cozumel, Dallas/Fort Worth, Denver, El Paso, Fort Myers, Gulfport/Biloxi, Harlingen, Houston, Las Vegas, Laughlin, Los Angeles, Manzanillo, Mazatlan, Miami, Minneapolis/St.Paul, New York, Orlando, Palm Springs, Phoenix, Portland, Puerto Vallarta, San Diego, San Francisco, San Juan, Seattle, St.Petersburg, St. Thomas.

Fleet

6 Boeing 737-800

Boeing 737-8CX TC-SUG (Lutz Schönfeld / Berlin-SXF)

SUN EXPRESS

P.O.Box 28, 07300 Antalya, Turkey, Tel. 0-2423102626,
Fax. 0-2423102650, www.sunexpress.com
E-mail: travelcenter@sunexpress.com.tr

Three- / Two- letter code	IATA No.	Reg'n prefix	ICAO callsign
SXS / XQ	564	TC	Sun Express

On 11th September 1989 Lufthansa (40% of the shares), Turkish Airlines (40%) and Turkish investors (20%) set up the airline Sun Express with its headquarters in Antalya. Operations started with a leased Boeing 737-300 on 4th April 1990; the first flight was from Nuremberg to Antalya. Two further leased Boeing 737-300s were added for 1991, and additional aircraft were available from Lufthansa or Turkish as required. Because of the Gulf War, Turkish tourism came almost to a standstill in 1991, and the planned additional destinations could not be taken on, but with the return of peace this situation was redressed.

In 1995 the Lufthansa shareholding was passed over to Condor, and this helped to stimulate German bookings. Sun Express is a typical niche carrier, operating charters from many of Europe's smaller airports to Turkish holiday destinations. In 2002, however, scheduled services were begun from Frankfurt and Munich to Antalya. During the same year, the fleet which had been built up with Boeing 737s, mainly series 400s, was turned over to the latest -800s. The German market represents the source of 75% of Sun Express' business, with over 15 airports served in high season.

Routes

Charter and scheduled services from airports in Germany, England, Luxembourg, the Netherlands, Austria, Poland, Switzerland and other European points to Antalya, Bodrum, Dalaman, and Izmir.

Fleet

8 Boeing 737-800

Douglas DC-9-51 N54642 (Christofer Witt collection)

SURINAM AIRWAYS

P.O.Box 2029, Coppenamestraat 136
Paramaribo, Surinam
Tel. 465700, Fax. 491213, www.slm.firm.sr

Three- / Two- letter code	IATA No.	Reg'n prefix	ICAO callsign
SLM / PY	192	PZ	Surinam

Surinaamse Luchtvaart Maatschappij NV was established in January 1955 with the objective of providing service from the capital, Paramaribo, to the little developed hinterland of Surinam. Initial service commenced with DC-3s and was at first scanty, but from 1964 routes to neighbouring countries – to Georgetown, Port of Spain and Curacao – were begun with the help of KLM as a pool partner. With Surinam's independence from the Netherlands in 1975 came the introduction of a service to Amsterdam, for which leased Douglas DC-8s were brought into use. In 1980 service was also begun to Miami. For short-range services, two 20-seater de Havilland Twin Otter 300s were acquired in 1979, and these have remained in the fleet ever since. At the beginning of 1993 the Amsterdam route was passed over to KLM, as Surinam Airways had no aircraft suitable for this long-distance route. Since then the airline has concentrated on regional services, for which a DHC-8 (in 1993) and an MD-87 (in 1996) were acquired. At the end of 1999 the MD-87 was replaced in the fleet by a DC-9-50 and the Dash 8 has also been returned to its lessor. An MD-82 was however added in February 2003. KLM remains an important partner and there is a codeshare agreement in place for the important tourist route to Amsterdam. There is a similar arrangement with Air France.

Routes

Aruba, Barbados, Belem, Cayenne, Curacao, Georgetown, Miami, Paramaribo, Port of Spain.

Fleet

2 De Havilland DHC-6- 300
1 Douglas DC-9-50
1 McDonnell Douglas MD-82

Airbus A319-112 HB-IPT (Author / Zürich)

SWISS INTERNATIONAL AIRLINES

Postfach, 4002 Basle, Switzerland
Tel. 61-58200, Fax. 61-5823333, E-mail:
communications@swiss.com, www.swiss.com

Three- / Two- letter code	IATA No.	Reg'n prefix	ICAO callsign
SWR / LX	724	HB	Swiss

When in October 2001 the myth of the indestructible Swissair was suddenly shattered, it was necessary to win back the trust of passengers, investors, the public and the authorities. The solution was to set up a new airline, under the guidance of successful Swissair subsidiary Crossair. This had been in business since 1979 and during this time it had brought many positive aspects to the Swiss air transport industry. The route to a new national airline was via the formal bankruptcy of Swissair (SAir Group) and the takeover of most of its assets by Crossair, which relinquished its name and became

Swiss International Airlines, beginning operations on 1st April 2002. All of the former Crossair aircraft were taken on, with the addition of many aircraft from the former Swissair fleet. Even though it was a new company, it was starting up in difficult times, and early profitability was not envisaged; it would need time to stabilise and success would probably need several years of continuous development. Apparently the expectation in Switzerland is somewhat different, where developments will be closely watched on the streets and by the media, which competent or not, will

always be looking for a headline.Operations have shown that some splitting of operations would be sensible, and from autumn 2003 Swiss Express has been set up, to look after regional services. For charter and tourist flights, Swiss Sun has been established. During late summer 2003 the fleet and workforce was being cut by about a third to try to redress the adverse financial situation. However, new Airbus A340s are to commence delivery over the next year, to replace the MD-11s.

Routes

Swiss has a wide network in Europe and worldwide, with a further 100 or so destinations in North and South America, Asia and Africa.

Fleet		Ordered
7 Airbus A319-100	3 McDonnell Douglas MD-83	13 Airbus A340
12 Airbus A320-200	19 BAe/Avro RJ 85/100	55 Embraer ERJ-175/195
6 Airbus A321-100	20 Embraer ERJ-145	
13 Airbus A330-200	20 Saab 2000	
12 McDonnell Douglas MD-11		

Airbus A320-232 YK-AKA (Stefan Schlick / Frankfurt)

SYRIANAIR

P.O.Box 417, Damascus, Syria
Tel. 2220700, Fax. 2214923
www.syrian-airlines.com/saa

Three- / Two- letter code	IATA No.	Reg'n prefix	ICAO callsign
SYR / RB	070	YK	Syrianair

The Syrian national airline was founded in October 1961 by the government after its predecessor Syrian Airways (founded on 21st December 1946) had united with Misrair to form United Arab Airlines. However, this union lasted for less than two years. Egyptian carrier Misrair had been renamed as UAA in February 1958 and Syrian Airways merged with it from 23rd December 1958. After Syria's break with Egypt, Syrian Arab Airlines, to give the airline its full name, took back its fleet and routes from UAA. Syrian Airways had operated domestic and regional routes from Damascus; Syrian Arab inherited these and

started operating into Europe with Douglas DC-6Bs, serving Paris and London from 1964 and also flying east to Karachi and Delhi. Depending on the political orientation of the government from time to time, both Western and Soviet-built aircraft were used. SE 210 Caravelles were introduced from 1965 and Boeing 747SPs in 1976. The first Boeing 727 was delivered in March 1976 to supplement the Caravelles, the latter only being retired at the beginning of 1996. During the early 1980s Tupolev Tu-134s were acquired, followed by Tu-154s. A well overdue fleet renewal was started in the later

part of 1998 and early 1999 when Airbus A320s were delivered, in a new colour scheme for the airline, to replace the Boeing 727s by mid-2000. In addition to the airline's 'proper' fleet, the Syrian Air Force operates a selection of Yak 40s, Antonov 26s and Ilyushin 76s in full Syrianair colours. During the annual times of pilgrimage, direct flights are made from most Syrian airports to Jeddah/Mecca. Syrianair is responsible for ground handling at these airports.

Routes

Abu Dhabi, Aleppo, Algiers, Amsterdam, Athens, Bahrain, Beirut, Berlin, Brussels, Bucharest, Budapest, Cairo, Damascus, Deirezzor, Delhi, Dharan, Doha, Dubai, Frankfurt, Istanbul, Jeddah, Kameshli, Karachi, Khartoum, Kuwait, Larnaca, Latakia, London, Madrid, Marseilles, Moscow, Mumbai, Munich, Muskat, Paris, Riyadh, Rome, Sanaa, Sharjah, Stockholm, Teheran, Tunis.

Fleet

6 Airbus A320
1 Antonov An-24
5 Antonov An-26
2 Boeing 747SP
2 Boeing 727-200Adv.

4 Ilyushin IL-76M
6 Tupolev Tu-134B
3 Tupolev Tu-154M
6 Yakovlev Yak-40

Boeing 737-2M2C D2-TBC (Bastian Hilker / Harare)

TAAG ANGOLA AIRLINES

Rua da Missao, C P 3010, Luanda, People's Republic of Angola, Tel. 2-336510
Fax. 2-392229, www.taag-airlines.com

Three- / Two- letter code	IATA No.	Reg'n prefix	ICAO callsign
DTA / DT	118	D2	DTA

Direccao de Exploracao dos Transportes Aeros (DTA) was established by order of the Portuguese government in September 1938. However, it was not possible to begin operations until 1940 because of a lack of infrastructure. With an initial fleet of three de Havilland Dragon Rapides, scheduled services were started on 17th July 1940 on domestic routes, and additionally on an international route between Luanda and Pointe Noire in the Congo Republic (then French Equatorial Africa), where connections were available to various European destinations. The name was changed also in this year to DTA – Linhas Aereas de Angola, in which form it remained until 1973. For political reasons operations, with a few exceptions, were suspended between late 1974 and the country's independence from Portugal in November 1975. When the airline was renamed TAAG – Linhas Aereas de Angola, it became the flag carrier of the new people's republic. Boeing 707s and 737s were acquired in the late 1970s and early 1980s, with Fokker F.27s forming the basis of the domestic fleet, though Soviet-built types were also acquired. A TriStar was leased from TAP from 1990 for long-range services, and a Boeing 747-300 was acquired for routes to South America and Europe, replacing the Ilyushin 62. From the late 1990s there has been co-operation with Air Namibia and SAA-South African Airways. After the 2002 peace treaty between the factions in the civil war, air transport in Angola again took on civilian form. Angola Air Charter is a fully-owned subsidiary and uses Boeing 727s and IL-76s on freight duties.

Routes

Benguela, Cabinda, Catumbela, Dundo, Harare, Huambo, Johannesburg, Kinshasa, Kuito, Lisbon, Luanda, Lubango, Lusaka, Malange, Menongue, Paris, Pointe Noire, Rio de Janeiro, Sal, Sao Tome, Soyo, Windhoek.

Fleet

5 Boeing 737-200Adv.
2 Boeing 747-300

Airbus A320-233 N458TA (Josef Krauthäuser / Miami)

TACA INTERNATIONAL AIRLINES

Edifico Altos 2 Piso, San Salvador, El Salvador
Tel. 2678888, Fax. 2233757,
www.taca.com

Three- / Two- letter code	IATA No.	Reg'n prefix	ICAO callsign
TAI / TA	202	YS	Taca

TACA International Airlines was founded in November 1939 in El Salvador as TACA El Salvador, at that time a division of TACA-Airways SA, a powerful multi-national organisation in Central America. The well-known airline pioneer Lowell Yerex had formed TACA originally in Honduras in 1931. Operations began on the Salvador-Tegucigalpa-Managua-San Jose trunk route. In 1942 flights started with DC-3s to Bilbao in the Panama Canal Zone and a year later to Havana. TACA International succeeded TACA El Salvador in 1950 and acquired all remaining assets of the original TACA Corporation in 1960. The airline used Douglas DC-4s and DC-6s and Vickers Viscounts until the first jet aircraft, a BAC One-Eleven, entered service in 1966. Twenty years later TACA added its first widebody, a Boeing 767. Investment in other airlines has become a feature, and the following airlines are all members of the TACA group, though with differing shareholdings: Aviateca, Islena Airlines, LACSA, NICA and TACA Peru. From 1998 a new marketing alliance was instituted within the group, evidenced externally by a new unified set of colour schemes for the aircraft. Co-operation within the group bring synergies and possibilities for savings, for instance in a group order of new equipment from Airbus. Fleet renewal began with the delivery of the first A320 in 1997, with the smaller A319 being delivered from Summer 1999. Aircraft are moved around within the group to meet changing demands. TACA International's base is at the El Salvador International airport in the capital, San Salvador.

Routes

Belize, Buenos Aires, Caracas, Cuzco, Dallas/Fort Worth, Flores, Guatemala City, Guayaquil, Houston, Iquitos, La Ceiba, La Paz, Lima, Los Angeles, Managua, Mexico City, Miami, Montego Bay, New Orleans, New York, Panama City, San Francisco, San Jose, San Pedro Sula, San Salvador, Sao Paulo, Tegucigalpa, Washington.

Fleet	Ordered
5 Airbus A319-100	12 Airbus A319
24 Airbus A320-200	5 Airbus A320
8 Boeing 737-200	

Tupolev Tu-154M EY-85651 (Albert Kuhbandner / Munich)

TAJIKISTAN AIRLINES

31/2 Titov, Dushanbe Airport 734006
Tajikistan Tel. 3772-212195, Fax. 3772-510091
www.tajikistanairlines.com

Three- / Two- letter code	IATA No.	Reg'n prefix	ICAO callsign
TZK / 7J	502	EY	Tajikistan

Also known as Tajik Air or Tajikair, the former Aeroflot regional directorate was taken over from the state in 1990 and reorganised. It was anticipated that the airline would operate schedules, cargo and charter flights, and provide special services for members of the government. Mil-8 helicopters are used to provide passenger and emergency service in inaccessible mountain areas, where they are often the only means of speedy connection with a major town. There is an alliance with Tajikistan International Airlines, which has no aircraft of its own, and thus relies on Tajikistan Airlines for its operations.

In 1998 all the other airlines were merged into Tajikistan Airlines. Because the country has economic problems and a shortage of foreign exchange, part of its extensive but ageing fleet is either unserviceable or has been sold, and new services are seldom added, but Munich was added on a weekly basis from the Summer of 1999. An intermediate stop is made in Istanbul for a crew-change; however they do not sleep in a hotel, but on the aircraft. Charter flights are undertaken for various reasons, and they serve to put money in the bank. The airline and country profited from the last Afghanistan conflict. As a

neighbouring country, Tajikistan was a stopover point on the way from and to northern Afghanistan.

Routes

Almaty, Bishek, Delhi, Dubai, Dushanbe, Istanbul, Ekaterinburg, Karachi, Mashad, Moscow, Munich, Novosibirsk, Sharjah, Teheran.

Fleet

6 Antonov An-24/26
4 Tupolev Tu-134A
8 Tupolev Tu-154B/M
4 Yakovlev Yak-40

Airbus A319-132 PT-MZA – Fokker 100 PT-MRG (Manfred Turek / Sao Paulo)

TAM

Rue Monsenhor Antonio Pepe 94, CEP
04357080 Sao Paulo, Brazil, Tel. 11-55828685,
Fax. 11-55828155, www.tam.com.br

Three- / Two- letter code	IATA No.	Reg'n prefix	ICAO callsign
TAM / JJ	8957	PT	TAM

TAM was set up by VASP and Taxi Aereo Marila on 12th May 1976 as Transportes Aereos Regionais to operate scheduled services in the interior of Sao Paulo state in Brazil. Operations began on 12th July 1976 with Fokker F.27s from Sao Paulo (Congonhas). For less well frequented routes, Brazilian-built, Embraer 110 Bandeirantes have been used. In October 1990 the first jet aircraft, Fokker 100s entered service. The airline continued its network expansion with a mix of Fokker F.27s, Fokker 50s and 100s, but following the demise of Fokker, a number of aircraft whose delivery had been anticipated would not now

be built, and an alternative fleet plan had to be made. The decision went in favour of Airbus, and so A319s, A320s and even A330s were ordered. Though in 1999 the airline had been active almost exclusively within Brazil, this was to change from 28th June 1999 with the delivery of the first A330, at the same time as two A320s. A daily service to Miami was instituted late in 1999, and European services have followed. TAM, together with regional companies TAM-Meridonal and TAM-Express, has developed to become Brazil's largest airline. Because of the continuingly difficult business situation in Brazil, there

has been co-operation with Varig on various services and an on-off plan during 2003 for the full merger of TAM and Varig. TAM is based at Sao Paulo's Congonhas airport.

Routes

Aracaju, Aracatuba, Bauru, Belem, Belo Horizonte, Brasilia, Buenos Aires, Cabo Frio, Campinas, Campo Grande, Corumba, Cuiaba, Florianopolis, Fortalezza, Iguacu Falls, Imperatiz, Londrina, Macapa, Maceio, Manaus, Maraba, Marilia, Miami, Natal, Paris-CDG, Port Alegre, Porto Seguro, Port Velho, Prudente, Punta del Este, Recife, Rio de Janeiro, Salvador, Sao Luiz, Sao Paulo, Teresina, Uberlandia, Una, Vitoria.

Fleet		Ordered
13 Airbus A319-100	48 Fokker 100	15 Airbus A319-100
31 Airbus A320-200		1 Airbus A330-200
9 Airbus A330-200		

Boeing 727-134 HC-BLE (Hans-Willi Mertens collection)

TAME - LINEA AEREA DEL ECUADOR

Avenida Amazonas 1354 Colon, Quito Ecuador, Tel. 2-509375, Fax. 2-509594, E-mail: tame1@tame.com.ec, www.tame.com.ec

Three- / Two- letter code	IATA No.	Reg'n prefix	ICAO callsign
TAE / EQ	269	HC	Tame

In 1962 the Ecuadorian Air Force set up an air transport service to try to improve the poor infrastructure within the country. Using two DC-3s Transportes Aereos Militares began its first routes from Quito and Guayaquil to the more isolated regions of Ecuador, which were not served by commercially-run airlines. Included were the Galapagos Islands in the Pacific, which would receive a TAM aircraft once or twice a month. Until the DC-6 took over this route, it was served by Douglas DC-3s fitted with additional fuel tankage. Some of the DC-3s were replaced from 1970 by more modern HS.748 turboprops, but others remained in service until the beginning of the 1990s. In 1970 the military partially withdrew and TAME was reconstituted as a joint stock company. Two years later TAME took over Compania Ecuatoriana de Aviacion and their regional route network. Further aircraft including Lockheed L-188 Electras and Douglas DC-7s came into use. The first jet came in 1980 with the Boeing 727-300, followed by a 737-200 in 1981. Further second hand 727s were added during 1984 and 1985. During the 1990s TAME has acted as a feeder airline for Lufthansa and Air France from Caracas, and has provided services to Havana and Miami. A Boeing 757 was used briefly in 1999, and the name has been demilitarised as Transportes Aéreos Mercantiles Ecuatorianas SA. Congress in Quito in 2002 gave permission for a part-privatisation, though 51% of the shares are to remain in state/military hands.

Routes

Bogota, Cuenca,Guayaquil, Havana, Lago Agrio, Lima, Machala, Macara, Manta, Quito, Santiago, Tulcan.

Fleet

2 Boeing 727-100
5 Boeing 727-200
1 Fokker F.28

Airbus A320-211 C-FMES (Thomas Kim / Toronto)

TANGO

P.O.Box 64239, Thorncliffe Outlet, 5512 4th Street NW
Calgary, Alberta T2K 6J0, Canada, Tel. 1-8003151390
Fax. 1-8665840380, www.flytango.com

Three- / Two- letter code	IATA No.	Reg'n prefix	ICAO callsign
AC Tango	–	C	Air Canada-Tango

Tango by Air Canada means low-cost/no-frills on flights and is Air Canada's attempt with a new marketing approach to put passengers on seats after 11th September. The whole air transport industry was shaken by that day's events, but the long-established, full-service carriers struggled more than the often more flexible low-cost operators. Especially in western Canada, Air Canada was facing severe competition from Westjet. Tango started operations on 1st November 2001 between the country's most important centres. Drinks and snacks can be bought on the aircraft, and electronic ticketing and internet bookings are the norm. The fleet was made up of six Airbus A320s seconded from the parent company and painted in a new colour scheme. Just a few days after Tango's start up, on 8th November, Canada 3000 became bankrupt and Tango took over a large part of their passengers; Tango accepted Canada 3000 tickets and in doing do gained public recognition. In February 2002 a total of 14 new routes, including to smaller towns such as Thunder Bay or Deer Lake, were announced. More A320s were added, and Boeing 737-200s ordered. In the winter timetable were shown for the first time, classic US leisure destinations including Las Vegas, Fort Lauderdale and Orlando. Competition returned at several airports and thus from Abbotsford, a small airport east of Vancouver, there were just too few passengers to fill the flights being offered to Toronto. Thus Tango was obliged to reduce its services to some destinations to remain cost-effective.

Routes

Calgary, Edmonton, Fredericton, Halifax, Montreal, Quebec City, Regina, Saskatoon, St. John, St. Johns, Toronto, Vancouver, Winnipeg.

Fleet

11 Airbus A320-200
 2 Boeing 737-200

Airbus A319-111 CS-TTC (Albert Kuhbandner / Munich)

TAP AIR PORTUGAL

Edifico 25, Aeroporto Lisboa 1704 Lisboa,
Portugal, Tel. 21-8415000, Fax. 21-8415881,
www.tap-airportugal.pt

Three- / Two- letter code	IATA No.	Reg'n prefix	ICAO callsign
TAP / TP	047	CS	Air Portugal

Transportes Aereos Portugueses – TAP was established on 14th March 1945 by the Portuguese government. Operations began on 19th September 1946 with a converted C-47 (DC-3) from Lisbon to Madrid, and Casablanca was served with a Lockheed Lodestar. Routes opened to Luanda and Laurenco Marques in Mozambique on 31st December 1946, followed in 1947 by London and Paris. All these were operated with Douglas DC-4s. TAP became a joint stock company, partly with private shareholders from 1st June 1953. L-1049 Constellations were used for long-distance routes. When Caravelles were commissioned in 1962, followed by Boeing 707s in

1966 as well as Boeing 727s a year later, this provided TAP with an all jet fleet. In 1972 TAP took on its first widebody, a Boeing 747. The turmoil of the revolution in Portugal in 1975 brought most TAP services to a standstill, but in 1977 after reorganisation it was possible to return flights to their full extent. The present name and colour scheme and logo were adopted in 1979. Two new types were integrated in 1984: the Lockheed L-1011 TriStar for long-range and the Boeing 737 for short and medium-haul. The first Airbus A320-200 arrived in 1992 and the TriStars were sold off during 1994/95 following the arrival of the Airbus A340 as a replacement.

Airbus A319s commenced delivery from December 1997. With the delivery of the Airbus A321 in 2001 the last Boeing 737s were retired, and TAP now has a pure Airbus fleet. TAP has holdings in Air Macau, Air Sao Tome and Yes Linhas Aereas, and ATA-Aerocondor flies Shorts 360s from Madeira on inter-island services under TAP flight numbers. In April 1999 the SAir Group took a 20% holding in TAP, which became a member of the Qualiflyer Group. Fortunately, TAP came out from the collapse of the SAir group unscathed and following some reconstruction, has developed positively.

Routes

Amsterdam, Barcelona, Bissau, Bologna, Brussels, Caracas, Copenhagen, Dakar, Faro, Fortaleza, Frankfurt, Funchal, Geneva, Horta, Johannesburg, Lisbon, London, Luanda, Luxembourg, Madrid, Maputo, Milan, Munich, New York, Nice, Paris, Ponta Delgada, Porto, Porto Santo, Punta Cana, Recife, Rio de Janeiro, Rome, Sal, Salvador, Sao Paulo, Sao Tomé, Stockholm, Terceira, Varadero, Zürich.

Fleet

16 Airbus A319-100
9 Airbus A320-200
3 Airbus A321-200

5 Airbus A310-300
4 Airbus A340-300

Ordered

3 Airbus A319
2 Airbus A320

Boeing 737-78J YR-BGG (Albert Kuhbandner / Munich)

TAROM

OTP A/P SOS Bucuresti Ploesti KM 16,5, 11181
Bucharest, Romania, Tel. 1-2014700, Fax. 1-2014761
E-mail: info@tarom.ro, www.tarom.ro

Three- / Two- letter code	IATA No.	Reg'n prefix	ICAO callsign
ROT / RO	281	YR	Tarom

Transporturile Aeriene Romana Sovietica (TARS) was established as a Romanian-Soviet airline in 1946 to succeed the pre-war state airline LARES. Operations began with a fleet of Lisunov Li-2s provided by the Russian partner. The Romanian state acquired the shares in 1954 and it was renamed as TAROM (Transporturile Aeriene Romane). Tarom flew Ilyushin IL-14s from 1958 to destinations in eastern and western Europe and the first IL-18s entered service in 1963. In 1968 Tarom took on its first BAC One-Eleven, a type which was later built under licence in Romania. Ilyushin IL-62s and Boeing 707s were commissioned in 1973 and 1974, the latter used to open a New York route. The IL-62s allowed extension of services to Africa and the Far East. Two Airbus A310s for long-distance routes were delivered late in 1992, with five Boeing 737-300s arriving in late 1993 and 1994. The intention was to bring the whole fleet up to 'western' standard by the mid-1990s, but this aim has been hindered by Romania's poor economic progress. Some of the older Soviet-built types which are more or less unsaleable were simply mothballed. A planned privatisation has also faltered and could only take place after further modernisation. ATR 42s replaced older Antonov 24s from 1997, with improved ATR 42-500s in use from 1998 and new generation Boeing 737s arrived during 2000/01. The new aircraft have allowed the network to be further developed. The last of the old Russian types and the noisy BAC One-Elevens have all gone, and the Boeing 737s are now augmented by the new -700 model.

Routes

Amman, Amsterdam, Arad, Athens, Beijing, Beirut, Berlin, Brussels, Budapest, Bucharest, Cairo, Chisinau, Constanza, Copenhagen, Damascus, Dubai, Düsseldorf, Frankfurt, Istanbul, Larnaca, London, Madrid, Moscow, Munich, New York, Paris, Prague, Rome, Satu Mare, Sibiu, Sofia, Stuttgart, Tel Aviv, Thessaloniki, Timisoara, Tripoli, Vienna, Warsaw.

Fleet	Ordered
2 Airbus A310-300	1 Boeing 737-700
7 ATR 42-500	4 Boeing 737-800
7 Boeing 737-300	
3 Boeing 737-700	

Boeing 747-4D7 HS-TGJ (Henry Holden / Los Angeles)

THAI AIRWAYS INTERNATIONAL

89 Vibhavachi Rangit Road, Bangkok 10900
Thailand, Tel. 02-5130121, Fax. 02-5130203
E-mail: public.info@thaiair.com, www.thaiair.com

Three- / Two- letter code	IATA No.	Reg'n prefix	ICAO callsign
THA / TG	217	HS	Thai

Thai Airways celebrated 40 years of service in May 2000. It was established in August 1959 as a joint venture between SAS (30%) and the Thai Airways Company (70%), which operated regionally, to take over Thai's international routes. Flights started in May 1960 to neighbouring countries, to Hong Kong and Tokyo, using three DC-6Bs. The change to jets came in 1963 with the SE 210 Caravelle, replaced from 1969 by DC-9-41s. When DC-8-33s arrived Thai expanded its network to Australia in April 1971, Copenhagen from June 1972, and Frankfurt from 1973. In May 1975, when the DC-10-30 was delivered, Thai introduced a new colour scheme. The airline has been in state ownership since April 1977 when SAS gave up its holding. Fleet expansion and updating has continued, with Airbus A300s in 1975 and Boeing 747s from 1979, allowing services to the USA to start from 1980. On 1st April 1980 Thai International and Thai Airways merged in preparation for a privatisation, which proved to be a long drawn out process. The older DC-10s were replaced during 1991/92 with new MD-11s and from 1995 the first Airbus A330 was added, with the first Boeing 777 arriving in the following Spring. The MD-11s are to be phased out with the delivery of the A340s on order for delivery from October 2004 (-500s) and October 2005 (-600s). The airline's headquarters and maintenance base are at Bangkok's Don Muang Airport, but preparations have begun for a move to the new Bangkok-Suvarnabhumi airport. In May 1997 Thai International became a founder member of the Star Alliance.

Routes

Abu Dhabi, Athens, Auckland, Bahrain, Bandar Seri Begawan, Bangkok, Beijing, Brisbane, Chengdu, Chittagong, Colombo, Copenhagen, Dacca, Da Nang, Delhi, Denpassar, Djakarta, Dubai, Frankfurt, Fukuoka, Geneva, Guangzhou, Hanoi, Ho Chi Minh City, Hong Kong, Karachi, Kathmandu, Kolkota, Kuwait, London, Los Angeles, Madrid, Manila, Melbourne, Mumbai, Munich, Muscat, Nagoya, Osaka, Paris, Penang, Perth, Pusan, Rome, Seoul, Shanghai, Singapore, Stockholm, Sydney, Taipei, Tokyo, Vientiane, Xiamen, Yangon, Zürich and about 15 domestic points.

Fleet

21 Airbus A300-600
12 Airbus A330-300
2 ATR 72-200
10 Boeing 737-400

2 Boeing 747-300
16 Boeing 747-400
14 Boeing 777-200/300
4 McDonnell Douglas MD-11

Ordered

3 Airbus A340-500
5 Airbus A340-600

Boeing 757-200 G-FCLE (Albert Kuhbandner / Salzburg)

THOMAS COOK AIRLINES

Commonwealth House, Chicago Avenue
Manchester Airport, M90 3FL, Great Britain
Tel. 161-4895757, Fax. 161-4895758
E-Mail: talktous@thomascook.com, www.thomascook.com

Three- / Two- letter code	IATA No.	Reg'n prefix	ICAO callsign
TCX / MT	-	G	Globe

In 1995 the British tour operator Flying Colours Leisure Group (Sunset Holidays,Priority Holidays, Club 18-30) set up its in-house airline, Flying Colours. Boeing 757s were used on routes to the usual Mediterranean holiday spots. During 1998 the Flying Colours Leisure Group was acquired by another tour company, Sunworld, and that operator's own airline, Airworld was merged with Flying Colours. Sunworld found itself in the ownership of Thomas Cook Holdings, one of Britain's largest travel groups, with interests worldwide. In 1998 this was in turn merged with the Carlson Leisure Group, whose house airline was Caledonian Airways, by then using Airbus A320s, McDonnell Douglas DC-10s and Lockheed L-1011 TriStars. The new group kept the established Thomas Cook name, but found itself with two successful charter airlines under its roof. The inevitable merger took place at the end of the 1999 summer season, but since there was no decision on which of the two names to keep, the new name of JMC (after James Mason Cook, son of the founder) was adopted for the concern and for its airline. The first aircraft appeared in the new colours in March 2000. Thomas Cook Holdings was again taken over by the German C & N Touristik AG in 2001 in a globalisation move in the travel industry. By autumn 2002 it had been decided to re-adopt the well-known Thomas Cook name for the group and the airline and its international partners. Thus JMC in Great Britain, Condor in Germany and Thomas Cook Airline in Belgium have all been given the new name and a common colour scheme, effective from 1st May 2003 in the case of JMC.

Routes

Alicante, Almeria, Antalya, Arrecife, Athens, Bergamo, Bodrum, Burgas, Calgary, Cancun, Catania, Chania, Corfu, Dalaman, Edmonton, Faro, Fuerteventura, Funchal, Geneva, Gerona, Halifax, Heraklion, Ibiza, Innsbruck, Izmir, Jerez de la Frontera, Kavala,Kos, Larnaca, Lyon, Malta, Monastir, Montreal, Naples, Nassau, Ottawa, Puerto Plata, Rhodes, Salzburg, Samos, Santorin, Skiathos, Toronto, Toulouse, Vancouver.

Fleet

8 Airbus A320-200
2 Airbus A330-200
17 Boeing 757-200

Tupolev Tu-204 SU-EAJ (Author's collection)

TNT AIRWAYS

Rue de l'Aéroport, 4460 Grace-Hollogone
Liège, Belgium, Tel. 4-2393000, Fax. 4-2393999
www.tnt-airways.be

Three- / Two- letter code	IATA No.	Reg'n prefix	ICAO callsign
TAY / 3V	163	Various	Quality

TNT, which originated in Australia in 1968, is one of the world's largest cargo organisations. TNT came to Europe in 1984 and in 1987 the European airfreight system was established with a special version of the BAe 146, the QT (or 'quiet trader'). This particularly quiet jet is not subject to night-flight restrictions and can therefore be used for overnight parcel services. TNT did not operate its own aircraft but chartered them to partners such as Air Foyle, Mistral Air, Sterling, Channel Express, Pan Air Lineas Aereas and Hunting Cargo. Until 1998 the hub was at Cologne/Bonn and cargoes were flown here from around 30 points in Europe for distribution, sorting and transfer, before being flown out to its destinations later in that same night. A similar hub was set up at Manila in1993 to cover the Far East region. In 1998 there was a change of ownership and the company became TPG Holdings. The new owner changed the airline name to TNT Airways and reorganised operations. Because of German environmental restrictions and a lack of space for long term growth, the European hub was moved in 1998 to a new superhub at Liège in Belgium. Airbus A300s enhanced capacity from 2000 and from 2002 the Russian-built Tupolev 204 was added on a sub-charter basis. As well as its own aircraft, partner airlines such as Panair fly in TNT colours on a contract basis.

Routes

TNT flies from its main hub in Liège to over 50 destinations within Europe.

Fleet

19 BAe 146-200/300 QT
1 Boeing 747F
2 Boeing 737-300F
6 Airbus A300F

Boeing 767-216 EI-CZD (Gerhard Schütz / Salzburg)

TRANSAERO AIRLINES

Smolenska Perenlok 3-4,2-ND, 121089, Moscow, Russia, Tel. 095-2411064, Fax.095- 2416209
E-mail: info@transaero.ru, www.transaero.ru

Three- / Two- letter code	IATA No.	Reg'n prefix	ICAO callsign
TSO / UN	670	RA	Transaero

Transaero was founded in late 1991 as one of the first private joint stock companies in Russia and the first non-Aeroflot airline approved for scheduled passenger services in Russia. The shareholders are Aeroflot and aircraft manufacturers Ilyushin and Yakovlev. Operations commenced in early 1992, using Tupolev Tu-154s. Thousands of emigrants were flown from Russia to Israel in a spectacular action which caught the attention of the media and gave the young airline publicity. Two Boeing 737-200s were leased in late 1992 and two Ilyushin IL-86s acquired, as well as IL-76s for cargo work. In April 1994 Transaero took

delivery of its first Boeing 757, and was admitted as a member of IATA. Further 757s were added during 1995, allowing more routes to be opened up. In 1996 the first routes to the United States in competition with Aeroflot were started. Leased ex-American Airlines DC-10s were used for the Moscow-Los Angeles route, with a further route to Orlando being added in the Autumn. More international services were added, and in 1997 the airline took a 30% stake in Latvian airline Riga Air, with whom some joint services were flown. However, Russia's mounting economic problems at the end of the 1990s had their effect on

Transaero; passenger numbers dropped dramatically and, far from implementing further expansion, the airline was forced to drop routes, including those to the USA, and return the DC-10s and 757s to their lessors. Two new Boeing 737-700s were however added on lease from mid-1998 and an Airbus A310-300 from September 2000, with a Boeing 767 from early 2003. Transaero announced orders in August 2003 for four Tupolev Tu-204s for delivery from the end of 2004 to mid-2005 on fifteen-year leases. Subsidiary Transaero Express flies Yak-40s on regional services and on VIP charters on behalf of Transaero.

Routes

Almaty, Astana, Baku, Ekaterinburg, Frankfurt, Irkutsk, Karaganda, Kiev, London, Nizhnvartovsk, Odessa, St. Petersburg, Strasbourg, Tashkent, Tel Aviv.

Fleet

3 Boeing 737-200
2 Boeing 737-300
2 Boeing 737-700
3 Boeing 767-200

1 Ilyushin IL-86

Ordered

4 Tupolev Tu-204-300

Airbus A321-131 B-22601 (Josef Krauthäuser collection)

TRANSASIA AIRWAYS

139 Cheng Chou Road, Taipei, Republic of China, Tel. 2-25575767, Fax. 2-25570631
E-mail: mail@tna.com.tw, www.tna.com.tw

Three- / Two- letter code	IATA No.	Reg'n prefix	ICAO callsign
TNA / GE	170	B	Transasia

Foshing Airlines, founded in 1951, experienced more downs than ups in its lifetime, and surrendered its operating licence in 1965. However, it was reactivated in 1990 by the Gold Sun Group and since then has made rapid progress. It was renamed as Transasia Airways in 1992 in order to better reflect the airline's ambitions with regard to an international network. The first jet aircraft was the Airbus A320, which was delivered in August 1992. In this same year international services were opened to Cambodia and the Philippines. The fast-growing company took delivery of more A320s in 1995 as well as the first of six larger A321s. Some of the 321s were given special colour schemes, incorporating advertising. Shorter-range services were flown by a fleet of ATR 42s introduced in 1989, but now replaced by ATR 72s, the first of which was delivered in November 1990.The company's main operating bases are at Taipei-Sung Shan and Kaoshiung. As well as scheduled flights, Transasia is also active in the holiday business with flights to Thailand and the Philippines. On the Chinese mainland there are partnerships with Shanghai Airlines and Xiamen Airlines.

Routes

Chiayi, Hualien, Kaoshiung, Kinmen, Kota Kinabalu, Macau, Makung, Pingtung, Phom Penh, Phuket, Tainan, Taipei, Taitung.

Fleet

12 ATR 72-200/500
 3 Airbus A320-200
 6 Airbus A321-100

Boeing 757-2K2 PH-TKD (Stefan Schlick/ Arrecife)

TRANSAVIA AIRLINES

Postbus 7777, 1118 ZM Schiphol, Netherlands
Tel. 020-6046427, Fax. 020-6484633
E-mail: contact@transavia.nl, www.transavia.nl

Three- / Two- letter code	IATA No.	Reg'n prefix	ICAO callsign
TRA / HV	979	PH	Transavia

Transavia Airlines, which was originally formed as Transavia Limburg in 1965 and changed its name to Transavia Holland in 1967 before becoming Transavia Airlines in 1986, has been in operation since 16th November 1966 when it carried out a charter to Naples. Initially flights to the Mediterranean were offered with three Douglas DC-6s. The airline acquired its first jet, a Boeing 707, followed by an SE 210 Caravelle in 1969; the Caravelles were replaced by the Boeing 737 in 1974. A scheduled service from Amsterdam to London was introduced on 26th October 1986 and there were also schedules to Spain, but by far the major activity was charter work, particularly a large share of the Dutch holiday market, and the leasing out to other airlines of some of its not insubstantial fleet of Boeing 737s and from early 1993, 757s. Since 1991, Transavia has been a subsidiary of KLM, which has an 80% holding, the balance being with a bank. The current colour scheme was adopted during the Summer of 1995. The first of the new Boeing 737-800s were received from June 1998, phasing out the older models; the fleet is now amongst the most modern in Europe. Seats on most Transavia services are now bookable by individuals; internet sales have become increasingly important. During 2002 Transavia established a low-cost division under the name 'Basiq', but the aircraft used for these services are flown in Transavia colours. The company has its base and maintenance facility at Amsterdam-Schiphol, from where scheduled services to London and Spain are also flown.

Routes

Alicante, Amsterdam, Antalya, Arrecife, Barcelona, Casablanca, Catania, Chambery, Djerba, Faro, Fuerteventura, Funchal, Heraklion, Innsbruck, Izmir, Kathmandu, Kavalla, Las Palmas, Lisbon, Malaga, Malta, Milan, Naples, Nice, Palma de Mallorca, Pisa, Porto, Rhodes, Rotterdam, Salzburg, Seville, Sharjah, Tenerife, Valencia, Zakynthos.

Fleet

```
 8 Boeing 737-700
17 Boeing 737-800
 1 Boeing 757-200
 2 Boeing 757-300
```

De Havilland DHC-6 Twin Otter 300 8Q-TMG (Ralf Lücke / Male)

TRANS MALDIVIAN AIRWAYS

P.O.B 2079, Male 20-06, Maldives
Tel. 325708, Fax. 323161
E-mail: mail@tma.com.mv

Three- / Two- letter code	IATA No.	Reg'n prefix	ICAO callsign
HUM / –	–	8Q	Hum

The Maldives total an area of only some 298 square kilometres, spread amongst over 2000 islands. Travel by boat between the widely-spaced islands is time-consuming and so more and more tourists use aircraft from the airport at Hulule to reach their destination resort. As the islands are so tiny and do not have runways, aircraft have to be float-equipped. Trans Maldivian Airways was set up in 1989 as Hummingbird Helicopters and used two Sikorsky S-61N helicopters for flights to the newly established tourist facilities on the islands. Supplies of all kinds and the tourists themselves were transferred relatively quickly.

However, the use of these helicopters, so far from servicing facilities, was very expensive and so the lease of these machines was given up after only a few months. Russian-built Mil Mi-8 helicopters were leased in as replacements and were in service for several years. They were more robust and more suitable for the operation, even if not so comfortable. Under new management in 1998, the company changed its name to Hummingbird Island Airways, and for the first time, fixed-wing aircraft were brought into use. The Cessna Caravan and DHC-6 Twin Otters were float-equipped. Following a tragic helicopter

accident, the use of this type of transport was banned by the authorities. Further fixed-wing aircraft were acquired and it was decided to standardise entirely on the Twin Otter, since it was best suited to the task. The current company name was adopted from 2001.

Routes

Air taxi services between the outlying islands and the airport at Male-Hulule.

Fleet

12 De Havilland DHC-6-100/300

Boeing 757-236 N521NA (Tony Stork / Baltimore)

TRANS MERIDIAN AIRLINES

680 Thornton Way, Lithia Springs, Georgia 30122, USA, Tel. 770-7326900, Fax. 770-7326956, E-mail: info@ transmeridian-airlines co, www.transmeridian-airlines.com

Three- / Two- letter code	IATA No.	Reg'n prefix	ICAO callsign
TRZ / T9	–	N	Transmeridian

This charter airline, founded in Atlanta in 1995, was licensed by the FAA and DoT in October of that year and began operations with the Boeing 727-200 on behalf of leading tour operators. Transmeridian concentrated for its traffic on the major conurbations in the north east of the United States and in the midwest, with Chicago as its leading departure airport. Year round, Transmeridian flies to the Americans' favourite holiday destinations, including of course Las Vegas and the Caribbean. In 1996 the fleet was expanded with an Airbus A320, and a further Boeing 727-200 was acquired. As well as its own aircraft, Trans Meridian also used A320s from the Irish airline Translift, renamed in 1998 as Transaer, on a seasonal basis. The Irish operator was a shareholder in Transmeridian. There was also a contract with Daimler Chrysler for the regular transport of employees between Stuttgart and Detroit, until the car giant acquired its own Airbus A319. Further A320s were acquired, the total eventually reaching four. When Transaer filed for bankruptcy in autumn 2000, Transmeridian was affected, as it suddenly found itself without most of its aircraft, being reduced to a single Boeing 727. The airline thus sought Chapter 11 bankruptcy protection for a long time, finally leaving this condition in mid-2002. New investors allowed for the acquisition of new aircraft and a new colour scheme was likewise introduced. Alongside the 727s, Boeing 757s have been added; the Airbus A320s are no longer in the fleet. Since June 2003, Transmeridian has also been flying scheduled services from Syracuse and Sanford to San Juan on the island of Puerto Rico. Principal bases are at Minneapolis and Des Moines, Iowa.

Routes

Charter services within the USA, and to destinations in Mexico and the Caribbean.

Fleet

5 Boeing 727-200
4 Boeing 757-200

Ordered

1 Boeing 757-200

ATR 42-300 D4-CBE (Hans Kasseckert / Sao Vicente)

TRANSPORTES AEREOS DE CABO VERDE

Caixa Postal 1, Praia, Republic of Cape Verde
Tel. 613215, Fax. 613585
E-mail: informacion@tacv.com, www.tacv.com

Three- / Two- letter code	IATA No.	Reg'n prefix	ICAO callsign
TCV / VR	696	D4	Transverde

Transportes Aereos de Cabo Verde (TACV) was founded on 27th December 1958 to succeed a local flying club which had provided some domestic air services from May 1955 using de Havilland Doves until its bankruptcy in 1958. TACV began operations in January 1959. In 1971 the first of three Britten-Norman Islanders was commissioned. Operations were suspended for a while in 1967, while re-organisation took place with the help of the Portuguese airline TAP. After the country gained independence from Portugal on 5th July 1975, TACV became the flag carrier of the newly established

republic. With the acquisition of a BAe HS.748 in 1973, a weekly service to Dakar in Senegal was set up; this was to remain TACV's sole international route for several years. In association with TAP Air Portugal there was a direct service to Lisbon under a TCV flight number, but operated by a TAP Airbus. As a more modern supplement to the HS.748, two ATR 42s were delivered at the end of 1994, and the arrival in March 1996 of the airline's own Boeing 757-200 allowed the route to Lisbon, and new routes to Frankfurt and Amsterdam, to be flown by TACV aircraft. A third ATR 42 was delivered in 1997, allowing the

retirement of the HS.748. The Cape Verde Islands are slowly developing as a tourist destination and so from 1998 further European airports were added to TACV's network, at the expense of some African services, which were dropped. A Boeing 737-300 became TCV's second jet at the end of 2002 and a fourth ATR 42 has been taken on to help with the growing inter-island traffic.

Routes

Amsterdam, Boa Vista, Bologna, Dakar, Las Palmas, Lisbon, Madrid, Maio, Mosteiros, Munich, Paris, Praia, Rome, Sal, Santo Antao, Sao Filipe, Sao Nicolau, Sao Vicente.

Fleet

4 ATR 42-300
1 Boeing 737-300
1 Boeing 757-200
1 De Havilland DHC-6 Twin Otter

Embraer ERJ-145ER N804HK (Author's collection)

TRANS STATES AIRLINES

11495 Natural bridge, Suite 340, Bridgeton Miss. 63044 USA, Tel. 314-2224300, Fax. 314-2224313
E-mail: info@transstates.net, www.transstates.net

Three- / Two- letter code	IATA No.	Reg'n prefix	ICAO callsign
LOF / 9N	414	N	Waterski

In May 1982 Resort Air was founded in St.Louis and it began operations in April 1983 with Fairchild-Swearingen Metros, serving regional destinations in the states of Illinois and Missouri. An agreement was reached with Trans World in 1985 for the TWA Express feeder service to be built up. In 1986 there was a change of ownership at Resort Air, but the airline remained in private hands and the current name of Trans States Airlines was adopted from 1989. Air Midwest also flew Metros on feeder services for TWA, and after this company encountered financial difficulties, Trans States took it over in 1991. At that time the most suitable aircraft for Trans States Airlines' services was the British Aerospace Jetstream 32, and a large fleet of this type was brought into use from 1990. Later, the fleet was augmented with ATR 42s and its larger brother the ATR 72, as well as the Jetstream 41. From 1993 co-operation with other major airlines – US Air, Northwest and Alaska Airlines – brought further work. Summer 1998 saw the delivery to Trans States of the first of their Embraer ERJ-145 regional jets. During early 2000 the airline closed its California operation for US Airways, Northwest and Alaska, and its Delta Connection operations from early 2001, launching instead a Pittsburgh-based operation for US Airways. With the takeover of failing TWA by American Airlines in 2002, other contracts were gained with American, for whom Trans States now operates under the American Connection banner. Though most flights now operate in the colours of the appropriate partner airline, some aircraft are still in the airline's own colours.

Routes

Albany, Baltimore, Birmingham, Bloomington/Normal, Boston, Burlington, Champaign, Chattanooga, Chicago, Cleveland, Columbia, Decatur, Detroit, Evansville, Fayetteville, Fort Wayne, Grand Rapids, Hartford, Joplin, Lexington, Madison,Memphis, Moline, New York, Norfolk, Peoria, Philadelphia, Pittsburgh, Raleigh/Durham, Rochester, Sioux City, South Bend, Springfield, St.Louis, Toledo, Washington.

Fleet		Ordered
5 ATR 42-300 3 ATR 72-200 25 BAe Jetstream 41	19 Embraer ERJ-145	5 Embraer ERJ-145

Boeing 737-4Y0 OK-TVS (Lutz Schönfeld / Berlin-SXF)

TRAVEL SERVICE AIRLINES

P.O.Box 119, 16008 Praha 6, Czech Republic
Tel. 2-6888661, Fax. 2-6888660
E-mail: trav_air@travelservis.cz

Three- / Two- letter code	IATA No.	Reg'n prefix	ICAO callsign
TVS / QS	–	OK	Skytravel

Travel Service Airlines has its origins in the government's air transport squadron, SLU Statni letecky utvar MA. After the dissolution of the former Czechoslovakia to form the Czech Republic and Slovakia, this was commercialised in 1997 and offered to conduct flights on behalf of tour operators. The former state monopoly travel organisation Cedok took 35% of the shares in Travel Service Airlines, and Canaria Travel was another shareholder. Initially a Tu-154 from the fleet of SLU was used in Travel Service's attractive colours to destinations in the Mediterranean area. The desires of customers in respect of comfort, safety and the efficiency of aircraft used by competitor airlines led to the acquisition as soon as 1998 of a Boeing 737-400, with a further example added in the following year. The company has continued to expand, both in terms of route network and fleet size. With the delivery of the first of the Boeing 737-800s, the Tupolev 154s were retired; for the 2002 summer season a further pair of 737-800s were added. A subsidiary, Travel Service Spain, was set up at the beginning of 2003 and also uses the 737-800 on charter work.

Routes

Charter flights to destinations in the Canary Isles, Mediterranean and Northern Africa. Additionally, ad hoc charters to European destinations, and as far as Bangkok.

Fleet

2 Boeing 737-400
4 Boeing 737-800

Airbus A319-114 TS-IMO (Daniel Hustedt / Hamburg)

TUNISAIR

Boulevard 7 Novembre, 1012 Tunis, Tunisia
Tel. 71-700100, Fax. 71-700897
www.tunisair.com.tn

Three- / Two- letter code	IATA No.	Reg'n prefix	ICAO callsign
TAR / TU	199	TS	Tunair

Tunisair was established in 1948 as a subsidiary of Air France by agreement with the Tunisian government. Operations began in 1949 with Douglas DC-3s, initially from Tunis to Corsica and Algiers. In 1954 Tunisair acquired its first Douglas DC-4 for services to Paris. By 1957 the government had acquired a controlling 51% interest; Air France's shareholding has gradually reduced. In 1961 the airline entered the jet era with the beginning of services with SE 210 Caravelles. As no successor to the Caravelle was available from a French manufacturer, the airline decided to acquire Boeing 727s and the first of these was added to the fleet in 1972, with the type giving long service into the 1990s. After the Caravelles had been taken out of service in late 1977, the Boeing 737-200 arrived in 1979. A swing back into favour for European aircraft manufacturers came in 1982 with the single Airbus A300, and the first A320 in 1990, the latter delivery prompting the introduction of the present, modern colour scheme. More A320s were added in 1994/95, with Boeing 737-500s between 1992 and 1995. New model 737-600s replaced some of the old 727s during 1999, and from February 2000 two Airbus A300-600Rs were added on lease. These are used for the best-patronised routes, but also on charters, many of which are flown for European tour operators. The Tunisian government now holds 45.2% of the shares and Air France 5.2%, with the rest in private hands. Tunisair has a shareholding in Tuninter, which operates domestic services and like Tunisair, is based at Tunis-Carthage. There is close co-operation with Air Algerie, Royal Air Maroc and Air France.

Routes

Algiers, Amman, Amsterdam, Athens, Barcelona, Beirut, Berlin, Bordeaux, Brussels, Budapest, Cairo, Casablanca, Copenhagen, Damascus, Dakar, Djerba, Düsseldorf, Frankfurt, Gafsa, Geneva, Graz, Hamburg, Istanbul, Jeddah, Lille, Lisbon, London, Luxembourg, Lyon, Madrid, Malta, Marseilles, Milan, Monastir, Munich, Nice, Nouakchott, Palermo, Paris, Prague, Rome, Salzburg, Sfax, Stockholm, Strasbourg, Tabarka, Toulouse, Tozeur, Tripoli, Tunis, Vienna, Warsaw, Zürich.

Fleet

3 Airbus A300-600	4 Boeing 737-200Adv.
3 Airbus A319-100	4 Boeing 737-500
12 Airbus A320-200	7 Boeing 737-600

Airbus A340-300 TC-JFF (Albert Kuhbandner/Amsterdam)

TURKISH AIRLINES

Genel Müdürlük Binsai, Atatürk Hava Limani
34830 Yesilköy Istanbul, Turkey, Tel. 212-6636300
Fax. 212-6634744, E-mail: customer@thy.com
www.turkishairlines.com

Three- / Two- letter code	IATA No.	Reg'n prefix	ICAO callsign
THY / TK	235	TC	Turkair

THY stems from Turkiye Devlet Hava Yollari (DHY), founded in 1933 and taken over by the state in 1956, along with its aircraft including Douglas DC-3s. The first new acquisition, the Vickers Viscount, was delivered from January 1958. In 1960 the first services to western Europe were started, including Frankfurt. The first Douglas DC-9 was delivered in August 1967 and the first widebody, the DC-10 on 1st December 1972. For regional services the Fokker F.27 and F.28 were used. Boeing 727-200s were taken on from 1974 and from 1984 the first Airbus A310. For a long time THY concentrated on the development of domestic rather than international services; only from the late 1960s were services to the major European cities to become a feature, no doubt influenced by the need to provide for the travel needs of the many expatriate Turkish workers. The first Airbus A310 was brought into service from 1985, and in 1990 came the first overseas destination, New York. In this year also, a new colour scheme was adopted for THY's aircraft. Capacity continued to be increased, with the Airbus A340 arriving in 1993, along with further Boeing 737s. Also from 1994 the Avro RJ100 was introduced for short and medium range services, replacing older DC-9s and Fokker F.28s; the latest model 737-800 was introduced from October 1998. The last of the Airbus A310s left the fleet in 2003. THY has shareholdings in Sun Express and Kibris Cyprus Turkish Airlines and is also quite active in the charter and freight business.

Routes

THY flies to more than 35 Turkish domestic destinations, and to Abu Dhabi, Algiers, Almaty, Amman, Amsterdam, Ashkhabad, Athens, Bahrain, Baku, Bangkok, Barcelona, Basle, Beijing, Beirut, Berlin, Bishkek, Brussels, Bucharest, Cairo, Capetown, Cologne, Copenhagen, Dubai, Düsseldorf, Frankfurt, Geneva, Hamburg, Hanover, Hong Kong, Jeddah, Johannesburg, Kuala Lumpur, Kuwait, London, Lyon, Madrid, Manchester, Milan, Munich, New York, Nice, Nuremberg, Osaka, Paris, Riyadh, Rome, Seoul, Shanghai, Singapore, Stockholm, Stuttgart, Tashkent, Teheran, Tel Aviv, Tokyo, Tunis, Vienna, Zagreb and Zürich.

Fleet		Ordered
7 Airbus A340-300	14 Boeing 737-400	5 Boeing 737-800
11 Avro RJ 70/100	2 Boeing 737-500	
1 Boeing 727-200F	28 Boeing 737-800	

Fokker 70 OE-LFH (Josef Krauthäuser / Frankfurt)

TYROLEAN AIRWAYS

Postfach 81 Flughafen, 6026 Innsbruck, Austria,
Tel. 512-22220, Fax. 512-22229005, E-mail:
communication@tyrolean.at, www.tyrolean.at

Three- / Two- letter code	IATA No.	Reg'n prefix	ICAO callsign
TYR / VO	734	OE	Tyrolean

Founded in 1958 as Aircraft Innsbruck, the airline operated non-scheduled services until 1980, when it acquired the rights to operate scheduled services from Innsbruck to Vienna. In preparation for these operations which began in April 1980, using de Havilland Canada DHC-7s, the company changed its name during 1979 to Tyrolean Airways. Also in 1980 further routes were opened to Zürich and Frankfurt. In 1994 the domestic arm of Austrian Airlines, Austrian Air Services, was integrated with Tyrolean following the acquisition by Austrian Airlines of a 43% stake in

Tyrolean Airways (Tiroler Luftfahrt AG). Since then Tyrolean has expanded strongly. New aircraft have been introduced: Fokker 70s from May 1995 and Canadair Regional Jets from May 1996 supplementing the previously all de Havilland Canada fleet of DHC-7s and DHC-8s. As well as scheduled services, Tyrolean operates charter flights quite extensively, some in connection with tour operators bringing holidaymakers to the Tyrol. Austrian Airlines took over the remaining shares in Tyrolean in 1998, and with its other partners in the AUA group, the airline has been

linked into the Star Alliance since March 2000. In October 2002 Rheintalflug, in which Austrian had been a majority shareholder, was merged into Tyrolean Airways.

Routes

Altenrhein, Amsterdam, Banja Luka, Berlin, Bologna, Bozen, Bremen, Brussels, Budapest, Chisinau, Cologne/Bonn, Dresden, Dublin, Dubrovnik, Düsseldorf, Elba, Florence, Frankfurt, Friedrichshafen,Gothenburg, Graz, Hamburg, Hanover, Helsinki, Innsbruck, Katowice, Klagenfurt, Kosice, Krakow, Leipzig, Linz, Ljubljana, Luxembourg, Lyon, Madrid, Milan, Minsk, Mostar, Munich, Nuremberg, Olbia, Oslo, Paris, Prague, Pristina, Rome, Salzburg, Strasbourg, Stuttgart, Timisoara, Tirana, Venice, Warsaw, Wroclaw, Zagreb, Zürich.

Fleet

15 Canadair CRJ200
12 De Havilland DHC-8-300
 8 De Havilland DHC-8-400

3 Embraer EMB145
6 Fokker 70

340

Boeing 737-500 UR-GAK (Marcus Baltes / Frankfurt)

UKRAINE INTERNATIONAL AIRLINES

Prospekt Pere Mogy 14, 01135 Kiev, Ukraine
Tel. 44-4615170, Fax. 44-2167994
www.ukraine-international.com

Three- / Two- letter code	IATA No.	Reg'n prefix	ICAO callsign
AUI / PS	566	UR	Ukraineinternational

This airline was formed in October 1992 as Air Ukraine International, a subsidiary company of Air Ukraine (which operates extensive domestic services with a large fleet of Soviet-built types) to operate international services. The newly-independent state of Ukraine took a 90% shareholding. Flights were started to Western Europe with a leased Boeing 737-400. In contrast with Air Ukraine, it was decided to operate modern aircraft which would appeal to western business travellers. However, the 737-400 proved to be expensive in leasing costs and was returned to its lessor in late 1994,

being replaced with an older 737-200, with a further 737-200 added in early 1995. The early hopes for the airline failed to be met and so the company, which was renamed as Ukraine International Airlines in 1995, developed only slowly, but in that year a positive sign was the acquisition of the first Boeing 737-300. Austrian Airlines, Guinness Peat Aviation and Swissair all took shareholdings and with the removal of the state influence the airline became more attractive to other investors. Two further Boeing 737-300s were leased and these were supplemented during 2001 and

2002 by 737-500s, with a corresponding increase in the route network. The airline is based at Kiev's Borispol airport, where it shares a maintenance facility with Air Ukraine.

Routes

Amsterdam, Barcelona, Berlin, Brussels, Donetsk, Frankfurt, Helsinki, Kiev, London, Lvov, Odessa, Paris, Rome, Simferopol, Vienna, Zürich.

Fleet

1 Boeing 737-200Adv.
3 Boeing 737-300
3 Boeing 737-500

Boeing 747-422 N180UA (Josef Krauthäuser / Los Angeles)

UNITED AIRLINES

P.O.Box 66100 Chicago, IL 60666, USA
Tel. 847-7004000, Fax. 847-7007345,
www.ual.com

Three- / Two- letter code	IATA No.	Reg'n prefix	ICAO callsign
UAL / UA	016	N	United

United Airlines Inc. was founded on 1st July 1931 as the new holding company of the former Boeing Air Transport, Varney Air Lines, National Air Transport and Pacific Air Transport. United flew Boeing 247s initially and then Douglas DC-3s. After the end of the war Douglas DC-4s and DC-6s were used, notably on the airline's route from New York to Chicago. In 1947 Hawaii was served for the first time and in 1959 the airline's first jet aircraft, a Douglas DC-8, was accepted into the fleet. United was the only US airline to order the French SE 210 Caravelle, with 20 for short and medium range routes. There were no follow-up orders however, and Boeing 727s were acquired. On 1st June 1961 Capital Airlines, one of America's largest airlines at the time, was taken over. The Boeing 747 joined the United fleet from June 1970. The Douglas DC-10 first appeared in United colours in 1972, with acquisitions up until 1987. In 1986 the rights to various routes in the Pacific and Lockheed TriStars were acquired from a struggling Pan Am. At the same time new aircraft were bought from Boeing; 737-300s and 767s have taken a major role since then, with the 757 increasing in numbers during the 1990s. Not insignificantly, United, with its strong Boeing associations, also ordered Airbus A320s and then A319s. It is also remarkable that United only began European services from 1990; from Autumn 1993 it entered into a partnership with Lufthansa, forming the basis of the worldwide Star Alliance, of which both airlines were founder members in May 1997. United was the launch customer for the Boeing 777, introduced in June 1995. In response to competition from low-cost airlines, United created a Shuttle by United division which operates on the US west coast and in other markets; around 60 Boeing 737-300s and -500s are earmarked for these 'no frills' services. United was particularly affected by the events of 11th September, with two aircraft lost. Subsequent cutbacks led to huge losses, so that from November 2002 United had to seek bankruptcy protection to allow reorganisation. Many aircraft were stored, and large staff cuts have been made.

Routes

United's most important hubs are Los Angeles, San Francisco, Chicago, Denver and Washington-Dulles with flights to over 200 destinations in the USA and worldwide.

Fleet

55 Airbus A319-100	96 Boeing 757-200
96 Airbus A320-200	55 Boeing 767-200/300
156 Boeing 737-300/500	61 Boeing 777-200
30 Boeing 747-400	

Fairchild/Dornier 328 N454FJ (Albert Kuhbandner / Oberpfaffenhofen)

UNITED EXPRESS

c/o United Airlines Customer Relations, WHQPW
P.O. Box 100, Chicago, Illinois 60666, USA
Tel. 847-7004000, Fax. 847-7007345, www.ual.com

Three- / Two- letter code	IATA No.	Reg'n prefix	ICAO callsign
UAL / UA	–	N	United Express

United Airlines has contracted smaller operators as partners in the United Express Feeder System. The object of setting up this system was to feed passengers from smaller airports into the airline's major hubs. Following the airline deregulation of the 1980s, this became an increasingly important activity. Established airlines used this as a method of keeping passengers loyal to their product and in order to be able to offer through services in the whole of the USA. United Airlines currently has contracts with four companies, in most of which it also has shareholdings. Air Wisconsin serves the Chicago O'Hare and Denver hubs, using BAe 146s and Canadair Regional Jets. Atlantic Coast Airlines serves the hub at Washington-Dulles with BAe Jetstream 41s and Canadair RJs. Mountain Air Express also operates out of Denver, using Fairchild/ Dornier 328 turboprops. Sky West Airlines comes originally from Salt Lake City and serves hubs at Los Angeles, San Francisco and Seattle on United's behalf, using Embraer Brasilias and Canadair Regional Jets. United expects more flexibility on these services from its partners than it would be able to manage itself. The trend is towards jets for these feeder services, with even the second generation turboprops being dropped. All United Express aircraft fly in a unified colour scheme, with only a small sticker on the aircraft identifying the actual operator.

Routes

Around 200 different destinations are served from the various hubs, with the different operators sometimes providing interconnecting services at the hubs.

Fleet

18 BAe 146-200/300
31 BAe Jetstream 41
145 Canadair CRJ200

48 Embraer EMB-120
23 Fairchild/Dornier 328

Ordered

55 Canadair RJ

Airbus A300-622F N139UP (Martin Kühn / Hahn)

UPS AIRLINES

1400 North Hurstbourne Parkway, Louisville
Kentucky 40223, USA, Tel. 502-3296500,
Fax. 502-3296550, www.ups.com

Three- / Two- letter code	IATA No.	Reg'n prefix	ICAO callsign
UPS / 5X	406	N	UPS

UPS – United Parcel Service was founded as long ago as 1907, and today is the largest company in the world in its sphere of business. In 1953 the two-day 'UPS-Air' service was set up. In 1982 UPS entered the overnight small package market and now serves more US points than any other carrier. It was only in 1987 that UPS established its own flight operations; up until then other airlines had been commissioned to carry out flights for UPS (even today a large number of outside companies still operate on its behalf). There are also regular flights to the European hub at Cologne, and there are further hubs in Hong Kong, Singapore, Miami and

Montreal, with the main US centre of operations in Louisville. Dedicated DC-8 freighters were initially the mainstay of the long-haul fleet and many are still in service today, but there is also a major fleet of Boeing 747 freighters which has been built up since 1984. UPS induced Boeing to build a cargo version of their 757-200 and was the first customer to receive the -200PF from 1987. Older Boeing 727s have been re-equipped with new, more powerful and more environmentally friendly Rolls-Royce Tay engines; these modified aircraft were first used in 1993, primarily to Europe where environmental regulations are more stringent. Some of the 727s were set up to be

able to fly passenger charters at weekends, with palletised, easily-installable seating. As with the 757PF, UPS was also the launch customer for the Boeing 767-300F, the first of 30 of which was delivered in October 1995. During 1999 UPS bought the South American routes of Challenge Air Cargo, in order to provide expansion in this market. The first of 30 new-build Airbus A300-600F freighters was delivered in July 2000; these also operate from the Europahub at Cologne/Bonn. This large contract for Airbus freighters will occupy the production line for some years. In 2002 the MD-11F was introduced; this type will gradually replace the DC-8s.

Routes

Regular cargo services to around 400 US domestic and 220 international airports. Over 1500 flights a day are operated.

Fleet

		Ordered
39 Airbus A300-600F	30 Boeing 767-300F	60 Airbus A300-600F
16 Boeing 747-100/200F	49 Douglas DC-8-70	15 McDonnell Douglas MD-11
58 Boeing 727-100/200F	5 McDonnell Douglas MD-11	(conversion programme)
75 Boeing 757-200F		

Tupolev Tu-154M RA-85807 (Florian Morasch / Salzburg)

URAL AIRLINES

Ul. Sputnikov 6, 620910 Ekaterinburg, Russia
Tel. 3432-268625, Fax. 3432-266221
www.uralairlines.com

Three- / Two- letter code	IATA No.	Reg'n prefix	ICAO callsign
SVR / U6	262	RA	Sverdlovsk Air

Using as a basis the former local Aeroflot division in the Ekaterinburg area, the Sverdlovsk Aviation Enterprise was established in 1993 as an independent airline. It took over from Aeroflot several aircraft and set about building up its own operations. Over the years employees have been able to acquire shares, or even to take part of their remuneration in the form of shares. Sverdlovsk Aviation Enterprise's operation was renamed in 1996 as Ural Airlines, to give the airline a more international positioning. A more appealing colour scheme also helped to establish a recognisable corporate identity. In addition to Russian domestic scheduled services, the airline is busy with charter work to western Europe and to the Middle East, and in freight work, for which the Antonov 24 and Ilyushin 86 are used. There is a codeshare with CSA-Czech Airlines on the Prague route.

Routes

Ekaterinburg, Moscow, Prague, St.Petersburg.

Fleet

3 Antonov 24
3 Ilyushin IL-86
16 Tupolev Tu-154

Airbus A319-112 N764US (Josef Krauthäuser / Phoenix)

US AIRWAYS

2345 Crystal Drive,Arlington Virginia 22227, USA, Tel. 540 872 7000, Fax. 540 872 5437, www.usairways.com

Three- / Two- letter code	IATA No.	Reg'n prefix	ICAO callsign
USA / US	037	N	US Air

All-American Aviation was set up on 5th March 1937 to provide postal services over a network of routes from Pittsburgh. Postal services ceased in 1949 and the concern changed its name to All American Airways on 7th March 1949 to coincide with the start of passenger services from Pittsburgh via Washington to Atlantic City using Douglas DC-3s. Martin 2-0-2s and Convair 340/440s replaced the DC-3s, the name was changed again to Allegheny Airlines and new routes opened, especially in the eastern United States. Lake Central Airlines was taken over on 1st July 1968 and on 7th April 1972 Mohawk Airlines followed, with its large route network and BAC One-Eleven aircraft. After deregulation, Pacific Southwest Airlines and the much larger Piedmont Airlines were also both taken over. US Air was adopted as the new, less parochial, name from 28th October 1979. Its first services to London were in 1988, followed in 1990 by Frankfurt, Paris and Zürich. Fokker 100s were introduced in 1989. US Air took over the New York to Washington and Boston shuttle services from Trump and shareholdings were taken in various US Air Express partner airlines. In January 1993 British Airways made a $400 million investment and operated joint services, but the partnership faltered and BA sold its holding in early 1997, at which time the airline took on the new identity of US Airways and new colours. Major fleet renewal, mostly courtesy of Airbus Industrie, began from 1998 with the introduction of A319s and A320s, with the A330 following in Spring 2000 and A321s from mid-2001. On 12th March 2002 US Airways entered Chapter 11 bankruptcy protection, and used the the time until March 2003 for radical change and reconstruction of the airline. Over 70 aircraft, including the Fokker 100 and MD-80 fleets were parked or sold, and other major cuts in routes and staff made. Fresh capital came from pension funds, banks and from savings made. Many services are flown under the US Airways Express banner (see page 347),

Routesl

US Airways' major hubs are at Pittsburgh, Philadelphia and Charlotte, with service to over 130 destinations in the USA, Caribbean and Europe.

Fleet

64 Airbus A319-100	82 Boeing 737-300
24 Airbus A320-200	46 Boeing 737-400
28 Airbus A321-200	34 Boeing 757-200
9 Airbus A330-300	11 Boeing 767-200ER

Embraer ERJ-145 N262SK (Thomas Kim)

US AIRWAYS EXPRESS

2345 Crystal Drive, Arlington, Virginia 22227, USA
Tel. 703-8727000, Fax. 703-8727064
www.usairways.com

Three- / Two- letter code	IATA No.	Reg'n prefix	ICAO callsign
USA / US	–	N	US Air Express

US Airways is contracted with several airlines under the 'Express' banner. Using a miscellany of types, flights are conducted under US Airways flight numbers. Air Midwest (AMW / ZV) has been a long-term US Airways Express carrier, using Beech 1900s out of its Kansas City base. The Allegheny Airlines (ALO / AL) name belonged to one of the founder companies of US Air, but has been retained and Allegheny flies from hubs in Pittsburgh and Philadelphia with DHC-8s. CC Air (CDL / ED) is based in Charlotte, and uses several BAe Jetstream 32s from here. Chautauqua Airlines (CHQ / RP) serves Indianapolis and Pittsburgh with a fleet of BAe Jetstream 31s, Embraer ERJ-145s and Saab 340s. Colgan Air (CJC / 9L) has been flying since 1999 for US Airways Express from New York, Boston and Washington using the Beech 1900 and Saab 340. Florida Gulf Airlines and Liberty Express, which belong to the Mesa group, serve Jacksonville and Philadelphia with Beech 1900s. Mesa Airlines (ASH / YV) is one of the largest commuter companies and looks after more than 40 destinations on the east coast, using the Embraer ERJ-145,de Havilland DHC-8 and Canadair RJ. Midway Airlines (MDW / JI) lost its independence after bankruptcy in 2002 and now flies its Canadair RJs as an Express Partner. The name Piedmont Airlines (HNA / US) also stems from the time of the merger of Allegheny into US Air. Piedmont is a fully-owned subsidiary and flies 60 DHC-8s from Fort Lauderdale and Washington. PSA Airlines (JIA / TF) is a further subsidiary, using Fairchild / Dornier 328s from Indianapolis, Dayton and Pittsburgh. Shuttle America (TCF / S5), an independent company in the late 1990s, also came under the Express banner after encountering financial difficulties. It operates Saab 340s and DHC-8s in the north-eastern USA. The final Express Partner is Trans States Airlines (LOF / 9N), with its BAe Jetstream 41s and Embraer ERJ-145s. US Airways Express plans to have over 300 regional jets, from both Embraer and Canadair, in service by 2006.

Routes

The various operators in the US Airways Express system conduct over 2000 flights a day to around 160 US destinations.

Fleet

Fleet		Ordered
12 BAe Jetstream 31	116 De Havilland DHC-8	85 Canadair CRJ200
15 BAe Jetstream 41	69 Embraer ERJ-145	120 Embraer ERJ-145
52 Beech 1900	30 Fairchild / Dornier 328	
9 Canadair CRJ200	38 Saab 340	

Airbus A320 N265AV (Stefan Schlick / Montego Bay)

USA3000

7 Campus Boulevard, Newton Square
Pennsylvania PA 19073, USA, Tel. 610-3251280,
Fax. 610-3251285, www.usa3000airlines.com

Three- / Two- letter code	IATA No.	Reg'n prefix	ICAO callsign
GWY / U5	–	N	Getaway

Apple Vacations is one of the largest operators of inclusive tours in the United States USA and had for some time had the ambition of owning its own in-house airline, as is the case with several British operators. However, instead of this, in the main travel season aircraft were leased from European charter airlines and used to fly to favourite winter destinations in the Caribbean. Founded at the beginning of 2000, Brendan Air did fulfil Apple's plan for its own airline. It was planned to undertake charters from the US east coast to Caribbean destinations.

Operations eventually began in October 2001 with leased Airbus A320s, but using the marketing name USA 3000. The airline's home base is at Philadelphia where there is co-operation with US Airways for aircraft handling and maintenance. Further aircraft were added in November and during early 2002. The company continues its growth, with scheduled services to Las Vegas and other destinations being added.

Routes

Charter flights in the Caribbean and to various destinations in Mexico and the USA.

Fleet

7 Airbus A320-200

Airbus A310-324 UK-31001 (Andreas Dabrowski / Hamburg)

UZBEKISTAN AIRWAYS

Movarounnakhr Kucasi 41, 700100 Tashkent, Uzbekistan
Tel. 71-337036, Fax. 71-331885, E-mail: info@
uzbekistan-airways.com, www.uzbekistan-airways.com

Three- / Two- letter code	IATA No.	Reg'n prefix	ICAO callsign
UZB / HY	250	UK	Uzbek

In 1992 the government of the newly independent state of Uzbekistan took responsibility for its air services. The aircraft of the former Aeroflot Tashkent directorate became the property of Uzbekistan, and were passed to Uzbekistan Airways, which was formed as the national airline. Some of the routes previously operated by Aeroflot were taken over and continued. Particular attention was paid to the new routes from western Europe via Tashkent to the Indian subcontinent and Far East and it was here that the airline with its particularly low priced tariffs entered into competition with established airlines. In order to be in a position to meet the higher expectations of Western travellers, Uzbekistan leased two Airbus A310-300s and concluded an agreement with Lufthansa for technical support. The first of these arrived in Tashkent in July 1993 and services started to London and Middle Eastern cities. In 1995 Kuala Lumpur and New Delhi were added as destinations, and in 1996 Jeddah and Tel Aviv came on line. As well as the schedules, there are numerous charters to Arab countries.

Modernisation and re-equipment with western aircraft started with the delivery in early 1997 of two leased Boeing 767-300s, and three Avro RJ 85s later in the year, with Boeing 757s added from September 1999. Uzbekistan is by far the largest airline operating in the country and has additional responsibilities for government tasks including patrol and agricultural work for which helicopters such as the Mil-8 are used.

Routes

Almaty, Amritsar, Ashkabad, Athens, Bahrain, Baku, Bangkok, Beijing, Birmingham, Bishkek, Bukhara, Chelyabinsk, Delhi, Dacca, Ekaterinburg, Frankfurt, Istanbul, Jeddah, Kazan, Kiev, Krasnodar, Krasnoyarsk, Kuala Lumpur, London, Mineralnye Vody, Moscow, New York, Novosibirsk, Nukus, Omsk, Osaka, Paris, Rome, Rostov, Samara, Samarkand, Seoul, Sharjah, Simferopol, St.Petersburg, Tashkent, Tel Aviv, Termez, Tyumen, Ufa, Urgench.

Fleet

3 Airbus A310-300
10 Antonov An-24
3 Avro RJ 85
3 Boeing 757-200
42 Boeing 767-300ER
8 Ilyushin IL-62

15 Ilyushin IL-76
10 Ilyushin IL-86
2 Ilyushin IL-114
17 Tupolev Tu-154
12 Yakovlev Yak 40

Boeing 777-2Q8(ER) PP-VRB (Richard Schmaus / London-LHR)

VARIG BRASIL

Avenida Almirante Silvio de Noronha 365,
CEP 20021-10 Rio de Janeiro, Brazil, Tel. 21-
8145644, Fax. 21-8145718, www.varig.com.br

Three- / Two- letter code	IATA No.	Reg'n prefix	ICAO callsign
VRG / RG	042	PP	Varig

Founded on 7th May 1927 by German immigrant Otto Ernst Meyer, Varig developed initially in the south of Brazil. The first aircraft was a Dornier Wal flying-boat which operated the first service on 3rd February 1928. First international service was in 1942 to Montevideo and Lockheed 10As were introduced in 1943. After the Second World War, Varig acquired 35 C-47/DC-3s and built up its network. In 1951 Aero Geral with its routes to Buenos Aires and Montevideo were taken over. Scheduled service to New York started in August 1955; from October 1959 the Caravelle was

substituted and from late 1960 Boeing 707s took over the route. REAL, a much larger airline, was taken over in 1961 and thus under its famous president Ruben Berta, Varig acquired new aircraft such as the CV 990, Lockheed L-188, C-46 and an extensive route network. The international network was also expanded in 1965 when it took over Panair do Brasil by government order. DC-10-30s came into service in May 1971. Cruzeiro do Sol, was bought in 1975 (and integrated in 1993) and in 1981 Airbus A300s and Boeing 747-200s were acquired. Boeing 767s, 747-400s, MD-11s and

Boeing 777s were all added later. Varig has majority shareholdings in Rio Sul and Nordeste Linhas Aereas. A dedicated cargo airline, Varig Log, was created in the latter part of 2000 to take on all Varig's cargo assets and services. South America's largest and most modern overhaul base is owned by Varig at Rio de Janeiro, the airline's main base. Varig has been a member of the Star Alliance since October 1997. In 2002 Varig celebrated its 75th anniversary in a difficult financial situation. On/off merger plans with TAM have been beset by legal battles and may or may not come to fruition.

Routes

Altamira, Aracaju, Asuncion, Belem, Belo Horizonte, Boa Vsta, Bogota, Brasilia, Buenos Aires, Campinas, Campo Grande, Cancun, Caracas, Copenhagen, Cordoba, Cuiaba, Curitiba, Florianopolis, Fortaleza, Frankfurt, Goiania, Iguacu Falls, Joao Pessoa, Joinville, La Paz, Lima, Lisbon, London, Londrina, Los Angeles, Macapa, Maceio, Madrid, Manaus, Miami, Milan, Montevideo, Nagoya, Natal, New York, Paris, Porto Allegre, Porto Seguro, Porto Velho, Recife, Rio Branco, Rio de Janeiro, Salvador, Santiago, Sao Luiz, Sao Paulo, Tabatinga, Tefe, Teresina, Tokyo, Uberlandia, Vitoria.

Fleet

29 Boeing 737-300
 2 Boeing 737-800
 2 Boeing 777-200
12 Boeing 767-200/300ER

2 Douglas DC-10-30F
14 McDonnell Douglas MD-11

Boeing 737-3L9 PP-SFN (Manfred Turek / Sao Paulo)

VASP

Praca Cte. Lineu Gomes sn, Ed. Sede VASP
Congonhas Airport, Sao Paulo CEP 04695, Brazil
Tel. 11-55323000, Fax. 11-55420880
E-mail: ascom@vasp.com.br, www.vasp.com.br

Three- / Two- letter code	IATA No.	Reg'n prefix	ICAO callsign
VSP / VP	343	PP	Vasp

Viacao Aerea Sao Paulo SA was founded on 4th November 1933 by the regional government of Sao Paulo and the municipal bank, with operations beginning on 16th April 1934. In 1935 two Junkers Ju 52/3s were acquired and scheduled service opened between Rio de Janeiro and Sao Paulo. The takeover of the Brazilian-German Aerolloyd Iguacu in 1939 added many routes. VASP used six Saab Scanias from 1950, and later all the aircraft of this type ever built, eighteen, were used until retired in 1966. Vickers Viscounts were used from 1958. Two more airlines, Loide

Aero Nacional and Navegaceo Aerea Brasileiro were taken over as part of a general rationalisation of Brazilian air service in 1962. The first jet, the BAC One-Eleven, arrived in December 1967, and eight NAMC YS-11s were acquired in late 1968; these replaced the Viscounts and DC-4s. VASP evolved over the years to become Brazil's second largest airline, continually modernising its fleet. The first four Boeing 737s were introduced in July 1969 and in the late 1970s the Brazilian-built Embraer Bandeirante regional aircraft came into service briefly, until the airline became all-jet.

Boeing 727s and Airbus A300s then formed the fleet, until MD-11s were added in 1992. During the late 1990s VASP took shareholdings in long-established South American carriers Ecuatoriana and Lloyd Aereo Boliviano, but early in 2000 VASP itself entered a period of financial difficulty. A reorganisation took place, and some aircraft returned to their lessors, with a consequent reduction in activity. A much slimmed airline is now active more regionally, with international services transferred to TAM or Varig. Subsidiary Vaspex uses the three Boeing 727 freighters.

Routes

Aracaju, Belem, Brasilia, Campinas, Campo-Grande, Culaba, Curitiba, Florianopolis, Fortalezza, Goiania, Iguacu, Ilheus, Joao Pessoa, Londrina, Macapa, Maceio, Manaus, Natal, Porto Allegre, Porto Seguro, Porto Velho, Recife, Ribeirao Preto, Rio de Janeiro, Salvador, Sao Jose do Porto Preto, Sao Luiz, Sao Paulo, Teresina, Uberlandia.

Fleet

```
 3 Airbus A300B2
 3 Boeing 727-200F
21 Boeing 737-200
 4 Boeing 737-300
```

Tupolev Tu-154M LZ-MIS (Frank Fielitz / Frankfurt)

VIA – AIR VIA BULGARIAN AIRWAYS

54 GM Dimitrov Blvd. Sofia, BG-1125 Bulgaria
Tel. 2-9712869, Fax. 2-9733454
E-mail: info@air-via.com, www.via-air.com

Three- / Two- letter code	IATA No.	Reg'n prefix	ICAO callsign
VIM / VL	–	LZ	Via Air

With the dissolution of the Warsaw Pact and moves to democratisation in Bulgaria, it became possible at the end of the 1980s to form private companies. A group of investors formed VIA-Air Via, or VIA est Vita, in 1990 as a private Bulgarian charter airline. The Black Sea beaches of Bulgaria, formerly a favourite with the denizens of East Germany and other eastern bloc countries, were to see a re-awakening of tourist interest. Bulgaria is a pleasant holiday destination, especially for families with children. Thus the increasing demand for travel could not be met by the state airline. Operations began with a Tupolev Tu-154 in spring 1990. Four further Tu-154s were acquired during 1990 as contracts were made with tour companies. The principal destination for VIA flights was the coastal airport at Varna, though there were also some services to the capital, Sofia. The bulk of the departures were from Belgium, Germany and France. VIA also carried out charter flights from Sofia to Beirut, Cairo or Dubai. During the peak season it was often necessary to lease in additional aircraft. In the medium term, fleet renewal is on the agenda, and discussions have taken place with Boeing and Airbus over a successor for the Tu-154.

Routes

Charter flights to Sofia and Varna on behalf of leading European tour operators.

Fleet

5 Tupolev Tu-154M

Airbus A320-214 S7-ASG (Thomas Kim / Bangkok)

VIETNAM AIRLINES

Gialem Airport, Hanoi, Socialist Republic of Vietnam, Tel. 4-8732732, Fax. 4-8272291, www.vietnamairlines.com

Three- / Two- letter code	IATA No.	Reg'n prefix	ICAO callsign
HVN / VN	738	VN	Vietnam Airlines

After the ending of the Vietnam war and the reunification of Vietnam, a new airline also came into existence in 1976: Hang Khong Vietnam. It took over the aircraft and staff of the former CAAV in the north and partly those of Air Vietnam. Air Vietnam had been 92.75% owned by the old southern government in 1975, shortly before the fall of Vietnam; it had been formed to take over the services of Air France in the area. Hang Khong Vietnam's fleet was very quickly changed over to Soviet standard as spare parts could not be obtained for the western-built aircraft and in the early and mid-1980s, Tupolev Tu-134As operated

several weekly services from Hanoi to Ho Chi Minh City (formerly Saigon), Phnom Penh, Bangkok and Vientiane. Only when the country opened up politically towards the West and the USA was possible in 1990 to place an order for western aircraft. As a replacement for Ilyushin IL-18s, two ATR 72s were ordered. Slow expansion of the route network was planned for the 1990s. In 1990 some Tu-134s were bought from Interflug stocks, the name changed to Vietnam Airlines and new colours were introduced. Political change also made it possible for Air France to acquire a stake in the airline and to provide

Airbus A320s from late 1993 for international flights as well as training and other support. As part of a plan to replace the Russian types, Boeing 767s and Fokker 70s were acquired to meet increased demand. The pace of growth has quickened and the network has expanded with routes to Australia and Europe and neighbouring countries which have large Vietnamese populations and where there is great demand for special flights during holiday and festival times. In April 2003 Vietnam Airlines took on its first Boeing 777-200ER, which are used for non-stop service to Paris.

Routes

Bangkok, Ban Me Throut, Berlin, Da Nang, Dalat, Dien Bien Phu, Dubai, Fukuoka, Guangzhou, Haiphong, Hanoi, Ho Chi Minh City, Hong Kong, Hue, Kaoshiung, Kuala Lumpur, Manila, Melbourne, Moscow, Na Trang, Osaka, Paris, Phnom Pen, Phuquoq, Pleiku, Quinhon, Rachgia, Seoul, Siem Reap, Singapore, Son La, Sydney, Taipei, Vientiane, Vinh City.

Fleet

10 Airbus A320-200
 2 Airbus A321-100
 9 ATR 72-300/500
 8 Boeing 767-300ER

2 Boeing 777-200
2 Fokker 70

Ordered

5 Airbus A321
3 ATR 72
4 Boeing 777-200

Airbus A340-313 G-VSUN (Klaus Brandmaier / London-LHR)

VIRGIN ATLANTIC

The Office, Crawley Business Quarter, W Sussex RH10 1DQ, Great Britain, Tel. 1293-562345 Fax. 1293-561721, www.virgin-atlantic.com

Three- / Two- letter code	IATA No.	Reg'n prefix	ICAO callsign
VIR / VS	932	G	Virgin

Virgin Atlantic has its origins in British Atlantic Airways founded in 1982, but which the CAA declined to licence. Richard Branson thus set up Virgin Atlantic through the Virgin Group. The collapsed Laker Airways was used by Branson as a model as there was an obvious demand for a 'cheap airline' to operate from London. Virgin Atlantic was granted a licence for London to New York (Newark) and the first flight was on 22nd June 1984. In November a daily connecting flight to Maastricht, Holland using BAC One-Elevens was started: this was later operated by Viscounts but ceased in 1990. With imaginative advertising and marketing the airline, offering only

cheap flights, attracted more sophisticated passengers. In 1986 another 747 was added, with four more in 1989 and further routes including Miami, New York JFK and Tokyo via Moscow were started. The Airbus A340 was introduced in late 1993 and used for routes to Hong Kong and Australia. During 1996 the Belgian airline EBA was bought and used as the basis for a European network under the Virgin Express name (see page 356). Also in 1996 the Johannesburg route was finally established. In 1998 Virgin was given authority to carry military personnel between London and Washington. In 1999 a Manchester-based charter airline was set up as

Virgin Sun, but this was closed in October 2001. Plans were made for an Australian low-cost airline, and this came to fruition in mid-2000 as Virgin Blue (see page 355). Virgin gained the strength of Singapore Airlines as a partner in December 1999 when SIA took a 49% holding in Virgin. Also in 1999 the current 'Silver Dream' colour scheme was introduced for Virgin's fleet. In the new century fleet renewal has moved ahead with Airbus A340-600s beginning delivery from 2002, replacing the 747-200s. In competition with British Airways, Virgin has gained more slots at Heathrow and increased services.

Routes

Antigua, Athens, Barbados, Boston, Brussels, Delhi, Hong Kong, Johannesburg, Lagos, Las Vegas, Los Angeles, Manchester, Miami, New York-JFK, New York-EWR, Orlando, Port Harcourt, San Francisco, Shanghai, St.Lucia, Tokyo, Washington.

Fleet	Ordered
18 Airbus A340-300/600	2 Airbus A340-600
13 Boeing 747-400	6 Airbus A380

Boeing 737-800 VH-VOF (Frank Schorr / Sydney)

VIRGIN BLUE

P.O.Box 1034, Spring Hill,QLD 4004, Australia
Tel. 7-32953000, Fax. 7-38394024, E-mail:
compliments@virginblue.com.au, www.virginblue.com

Three- / Two- letter code	IATA No.	Reg'n prefix	ICAO callsign
VOZ / DJ	–	VH	Virgin Blue

The Virgin Group set out to apply the successful recipe for its Virgin Atlantic and Virgin Express airlines in Australia; thus in 1999 Virgin Blue was established in Brisbane. Services began between Brisbane and Sydney on 31st August 2000 using a Boeing 737-400. Thanks to the bankruptcy of Ansett Australia, Virgin Blue was able to grow quickly to become a credible competitor for the quasi-monopolistic Qantas. Previously, Ansett and Qantas had dominated the Australian market and smaller companies had become their sub-contractors. When Ansett filed for bankruptcy, other airlines were affected and there was no competition for Qantas. Only Impulse Airlines had in 2000 started up as a low-cost airline with Boeing 717s, but it had succumbed to Qantas takeover barely a year later. Virgin sees itself as a thorn in the side of large, monopolistic companies and has for instance campaigned for many years against the planned alliance between American Airlines and British Airways. Virgin Blue thus won approval from passengers and in a short time was able to build up its fleet and open up more routes, including the principal business centres and tourist areas. After only three years the company has grown enormously and enjoys great popularity, but more to the point is successful in its business. It has been granted approval to launch international flights to Fiji, New Zealand and Vanuatu from October 2003.

Routes

Adelaide, Alice Springs, Brisbane, Broome, Cairns, Canberra, Coffs Harbour, Darwin, Goldcoast, Hobart, Launceston, Mackay, Melbourne, Perth, Rockhampton, Sunshinecoast, Sydney, Townsville.

Fleet

28 Boeing 737-400/700/800	10 Boeing 737-800

Boeing 737-4Y0 OO-VJO (Jan-Alexander Lück / Malaga)

VIRGIN EXPRESS

Building 116 Airport, B-1820 Melsbroek, Belgium
Tel. 2-7520511, Fax. 2-7520506, E-mail: communication@
virgin-express.com, www.virgin-express.com

Three- / Two- letter code	IATA No.	Reg'n prefix	ICAO callsign
VEX / TV	665	OO	Virgin Express

In November 1991 EuroBelgian Airlines was set up by the City Hotels Group and it began operations from 1st April 1992 with Boeing 737-300s as a general European charter airline, partly in the expectation of providing some of the capacity which would be needed in the wake of the collapse of Air Europe. Richard Branson, founder and head of the British airline Virgin Atlantic took over EBA in April 1996 to form a basis for his European expansion plans, renamed it as Virgin Express and set about building a low-cost airline operating scheduled services within Europe. Until that time, 'low-cost' in Europe had been equated with the use of old, less reliable aircraft, but Virgin Express took over EBA's modern Boeing 737-300s and augmented them with further examples. Likewise, EBA's existing network formed a good basis, with some modifications, and its charter operations were also continued. Rather than enter into head-on competition, a strong partnership was quickly established with Sabena and the national airline's London service taken over, flown by Virgin Express aircraft on a codeshare basis, several times a day. The first brand new Boeing 737-300 for Virgin – painted in an unmistakable red colour scheme complementary to that of Virgin Atlantic – was delivered at the end of 1996. In 1997 49% of Virgin Express shares were sold via the stock market: the balance remains with Branson. The main hub is Brussels-National, from where most of the charters are flown. The scheduled services have suffered some setbacks, with Virgin Express failing in its attempt to build up the German market, withdrawing from operations at Cologne/Bonn in 2002 because of strong competition, though it has expanded elsewhere.

Routes

Amsterdam, Athens, Barcelona, Bordeaux, Brussels, Copenhagen, Faro, Geneva, Gothenburg, Lisbon, Madrid, Malaga, Milan, Nice, Palma de Mallorca, Rome, Stockholm.

Fleet

6 Boeing 737-300
8 Boeing 737-400

Fokker 50 OO-VLK (Daniel Klein / Düsseldorf)

VLM

Luchthaven, Gebouw Bus 50 Antwerp Airport, B-2100
Deurne, Belgium, Tel.3-2309000, Fax. 3-2813200
E-mail: info@vlm-airlines.com, www.vlm-air.com

Three- / Two- letter code	IATA No.	Reg'n prefix	ICAO callsign
VLM / VG	978	OO	Rubens

Vlaamse Luchttransportmaatschappij NV was set up in Antwerp, the main city and business centre of Flanders, in February 1992. It took fifteen months for operations to get under way on 15th May 1993 with the first scheduled flight from Antwerp to London-City Airport. VLM is a typical niche carrier, offering services from smaller airports. Thus it flies from Rotterdam and from Mönchengladbach, which now has retitled itself with the somewhat more fancy name of Düsseldorf-Express-Airport. For a while the London-City service was extended with a British domestic leg to Liverpool, but this experiment was not a success and was dropped. The fleet has been expanded with the acquisition of further Fokker 50s, the airline's standard type, and the airline has expanded carefully in new markets. It also flies subcharters for other airlines. The original aircraft was acquired from the Norwegian operator Busy Bee, and retained their basic yellow and white colours, but in 1998 a new dark blue and white scheme was adopted, with the Flanders lion in gold on the fin. New seasonal routes to Guernsey and Jersey were introduced, and Manchester and Hanover were also added to the network. VLM is now Antwerp's leading operator with over 150 departures a week. It concentrates on only a few routes, but with high frequencies, being also the leading operator at London-City. Despite the various crises affecting air transport, it has managed to remain loss-free for some years. There is co-operation with KLM, Luxair, Virgin Express and European Air Express.

Routes

Antwerp, Brussels, Guernsey, Jersey, London-City, Luxembourg, Manchester, Milan, Rotterdam.

Fleet

11 Fokker 50

Airbus A320-214 I-VLEA (Jörg Thiel / Berlin-TXL)

VOLARE AIRLINES

Corso Garibaldi 186, 36016 Vicenza, Italy
Tel. 0445-800100, Fax. 0445-800101
www.volare-airlines.it

Three- / Two- letter code	IATA No.	Reg'n prefix	ICAO callsign
VLE / VA	263	I	Revola

Volare Airlines was established in 1997 by a group of people from the travel industry. A leased Airbus A320 was used to begin services in April 1998 for the summer season from airports in the North of Italy including Bergamo, Milan and Verona. Two more A320s were added during 1998 and scheduled services were also begun from Milan to Olbia. The SAir Group took a 34% shareholding in the young airline from September 1998. During 1999 more scheduled services were added, including to Rome, and more A320s were added. There was naturally co-operation with the other members of the SAir Group, particularly fellow Italian Air Europe and Swissair was responsible for aircraft technical matters. The growth continued into the new millennium and more destinations and increased frequencies were added, particularly with a boom in the Italian charter market. With the failure of the SAir Group, the ownership passed back into Italian hands, and from 2001 there was marked investment in the fleet. Airbus A330-200s were acquired for longer-range routes and Air Europe joined the Volare Group. Several of the Air Europe routes and aircraft were integrated into Volare by the end of 2002. Additionally the Spanish LTU subsidiary, LTE, was taken over by the Volare Group in 2001. A low-cost operation, Volareweb was set up at the beginning of 2003 for European services, and all of the group's activities are being expanded.

Routes

Alghero, Antalya, Athens, Barcelona, Bari, Beauvais, Bergamo, Berlin, Bilbao, Brussels, Cagliari, Cancun, Catania, Cayo Largo, Colombo, Hahn, Havana, Istanbul, Las Palmas, London, Madrid, Male, Mauritius, Milan, Olbia, Palma de Mallorca, Prague, Punta Cana, Rimini, Rome, Tirana, Valencia, Zürich.

Fleet	Ordered
17 Airbus A320-200	2 Airbus A330-200
2 Airbus A321-100	2 Airbus A320
6 Airnus A330-200	
2 Boeing 767-200	

Fokker F.27 Friendship 600 D-AISY (Lutz Schönfeld / Berlin-SFX)

WDL AVIATION

Postfach 980267, 51130 Cologne-airport
Germany, Tel. 02203-9670, Fax. 02203-967105
E-mail: info@wdl-aviation.de, www.wdl-aviation.de

Three- / Two- letter code	IATA No.	Reg'n prefix	ICAO callsign
WDL	–	D	WDL

Westdeutsche Luftwerbung WDL was established in 1955, with the objective of aerial advertising, be it with banners towed by aircraft, or with airships operating as flying billboards. The firm's headquarters were at the Essen-Mülheim airport. Charter and sightseeing flights were also offered and proved very popular at weekends. From this developed non-scheduled services, for which four to six-seater aircraft were used. The step to larger aircraft came in 1974 with the first Fokker F.27, and this type was used for both freight and passenger work. WDL-Flugdienst GmbH was created in 1991 for the operation of the

larger aircraft and took over all the F.27s. DLT was building up a regional network on behalf of Lufthansa, and WDL helped with this. Aircraft and crews were provided for several years for the network of this predecessor of Lufthansa Cityline. As the F.27 fleet continued to grow, so the company acquired new contracts. The new package companies such as TNT and UPS often contracted national companies to fly regional services from their central hubs, and Cologne/Bonn's airport is one of these hub airports. In 1991 the newly-formed1991 WDL Aviation GmbH moved its headquarters and

base to this airport and provided German and European distribution for these freight companies. In 1998 WDL took on its first BAe 146 jet, a series 100 which was used for passenger charter work; more of the type have been added since. The F.27 is getting long in the tooth and some decision about its successor must be imminent. Some WDL aircraft are leased out long-term to other airlines and painted in their colours, including three BAe 146s with Air Berlin

Routes

Regular freight flights on behalf of UPS, within Germany and Europe. Passenger services as charters or ad hoc, or for Eurowings and other companies.

Fleet

1 BAe 146-100
2 BAe 146-200
1 BAe 146-300
14 Fokker F.27

Boeing 737-2T4 C-GEWJ (Daniel Klein / Victoria)

WESTJET AIRLINES

5955 11th Street NE, Calgary, Alberta T2E 8N4
Canada, Tel. 403-4442600, Fax. 403-4442301
www.westjet.com

Three- / Two- letter code	IATA No.	Reg'n prefix	ICAO callsign
WJA / W5	–	C	Westjet

The notion of a low-cost airline for the West of Canada was mooted in 1994 by a group of businessmen in Calgary and set out in a master plan for interested investors. Thus Westjet was set up in June 1995 after the successful model of US companies Morris Air and Southwest Airlines. David Neeleman, who had been a leading light at both Morris Air and Southwest, and was founder of JetBlue Airlines, was an adviser. Services began on 29th February 1996 with two Boeing 737-200s from Calgary, at first serving Edmonton, Kelowna, Vancouver and Winnipeg. During 1996 two further 737-200s

were added to the fleet, which continued to grow steadily in the following three years. 1999 was a year of considerable change on the Canadian airline scene, after Canadian was taken over by Air Canada, and Westjet seized the newly-offered opportunities to expand its services into the east of the country, with services to Thunder Bay and Moncton. Also in 1999 a share offering was made in order to increase the capital base, in turn allowing the building of a new headquarters and hangars in Calgary as well as further fleet expansion. From early 2000 Hamilton was established as a hub

for services in Eastern Canada, with flights to Halifax, Montreal and Ottawa following. By 2003 Westjet had more or less doubled the size of its aircraft fleet and its number of routes, with expansion into the USA envisaged. Pending delivery of its own aircraft, many jets have been leased in on a seasonal basis. Westjet's success has been met by several newcomers on the scene, including Air Canada with its Tango and Zip brands.

Routes

Abbotsford, Calgary, Comox, Edmonton, Fort McMurry, Gander, Grande Prairie, Halifax, Hamilton, Kelowna, London, Moncton, Montreal, Ottawa, Prince George, Regina, Saskatoon, Sault St. Marie, St. Johns, Sudbury, Thunder Bay, Toronto, Vancouver, Victoria, Windsor, Winnipeg.

Fleet

21 Boeing 737-200
24 Boeing 737-700

Ordered

8 Boeing 737-600/700

De Havilland DHC-8-311 LN-WFS (Marcus Baltes / Frankfurt)

WIDEROE

P.O.Box 247, Langstranda 6, 8001 Bodo, Norway, Tel. 75-513500, Fax. 75-513581, E-mail: postmaster@wideroe.no, www.wideroe.no

Three- / Two- letter code	IATA No.	Reg'n prefix	ICAO callsign
WIF / WF	701	LN	Wideroe

Viggo Wideroe founded his Wideroe's Flyveselskap A/S on 19th February 1934. First he obtained a licence to open a route from Oslo to Haugesund. On behalf of DNL, the established Norwegian airline of the time and one of the predecessors of SAS, he opened a postal service in 1936 to Kirkenes in the north of Norway. After the Second World War, Wideroe started charter and supply flights again. It took over the Narvik-based Polarfly in 1950 and made a particular contribution to the opening up of the north of Norway. The first de Havilland DHC-6 Twin Otters were received in 1968 and used to open scheduled services on local routes. With government support a network from Bodo and Tromso was built up and this was extended over the years to around 30 to 40 smaller airfields, all of them standardised with similar landing aids and a runway of between 800 and 1,000 metres. In this way the necessary infrastructure was created in this inaccessible area crisis-crossed with fjords. Towns such as Kirkenes and Hammerfest had only been accessible by ship until the air services began. From 1993 to 1996 almost the entire fleet, including the DHC-7s which had served for some years, was replaced by modern DHC-8s and international service was opened for the first time to Sumburgh in the Shetland Islands and to Copenhagen. Wideroe also undertakes charter work. Other airlines, Fred Olsen, SAS and Braathens S.A.F.E. all had shares in Wideroe but in the late 1990s SAS took over the majority holding and Wideroe has since then been more closely involved and co-ordinated with SAS. The latest aircraft in the fleet is the lengthened Dash 8Q-400, the first of which was delivered in November 2002 and used from Stavanger to Aberdeen.

Routes

Aberdeen, Alta, Batsfjord, Billund, Bergen, Bervelag, Bodoe, Bromnoysund, Copenhagen, Forde, Gothenburg, Hamburg, Hammerfest, Harstad, Hasvik, Honningsvag, Kirkenes, Leknes, Melamn, Mo i Rana, Mosjoen, Namsos, Oslo, Roervik, Sandane, Sandefjord, Sorkjosen, Sogndal, Stavanger, Stockholm, Stokmarknes, Svolvaer, Tromsoe, Trondheim, Vadso, Vardoe, Volda.

Fleet

17 De Havilland DHC-8-100
9 De Havilland DHC-8-300
4 De Havilland DHC-8Q-400

McDonnell Douglas MD-11 N271WA (Marcus Baltes / Frankfurt)

WORLD AIRWAYS

101 World Drive, HLH Building, Peachtree City, Georgia 30269, USA, Tel. 770-6328000, Fax. 770-6328075
E-mail: service@worldair.com, www.worldair.com

Three- / Two- letter code	IATA No.	Reg'n prefix	ICAO callsign
WOA / WO	468	N	World

World Airways was founded on 29th March 1948 and began charter flights with a Boeing 314 flying boat from the US east coast. A year later flights moved from water to land; two Curtiss C-46s were used. Edward Daly acquired an 81% interest in the airline and made it into a large and well-known supplemental charter airline. From 1960 World took over an increasing number of flights for the USAF's Military Airlift Command, and DC-4s, DC-6s and Lockheed 1049 Constellations were bought or leased. The first Boeing 707s were acquired in 1963 and regular flights to Europe were introduced using these aircraft, as well as services to

the Caribbean and South America. In May 1973 charter flights to London began from Oakland, using Boeing 747s. World linked Newark and Baltimore/Washington with Los Angeles and Oakland from April 1979. Scheduled flights were further expanded with the introduction of DC-10s, and the Hawaii-Los Angeles-Baltimore-London-Frankfurt flights were the lowest priced charters to these destinations for many years. After restructuring in 1988 World abruptly withdrew from scheduled services. Malaysian Helicopter took over 25% of the shares in 1994 and invested in the company. From 1993, passenger services were restarted to

Israel and charters were resumed under the airline's own name to Great Britain and other European destinations. However, yet again these were withdrawn after the 1996 summer season, and the airline was to concentrate in future on ad hoc charters and freight flights. The airline moved towards a specialisation in wet-leasing their aircraft out, with World Airways aircraft thus flying in other airlines' colours. New owners in 2001 brought about a move to Georgia and numerous new contracts, including intensive flying for the US military in support of the conflicts in Afghanistan and Iraq.

Routes

Charter and freight flights worldwide.

Fleet

6 Douglas DC-10-30
9 McDonnell Douglas MD-11

Boeing 757-200 B-2829 (Jan-Alexander Lück / Beijing)

XIAMEN AIRLINES

Gaoqi Airport 361009 Xiamen, Fujian
People's Republic of China, Tel. 592-6022961
Fax. 592-6028263, www.xiaminair.com.cn

Three- / Two- letter code	IATA No.	Reg'n prefix	ICAO callsign
CXA / MF	731	B	Xiamen Airlines

Xiamen Airlines was founded in 1991 by China Southern Airlines (with 60% of the shares) and the regional governments of Xiamen and Fujian, and is virtually a subsidiary of CSA but with its own fleet and operating area. Operations began in 1992 with a leased Boeing 737-200. More 737s have been added, including -500 series from 1992 onwards, and Boeing 757s were added to the fleet with deliveries from August 1992 to February 1996. There are services to the South and East of the People's Republic. In late 1992 a route to Hong Kong was opened, the first international destination. During 1998 Xiamen Airlines received four Boeing 737-700s to replace the older -200s. The fleet has developed slowly but steadily and new routes added. The airline is based at Xiamen, where maintenance also takes place, and works closely with the companies in the China Southern group. Xiamen Airlines is a shareholder in Fujian Airlines, which leases aircraft from Xiamen as required.

Routes

Anqing, Bangkok, Beijing, Changchun, Changsha, Chengdu, Chongqing, Dalian, Fuzhou, Guangzhou, Guilin, Guiyang, Haikou, Hangzhou, Harbin, Hefei, Jinan, Jinjiang, Kunming, Lanzhou, Macau, Nanchang, Nanjing, Nanning, Nantong, Ningbo, Qingdao, Shanghai, Shantou, Shenyang, Shenzen, Shijiazhuang, Tianjin, Wenzhou, Wuhan, Wuyshan, Xian, Xiamen, Zhengzhou, Zhousan, Zhuhai.

Fleet		Ordered
2 Boeing 737-200Adv.	9 Boeing 737-700	1 Boeing 737-700
4 Boeing 737-300	7 Boeing 757-200	
6 Boeing 737-500		

Boeing 747SP-27 7O-YMN (Klaus Brandmaier / Salzburg)

YEMENIA

P.O.Box 1183, Sanaa, Republic of Yemen
Tel. 232380, Fax. 252963,
www.yemenia.com.ye

Three- / Two- letter code	IATA No.	Reg'n prefix	ICAO callsign
IYE / IY	635	7O	Yemeni

The 'new' Yemenia is the result of the amalgamation of the former Alyemen and Yemenia, respectively the two national airlines of the North and South Yemen, now merged into one nation again. Saudi Arabian Airlines is a 40% shareholder in the new airline. The two precursors were completely dissolved, bringing aircraft, routes, handling etc all completely into the new airline. The original Yemenia can be traced back to 1961 when it was established as Yemen Airlines, whilst Alyemen was set up soon after the split of the country into North and South in 1971. Several aircraft are also used for transport roles by the country's air force. The mixed fleet arising from the merger includes two DHC-7s delivered in 1996 to augment two earlier examples, and two Airbus A310s leased from Spring 1997 to give a modern image to international routes. A Boeing 747SP is used predominantly for government transport tasks, being fitted out in VIP configuration. Further fleet renewal has seen the arrival of the Boeing 737-800 to replace the older -200 models. An alliance was formed with Daallo Airlines in 1998, and some flights operated under a codeshare arrangement.

Routes

Abu Dhabi, Addis Ababa, Aden, Albuq, Al Gaydah, Amman, Asmara, Ataq, Bahrain, Cairo, Damascus, Djibouti, Doha, Dubai, Frankfurt, Hodeidah, Jeddah, Karachi, Khartoum, Larnaca, London, Moroni, Mumbai, Nairobi, Paris, Riyadh, Rome, Sanaa, Seiyun, Sharjah, Taiz.

Fleet

4 Airbus A310-300
3 Boeing 737-800
3 Boeing 737-200Adv.
2 Boeing 727-200Adv.
1 Boeing 747SP

2 De Havilland DHC-6 Twin Otter
4 De Havilland DHC-7
2 Lockheed L-382 Hercules
2 Ilyushin IL-76

Boeing 737-300 B-2936 (Author's collection/ Beijing)

ZHONGYUAN AIRLINES

No.106 Jinshua Rd, Zhengzhou,
Henan 450003, People's Republic of China
Tel. 371-6222542, Fax. 371-62222542

Three- / Two- letter code	IATA No.	Reg'n prefix	ICAO callsign
CYN / Z2	–	B	Zhongyuan

Zhongyuan Airlines was formed in 1991 in the Chinese province of Henan, and began operations in that same year with two Yunshuji Y7s, Chinese licence-built versions of the proven Antonov 24, though with some improvements over the Russian original. Initially the two Y7s served 15 destinations. As propeller driven types were taking too long to fly some of the longer routes, a Boeing 737-300 was acquired in April 1994. Some airports were also not allowing the use of propeller aircraft on safety grounds, and so the airlines were being influenced to acquire modern jets. Later in 1994 more 737-300s arrived and

expansion continued by the acquisition of further examples in 1999. Zhongyuan built up an alliance with Hainan Airlines, Shandong Airlines, Shenzen Airlines, Sichuan Airlines and Wuhan Air Lines to compete with China's larger airlines, but in mid-2000 was acquired by China Southern as an early move under the great new Chinese airline consolidation plan. It is however not yet clear whether Zhongyuan will be fully merged into China Southern; for the moment it continues to operate under its own identity.

Routes

Beijing, Changsha, Chengdu, Chongging, Guilin, Guiyang, Haikou, Harbin, Huangyan, Jingdezhen, Kunming, Nanjing, Ningbo, Shanghai, Shenyang, Shenzen, Wenzhou, Wuhan, Xiamen, Yantai.

Fleet

2 Yunshuji Y7
2 Boeing 737-300

Boeing 737-217 C-GCPO (Henry Tenby / Vancouver)

ZIP

Hangar 191, 8050. 22nd Street NE, Calgary
Alberta, T2E 7H6, Canada, Tel. 866-4636947
E-mail: info@4321zip.com, www.4321zip.com

Three- / Two- letter code	IATA No.	Reg'n prefix	ICAO callsign
WZP / 3J	–	C	Zipper

Zip is Air Canada's answer to the numerous low-cost airlines springing up in Canada in competition on low fares with the established national carrier. Especially in the west of the country, Westjet has been very successful, so that retaliation by the setting up of its own low-cost carrier by Air Canada was decided upon. Zip took to the skies on 8th September 2002, with its first route from Vancouver to Calgary, using the Boeing 737-200. All routes are served several times daily. The colour scheme of the aircraft is attractive and comes in various hues, including orange, blue, green and lilac, somewhat reminiscent of the old Braniff colours. Further routes were added quickly and the fleet, at first six aircraft, grew to eight and then eleven. Zip now flies not only in the west of Canada, but also to Montreal or London in the east. The network continues to be expanded.

Routes

Abbotsford, Calgary, Edmonton, London, Montreal, Ottawa, Saskatoon, Vancouver, Victoria, Winnipeg.

Fleet

11 Boeing 737-200

Airport Abbreviations/Codes

IATA	Place / Airport	Country
AAA	Anaa, Tuamotu	French-Polynesia
AAC	Al Arish	Egypt
AAE	Annaba	Algeria
AAK	Aranka	Kiribati
AAL	Aalborg	Denmark
AAN	Al Ain	UAE
AAQ	Anapa	Russia
AAR	Aarhus	Denmark
AAT	Altay	China
AAY	Al Gaydah	Yemen
ABA	Abakan	Russia
ABD	Abadan	Iran
ABE	Allentown, PA	USA
ABF	Abaiang	Kiribati
ABI	Abilene, Tx	USA
ABJ	Abidjan	Ivory Coast
ABL	Ambler, AK	USA
ABM	Bamaga, QL	Australia
ABQ	Albuquerque, NM	USA
ABR	Aberdeen, SD	USA
ABS	Abu Simbel	Egypt
ABT	Al-Baha	Saudi Arabia
ABV	Abuja	Nigeria
ABX	Albury, NSW	Australia
ABY	Albany, GA	USA
ABZ	Aberdeen	Great Britain
ACA	Acapulco	Mexico
ACC	Accra	Ghana
ACE	Arrecife, Lanzarote	Spain
ACH	Altenrhein	Switzerland
ACI	Alderney	Great Britain
ACK	Nantucket, MA	USA
ACT	Waco, TX	USA
ACV	Arcata / Eureka, CA	USA
ACY	Atlantic City, NJ	USA
ADA	Adana	Turkey
ADB	Izmir	Turkey
ADD	Addis Ababa	Ethiopia
ADE	Aden	Yemen
ADF	Adiyaman	Turkey
ADK	Adak, AK	USA
ADL	Adelaide, SA	Australia
ADQ	Kodiak, AK	USA
ADU	Ardabil	Iran
ADZ	San Andres	Columbia
AEA	Abemama Atoll	Kiribati
AEP	Buenos Aires AP J.N.	Argentina
AER	Adler / Sochi	Russia
AES	Alesund	Norway
AET	Allakaket, AK	USA
AEX	Alexandria, LA	USA
AEY	Akureyri	Iceland
AFA	San Rafael	Argentina
AFI	Amalfi	Columbia
AFL	Alta Floresta	Brazil
AFR	Afore	Papua New Guinea
AFW	Forth Worth-Alliance	USA
AFT	Afutara	Solomon Islands
AGA	Agadir	Morocco
AGB	Augsburg	Germany
AGF	Agen	France
AGH	Helsingborg	Sweden
AGJ	Aguni	Japan
AGK	Kagua	Papua New Guinea
AGL	Wanigela	Papua New Guinea
AGM	Tasiilaq	Greenland
AGP	Malaga	Spain
AGR	Agra	India
AGS	Augusta, GA	USA
AGT	Ciudad del Este	Paraguay
AGU	Aguascalientes	Mexico
AGV	Acarigua	Venezuela
AHO	Alghero	Italy
AHS	Ahuas	Honduras
AHU	Al Hoceima	Morocco
AIA	Alliance, NE	USA
AIC	Airok	Marshall Islands
AIE	Aiome	Papua New Guinea
AIM	Ailuk	Marshall Islands
AIR	Aripuana	Brazil
AIS	Arorae	Kiribati
AIT	Aitutaki	Cook Islands
AIU	Atiu	Cook Islands
AIW	Ai-Ais	Namibia
AJA	Ajaccio	France
AJF	Jouf	Saudi Arabia
AJL	Aizawi	India
AJN	Anjouan	Comores
AJR	Arvidsjaur	Sweden
AJU	Aracaju	Brazil
AJY	Agades	Niger
AKA	Ankang	China
AKB	Atka, AK	USA
AKC	Akron / Canton, OH	USA
AKD	Akola	India
AKF	Kufrah	Libya
AKG	Anguganak	Papua New Guinea
AKI	Akiak, AK	USA
AKJ	Asahikawa	Japan
AKK	Akhiok, AK	USA
AKL	Auckland	New Zealand
AKN	King Salmon, AK	USA
AKS	Auki	Solomon Islands
AKU	Aksu	China
AKX	Aktyubinsk	Kazakstan
ALA	Almaty	Kazakstan
ALB	Albany, NY	USA
ALC	Alicante	Spain
ALD	Alerta	Peru
ALF	Alta	Norway
ALG	Algiers	Algeria
ALH	Albany, WA	Australia
ALI	Alice, TX	USA
ALJ	Alexander Bay	South Africa
ALM	Alamogordo, NM	USA
ALP	Aleppo	Syria
ALR	Alexandra	New Zealand
ALW	Walla Walla, WA	Australia
ALY	Alexandria	Egypt
AMA	Amarillo, Tx	USA
AMB	Ambilobe	Madagascar
AMD	Ahmedabad	India
AMG	Amboin	Papua New Guinea
AMM	Amman, Queen Alia	Jordan
AMQ	Ambon	Indonesia
AMS	Amsterdam	Netherlands
AMZ	Ardmore	New Zealand
ANC	Anchorage, AK	USA
ANF	Antofagasta	Chile
ANI	Aniak, AK	USA
ANK	Ankara	Turkey
ANL	Andulo	Angola
ANM	Antalaha	Madagascar
ANR	Antwerp	Belgium
ANS	Andahuaylas	Peru
ANU	Antigua	
ANX	Andennes	Norway
AOC	Altenburg-Nobitz	Germany
AOI	Ancona	Italy
AOJ	Aomori	Japan
AOK	Karpathos	Greece
APF	Naples; FL	USA
APL	Nampula	Mozambique
APO	Apartada	Columbia
APS	Anapolis	Brazil
APW	Apia	Samoa
AQI	Qaisumah	Saudi Arabia
AQJ	Aqaba	Jordan
AQP	Arequipa	Peru
ARH	Archangelsk	Russia
ARI	Arica	Chile
ARK	Arusha	Tanzania
ARM	Armindale, NSW	Australia
ARN	Stockholm-Arlanda	Sweden
ARQ	Arauquita	Columbia
ART	Watertown, NY	USA
ARU	Aracatuba	Brazil
ARW	Arad	Romania
ASA	Assab	Eritrea
ASB	Ashkahbad	Turkmenistan
ASC	Ascension	Bolivia
ASD	Andros	Bahamas
ASE	Aspen, CO	USA
ASF	Astrachan	Russia
ASM	Asmara	Eritrea
ASO	Asosa	Ethiopia
ASP	Alice Springs, NT	Australia
ASR	Kayserie	Turkey
ASU	Asuncion	Paraguay
ASV	Amboseli	Kenya
ASW	Aswan	Egypt
ATA	Anta	Peru
ATB	Atbara	Seychelles
ATH	Athens	Greece
ATK	Atqasuk, AK	USA
ATL	Atlanta-Hartsfield, GA	USA
ATM	Altamira	Brazil
ATP	Aitape	Papua New Guinea
ATQ	Amritsar	India
ATR	Atar	Mauritania
ATV	Atiu	Chad
ATW	Appleton, MI	USA
AUA	Aruba	
AUG	Augusta, ME	USA
AUH	Abu Dhabi	UAE
AUR	Aurillac	France
AUS	Austin, TX	USA
AUT	Atauro	Indonesia
AUW	Wausau, WI	USA
AUY	Aneityum	Vanuatu
AVI	Ciego de Avila	Cuba
AVP	Wilkes-Barre,PA	USA
AVU	Avu Avu	Solomon Islands
AWD	Aniwa	Vanuatu
AWK	Wake Island	Midway Island
AWZ	Ahwaz	Iran
AXA	Anguilla	
AXD	Alexandroupolis	Greece

IATA	Place / Airport	Country	IATA	Place / Airport	Country	IATA	Place / Airport	Country
AXM	Armenia	Columbia	BIL	Billings, MT	USA	BTS	Bratislava	Slovakia
AXT	Akita	Japan	BIM	Bimini	Bahamas	BTV	Burlington,VT	USA
AYC	Ayacucho	Columbia	BIO	Bilbao	Spain	BUA	Buka	Papua New Guinea
AYK	Arkalyk	Kazakstan	BIQ	Biarritz	France	BUD	Budapest	Hungary
AYP	Ayacucho	Peru	BIS	Bismarck, ND	USA	BUE	Buenos Aires Intl.	Argentina
AYQ	Ayers Rock, NT	Australia	BJA	Bejaja	Algeria	BUF	Buffalo, NY	USA
AYR	AYR	Australia	BJL	Banjul	Gambia	BUG	Benguela	Angola
AYT	Antalya	Turkey	BJM	Bujumbura	Burundi	BUH	Bucharest	Romania
AZD	Yazd	Iran	BJS	Beijing	China	BUQ	Bulawayo	Zimbabwe
AZO	Kalamazoo, MI	USA	BJX	Leon	Mexico	BUR	Burbank, CA	USA
AZR	Adrar	Algeria	BKA	Moscow-Bykovo	Russia	BUS	Batumi	Georgia
BAG	Baguio	Philippines	BKI	Kota Kinabalu	Malaysia	BUZ	Bushehr	Iran
BAH	Bahrain		BKK	Bangkok	Thailand	BVA	Beauvais	France
BAK	Baku	Azerbaijan	BKM	Bakalalan	Malaysia	BVB	Boa Vista	Brazil
BAL	Batman	Turkey	BKO	Bamako	Mali	BVC	Boa Vista	Cape Verde Rep
BAQ	Barranquilla	Columbia	BKS	Bengkulu	Indonesia	BVG	Berlevag	Norway
BAY	Baia Mare	Romania	BKY	Bukavu	Congo	BVI	Birdsville, QL	Australia
BBA	Balmaceda	Chile	BLA	Barcelona	Venezuela	BVR	Brava	Cape Verde Rep
BBG	Butaritari	Kiribati	BLE	Borlange	Sweden	BWE	Braunschweig	Germany
BBK	Kasane	Botswana	BLI	Bellingham, WA	USA	BWI	Baltimore, MD	USA
BBM	Battambang	Cambodia	BLK	Blackpool	Great Britain	BWN	BandarSeri Begawan	Brunei
BBO	Berbera	Somalia	BLL	Billund	Denmark	BXN	Bodrum	Turkey
BBQ	Barbuda	Leeward Island	BLP	Bellavista	Peru	BXU	Butuan	Philippines
BBU	Bucharest	Romania	BLQ	Bologna	Italy	BYU	Bayreuth	Germany
BCA	Baracoa	Cuba	BLR	Bangalore	India	BZE	Belize City	Belize
BCD	Bacolod	Philippines	BLT	Blackwater, QL	Australia	BZN	Bozeman, MT	USA
BCN	Barcelona	Spain	BLV	Belleville, IL	USA	BZV	Brazzaville	Congo
BDA	Bermuda		BLZ	Blantyre	Malawi	CAB	Cabinda	Angola
BDB	Bundaberg, QL	Australia	BMA	Stockholm-Bromma	Sweden	CAE	Columbia, SC	USA
BDJ	Banjarmassin	Indonesia	BME	Broome, WA	Australia	CAG	Cagliari	Italy
BDL	Windsor-Locks	USA	BMG	Bloomington, In	USA	CAI	Cairo	Egypt
BDO	Bandung	Indonesia	BMI	Bloomington-Normal, IL	USA	CAK	Akron / Canton, OH	USA
BDP	Bhadrapur	Nepal	BMO	Bhamo	Myanmar	CAN	Guangzhou	China
BDR	Bridgeport, CT	USA	BNA	Nashville, TN	USA	CAP	Cap Haitien	Haiti
BDS	Brindisi	Italy	BND	Bandar Abbas	Iran	CAY	Cayenne	French-Guyana
BDU	Bardufoss	Norway	BNE	Brisbane, QL	Australia	CBB	Cochabamba	Bolivia
BEB	Benbecula	Great Britain	BOB	Bora Bora	Tahiti	CBG	Cambridge	Great Britain
BEF	Bluefields	Nicaragua	BOD	Bordeaux	France	CBL	Ciudad Bolivar	Venezuela
BEG	Belgrade	Serbia	BOG	Bogota	Columbia	CBO	Cotabato	Philippines
BEI	Beica	Ethiopia	BOH	Bornemouth	Great Britain	CBR	Canberra	Australia
BEL	Belem	Brazil	BOI	Boise, ID	USA	CCC	Cayo Coco	Cuba
BEO	Newcastle-Belmont	Australia	BOJ	Bourgas	Bulgaria	CCF	Carcassonne	France
BES	Brest	France	BOM	Mumbai	India	CCK	Cocos Island	Australia
BET	Bethel, AK	USA	BON	Bonaire	Neth. Antilles	CCP	Concepcion	Chile
BEW	Beira	Mozambique	BOO	Bodo	Norway	CCS	Caracas	Venezuela
BEI	Beirut	Lebanon	BOS	Boston, MA	USA	CCU	Kolkata	India
BFD	Bradford, PA	USA	BPF	Batuna	Solomon Islands	CDB	Cold Bay, AK	USA
BFI	Seattle-Boeing Field	USA	BPN	Balikpapan	Indonesia	CDG	Paris-Ch. De Gaulle	France
BFL	Bakersfield, CA	USA	BPS	Porto Seguro	Brazil	CDV	Cordova, AK	USA
BFN	Bloemfontein	South Africa	BPT	Beaumont, TX	USA	CEB	Cebu	Philippines
BFS	Belfast	Great Britain	BQN	Aguadilla	Puerto Rico	CEI	Chiang Rai	Thailand
BGA	Bucamaranga	Columbia	BQT	Brest	Belarus	CEN	Ciudad Obregon	Mexico
BGF	Bangui	Cental African Rep	BRC	San Carlos de Baril.	Argentina	CEZ	Cortez,CO	USA
BGI	Barbados		BRE	Bremen	Germany	CFE	Clermont-Ferrand	France
BGO	Bergen	Norway	BRI	Bari	Italy	CFN	Donegal	Ireland
BGR	Bangor, ME	USA	BRK	Bourke.NSW	Australia	CFS	Coffs Harbour, NSW	Australia
BGY	Milan - Bergamo	Italy	BRL	Burlington, IA	USA	CFU	Corfu	Greece
BHB	Bal Harbor, ME	USA	BRN	Berne	Switzerland	CGH	Sao Paulo-Congonhas	Brazil
BHE	Blenheim	New Zealand	BRO	Brownsville, TX	USA	CGK	Jakarta-Soekarno	Indonesia
BHH	Bisha	Saudi Arabia	BRQ	Brno	Czech Republic	CGN	Cologne / Bonn	Germany
BHI	Bahia Blanca	Argentina	BRR	Barra	Great Britain	CGO	Zengzhou	China
BHK	Bukhara	Uzbekistan	BRS	Bristol	Great Britain	CGP	Chittagong	Bangladesh
BHM	Birmingham, AL	USA	BRU	Brussels	Belgium	CGR	Campo Grande	Brazil
BHO	Bhopal	India	BRW	Barrow, AK	USA	CGY	Cagayan de Oro	Philippines
BHQ	Broken Hill, NSW	Australia	BSB	Brasilia	Brazil	CHA	Chattanooga, TN	USA
BHR	Bharatpur	Nepal	BSK	Biskra	Algeria	CHC	Christchurch	New Zealand
BHS	Bathurst, NSW	Australia	BSL	Basle-Mulhouse	Switzerland	CHQ	Chania	Greece
BHX	Birmingham	Great Britain	BTH	Batu Besar	Indonesia	CHS	Charleston, SC	USA
BHZ	Belo Horizonte	Brazil	BTM	Butte, MT	USA	CIA	Rome-Ciampino	Italy
BIA	Bastia	France	BTR	Baton Rouge, LA	USA	CID	Cedar Rapids, IA	USA

IATA	Place / Airport	Country	IATA	Place / Airport	Country	IATA	Place / Airport	Country
CIX	Chiclayo	Peru	DAY	Dayton, OH	USA	ERC	Erzincan	Turkey
CJA	Cajamarca	Peru	DBV	Dubrovnik	Croatia	ERF	Erfurt	Germany
CJS	Ciudad Juarez	Mexico	DCA	Washington-National	USA	ERS	Windhoek-Eros	Namibia
CJU	Cheju	South Korea	DDC	Dodge City, KS	USA	ERZ	Erzurum	Turkey
CKG	Chongqing	China	DEC	Decatur, Il	USA	ESB	Ankara-Esenboga	Turkey
CKY	Conakry	Guinea	DEL	Delhi	India	ESM	Esmeraldas	Ecuador
CLD	Carlsbad, CA	USA	DEN	Denver, CO	USA	ESR	El Salvador	Chile
CLE	Cleveland Intl, OH	USA	DFW	Dallas / Forth Worth	USA	ETH	Eilat	Israel
CLO	Cali	Columbia	DGO	Durango	Mexico	EUG	Eugene, OR	USA
CLQ	Colima	Mexico	DHA	Dhahran	Saudi Arabia	EUX	St.Eustatius	Netherlands Antilles
CLT	Charlotte, NC	USA	DHN	Dothan, AL	USA	EVN	Yerevan	Armenia
CLY	Calvi	France	DIJ	Dijon	France	EVV	Evansville, IN	USA
CMB	Colombo	Sri Lanka	DIL	Dilli	East-Timor	EWN	New Bern, NC	USA
CME	Ciudad del Carmen	Mexico	DIN	Dien Bien Phu	Vietnam	EWR	New York-Newark, NJ	USA
CMF	Chambery	France	DIR	Dire Dawa	Ethiopia	EXT	Exeter	Great Britain
CMH	Columbus, OH	USA	DIY	Diyarbakir	Turkey	EYW	Key West. FL	USA
CMN	Casablanca -Moh. V	Morocco	DJE	Djerba	Tunisia	EZE	Buenos Aires-M.Pista.	Argentina
CMW	Camaguey	Cuba	DJJ	Jaayapura	Indonesia	EZS	Elazig	Turkey
CNF	Belo Horizonte Intl.	Brazil	DKR	Dakar	Senegal	FAE	Faroe Islands	Denmark
CNJ	Cloncurry, QL	Australia	DLA	Douala	Cameroon	FAI	Fairbanks, AK	USA
CNM	Carlsbad, NM	USA	DLC	Dalian	China	FAN	Farsund	Norway
CNS	Cairns, QL	Australia	DLH	Duluth, MN	USA	FAO	Faro	Portugal
CNX	Chiang Mai	Thailand	DLI	Dalath	Vietnam	FAT	Fresno, CA	USA
COK	Cochin	India	DLM	Dalaman	Turkey	FAV	Fakarava	French-Polynesia
COO	Cotonou	Benin	DME	Moscow-Domodedovo	Russia	FAY	Fayetteville, NC	USA
COR	Cordoba	Argentina	DMU	Dimapur	India	FBM	Lubumbashi	Congo
COS	Colorado Springs, CO	USA	DNR	Dinard	France	FBU	Oslo-Fornebu	Norway
CPD	Coober Pedy, SA	Australia	DNZ	Denizli	Turkey	FCO	Rome-Leon. da Vinci	Italy
CPE	Campeche	Mexico	DOH	Doha	Qatar	FDF	Fort de France	Martinique
CPH	Copenhagen	Denmark	DOK	Donetsk	Ukraine	FDH	Friedrichshafen	Germany
CPQ	Campinas	Brazil	DOM	Dominica-Melville	Dominica	FEN	Fernando De Noronha	Brazil
CPR	Casper, WY	USA	DPS	Denpasar	Indonesia	FEZ	Fez	Morocco
CPT	Capetown	South Africa	DRS	Dresden	Germany	FIH	Kinshasa	Congo
CRD	Comodoro Rivadavia	Argentina	DRT	Del Rio, TX	USA	FJR	Al-Fujairah	UAE
CRL	Charleroi	Belgium	DRW	Darwin, NT	Australia	FKI	Kisangani	Congo
CRP	Corpus Christi, TX	USA	DSM	Des Moines, IA	USA	FKS	Fukushima	Japan
CSU	Santa Cruz Do Sul	Brazil	DTM	Dortmund	Germany	FLG	Flagstaff, AZ	USA
CSX	Changsha	China	DTW	Detroit Intl, MI	USA	FLL	Fort Lauderdale, FL	USA
CTA	Catania	Italy	DUB	Dublin	Ireland	FLN	Florianopolis	Brazil
CTG	Cartagena	Columbia	DUD	Dunedin	New Zealand	FLR	Florence	Italy
CTM	Chetumal	Mexico	DUR	Durban	South Africa	FLS	Flinders Island, TS	Australia
CTU	Chengdu	China	DUS	Düsseldorf	Germany	FLW	Flores, Azores	Portugal
CUC	Cucuta	Columbia	DUT	Dutch Harbor, AK	USA	FMO	Münster / Osnabrück	Germany
CUE	Cuenca	Ecuador	DVO	Davao	Philippines	FMY	Fort Myers, FL	USA
CUL	Culiacan	Mexico	DXB	Dubai	UAE	FNA	Freetown	Sierra Leone
CUN	Cancun	Mexico	DYR	Anadyr	Russia	FNB	Neubrandenburg	Germany
CUR	Curacao	Netherlands Antilles	DYU	Duushanbe	Tajikistan	FNC	Funchal, Madeira	Portugal
CUU	Chihuahua	Mexico	EAS	San Sebastian	Spain	FNI	Nimes	France
CUZ	Cuzco	Peru	EBB	Entebbe / Kampala	Uganda	FNJ	Pyongyang	North Korea
CVG	Cincinnati Intl, OH	USA	EBD	El Obeid	Sudan	FNT	Flint, MI	USA
CVJ	Cuernavaca	Mexico	EBJ	Esbjerg	Denmark	FOC	Fuzhou	China
CVM	Ciudad Victoria	Mexico	EBU	St.Etienne	France	FOD	Fort Dodge, IA	USA
CWB	Curitiba	Brazil	ECN	Ercan	Cyprus	FOR	Fortaleza	Brazil
CWL	Cardiff	Great Britain	EDI	Edinburgh	Great Britain	FPO	Freeport	Bahamas
CXB	Cox's Bazaar	Bangladesh	EFL	Kefallinia	Greece	FRA	Frankfurt	Germany
CXI	Christmas Island	Kiribati	EGE	Vail, CO	USA	FRJ	Frejus	France
CYB	Cayman Brac	Cayman Island	EGS	Egilsstadir	Iceland	FRL	Forli	Italy
CYI	Chiayi	Taiwan	EIN	Eindhoven	Netherlands	FRM	Fairmont, MN	USA
CYS	Cheyenne, WY	USA	EJA	Barrancabermeja	Columbia	FRO	Floro	Norway
CYU	Cuyo	Philippines	EKO	Elko, NV	USA	FRS	Flores	Guatemala
CZL	Constantine	Algeria	ELP	El Paso, TX	USA	FRU	Bishkek	Kyrghyzstan
CZM	Cozumel	Mexico	ELS	East London	South Africa	FSM	Fort Smith, AR	USA
CZS	Cruzeiro do Sul	Brazil	ELU	El Qued	Algeria	FSP	St.Pierre	St.Pierre &.Miquelon
CZX	Changzhou	China	EMA	East Midlands	Great Britain	FUE	Fuerteventura	Spain
DAB	Daytona Beach, FL	USA	EMN	Nema	Mauritania	FUJ	Fukue	Japan
DAC	Dacca	Bangladesh	EMS	Embessa	Papua New Guinea	FUK	Fukuoka	Japan
DAD	Da Nang	Vietnam	ENA	Kenai, AK	USA	FUN	Funafuti	Tuvalu
DAL	Dallas-Love Field, TX	USA	ENT	Enewetak Island	Marshall Islands	FWA	Fort Wayne, IN	USA
DAM	Damascus	Syria	NEU	Enugu	Nigeria	FYV	Fayetteville, AR	USA
DAR	Dar Es Salaam	Tanzania	EOH	Medellin E.O.Herrera	Columbia	GAJ	Yamagata	Japan

IATA	Place / Airport	Country	IATA	Place / Airport	Country	IATA	Place / Airport	Country
GAN	Gan	Maldives	GWY	Galway	Ireland	HZG	Hanzhong	China
GAO	Guantanamo	Cuba	GYE	Guayaquil	Ecuador	HZK	Husavik	Iceland
GAU	Gauahati	India	GYM	Guaymas	Mexico	IAD	Washington-Dulles	USA
GAX	Gamba	Gabon	GYN	Goiania	Brazil	IAH	Houston - G.Bush, TX	USA
GBE	Gaborone	Botswana	GYY	Gary, IN	USA	IBZ	Ibiza	Spain
GBJ	Marie Galante	Guadeloupe	GZT	Gaziantep	Turkey	ICT	Wichita, KS	USA
GCI	Guernsey	Great Britain	HAA	Hasvik	Norway	IDA	Idaho Falls, ID	USA
GCM	Grand Cayman	Cayman Islands	HAH	Moroni Intl.	Comores	IEV	Kiev-Zhulyany	Ukraine
GCN	Grand Canyon, AZ	USA	HAJ	Hanover	Germany	IFN	Isfahan	Iran
GDL	Guadalajara	Mexico	HAK	Haikou	China	IGM	Kingman, AZ	USA
GDN	Gdansk	Poland	HAM	Hamburg	Germany	IGR	Iguazu	Argentina
GDT	Grand Turk	Turks & Caicos	HAN	Hanoi	Vietnam	IGU	Iguacu Falls	Brazil
GDX	Magadan	Russia	HAR	Harrisburg, PA	USA	IIA	Inishmaan	Ireland
GEA	Noumea-Magenta	New Caledonia	HAU	Haugesund	Norway	IKT	Irkutsk	Russia
GEG	Spokane, WA	USA	HAV	Havana	Cuba	ILG	Wilmington, NC	USA
GEO	Georgetown	Guyana	HBA	Hobart, TS	Australia	ILO	Iloilo	Philippines
GER	Nueva Gerona	Cuba	HDD	Hyderabad	Pakistan	ILQ	Ilo	Peru
GES	General Santos	Philippines	HDY	Hat Yai	Thailand	IMF	Imphal	India
GFF	Griffith, NSW	Australia	HEL	Helsinki	Finland	INC	Yinchuan	China
GFK	Grand Forks, ND	USA	HER	Heraklion	Greece	IND	Indianapolis, IN	USA
GFN	Grafton, NSW	Australia	HFD	Hartford, CT	USA	ING	Lago Argentino	Argentina
GGG	Longview, TX	USA	HFE	Hefei	China	INN	Innsbruck	Austria
GHB	Governors Harbour	Bahamas	HFN	Hornafjordur	Iceland	INQ	Inisheer	Ireland
GIB	Gibraltar		HFT	Hammerfest	Norway	INT	Winston / Salem, NC	USA
GIG	Rio de Janeiro Intl.	Brazil	HGH	Hangzhou	China	INU	Nauru	
GIS	Gisborne	New Zealand	HGN	Mae Hong Son	Thailand	INV	Inverness	Great Britain
GIZ	Gizan	Saudi Arabia	HGU	Mont Hagen	Papua New Guinea	IOA	Ioannina	Greece
GJT	Grand Junction, CO	USA	HHA	Huanghua	China	IOM	Isle of Man	Great Britain
GKA	Goroka	Papua New Guinea	HHN	Hahn	Germany	IOR	Inishmore	Ireland
GKL	Great Keppel Isl, QL	Australia	HHQ	Hua Hin	Thailand	IPA	Ipota	Vanuatu
GLA	Glasgow	Great Britain	HII	Lake Havasu City, AZ	USA	IPC	Osterinseln	Chile
GLT	Gladstone, QL	Australia	HIJ	Hiroshima	Japan	IPH	Ipoh	Malaysia
GMB	Gambela	Ethiopia	HIN	Jinju	South Korea	IQT	Iquitos	Peru
GME	Gomel	Belarus	HIR	Honiara	Solomon Islands	IRA	Kira Kira	Solomon Islands
GNB	Grenoble	France	HIS	Hayman Island, QL	Australia	ISA	Mount Isa, QL	Australia
GND	Grenada		HKD	Hakodate	Japan	ISB	Islamabad	Pakistan
GNR	General Roca	Argentina	HKG	Hong Kong	China	ISC	Isle of Scilly	Great Britain
GNV	Gainesville, FL	USA	HKT	Phuket	Thailand	ISG	Ishigaki	Japan
GOA	Genoa	Italy	HLN	Helena, MT	USA	ISP	Long Island-McArthur	USA
GOE	Gonalia	Papua New Guinea	HLZ	Hamilton	New Zealand	IST	Istanbul	Turkey
GOH	Nuuk	Greenland	HMO	Hermosillo	Mexico	ITM	Osaka-Itami	Japan
GOI	Goa	India	HNA	Morioka	Japan	ITO	Hilo, HI	USA
GOJ	Nizhniy Novgorod	Russia	HND	Tokyo-Haneda	Japan	IVC	Invercargill	New Zealand
GOM	Goma	Congo	HNL	Honolulu, HI	USA	IVL	Ivalo	Finland
GOR	Gore	Ethiopia	HNM	Hana, HI	USA	IWJ	Iwami	Japan
GOT	Gothenburg-Landvetter	Sweden	HOB	Hobbs, NM	USA	IXA	Agartala	India
GOU	Garoua	Cameroon	HOD	Hodeidah	Yemen	IXE	Mangalore	India
GPT	Gulfport / Biloxi, MS	USA	HOG	Holguin	Cuba	IXJ	Jammu	India
GPZ	Grand Rapids, MN	USA	HOM	Homer, AK	USA	IXM	Mandurai	India
GRP	Gurupi	Brazil	HOQ	Hof	Germany	IXU	Aurangabad	India
GRQ	Groningen	Netherlands	HOR	Horta, Azores	Portugal	IZM	Izmir	Turkey
GRR	Grand Rapids, MI	USA	HOU	Houston-Hobby, TX	USA	IZO	Izumo	Japan
GRU	Sao Paulo-Guarulhos	Brazil	HPV	Kaui, HI	USA	JAI	Jaipur	India
GRW	Graciosa, Azores	Portugal	HRB	Harbin	China	JAN	Jackson, MS	USA
GRX	Granada	Spain	HRE	Harare	Zimbabwe	JAT	Jabot	Marshall Islands
GRZ	Graz	Austria	HRG	Hurghada	Egypt	JAV	Ilulissat	Greenland
GSE	Gothenburg-Saeve	Sweden	HRK	Kharkov	Ukraine	JAX	Jacksonville, FL	USA
GSO	Greensboro-High Point	USA	HRL	Harlingen, TX	USA	JDH	Jodhpur	India
GSP	Greenville / Spartanb.	USA	HSV	Huntsville, AL	USA	JDO	Juazeiro Do Norte	Brazil
GTA	Gatokae	Solomon Islands	HTI	Hamilton Island, QL	Australia	JED	Jeddah	Saudi Arabia
GTF	Great Falls, MT	USA	HUF	Terre Haute, IN	USA	JER	Jersey	Great Britain
GUA	Guatemala City	Guatemala	HUI	Hue	Vietnam	JFK	New York J.F.K. Intl.	USA
GUB	Guerrero Negro	Mexico	HUN	Hualien	Taiwan	JHE	Helsingborg	Sweden
GUM	Guam		HUU	Huanuco	Peru	JHG	Jinghong	China
GUP	Gallup, NM	USA	HUV	Hudiksvall	Sweden	JIB	Djibouti	
GUR	Alotau	Papua New Guinea	HUX	Huatulco	Mexico	JIL	Jilin	China
GUW	Atyrau	Kazakstan	HVG	Honningsvag	Norway	JIU	Jiujiang	China
GVA	Geneva	Switzerland	HVN	New Haven, CT	USA	JJI	Juanjui	Peru
GWL	Gwalior	India	HYD	Hyderabad	India	JKG	Jonköping	Sweden
GWT	Westerland	Germany	HYN	Huanyang	China	JKH	Chios	Greece

IATA	Place / Airport	Country	IATA	Place / Airport	Country	IATA	Place / Airport	Country
JKR	Janakpur	Nepal	KKJ	Kita Kyushu	Japan	LAF	Lafayette, IN	USA
JMK	Mykonos	Greece	KKN	Kirkenes	Norway	LAI	Lannion	France
JMS	Jamestown, ND	USA	KKZ	Koh Kong	Cambodia	LAJ	Lages	Brazil
JNB	Johannesburg	South Africa	KLO	Kalibo	Philippines	LAN	Lansing, MI	USA
JNS	Narsassuaq	Greenland	KLU	Klagenfurt	Austria	LAO	Laoag	Philippines
JNU	Juneau, AK	USA	KLX	Kalamata	Greece	LAP	La Paz	Mexico
JNX	Naxos	Greece	KMG	Kunming	China	LAR	Laramie, WY	USA
JNZ	Jinzhou	China	KMI	Miyazaki	Japan	LAS	Las Vegas, NV	USA
JOE	Joensuu	Finland	KMJ	Kumamoto	Japan	LAU	Lamu	Kenya
JOG	Jogjakarta	Indonesia	KMP	Keetmanshoop	Namibia	LAW	Lawton, OK	USA
JON	Johnston Island	USA	KMQ	Komatsu	Japan	LAX	Los Angeles Intl, CA	USA
JRH	Jorhat	India	KMV	Kalemyo	Myanmar	LBA	Leeds Bradford	Great Britain
JRO	Killimanjaro	Tanzania	KND	Kindu	Congo	LBB	Lubbock, TX	USA
JSH	Sitia	Greece	KNH	Kinmen	Taiwan	LBC	Lübeck	Germany
JSI	Skiathos	Greece	KNQ	Kone	New Caledonia	LBQ	Lambarene	Gabon
JSR	Jessore	Bangladesh	KNX	Kununurra, WA	Australia	LBU	Labuan	Malaysia
JSY	Syros	Greece	KOA	Kona, HI	USA	LBV	Libreville	Gabon
JTR	Thira	Greece	KOC	Koumac	New Caledonia	LBX	Lubang	Philippines
JUL	Juliaca	Peru	KOE	Kupang	Indonesia	LCA	Larnaca	Cyprus
JUM	Jumla	Nepal	KOI	Kirkwall	Great Britain	LCE	La Ceiba	Honduras
JUZ	Juzhou	China	KOJ	Kagoshima	Japan	LCG	La Coruna	Spain
KAB	Kariba	Zaire	KOK	Kokkola / Pietarsaari	Finland	LCH	Lake Charles, LA	USA
KAC	Kahmeshli	Syria	KOS	Sihanoukville	Cambodia	LCY	London City-Airport	Great Britain
KAD	Kaduna	Nigeria	KOW	Ganzhou	China	LDB	Londrina	Brazil
KAG	Kangnung	South Korea	KPO	Pohang	South Korea	LDE	Lourdes / Tarbes	France
KAJ	Kajaani	Finland	KRK	Krakow	Poland	LDK	Lidköping	Sweden
KAN	Kano	Nigeria	KRN	Kiruna	Sweden	LDY	Londonderry	Great Britain
KAO	Kuusamo	Finland	KRR	Krasnodar	Russia	LEA	Learmonth, WA	Australia
KAW	Kawthaung	Myanmar	KRS	Kristansand	Norway	LED	St.Petersburg	Russia
KBL	Kabul	Afghanistan	KRT	Khartoum	Sudan	LEI	Almeria	Spain
KBP	Kiev-Borispol	Ukraine	KRW	Krasnovodsk	Turkmenistan	LEJ	Leipzig	Germany
KBR	Kota Bharu	Malaysia	KRY	Karamay	China	LEX	Lexington, KY	USA
KCH	Kuching	Malaysia	KSA	Kosrae	Caroline Islands	LFT	Lafayette, LA	USA
KCZ	Kochi	Japan	KSC	Kosice	Slovakia	LFW	Lome	Togo
KDI	Kendari	Indonesia	KSD	Karlstad	Sweden	LGA	New York La-Guardia	USA
KDN	N'dende	Gabon	KSH	Kormanshah	Iran	LGB	Long Beach, CA	USA
KDV	Kandavu	Fiji Islands	KSJ	Kasos	Greece	LGK	Langkawi	Malaysia
KEF	Keflavik	Iceland	KSN	Kostanay	Kazakhstan	LGP	Legaspi	Philippines
KEH	Kenmore, WA	USA	KSO	Kastoria	Greece	LGQ	Lago Agrio	Ecuador
KEJ	Kemerovo	Russia	KSU	Kristiansund	Norway	LGS	Malargue	Argentina
KEL	Kiel	Germany	KSY	Kars	Turkey	LGW	London - Gatwick	Great Britain
KER	Kerman	Iran	KTM	Kathmandu	Nepal	LHE	Lahore	Pakistan
KFA	Kiffa	Mauritania	KTN	Ketchikan, AK	USA	LHR	London - Heathrow	Great Britain
KGA	Kananga	Congo	KTW	Katowice	Poland	LHW	Lanzhou	China
KGD	Kaliningrad	Russia	KUA	Kuantan	Malaysia	LIG	Limoges	France
KGF	Karaganda	Kazakstan	KUC	Kuria	Kiribati	LIH	Lihue-Kaui Island, HI	USA
KGG	Kedougou	Senegal	KUD	Kudat	Malaysia	LIL	Lille	France
KGI	Kalgoorlie, WA	Australia	KUF	Samara	Russia	LIM	Lima	Peru
KGL	Kigali	Rwanda	KUH	Kushiro	Japan	LIN	Milan - Linate	Italy
KGO	Kirovograd	Ukraine	KUL	Kuala Lumpur	Malaysia	LIR	Liberia	Costa Rica
KGS	Kos	Greece	KUM	Yakushima	Japan	LIS	Lisbon	Portugal
KHH	Kaohsiung	Taiwan	KUN	Kaunas	Lithuania	LIT	Little Rock, AR	USA
KHI	Karachi	Pakistan	KUO	Kuopio	Finland	LJG	Lijiang City	China
KHM	Khamti	Myanmar	KUU	Kulu	India	LJU	Ljubljana	Slovenia
KHN	Nanchang	Chiina	KUV	Kunsan	South Korea	LKL	Lakselv	Norway
KHS	Khasab	Oman	KVA	Kavala	Greece	LKN	Leknes	Norway
KHV	Khabarovsk	Russia	KVX	Kirov	Russia	LKO	Lucknow	India
KID	Kristianstad	Sweden	KWA	Kwajalein	Marshall Islands	LLA	Lulea	Sweden
KIJ	Niigata	Japan	KWE	Guiyang	China	LLI	Lalibela	Ethiopia
KIM	Kimberley	South Africa	KWI	Kuwait		LLW	Lilongwe	Malawi
KIN	Kingston	Jamaica	KWJ	Kwangju	South Korea	LML	Lae Island	Marshall Islands
KIO	Kili Island	Marshall Islands	KWL	Guilin	China	LMN	Limbang	Malaysia
KIR	Kerry County	Ireland	KYA	Konya	Turkey	LMP	Lampedusa	Italy
KIS	Kisumu	Kenya	KYS	Kayes	Mali	LNE	Lonorore	Vanuatu
KIT	Kithira	Greece	KZI	Kozani	Greece	LNO	Leonora, WA	Australia
KIV	Kishinev	Moldavia	KZN	Kazan	Russia	LNY	Lanai City, HI	USA
KIX	Osaka-Kansai	Japan	KZO	Kzyl Orda	Kazakhstan	LNZ	Linz	Austria
KJA	Krasnoyarsk	Russia	KZS	Kastelorizo	Greece	LOI	Lontras	Brazil
KJP	Kerama	Japan	LAD	Luanda	Angola	LOS	Lagos	Nigeria
KKC	Khon Kaen	Thailand	LAE	Lae	Papua New Guinea	LPB	La Paz	Bolivia

IATA	Place / Airport	Country	IATA	Place / Airport	Country	IATA	Place / Airport	Country
LPI	Linköping	Sweden	MED	Medina	Saudi Arabia	MSQ	Minsk Intl.	Belarus
LPL	Liverpool	Great Britain	MEG	Malange	Angola	MST	Maastricht	Netherlands
LPQ	Luan Prabang	Laos	MEL	Melbourne, VI	Australia	MSU	Maseru	Lesotho
LPT	Lampang	Thailand	MEM	Memphis, TN	USA	MSY	New Orleans Intl. LA	USA
LRD	Laredo,TX	USA	MES	Medan	Indonesia	MTS	Manzini	Swaziland
LRE	Longreach, QL	Australia	MEX	Mexico City Intl.	Mexico	MTY	Monterrey	Mexico
LRH	La Rochelle	France	MFM	Macau	China	MUB	Maun	Botswana
LRM	La Romana	Dominican Rep	MFN	Milford Sound	New Zealand	MUC	Munich	Germany
LRS	Leros	Greece	MFT	Machu Picchu	Peru	MUW	Maskara	Algeria
LSC	La Serena	Chile	MAG	Managua	Nicaragua	MVB	Franceville	Gabon
LSH	Lashio	Myanmar	MGF	Maringa	Brazil	MVD	Montevideo	Uruguay
LSI	Shetland-Sumburgh	Great Britain	MGH	Margate	South Africa	MVY	Marthas Vineyard, MA	USA
LSP	Las Piedras	Venezuela	MGL	Mönchengladbach	Germany	MWH	Moses Lake, WA	USA
LSS	Terre Haute	Guadeloupe	MGM	Montgomery, AL	USA	MWV	Mundulkin	Cambodia
LST	Launceston	Australia	MGQ	Mogadishu	Somalia	MWZ	Mwanza	Tanzania
LTK	Latakia	Syria	MHD	Mashad	Iran	MXL	Mexicali	Mexico
LTN	London Luton	Great Britain	MHG	Mannheim	Germany	MXP	Milan Malpensa	Italy
LTO	Loreto	Mexico	MHH	Marsh Harbour	Bahamas	MXX	Mora	Sweden
LUA	Lukla	Nepal	MHQ	Marieham	Finland	MYD	Malindi	Kenya
LUD	Lüderitz	Namibia	MHT	Manchester, NH	USA	MYJ	Matsuyama	Japan
LUG	Lugano	Switzerland	MIA	Miami, FL	USA	MYR	Myrtle Beach, SC	USA
LUN	Lusaka	Zambia	MID	Merida	Mexico	MZG	Makung	Taiwan
LUO	Luena	Angola	MIK	Mikkeli	Finland	MZI	Mopti	Mali
LUQ	San Luis	Argentina	MIR	Monastir	Tunisia	MZL	Manizales	Columbia
LUX	Luxembourg		MJC	Man	Ivory Coast	MZT	Mazatlan	Mexico
LVB	Livramento	Brazil	MJF	Mosjoen	Norway	NAG	Nagpur	India
LVI	Livingston	Zambia	MJN	Majunga	Madagascar	NAN	Nadi	Fiji
LWB	Lewisburg, WV	USA	MJT	Mytilene	Greece	NAP	Naples	Italy
LWK	Shetland-Lerwick	Great Britain	MJV	Murcia	Spain	NAS	Nassau	Bahamas
LWO	Lvov	Ukraine	MKB	Mekambo	Gabon	NAT	Natal	Brazil
LWS	Lewiston, ID	USA	MKC	Kansas City, MO	USA	NBO	Nairobi	Kenya
LXA	Lhasa	China	MKE	Milwaukee, WI	USA	NCA	North Caicos	Turks & Caicos
LXG	Luang Namtha	Laos	MKK	Kaunakakai, HI	USA	NCE	Nice	France
LXR	Luxor	Egypt	MKL	Jackson, TN	USA	NCL	Newcastle	Great Britain
LXS	Lemnos	Greece	MKY	Mackay, QL	Australia	NCR	San Carlos	Nicaragua
LYA	Luoyang	China	MLA	Malta		NCU	Nukus	Uzbekistan
LYB	Little Cayman	Cayman Island	MLE	Male	Maldives	NCY	Annecy	France
LYG	Lianyungang	China	MLI	Moline, IL	USA	NDB	Nouadhibou	Mauritania
LYH	Lynchburg, VA	USA	MLN	Melilla	Spain	NDJ	Ndjamena	Chad
LYR	Longyearbyen	Norway	MLO	Milos	Greece	NEG	Negril	Jamaica
LYS	Lyon	France	MLW	Monrovia	Liberia	NEV	Nevis	St.Kitts & Nevis
LZC	Lazaro Cardenas	Mexico	MLX	Malatya	Turkey	NFO	Niuafo'ou	Tonga
LZH	Lizhou	China	MMA	Malmö	Sweden	NGB	Ningbo	China
LZO	Luzhou	China	MME	Teesside	Great Britain	NGE	Ngaoundere	Cameroon
MAA	Chennai / Madras	India	MMJ	Matsumoto	Japan	NGO	Nagoya	Japan
MAB	Maraba	Brazil	MMK	Murmansk	Russia	NGS	Nagasaki	Japan
MAD	Madrid	Spain	MMO	Maio	Cape Verde	NHA	Nha-Trang	Vietnam
MAF	Midland Odessa, TX	USA	MMY	Miyako Shima	Japan	NIG	Nikunau	Kiribati
MAG	Madang	Papua New Guinea	MNI	Montserrat		NIM	Niamey	Niger
MAH	Menorca	Spain	MNL	Manila	Philippines	NIX	Nioro	Mali
MAJ	Majuro	Marshall Islands	MNU	Moulmyne	Myanmar	NKC	Nouakchott	Mauritania
MAM	Matamoros	Mexico	MOB	Mobile, AL	USA	NKG	Nanjing	China
MAN	Manchester	Great Britain	MON	Mount Cook	New Zealand	NLD	Nuevo Laredo	Mexico
MAO	Manaus	Brazil	MPK	Mokpo	South Korea	NLK	Norfolk Island	Australia
MAR	Maracaibo	Venezuela	MPL	Montpellier	France	NLP	Nelspruit	South Africa
MAZ	Mayaguez	Porto Rico	MPM	Maputo	Mozambique	NLV	Nikolaev	Ukraine
MBA	Mombasa	Kenya	MPM	Mount Pleasant	Falkland, GB	NNG	Nanning	China
MBJ	Montego Bay	Jamaica	MPW	Mariupol	Ukraine	NNY	Nanyang	China
MCI	Kansas City Intl, MO	USA	MQL	Mildura, VI	Australia	NOU	Noumea	New Caledonia
MCN	Macon, GA	USA	MQS	Mustique	Grenadines	NOV	Huambo	Angola
MCO	Orlando, FL	USA	MQT	Marquette, MI	USA	NOZ	Novokuznetsk	Russia
MCT	Muscat	Oman	MRD	Merida	Venezuela	NPE	Napier-Hastings	New Zealand
MCY	Sunshine Coast, QL	Australia	MRS	Marseilles	France	NQN	Neuquen	Argentina
MDE	Medellin J.M.Cordova	Columbia	MRU	Mauritius		NRK	Norrköping	Sweden
MDL	Mandalay	Myanmar	MRV	Mineralnye Vody	Russia	NRL	North Ronaldsay	Great Britain
MDQ	Mar del Plata	Argentina	MRY	Monterey, CA	USA	NRN	Niederrhein	Germany
MDS	Middle Caicos	Turks & Caicos	MSH	Masirah	Oman	NRT	Tokyo - Narita	Japan
MDT	Harrisburg Intl, PA	USA	MSJ	Misawa	Japan	NSB	Bimini North	Bahamas
MDW	Chicago Midway, IL	USA	MSO	Missoula, MT	USA	NSI	Yaounde	Cameroon
MDZ	Mendoza	Argentina	MSP	Minneapolis / St.Paul	USA	NSK	Norilsk	Russia

IATA	Place / Airport	Country	IATA	Place / Airport	Country	IATA	Place / Airport	Country
NSN	Nelson	New Zealand	PBX	Porto Alegre do Norte	Brazil	PRI	Praslin Island	Seychelles
NTE	Nantes	France	PCL	Pucallpa	Peru	PRN	Pristina	Kosovo
NTL	Newcastle, NSW	Australia	PCM	Playa del Carmen	Mexico	PSA	Pisa	Italy
NTO	Santo Antao	Cape Verde	PDG	Padang	Indonesia	PSE	Ponce	Puerto Rico
NTY	Sun City	South Africa	PDL	Ponta Delgada, Azor.	Portugal	PSP	Palm Springs, CA	USA
NUE	Nuremberg	Germany	PDP	Punta del Este	Uruguay	PSR	Pescara	Italy
NVK	Narvik	Norway	PDX	Portland, OR	USA	PSS	Posadas	Argentina
NWI	Norwich	Great Britain	PEE	Perm	Russia	PTH	Port Heiden, AK	USA
NYM	Nyngan	Russia	PEG	Perugia	Italy	PTP	Pointe-a-Pitre	Guadeloupe
OAK	Oakland, CA	USA	PEI	Pereira	Columbia	PTY	Panama City Intl.	Panama
OAX	Oaxaca	Mexico	PEK	Beijing Capital	China	PUD	Puerto Deseado	Argentina
OCJ	Ocho Rios	Jamaica	PEM	Puerto Maldano	Peru	PUJ	Punta Cana	Dominican Rep
ODE	Odense	Denmark	PEN	Penang	Malaysia	PUQ	Punta Arenas	Chile
ODS	Odessa	Ukraine	PER	Perth, WA	Australia	PUS	Pusan	South Korea
OGG	Kahului, HI	USA	PET	Pelotas	Brazil	PUU	Puerto Asis	Columbia
OHD	Ohrid	Macedonia	PEW	Peshawar	Pakistan	PUY	Pula	Croatia
OIM	Oshima	Japan	PFO	Paphos	Cyprus	PVA	Providencia	Columbia
OIT	Oita	Japan	PGF	Perpignan	France	PVC	Provincetown, MA	USA
OKA	Okinawa	Japan	PHC	Port Harcourt	Nigeria	PVD	Providence, RI	USA
OKC	Oklahoma City,OK	USA	PHE	Port Hedland, WA	Australia	PVK	Preveza / Lefkas	Greece
OKD	Sapporo	Japan	PHF	Newport News, VA	USA	PVR	Puerto Vallarta	Mexico
OKI	Oki	Japan	PHL	Philadelphia, PA	USA	PXO	Porto Santo, Madeira	Portugal
OKJ	Okajama	Japan	PHR	Pacific Harbour	Fiji	PXU	Pleiku	Vietnam
OKN	Okondja	Gabon	PHX	Phoenix, AZ	USA	PYH	Puerto Ayacucho	Venezuela
OLB	Olbia	Italy	PIA	Peoria, IL	USA	PZB	Pietermaritzburg	South Africa
OMA	Omaha, NE	USA	PIE	St.Petersburg, FL	USA	PZO	Puerto Ordaz	Venezuela
OMB	Omboue	Gabon	PIF	Pingtung	Taiwan	PZU	Port Sudan	Sudan
OME	Nome, AK	USA	PIH	Pocatello, ID	USA	RAB	Rabaul	Papua New Guinea
OMS	Omsk	Russia	PIK	Glasgow - Prestwick	Great Britain	RAH	Rafha	Saudi Arabia
ONT	Ontario, CA	USA	PIT	Pittsburgh, PA	USA	RAI	Praia	Cape Verde
ONX	Colon	Panama	PJM	Puerto Jiminez	Costa Rica	RAK	Marrakech	Morocco
OOL	Goldcoast, QL	Australia	PKC	Petropavlovsk	Russia	RAP	Rapid City, SD	USA
OOM	Cooma, NSW	Australia	PKR	Pokhara	Nepal	RBA	Rabat	Morocco
OPO	Porto	Portugal	PKZ	Pakse	Laos	RBM	Straubing	Germany
OPS	Sinop	Brazil	PLM	Palambang	Indonesia	RBR	Rio Branco	Brazil
ORB	Orebro	Sweden	PLP	La Palma	Panama	RDU	Raleigh / Durham, NC	USA
ORD	Chicago O'Hare Intl.	USA	PLQ	Palanga	Lithuania	REC	Recife	Brazil
ORF	Norfolk, VA	USA	PLS	Providenciales	Turks & Caicos	REG	Reggio Calabria	Italy
ORK	Cork	Ireland	PLW	Palu	Indonesia	REK	Reykjavik	Iceland
ORL	Orlando, FL	USA	PLX	Semipalatinsk	Kazakstan	REN	Orenburg	Russia
ORN	Oran	Algeria	PLZ	Port Elizabeth	South Africa	REP	Siem Rap	Cambodia
ORW	Ormara	Pakistan	PMA	Pemba	Tanzania	RES	Resistencia	Argentina
ORY	Paris -Orly	France	PMC	Puerto Montt	Chile	REU	Reus	Spain
OSD	Ostersund	Sweden	PMF	Parma	Italy	RFS	Rosita	Nicaragua
OSH	Oshkosh, WI	USA	PMI	Palma de Mallorca	Spain	RGL	Rio Gallegos	Argentina
OSL	Oslo	Norway	PMO	Palermo	Italy	RGN	Yangon	Myanmar
OSR	Ostrava	Czech Republic	PMV	Porlamar	Venezuela	RHE	Reims	France
OSS	Osh	Kyrghyzstan	PNA	Pamplona	Spain	RHO	Rhodes	Greece
OST	Ostend	Belgium	PNH	Phnom Penh	Cambodia	RIC	Richmond, VA	USA
OSW	Orsk	Russia	PNL	Pantelleria	Italy	RIG	Rio Grande	Brazil
OSY	Namsos	Norway	PNQ	Poona	India	RIX	Riga	Lithuania
OTP	Bucharest - Otopeni	Romania	PNR	Point Noire	Congo	RJK	Rijeka	Croatia
OUD	Oujda	Morocco	PNS	Pensacola, FL	USA	RKT	Ras Al khaimah	UAE
OUL	Oulu	Finland	POA	Porto Alegre	Brazil	RLG	Rostock - Laage	Germany
OUZ	Zouerate	Mauritania	POG	Port Gentil	Gabon	RMF	Marsa Alam	Egypt
OVB	Novosibirsk	Russia	POI	Potosi	Bolivia	RNB	Ronneby	Sweden
OVD	Asturias	Spain	POL	Pemba	Mozambique	RNJ	Yoronjima	Japan
OXB	Bissau	Guinea - Bissau	POM	Port Moresby	Papua New Guinea	RNN	Bornholm	Denmark
OZZ	Ouarzazate	Morocco	POP	Puerto Plata	Dominican. Rep.	RNO	Reno, NV	USA
PAC	Panama City	Panama	POR	Pori	Finland	RNS	Rennes	France
PAD	Paderborn	Germany	POS	Port of Spain	Trinidad & Tobago	ROA	Roanoke, VA	USA
PAP	Port au Prince	Haiti	POZ	Poznan	Poland	ROC	Rochester, NY	USA
PAS	Paros	Greece	PPG	Pago Pago	Samoa	ROK	Rockhampton, QL	Australia
PAT	Patna	India	PPK	Petropavlovsk	Kazakstan	ROS	Rosario	Argentina
PBC	Puebla	Mexico	PPN	Popayan	Columbia	ROT	Rotorua	New Zealand
PBD	Porbandar	India	PPS	Puerto Princesa	Philippines	ROV	Rostov	Russia
PBE	Puerto Berrio	Columbia	PPT	Papeete	Tahiti	ROW	Roswell, NM	USA
PBH	Paro	Bhutan	PRC	Prescott, AZ	USA	RRG	Rodrigues Island	Mauritius
PBI	West Palm Beach, FL	USA	PRG	Prague	Czech Republic	RSA	Santa Rosa	Argentina
PBM	Paramaribo	Surinam	PRH	Phrea	Thailand	RST	Rochester, MN	USA

373

IATA	Place / Airport	Country	IATA	Place / Airport	Country	IATA	Place / Airport	Country
RSU	Josu	South Korea	SKB	St. Kitts	St.Kitts & Nevis	TAI	Taiz	Yemen
RSW	Fort Myers, FL	USA	SKD	Samarkand	Russia	TAK	Takamatsu	Japan
RTM	Rotterdam	Netherlands	SKG	Thessaloniki	Greece	TAM	Tampico	Mexico
RTW	Saratov	Russia	SKN	Stokmarknes	Norway	TAO	Qingdao	China
RUH	Riyadh	Saudi Arabia	SKP	Skopje	Macedonia	TAS	Tashkent	Uzbekistan
RUN	St.Denis de la Reunion	F-Reunion	SKZ	Sukkur	Pakistan	TBO	Tabora	Tanzania
RVA	Farafangana	Madagascar	SLC	Salt Lake City, UT	USA	TBS	Tiflis	Georgia
RVN	Rovaniemi	Finland	SLL	Salalah	Oman	TBU	Tongatapu	Tonga
RXS	Roxas	Philippines	SLM	Salamanca	Spain	TBZ	Tabriz	Iran
SAB	Saba	Netherlands Antilles	SLP	San Luis Potosi	Mexico	TCP	Taba	Egypt
SAC	Sacramento, CA	USA	SLU	St. Lucia		TCL	Tuscaloosa, AL	USA
SAF	Santa Fe, NM	USA	SLW	Saltillo	Mexico	TER	Terceira, Azores	Portugal
SAH	Sanaa	Yemen	SMA	Santa Maria, Azores	Portugal	TET	Tete	Mozambique
SALI	San Salvador	El Salvador	SMI	Samos	Greece	TEU	The Anau	New Zealand
SAN	San Diego, CA	USA	SMO	Santa Monica, CA	USA	TEZ	Tezpur	India
SAP	San Pedro Sula	Honduras	SNA	Santa Ana, CA	USA	TFF	Tefe	Brazil
SAQ	San Andros	Bahamas	SNN	Shannon	Ireland	TFN	Tenerife, Nord	Spain
SAT	San Antonio, TX	USA	SOF	Sofia	Bulgaria	TFS	Tenerife, Süd	Spain
SAV	Savannah, GA	USA	SON	Espiritu Santo	Vanuatu	TGU	Tegucigalpa	Honduras
SBA	Santa Barbara, CA	USA	SOU	Southampton	Great Britain	THF	Berlin Tempelhof	Germany
SBH	St. Barthelemy		SPB	St.Thomas	US Virgin Islands	THR	Tehran	Iran
SBP	San Luis Obispo, CA	USA	SPC	Santa Cruz	Spain	TIA	Tirana	Albania
SBW	Sibu	Malaysia	SPD	Saidpur	Bangladesh	TIE	Tippi	Ethiopia
SBZ	Sibiu	Romania	SPI	Springfield, IL	USA	TIF	Taif	Saudi Arabia
SCL	Santiago	Chile	SPK	Sapporo	Japan	TIJ	Tijuana	Mexico
SCN	Saarbrücken	Germany	SPN	Saipan	US-Marianas	TIV	Tivat	Serbia
SCQ	Sant. de Campostella	Spain	SPS	Wichita Falls, TX	USA	TJK	Tokat	Turkey
SCU	Santiago	Cuba	SPU	Split	Croatia	TJM	Tyumen	Russia
SCY	San Christobal	Ecuador	SQO	Storuman	Sweden	TKK	Truk	Caroline Islands
SCZ	Santa Cruz Island	Solomon Islands	SRA	Santa Rosa	Brazil	TKS	Tokushima	Japan
SDD	Lubango	Angola	SRE	Sucre	Brazil	TKU	Turku	Finland
SDF	Louisville, KY	USA	SRP	Stord	Norway	TLH	Tallahassee, FL	USA
SDJ	Sendai	Japan	SRQ	Sarasota / Bradenton	USA	TLL	Tallinn	Estonia
SDK	Sandakan	Malaysia	SRZ	Santa Cruz	Bolivia	TLN	Toulon	France
SDL	Sundsvall	Sweden	SSA	Salvador	Brazil	TLS	Toulouse	France
SDQ	Santo Domingo	Dominican. Rep.	SSB	St.Croix	US Virgin Islands	TLV	Tel Aviv	Israel
SDR	Santander	Spain	SSH	Sharm El Sheik	Egypt	TME	Tame	Columbia
SDU	Rio de Jan. Sant.Dumt.	Brazil	SSX	Samsun	Turkey	TMP	Tampere	Finland
SEA	Seattle-Tacoma, WA	USA	STD	Santo Domingo	Venezuela	TMR	Tamanrasset	Algeria
SEL	Seoul	South Korea	STL	St. Louis, MO	USA	TMS	Sao Tomé	
SEZ	Mahe	Seychelles	STN	London Stansted	Great Britain	TMU	Tambor	Costa Rica
SFA	Sfax	Tunisia	STR	Stuttgart	Germany	TMW	Tamworth, NSW	Australia
SFB	Sanford, FL	USA	STW	Stavropol	Russia	TNA	Jinan	China
SFD	San Fernando	Venezuela	SUB	Surabaya	Indonesia	TNG	Tangier	Morocco
SFG	San Martin	French Antilles	SUF	Lamezia Terme	Italy	TNN	Tainan	Taiwan
SFL	Sao Filipe	Cape Verde	SUH	Suhr	Oman	TNR	Antananarivo	Madagascar
SFN	Santa Fe	Argentina	SUV	Suva	Fiji	TOE	Tozeur	Tunisia
SFO	San Francisco, CA	USA	SUX	Sioux City, IA	USA	TOL	Toledo, OH	USA
SFS	Subic Bay	Philippines	SVD	St. Vincent		TOM	Timbuktu	Mali
SGC	Surgut	Russia	SVG	Stavanger	Norway	TOS	Tromso	Norway
SGD	Sonderburg	Denmark	SVJ	Svolvaer	Norway	TPA	Tampa, FL	USA
SGE	Siegerland	Germany	SVO	Moscow Sheremetyevo	Russia	TPE	Taipei	Taiwan
SGN	Ho Chi Minh City	Vietnam	SVQ	Seville	Spain	TRC	Torreon	Mexico
SHA	Shanghai	China	SVX	Ekaterinburg	Russia	TRD	Trondheim	Norway
SHE	Shenyang	China	SVZ	San Antonio	Venezuela	TRF	Sandeford (Torp)	Norway
SHJ	Sharjah	UAE	SWA	Shantou	China	TRI	Tri-Cities, TN	USA
SHO	Sokcho	South Korea	SWP	Swakopmund	Namibia	TRN	Turin	Italy
SHV	Shreveport, LA	USA	SXB	Strasbourg	France	TRS	Trieste	Italy
SIA	Xian	China	SXF	Berlin Schönefeld	Germany	TRU	Trujillo	Peru
SID	Sal	Cape Verde	SXL	Sligo	Ireland	TRV	Trivandrum	India
SIN	Singapore		SXM	St Maarten	Netherlands Antilles	TRW	Tarawa	Kiribati
SIP	Simferopol	Russia	SXR	Srinagar	India	TSA	Taipei Sung Shan	Taiwan
SIT	Sitka, AK	USA	SYD	Sydney, NSW	Australia	TSJ	Tsushima	Japan
SJB	San Joaquin	Bolivia	SYR	Syracuse, NY	USA	TSN	Tianjin	China
SJC	San Jose, CA	USA	SYZ	Shiraz	Iran	TSR	Timisoara	Romania
SJJ	Sarajevo	Bosnia	SZG	Salzburg	Austria	TST	Trang	Thailand
SJK	Sao Jose dos Campos	Brazil	SZX	Shenzen	China	TSV	Townsville, QL	Australia
SJL	Sao Gabriel	Brazil	SZZ	Szczecin	Poland	TTT	Taitung	Taiwan
SJO	San Jose	Costa Rica	TAC	Tacloban	Philippines	TTU	Tetouan	Morocco
SJU	San Juan Intl.	Puerto Rico	TAE	Taegu	South Korea	TUC	Tucuman	Argentina

IATA	Place / Airport	Country	IATA	Place / Airport	Country	IATA	Place / Airport	Country
TUF	Tours	France	VXE	Sao Vicente	Cape Verde	YSB	Sudbury	Canada
TUL	Tulsa, OK	USA	VXO	Vaxjo	Sweden	YSJ	St. John	Canada
TUN	Tunis	Tunisia	WAT	Waterford	Ireland	YSM	Fort Smith, NT	Canada
TUS	Tucson, AZ	USA	WAW	Warsaw	Poland	YTS	Timmins	Canada
TXG	Taichung	Taiwan	WDH	Windhoek	Namibia	YTZ	Toronto City Centre	Canada
TXK	Texarkana, AR	USA	WEF	Weifang	China	YUL	Montreal - Dorval	Canada
TXL	Berlin Tegel	Germany	WGA	Wagga Wagga, NSW	Australia	YUM	Yuma, AZ	USA
TYL	Talara	Peru	WIL	Nairobi Wilson	Kenya	YUT	Repulse Bay, NT	Canada
TYN	Taiyuan	China	WKA	Wanaka	New Zealand	YVA	Moroni	Comores
TYS	Knoxville, TN	USA	WLG	Wellington	New Zealand	YVO	Val d'Or	Canada
TZN	South Andros	Bahamas	WNZ	Wenzhou	China	YVR	Vancouver	Canada
TZX	Trabzon	Turkey	WRO	Wroclaw	Poland	YWG	Winnipeg	Canada
UAK	Narsarsuaq	Greenland	WUH	Wuhan	China	YWK	Wabush, NF	Canada
UBJ	Ube	Japan	WUZ	Wuzhou	China	YXE	Saskatoon	Canada
UCA	Utica, NY	USA	WVB	Walvis Bay	Namibia	YXT	Terrace, BC	Canada
UDI	Uberlandia	Brazil	WXN	Wanxian	China	YXU	London, OT	Canada
UDR	Udaipur	India	WYN	Wyndham, WA	Australia	YXX	Abbotsford, BC	Canada
UET	Quetta	Pakistan	XCH	Christmas Island	Australia	YXY	Whitehorse	Canada
UFA	Ufa	Russia	XFN	Xiangfan	China	YYB	North Bay	Canada
UIO	Quito	Ecuador	XMN	Xiamen	China	YYC	Calgary	Canada
UIP	Quimper	France	XNN	Xining	China	YYJ	Victoria	Canada
ULB	Ulei	Vanuatu	XRY	Jerez de la Frontera	Spain	YYQ	Churchill	Canada
ULN	Ulaanbataar	Mongolia	XSP	Singapore Seletar		YYR	Goose Bay	Canada
UMD	Uummannag	Greenland	YAB	Arctic Bay	Canada	YYT	St.Johns	Canada
UME	Umea	Sweden	YAM	Sault St.Marie, OT	Canada	YYZ	Toronto Lester Pearson	Canada
UMR	Woomera, SA	Australia	YAO	Yaounde	Cameroon	YZF	Yellowknife	Canada
URA	Uralsk	Kazakstan	YAP	Yap	Caroline Islands	YZR	Sarnia	Canada
URC	Urumqi	China	YBA	Banff, AL	Canada	YZV	Sept-Iles	Canada
URO	Rouen	France	YBC	Baie Comeau, QU	Canada	ZAD	Zadar	Croatia
URT	Surat Thani	Thailand	YBE	Uranium City	Canada	ZAG	Zagreb	Croatia
URY	Gurayat	Saudi Arabia	YBL	Campbell River	Canada	ZAM	Zamboango	Philippines
USH	Ushuaia	Argentina	YBX	Blanc Sablon	Canada	ZAZ	Zaragoza	Spain
USM	Koh Samui	Thailand	YDA	Dawson City	Canada	ZBF	Bathurst	Canada
USN	Ulsan	South Korea	YDF	Deer Lake	Canada	ZCC	Baden-Baden	Germany
UTP	Utapao	Thailand	YDQ	Dawson Creek	Canada	ZCO	Temuco	Chile
UUD	Ulan Ude	Russia	YEG	Edmonton	Canada	ZHA	Zhanjiang	China
UYN	Yulin	China	YEV	Inuivik	Canada	ZLO	Manzanillo	Mexico
VAA	Vaasa	Finland	YFB	Iqualit	Canada	ZNE	Newman, WA	Australia
VAN	Van	Turkey	YFC	Fredericton	Canada	ZNZ	Zanzibar	Tanzania
VAR	Varna	Bulgaria	YFS	Fort Simpson	Canada	ZQN	Queenstown	New Zealand
VAS	Sivas	Turkey	YGP	Gaspe, QU	Canada	ZRH	Zürich	Switzerland
VBY	Visby	Sweden	YHG	Charlottetown, NF	Canada	ZTH	Zakhinthos	Greece
VCE	Venice	Italy	YHM	Hamilton	Canada	ZUH	Zhuhai	China
VCT	Victoria, TX	USA	YHY	Hay River	Canada	ZZU	Mzuzu	Malawi
VDB	Fagernes	Norway	YHZ	Halifax	Canada			
VER	Vera Cruz	Mexico	YJT	Stephanville, NF	Canada			
VEY	Vestmannaeyjar	Iceland	YKA	Kamloops	Canada			
VFA	Victoria Falls	Zimbabwe	YKL	Schefferville	Canada			
VGO	Vigo	Spain	YKM	Yakima, WA	USA			
VIE	Vienna	Austria	YKS	Yakutsk	Russia			
VIX	Vitoria	Brazil	YLW	Kelowna	Canada			
VKO	Moscow Vnukovo	Russia	YMM	Fort McMurray, AB	Canada			
VKT	Vorkuta	Russia	YMX	Montreal - Mirabel	Canada			
VLC	Valencia	Spain	YNJ	Yanji	China			
VLI	Port Vila	Vanuatu	YNT	Yantai	China			
VLN	Valencia	Venezuela	YOL	Yola	Nigeria			
VON	Vilnius	Lithuania	YOW	Ottawa	Canada			
VNS	Varanasi	India	YPA	Prince Albert	Canada			
VNY	Van Nuys, CA	USA	YPR	Prince Rupert	Canada			
VOG	Volgograd	Russia	YQB	Quebec	Canada			
VOZ	Voronzesh	Russia	YQI	Yarmouth, NS	Canada			
VPZ	Valparaiso, IN	USA	YQG	Windsor	Canada			
VRA	Varadero	Cuba	YQK	Kenora	Canada			
VRN	Verona	Italy	YQL	Lethbridge, AL	Canada			
VSA	Villahermosa	Mexico	YQL	Monton, NB	Canada			
VST	Vasteras	Sweden	YQQ	Comox, BC	Canada			
VTE	Vientiane	Laos	YQR	Regina	Canada			
VVC	Villavicencio	Columbia	YQT	Thunder Bay	Canada			
VVI	Santa Cruz Viru Viru	Bolivia	YQU	Grande Prairie, AB	Canada			
VVO	Vladivostok	Russia	YQX	Gander	Canada			

Code	Airline	Code	Airline	Code	Airline
AAH	Aloha Airlines (AQ)	ALK	Srilankan (UL)	AXX	Avioimpex (M4)
AAL	American Airlines (AA)	ALO	Allegheny Airlines (US)	AYZ	Atlant Soyuz Airlines (3G)
AAR	Asiana (OZ)	ALX	HBA Hewa Bora	AZA	Alitalia (AZ)
AAW	Afriqiyah Airways (8U)	AMC	Air Malta (KM)	AZI	Azzurraair (ZS)
AAY	Allegiant Air (G4)	AMF	Ameriflight	AZL	Air Zanzibar
ABD	Air Atlanta Iceland (CC)	AMI	Air Maldives (L6)	AZM	Aerocozumel (AZ)
ABG	Abakan-Avia	AMK	Amerer Air	AZW	Air Zimbabwe (UM)
ABH	Aebal (DF)	AML	Air Malawi (QM)	BAG	Deutsche BA (DI)
ABO	APSA Colombia	AMM	Air 2000 (DP)	BAL	Britannia Airways (BY)
ABR	Air Contractors (AG)	AMO	Air Montreal (F8)	BAW	British Airways (BA)
ABX	ABX Air (GB)	AMT	American Trans Air (TZ)	BBC	Biman Bangladesh (BG)
ACA	Air Canada (AC)	AMU	Air Macau (NX)	BBR	Santa Barbara Airlines (BJ)
ACD	Academy Airlines	AMC	Aeromexico (AM)	BCS	European Air Transport (QY)
ACI	Air Caledonie Intl. (SB)	AMV	AMC Aviation	BCY	City Jet (WX)
ACO	Air Colombia	AMW	Air Midwest (ZV)	BER	Air Berlin (AB)
ACQ	Aerocontinente (N6)	AMX	Aeromexico (AM)	BES	Aero Services Executive (W4)
ADB	Antonov Airlines	ANA	ANA-All Nippon Airways (NH)	BFC	Basler Airlines
ADH	Air One (AP)	ANG	Air Niugini (PX)	BFF	Air Nunavut
ADK	ADC Airlines	ANI	Air Atlantic Cargo	BFL	Buffalo Airways (J4)
ADO	Air Hokkaido Intl. (HD)	ANK	Air Nippon (EL)	BGA	Airbus Transport International
ADR	Adria Airways (JP)	ANO	Air North Regional (TL)	BGM	Tatarstan Air Enterprise
AEA	Air Europa (UX)	ANS	Air Nostrum (YW)	BHO	Bhoja Airlines (B4)
AEE	Aegean Aviation	ANT	Air North (4N)	BHS	Bahamasair (UP)
AEF	Aero Lloyd (YP)	ANZ	Air New Zealand (NZ)	BIE	Air Mediterranee
AEH	Aviaexpress (RX)	AOD	Aero Vodochody	BIM	Binter Mediterraneo (AX)
AER	Alaska Central Express (KO)	AOK	Aeroatlantico	BKL	Baikal Airlines (X3)
AES	ACES Colombia (VX)	AOO	AS Aviakompania	BKP	Bangkok Airways (PG)
AEU	Astraeus	APB	Air Atlantique (KI)	BKU	Bykovo Avia
AEW	Aerosvitt Airlines (VV)	APC	Airpac Airlines (LQ)	BLC	TAM-Express (JJ)
AFE	Airfast Indonesia	APO	Aeropro	BLI	Belair
AFG	Ariana Afghan Airlines (FG)	APP	Aeroperlas (WL)	BLL	Baltic Airlines
AFK	Afrik Airlines	APR	Air Provence International	BLR	Atlantic Coast Airlines (DH)
AFL	Aeroflot Russian Airlines (SU)	APT	LAP Colombia	BLS	Bearskin Airlines (JV)
AFM	Affretair (ZL)	ARB	Avia Air (8R)	BLV	Bellview Airlines (B3)
AFO	Aero Empresa Mexicana	ARE	Aires Colombia (4C)	BLX	Britannia Airways (6B)
AFP	TAM	ARG	Aerolineas Argentinas (AR)	BMA	British Midland (BD)
AFR	Air France (AF)	ARK	Ararat Avia (4A)	BOA	Boniair
AGL	Air Angouleme	ARN	Air Nova (QK)	BOI	Aboitiz Air
AGN	Air Gabon (GN)	ARP	L'Aeroposte	BON	Air Bosna (JA)
AGO	Angola Air Charter (C3)	ASA	Alaska Airlines (AS)	BOT	Air Botswana (BP)
AGU	Air Guadeloupe (OG)	ASE	ASA-Delta Connection (EV)	BOU	Bouraq Indonesia (BO)
AGV	Air Glaciers (GB)	ASF	Air Schefferville	BPA	Blue Panorama (9S)
AGX	Aviogenex (JJ)	ASH	Mesa Airlines (YU)	BRA	Braathens (BU)
AHA	Air Alpha (GD)	ASJ	Air Satellite	BRD	Brock Air Service
AHC	Azal Cargo Air	ASM	Air Saint Martin (S6	BRG	Bering Air (8E)
AHG	Aerochaga Airlines	ASU	Aerosur	BRO	Base Airlines (5E)
AHK	Air Hong Kong (LD)	ASW	Air Southwest	BRT	British Regional Airlines (TH)
AHR	Air Adriatic	ATC	Air Tanzania (TC)	BRU	Belavia (B2)
AHY	Azerbaijan Airlines (J2)	ATK	Aerotaca Colombia	BRY	Brymon European Airw. (BC)
AIC	Air India (AI)	ATN	Air Transport International (8C)	BRZ	Samara Airlines (E5)
AIE	Air Inuit (3H)	ATT	Aer Turas Teoranta	BSK	Miami Air (GL)
AIG	Air Inter Gabon	AUA	Austrian Airlines (OS)	BSY	Big Sky Airlines (GQ)
AIK	African Airlines International	AUB	Augsburg Airways (IQ)	BTA	Continental Express (CO)
AIN	African International Airways	AUI	Ukraine International Airlines (PS)	BTC	BAL-Bashkirski (V9)
AIP	Alpine Air (5A)	AUL	AVL (5N)	BTH	Air Saint Barthelmy (OJ)
AIS	Aeris (SH)	AUR	Aurigny Air Services (GR)	BTI	Air Baltic (BT)
AIX	Aircruising Australia	AVA	Avianca Columbia (AV)	BUK	Buckley Air
AIZ	Arkia (IZ)	AVE	Avensa (VE)	BVT	Berjaya Air (J8)
AJI	Ameristar Jet Charter	AVN	Air Vanuatu (NF)	BVU	Bellview Airlines
AJM	Air Jamaica (JM)	AVZ	Aeroservice Kazakstan	BWA	BWIA International (BW)
AJT	Amerijet (JH)	AWC	Titan Airways	BZH	Brit Air (DB)
AJX	Air Japan (NQ)	AWE	America West Airlines (HP)	CAG	CNAC-Zhejiang Airlines (F6)
AKK	Aklak Air (6L)	AWI	Air Wisconsin-United Express	CAL	China Airlines (CI)
AKL	Air Kilroe	AWS	Arab Wings	CAM	Camai Air (R9)
AKN	Alkan Air	AWT	Air West	CAV	Calm Air (MO)
AKR	Arctic Air (8A)	AXF	Asian Express Airlines (HJ)	CAW	Comair (MN)
AKT	Karat (2U)	AXL	KLM Exel (4X)	CAY	Cayman Airways (KX)
ALG	Air Logistics	AXM	Air Asia (AK)	CBB	Air Caribbean (C2)

CBE	Aerocaribe (QA)	CXJ	China Xinjiang Airlines (XO)	FAO	Falcon Air Express (F2)
CBF	China Northern Airlines (CJ)	CXN	China Southwest Airl. (SZ)	FAT	Farner Air Transport
CBJ	Caribjet	CXP	Casino Express (XP)	FBF	Fine Air (FB)
CCA	Air China (CA)	CXT	Coastal Air Transport (DQ)	FCN	Falcon Aviation (IH)
CCI	Capital Cargo International (PT)	CYH	ChinaYunnan Airlines (3Q)	FDX	Fed Ex (FX)
CCM	Compagnie Corse Mediterranee (XK)	CYN	Zhongyuan Airlines (Z2)	FEA	Far Eastern Air Transp. (EF)
CCP	Champion Air (MG	CYP	Cyprus Airways (CY)	FFR	Fischer Air (8F)
CDG	Shandong Airlines (SC)	DAG	Daghestan Airlines	FFT	Frontier Airlines (F9)
CDL	CC Air (ED)	DAH	Air Algerie (AH)	FIN	Finnair (OY)
CDP	Aero Condor (P2)	DAL	Delta Air Lines (DL)	FJI	Air Pacific (FJ)
CDS	Central District Airlines	DAN	Maersk Air (DM)	FLI	Atlantic Airways (RC)
CES	China Eastern Airlines (MU)	DAO	Daallo Airlines (D3)	FOM	Freedom Air Intl.
CET	Centralafrican Airlines (GC)	DAT	DAT Delta Air Transport	FRN	Tulip Air Charter
CFG	Condor (DE)	DAZ	DAS Air Cargo	FRS	Flandre Air (IX)
CFJ	Fujian Airlines (IV)	DBY	Britannia Airways (BN)	FSC	Four Star Aviation (HK)
CFZ	Zhongfei Airlines	DHL	DHL Airways (ER)	FUA	Futura Intl.Airways (FH)
CGH	Air Guizhou	DHX	DHL Aviation (ES)	FWI	Air Guadeloupe (TX)
CGT	CNG Transavia	DJU	Air Dijibouti (DY)	FWL	Florida West Airlines (RF)
CHB	Chelyabinsk Air Enterprise (H6)	DLA	Air Dolomiti (EN)	FWQ	Flight West Airlines (YC)
CHH	Hainan Airlines (H4)	DLH	Lufthansa (LH)	FXI	Flugfelag Islands (NY)
CHJ	Chaika Aircompany	DMO	Domodedovo Airlines (E3)	GAP	Air Philippines (2P)
CHP	Aviacsa (6A)	DNM	Denim Air (3D)	GAW	Gambia Airways
CHQ	Chautauqua Airlines (US)	DNV	Donavia (D9)	GBL	GB Airways (GT)
CIB	Condor-Berlin	DOA	Dominicana de Aviacion (DO)	GBU	Air Bissau (YZ)
CIC	ICC Air Cargo Canada	DOB	Dobrolet Airlines	GCO	Gemini Air Cargo (GR)
CIM	Cimber Air (QI)	DRG	Italair (B8)	GDI	Grandair (8L)
CIR	Artic Circle Air Service	DRK	Druk Air (KB)	GEC	Lufthansa Cargo (LH)
CKS	Kalitta American Intl. Airw. (CB)	DSB	Air Senegal (DS)	GFA	Gulf Air (GF)
CLC	Classic Air	DSR	DAS Air Cargo (SE)	GFT	Gulfstream International (3M)
CLG	Chalair (M6)	DTA	TAAG Angola Airlines (DT)	GHA	Ghana Airways (GH)
CLH	Lufthansa Cityline (CL)	DTR	Danish Air Transport (DX)	GIA	Garuda Indonesia (GA)
CLT	Air Caribbean (XC)	EAA	TAAN	GIB	Air Guinee (GI)
CLX	Cargolux (CV)	EAQ	Eastern Australia Airlines	GIL	Gill Airways (9C)
CMI	Continental Micronesia (GS)	EAT	Air Transport Europe	GIO	Regionair (RH)
CMP	Copa Panama (CM)	EAV	Eagle Airlines (ZN)	GLA	Great Lakes Airlines (ZK)
CNA	Centennial Airlines (BE)	ECA	Eurocypria Airlines (UI)	GLB	Trans Global
CNJ	Nanjing Airlines (3W)	ECC	Crossair Europe (QE)	GMI	Germania Fluggesellschaft (ST)
CNK	Sunwest International	EDW	Edelweiss Air	GNT	British Midland Commuter
CNM	Canarias Regional (FW)	EEA	Ecuatoriana (EU)	GRL	Groenlandsfly (GL)
CNW	China Northwest Airl. (WH)	EEU	Eurofly Service	GRO	Allegro Air
COA	Continental Airlines (CO)	EEX	Avanti Air	GTI	tlas Air (5Y)
COM	Comair (OH)	EEZ	Eurofly (GJ)	GTV	Aerogaviota
CPA	Cathay Pacific (CX)	EGF	American Eagle Airlines	GUG	Aviateca (GU)
CPI	Cebu Pacific Air (5J)	EIA	Evergreen Intl.Airlines (EZ)	GYA	Guyana Airways (GY)
CRC	Conair Aviation	EIN	Aer Lingus (EI)	GZP	Gazpromavia
CRF	Crimea Air (OR)	ELG	Alpi Eagles (E8)	HAL	Hawaiian Air (HA)
CRG	City Link Airlines	ELK	Elk Airways (S8)	HAR	Harbour Airlines (HB)
CRL	Corse Air (SS)	ELL	Estonian Air (OV)	HCB	Helenair
CRN	Aero Caribbean	ELO	Eurolot	HDA	Dragonair (KA)
CRQ	Air Creebec (YN)	EKP	Aerolineas Ejecutivas	HHI	Hamburg International
CRX	Crossair (LX)	ELV	TANS	HJA	Air Haiti
CSA	CSA (OK)	ELY	EL AL Israel Airlines (LY)	HLF	Hapag-Lloyd Flug (HF)
CSB	Air Commerce	ENI	Enimex	HLQ	Harlequin Air
CSC	Sichuan Airlines (3U)	ENW	Airnor	HMS	Hemus Air (DU)
CSH	Shanghai Airlines (FM)	EQA	Eagle Aviation (Y4)	HRH	Royal Tongan Airlines (WR)
CSN	China Southern Airl. (CZ)	EQL	Air Sao Tomé & Principe (KY)	HTT	Air Tchad
CSO	Casino Airlines	ERG	Aviaenergo	HVN	Vietnam Airlines (VN)
CSZ	Shenzhen Airlines (4G)	ERH	ERA Aviation (7H)	IAC	Indian Airlines (IC)
CTH	China General Aviation (GP)	ERT	Red Sea Air	IAW	Iraqi Airways (IA)
CTN	Croatia Airlines (OU)	ESL	East Line Airlines (P7)	IBB	Binter Canaris (NT)
CTP	Tapo Avia (PQ)	ETH	Ethiopian Airlines (ET)	IBE	Iberia (IB)
CTZ	CATA-Lineas Aerea	EUA	ERA (E5)	ICB	islandsflug (HH)
CUA	China United Airlines (HR)	EUL	Euralair (RN)	ICE	Icelandair (FI)
CUB	Cubana (CU)	EVA	Eva Air (BR)	ICL	CAL Cargo Air Lines
CUT	Court Air	EWG	Eurowings (EW)	ILM	Inter Air (D6)
CVA	Air Chathams (CV)	EWW	Emery Worldwide (GJ)	IMX	Zimex Aviation (MF)
CVU	Grand Canyon Airlines	EXS	Channel Express (LS)	INI	Benair
CWC	Challenge Air Cargo (WE)	EXT	Night Express Luftverkehr	IRA	Iran Air (IR)
CWU	Wuhan Air Lines (WU)	EXY	South African Express Airways	IRB	Iran Airtours
CXA	Xiamen Airlines (MF)	EZY	Easyjet Airline (U2)	IRC	Iran Aseman Airlines
CXH	China Xinhua Airlines (X2)	FAB	First Air (7F)	IRK	Kish Air (KN)
CXI	Shanxi Aviation (BC)	FAJ	Air Fiji (PC)	IRM	Mahan Air

ISR	Israir	LOT	LOT Polish Airlines (LO)	ORM	Orel Air Enterprise
ISS	Meridiana (IG)	LPR	LAPA (MJ)	ORZ	Zorex Air Transport
IST	Istanbul Airlines (IL)	LRC	Lacsa (LR)	OSL	Sosoliso Airlines
ISV	Islenia Airlines	LTP	Latpass Airlines (QI)	OST	Alania Airline
IWD	Iberworld (TY)	LTU	LTU Intl. Airways (LT)	OVA	Aeronova
IYE	Yemenia Airways (IY)	LYC	Lynden Air Cargo (L2)	OWL	Miami Valley Aviation
JAA	Japan Asia Airways (EG)	MAA	MAS Air Cargo (MY)	OXE	Gregg Air
JAC	Japan Air Commuter (JN)	MAH	Malev Hungarian Airl. (MA)	OZU	Khozu-Avia
JAI	Jet Airways Ltd. (9W)	MAK	MAT-Macedonian Airlines (M7)	PAA	Pan Am
JAK	Jana Arka	MAS	Malaysia Airlines (MH)	PAC	Polar Air Cargo (PO)
JAL	Japan Airlines (JL)	MAU	Air Mauritius (MK)	PAL	Philippines (PR)
JAT	JAT-Yugoslav Airlines (JU)	MDG	Air Madagascar (MD)	PAO	Polynesian Airlines (PH)
JAZ	Japan Air Charter (JZ)	MDJ	JARO International (JT)	PAR	Spair Air Transport (S4)
JEA	Jersey European Airw. (JY)	MDL	Mandala Airlines (RI)	PAS	Pelita Air Service (EP)
JEM	Emerald Airways (G3)	MDS	MED Airlines (M8)	PAV	VIP Avia
JEX	JAL Express (JC)	MDV	Moldavian Airlines (2M)	PAX	Pan Air
JKK	Spanair (JK)	MEA	Middle East Airlines (ME)	PBU	Air Burundi (PB)
JLH	Jet Link Holland	MEP	Midwest Express (YK)	PCO	Pacific Coastal (8P)
JMC	JMC Airlines	MES	Mesaba (XJ)	PEG	Pelangi Air (9P)
JMX	Air Jamaica Express	MFZ	Mofaz Air	PFC	Pacific Intl. Airlines
JSC	Airstan	MGL	Miat Mongolian Airl. (OM)	PGA	PGA-Portugalia (NI)
JTA	Japan Transocean Air	MKA	MK Airlines (7G)	PGP	Perm Airlines
JUS	USA Jet Airlines	MLD	Air Moldova (9U)	PGT	Pegasus Airlines
KAC	Kuwait Airways (KU)	MLI	Air Mali (L9)	PIA	Pakistan Intl.Airlines (PK)
KAL	Korean Air (KE)	MLV	Air Modova Intl. (3R)	PLA	Polynesian Airways (PH)
KBA	Ken Borek Airlines (4K)	MNA	Merpati (MZ)	PLK	Pulkovo Aviation (Z8)
KDA	Kendell Airlines (KD)	MNB	MNG Cargo Airlines (MB)	PMI	Air Europa Express
KFA	Kelowna Flightcraft	MNX	Manx Airlines (JG)	PNW	Palestinian Airlines (PF)
KFB	Air Botnia (KF)	MON	Monarch Airlines (ZB)	PRH	Pro Air (P9)
KGA	Kyrghyzstan Airlines (K2)	MPD	Air Plus Comet (2Z)	PTB	Passaredo (Y8)
KHA	Kitty Hawk Air Cargo (KR)	MPH	Martinair Holland (MP)	PTN	Pantanal (P8)
KHB	Dalavia (H8)	MRS	Air Marshall Islands (CW)	PUA	Pluna (PU)
KIL	Kuban Airlines (GW)	MRT	Air Mauritanie (MR)	PUB	Aeropublic
KIS	Contact Air (3T)	MSK	Maersk Air(VB)	PVV	Continental Airways (PC)
KJC	Kras Air	MSR	Egypt Air (MS)	PXA	Pecotox Air
KKB	Air South (WV)	MTL	RAF Avia	PYR	Pyramid Airlines
KLA	Air Lithuania (TT)	MTM	MTM Aviation	QAC	Qatar Air Cargo
KLC	KLM Cityhopper (HN)	MVD	KMV (KV)	QAF	Qatar Amiri Flight
KLM	KLM Royal Dutch Airl. (KL)	MWT	Midwest Aviation	QFA	Qantas (QF)
KLN	Kaliningrad Avia (K8)	MXA	Mexicana (MX)	QLA	Aviation Quebec Labrador (QC)
KOR	Air Koryo (JS)	MTS	Mahfooz Aviation (M2)	QNK	Kabo Air (9H)
KQA	Kenya Airways (KQ)	NAC	Northern Air Cargo (HU)	QQA	Alliance Airlines (QQ)
KRE	Aerosucre	NAO	North American Airl. (XG)	QSC	ASA African Safari
KSM	Kosmos Aviakompania	NCA	Nippon Cargo Airlines (KZ)	QTR	Qatar Airways Co. (Q7)
KYV	Kibris Turkish Airlines (YK)	NGA	Nigeria Airways (WT)	QXE	Horizon Air (QX)
KZK	Air Kazakstan	NIS	Nica (6Y)	RAM	Royal Air Maroc (AT)
LAA	Libyan Arab Airlines (LN)	NJS	National Jet Systems (NC)	RBA	Royal Brunei (BI)
LAJ	British Mediterranean (KJ)	NKS	Spirit Airlines (NK)	RDN	Dinar (D7)
LAL	Air Labrador (WJ)	NMB	Air Namibia (SW)	RGI	Regional Airlines (VM)
LAM	Linhas Aereas Mocambique (TM)	NRX	Filder Air Service	RIT	Asian Spirit
LAN	LAN Chile (LA)	NTR	TNT Intl. Aviation Service	RJA	Royal Jordanian (RJ)
LAO	Lao Aviation (QV)	NTS	Cirrus Air	RKA	Air Afrique (RK)
LAP	TAM Paraguayas (PZ)	NTW	Nationwide Airlines (CE)	RLD	RAS-Flug (RW)
LAV	Aeropostal (VH)	NWA	Northwest Airlines (NW)	RME	Armenian Airlines (R3)
LBC	Albanian Airlines (7Y)	NZM	Mount Cook Airline (NM)	RMV	Romavia (VQ)
LBT	Nouvelair Tunisie	OAC	Oriental Airways	RNA	Royal Nepal Airlines (RA)
LCI	Lufthansa Hinduja Cargo India (LF)	OAE	Omni Air (X9)	ROM	Aeromar Airlines (BQ)
LCO	Ladeco (UC)	OAL	Olympic Airways (OA)	RON	Air Nauru (ON)
LDA	Lauda Air (NG)	OCA	Aserca Airlines (R7)	ROT	Tarom (RO)
LDE	LADE (LD)	ODS	Odessa Airlines (5K)	RPB	Aerorepublica (P5)
LDI	Lauda Air SpA (L4)	OEA	Orient Thai Airlines (OX)	RQX	Air Engadina/ KLM Alps (RQ)
LFA	Alfa Hava Yollari (H7)	OHY	Onur Air (8Q)	RSL	Rio Sul (SL)
LGL	Luxair (LG)	OIR	Slov Air	RSN	Royal Swazi Natl. Airways
LGW	Luftfahrtgesellschaft Walther (HE)	OKJ	Okada Air (9H)	SAM	Sam Columbia (MM)
LHN	Express One Intl. (EO)	OLT	Ostfriesische Lufttransport (OL)	SAS	Scandinavian (SK)
LIA	Liat Caribbean Airlines (LI)	OLY	Olympic Aviation (7U)	SAT	Sata Air Acores (SP)
LIL	Lithuanian Airlines (TE)	OMA	Oman Air	SAY	Scott Airways (CB)
LIT	Air Littoral (FU)	OMS	Omsk Avia	SBI	Sibir Airlines (S7)
LKR	Laker Airways (6F)	ONT	Air Ontario (GX)	SBY	Tempelhof Express (FC)
LLB	Lloyd Aereo Boliviano (LB)	ORB	Orenburg Airlines	SBZ	Scibe Airlift Zaire (ZM)
LOF	Trans States Airlines (9N)	ORC	Air Cordial	SCH	Schreiner Airways (AW)
LOG	Loganair (LC)	ORF	Oman Royal Flight (RS)	SCI	Special Cargo Airways (C7)

RTL	Rheintalflug (WG)	TUD	Flight Alaska (4Y)	XJC	Xclusive Jet Charter
RUS	Cirrus Airlines (C9)	TUI	Tuninter (UG)	XKX	Asenca
RVV	Reeve Aleutian Airways (RV)	TUL	Tulpair Av. Company	XLA	Excel Airways (JN)
RWD	Alliance Air Express	TYM	Tyumen Airlines	XME	Australian Air Express (XM)
RYN	Ryan International Airlines	TYR	Tyrolean Airways (VO)	XNA	Express Net Airlines
RYR	Ryanair (FR)	TZK	Tajikistan Airlines (7J)	XST	Skyteam
RZO	SATA International (S4)	UAE	Emirates (EK)	YRG	Air Yugoslavia
SAA	South African Airways (SA)	UAL	United Airlines (UA)	YRR	Scenic Airlines (YR)
SAI	Shaheen International (NL)	UBA	Myanma Airways (UB)	YSS	Yes - Linhas Aéras Charter S.A.
SCW	Braathens Malmö Aviation (BU)	UCA	USAir Express-Commutair	YXA	Airports Authority of India
SCX	Sun Country Airlines (SY)	UGA	Uganda Airlines (QU)	YZR	Yangtze River Express LLC
SER	Aero California (JR)	TPC	Air Caledonie (TY)	ZAK	Zambia Skyways (X7)
SEU	Star Airlines (2R)	TRA	Transavia Airlines (HV)	ZAN	Zantop International Airlines
SEY	Air Seychelles (HM)	TRJ	Tyumen Airways (VO)	ZBA	ZB Air
SFB	Air Sofia (CT)	TRS	Air Tran Airways (FL)		
SFR	Safeair (FA)	TRZ	Transmeridian Airlines (T9)		
SGL	Senegal Air	TSC	Air Transat (TS)		
SHK	Shoruk Air (7Q)	TSO	Trans Aero (4J)		
SIA	Singapore Airlines (SQ)	TTR	Tatra Air (QS)		
SIB	Sibaviatrans (5M)	TUI	Tuninter (UG)		
SIC	Air Sicilia (BM)	UKR	Air Ukraine (GU)		
SKW	Skywest-Delta Connection (OO)	UPA	Air Foyle (GS)		
SKY	Skymark Airlines (BC)	UPS	UPS Airlines (5X)		
SLK	Silkair (MI)	USA	US Airways (US)		
SLL	Slovak Airlines (6Q)	USS	USAir Shuttle (TB)		
SLM	Surinam Airways (PY)	UYA	Yute Air Alaska (4Y)		
SLR	Sobelair (S3)	UYC	Cameroon Airlines (UY)		
SNB	Sterling European Airl. (NB)	UZB	Uzbekistan Airways (HY)		
SNZ	Santa Cruz Imperial	VAL	Voyageur Airways		
SOL	Solomon Airlines (IE)	VAP	Phuket Airlines (9R)		
SPA	Sierra Pacific Airlines (SI)	VAS	Atran (V8)		
STU	STAF (FS)	VAZ	Airlines 400		
SUD	Sudan Airways (SD)	VBW	Air Burkina (VH)		
SUF	Sunflower Airlines (PI)	VDA	Volga Dnepr Cargo Airl. (VI)		
SUZ	Premiair Charter	VEC	Vensecar International (V4)		
SVA	Saudia (SV)	VEE	Victor Echo		
SVR	Ural Airlines (U6)	VEX	Virgin Express (TV)		
SVV	Servivensa (VC)	VGA	Air Vegas Airlines (6V)		
SWA	Southwest Airlines (WN)	VHM	VHM Schul- and Charterflug		
SWD	Southern Winds (A4)	VID	Aviaprad		
SWL	SAE Swe Aviation	VIF	VIF Luftfahrtgesellschaft		
SXS	Sunexpress (XQ)	VIH	Vichi Air Company		
SYR	Syrianair (RB)	VIK	Viking Airlines		
TAB	Taba (TT)	VGD	Vanguard Airlines (NJ)		
TAE	Tame (EQ)	VIM	VIA (VL)		
TAI	TACA Intl. Airlines (TA)	VIR	Virgin Atlantic Airways (VS)		
TAJ	Tunisavia	VKO	Vnukovo Airlines (V5)		
TAM	TAM Brasil (KK)	VLE	Voloare Airlines (8D)		
TAO	Aeromar Airlines (VW)	VLM	VLM (V4)		
TAP	TAP Air Portugal (TP)	VRG	Varig (RG)		
TAR	Tunis Air (TU)	VSP	VASP (VP)		
TAS	Lotus Air	VTA	Air Tahiti (VT)		
TBA	Transbrasil (TR)	VTR	Air Ostrava (8K)		
TCF	Shuttle America (S5)	VTS	Everts Air Alaska / Cargo (3K)		
TCV	TACV Cabo Verdes (VR)	VUN	Air Ivoire (VU)		
TEP	Transeuropean Airlines (UE)	VUR	VIP		
THA	Thai Airways Intl. (TG)	VVI	Vivant Air		
THT	Air Tahiti Nui (TN)	VXG	Avirex (G2)		
THY	Turkish Airlines (TK)	VXP	Avion Express		
TII	ATI Aircompany	VXX	Aviaekspress Airlines		
TMA	TMA of Lebanon (TL)	VZR	Aviazur		
TPA	TAMPA Columbia (QT)	WDL	WDL Aviation		
TRA	Transavia Airlines (HV)	WDY	Chicago Express Airlines (C8)		
TRJ	AJT Air International(E9)	WIF	Wideroe (WF)		
TRQ	Cityconnect (6N)	WOA	World Airways (WO)		
TRS	Airtran Airways (FL)	WSG	Wasaya Airways		
TRZ	Transmeridian Airlines (T9)	WTA	Africa West (FK)		
TSC	Air Transat (TS)	WTC	Weasua Airtransport		
TSE	Transmile Air Service (TH)	WTV	Western Aviators		
TSG	Trans Air Congo TAC (Q8)	WYC	Wycombe Air Centre		
TSO	Transaero Airlines (UN)	WZP	Zip Air		
TUA	Turkmenistan Airlines (T5)	XAX	Airx		

International Aircraft Registration Prefixes

By Prefix

Prefix	Country		Prefix	Country		Prefix	Country
AP	Pakistan		LX	Luxembourg		V4	St. Kitts & Nevis
A2	Botswana		LY	Lithuania		V5	Namibia
A3	Tonga Islands		LZ	Bulgaria		V6	Micronesia
A4O	Oman		N	USA		V7	Marshall Islands
A5	Bhutan		OB	Peru		V8	Sultanate of Brunei
A6	United Arab Emirates		OD	Lebanon		XA/B/C	Mexico
A7	Qatar		OE	Austria		XT	Burkina Faso
A8	Liberia		OH	Finland		XU	Cambodia
A9C	Bahrain		OK	Czech Republic		XY	Myanmar
B	People's Republic of China		OM	Slovakia		YA	Afghanistan
B-H	Hong Kong		OO	Belgium		YI	Iraq
B-M	Macau		OY	Denmark		YJ	Vanuatu
B	Republic of China (Taiwan)		P	North Korea		YK	Syria
C	Canada		PH	Netherlands		YL	Latvia
CC	Chile		PJ	Netherlands Antilles		YN	Nicaragua
CCCP	former Soviet Union		PK	Indonesia		YR	Romania
CN	Morocco		PP	Brazil		YS	El Salvador
CP	Bolivia		PR	Brazil		YU	Serbia and Montenegro
CS	Portugal		PT	Brazil		YV	Venezuela
CU	Cuba		PZ	Surinam		Z	Zimbabwe
CX	Uruguay		P2	Papua New Guinea		ZA	Albania
C2	Nauru		P4	Aruba		ZK	New Zealand
C3	Andorra		RA	Russia		ZP	Paraguay
C5	Gambia		RDPL	Laos		ZS	South Africa
C6	Bahamas		RP	Philippines		ZR	Macedonia
C9	Mozambique		SE	Sweden		3A	Monaco
D	Germany		SP	Poland		3B	Mauritius
DQ	Fiji Islands		ST	Sudan		3C	Equatorial Guinea
D2	Angola		SU	Egypt		3D	Swaziland
D4	Cape Verde Islands		SU-Y	Palestine		3X	Guinea
D6	Comores Islands		SX	Greece		4K	Azerbaijan
EC	Spain		S2	Bangladesh		4L	Georgia
EI	Ireland		S5	Slovenia		4R	Sri Lanka
EK	Armenia		S7	Seychelles		4X	Israel
EP	Iran		S9	Sao Tome & Principe		5A	Libya
ER	Moldavia		TC	Turkey		5B	Cyprus
ES	Estonia		TF	Iceland		5H	Tanzania
ET	Ethiopia		TG	Guatemala		5N	Nigeria
EW	Belarus		TI	Costa Rica		5R	Madagascar
EX	Kyrgyzstan		TJ	Cameroon		5T	Mauritania
EY	Tajikistan		TL	Central Africa		5U	Niger
EZ	Turkmenistan		TN	Congo		5V	Togo
E3	Eritrea		TR	Gabon		5W	Samoa
F	France		TS	Tunisia		5X	Uganda
G	Great Britain		TT	Chad		5Y	Kenya
HA	Hungary		TU	Ivory Coast		6O	Somalia
HB	Switzerland (including Lichtenstein)		TY	Benin		6V	Senegal
HC	Ecuador		TZ	Mali		6Y	Jamaica
HH	Haiti		T2	Tuvalu		7O	Yemen
HI	Dominican Republic		T3	Kiribati		7P	Lesotho
HK	Columbia		T7	San Marino		7Q	Malawi
HL	South Korea		T8A	Palau		7T	Algeria
HP	Panama		T9	Bosnia-Herzegovina		8P	Barbados
HR	Honduras		UK	Uzbekistan		8Q	Maldives
HS	Thailand		UN	Kazakstan		8R	Guyana
HZ	Saudi Arabia		UR	Ukraine		9A	Croatia
H4	Solomon Islands		VH	Australia		9G	Ghana
I	Italy		VN	Vietnam		9H	Malta
JA	Japan		VP-A	Anguilla		9J	Zambia
JU	Mongolia		VP-B	Bermuda		9K	Kuwait
JY	Jordan		VP-C	Cayman Islands		9L	Sierra Leone
J2	Djibouti		VP-F	Falkland Islands		9M	Malaysia
J3	Grenada		VP-G	Gibraltar		9N	Nepal
J5	Guinea Bissau		VP-L	British Virgin Islands		9Q	Congo/Kinshasa
J6	St.Lucia		VP-M	Montserrat		9U	Burundi
J7	Dominica		VQ-T	Turks & Caicos Islands		9V	Singapore
J8	St.Vincent and Grenadines		VT	India		9XR	Rwanda
LN	Norway		V2	Antigua and Barbuda		9Y	Trinidad and Tobago
LV	Argentina		V3	Belize			

By Country

Country	Code	Country	Code	Country	Code
Afghanistan	YA	Georgia	4L	Niger	5U
Albania	ZA	Germany	D	Nigeria	5N
Algeria	7T	Ghana	9G	Norway	LN
Andorra	C3	Gibraltar	VP-G	Oman	A4O
Angola	D2	Grenada	J3	Pakistan	AP
Anguilla	VP-A	Greece	SX	Palau	T8A
Antigua & Barbuda	V2	Great Britain	G	Palestine	SU-Y
Argentina	LV	Guam	N	Panama	HP
Armenia	EK	Guinea	3X	Papua New Guinea	P2
Aruba	P4	Guinea Bissau	J5	Paraguay	ZP
Australia	VH	Guyana	8R	Peru	OB
Austria	OE	Haiti	HH	Philippines	RP
Azerbaijan	4K	Honduras	HR	Poland	SP
Bahamas	C6	Hong Kong	B-H	Portugal	CS
Bahrain	A9C	Iceland	TF	Puerto Rico	N
Bangladesh	S2	India	VT	Qatar	A7
Barbados	8P	Indonesia	PK	Romania	YR
Barbuda	V2	Iran	EP	Russia	RA
Belarus	EW	Iraq	YI	Rwanda	9XR
Belgium	OO	Israel	4X	Samoa	5W
Belize	V3	Italy	I	San Marino	T7
Benin	TY	Ivory Coast	TU	Sao Tomé & Principe	S9
Bermuda	VP-B	Jamaica	6Y	Saudi Arabia	HZ
Bhutan	A5	Japan	JA	Senegal	6V
Bolivia	CP	Jordan	JY	Serbia & Montenegro	YU
Bosnia-Herzegovina	T9	Kazakstan	UN	Seychelles	S7
Botswana	A2	Kenya	5Y	Sierra Leone	9L
Brazil	PP/PT/PR	Kiribati	T3	Singapore	9V
British Virgin Islands	VP-L	Korea, North	P	Slovakia	OM
Brunei	V8	Korea, South	HL	Slovenia	S5
Bulgaria	LZ	Kuwait	9K	Solomon Islands	H4
Burkina Faso	XT	Kyrgyzstan	EX	Somalia	6O
Burundi	9U	Laos	RDPL	South Africa	ZS
Cambodia	XU	Latvia	YL	Spain	EC
Cameroon	TJ	Lebanon	OD	Sri Lanka	4R
Canada	C	Lesotho	7P	St.Kitts & Nevis	V4
Cape Verde Islands	D4	Liberia	A8	St.Lucia	J6
Cayman Islands	VP-C	Libya	5A	St.Vincent and Grenadines	J8
Central African Republic	TL	Liechtenstein	HB	Sudan	ST
Chad	TT	Lithuania	LY	Surinam	PZ
Chile	CC	Luxembourg	LX	Swaziland	3D
China, People's Republic of	B	Macau	B-M	Sweden	SE
China, Republic (Taiwan)	B	Macedonia	Z3	Switzerland	HB
Columbia	HK	Madagascar	5R	Syria	YK
Comores	D6	Malawi	7Q	Taiwan (Republic of China)	B
Congo Brazzaville	TN	Malaysia	9M	Tajikistan	EY
Congo/Kingshasa	9Q	Maldives	8Q	Tanzania	5H
Costa Rica	TI	Mali	TZ	Thailand	HS
Croatia	9A	Malta	9H	Togo	5V
Cuba	CU	Marshall Islands	V7	Tonga	A3
Cyprus	5B	Mauritania	5T	Trinidad and Tobago	9Y
Czech Repulic	OK	Mauritius	3B	Tunisia	TS
Denmark	OY	Mexico	XA/XB/XC	Turkey	TC
Djibouti	J2	Micronesia	V6	Turkmenistan	EZ
Dominica	J7	Moldova	ER	Turks & Caicos	VQ-T
Dominican Republic	HI	Monaco	3A	Tuvalu	T2
Ecuador	HC	Mongolia	JU	Uganda	5X
Egypt	SU	Montenegro	YU	Ukraine	UR
El Salvador	YS	Montserrat	VP-M	United Arab Emirates	A6
Equatorial Guinea	3C	Morocco	CN	Uruguay	CX
Eritrea	E3	Mozambique	C9	USA	N
Estonia	ES	Myanmar	XY	Uzbekistan	UK
Ethiopia	ET	Namibia	V5	Vanuatu	YJ
Falkland Islands	VP-F	Nauru	C2	Venezuela	YV
Fiji	DQ	Nepal	9N	Vietnam	VN
Finland	OH	Netherlands	PH	Yemen	7O
France	F	Netherlands Antilles	PJ	Zambia	9J
Gabon	TR	New Zealand	ZK	Zimbabwe	Z
Gambia	C5	Nicaragua	YN		

WRECKS & RELICS
THE ALBUM

Ken Ellis

WRECKS & RELICS
18th Edition

Ken Ellis

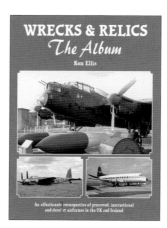

The continuing popularity of the biennial *Wrecks & Relics*, recording preserved, instructional and derelict airframes in the UK and Ireland is well known. Ken Ellis has amassed an extensive archive of unpublished photos from the last forty-some years of *W&R* publication, and following a brief introductory narrative covering *W&R* itself, and the general preservation scene over the years, the body of the book is a gloriously nostalgic collection of photos with extended captions explaining the histories and linking the themes. As *W&R* was a black and white publication for so many years, most of the fascinating subject matter has not appeared in colour before.

The themes include: Airliners; Alas, No More (RIP Museums); Duxford's Early Days; Founding Fathers; Hulks; Light and General; Military Miscellany; Mr Nash; Mr Shuttleworth; Navy First!; Ones That Got Away; On Guard; RAF Museum; Time Capsule (Cranfield); V-Bombers; Warbird Origins; plus a types and locations index. A must for regular W&R readers and an outstanding overview of the UK preservation scene over the years.

Sbk, 280 x 215 mm, 128 pages
340 mostly colour photographs
1 85780 166 0   Published May 2003
£16.99

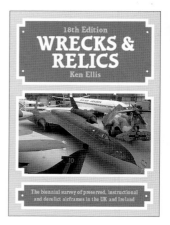

Now in its 41st year of publication, this standard reference work takes the reader on a county-by-county and province-by-province journey through the fascinating world of museums, military stores and dumps, 'geriatric' airliners awaiting the axe, restoration workshops, technical schools, treasures in garages and barns and much more. Within the wealth of detailed information supplied on thousands of aircraft can be found commentary, items to raise the eyebrow and myriad 'I never knew that', expressions!

Fully revised and updated, this latest edition has an array of appendices to take the subject further and the usual extensive indexing and cross-referencing.

In full colour again for this edition, the 64 page photographic section is packed with fascinating and obscure subjects and is as wide-ranging and comprehensive as ever.

Hardback
210 x 148mm, 320 pages
192 colour photographs
1 85780 133 4
Published May 2002
£15.99